D1288999

BARGAINING

BARGAINING
Formal Theories of Negotiation

Edited and with contributions by
ORAN R. YOUNG

University of Illinois Press
Urbana   Chicago   London

Daniel Ellsberg, "Theory of the Reluctant Duelist," reprinted with permission from *The American Economic Review*, XLVI (1956), 909–923.

John F. Nash, Jr., "The Bargaining Problem," reprinted with permission from *Econometrica*, XVIII (1950), 155–162.

John F. Nash, Jr., "Two-Person Cooperative Games," reprinted with permission from *Econometrica*, XXI (1953), 128–140.

John C. Harsanyi, "Bargaining and Conflict Situations in the Light of a New Approach to Game Theory," reprinted with permission from *The American Economic Review*, LV (1965), 447–457.

Robert L. Bishop, "Game-Theoretic Analyses of Bargaining," reprinted with permission from *The Quarterly Journal of Economics*, LXXVII (1963), 559–602.

Frederik Zeuthen, "Economic Warfare," from *Problems of Monopoly and Economic Warfare* (London: Routledge and Kegan Paul, Ltd., 1930, 1968), pp. 104–135, reprinted with permission.

Jan Pen, "A General Theory of Bargaining," reprinted with permission from *The American Economic Review*, XLII (1952), 24–42.

Robert L. Bishop, "A Zeuthen-Hicks Theory of Bargaining," reprinted with permission from *Econometrica*, XXXII (1964), 410–417.

John G. Cross, "A Theory of the Bargaining Process," reprinted with permission from *The American Economic Review*, LV (1965), 67–94.

Alan Coddington, "A Theory of the Bargaining Process: Comment," reprinted with permission from *The American Economic Review*, LVI (1966), 522–530.

John G. Cross, "A Theory of the Bargaining Process: Reply," reprinted with permission from *The American Economic Review*, LVI (1966), 530–533.

M. B. Nicholson, "The Resolution of Conflict," reprinted with permission from *The Journal of the Royal Statistical Society*, Series A (General), CXXX (1967), 529–540.

John C. Harsanyi, "Approaches to the Bargaining Problem before and after the Theory of Games," reprinted with permission from *Econometrica*, XXIV (1956), 144–157.

Jan Pen, "Comment on the Bargaining Problem," from *The Wage Rate under Collective Bargaining* (Cambridge: Harvard University Press, 1959), pp. x–xiii, reprinted with permission.

Harvey M. Wagner, "A Unified Treatment of Bargaining Theory," reprinted with permission from the *Southern Economic Journal*, XXIII (1957), 380–397.

John C. Harsanyi, "Notes on the Bargaining Problem," reprinted with permission from the *Southern Economic Journal*, XXIV (1958), 471–476.

Harvey M. Wagner, "Rejoinder on the Bargaining Problem," reprinted with permission from the *Southern Economic Journal*, XXIV (1958), 476–482.

Thomas C. Schelling, "An Essay on Bargaining," reprinted with permission from *The American Economic Review*, XLVI (1956), 281–306, and *The Strategy of Conflict* (Cambridge: Harvard University Press, 1960), pp. 21–52.

Daniel Ellsberg, "The Theory and Practice of Blackmail," reprinted with permission of the author. This essay was originally a public lecture delivered in Boston under the auspices of the Lowell Institute on March 10, 1959. It was distributed in mimeographed form by the RAND Corporation (RAND P-3883) in 1959 and again in 1968. It has not, however, been formally published previously.

LIBRARY OF CONGRESS CATALOGING IN PUBLICATION DATA

Main entry under title:

Bargaining: formal theories of negotiation.

   Bibliography: p.
   Includes index.
   1. Negotiation—Addresses, essays, lectures.
I. Young, Oran R.
BF637.N4B35   658.4'03   72-75493
ISBN 0-252-00273-3

BF
637
N4
B 35

PREFACE

In assembling materials for this book, I have been guided by the following objectives: (1) to take stock of the corpus of deductive work on bargaining, (2) to clarify several conceptual problems that commonly arise in analyses of bargaining, and (3) to evaluate the prospects for further theoretical work on the bargaining problem in the foreseeable future. Throughout this work, I have tried to come to grips with the various models of bargaining from the point of view of their ultimate application to real-world situations. That is, it has not been my intention to deal with these models solely or even primarily as logical constructs without reference to their empirical applicability, though the reader will find numerous comments on logical problems which they generate. In addition, I have been concerned, for the most part, with the potential of the bargaining models as "descriptive" or "positive" theory in contrast to "prescriptive" theory. I certainly do not wish to deny that the analysis of bargaining raises a number of interesting and important normative issues. Nevertheless, my basic concern in putting this book together has been with problems of explanation and prediction rather than with criteria of fair division or procedures for adjudication.

I should perhaps say a few words here about the coverage of this book. It is still just possible to deal with the major streams of work associated with the construction of deductive models of bargaining within the confines of a single volume. Accordingly, I have not consciously omitted any major approach to the analysis of bargaining in deductive terms even though I have not been able to include all of the efforts that fall within the major approaches. As it happens, my task in selecting specific items for inclusion has been facilitated by the fact that many of those who have contributed to the analysis of bargaining in deductive terms have formulated their basic models in self-contained essays, despite some of them having also presented their ideas at greater length in full-scale monographs on bargaining. Consequently, I have generally been able to select material that originally appeared in article form for inclusion in this book even though I have discussed some of the more extended arguments set forth in the monographs in my introductory essays.

No advanced knowledge of mathematics is required to understand the essays in this book. On the contrary, the mathematics employed in these essays is generally quite straightforward and easy to follow. Nevertheless, a general familiarity with some of the principal techniques utilized in game-theoretic and economic models will certainly prove helpful to the reader. An introductory discussion of these techniques has not been included in the book because it would be too cumbersome, because many readers would find it unnecessary and tiresome, and because it is easy to locate excellent discussions in other places. For those readers unfamiliar with the analytic techniques in question, however, the following references may prove useful. On the concepts of utility theory and rational choice employed in game theory consult: (1) Ward Edwards, "The Theory of Decision Making," *Psychological Bulletin,* LI (1954), 380–417, (2) L. J. Savage, *The Foundations of Statistics* (New York, 1954), and (3) R. Duncan Luce and Howard Raiffa, *Games and Decisions* (New York, 1957). Discussions of the relevant economic techniques can be found in many standard economic texts. But for a consistently helpful introductory treatment consult Paul Samuelson, *Economics* (New York, any edition).

It is somewhat unusual for a political scientist to undertake a work of this kind. The great bulk of deductive work on bargaining has been done by economists or mathematicians interested in the theory of games. Consequently, the empirical illustrations and applications included in many analyses of bargaining are weighted heavily toward various phenomena arising in the field of economics, such as the establishment of the price level among oligopolists and the setting of the wage rate in labor-management negotiations. Nevertheless, bargaining is common in a great many sociopolitical relationships ranging from the interactions of the members of family units to the interactions of nation states. Under the circumstances, there is an important need for theoretical work on bargaining on the part of students of all the social sciences. It is my hope to encourage a greater exchange of ideas among scholars in the several social sciences concerned with the study of bargaining.

It is a pleasure to acknowledge a number of debts at this time. Above all, I am grateful to Princeton University and to the John Simon Guggenheim Memorial Foundation for allowing me to enjoy a sabbatical leave during the academic year 1969–1970. I spent a pleasant summer at the Center for Advanced Study in the Behavioral Sciences in 1969 during which I began to select materials for this book on a systematic basis. During the fall of 1969, I had the good fortune to be a research fellow at The London School of Economics and Political Science. I suspect my acquaintances at the LSE do not realize how helpful they were in stimulating my thinking on what undoubtedly seemed to them a rather abstruse enterprise. The International House of Japan was helpful to me in many ways during the spring of 1970. I am especially grateful to Yukio Fujino, librarian of the International House, for his willing assistance in helping me to locate materials. I am also happy to acknowledge my debt to The Australian National University and to Hedley Bull, head of the Department of International Relations at the ANU. As a visiting fellow at the ANU during June, 1970, I was able to continue my analysis of the bargaining problem in highly pleasant surroundings.

Finally, I wish to offer my thanks publicly to Norman Frohlich and Joe A. Oppenheimer, my collaborators in the pursuit of theory concerning political leadership and the supply of collective goods and my intellectual companions throughout the last several years. To them I owe a major debt for general intellectual stimulation as well as detailed criticisms of draft material for this book.

CONTENTS

INTRODUCTION

STRATEGIC INTERACTION AND BARGAINING

Oran R. Young

This is a book about bargaining in a wide variety of economic, political, and social situations. More specifically, it deals with the principal deductive models that have been constructed from time to time to explain the phenomenon of bargaining. As such, it constitutes an attempt both to evaluate the existing theories of bargaining and to assess the prospects for future research on this subject.

The proposition that bargaining is an important social phenomenon is extremely widespread in the literature of the social sciences. At the most general level, the concept of bargaining occupies an important place in the theory of games which is, in principle, applicable to a wide range of human interactions. And informal references to bargaining as a major feature of human exchange relationships can be found in discussions of topics ranging all the way from interactions among the members of family units to interactions among the actors in the international system.

The most extensive deductive analyses of bargaining have been carried out in the field of economics. In brief, bargaining may occur in economic exchange relationships whenever imperfect competition prevails. Consequently, bargaining constitutes an important aspect of such well-known subjects as bilateral monopoly and oligopoly. This means, for example, that bargaining will often be a major determinant of such matters as the wage rate in labor-management negotiations and the price level in oligopolistic markets. For a long time economists argued that while it was possible for economic analysis to place certain limits on the bargaining range,[1] the bargaining problem itself was either insoluble or properly a subject for sociologists or political scientists rather than economists.[2] More recently, however, a number of economists have taken up the challenge posed by the bargaining problem with the result that we now have a number of interesting economic models of bargaining.[3] For all practical purposes, this development in the field of economics can be dated from the pioneering work of Zeuthen and Hicks in the early 1930s.[4]

In other substantive fields, work on the development of deductive models of bargaining has lagged far behind this work in economics. Nevertheless, the bargaining problem has recently become a major focus of less formal analyses

---

[1] Well-developed ideas concerning the bargaining range go back at least to the latter part of the nineteenth century and the work of Edgeworth. For a straightforward discussion of the bargaining range in terms of the Edgeworth box diagram see James M. Buchanan and Gordon Tullock, *The Calculus of Consent* (Ann Arbor, 1962), pp. 97–105.

[2] This early conclusion among economists has been commented upon by a number of scholars. For a helpful summary of the relevant arguments see J. Pen, "A General Theory of Bargaining," reprinted herein.

[3] The most important of these models are included in Part Two of this book.

[4] See, in particular, Frederik Zeuthen, *Problems of Monopoly and Economic Warfare,* partially reprinted herein, and J. R. Hicks, *The Theory of Wages* (London, 1932).

in a number of other fields. This is particularly true of international relations, a field in which bargaining activities are of central importance,[5] and of political science, a field in which bargaining among organized political parties, among interest groups, and within bureaucracies constitutes a major focus of attention. In addition, there are other fields whose subject matter is, in principle, susceptible to analysis in terms of the concept of bargaining and whose practitioners are beginning to formulate some of their major research interests along these lines. This is especially true of sociology in which a variety of problems, from the interactions among the members of family units to the relations among different ethnic and class groupings, tend to involve extensive bargaining activities.

Thus, the concept of bargaining occupies an influential position throughout the social sciences. Unfortunately, however, the concept is beset by severe definitional difficulties. General definitions of bargaining tend to be imprecise, and there is no consensus among scholars on the fundamental content of the concept.[6] This has occasionally proved advantageous in the sense that it has facilitated the introduction of new and imaginative ideas in the study of bargaining. Nevertheless, it has also produced serious problems because it means that the concept of bargaining is a highly ambiguous one and that generalizations about bargaining are always difficult to evaluate.

Even more serious, the principal conceptions of bargaining tend to direct attention toward qualitatively different problems, and in some cases they actually conflict with each other. A few examples will serve to indicate the resultant difficulties. First, some conceptions of bargaining focus primarily on outcomes and lead to the formulation of static theories while others are more concerned with the processes through which outcomes are achieved by bargaining and lead to the development of dynamic theories.[7] Second, though some scholars define bargaining in such a way that it is relevant only in situations involving some element of conflict among the actors, others see nothing incompatible about the conjunction of bargaining and pure cooperation in-

---

[5] For a well-known effort by an economist to move in the direction of formal models in the analysis of international bargaining see Thomas C. Schelling, *The Strategy of Conflict* (Cambridge, 1960).

[6] A few examples should help to indicate the nature of these problems. Rapoport defines bargaining rather broadly as "Negotiation among partners or opponents in which no disinterested parties participate and no principles of equity are invoked"— Anatol Rapoport, *Strategy and Conscience* (New York, 1964), p. 308. Mitchell employs the language of economics in defining bargaining as "A means of exchange in which the terms of settlement are within the control of the partners to the exchange"—William C. Mitchell, *Public Choice in America* (Chicago, 1971), p. 383. And Cross tends to employ the terms "negotiation" and "bargaining" interchangeably although he goes on to say that "When a distinction does arise, the term 'bargaining' will refer to the process of demand formation and revision which provides the basic mechanism whereby the parties converge toward an agreement, while 'negotiation' will refer to the whole situation within which bargaining occurs"—John G. Cross, *The Economics of Bargaining* (New York, 1969), p. 7.

[7] The static models of bargaining included in the theory of games exemplify the focus on outcomes while the dynamic economic models of bargaining illustrate the emphasis on processes. For a detailed analysis of these models see Parts One and Two.

volving two or more purposive actors.[8] Third, although the classic conception of bargaining relates to competitive-cooperative or mixed motive interactions, some notions of bargaining permit the occurrence of bargaining activities in situations characterized by pure (or zero-sum) conflict as well.[9] Fourth, some analysts discuss bargaining in situations where the actors possess perfect or complete information along all dimensions while others regard imperfect information as a necessary condition for the occurrence of bargaining.[10] Fifth, conceptions of bargaining vary greatly in the extent to which they include possible changes in the basic parameters of bargaining situations within the bargaining problem itself. In some conceptions, for example, bargaining takes place only when the utility functions of the players as well as the alternatives available to each player are fixed and known[11] while in other conceptions efforts to manipulate these factors may play a central role in the bargaining process itself.[12]

Under the circumstances, it is not feasible to speak of *the* theory of bargaining. Accordingly, this book deals with the most important conceptions of bargaining as well as the major theories that have been constructed from time to time to explain the phenomenon of bargaining. There is, however, a crucial common theme that ties all these conceptions and theories of bargaining together. In every case, bargaining is conceptualized as a means (though not the only one) through which purposive actors can reach specific settlements or outcomes under conditions of strategic interaction or interdependent decision making. Bargaining can therefore be defined as a means by which two or more purposive actors arrive at specific outcomes in situations in which: (1) the choices of the actors will determine the allocation of some value(s), (2) the outcome for each participant is a function of the behavior of the other(s), and (3) the outcome is achieved through negotiations between or among the players.

A. STRATEGIC INTERACTION

It follows from this argument that strategic interaction is a central feature of all situations involving bargaining, no matter how the phenomenon of bargaining is conceptualized in detail. Strategic behavior is the behavior of

---

[8] The idea that bargaining ordinarily occurs in conjunction with conflict is widely held. But see Schelling, *Strategy of Conflict,* Chapter 4, for a discussion of activities that can be characterized as bargaining under conditions of pure cooperation.

[9] For an analysis of zero-sum interactions that appears to leave room for activities that can be regarded as bargaining see Daniel Ellsberg, "Theory of the Reluctant Duelist," reprinted herein.

[10] Game-theoretic analyses of bargaining games, for example, often include assumptions that have the effect of giving the players perfect information along all dimensions, though they generally do not involve explicit assumptions of perfect information. The manipulative conception of bargaining, on the other hand, establishes imperfect information as a necessary condition for bargaining. Compare the models set forth in Parts One and Four of this book on this point.

[11] These conditions constitute standard assumptions in game-theoretic models.

[12] Activities of this kind occupy an important position in the manipulative conception of bargaining. For specific illustrations see Part Four.

any individual member of a group[13] involving a choice of action contingent upon that individual's estimates of the actions (or choices) of others in the group, where the actions of each of the relevant others are based upon a similar estimate of the behavior of group members other than himself.[14] Thus, strategic behavior will occur whenever two or more individuals all find that the outcomes associated with their choices are partially controlled by each other.[15] Strategic *interaction,* then, is simply the set of behavior patterns manifested by individuals whose choices are interdependent in this fashion. In this context, note that the concept of individual choice or decision making is central to the meaning of strategic interaction. Hence, let us say that an individual makes a choice whenever he selects a specific alternative from some set of differentiated alternatives. The central roll of individual choice in strategic interaction undoubtedly accounts for the fact that situations involving interaction of this kind are often described in terms of the notion of interdependent decision making.[16]

This definition of strategic interaction subsumes as a special case situations in which only two individuals are involved.[17] That is, whenever one individual's choices are contingent upon his estimate of the actions (or choices) of only one other individual, who likewise finds his choices contingent upon an estimate of the first individual's choices, a special and limited form of strategic interaction occurs. The only difference between the general case of strategic interaction and the special, two-actor case is that in the latter each individual must estimate the behavior of a single specified individual while in the general case each individual must estimate (and ultimately aggregate) the behavior of a number of relevant others, all of whom find themselves in symmetrically interdependent positions with respect to their choices. In all situations involving strategic interaction, therefore, each individual's evaluation of his alternatives is a function of his assessment of the probable behavior of a subgroup excluding himself but including all the other members of the group. If the group contains only two members, the relevant subgroups will both be single-member subgroups. When the group contains more than two members, on the other hand, both the number and the size of the subgroups will increase proportionately. In both cases, however, all the members of the group will find themselves in interdependent situations with respect to the evaluation of their alternatives.

---

[13] For the sake of simplicity this discussion is couched in terms of individual human beings as actors. However, the basic argument is relevant to any decision-making unit, though the introduction of collective actors produces additional analytic complexities of an interesting nature.

[14] This definition is adapted from the discussion in Norman Frohlich, Joe A. Oppenheimer, and Oran R. Young, *Political Leadership and Collective Goods* (Princeton, 1971), pp. 122–123.

[15] This phraseology is employed by Rapoport, *Strategy and Conscience,* Chapter 4.

[16] Schelling, in particular, has employed this concept extensively in discussing strategic interaction. See Schelling, *The Strategy of Conflict,* Chapter 4.

[17] The argument of this paragraph is also discussed in Frohlich, Oppenheimer, and Young, *Political Leadership and Collective Goods,* Chapter 5.

Given the conceptual link between strategic interaction and bargaining, the first step in the analysis of bargaining is to identify the types of situation in which strategic interaction can be expected to occur. The remainder of this section deals with this problem under the assumption that individuals behave in a rational fashion.[18] In the course of the discussion, it should become clear that a number of important economic, political, and social phenomena will ordinarily be significantly affected by the presence of strategic interaction.

To facilitate this analysis let us define an individual's decision-making environment as all those factors extrinsic to the individual himself which affect his ability to make choices in such a way as to maximize his utility. Thus, any individual's decision-making environment may include other purposive actors as well as a variety of inanimate factors (that is, nature). An individual attempting to make a rational choice will have to take into account the effects of strategic interaction whenever his decision-making environment is not fixed or cannot be treated as if it were fixed due to the actions of others who are facing analogous decision-making problems. This is so because only those individuals who can treat their decision-making environment as fixed can safely assume that the choices of relevant others are not contingent upon their own behavior. Consequently, it is crucial to the present analysis of the occurrence of strategic interaction to identify those situations in which the individual can reasonably proceed on the assumption that his decision-making environment is fixed.

In dealing with this question, let us proceed from the distinction between private goods and collective goods.[19] In the case of private goods, there are two types of situation in which the individual can safely assume that his decision-making environment is fixed. First, individuals regularly make choices that are affected only by nature and that are in no way contingent upon the actions of other purposive or intelligent actors. The well-known problem of the man appraising the weather to decide whether or not to carry an umbrella to work exemplifies situations of this kind.[20] In the simplest cases, it is reason-

---

[18] Rational behavior involves the following conditions: (1) the individual evaluates alternatives in his environment on the basis of his preferences among them, (2) his preference ordering is consistent and transitive, and (3) he always chooses the preferred alternative.

All the essays in this book employ some assumption of rational choice even though they differ significantly with respect to both the formal requirements of rational choice and the problems of behaving rationally under conditions of strategic interaction. Note, however, that strategic interaction can occur even in the absence of rational behavior. In fact, the occurrence of strategic interaction is compatible with a variety of behavioral assumptions.

[19] A private good is any good that can be supplied through a market mechanism on an individualistic basis. A collective good, by contrast, is any good that cannot be withheld from any member of a specified group once it is supplied to some member of the group. Some writers also include the notion of "jointness of supply" (that is, the ability of a single production unit to support many consumption units) in the definition of the concept "collective good." The present discussion, however, is concerned with the consequences of nonexcludability rather than jointness of supply.

[20] For a specific example together with an illustrative payoff matrix see Rapoport, *Strategy and Conscience*, pp. 31–33.

able to regard nature as having a fixed value that never changes (for example, it is sunny every day all year round). In more complex cases, nature can be conceptualized in terms of a probability distribution (for example, on any given day there is a fixed probability of sunshine and rain). In all of these cases, however, there is no scope for strategic interaction since the individual's decision-making environment is fixed and the situation does not involve inter-actions between two or more purposive actors whose choices are reciprocally contingent.[21]

Second, in certain cases it is reasonable for the individual to proceed as if his decision-making environment were fixed even though it contains other purposive actors. In essence, this possibility arises from an application of the law of large numbers. Thus, such a procedure may be justified in situations where large numbers of individuals participate in a given activity in such a way that the impact of the actions of each individual is perceived as insigni-ficant in the absence of coordination and the scope for coordination among individuals is negligible. Perhaps the most prominent examples of the use of assumptions of this kind occur in the models of the behavior of consumers and entrepreneurs under conditions of perfect competition which form the core of classical economics. In any given market, it is assumed that the individual consumer faces a fixed price which he is powerless to alter because he is only a single individual among a large mass of undifferentiated consumers who have no ability to coordinate their actions. Consequently, the only course open to the individual consumer is to treat the market price as a given and to decide whether or not to purchase the good in question by examining his personal preference ordering and his resource endowment. The situation is much the same for individual entrepreneurs calculating whether they can make a profit in a given perfect-competition market. In effect, the price the entre-preneur can charge for the good in question is fixed by the operation of the market mechanism over which he is assumed to have no control. In con-templating the profitability of entering a given market, therefore, the only thing the entrepreneur can hope to manipulate is the cost side of his equation. In addition to these well-known models of economics, it is worth noting that several scholars have recently constructed models of voting in situations in-volving very large electorates which also make use of the law of large numbers to reduce the choice problem of the individual to one in which he can treat his decision-making environment as if it were fixed.[22] In essence, all the models referred to in this paragraph exclude strategic interaction and, therefore, bar-gaining because they do not allow for direct interactions among purposive individuals even though the aggregate behavior of the participants will deter-

---

[21] Note, however, that the individual will not necessarily possess perfect information about his decision-making environment just because it is fixed. The man appraising the weather, for example, may not know the probability of sunshine and of rain.

[22] The most important examples can be found in Anthony Downs, *An Economic Theory of Democracy* (New York, 1957), and Gordon Tullock, *Toward a Mathematics of Politics* (Ann Arbor, 1967). Unlike many of the models of classical economics, however, these voting models do not always assume that the individual voter possesses perfect information along all dimensions.

mine the market price and the effectiveness of casting a vote. In such models, therefore, each individual's choices reduce to "simple" maximizing problems unaffected by the phenomenon of strategic interaction.

In the case of collective goods, on the other hand, strategic interaction will always occur so long as individuals do not possess perfect information along all dimensions and coordination among individuals is not ruled out altogether by assumption. A formal demonstration of this proposition is set forth in *Political Leadership and Collective Goods.*[23] In essence, however, this conclusion stems from the collective nature of such goods, which insures that the amount of a given collective good received by any individual will be partially determined by the actions of others with respect to the supply of the good in question while the amount received by the others will, in turn, be a function of the actions of the first individual. And in the absence of perfect information, no participant will be able to make certain predictions or form confident expectations about the probable behavior of others in situations of this kind. Under the circumstances, the rational individual will find his choices contingent upon the choices of others which are, in turn, contingent upon his own choices, and the impact of strategic interaction will affect his decision-making problem.

Even in the field of economics in which models based on the assumption of a fixed decision-making environment have enjoyed considerable success, there are numerous substantive problems that cannot be treated adequately without coming to grips with the phenomenon of strategic interaction. Such prominent subjects as bilateral monopoly and oligopoly illustrate this point. Moreover, in the other social sciences, the range of problems that *can* be analyzed without taking strategic interaction into account is severely restricted. It may make sense, as mentioned previously, to ignore strategic interaction in certain voting situations where the electorate is very large and coordination among individual voters is very costly and/or not valued by anyone.[24] But numerous important phenomena, such as the interactions among the members of family units, among decision makers in bureaucracies, among interest groups and associations, among political parties, and among nation states will generally be significantly affected by strategic interaction. Consequently, it seems safe to conclude as an empirical generalization that strategic interaction is relevant to a very large class of important real-world phenomena.

B. THE PROBLEM OF STRATEGIC INTERACTION

Just as the concept of individual choice is central to the meaning of strategic interaction, the availability of information plays a crucial role in all situations

---

[23] Frohlich, Oppenheimer, and Young, *Political Leadership,* Chapter 5.

[24] The secret ballot, for example, has always been supported by those who believe that coordination among individual voters should be made impossible or extremely costly. But even when the secret ballot is employed, political parties and interest groups often play a highly influential role in coordinating the actions of individual voters in democratic elections.

involving choices among differentiated alternatives. This point is sometimes obscured by the widespread habit of assuming perfect information along all dimensions at the outset in constructing models of rational decision making.[25] This assumption cannot be allowed to pass unquestioned in the analysis of interdependent decision making, however, since the introduction of strategic interaction generates qualitatively new problems concerning information for the individual decision maker. In this connection, the present section elaborates on the argument that whereas the concept of information is reasonably straightforward in choice situations involving a decision-making environment that is fixed or that can be treated as if it were fixed, the concept itself becomes logically ambiguous under conditions of strategic interaction and, consequently, in the analysis of bargaining.

For purposes of this analysis let us define information as knowledge about all those factors (whether intrinsic to the individual decision maker or aspects of his decision-making environment) which affect the ability of an individual to make choices in any given situation in such a way as to maximize his utility.[26] Even when his decision-making environment is fixed so that strategic interaction does not occur, an individual needs information about several distinguishable factors in order to make choices in a rational fashion.[27] In the first instance, there is the problem of identifying the decision-making context, in the sense of specifying the range of distinct alternatives among which the individual can choose. In deductive models of decision making, this problem is ordinarily handled by assumption.[28] But in many real-world situations, it is a source of severe difficulties for the individual decision maker. Assuming that he can identify his decision-making context, the individual still requires information about several more specific factors. First, he must have complete knowledge of his own preference ordering or utility function. That is, the individual must be able to construct a confident ranking of the alternatives in his environment in terms of his preferences among them. So long as each of his alternatives represents a certain outcome, however, the individual need

---

[25] As a result, explicit analyses of the role of information in models of choice, especially in the field of economics, are few and far between. For some interesting exceptions, which at least raise the possibility of introducing imperfect information into various economic models, see Armen A. Alchian, "Uncertainty, Evolution, and Economic Theory," *Journal of Political Economy,* LVIII (1950), 211–221; Martin Shubik, "Information, Theories of Competition, and the Theory of Games," *Journal of Political Economy,* LX (1952), 145–150; and Martin Shubik, "Information, Risk, Ignorance, and Indeterminacy," *Quarterly Journal of Economics,* LXVIII (1954), 629–640.

[26] Consequently, information can be described with respect to a number of distinguishable dimensions. This point will be particularly important when we discuss the concept of perfect information.

[27] For a standard treatment of the issues under discussion in this paragraph consult L. J. Savage, *The Foundations of Statistics* (New York, 1954).

[28] That is, formal models of choice commonly begin by specifying a set range of alternatives for the individual decision maker on an *a priori* basis. Note that this procedure abstracts away all the problems associated with shifts in the range of available alternatives arising either from the removal of previously viable alternatives or the introduction of new alternatives.

only be able to specify his preference ordering in ordinal terms to choose among his alternatives in such a way as to maximize his utility.[29] Second, when the presence of risk makes it impossible to characterize the individual's alternatives in terms of certain outcomes, he requires information about the probabilities associated with the various outcomes in order to make rational choices. That is, he must be able to describe his decision-making environment in terms of fixed probabilities, if not certain outcomes. This requirement implies that the individual must act as if he:[30] (1) understands the nature of expected-utility calculations, (2) is able to specify his preference ordering in cardinal rather than ordinal terms,[31] and (3) accepts the implications of expected-utility calculations with respect to the phenomenon of risk.[32] Third, in cases where it is not possible to calculate probabilities in terms of mathematical ratios or numerical frequencies, the individual requires knowledge of some technique(s) for coming to grips with uncertainty in the technical sense.[33] Problems of this kind are particularly severe in dealing with phenomena that are intrinsically non-iterative because it is not very meaningful even to attempt to calculate probabilities in terms of empirical frequencies in such cases.[34]

Under the circumstances, it is apparent that the problems of information even in cases where it is reasonable to treat the decision-making environment as fixed will often be extensive.[35] But none of them is insurmountable, at least in logical terms.[36] The introduction of strategic interaction, however, compli-

[29] It should be emphasized that this conclusion also requires the assumptions that the preference ordering of the individual will be transitive and consistent over time.

[30] For a careful analysis of each of these points see Ward Edwards, "The Theory of Decision Making," *Psychological Bulletin*, LI (1954), 380–417.

[31] In a sense, the lottery system of calculating utilities under conditions of risk constitutes an alternative to the requirement that preference orderings be stated in cardinal terms. But it produces a number of analytic problems of its own. For a particularly straightforward discussion of these issues see Anatol Rapoport, *Two-Person Game Theory* (Ann Arbor, 1966), Chapter 2.

[32] Thus, most formulations of the concept of expected utility assume a neutral valuation of risk. For a helpful summary of the implications of this assumption see *ibid.*, pp. 32–39.

[33] The distinction between risk and uncertainty is due originally to Frank Knight. Under conditions of risk, the individual is able to identify the outcomes associated with each of his alternatives at least in terms of specific probability distributions. Under conditions of uncertainty, however, the individual lacks any clear-cut basis for the assignment of probability distributions of this kind. The introduction of uncertainty obviously produces severe analytic problems in the context of formal models of choice. For a useful survey of efforts to deal with the problem of uncertainty see R. Duncan Luce and Howard Raiffa, *Games and Decisions* (New York, 1957), Chapter 13.

[34] For a discussion that emphasizes this point see Rapoport, *Strategy and Conscience*, Chapter 3. And for a well-known attack on various economic models along these lines consult G. L. S. Shackle, *Expectation in Economics* (Cambridge, 1949). It is always possible to solve this problem by assuming that the individual employs "subjective probabilities." But this abstracts away the whole question of how the individual obtains specific values for subjective probabilities, especially with respect to occurrences that are non-iterative in some intrinsic sense.

[35] For an impressive catalog of these problems see Rapoport, *Strategy and Conscience*, Part II.

[36] In actual empirical situations, some of these problems may well prove practically insurmountable. But this does not alter the fact that they are logically surmountable.

cates this picture in a qualitative fashion because it means that the rational individual must take into account the probable choices of others, whose choices are in turn contingent upon his own, in making his choices. That is, the introduction of strategic interaction means that each individual is faced with the new problems of identifying the others upon whose choices his own choices are contingent and of acquiring information about the probable behavior of these individuals.

Ideally, any individual who discovers that his choices are interdependent with those of one or more other individuals would desire to acquire enough information about the relevant other(s) to be able to make accurate predictions of their choices or at least to form confident expectations concerning their probable behavior. If this were possible, the individual's choice problem would become strictly analogous to a game against nature. That is, the complications associated with strategic interaction would disappear since the choices of the relevant other(s) would no longer be contingent, strictly speaking, upon the choices of the first individual so that he would be able to treat his decision-making environment as if it were fixed. Logically, however, this result can only be achieved through the introduction of restrictive assumptions that eliminate the impact of strategic interaction since the concept of strategic interaction means (by definition) that the choices of the relevant other(s) will be contingent upon the choices of the first individual. Consequently, it seems clear that the introduction of strategic interaction produces problems that are qualiatively different from those included in the traditional model of rational choice.[37]

What information about the relevant other(s) would help the individual to make predictions or form expectations about their probable behavior, thereby eliminating the impact of strategic interaction? Assuming that the identity of the other individual was known and that it was reasonable to rely on the rationality of the other, the first individual would still have a need for information about the following factors. First, he would need to know the range of alternatives available to the other. Second, he would require knowledge of the other's preference ordering or utility function. Third, he would need information about any probability distributions affecting the other individual's choices and attributable to nature rather than to the presence of strategic interaction. Fourth, he would require information about the other's reactions to and techniques for coping with strategic interaction itself since the other individual would be facing the same problems of prediction as the first individual.

Each of these requirements is likely to pose severe problems in specific decision-making situations.[38] Even if we assume that the rational individual is

---

[37] This is evidently the source of the professed rejection of rational choice models by some scholars, such as Jan Pen, who have tried to deal with the bargaining problem. For the details of his somewhat ambivalent attitude toward the concept of rationality see Pen, "A General Theory of Bargaining," reprinted herein.

[38] In some real-world situations, the individual would consider himself fortunate to be able to identify the relevant others precisely, let alone to be able to specify their alter-

somehow able to acquire complete knowledge about the first three of these factors, however, he still faces a genuine dilemma. The crucial problem is, of course, that the second individual's efforts to cope with strategic interaction will be contingent upon the behavior of the first individual which will, in turn, be contingent upon the behavior of the second individual. Consequently, given the general model of rational choice under discussion here, two individuals engaged in strategic interaction will become involved in an "outguessing" regress[39] that can never produce accurate predictions or confident expectations concerning the choices of either party so long as the relationship continues to be characterized by the presence of strategic interaction. In fact, if one or both of the participants did achieve accurate predictions or confident expectations of the choices of the other, the situation would (*ipso facto*) cease to be characterized by the presence of strategic interaction.[40]

The concept "perfect information" is widely employed in models of rational decision making. This concept stems directly from the models of classical economics in which it generally figures prominently as an explicit assumption. And some such assumption is at least implicit in most formal models of choice (including the models of game theory). In the context of situations involving fixed decision-making environments and, therefore, no strategic interaction, the meaning of perfect information is relatively straightforward. It refers to situations in which the decision maker has complete knowledge of the alternatives available to him, his own preference ordering or utility function, and the probability distributions associated with any of his alternatives affected by risk.[41] In such situations, the choice problem of the individual reduces to a matter of straightforward calculation and the problems of strategic interaction and bargaining never arise. If risk is not a factor, the individual simply selects his most preferred alternative. And even under conditions of risk, determinate solutions are not difficult to derive so long as the individual understands and accepts the procedures involved in expected-utility calculations.

With the introduction of strategic interaction, however, the concept of perfect information immediately becomes highly ambiguous. In fact, it is even difficult to discuss the concepts of strategic interaction and perfect information together. The problem is that strategic interaction and perfect information are fundamentally and irrevocably incompatible. Perfect in-

---

natives and utility functions in detail. Problems of this kind are particularly likely to prove troublesome when strategic interaction occurs among large groups of individuals.

[39] That is, a relationship that produces sequences in the form of he thinks, I think, he thinks, I think, and so forth.

[40] Interestingly, if one of the individuals is identifiably irrational, there is at least a *chance* that an "outguessing" regress will not occur. Thus, the irrational individual may ignore the fact that his choices are contingent upon the choices of the other individual or respond to the presence of strategic interaction in a highly stylized fashion, thereby allowing the rational individual to make accurate predictions or form confident expectations about his behavior.

[41] Note again that an individual employs information along several distinguishable dimensions in his decision-making processes. Perfect information is defined here, therefore, as complete knowledge along all relevant dimensions.

formation requires either that the individual's decision-making environment be fixed (at least in terms of probability distributions) or that he be able to make accurate predictions or develop confident expectations concerning the probable behavior of any other purposive actor(s) whose choices affect his own choice problem.[42] But this is precisely what the presence of strategic interaction precludes. Strategic interaction means (by definition) that the choices of two or more individuals are reciprocally contingent and it leads inevitably to an "outguessing" regress. As a result, any individual engaged in a situation involving strategic interaction will find it impossible to make accurate predictions concerning the probable behavior of the relevant other(s). Thus, strategic interaction always produces an irreducible gap in the information of the individuals involved, a fact that accounts for the occurrence of uncertainty in the technical sense in any situation affected by strategic interaction.[43] Consequently, it is impossible to construct models of choice which assume the presence of strategic interaction and perfect information at the same time.[44]

C. RESOLVING THE PROBLEM

Though the presence of strategic interaction poses a logical dilemma, it does not necessarily produce an insurmountable practical problem. Despite

---

[42] There is an alternative definition of perfect information employed by some game theorists. Rapoport, for example, has defined perfect information as follows: "If the player is always in a position to know the actual choices made by all the players who have already moved, then the game is called a *game of perfect information.*" Anatol Rapoport, *N-Person Game Theory* (Ann Arbor, 1970), p 54 (emphasis in original). Note that this definition differs significantly from the definition of perfect information employed in this book since it is not sufficient to allow the rational individual to make accurate predictions of the future choices of the relevant other(s) in situations initially characterized by strategic interaction.

[43] That is, there is no clear-cut way of assigning probabilities to the choices of the relevant other(s) so long as strategic interaction is present. It is worth emphasizing, however, that various levels or degrees of information short of perfect information are compatible with the presence of strategic interaction. At one extreme, it is possible to assume that the individual possesses complete knowledge of the relevant other's available alternatives, utility function, and probability distributions attributable to natural factors so that he lacks complete knowledge only about the other's behavior with respect to the phenomenon of strategic interaction *per se*. Some such position is often adopted in studies of interdependent decision making, including many analyses of bargaining. At the other extreme, it is possible to imagine situations involving strategic interaction in which the individual has trouble even identifying the relevant other, let alone specifying his range of alternatives, utility function, and so forth. And it is evident that various intermediate situations may occur. Under the circumstances, the level of information available to individuals engaged in interdependent decision making has the effect of determining the range of factors that may become involved in "outguessing" activities and that may be subject to deliberate manipulation on the part of the participants. As will become clear in later parts of this book, variations along these lines are responsible for some of the important differences among existing analyses of bargaining.

[44] Note, however, that it is perfectly possible to have imperfect information without strategic interaction. In fact, decision-making situations of this type occur regularly. And when the problem of imperfect information has been discussed by economists, it has usually been in the context of choice problems unaffected by strategic interaction.

the fact that there is no logical solution to the regress generated by strategic interaction,[45] there is no reason to conclude that individuals will be incapable of making choices under conditions of strategic interaction. There is no empirical evidence to suggest that individuals are typically paralyzed or incapacitated with respect to their choice problems in situations initially characterized by the presence of strategic interaction. And whenever an individual actually makes a choice in a situation of this kind, he automatically eliminates the strategic aspect of the situation in the process.

Under the circumstances, two closely related questions arise. The basic question is how do individuals actually solve the problem of strategic interaction in various real-world situations? And related to this is the question of what sorts of models can be constructed to explain or predict these procedures and their results? That is, how can the outside observer theorize successfully about human behavior in response to the phenomenon of strategic interaction? There are in fact several distinguishable ways in which individuals can handle the problem of strategic interaction in specific situations. And not all of them produce activities that can be meaningfully described in terms of the concept of bargaining. This is why strategic interaction is not a sufficient condition (though it is a necessary condition) for the occurrence of bargaining. Consequently, a brief description of the principal methods of handling the problem of strategic interaction will serve to place the bargaining problem in perspective and to set the stage for the more detailed analyses of the several existing conceptions of bargaining to be undertaken in later parts of this book.

First, the individual faced with a situation that actually involves strategic interaction may simply ignore this aspect of his choice problem. That is, he can respond to such a situation as if his decision-making environment were fixed, assigning specific values or expected values to the alternatives he faces without reference to the impact of other purposive actors on his choice problem.[46] Under these conditions, the individual treats his decision-making problem as if it were a game against nature, and no activities that can be described in terms of the concept of bargaining arise. Note, however, that the use of this procedure is likely to yield poor results for the individual unless the impact of strategic interaction on his choice problem is negligible. Hence, it seems reasonable to conclude that this procedure for solving the problem of strategic interaction will not be employed extensively except in cases where the impact of strategic interaction is slight.

Second, strategic interaction does not arise when the participants move (that is, make their choices) sequentially rather than simultaneously or independently and their relationship is restricted to a one-move (or once-and-

---

[45] That is, in the absence of additional assumptions of a restrictive nature, the regress becomes infinite and no outcome can occur.

[46] That is, he can simply employ some autonomous procedure to assign certain values to the probabilities associated with the outcomes involved in his alternatives as well as the worth to him of each outcome if it is realized.

for-all) interaction.[47] To see this consider a two-person interaction (between players A and B) in which A is to move first and B is to respond. Here B can safely treat his decision-making environment as fixed since he does not have to regard A's choice as contingent upon his own choice and he need not worry about future moves on A's part. Accordingly, B simply chooses in such a way as to maximize his utility, taking into account A's actual choice. By the same token, A is now able to predict with confidence B's response to any given choice on his (A's) part. Therefore, A will choose among his own alternatives in such a way as to maximize his utility, taking into account his ability to predict B's response. Situations of this kind are analogous to the minorant or majorant game in game theory,[48] and they do not produce either an "out-guessing" problem in the calculations of the individual participants or any incentives for the players to engage in negotiations. For this reason, such sequential-move situations do not lead to any activities that can be thought of as bargaining.

Third, the individual may deal with strategic interaction by making sub-jective estimates of the probable choices of the relevant other(s). Assuming that the individual succeeds in establishing such estimates, the consequences are straightforward. His decision-making environment becomes fixed, strategic interaction vanishes, and there is no need for anything resembling bargaining. The use of this procedure to solve the problem of strategic interaction is un-doubtedly common in real-world situations, especially when negotiation is regarded as a costly activity and when the individual must interact simul-taneously[49] with a large number of others. Nevertheless, the formulation of subjective estimates in such situations raises serious problems. Although there are numerous rules of thumb that can be employed in the process of making these estimates,[50] the results will always be highly subjective since they will inevitably be based on guesses concerning the probable choices of others whose choices will, in turn, be based on guesses about the probable choices of the first individual. Consequently, the formation of subjective estimates may involve a certain amount of silent "outguessing," even though this procedure does not produce any activities that can be labeled "bargaining."[51]

Fourth, the participants in a situation involving strategic interaction may negotiate a settlement between or among themselves. This procedure gives rise

[47] In principle, strategic interaction can be avoided so long as the sequence of moves is finite. This is so because any finite sequence can be normalized into a "one-shot" sequence in which one of the players is to move first and the other is to respond.

[48] For a discussion of the minorant and majorant game which is helpful in this context, see Ellsberg, "Theory of the Reluctant Duelist," reprinted herein.

[49] For a discussion that emphasizes the costs of negotiation consult Gordon Tullock, *Private Wants, Public Means* (New York, 1970), pp. 55–70.

[50] For some general comments on rules of thumb which are suggestive in this con-nection, see Alchian, "Uncertainty, Evolution, and Economic Theory."

[51] That is, individuals may attempt to outguess the relevant others in forming sub-jective estimates of their probable choices, though they do not engage in any negotiations (or communicate in any way) with the relevant others. For a helpful discussion of this possibility see Schelling, *Strategy of Conflict*, pp. 54–67.

to the classic case of bargaining. It is possible to analyze interactions of this type by introducing assumptions that either specify how the individual participants will behave in the resultant negotiations or lay down detailed criteria that an outcome or settlement must fulfill. Two sets of models that are of great importance in the analysis of bargaining have been constructed along these lines. In the first instance, some scholars have introduced criteria that permit the prediction of determinate outcomes.for such interactions on the assumption that the participants behave *as if* they accepted these criteria. This practice has led to the static models of bargaining associated with the theory of games, which focus on the distribution of rewards or payoffs among the players. At the same time, other scholars have emphasized the use of assumptions that have the effect of allowing each participant to form confident expectations about the behavior of the relevant other(s) at any given moment in time but that also permit the adjustment or correction of these expectations over time through the working of some well-defined adaptation mechanism. This procedure has led to the construction of several dynamic models of bargaining in the field of economics, which tend to concentrate on the interaction processes leading toward a settlement. There is no doubt that these two sets of models constitute the mainstream in the development of deductive theories of bargaining. Accordingly, subsequent parts of this book will deal with these models in considerable detail.[52]

Fifth, the individual may react to the uncertainties associated with strategic interaction by attempting to manipulate his decision-making environment. That is, one way to make the choices of the relevant other(s) more predictable is to gain as much influence or leverage over their behavior as possible. And if an individual is able to gain complete control over the behavior of the relevant other(s), he can predict their behavior accurately so that the problem of strategic interaction disappears as far as he is concerned. The principal method of gaining control over the behavior of others under conditions of strategic interaction is to manipulate the information they utilize in their decision-making processes. There are many distinguishable tactics that may be employed to achieve this objective in specific situations, though the effectiveness of any given tactic will be influenced by the fact that the relevant other(s) may well be attempting to manipulate the information of the first individual at the same time. Models arising from this approach to the problem of strategic interaction also occupy an important position in the analysis of bargaining; they focus on the manipulative activities that are often associated with bargaining in informal discussions. Therefore, these models will also be discussed in some detail in a subsequent part of this book.[53]

Sixth, the problem of strategic interaction can always be resolved by transforming a given relationship qualitatively. Thus, some outside actor or

---

[52] The game-theoretic models are dealt with in Part One and the economic models in Part Two.

[53] See Part Four.

third party can intervene in such a way as to impose a settlement of the issues at stake on the original participants. In such cases, the settlement flows from the intervention of the outside party who imposes his will on the participants rather than from the activities of the participants themselves. In real-world situations, transformation of this type occurs frequently when a government intervenes to impose a settlement on the parties to a dispute. Similarly, judicial procedures accompanied by prior agreement to accept the results or by effective enforcement mechanisms can be interpreted in much the same light. In all these cases, the problem of strategic interaction is overcome through a qualitative transformation of the initial situation which has the effect of eliminating the impact of strategic interaction so far as the original participants are concerned. When it is successful, this procedure for handling the problem constitutes an alternative to bargaining since the concept of bargaining ordinarily refers to the settlement of situations involving strategic interaction through the activities of the original participants themselves. It is worth noting, however, that situations characterized by interdependent decision making can be *partially* transformed in the sense that the procedures referred to in this paragraph are employed with some effect but without producing a determinate settlement for the issues at stake. In such cases, bargaining may occur together with the use of such transforming procedures, and the two techniques for handling the problem of strategic interaction may interact with each other in interesting ways.[54] This often occurs, for example, when an outside mediator who lacks the power of compulsory arbitration attempts to facilitate the settlement of a given dispute.[55]

Finally, it is worth mentioning two other courses of action that often occur in the context of efforts to handle the problem of strategic interaction, though they do not produce resolutions of the problem in themselves. In the first instance, an individual engaged in strategic interaction may expend some of his resources on the acquisition of additional information about the relevant other(s).[56] This procedure may well prove helpful in the formulation of subjective estimates or in the selection of bargaining tactics for specific negotiations. But it cannot resolve the problem of strategic interaction in itself since the choices of the relevant other(s) will remain reciprocally contingent with those of the first individual no matter how much he spends on research concerning their probable behavior. Beyond this, individuals who find themselves strategically interrelated may collude, particularly when it is possible for them all to satisfy their own aspirations at the expense of some outside actor or

---

[54] For a useful discussion of one specific set of possibilities along this line (under the somewhat misleading heading of "arbitration") consult Cross, *Economics of Bargaining,* Chapter 5.

[55] For an analysis of various roles for third parties in facilitating the termination of disputes which adopts this perspective see Oran R. Young, *The Intermediaries* (Princeton, 1967).

[56] For general discussions of investing in information, which do not deal explicitly with the problem of strategic interaction, see Downs, *An Economic Theory of Democracy,* and Tullock, *Toward a Mathematics of Politics.*

third party.[57] This undoubtedly occurs in many real-world situations. But such collusion cannot in itself resolve, the problem of strategic interaction among the original participants because at some point they will still face the problem of dividing the spoils among themselves. Thus, initial collusion will always generate another strategic-interaction problem that must be handled through some procedure such as negotiation among the participants.

[57] In this connection, collusion refers to efforts on the part of the participants to increase the size of the prize as an alternative to focusing on the division of the original prize.

PART ONE
Game-Theoretic Models of Bargaining

INTRODUCTION

Recognizing the limitations of the perfect-competition assumption of classical economics, a number of scholars have sought in recent decades to construct models of rational choice which affirm, at least at the outset, the importance of strategic interaction. Perhaps the most well-known approach to rational choice under conditions of strategic interaction is the theory of games.[1] Inasmuch as all the models of game theory deal with situations involving interdependent decision making, it would be plausible to adopt the view that all of game theory has some bearing on the analysis of bargaining. But this is not the position generally adopted by the game theorists themselves. As this introductory essay seeks to demonstrate in some detail, most game theorists regard the bargaining problem as a special case of interdependent decision making, with the result that the concept of bargaining is relevant only to a subset of the whole collection of game-theoretic models.

All the models of game theory share a number of important features. Though game theory affirms the importance of strategic interaction at the outset, *all* formal models of this type include a series of assumptions that operate to circumscribe the scope for strategic interaction. Specifically, all game-theoretic models incorporate at least the following assumptions.[2] First, both the number of players and their identity are assumed to be fixed and known to everyone. Second, all the players are assumed to be fully rational, and each player knows that the others are rational.[3] Third, the payoff function of each player is assumed to be fixed and known at the outset. This assumption subsumes several subsidiary points. Each player's range of alternatives (or strategies) is fixed and known by assumption. The utility function of each player is fixed and known. And under conditions of risk arising from natural (that is, inanimate) sources, the results of each player's expected-utility calculations are fixed and known. It is this complex of assumptions which makes it possible to specify the characteristic payoff matrixes of game-theoretic models. Fourth, the formal models of game theory restrict the role of communication among the players in a highly stylized fashion. In particular, communication can never affect either the form or the content of a game's payoff matrix once it is initially established.

These assumptions are extremely powerful ones in the sense that they

---

[1] The classic work on the theory of games is John von Neumann and Oskar Morgenstern, *Theory of Games and Economic Behavior* (Princeton, 1944, 1947). The best general survey of game theory, written in straightforward language, is still R. Duncan Luce and Howard Raiffa, *Games and Decisions* (New York, 1957).

[2] For a more detailed discussion of these assumptions see Luce and Raiffa, *Games and Decisions*, Chapter 3.

[3] The term "rationality" is employed here as a formal concept. In addition to a general interest in matching means and ends purposely, it implies that: (1) the individual evaluates alternatives in his environment on the basis of his preferences among them, (2) his preference ordering is consistent and transitive, and (3) he always chooses the preferred alternative.

reduce the scope for strategic interaction drastically and that they abstract away a number of problems that many students of decision making regard as highly important in a wide variety of real-world situations.[4] Nevertheless, they are not sufficient to yield a general model of interdependent decision making capable of producing determinate solutions. This is the case because they do not rule out altogether the impact of strategic interaction. That is, even after the introduction of these assumptions, the players may still find themselves engaged in an "outguessing" regress with respect to the strategic or interdependent aspect of their relationship.

Consequently, though game theory rests upon an explicit affirmation of the importance of strategic interaction or interdependent decision making, it cannot generate determinate solutions for choice problems of this kind so long as there is any remaining scope for strategic interaction. To date, game theorists have responded to this difficulty in two distinct ways. Some analysts have chosen to turn aside from the search for determinate solutions, at least temporarily, and to direct their attention either toward reconceptualization or toward the production of empirical generalizations that can be employed as premises in models of interdependent decision making. Thus, they have avoided introducing at the outset additional restrictive assumptions capable of eliminating strategic interaction once and for all. In very different ways, this approach to the problem is exemplified in the work of Schelling[5] and Rapoport.[6] Other analysts, however, have continued to emphasize the early achievement of determinate solutions as their primary goal. Accordingly, they have introduced various devices designed to absorb the remaining vestiges of strategic interaction in the basic assumptions of their models. For the most part, these devices involve either the suppression of strategic interaction by means of assumptions that permit each player to make fully accurate predictions of the (probable) choices of the others[7] or the avoidance of strategic

---

[4] For a work that employs the language of game theory but that ultimately amounts to a powerful argument in favor of this proposition, see Thomas C. Schelling, *The Strategy of Conflict* (Cambridge, 1960).

[5] Schelling's work amounts in essence to an imaginative set of efforts to reconceptualize the theory of games. In this connection, see especially *ibid.*

[6] Although Rapoport has often discussed the formal models of game theory, his most distinctive contribution lies in his systematic inductive work on various gamelike situations. Among his many publications in this field, see especially Anatol Rapoport and Albert Chammah, *Prisoner's Dilemma* (Ann Arbor, 1965). And for an explicit statement by Rapoport concerning the importance of introducing empirical premises, see Anatol Rapoport, *Two-Person Game Theory* (Ann Arbor, 1966), Chapter 10.

[7] The effect of these assumptions is to give the players perfect or complete information along all dimensions, even though perfect information frequently is not introduced as an explicit assumption. Considering the crucial importance of these assumptions in eliminating strategic interaction, it is interesting to note how casually many game theorists have treated the question of perfect information in their work. Nash, for example, refers only in passing to his "assumption of complete information," which makes such things as "bargaining ability" and "the usual haggling process" irrelevant (John F. Nash, "Two-Person Cooperative Games," p. 138, reprinted herein). Similarly, see also John A. Harsanyi, "Approaches to the Bargaining Problem before and after the Theory of Games," p. 157n, reprinted herein.

interaction by means of assumptions that specify conditions that a solution must meet.[8]

The resultant search for determinate solutions within the framework of game theory has not led to a general model governing rational choice in interdependent situations. Instead, it has produced a number of special models applicable to specific types of interdependent decision making. The purest and most well-known game-theoretic solutions are those associated with the von Neumann-Morgenstern analysis of two-person, zero-sum interactions.[9] By definition, situations of this kind involve pure conflict so that each player's choices are affected only by the actions of the other player who is perfectly malevolent as far as he is concerned. The von Neumann-Morgenstern solution for such games arises from the proposition that when these new factors are combined with the basic assumptions of all game theory, it turns out that the individual player in a two-person, zero-sum game can maximize his own payoff without becoming engaged in an "outguessing" regress with the other player. This proposition follows, according to the analysis of von Neumann and Morgenstern, because the rational individual must assume that his opponent will "do his worst," whatever strategy he himself selects. Thus, each player can maximize his payoffs by choosing that strategy which contains the best of the worst payoffs for himself.[10] When the payoff matrix of the game exhibits a saddlepoint, the rational individual can achieve this result by selecting a pure strategy based on the maximin (or minimax) principle. When the payoff matrix does not exhibit a saddlepoint, on the other hand, he can still maximize his payoff by selecting an appropriate mixed strategy, making sure to randomize his choice in specific plays of the game.[11]

The key point in this analysis is the proposition that the rational player in a two-person, zero-sum game can predict the (probable) choices of his opponent accurately so that his choice problem becomes fundamentally analogous to a game against nature in which there is no strategic interaction.[12] Note, however, that the use of the maximin principle will not allow the ra-

---

[8] By specifying required characteristics of a solution it is possible to reach determinate conclusions concerning the distribution of payoffs between or among the players. To treat these conclusions as positive predictions it is necessary to assume that the players behave *as if* they take these characteristics into account in their decision making.

[9] A constant-sum game is one in which the sum of the payoffs to the players remains constant over all possible outcomes of the game. Two-person, zero-sum games are a subset of constant-sum games in which there are only two players and the sum of the payoffs is always zero. For the basic presentation of the von Neumann-Morgenstern analysis of these games see von Neumann and Morgenstern, *Theory of Games and Economic Behavior.*

[10] The resultant outcome is commonly referred to as the player's security level since it represents the best outcome he can guarantee for himself no matter how his opponent behaves.

[11] For a particularly straightforward explanation of these rules see Anatol Rapoport, *Strategy and Conscience* (New York, 1964), Chapter 5. For a fuller treatment consult Luce and Raiffa, *Games and Decisions,* Chapter 4.

[12] There is no remaining scope for strategic interaction because the choices of each player's opponent are no longer strictly contingent upon his own choices.

tional individual to maximize his payoff in such games unless all the basic assumptions of game theory hold. If any of the utility values are unknown or the opponent fails to behave in a fully rational fashion, for example, an individual who employs this principle will not necessarily maximize his payoff. Similarly, if the interaction is not actually zero-sum in nature, the use of zero-sum rules to guide decision making can lead to bizarre results, as Rapoport has demonstrated in the case of the prisoner's dilemma.[13]

Although the von Neumann-Morgenstern solution for two-person, zero-sum games is clearly elegant, its logical status has been challenged on a number of grounds.[14] Perhaps the most persuasive of these challenges is the one set forth by Ellsberg. In brief, Ellsberg argues that the von Neumann-Morgenstern solution is actually built up from an analysis of the best strategies for the players in the minorant and majorant games, which involve decision making under conditions of certainty.[15] That is, having ascertained the optimal choice for each player under the assumption that he is required to move first, von Neumann and Morgenstern simply transfer the resultant choices to the game in normal form involving simultaneous choices. But this raises a problem since, as Ellsberg argues, in the normalized game "The fact that one's choice is hidden from the opponent means that the opponent's choice, and hence the outcome of one's strategy, is uncertain."[16] Consequently, "It can not simply be taken for granted (in fact, it does not seem to be true) that what is uniquely reasonable in the minorant or majorant games will still be uniquely reasonable in the normalized game."[17] Ellsberg therefore concludes that even though a player has a unique and logically obvious choice in a two-person, zero-sum interaction in which he is required to move first, there is no conclusive reason why the rational individual must accept this choice as the best strategy when the game is played on a normalized or simultaneous-move basis.

Under the circumstances, Ellsberg argues that the logical status of the von Neumann-Morgenstern solution can only be saved by introducing an additional assumption to the effect that the players participate in the normalized

---

[13] Rapoport has emphasized this point tirelessly in recent years. For a particularly clear and succinct statement of his findings, however, see Rapoport, *Strategy and Conscience*, Chapter 6.

[14] See, for example, Hans Neisser, "The Strategy of Expecting the Worst," *Social Research*, XIX (1952), 346–362; Karl Kaysen, "The Minimax Rule of the Theory of Games and the Choices of Strategy under Conditions of Uncertainty," *Metroeconomica* (April, 1952), 5–14; and Daniel Ellsberg, "Theory of the Reluctant Duelist," reprinted herein. For a defense of the von Neumann-Morgenstern solution against these challenges, consult Anthony Y. C. Koo, "Recurrent Objections to the Minimax Strategy," *The Review of Economics and Statistics*, XLI (1959), 36–41.

[15] A game in normal form is one in which the strategies of the players can be represented in a single matrix and in which the players make their choices simultaneously (or at least in ignorance of each other's choice). The minorant and majorant games are similar to games in normal form except that one or the other of the players must make and indicate his choice first.

[16] Ellsberg, "The Reluctant Duelist," p. 914, reprinted herein.

[17] *Ibid.*

game *as if* it were a minorant or majorant game. The price of introducing this assumption, however, is substantial since it implies, as Ellsberg points out, that the players behave on the basis of a kind of "cautious pessimism."[18] And this restriction is neither a realistic description of the way individuals actually behave in many real-world situations nor a prescription that would meet with general acceptance. Alternatively, it would be possible to avoid this assumption, embark on a search for alternatives to the von Neumann-Morgenstern solution, and reopen the problem of strategic interaction in two-person, zero-sum games. Such a course would make it possible to introduce into such situations a number of dynamic activities commonly associated with the concept of bargaining, but it would also produce a need for fundamental alterations in the existing models of game theory.

Two-person, zero-sum games are particularly attractive in analytic terms since they are defined in such a way as to facilitate the efforts of the rational individual to predict the (probable) choices of the other player. That is, the remaining vestiges of strategic interaction are excluded through the introduction of several relatively straightforward assumptions in such cases: that there are only two players, that the situation constitutes a zero-sum relationship, and (if one accepts Ellsberg's argument) that the players behave as if they were engaged in a minorant or majorant game. The achievement of determinate solutions is not so easy, however, in two-person, nonzero-sum interactions.[19] Faced with a nonzero-sum relationship, the rational individual will still have to come to grips with the impact of strategic interaction since his choices and those of the other player will remain reciprocally contingent. Consequently, to eliminate strategic interaction from nonzero-sum situations it is necessary to introduce some new set of restrictive assumptions.[20] At this point, game theory divides into a number of separate domains distinguished by the specific assumptions they employ to suppress or circumvent the problem of strategic interaction.[21] Nevertheless, these domains can be grouped into several major categories, and this is of considerable importance in identifying the game-theoretic conception of bargaining, since game theorists ordinarily apply the term "bargaining" to only one of these categories.   ·

First, some game theorists (notably Harsanyi) have sought to achieve determinate solutions for nonzero-sum games by introducing the notion that each player may be able to assign "subjective probabilities" to the choices of the other participant.[22] That is, it is possible to suppose that each individual

---

[18] On "cautious pessimism" see *ibid.,* p. 921. Note also Ellsberg's argument on p. 915.

[19] Strictly speaking, a nonzero-sum game is any game in which the payoffs to the players do not always sum to zero. In common usage, however, the term "nonzero-sum game" is employed to refer to all nonconstant-sum games.

[20] For a related discussion of the game-theoretic approach to nonzero-sum games, see Alan Coddington, *Theories of the Bargaining Process* (London, 1968), Chapter 5.

[21] For an excellent survey that covers most of the resultant models, consult Luce and Raiffa, *Games and Decisions,* Chapters 5–7.

[22] See, for example, John C. Harsanyi, "A General Theory of Rational Behavior in Game Situations," *Econometrica,* XXXIV (1966), 613–634. Note that this usage of the term "subjective probabilities" differs somewhat from another (and more common) usage

proceeds in some subjective fashion to estimate the probable choices of the other player. Assuming that the individual succeeds in attaching a specific set of probabilities to the choices of the other, the consequences are clear. In essence, the individual acquires perfect information in the process[23] so that his choice problem reduces to a situation that is fundamentally analogous to a game against nature. This is so because he is no longer actually interacting with another purposive individual whose choices are mutually contingent with his own.[24] Accordingly, strategic interaction vanishes and determinate solutions become a matter of straightforward calculation.

This procedure, however, is difficult to combine with the basic perspective of game theory. The central problem is to formulate some decision rule that will allow the individual to assign subjective probabilities to the choices of the other players in a rational fashion. Harsanyi and others have attempted to deal with this problem by introducing the notion of "symmetrical rationality." This notion suggests that the rational individual should assign probabilities to the choices of the other player by placing himself in the position of the other player on the grounds that it must be assumed that all rational individuals will do the same thing under the same circumstances.[25] Unfortunately, however, this proposal only begs the dilemma associated with the presence of strategic interaction. Thus, no rational individual can arrive at definitive decisions concerning his own choices or the choices he would make if he were in the position of the other player whenever strategic interaction is present because of the impact of the "outguessing" regress. Consequently, the individual engaged in a nonzero-sum interaction cannot get anywhere in assigning probabilities to the choices of the other player by attempting to place himself in the other player's position.[26]

This means that the achievement of determinate solutions for two-person, nonzero-sum games through the estimation of subjective probabilities requires the introduction of an assumption to the effect that the individual employs some specified rules of thumb in assigning probabilities to the choices

---

of the term in which subjective probabilities are the probabilities that individuals assign to their own outcomes under conditions of risk when it is difficult or impossible to calculate objective probabilities in terms of ratios or empirical frequencies. For a clear discussion of this latter usage of the term, see Ward Edwards, "The Theory of Decision Making," *Psychological Bulletin*, LI (1954), 388–417.

[23] That is, he now possesses certain values for all the terms in his decision-making equation. In the present context, it might be argued that the individual has not actually acquired perfect information in some deeper sense and that the subjective probabilities he employs are little more than a means of covering up his ignorance. This raises a number of interesting questions, but it does not alter the conclusion stated in the text.

[24] Once the individual acquires specific estimates of the probabilities of the other's choices, he no longer has to concern himself with the *actual* calculations of the other player.

[25] On this point see John C. Harsanyi, "On the Rationality Postulates Underlying the Theory of Cooperative Games," *Journal of Conflict Resolution*, V (1961), 179–196.

[26] For another discussion of this point see Rapoport, *Two-Person Game Theory*, pp. 139–140.

of the other player.[27] But this is not a very satisfactory position to adopt within the framework of the theory of games. Logically speaking, there is an infinite variety of rules of thumb that could be used in assigning subjective probabilities, and game theory offers no persuasive reason to select any one of these rules over the others. This problem can be handled by introducing new assumptions (or empirical premises) about such things as the personality traits of the players. But such a course would carry the analyst far outside the basic structure of the theory of games, requiring a fundamental revision of the basic perspective of game theory.

Second, game theorists have sought to predict outcomes in nonzero-sum interactions by searching for solutions that seem particularly stable. The best-known solution concept of this kind involves the notion of equilibrium points. An equilibrium point can be defined as "an outcome such that if either player (unilaterally) departs from it by choosing another strategy he does not improve his payoff and, in general, impairs it."[28] The resultant outcome can be thought of as a solution to the game in the sense that it represents a specific point from which no rational player will be motivated to move on his own initiative.[29] This solution concept for nonzero-sum games has received a good deal of attention, especially since Nash proved that all nonzero-sum games exhibit at least one equilibrium point.[30]

In some nonzero-sum games, the idea of the equilibrium point as the solution is easily understandable in intuitive terms. However, there are several serious objections to the equilibrium point as a general solution for two-person, nonzero-sum games. To begin with, many nonzero-sum games exhibit several equilibrium points which are not equivalent and interchangeable. This is true, to take a well-known example, of any interaction that displays the structural features of the game of chicken.[31] In such cases, the notion of the equilibrium point is not sufficient to yield determinate solutions within the framework of the basic assumptions of game theory. This problem can be

---

[27] For a preliminary discussion of rules of thumb which is suggestive, even though it is not framed in terms of the problem of interdependent decision making, see Armen A. Alchian, "Uncertainty, Evolution, and Economic Theory," *Journal of Political Economy,* LVIII (1950), 211–221.

[28] Anatol Rapoport and Albert Chammah, "The Game of Chicken," *American Behavioral Scientist,* X (1966), 10.

[29] For a helpful discussion of a number of the points raised in this paragraph and the next one see Rapoport, *Two-Person Game Theory,* Chapter 9.

[30] On the significance of Nash's result see *ibid.,* p. 128.

[31] On this point see Rapoport and Chammah, "The Game of Chicken," pp. 10–11.

The defining characteristics of the game of chicken can be spelled out in terms of the following matrix:

	C_2	D_2
C_1	R, R	S, T
D_1	T, S	P, P

A situation with the basic features of a game of chicken occurs whenever $T > R > S > P$. For a discussion of this point see Rapoport and Chammah, *Prisoner's Dilemma,* pp. 226–227.

solved by introducing further assumptions that permit the selection of one of the equilibrium points as a unique solution. Schelling's concept of salience or prominence, for example, has sometimes been employed for this purpose.[32] But such additions carry us outside the basic structure of the theory of games. Next, it is not uncommon for nonzero-sum games to display no equilibrium points based on pure strategies. In such cases, the idea of the equilibrium point as the solution takes on a certain ambiguity in "one-shot" situations. And it is unlikely to produce good descriptive results since the identification of the equilibrium point is apt to place unrealistic demands on the computational capacity of the players.

Finally, the equilibrium point as the solution for nonzero-sum games leads to peculiar or even bizarre results in a number of nonzero-sum games. Any game with the essential structural features of the prisoner's dilemma illustrates this point.[33] In the prisoner's dilemma, there is a perfectly stable equilibrium point, but it yields outcomes that are not Pareto optimal.[34] And players who violate the rationality postulates of game theory can consistently do better than players who adhere to the equilibrium point as required by these postulates. This paradox stems from the fact that players who can jointly negotiate a settlement may both be able to improve on the payoffs associated with the equilibrium point in a nonzero-sum game even though neither player is motivated to depart unilaterally from the equilibrium point.[35] Consequently, the equilibrium point cannot be regarded as an adequate solution concept for nonzero-sum games in which the players are permitted to negotiate a settlement (that is, cooperative games).

Third, a number of game theorists have sought to circumvent the "out-guessing" regress associated with strategic interaction in the context of two-person, nonzero-games by introducing fixed decision rules, whose application yields unique predictions concerning the distribution of payoffs between the players. These decision rules are based on specific criteria concerning the worth or "power" of the individual players[36] and/or on certain desirable at-

---

[32] For Schelling's original discussion of salience, see Schelling, *Strategy of Conflict*, Chapter 3. It should be emphasized that no one has yet produced a formalization of the concept of salience for the purpose of choosing among alternative equilibrium points.

[33] For a brief account of the peculiar problems associated with the prisoner's dilemma see Rapoport, *Strategy and Conscience*, Chapter 6.

The defining characteristic of the prisoner's dilemma game can be spelled out in terms of the matrix set forth in footnote 30. A situation with the basic features of a prisoner's dilemma game will occur whenever $S < P < R < T$ and $2R > S + T$. For a discussion of this point see Rapoport and Chammah, *Prisoner's Dilemma*, pp. 33–36.

[34] From a purely descriptive point of view, the fact that the outcomes are not Pareto optimal is not necessarily damaging. From the prescriptive point of view (which has motivated many game theorists), however, it is difficult to justify outcomes that are not Pareto optimal.

[35] Note, however, that a negotiated settlement is not likely to be an equilibrium point even though it yields better payoffs for both players than the equilibrium point. Consequently, there are apt to be incentives to cheat associated with negotiated settlements so that the notion of enforcement mechanisms becomes important when negotiated settlements are feasible.

[36] There are numerous criteria that can be used to determine the worth or relative

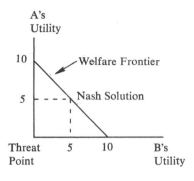

Figure I

tributes of a solution (for example, Pareto optimality, symmetry). Such procedures for circumventing strategic interaction in two-person, nonzero-sum
games have generally been applied to situations "where two individuals can
obtain certain prizes if they can agree on how these should be divided between
them; while if they cannot agree, then a conflict situation will arise with specified payoffs to both parties."[37] Games of this kind are known as cooperative
games (or bargaining games) since they permit negotiation between the
players, and it is the solutions that have been proposed for such games that are
commonly described in terms of the concept of bargaining by game theorists.

Figure I illustrates this type of interaction in graphic form.[38] Here the
problem is for players A and B to divide the value under the welfare
frontier between themselves, with the proviso that each will receive nothing if
they fail to reach agreement on a specific point of division.[39] Accordingly,
each player is motivated simultaneously by the incentive to agree on some
point of division and by the incentive to get as large a portion of the prize for
himself as possible.

The specific schemes that have been devised to generate predictions concerning the distribution of payoffs in such bargaining games all take the
form of detailed decision rules (or sets of conditions) that produce de-

---

"power" of the individual player. These include such yardsticks as the amount the
player would lose from an outcome of no agreement, the player's security level or
amount he can guarantee himself regardless of the behavior of the other player, and
the player's ability to damage or inflict losses on the other player.

[37] Harsanyi, "On the Rationality Postulates Underlying the Theory of Cooperative
Games," p. 181.

[38] As is common practice, the utility scales of both players in Figure I have been
arbitrarily transformed so that the threat point can be represented as zero on each
player's utility scale.

[39] It is not necessary, in situations of this kind, to assume that the players will receive
nothing if they fail to reach a specific agreement or even that their payoffs will be
symmetrical in such situations. Given the possibility of transforming the utility scales in
an arbitrary fashion together with the avoidance of interpersonal comparisons of utility,
however, the threat point can be conveniently represented as zero on the utility scale of
each player.

terminate outcomes[40] in the event that both players accept them or behave *as if* they accepted them.[41] The most well known of these schemes is the Nash solution whose application is illustrated in Figure I.[42] But there are a number of other solutions of this general type associated with the names of such scholars as Shapley, Raiffa, Braithwaite, and Harsanyi.[43]

Though these decision rules yield determinate solutions, they exhibit serious limitations as devices for handling the bargaining problem. Logically, an infinite number of decision rules of this type could be developed, and many of them (though not all) would produce differential results for the parties involved in any specific bargaining game.[44] Consequently, it is hardly surprising that none of these solutions yields good results when treated as "descriptive" theory rather than "prescriptive" theory. It is true that each player could proceed by assuming that the other will behave on the basis of some one of these decision rules and select his own optimal strategy accordingly. This would effectively eliminate the remaining vestiges of strategic interaction, thereby reducing the individual's choice problem once again to a situation fundamentally analogous to a game against nature. But this procedure could only produce rational results for the individual employing it if the other player were prepared to accept a relatively unfavorable (and therefore irrational from his perspective) rule from the set of such decision rules *and* the individual using the procedure could count on such cooperation from his partner (opponent).[45] This conclusion follows from that fact that as long as there exist several decision rules that yield differential results for the players, there

---

[40] These solution schemes generally assume infinitely divisible payoffs. The occurrence of indivisible or lumpy payoffs can be handled analytically by introducing the possibility of side payments. But this procedure generates problems. The introduction of side payments raises the problem of interpersonal comparisons of utility since it is difficult to arrange side payments without a common medium of exchange (such as money). In addition, when side payments are employed, it is necessary to introduce some mechanism to determine the size and distribution of side payments between the players.

[41] In this context, the fact that the resultant "solutions" do not correspond well with the actual outcomes of analogous real-world situations counts as evidence against the assumption that the players behave as if they accepted these decision rules.

[42] See John F. Nash, "The Bargaining Problem" and "Two-Person Cooperative Games," both reprinted herein.

[43] On the Shapley solution for nonzero-sum games, see L. S. Shapley, "A Value for N-Person Games," in H. W. Kuhn and A. W. Tucker, eds., *Contributions to the Theory of Games*, Vol. II (Princeton, 1953), and Rapoport, *Two-Person Game Theory*, pp. 94–122. On the other solutions consult, *inter alia*, Howard Raiffa, "Arbitration Schemes for Generalized Two-Person Games," in Kuhn and Tucker, eds., *Contributions to the Theory of Games;* R. B. Braithwaite, *Theory of Games as a Tool for the Moral Philosopher* (Cambridge, 1955); John C. Harsanyi, "A General Theory of Rational Behavior in Game Situations" and his "Bargaining and Conflict Situations in the Light of a New Approach to Game Theory," reprinted herein. The bargaining model of Frederik Zeuthen is sometimes included in this category. The reasons why this practice is not followed here are set forth in considerable detail in the Introductions to Parts Two and (especially) Three of this book.

[44] Though the number of rules of this type which have been formalized is relatively small, it is sufficient to display the potential for variation in the results.

[45] For another discussion of this point see Harvey Wagner, "Rejoinder on the Bargaining Problem," reprinted herein.

cannot be a single rule that maximizes the payoffs of both players simultaneously.[46]

For some time there has been a controversy concerning the extent to which these solutions for nonzero-sum games should be described in terms of the descriptive concept of bargaining or the prescriptive notion of arbitration.[47] In general, the resultant debate has focused on the presence or absence of concepts of equity in these solution schemes. Those who have interpreted the schemes as guidelines for arbitration have generally maintained that they all hinge on some notion of equity, even if it is only an implicit affirmation of the principle that some measure of the relative "power" positions of the players[48] should be the decisive factor in determining the outcome.[49] Other scholars, on the other hand, have argued that some of these schemes must be regarded as descriptively significant bargaining solutions on the grounds that they do not involve any conception of equity, even though it is undoubtedly true that there are decision rules of this kind that do amount to prescriptive principles that are more suitable for efforts at arbitration.[50] It is worth emphasizing here, however, that this debate concerning the role of equity in these schemes obscures another issue that is highly relevant to the distinction between descriptive bargaining solutions and prescriptive arbitration solutions. For reasons set forth in the preceding paragraph, it seems reasonable to conclude that any specific solution along these lines will ordinarily have to be imposed on at least one of the players in a two-person, nonzero-sum game of the cooperative type. Consequently, insofar as bargaining is conceptualized as a mechanism for coming to grips with the problem of strategic interaction by means of negotiations between the initial participants rather than the imposition of a solution by an outside party,[51] it is difficult to escape the conclusion that the solution schemes under discussion here are more relevant to

[46] Although some have argued that the Nash solution is uniquely attractive, it is hard to find any decisive basis for this conclusion. There is nothing intrinsically superior about the Nash solution just because it leads to the maximization of the product of the player's utility gains. This solution leads to outcomes in some cases (as Braithwaite has argued) that are incompatible with widely held ideas of fairness or justice, and there is no *a priori* reason to assume that the maximization of the product of utility gains will generally occur in real-world situations. In the case of identical bargainers, moreover, the attractiveness of the Nash solution evidently stems more from the impact of symmetry than the terms of the solution itself.

[47] See, for example, the exchange between Wagner and Harsanyi: Harvey Wagner, "A Unified Treatment of Bargaining Theory"; John C. Harsanyi, "Notes on the Bargaining Problem"; and Wagner, "Rejoinder on the Bargaining Problem," all three reprinted herein.

[48] Since there are numerous possible measures of the relative "power" positions of the players, there is nothing uniquely attractive about any particular solution based on a criterion of this kind.

[49] Rapoport, for example, has taken this position. See Rapoport, *Two-Person Game Theory*, pp. 210–211.

[50] Perhaps the most tireless exponent of this view is Harsanyi. For a clear example see Harsanyi, "Notes on the Bargaining Problem."

[51] For a discussion of this characteristic of bargaining see the general Introduction to this book, p. 18.

the problem of arbitration than to the problem of predicting the results of bargaining.[52]

The preceding discussion focuses entirely on two-person games. However, there is also a large game-theoretic literature dealing with N-person interactions (both zero-sum and nonzero-sum), and some of this literature raises issues that are distinctly relevant to the bargaining problem.[53] In general, analyses of N-person games concentrate on two distinguishable issues: (1) the formation of coalitions in games involving three or more players and (2) the payoffs to the individual players in an N-person interaction.

In games involving three or more players where some subset of the players can increase their payoffs by banding together, the formation of coalitions tends to become a central feature of the interaction.[54] And it seems reasonable to associate the concept of bargaining with the formation of specific coalitions in such situations.[55] A number of game theorists have sought to deal with the issues that arise in this context by introducing the concepts of characteristic functions and imputations.[56] The characteristic function of an N-person game is a payoff vector specifying the payoffs to all possible coalitions in the game. Given the characteristic function of a specific game, an imputation is a set of payments to the players in the game which do not violate the criteria of individual rationality and group rationality. It follows that it is possible to identify an infinite range of imputations for any specific game in characteristic function form. This line of thinking has led to a number of proposals concerning the identity of stable sets of imputations for games in characteristic function form such as the core, the von Neumann-Morgenstern solution, the Aumann-Maschler bargaining set, and the idea of psi-stability.[57] It is worth emphasizing that these proposals single out sets (often infinite sets) of stable imputations rather than a single, uniquely stable imputation for N-person games. The von Neumann-Morgenstern solution, for example, identifies sets of imputations such that no imputation in a stable set dominates any other

[52] This conclusion helps to explain the fact that these solution schemes all involve certain criteria, such as Pareto optimality, which are frequently violated in real-world cases of bargaining.

[53] For general discussions of N-person game theory see Luce and Raiffa, *Games and Decisions,* Chapters 7 to 12 and, especially, Anatol Rapoport, *N-Person Game Theory* (Ann Arbor, 1970).

[54] A coalition arises whenever two or more players in an N-person interaction join together in the interests of increasing their payoffs over what they could command on the basis of uncoordinated behavior.

[55] For a preliminary discussion of the role of bargaining in coalition formation, see E. W. Kelley, "Bargaining in Coalition Situations," in Sven Groennings, E. W. Kelley, and Michael Leiserson, eds., *The Study of Coalition Behavior* (New York, 1970), pp. 273-296.

[56] For formal definitions of these concepts, together with a discussion of their analytic implications, consult Luce and Raiffa, *Games and Decisions,* pp. 180-198.

[57] For an excellent survey of all these models see Rapoport, *N-Person Game Theory.* A brief, nontechnical discussion of these models can be found in Michael Leiserson, "Game Theory and the Study of Coalition Behavior," in Groennings, Kelley, and Leiserson, eds., *The Study of Coalition Behavior,* pp. 255-272.

member of the set while at least one imputation in the set dominates any given imputation not in the stable set.[58] Consequently, this approach to N-person games focuses on sets of reasonable outcomes rather than unique outcomes for games in characteristic function form. Moreover, these models have little to say about the processes of interaction among the players which ultimately lead to the formation of a specific coalition, though some of them include restrictive assumptions that rule out the formation of certain coalitions that are logically possible.

By contrast, some scholars have attempted to determine the expected value or worth of the individual player in an N-person interaction instead of elaborating on the problem of coalition formation. This line of thinking is fundamentally similar to the search for determinate solutions in cooperative, two-person games. That is, the resultant models introduce detailed decision rules concerning such things as the relative "power" of the players as a means of circumventing the difficulties associated with strategic interaction.[59] Accordingly, it is not unreasonable to conceptualize the outcomes specified by such models in terms of the notion of bargaining. The most well-known solution concepts of this type are the Shapley value and Harsanyi's generalization of the Nash solution to cover N-person games.[60] Like the solutions for two-person, bargaining games, however, these concepts deal only with the distribution of payoffs among the players and not with the processes of interaction through which the players arrive at these distributions. Moreover, it can be argued that these solutions are more relevant to the prescriptive problem of arbitration than to the descriptive problem of predicting bargaining outcomes for the same reasons that this is so with respect to the analogous solutions for two-person bargaining games.

Although a substantial part of N-person game theory is clearly relevant to the bargaining problem, the formal results are severely limited. Many of the conclusions seem more applicable to prescriptive analysis than to the production of descriptive theory. The results often identify only sets of reasonable outcomes in contrast to unique outcomes. And none of the models of N-person game theory focuses directly on the processes of coalition formation among the players. Thus, the theory of games does not constitute the basis of a general theory of bargaining in N-person interactions. Under the circumstances, it is not surprising that the phenomenon of coalition formation has recently begun to attract increasing attention from scholars whose work is

[58] For a detailed discussion of the von Neumann-Morgenstern solution see Rapoport, *N-Person Game Theory,* Chapter 4.

[59] In N-person games, such decision rules may yield negative payoffs to specific players. Nevertheless, they are similar to the solution concepts for cooperative, two-person games in the sense that they involve detailed decision rules that produce determinate solutions on the assumption that the players behave *as if* they accepted them.

[60] On these solution concepts see Shapley, "A Value for N-Person Games," and John C. Harsanyi, "A Bargaining Model for the Cooperative N-Person Game," in R. D. Luce and A. W. Tucker, eds., *Contributions to the Theory of Games,* Vol. IV (Princeton, 1959). For straightforward discussions of these solutions consult Rapoport, *N-Person Game Theory,* Chapters 5 and 11.

either not based on game-theoretic concepts[61] or only loosely connected to the central ideas of game theory.[62]

In concluding this introductory discussion, it may be helpful to set forth several summary statements concerning the utility of game theory in the analysis of bargaining. The theory of games has several important virtues in this context. Most of the models of game theory exhibit logical closure, and many of them are characterized by mathematical elegance as well. The language of game theory permits the formulation of sharp definitions of important problems that tend to remain ambiguous within other conceptual frameworks. And a great many scholars have found game theory attractive for its conceptual richness and provocativeness.

As the basis of a general theory of bargaining, however, game theory displays a number of severe limitations and drawbacks. The concept of bargaining occupies a highly restricted place in the theory of games. Thus, bargaining is associated primarily with proposed solutions for certain types of cooperative or negotiable games. And even in such cases, it is possible to argue cogently that the prescriptive concept of arbitration is more relevant than the descriptive concept of bargaining in characterizing the conclusions of game theory. Raising questions about some of the conclusions of orthodox game theory makes it possible to see greater potential scope for the notion of bargaining within the conceptual framework established by game theory. This is the case, for example, with the line of thought initiated by Ellsberg's critique of the von Neumann-Morgenstern solution for two-person, zero-sum games. But analyses proceeding along such lines also serve to demonstrate the limitations of the existing models of game theory for efforts to deal with important aspects of the bargaining problem.

The assumptions upon which the models of game theory are founded also have the effect of abstracting away a number of problems that are widely regarded as important in the context of bargaining.[63] This is true, for example, of a variety of activities associated with the specification of the payoff matrix for particular interactions as well as the uses of communications by the players. Above all, it is true with respect to the efforts of players to manipulate each other's information concerning such things as the availability of specific alternatives, utility functions, and behavior relating to the problem of strategic interaction itself. Accordingly, the models of game theory are simply not relevant to a number of questions that are often asked in analyses of bargaining.

[61] In this connection, the work of Caplow and Gamson is particularly well known. For a helpful introductory survey of this work, see Jerome M. Chertkoff, "Sociopsychological Theories and Research on Coalition Formation," in Groennings, Kelley, and Leiserson, eds., *The Study of Coalition Behavior*, pp. 297–322.

[62] Here the work of Riker is particularly prominent. See William Riker, *The Theory of Political Coalitions* (New Haven, 1962).

[63] Perhaps the most important abstraction employed in the theory of games is the complex of assumptions which makes it possible to specify the payoff matrix for particular games. But the assumption of rational choice, without reference to time and decision costs, also exerts a powerful impetus in this direction.

Beyond this, the models of game theory are fundamentally static models in the sense that they focus on outcomes in contrast to processes.[64] That is, while it is perfectly possible to discuss the ultimate distribution of payoffs between or among the players in terms of the models of game theory, this conceptual foundation has little to offer in analyzing the sequences of actions and reactions (or offers and counteroffers) through which the participants ultimately arrive at a specific bargain. And this too produces difficulties in the study of bargaining since the concept is frequently understood explicitly in terms of processes involving sequences of offers and counteroffers together with the utilization of various bargaining tactics.

Finally, the models of game theory have not produced good predictions in empirical terms. That is, the outcomes predicted by these logical models do not correspond well with the actual outcomes that occur in related real-world situations even though a number of the models are logically and mathematically elegant.[65] In fact, the descriptive accuracy of the models is poor even in carefully controlled experiments specifically designed to test the extent to which the predictions of the models correspond to actual outcomes.[66] This raises the distinction between descriptive theory and prescriptive theory once again in a particularly forceful fashion. There is certainly no reason to denigrate the value of the models of game theory for prescriptive purposes, though in many cases there is no one solution concept that seems uniquely attractive in normative terms. However, it is difficult to see how these models can be regarded as adequate for descriptive purposes, except in extremely limited situations that do not encompass a significant portion of the bargaining problem.

[64] For an account that stresses this aspect of the game-theoretic approach to bargaining, see John G. Gross, *The Economics of Bargaining* (New York, 1969), especially Chapters 1 and 2.

[65] In the case of zero-sum games, it is even difficult to locate real-world analogues.

[66] For an excellent survey of experimental work in this area, see Anatol Rapoport and Carol Orwant, "Experimental Games: A Review," *Behavioral Science,* VII (1962), 1–37.

THEORY OF THE RELUCTANT DUELIST
Daniel Ellsberg

> We wish to find the mathematically complete principles which define "rational behavior" for the participants in a social economy, and to derive from them the general characteristics of that behavior.

Thus von Neumann and Morgenstern defined their goal in the *Theory of Games and Economic Behavior*.[1]

Their analysis of the problem, their model, their approach to it were brilliantly conceived; they invented an array of new concepts and new techniques of analysis to examine what has come to be known as the game situation. But they aimed beyond. With respect at least to the special situation of the "zero-sum two-person" game they offered not merely a new way of looking at an old problem but "a precise theory . . . which gives complete answers to all questions."[2]

Rarely is it kind to remind a theorist of such a statement ten years later. Yet the fact is that for more than a decade their solution of the special problem has stood without serious challenge. Critics of game theory have indeed questioned the assumptions, the concepts, the importance of the model; but they have published few complaints about the conclusions drawn from the model. Game theorists have gone on to new problems. They have abandoned some assumptions and developed more complex and versatile models. But they have rarely derived results so elegant, determinate or general as those claimed for the two-person zero-sum game. The solution associated with that model has come to represent game theory: its most solid achievement, the best measure of its promise. No one has cared to question its status as *the* theory of the two-person zero-sum game.

Is it a satisfactory theory, within the limits of its own model and assumptions? I do not believe it is. I do not think it would be useful in

* This article was originally part of an honors thesis entitled "Theories of Rational Choice Under Uncertainty" submitted at Harvard College, April 1952. The author wishes particularly to thank John Chipman (who supervised the original writing), Carl Kaysen, Wassily Leontief, Martin Shubik and Oskar Morgenstern for their valuable criticism. The author is presently serving with the United States Marine Corps, on leave of absence from Harvard University.

[1] John von Neumann and Oskar Morgenstern (Princeton, 1944), p. 31. All citations in this paper will refer to this work, unless otherwise noted.

[2] P. 101.

predicting behavior in the situations it considers, nor does it seem acceptable as a general norm of behavior.

Von Neumann and Morgenstern approach a particular context of rational choice under uncertainty: in which the outcome of an action is uncertain because it depends on the interaction of a small number of conflicting wills. Because rational choice has been undefined for situations involving uncertainty, orthodox theory, premised on rational behavior, has been correspondingly "indeterminate" for these situations.

By *certainty* is meant a situation in which each available action is associated in the actor's mind with a single, certain consequence. The rule of rational choice under certainty, to which we will refer frequently, requires him to choose that action whose consequence he most prefers. The rule is meaningless when an individual must act under uncertainty, *i.e.,* when he associates with a given action a *set* of possible outcomes, some of which may be favorable and some unfavorable.

It is not difficult to devise various rules of choice that can be applied in this situation, any one of which might be termed, more or less arbitrarily, "rational." To discover a rule with general usefulness in predicting or prescribing behavior under uncertainty is something else again. It is this at which von Neumann and Morgenstern aim. "The superiority of 'rational behavior' over any other kind is to be established . . . for all conceivable situations—including those where 'the others' behave irrationally, in the sense of the standards which the theory will set for them."[3]

We might consider a principle to be a "useful" definition of rational choice under uncertainty if most people who were rational under certainty would reject any decision inconsistent with the principle.[4] With this criterion we can probe the von Neumann-Morgenstern conclusions. If it should appear that a large number of reasonable people will accept some decisions inconsistent with the particular rule that the authors propose, and if their reasons are not random or foolish, then the von Neumann-Morgenstern principle could not be satisfactory as the unique definition of rational behavior in the game situation.

Some familiarity with the model and concepts of the zero-sum two-person game will be taken for granted, but the abstract model can be described briefly. Player A selects a strategy i from the set of strategies open to him by the rules of the game. Simultaneously, in ignorance of A's choice, player B selects a strategy j from his set of admissible strategies. Then, after the choices are revealed, A receives an amount a_{ij} and B receives an amount $-a_{ij}$ (or, B pays A an amount a_{ij}). The

[3] P. 32.

[4] This proposition has been adapted from one in an unpublished paper by Jacob Marschak.

subscripts indicate that the payoff is a function of both strategies. The rules of the game prescribe a pair of outcomes corresponding to each possible pair of strategies. The sum of the outcomes is zero; what one player wins, the other loses.

In this model, each player makes but one "move." Thus, the analysis applies directly to such simple games as matching pennies, in which each player chooses between the alternatives, heads or tails. To generalize the results to more complex games such as poker or chess, the authors interpret the player's single move as the choice of a strategy, a concept which they define: " a plan which specifies what choices he will make in every possible situation, for every possible actual information which he may possess at that moment. . . ."[5] When both players have chosen strategies in this sense, the outcome of the game is determined. Thus, complex games can be analyzed in static terms, as though the outcome were determined by a single choice on the part of each player.

To "divide the difficulties" of the analysis, the authors make some important simplifying assumptions. First, the outcomes are represented not in utilities, cardinal or otherwise, but unequivocally in money.[6] Second, von Neumann and Morgenstern abstract from uncertainties concerning the rules of the game. Each player knows with certainty: (a) what strategies he is allowed; (b) what strategies his opponent is allowed; (c) the outcome corresponding to any pair of opposing strategies. Finally, there is a significant tacit assumption that each player knows his opponent has the same rules of the game in mind.

The strategies and payoff function, which comprise the rules of the game, can be represented by a matrix, each row corresponding to one of A's possible strategies, each column, one of B's strategies, the matrix elements being the payoffs corresponding to pairs of opposing strategies. There is no need to show B's outcomes explicitly, since they are merely the negatives of A's.

The model described above is the "normalized" version of the game. It expresses just those elements of uncertainty which von Neumann and Morgenstern wish to emphasize. Since each player must choose in ignorance of his opponent's choice, and since the outcome of any strategy depends on that unknown choice, there is a *set* of possible outcomes corresponding to each possible strategy, rather than a single, certain outcome. The problem is to prescribe a unique "rational" choice among these *sets* of uncertain outcomes.

In special cases the choice may be easy. If the payoff function hap-

[5] P. 79.
[6] P. 8.

pens to be such that the outcome of one particular strategy is better than the outcome of another for every one of the opponent's possible strategies, the first will be said to "dominate" the second. In terms of the matrix, if each element in one row is greater than the corresponding element in another row, the first strategy dominates the second. To choose a strategy which is dominated by another would be to accept an outcome which is certain to be less favorable than if the dominant strategy were to be chosen. The rule seems indicated that the rational player will never choose a dominated strategy.

The hard choices come when (a) sets of outcomes overlap, so that the opponent's choice determines whether the outcome of one strategy is better or worse than that of another, and when (b) the opponent's choice is uncertain, being made simultaneously with one's own. These are conditions of the normalized game, which is the target of the analysis.

Von Neumann and Morgenstern approach this target indirectly, via two models which depart from the conditions of the normalized game and which are in themselves of much less significance. They explain their approach:

> The introduction of these two games . . . achieves this: It ought to be evident by common sense—and we shall also establish it by an exact discussion—that for [these games] the "best way of playing"—*i.e.* the concept of rational behavior—has a clear meaning.[7]

In one of these modified games, called the minorant game, A must make his choice first, after which B chooses in full knowledge of A's choice. Since B, in this game, acts under certainty, the basic principle of rationality under certainty prescribes his choice. Given strategy i by A, then to each strategy available to B there corresponds a single, certain outcome, and his unique rational choice is that strategy associated with the outcome: $\text{Min}_j a_{ij}$, where i is given.[8] That is, he should pick the column corresponding to the minimum element in the row selected by A.

Now if A, moving first, knows literally nothing about B's "mentality," then A must choose under uncertainty. But in this model, if A has the relatively small scrap of information that B is rational under certainty, then A too acts under certainty. Operationally, the statement that B is known to be rational under certainty is equivalent to the statement that B, moving second, is certain to choose the minimum element in any row picked by A. If A thus considers it impossible

---

[7] P. 100.

[8] B will be described as minimizing a_{ij}, since his outcome is $-a_{ij}$. He could equally well be described as maximizing $-a_{ij}$.

that a given strategy should have any but its minimum outcome, the rule is inevitable that it is irrational for A to pay any attention to the $m(n\text{-}1)$ matrix elements which are not row minima. A should choose the "maximin" strategy corresponding to the largest of the row minima.

In the second special model, the majorant game, B must choose before A, who then chooses with certainty of the outcome. As above, if B does know A to be rational under certainty, this is equivalent to knowing that elements which are not column maxima are not possible outcomes. Hence under this special assumption B also acts under certainty, associating a single, certain outcome ($\text{Max}_i a_{ij}$, for given j) with each strategy. The only strategy which is rationally consistent with his belief about A is his "minimax" strategy, *i.e.*, the strategy corresponding to the outcome $\text{Min}_j \text{Max}_i a_{ij}$, which guarantees him the best of the "possible" outcomes.

Thus, the authors' assertion is justified. In these special models, in which one player possesses, and is known to possess, knowledge of the other's choice, certain rules of rational choice for both players do appear uniquely valid.

In the normalized game, to which we now return, neither player knows with certainty his opponent's choice beforehand, since both choose simultaneously. The principle of choice which von Neumann and Morgenstern propose is essentially this: each player should choose *as though* he were moving first in a minorant (or majorant) game, and *as if* he were certain that his opponent were rational and informed. Thus, player A should consider only the minimum element in each row: *i.e.*, the worst that could happen to him under that strategy. He should then choose the strategy with best minimum outcome. This particular outcome may be expressed as $\text{Max}_i \text{Min}_j a_{ij}$, his maximin strategy; the corresponding policy for player B is to choose the column with the lowest maximum outcome ($\text{Min}_j \text{Max}_i a_{ij}$), or minimax.[9]

The nature of this prescription differs markedly from that applying in the minorant or majorant games. In those, the first player knows that the second acts with certainty of the outcome, and knows (we assume) that the second is rational under certainty; thus he too acts under certainty. The conclusion that he should choose his minimax strategy then follows directly from the principle of rational choice under certainty (there is, in fact, no problem of uncertainty). It is

---

[9] For convenience, this rule of choice for the normalized game will hereafter be referred to as the minimax principle. Either player may be said to choose his minimax strategy— *i.e.*, the one prescribed by this principle—though the context may indicate, for a particular player, that a maximin strategy is involved.

precisely this property that is missing from the normalized game. There, knowledge that one's opponent is rational under certainty has no immediate bearing on the outcome to be expected from different strategies, for it is known that the opponent himself must act under uncertainty. The fact that one's own choice is hidden from the opponent means that the opponent's choice, and hence the outcome of one's strategy, is uncertain.

Von Neumann and Morgenstern instruct the player in the normalized game to act as if he were certain of the consequences, although in fact he is not and cannot be certain. Note that these particular "as if" assumptions are not *mandatory* on the players merely because of the game situation and the conflict of interest between them. Each player knows that his opponent would like to inflict the maximum possible loss on him; but he also knows that his opponent, moving simultaneously and in ignorance of his own choice, cannot be certain of succeeding.

Unless the player believes that his opponent is gifted with extra-sensory perception, the knowledge that he is hostile, "reasonable" and informed cannot make his strategy certain. Uncertainty is a state of mind, a property of belief or expectation; if it is present it cannot simply be "assumed away." The "as if" or minimax policy proposed by von Neumann and Morgenstern is not a method for exorcising uncertainty but is one among several principles for acting in the presence of uncertainty. Its provisional nature is mentioned here not as a criticism but because that aspect is obscured in *The Theory of Games*. Von Neumann and Morgenstern leave the impression that the minimax principle for the normalized game follows logically (and inevitably) from the similar principle in the minorant and majorant games: hence, that it is derived eventually from the notion of rational choice under certainty.

They do not, indeed, begin in that vein. They first present the advantages (from a conservative point of view) of the minimax principle, concluding: "It is *reasonable* to define *a* good way for 1 to play the game" as that strategy which guarantees him at least the maximin outcome. Similarly, "it is reasonable to define *a* good way for 2 to play the game as one which guarantees him a gain" corresponding to the minimax outcome.[10] Or as paraphrased above, it is reasonable to define a good way for a player to behave: play as though moving first in a minorant or majorant game. This method might indeed be considered sound conservative behavior. But the authors continue:

[10] Both quotations are from p. 108; italics added.

"So we have:
(14:C:a) *The* good way (strategy) for 1 to play the game" (my italics) is maximin. And:
"(14:C:b) *The* good way (strategy) for 2 to play the game" (my italics) is minimax. The next paragraph begins: "Finally, our definition of *the* good way of playing, as stated at the beginning of this section, yields immediately. . . ."[11] The fact is that their statement at the beginning of the section did not define *the* good way of playing. It defined *a* good way. Yet the authors are ready to start the next section with: "(14:C:a) − (14:C:f) . . . settle everything as far as the strictly determined two-person games are concerned."[12]

It is not to confront the authors with a petty lapse that the metamorphosis of *a* into *the* has been plotted in detail. That passage plays no minor role. Keystone of the whole "determinate" theory of the normalized game is a uniquely valid principle of rational behavior: enthroned, in the citation above, by a bit of sleight-of-hand. It cannot simply be taken for granted (in fact, it does not seem to be true) that what is uniquely reasonable in the minorant or majorant games will still be uniquely reasonable in the normalized game.

Rejecting any such easy conclusion, it still remains to judge the von Neumann-Morgenstern principle on its merits. The maximin rule does offer a type of security—the certainty of achieving an outcome which is at least better than the worst possible (*i.e.*, the lowest element in the matrix). But this security is purchased at a price. Along with it goes the certainty that the outcome will not *exceed* a certain sum (namely, the best element in the set containing the maximin outcome). This upper limit may be only slightly better than the maximin outcome, which in turn may be only a shade better than the worst possible outcome. At the same time, other strategies may offer the possibility of dazzlingly superior outcomes, combined with minimum outcomes barely below the maximin. With such a payoff function, it is not obvious that simple "reasonableness" prescribes uniquely the choice of the maximin strategy.

The key question of this paper may be phrased: Is it useful to call a player irrational because he decides to use a nonminimax strategy? Consider the payoff matrix shown in Figure 1. In this game, A's maximin strategy is A-2; B's minimax strategy is B-2. According to von Neumann and Morgenstern, these are "the rational" choices for A and B. Any other choice would expose the player to the chance of losing 10. On the other hand, the "rational" strategy also guarantees that the

[11] All quotations are from *loc. cit.*; italics added.
[12] P. 109.

player will not get more than 0.

Would most people who were rational under certainty reject any other choice of strategy? Suppose that A were to play a nonmaximin strategy, A-1 or A-3. If B played his "rational" strategy B-2, A would do exactly as well as if he had used his own "rational" strategy A-2. If B were not certain to use B-2, then A would stand to win or to lose 10. Player A might prefer this uncertainty to the certainty of winning 0.

A similar argument holds for B. In this game, both might use nonminimax strategies even though each knew his opponent to be rational under certainty and informed as to the payoff matrix. And there seem to be no convincing grounds for saying that these choices would be unreasonable.

In this game there is no way for one player to be sure of "punish-

	B-1	B-2	B-3
A-1	10	0	−10
A-2	0	0	0
A-3	−10	0	10

Figure 1

ing" the other for using a "bad" strategy; in fact, to have a chance of inflicting any loss on the other he must use a "nonrational" strategy himself.[13] There is another implication that deserves some thought. In this game[14] the behavior of a man "rational" in the von Neumann-Morgenstern sense would be unaffected if every element in the payoff matrix were multiplied by a constant. But are not most people interested in comparing the differential gains that they might make (by choosing a nonminimax strategy over a minimax strategy) with the differential losses they would risk? A player who was willing to accept the uncertainty of receiving either 10¢, 0¢ or −10¢ might be unwilling to risk the loss of $100, even if combined with the possibility of winning $100.[15] Such a player, in contrast to the von Neumann-

[13] This matrix is by no means a mere oddity. Von Neumann and Morgenstern spend considerable time analyzing games with precisely these characteristics; *e.g.*, see the case on page 164: "If the opponent played the good strategy, then the player's mistake would not matter."

[14] And in every "specially strictly determined" game, as defined below.

[15] This point would not be met by replacing the money outcomes which the authors do use by "von Neumann-Morgenstern utilities," of the sort they discuss in their opening pages. The latter are relevant, if they can be found at all, only to situations involving

Morgenstern "rational" player, is taking into account outcomes other than minimum payoffs. He does not believe, and is not assuming, that his opponent is certain to succeed in enforcing the minimum. Is this irrational? Unlike the minorant and majorant games, there is no clear basis for certainty that the nonminimum outcomes are impossible.

It would appear that von Neumann and Morgenstern fail their own criterion; their rule of rational behavior fails to be superior in face of the possibility that the opponent may behave "irrationally." They do make an effort to avoid this test:

> It is possible to argue that in a zero-sum two-person game the rationality of the opponent can be assumed, because the irrationality of his opponent can never harm a player. Indeed, since there are only two players and since the sum is zero, every loss which the opponent—irrationally— inflicts upon himself, necessarily causes an equal gain to the other player.[16]

The defense is inadequate. Their conception of "harm" seems to exclude any element of "opportunity cost," "regret," any notion of the pain incurred in passing up a real chance of great gains or in discovering, afterwards, that one could have done much better than he did (by risking slightly worse). The very mention of the possibility that an opponent will violate any given set of rules suggests that any element in the whole matrix is *possible*. If there is indeed a chance that the opponent will make a "mistake," why not help him to inflict a *large* loss on himself?

The particular game discussed above belongs to a class of games known as "specially strictly determined."[17] With respect to these games at least, von Neumann and Morgenstern regard it as obvious and un-questionable that their minimax principle is solely rational. The criticisms presented so far might tend to unpin such faith in the unique claims of the rule, even in this most favorable context. It is time now to consider their efforts to extend the application of their principle and their concept of the "solution" or "value" of a game.

In the minorant and majorant games the assumptions (a) that both players are rational under certainty, and (b) that the player moving first knows that his opponent is rational under certainty, are sufficient to make the outcome of the play uniquely determined. Given these assumptions, the outcome to A in the minorant game will be $v_1 =$

---

risk, *i.e.*, known probabilities. (See "Classic and Current Notions of 'Measurable Utility,' " *Econ. Jour.*, Sept. 1954, LXIV, 528-56.) The situation described so far involves no probabilities. The authors insist that it is conceptually impossible to measure uncertainty as to the opponent's choice in terms of numerical probabilities.

[16] P. 128.

[17] Defined below.

$\text{Max}_i\text{Min}_j a_{ij}$ and the outcome to B is $-v_1$. In the majorant game (A moving second) the outcome to A is $v_2 = \text{Min}_j\text{Max}_i a_{ij}$, the outcome to B is $-v_2$. These payoffs are plausibly defined as "values" of the games for the players in two distinct senses: (a) if the assumptions apply, these are the outcomes that will actually result; (b) given the assumptions, they represent the maximum amounts which the players rationally should be willing to pay for the privilege of playing the game.

It can be proven that v_1 (maximin) is always less than or equal to v_2 (minimax). If $v_1 = v_2$, $\text{Max}_i\text{Min}_j a_{ij} = \text{Min}_j\text{Max}_i a_{ij}$, a "saddlepoint" is said to exist in the payoff function. This condition is of no interest at all in the minorant and majorant games, so far as the players' choices are concerned. However, it does play a role in the authors' attempt to derive a numerical value of a play in the normalized game.

They follow two parallel lines of argument. The first proceeds thus: (a) definite "values" can be assigned to the minorant and majorant games: (b) moving first is less advantageous than moving second, and moving simultaneously (as in the normalized game) must lie in between; (c) therefore if a "value" for the normalized game can be found at all, it must lie between the values of the minorant and majorant games, *i.e.*, v must be between v_1 and v_2; (d) thus, if the payoff matrix has a saddlepoint, $v_1 = v_2$, this outcome must constitute the unique value v of the normalized game.[18]

This is supported by an "heuristic" argument that the numbers v_1 and v_2, defined as above but no longer associated with the minorant or majorant games, have a practical significance in connection with the normalized game. Although in this game both players choose simultaneously,

> It is nevertheless conceivable that one of the players, say 2, "finds out" his adversary; i.e., that he has somehow acquired the knowledge as to what his adversary's strategy is. The basis for this knowledge does not concern us. . . .[19]

They assert that in this case, conditions "become exactly the same as if" the game were a minorant game. Likewise, if player 1 "finds out" his adversary, conditions become "exactly the same as if" the game were the majorant game.[20] In either of these cases, they claim, the "value" of the normalized game becomes a "well-defined quantity":

[18] A game with a saddlepoint corresponding to two strategies of the type we have considered so far ("pure" strategies) is said to be "specially strictly determined." The matrix in Figure 1 is an example.

[19] P. 105.

[20] P. 106.

v_1 in the first case, v_2 in the second. Moreover, finding out is better than being found out, and the case in which neither occurs is in between; therefore the value of the normalized game must be bounded by v_1 and v_2, and if they are equal it is uniquely determined.

In both arguments the key proposition is that v, if it can be defined at all, must lie between v_1 and v_2, so that if they are equal the value is uniquely determined. Yet each overlooks a vital difference between the minorant-majorant games and the normalized game. In talking about the latter, we must assume that neither player is certain beforehand that he will be found out. After all, if B, for example, knew with certainty that he would be found out, it would not be "as if" A and B were playing the majorant game; they *would* be playing the majorant game.

Recognizing this, our whole previous discussion points to the possibility that B, *even though reasonable and informed,* might be "found" playing some nonminimax strategy. The potential reward to A of "finding out" B is thus not limited to v_2 (minimax). With foreknowledge in the normalized game, A might be able to achieve the very highest outcome in the matrix.

In other words, if A had a crystal ball that foretold B's strategies, a normalized game would not become "exactly the same as" a majorant game; it would be better. Even without the crystal ball, A might well prefer to play the normalized version of a game (which might offer the chance, if not the certainty, of higher payoff) to the majorant game: which is to say that v_2 is not a meaningful upper bound to the "value" of the normalized game for A.

Similarly, the possibility that B may find out A implies that the final outcome may range anywhere from maximin down to "minimin," the lowest element in the matrix. Under these circumstances, B might be willing to pay more than $-v_1$ to play the game. In terms of the payoff function in Figure 1, the "value" to either player of the minorant or majorant game corresponding to the matrix is 0. Yet either might be willing to pay, say, 1 for the privilege of playing the normalized game, which offers a chance of winning 10; and one of them might end up with an outcome of 10, rather than 0. Thus the value of the normalized game, either in the sense of actual outcome or of reasonable "worth" to the player, is not necessarily bounded by v_1-v_2.

This conclusion is crippling to the von Neumann-Morgenstern argument. If v_1 and v_2 separately have little relevance to the normalized game, they are no more relevant when they happen to be equal. This removes most of the interest from the question, regarded by von Neumann and Morgenstern as the central problem of the two-person zero-sum game, as to the general conditions for the existence of a saddlepoint. Von Neumann's early solution to this problem does nothing to increase the *significance* of the saddlepoint.[21]

It is true that the existence of a saddlepoint is not entirely without interest, given certain hypothetical conditions:

1. If a player actualy did expect with certaintly that his opponent would "find him out," then he could do no better (in games with a saddlepoint) than to use his maximin strategy; in effect he would be playing a minorant game. But it would seem distinctly paranoid to feel certain that one would be found out on a·single play (and von Neumann and Morgenstern insist again and again that their analysis is developed entirely with reference to a single play).[22]

2. Although von Neumann and Morgenstern never consider aspects of a dynamic sequence of plays of two-person games, it might be argued that in such a sequence a saddlepoint would represent an equilibrium position, if both players had particular expectations. Specifically, if each player expected with certainty that his opponent would *go on* playing his minimax strategy, he himself would have no incentive to depart from his own minimax strategy. Aside from the fact that this seems definitely to involve a belief in the opponent's "rationality" such an argument, to earn a hearing, should be accompanied by assurances as to stability. If one player, for whatever reason, were in one play to depart from his minimax strategy, this in itself would tend to destroy the expectations which gave the saddlepoint the nature of an equilibrium. Henceforth both players would have incentives to use non-minimax strategies. Thus, let one small "shock" displace the outcome from the saddlepoint and it would show no tendency to return. Even as a dynamic equilibrium the saddlepoint would have no obvious interest, for it would be unstable.

Moreover, any appeal to dynamic considerations opens the door to new reasons for the employment of nonminimax strategies, strategies of a type the authors necessarily failed to consider: *e.g.,* strategies chosen to confuse the opponent as to one's own intentions, rationality or knowledge of the payoff matrix. Creating doubts by deliberately

[21] He proves that if "mixed" strategies (probability combinations of the "pure" strategies we have considered) are regarded as included in the payoff function, every game will have a saddlepoint. But the saddlepoint is certainly no more significant when it corresponds to a pair of mixed strategies than when the game is "specially strictly determined," as is the example we have discussed.

[22] "We have always insisted that our theory is a static one, and that we analyze the course of one play and not that of a sequence of successive plays" (p. 146); "We have repeatedly professed that our considerations must be applicable to one isolated play and also that they are strictly statical" (p. 189n). This paper has considered the theory on the authors' own terms, as applying to a single play. Besides providing a foundation for a dynamic theory, the case is far from trivial. There are many important real situations in which only one play of a game is possible.

erratic or "foolish" choices, one could tempt the opponent to pursue (for sound, profit-seeking motives) into the regions where big killings were possible. There would also be strategies designed to "find out" the opponent's future intentions or pattern of play. The fact is that there is not, in any real sense, a dynamic theory of games. To debate whether the saddlepoint may not be a stationary solution in this nonexistent theory seems premature.

3. A saddlepoint represents an outcome v such that by acting appropriately A can be sure of receiving at least v no matter what B does, and B can keep A from receiving more than v no matter what A does. This fact is frequently cited as the basis for calling the saddlepoint the "value" of the normalized game. Yet to imply either that the saddlepoint will be achieved or that it represents the "worth" of the game to the players is to specify a very particular sort of player. Both must be "cautious pessimists," exclusively concerned with best *guaranteed* income.

Perhaps the bulk of recent work on the theory of the two-person zero-sum game has been concerned with the numerical computation of von Neumann's saddlepoint "solution." The question raised by our discussion is: Just what problem does this "solution" solve? We can make at least a partial answer as to what it does *not* solve. If no assumptions are made about the psychology of the players other than that they are reasonable and informed, then the saddlepoint represents neither an outcome that will necessarily be achieved nor the maximum amount that a player might reasonably offer to play the game. It fits neither of the two senses in which an outcome might usefully be defined as the "value" of a game.

In particular, we must reject the authors' statement: "Nor are our results for one player based upon any belief in the rational conduct of the other—a point the importance of which we have repeatedly stressed."[23] In nearly all games, if the possibility is considered that the opponent will not be "rational" in the von Neumann-Morgenstern sense, there will be nonminimax strategies which offer the chance of doing better than one could possibly do by choosing the minimax strategy. Surely there are many players, rational under certainty, who would regard these "bad" strategies as "superior," given this possibility.

At one point in their book, briefly, von Neumann and Morgenstern concede this aspect of their theory in a highly significant (and little noticed) sentence:

While our good strategies are perfect from the defensive point of view,

[23] P. 160.

they will (in general) not get the maximum out of the opponent's (possible) mistakes—*i.e.,* they are not calculated for the offensive.[24]

This statement is decisive in establishing the character and the limitations of the theory. Swiftly leaving behind the admission so casually introduced, the authors hasten to point out: "It should be remembered, however, that . . . a theory of the offensive, in this sense, is not possible without essentially new ideas."[25] This may be no recommendation of the old ideas. Is it not likely that what they term a "theory of the offensive" is precisely what would appeal to many as a theory of rationality? More broadly, should there not be within a proper theory of rational behavior room for both offensive and defensive points of view? When did "rational" become synonymous with "defensive"?

Consider any matrix in which each row contains at least one negative element: *i.e.,* a game in which each one of A's strategies offers him a chance of some loss. The matrix in Figure 1 would be an example if its middle row were deleted (it would then look like the payoff function for matching dimes). Suppose that A were offered a new strategy which gave him the certainty of standing pat, neither winning nor losing. This would amount to adding a row of zeros to the matrix (as in Figure 1). To make the new strategy concrete, we might let the row of zeros correspond to the option of passing up particular plays of the game without penalty. If he were a disciple of von Neumann and Morgenstern, A's problem of choice would be solved. He would never play. No matter how slight the possible losses or how rich the potential gains with his other strategies, A would clutch at the row of zeros.

One might well ask: Why bother to play the game at all, if one prefers the certainty of zero to the chance of winning or losing? This question once was put to a prominent game theorist; his unconsidered reply, presumably intended as no more than a partial answer, was that in many situations one *must* play a game, even against one's wishes.

The vital orientation of game theory is implicit in that remark. If we should suppose—as no game theorist has in fact proposed—that the game models under consideration all represent uncertainty situations in which an individual is forced, reluctantly, to make decisions, the rationale for the minimax principle becomes immediately far more convincing. The behavior of their "rational" player may well be described as that of a man whose sole concern is to come out with as little loss as possible. The minimax strategy, to him, is the least

[24] P. 164. In other words, if B should use a nonminimax strategy, A generally could not enforce the maximum element in that column by choosing his own maximin strategy.
[25] P. 164.

ominous choice in a game he would rather not play. His is not the attitude, to be sure, of one playing a game for entertainment or profit. It is, in fact, the psychology of a timid man pressed into a duel.

This is not to deny that cautious pessimists do exist or that a defensive policy is often desirable. A theory of reluctant duelists is not a small achievement. But it could not be reliable in predicting behavior in situations corresponding to the zero-sum two-person game; nor is it plausible that players should be advised to conform to it against their inclinations. It is certainly not a theory of games. It is not a theory of rational behavior under game-uncertainty; that theory lies in the future. If it comes, I believe it will show an immense debt to the insights and theoretical framework provided by von Neumann and Morgenstern. But it will not come the faster for a misbelief that its place was filled a dozen years ago.

THE BARGAINING PROBLEM

John F. Nash

A new treatment is presented of a classical economic problem, one which occurs in many forms, as bargaining, bilateral monopoly, etc. It may also be regarded as a nonzero-sum two-person game. In this treatment a few general assumptions are made concerning the behavior of a single individual and of a group of two individuals in certain economic environments. From these, the solution (in the sense of this paper) of the classical problem may be obtained. In the terms of game theory, values are found for the game.

INTRODUCTION

A TWO-PERSON bargaining situation involves two individuals who have the opportunity to collaborate for mutual benefit in more than one way. In the simpler case, which is the one considered in this paper, no action taken by one of the individuals without the consent of the other can affect the well-being of the other one.

The economic situations of monopoly versus monopsony, of state trading between two nations, and of negotiation between employer and labor union may be regarded as bargaining problems. It is the purpose of this paper to give a theoretical discussion of this problem and to obtain a definite "solution"—making, of course, certain idealizations in order to do so. A "solution" here means a determination of the amount of satisfaction each individual should expect to get from the situation, or, rather, a determination of how much it should be worth to each of these individuals to have this opportunity to bargain.

This is the classical problem of exchange and, more specifically, of bilateral monopoly as treated by Cournot, Bowley, Tintner, Fellner, and others. A different approach is suggested by von Neumann and Morgenstern in *Theory of Games and Economic Behavior*[2] which permits the identification of this typical exchange situation with a nonzero sum two-person game.

In general terms, we idealize the bargaining problem by assuming that the two individuals are highly rational, that each can accurately compare his desires for various things, that they are equal in bargaining skill, and that each has full knowledge of the tastes and preferences of the other.

[1] The author wishes to acknowledge the assistance of Professors von Neumann and Morgenstern who read the original form of the paper and gave helpful advice as to the presentation.

[2] John von Neumann and Oskar Morgenstern, *Theory of Games and Economic Behavior*, Princeton: Princeton University Press, 1944 (Second Edition, 1947), pp. 15–31.

In order to give a theoretical treatment of bargaining situations we abstract from the situation to form a mathematical model in terms of which to develop the theory.

In making our treatment of bargaining we employ a numerical utility, of the type developed in *Theory of Games*, to express the preferences, or tastes, of each individual engaged in bargaining. By this means we bring into the mathematical model the desire of each individual to maximize his gain in bargaining. We shall briefly review this theory in the terminology used in this paper.

UTILITY THEORY OF THE INDIVIDUAL

The concept of an "anticipation" is important in this theory. This concept will be explained partly by illustration. Suppose Mr. Smith knows he will be given a new Buick tomorrow. We may say that he has a Buick anticipation. Similarly, he might have a Cadillac anticipation. If he knew that tomorrow a coin would be tossed to decide whether he would get a Buick or a Cadillac, we should say that he had a $\frac{1}{2}$ Buick, $\frac{1}{2}$ Cadillac anticipation. Thus an anticipation of an individual is a state of expectation which may involve the certainty of some contingencies and various probabilities of other contingencies. As another example, Mr. Smith might know that he will get a Buick tomorrow and think that he has half a chance of getting a Cadillac too. The $\frac{1}{2}$ Buick, $\frac{1}{2}$ Cadillac anticipation mentioned above illustrates the following important property of anticipations: if $0 \leqslant p \leqslant 1$ and A and B represent two anticipations, there is an anticipation, which we represent by $pA + (1 - p) B$, which is a probability combination of the two anticipations where there is a probability p of A and $1 - p$ of B.

By making the following assumptions we are enabled to develop the utility theory of a single individual:

1. An individual offered two possible anticipations can decide which is preferable or that they are equally desirable.

2. The ordering thus produced is transitive; if A is better than B and B is better than C then A is better than C.

3. Any probability combination of equally desirable states is just as desirable as either.

4. If A, B, and C are as in assumption (2), then there is a probability combination of A and C which is just as desirable as C. This amounts to an assumption of continuity.

5. If $0 \leqslant p \leqslant 1$ and A and B are equally desirable, then $pA + (1 - p) C$ and $pB + (1 - p) C$ are equally desirable. Also, if A and B are equally desirable, A may be substituted for B in any desirability ordering relationship satisfied by B.

These assumptions suffice to show the existence of a satisfactory utility function, assigning a real number to each anticipation of an individual. This utility function is not unique, that is, if u is such a function then so also is $au + b$, provided $a > 0$. Letting capital letters represent anticipations and small ones real numbers, such a utility function will satisfy the following properties:

(a) $u(A) > u(B)$ is equivalent to A is more desirable than B, etc.

(b) If $0 \leqslant p \leqslant 1$ then $u[pA + (1 - p) B] = pu(A) + (1 - p) u(B)$.

This is the important linearity property of a utility function.

TWO PERSON THEORY

In *Theory of Games and Economic Behavior* a theory of n-person games is developed which includes as a special case the two-person bargaining problem. But the theory there developed makes no attempt to find a value for a given n-person game, that is, to determine what it is worth to each player to have the opportunity to engage in the game. This determination is accomplished only in the case of the two-person zero sum game.

It is our viewpoint that these n-person games should have values; that is, there should be a set of numbers which depend continuously upon the set of quantities comprising the mathematical description of the game and which express the utility to each player of the opportunity to engage in the game.

We may define a two-person anticipation as a combination of two one-person anticipations. Thus we have two individuals, each with a certain expectation of his future environment. We may regard the one-person utility functions as applicable to the two-person anticipations, each giving the result it would give if applied to the corresponding one-person anticipation which is a component of the two-person anticipation. A probability combination of two two-person anticipations is defined by making the corresponding combinations for their components. Thus if $[A, B]$ is a two-person anticipation and $0 \leqslant p \leqslant 1$, then

$$p[A, B] + (1 - p)[C, D]$$

will be defined as

$$[pA + (1 - p)C, pB + (1 - p)D].$$

Clearly the one-person utility functions will have the same linearity property here as in the one-person case. From this point onwards when the term anticipation is used it shall mean two-person anticipation.

In a bargaining situation one anticipation is especially distinguished; this is the anticipation of no cooperation between the bargainers. It is natural, therefore, to use utility functions for the two individuals which assign the number zero to this anticipation. This still leaves each individual's utility function determined only up to multiplication by a positive real number. Henceforth any utility functions used shall be understood to be so chosen.

We may produce a graphical representation of the situation facing the two by choosing utility functions for them and plotting the utilities of all available anticipations in a plane graph.

It is necessary to introduce assumptions about the nature of the set of points thus obtained. We wish to assume that this set of points is compact and convex, in the mathematical senses. It should be convex since an anticipation which will graph into any point on a straight line segment between two points of the set can always be obtained by the appropriate probability combination of two anticipations which graph into the two points. The condition of compactness implies, for one thing, that the set of points must be bounded, that is, that they can all be inclosed in a sufficiently large square in the plane. It also implies that any continuous function of the utilities assumes a maximum value for the set at some point of the set.

We shall regard two anticipations which have the same utility for any utility function corresponding to either individual as equivalent so that the graph becomes a complete representation of the essential features of the situation. Of course, the graph is only determined up to changes of scale since the utility functions are not completely determined.

Now since our solution should consist of *rational* expectations of gain by the two bargainers, these expectations should be realizable by an appropriate agreement between the two. Hence, there should be an available anticipation which gives each the amount of satisfaction he should expect to get. It is reasonable to assume that the two, being rational, would simply agree to that anticipation, or to an equivalent one. Hence, we may think of one point in the set of the graph as representing the solution, and also representing all anticipations that the two might agree upon as fair bargains. We shall develop the theory by giving conditions which should hold for the relationship between this solution point and the set, and from these deduce a simple condition determining the solution point. We shall consider only those cases in which there is a possibility that both individuals could gain from the situation. (This does not exclude cases where, in the end, only one individual could have benefited because the "fair bargain" might consist of an agreement to use a probability method to decide who is to gain in the end. Any probability combination of available anticipations is an available anticipation.)

Let u_1 and u_2 be utility functions for the two individuals. Let $c(S)$ represent the solution point in a set S which is compact and convex and includes the origin. We assume:

6. If α is a point in S such that there exists another point β in S with the property $u_1(\beta) > u_1(\alpha)$ and $u_2(\beta) > u_2(\alpha)$, then $\alpha \neq c(S)$.

7. If the set T contains the set S and $c(T)$ is in S, then $c(T) = c(S)$.

We say that a set S is symmetric if there exist utility operators u_1 and u_2 such that when (a, b) is contained in S, (b, a) is also contained in S; that is, such that the graph becomes symmetrical with respect to the line $u_1 = u_2$.

8. If S is symmetric and u_1 and u_2 display this, then $c(S)$ is a point of the form (a, a), that is, a point on the line $u_1 = u_2$.

The first assumption above expresses the idea that each individual wishes to maximize the utility to himself of the ultimate bargain. The third expresses equality of bargaining skill. The second is more complicated. The following interpretation may help to show the naturalness of this assumption: If two rational individuals would agree that $c(T)$ would be a fair bargain if T were the set of possible bargains, then they should be willing to make an agreement, of lesser restrictiveness, not to attempt to arrive at any bargains represented by points outside of the set S if S contained $c(T)$. If S were contained in T this would reduce their situation to one with S as the set of possibilities. Hence $c(S)$ should equal $c(T)$.

We now show that these conditions require that the solution be the point of the set in the first quadrant where $u_1 u_2$ is maximized. We know some such point exists from the compactness. Convexity makes it unique.

Let us now choose the utility functions so that the above-mentioned point is transformed into the point $(1, 1)$. Since this involves the multiplication of the utilities by constants, $(1, 1)$ will now be the point of maximum $u_1 u_2$. For no points of the set will $u_1 + u_2 > 2$, now, since if there were a point of the set with $u_1 + u_2 > 2$ at some point on the line segment between $(1, 1)$ and that point, there would be a value of $u_1 u_2$ greater than one (see Figure 1).

We may now construct a square in the region $u_1 + u_2 \leqslant 2$ which is symmetrical in the line $u_1 = u_2$, which has one side on the line $u_1 + u_2 = 2$, and which completely encloses the set of alternatives. Considering the square region formed as the set of alternatives, instead of the older set, it is clear that $(1, 1)$ is the only point satisfying assumptions (6) and (8). Now using assumption (7) we may conclude that $(1, 1)$ must also be the solution point when our original (transformed) set is the set of alternatives. This establishes the assertion.

We shall now give a few examples of the application of this theory.

Let us suppose that two intelligent individuals, Bill and Jack, are in a position where they may barter goods but have no money with which

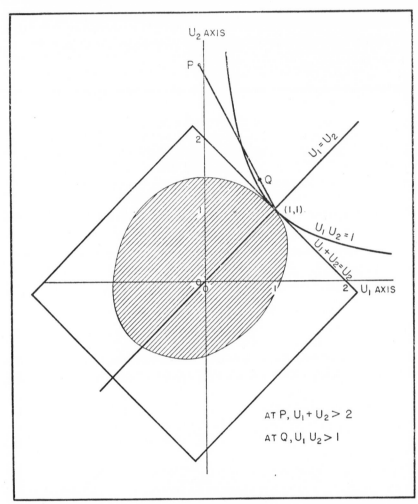

FIGURE 1

to facilitate exchange. Further, let us assume for simplicity that the utility to either individual of a portion of the total number of goods involved is the sum of the utilities to him of the individual goods in that portion. We give below a table of goods possessed by each individual with the utility of each to each individual. The utility functions used for the two individuals are, of course, to be regarded as arbitrary.

Bill's goods	Utility to Bill	Utility to Jack
book	2	4
whip	2	2
ball	2	1
bat	2	2
box	4	1
Jack's goods		
pen	10	1
toy	4	1
knife	6	2
hat	2	2

The graph for this bargaining situation is included as an illustration (Figure 2). It turns out to be a convex polygon in which the point where the product of the utility gains is maximized is at a vertex and where there is but one corresponding anticipation. This is:

> *Bill gives Jack:* book, whip, ball, and bat,
> *Jack gives Bill:* pen, toy, and knife.

When the bargainers have a common medium of exchange the problem may take on an especially simple form. In many cases the money equiva-

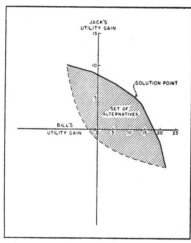

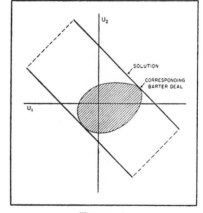

FIGURE 2   FIGURE 3

FIGURE 2—The solution point is on a rectangular hyperbola lying in the first quadrant and touching the set of alternatives at but one point.

FIGURE 3—The inner area represents the bargains possible without the use of money. The area between parallel lines represents the possibilities allowing the use of money. Utility and gain measured by money are here equated for small amounts of money. The solution must be formed using a barter-type bargain for which $u_1 + u_2$ is at a maximum and using also an exchange of money.

lent of a good will serve as a satisfactory approximate utility function. (By the money equivalent is meant the amount of money which is just as desirable as the good to the individual with whom we are concerned.) This occurs when the utility of an amount of money is approximately a linear function of the amount in the range of amounts concerned in the situation. When we may use a common medium of exchange for the utility function for each individual the set of points in the graph is such that that portion of it in the first quadrant forms an isosceles right triangle. Hence the solution has each bargainer getting the same money profit (see Figure 3).

Princeton University

TWO-PERSON COOPERATIVE GAMES
John F. Nash

In this paper, the author extends his previous treatment of "The Bargaining Problem" to a wider class of situations in which threats can play a role. A new approach is introduced involving the elaboration of the threat concept.

INTRODUCTION

THE THEORY presented here was developed to treat economic (or other) situations involving two individuals whose interests are neither completely opposed nor completely coincident. The word cooperative is used because the two individuals are supposed to be able to discuss the situation and agree on a rational joint plan of action, an agreement that should be assumed to be enforceable.

It is conventional to call these situations "games" when they are being studied from an abstract mathematical viewpoint. Here the original situation is reduced to a mathematical description, or model. In the abstract "game" formulation only the minimum quantity of information necessary for the solution is retained. What the actual alternative courses of action are among which the individuals must choose is not regarded as essential information. These alternatives are treated as abstract objects without special qualities and are called "strategies." Only the attitudes (like or dislike) of the two individuals towards the ultimate results of the use of the various possible opposing pairs of strategies are considered; but this information must be well utilized and must be expressed quantitatively.

The theory of von Neumann and Morgenstern applies to some of the games considered here. Their assumption that it is possible for the players to make "side-payments" in a commodity for which each individual (player) has a linear utility narrows the range of their theory's applicability. In this paper there is no assumption about side-payments. If the situation permits side-payments then this simply affects the set of possible final outcomes of the game; side-payments are treated just like any other activity that may take place in the actual playing of the game—no special consideration is necessary. The von Neumann and Morgenstern approach also differs by giving a much less determinate solution. Their approach leaves the final situation only determined up to a side-payment. The side-payment is generally not determined but is restricted to lie in a certain range.

An earlier paper by the author [3] treated a class of games which are in one sense the diametrical opposites of the cooperative games. A game is

¹ This paper was written with the support of The RAND Corporation. It appeared in an earlier form as RAND P–172, August 9, 1950.

non-cooperative if it is impossible for the players to communicate or collaborate in any way. The non-cooperative theory applies without change to any number of players, but the cooperative case, which is analyzed in this paper, has only been worked out for two players.

We give two independent derivations of our solution of the two-person cooperative game. In the first, the cooperative game is reduced to a non-cooperative game. To do this, one makes the players' steps of negotiation in the cooperative game become moves in the non-cooperative model. Of course, one cannot represent all possible bargaining devices as moves in the non-cooperative game. The negotiation process must be formalized and restricted, but in such a way that each participant is still able to utilize all the essential strengths of his position.

The second approach is by the axiomatic method. One states as axioms several properties that it would seem natural for the solution to have and then one discovers that the axioms actually determine the solution uniquely. The two approaches to the problem, via the negotiation model or via the axioms, are complementary; each helps to justify and clarify the other.

THE FORMAL REPRESENTATION OF THE GAME

Each of the players (one and two) has a compact convex metrizable space S_i of mixed strategies s_i (those readers who are unacquainted with the mathematical technicalities will find that they can manage quite well by ignoring them). These mixed strategies represent the courses of action player i can take independently of the other player. They may involve deliberate decisions to randomize, to decide between alternative possibilities by using a randomizing process involving specified probabilities. This randomizing is an essential ingredient in the concept of a mixed strategy. By beginning with a space of mixed strategies instead of talking about a sequence of moves, etc., we presuppose a reduction of the strategic potentialities of each player to the normal form [4].

The possible joint courses of action by the players would form a similar space. But the only important thing is the set of those pairs (u_1, u_2) of utilities which can be realized by the players if they cooperate. We call this set B and it should be a compact convex set in the (u_1, u_2) plane.

For each pair (s_1, s_2) of strategies from S_1 and S_2, there will be the utility to each player of a situation where these strategies are to be employed or carried out. These utilities (pay-offs in game theoretic usage) are denoted by $p_1(s_1, s_2)$ and $p_2(s_1, s_2)$. Each p_i is a linear function of s_1 and of s_2, although it cannot be expected to depend linearly on the two varying simultaneously; in other words, p_i is a bilinear function of s_1 and s_2. Basically this linearity is a consequence of the type of utility we assume for the players; it is thoroughly discussed in an early chapter of von Neumann and Morgenstern [4].

And of course each point in the (u_1, u_2) plane of the form $[p_1(s_1, s_2),$ $p_2(s_1, s_2)]$ must be a point in B because every pair (s_1, s_2) of independent strategies corresponds to a joint policy (probably an inefficient one). This remark completes the formal, or mathematical, description of the game.

THE NEGOTIATION MODEL

To explain and justify the negotiation model used to obtain the solution we must say more about the general assumptions about the situation facing the two individuals, or, what it amounts to, about the conditions under which the game is to be played.

Each player is assumed fully informed on the structure of the game *and* on the utility function of his co-player (of course he also knows his own utility function). (This statement must not be construed as inconsistent with the indeterminacy of utility functions up to transformations of the form $u' = au + b,\ a > 0$.) These information assumptions should be noted, for they are not generally perfectly fulfilled in actual situations. The same goes for the further assumption we need that the players are intelligent, rational individuals.

A common device in negotiation is the threat. The threat concept is really basic in the theory developed here. It turns out that the solution of the game not only gives what should be the utility of the situation to each player, but also tells the players what threats they should use in negotiating.

If one considers the process of making a threat, one sees that its elements are as follows: A threatens B by convincing B that if B does not act in compliance with A's demands, then A will follow a certain policy T. Supposing A and B to be rational beings, it is essential for the success of the threat that A be *compelled* to carry out his threat T if B fails to comply. Otherwise it will have little meaning. For, in general, to execute the threat will not be something A would want to do, just of itself.

The point of this discussion is that we must assume there is an adequate mechanism for forcing the players to stick to their threats and demands once made; and one to enforce the bargain, once agreed. Thus we need a sort of umpire, who will enforce contracts or commitments.

And in order that the description of the game be complete, we must suppose that the players have no prior commitments that might affect the game. We must be able to think of them as completely free agents.

THE FORMAL NEGOTIATION MODEL

Stage one: Each player (i) chooses a mixed strategy t_i which he will be forced to use if the two cannot come to an agreement, that is, if their demands are incompatible. This strategy t_i is player i's threat.

Stage two: The players inform each other of their threats.

Stage three: In this stage the players act independently and without communication. The assumption of independent action is essential here, whereas no special assumptions of this type are needed in Stage one, as it turns out. In Stage three, each player decides upon his demand d_i, which is a point on his utility scale. The idea is that player i will not cooperate unless the mode of cooperation has at least the utility d_i to him.

Stage four: The pay-offs are now determined. If there is a point (u_1, u_2) in B such that $u_1 \geqslant d_1$ and $u_2 \geqslant d_2$, then the pay-off to each player i is d_i. That is, if the demands can be simultaneously satisfied, then each player gets what he demanded. Otherwise, the pay-off to player i is $p_i(t_1, t_2)$; i.e., the threats must be executed.

The choice of the pay-off function in the case of compatible demands may seem unreasonable, but it has its advantages. It cannot be accused of contributing a bias to the final solution and it gives the players a strong incentive to increase their demands as much as is possible without losing compatibility. But it can be embarrassingly accused of picking points that are not in the set B. Effectively, we have enlarged B to a set including all utility pairs dominated (weakly; $u_1' \leqslant u_1$, $u_2' \leqslant u_2$) by a pair in B.

What we have is actually a two move game. Stages two and four do not involve any decisions by the players. The second move choices are made with full information about what was done in the first move. Therefore, the game consisting of the second move alone may be considered separately (it is a game with a variable pay-off function determined by the choices made at the first move). The effect of the choice of threats on this game is to determine the pay-offs if the players do not cooperate.

Let N be the point $[p_1(t_1, t_2), p_2(t_1, t_2)]$ in B. This point N represents the effect of the use of the threats. Let u_{1N} and u_{2N} abbreviate the coordinates of N. If we introduce a function $g(d_1, d_2)$ which is $+1$ for compatible demands and 0 for incompatible demands, then we can represent the pay-offs as follows:

to player one $d_1g + u_{1N}(1 - g)$,
to player two $d_2g + u_{2N}(1 - g)$.

The demand game defined by these pay-off functions will generally have an infinite number of inequivalent equilibrium points [3]. Every pair of demands which graphs as a point on the upper-right boundary of B and which is neither lower nor to the left of N will form an equilibrium point. Thus the equilibrium points do not lead us immediately to a solution of the game. But if we discriminate between them by studying their relative stabilities we can escape from this troublesome non-uniqueness.

To do this we "smooth" the game to obtain a continuous pay-off function and then study the limiting behavior of the equilibrium points of the smoothed game as the amount of smoothing approaches zero.

A certain general class of natural smoothing methods will be considered here. This class is broader than one might at first think, for many other methods that superficially seem different are actually equivalent.

To smooth the game we approximate the discontinuous function g by a continuous function h, which has a value near to g's value except at the points near the boundary of B, where g is discontinuous. The function $h(d_1, d_2)$ should be thought of as representing the probability of compatibility of the demands d_1 and d_2. It can be thought of as representing uncertainties in the information structure of the game, the utility scales, etc. For convenience, let us assume that $h = 1$ on B and that h tapers off very rapidly towards zero as (d_1, d_2) moves away from B, without ever actually reaching zero. Another simplification can be had by assuming the utility functions properly transformed so that $u_{1N} = u_{2N} = 0$. Then we can write the pay-off functions for the smoothed game as $P_1 = d_1 h$, $P_2 = d_2 h$. For the original game h is replaced by g.

A pair of demands (d_1, d_2) viewed as a pair of pure strategies in the demand game, will be an equilibrium point if p_1, which is $d_1 h$, is maximized here for constant d_2 and if $p_2 = d_2 h$ is maximized for constant d_1. Now suppose (d_1, d_2) is a point where $d_1 d_2 h$ is maximized over the whole region in which d_1 and d_2 are positive. Then $d_1 h$ and $d_2 h$ will be maximized for constant d_2 and d_1, respectively, and (d_1, d_2) must be an equilibrium point.

If the function h decreases with increasing distance from B in a wavy or irregular way, there may be more equilibrium points and perhaps even more points where $d_1 d_2 h$ is a maximum. But if h varies regularly there will be only one equilibrium point coinciding with a unique maximum of $d_1 d_2 h$. However, we do not need to appeal to a regular h to justify the solution.

Let P be any point where $d_1 d_2 h$ or, what is the same thing, $u_1 u_2 h$ is maximized as above described and let ρ be the maximum of $u_1 u_2$ on the part of B lying in the region $u_1 \geqslant 0$, $u_2 \geqslant 0$. The value of $u_1 u_2$ at P must be at least ρ, since $0 \leqslant h \leqslant 1$ and since $h = 1$ on B. Figure 1 illustrates this situation. In it, Q is the point where $u_1 u_2$ is maximized on B (in the first quadrant about N) and $\alpha\beta$ is the hyperbola $u_1 u_2 = \rho$, which touches B at Q.

The important observation is that P must lie above $\alpha\beta$ but still be near enough to B for h to nearly equal 1. And as less and less smoothing is used, h will decrease more and more rapidly on moving away from B; hence any maximum point P of $u_1 u_2 h$ will have to be nearer and nearer to B. In the limit all such points must approach Q, the only contact point of B and the area above $\alpha\beta$. Thus Q is a necessary limit of equilibrium points, and Q is the only one.

We take Q for the solution of the demand game, characterized as the *only necessary limit of the equilibrium points of smoothed games.* The values of u_1 and u_2 at Q will be taken as the values of the demand game and as the optimal demands.

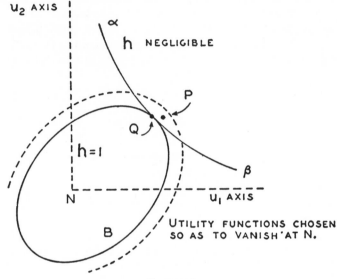

FIGURE 1

The discussion above implicitly assumed that B contained points where $u_1 > 0$, $u_2 > 0$ (after the normalization which made $u_1 = u_2 = 0$ at N). The other cases can be treated more simply without resource to a smoothing process. In these "degenerate cases" there is only one point of B which dominates the point N and is not itself dominated by some other point of B. (A point (u_1, u_2) is dominated by another point (u_1', u_2') if $u_1' \geqslant u_1$ and $u_2' \geqslant u_2$) [see Figure 3]. This gives us the natural solution in these cases.

One should note that the solution point Q of the demand game varies as a continuous function of the threat point N. Also there is a helpful geometrical characterization of the way Q depends on N. The solution point Q is the contact point with B of a hyperbola whose asymptotes are the vertical and horizontal lines through N. Let T be the tangent at Q to this hyperbola (see Figure 2).

If linear transformations are applied to the utility functions, N can be made the origin and Q the point $(1, 1)$. Now T will have slope -1 and the line NQ will have slope $+1$. The essential point is that slope $T = $ minus slope NQ, because this is a property that is not destroyed by linear transformations of the utilities. T will be a support line for the set B (that is, a line such that all points of B are either on the lower left side of T or are on T itself; for a proof, see reference [2] where the same situation arises).

We can now state the criterion: if NQ has positive slope and a support line T for B passes through Q with a slope equal but opposite to NQ's slope, then Q is the solution point for the threat point N. If NQ is horizontal/vertical and is itself a support line for B and if Q is

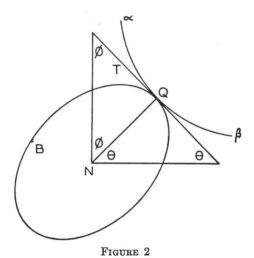

FIGURE 2

the rightmost/uppermost of the points common to B and NQ, then again Q is the solution point for N (see Figure 3), and one of these cases must hold if Q is N's solution point; the criterion is a necessary and sufficient one.

Any support line of B with a contact point Q on the upper-right boundary of B determines a complementary line through Q with equal but opposite slope. All points on the line segment in which this complementary line intersects B are points which, as threat points, would have Q as corresponding solution point. The class of all these line segments is a ruling of B by line segments which intersect, if at all, only on the upper-right boundary of B. Given a threat point N, its solution point is the upper-right end of the segment passing through it (unless perhaps N is on more than one ruling and hence is on the upper-right boundary and is its own solution point).

We can now analyze the threat game, the game formed by the first move and with pay-off function determined by the solution of the demand game. This pay-off is determined by the location of N, specifically by the ruling on which N falls. A ruling that is higher (or farther left) is more favorable to player two (let us definitely think of u_2 as measured on the vertical axis of the utility plane) and less favorable to player one.

Now if one player's threat is held fixed, say player one's at t_1, then the position of N is a function of the other player's threat, t_2. The co-ordinates of N, $p_1(t_1, t_2)$ and $p_2(t_1, t_2)$ are linear functions of t_2. Hence the transformation, t_2 goes into N, defined by this situation is a linear transformation of the space S_2 of player two's threats into B. That part of the image of S_2 that falls on the most favorable (for player two) ruling will contain the images of the threats that would be best as replies to player one's fixed particular threat t_1. And this set of best replies

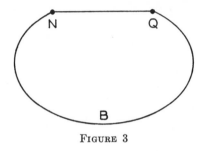

FIGURE 3

must be a convex compact subset of S_2 because of the linearity and continuity of the transformation of S_2 into B.

The continuity of N as a function of t_1 and t_2 and the continuity of Q as a function of N insure that the pay-off function defined for the threat game by solving the demand game is a continuous function of the threats. And this suffices to make each player's set of best replies what is called an upper semi-continuous function of the threat being replied to. Now consider any pair of threats (t_1, t_2). For each threat of the pair the other player has a set of best replies. Let $R(t_1, t_2)$ be the set of all pairs which contain one threat from each of the two sets of replies. R will be an upper semi-continuous function of (t_1, t_2) in the space of opposed pairs of threats, and $R(t_1, t_2)$ will always be a convex set in this space, $S_1 \times S_2$.

We are now ready to use the Kakutani fixed point theorem, as generalized by Karlin [1, pp. 159–160]. This theorem tells us that there is some pair (t_{10}, t_{20}) that is contained in its set $R(t_{10}, t_{20})$, which amounts to saying that each threat is a best reply to the other. Thus we have obtained an equilibrium point in the threat game. It is worth noting that this equilibrium point is formed by pure strategies in the threat game (a mixed strategy here would involve randomization over several threats).

The pair (t_{10}, t_{20}) also has minimax and maximin properties. Since the final pay-off in the game is determined by the position of Q on the upper-right boundary of B, which is a negatively sloping curve, each player's pay-off is a monotone decreasing function of the others. So if player one sticks to t_{10}, player two cannot make one worse off than he does by using t_{20} without improving his own position, and he can't do this because (t_{10}, t_{20}) is an equilibrium point [3]. Thus t_{10} *assures* player one the equilibrium pay-off and t_{20} accomplishes the same for player two.

The threat game is now revealed to be very much like a zero-sum game, and one can readily see that if one player were to choose his threat first and inform the other, rather than their simultaneously choosing threats, this would not make any difference because there is a "saddle-point" in pure strategies. It is rather different with the demand game. The right to make the first demand would be quite valuable, so the simultaneity here is essential.

To summarize, we have now solved the negotiation model, found the values of the game to the two players, and shown that there are optimal threats and optimal demands (the optimal demands are the values).

THE AXIOMATIC APPROACH

Rather than solve the two-person cooperative game by analyzing the bargaining process, one can attack the problem axiomatically by stating general properties that "any reasonable solution" should possess. By specifying enough such properties one excludes all but one solution.

The axioms below lead to the same solution that the negotiation model gave us; yet the concepts of demand or threat do not appear in them. Their concern is solely with the relationship between the solution (interpreted here as the value) of the game and the basic spaces and functions which give the mathematical description of the game.

It is rather significant that this quite different approach yields the same solution. This indicates that the solution is appropriate for a wider variety of situations than those which satisfy the assumptions we made in the approach via the model.

The notation used below is the same as before, except for a few additions. A triad (S_1, S_2, B) stands for a game and $v_1(S_1, S_2, B)$ and $v_2(S_1, S_2, B)$ are its values to the two players. Of course the triadic representation, (S_1, S_2, B), leaves implicit the payoff functions $p_1(s_1, s_2)$ and $p_2(s_1, s_2)$ which must be given to determine a game.

AXIOM I: For each game (S_1, S_2, B) there is a unique solution (v_1, v_2) which is a point in B.

AXIOM II: If (u_1, u_2) is in B and $u_1 \geqslant v_1$ and $u_2 \geqslant v_2$ then $(u_1, u_2) = (v_1, v_2)$; that is, the solution is not weakly dominated by any point in B except itself.

AXIOM III: Order preserving linear transformations of the utilities $(u_1' = a_1 u_1 + b_1, u_2' = a_2 u_2 + b_2$ with a_1 and a_2 positive) do not change the solution. It is understood that the numerical values will be changed by the direct action of the utility transformations, but the relative position of (v_1, v_2) in B should stay the same.

AXIOM IV: The solution does not depend on which player is called player one. In other words, it is a symmetrical function of the game.

AXIOM V: If a game is changed by restricting the set B of attainable pairs of utilities and the new set B' still contains the solution point of the original game, then this point will also be the solution point of the new game. Of course the new set B' must still contain all points of the form $[p_1(s_1, s_2), p_2(s_1, s_2)]$, where s_1 and s_2 range over S_1 and S_2, to make (S_1, S_2, B') a legitimate game.

AXIOM VI: A restriction of the set of strategies available to a player cannot increase the value to him of the game. Symbolically, if S_1' is contained in S_1, then $v_1(S_1', S_2, B) \leqslant v_1(S_1, S_2, B)$.

AXIOM VII: There is some way of restricting both players to single strategies without increasing the value to player one of the game. In symbols, there exist s_1 and s_2 such that $v_1(s_1, s_2, B) \leqslant v_1(S_1, S_2, B)$. Similarly, there is a way to do the same for player two.

There is little need to comment on Axiom I; it is just a statement on the type of solution desired. Axiom II expresses the idea that the players should succeed in cooperating with optimal efficiency. The principle of noncomparability of utilities is expressed in Axiom III. Each player's utility function is regarded as determined only up to order preserving linear transformations. This indeterminacy is a natural consequence of the definition of utility [4, chapter 1, part 3]. To reject Axiom III is to assume that some additional factor besides each individual's relative preferences for alternatives is considered to make the utility functions more determinate and to assume that this factor is significant in determining the outcome of the game.

The symmetry axiom, Axiom IV, says that the only significant (in determining the value of the game) differences between the players are those which are included in the mathematical description of the game, which includes their different sets of strategies and utility functions. One may think of Axiom IV as requiring the players to be intelligent and rational beings. But we think it is a mistake to regard this as expressing "equal bargaining ability" of the players, in spite of a statement to this effect in "The Bargaining Problem" [2]. With people who are sufficiently intelligent and rational there should not be any question of "bargaining ability," a term which suggests something like skill in duping the other fellow. The usual haggling process is based on imperfect information, the hagglers trying to propagandize each other into misconceptions of the utilities involved. Our assumption of complete information makes such an attempt meaningless.

It is probably harder to give a good plausibility argument for Axiom V than for any of the others. There is some discussion of it in "The Bargaining Problem" [2]. This axiom is equivalent to an axiom of "localization" of the dependence of the solution point on the shape of the set B. The location of the solution point on the upper-right boundary of B is determined only by the shape of any small segment of the boundary that extends to both sides of it. It does not depend on the rest of the boundary curve.

Thus there is no "action at a distance" in the influence of the shape of B on the location of the solution point. Thinking in terms of bargaining, it is as if a proposed deal is to compete with small modifications of itself and that ultimately the negotiation will be understood to be restricted to a narrow range of alternative deals and to be unconcerned with more remote alternatives.

The last two axioms are the only ones that are primarily concerned with the strategy spaces S_1 and S_2, and the only ones that are really new. The other axioms are simply appropriate modifications of the axioms used in "The Bargaining Problem." Axiom VI says that a player's position in the game is not improved by restricting the class of threats available to him. This is surely reasonable.

The need for Axiom VII is not immediately obvious. Its effect is to remove the possibility that the value to a player of his space of threats should be dependent on collective or mutual reinforcement properties of the threats. The way Axiom VII is used in the demonstration of the adequacy of the axioms probably reveals its real content better than any heuristic discussion we might give here.

We can shortcut some of the arguments needed to show that the axioms accomplish their purpose and characterize the same solution we obtained with the model by appealing to the results of "The Bargaining Problem." We first consider games where each player has but one possible threat. Such a game is essentially a "bargaining problem," and for that sort of game our Axioms I, II, III, IV, and V are the same as the axioms of "The Bargaining Problem."

This determines the solution in the case where each player has but one strategy available. It must be the same solution obtained in "The Bargaining Problem," which was the same as the solution we got for the demand game (which is played after each player has chosen a threat) in the preceding approach. This solution is characterized by the maximization of the product, $[v_1 - p_1(t_1, t_2)] [v_2 - p_2(t_1, t_2)]$, of the differences between the values of the game and the utilities of the situation where the players do not cooperate.

However, we are obliged to remark that the situation to be treated here is more general than that in "The Bargaining Problem" because it was assumed in that paper that there was some way for the players to cooperate with mutual benefit. Here it may be the case that only one, or neither, of the players can actually gain by cooperation. To show that the axioms handle this case seems to require a more complicated argument using Axioms VI and VII. But this is a minor point and we shall not include that argument, which is long out of proportion to its significance.

The primary function of Axioms VI and VII is to enable us to reduce the problem of games where each player may have a non-trivial space of strategies (threats) to the case we have just dealt with, where each has but one possible threat. Suppose player one is restricted to a strategy t_{10} which would be an optimal threat in the threat game discussed before in the non-axiomatic approach. Then from Axiom VI, we have

$$v_1(t_{10}, S_2, B) \leqslant v_1(S_1, S_2, B).$$

Now we apply Axiom VII to restrict S_2 to a single strategy (S_1 is already restricted) without increasing the value of the game to player one. Let t_2^* stand for the single strategy that S_2 is restricted to, then

$$v_1(t_{10}, t_2^*, B) \leqslant v_1(t_{10}, S_2, B).$$

Now we know that the value of a game where each player has but one threat is the same value obtained in the first part of this paper. Hence we know that against the threat t_{10} there is no better threat for player two, and no threat more unfavorable for player one, than t_{20} (i.e., an optimal threat for player two). So we may write

$$v_1(t_{10}, t_{20}, B) \leqslant v_1(t_{10}, t_2^*, B).$$

Combining the three inequalities we have

$$v_1(t_{10}, t_{20}, B) \leqslant v_1(S_1, S_2, B).$$

Similarly, we have

$$v_2(t_{10}, t_{20}, B) \leqslant v_2(S_1, S_2, B).$$

And now we observe, by Axiom II, that the last two inequalities may be replaced by equalities, because $v_1(t_{10}, t_{20}, B)$ and $v_2(t_{10}, t_{20}, B)$ are the coordinates of a point on the upper-right boundary of B. Thus the axiomatic approach gives the same values as the other approach.

Massachusetts Institute of Technology

REFERENCES

[1] KUHN, H. W. AND A. W. TUCKER, eds., *Contributions to the Theory of Games (Annals of Mathematics Study No. 24)*, Princeton: Princeton University Press, 1950, 201 pp.

[2] NASH, JOHN, "The Bargaining Problem," ECONOMETRICA, Vol. 18, April, 1950, pp. 155–162.

[3] NASH, JOHN, "Non-Cooperative Games," *Annals of Mathematics*, Vol. 54, September, 1951, pp. 286–295.

[4] VON NEUMANN, J. AND O. MORGENSTERN, *Theory of Games and Economic Behavior*, 2nd edition, Princeton: Princeton University Press, 1947, 641 pp.

BARGAINING AND CONFLICT SITUATIONS IN LIGHT OF A NEW APPROACH TO GAME THEORY

John C. Harsanyi

I

Classical economic theory is based on the assumption that in most economic situations people will act in a rational manner; that is, in accordance with certain consistency requirements called "rationality postulates"—or at least that their deviations from rationality in this sense will not be very important. Economic theory then shows that, as far as a person's actions satisfy the relevant rationality postulates, his behavior will be equivalent to maximizing his (ordinal) utility function. (The rationality postulates needed require that his choices should be transitive and connected and should satisfy an appropriate continuity requirement.)

This concept of rational behavior—assuming that it leads to realistic predictions—is an extremely powerful explanatory principle because it enables us to account for a large number of possibly quite complex empirical facts about people's behavior, in terms of a few relatively simple assumptions about their preferences or equivalently about their utility functions.

This rational behavior concept of classical economic theory, however, fails to furnish sufficiently specific predictions in situations involving risk or uncertainty, such as insurance, gambling, speculation, and in general entrepreneurial behavior; as well as in situations involving strategic interaction between two or more persons or organizations, such as individual and collective bargaining, bilateral monopoly, duopoly, oligopoly, situations involving political pressure and counterpressure, etc.

More particularly, in analyzing the concept of rational behavior, we have to distinguish the following cases:

1. Rational behavior of an isolated individual: (*a*) under certainty (where the outcome of any possible action he may take is fully known to him in advance); (*b*) under risk (where he knows at least the objective probabilities associated with alternative possible outcomes); (*c*)

under uncertainty (where even some or all of these objective probabilities are unknown to him, or where these objective probabilities are
not even defined in any straightforward sense).

2. Rational behavior by two or more interacting individuals, where
each individual is rationally pursuing his own personal interests (i.e.,
all his objectives, both selfish and unselfish, to which he assigns positive utility) against other individuals rationally pursing their own personal interests (again both selfish and unselfish)—the basic problem of
game theory. For some purposes it is convenient to include also:

3. The rational pursuit of the long-run interests of the society as a
whole—the basic problem of ethics,[1] and of welfare economics, which
for our purposes is essentially a branch of ethics.

The rational behavior concept of classical economics corresponds to
case 1*a* (certainty). It has remained for modern decision theory to develop satisfactory definitions for rational behavior in cases 1*b* and 1*c*
(risk and uncertainty), by means of supplementing the rationality assumptions of classical economics by a few additional rationality postulates. The most important additional postulate needed is the Sure-
Thing (or Dominance) Principle: If action X cannot yield worse results than action Y but can possibly yield better results, then a rational
individual will choose X in preference to Y.

It can be shown that if a given individual acts in accordance with
this enlarged set of rationality postulates, then his behavior will be
equivalent to maximizing his expected utility[2]; i.e., to maximizing the
mathematical expectation of his cardinal utility function. (Unlike an
ordinal utility function, a person's cardinal utility function is uniquely
determined once a zero point and a unit of measurement are chosen for
his utility.)

More particularly, in the case of risk, where the individual concerned knows all the relevant objective probabilities, he will maximize
his expected utility as defined in terms of these objective probabilities;
whereas in the case of uncertainty, where he has to act without knowing all these objective probabilities, he will maximize his expected utility as defined partly or wholly in terms of his own subjective probabilities (which intuitively can be interpreted as his personal estimates of
the objective probabilities unknown to him). This definition of rational
behavior, making use of subjective probabilities, is often called the
"Bayesian" concept of rationality.

[1] This is true at least under a utilitarian concept of ethics.
[2] For a proof of the expected-utility maximization theorem in the case of risk, see,
e.g. [11]. For a proof in the case of uncertainty, see [17] or [1]. The last paper shows
that even for uncertainty the assumptions needed do not go essentially beyond a certain
form of the sure-thing principle.

II

We have already mentioned that classical economic theory fails to furnish determinate predictions in game situations, at least in those where there is significant strategical interdependence between the various participants' behavior. To take a very simple example, suppose a seller and a buyer try to settle the price of a house by bargaining. The seller's reservation price (supply price) is $20,000 while the buyer's demand price is $30,000. Then classical economic theory can predict only that the price will lie somewhere between $20,000 and $30,000. But it cannot predict where the price will in fact lie between these two limits—indeed it cannot even specify the variables actually determining the price within this range.

Even worse types of indeterminacy arise in slightly more complex situations, such as duopoly, where the space of possible outcomes has more than one dimension. Many eminent economists, starting with Cournot, have tried to obtain more determinate predictions for duopoly situations on the basis of various more or less *ad hoc* assumptions, but it is now generally agreed that their duopoly models were rather unsatisfactory. In particular, though all of them started out with the aim of predicting how two rational duopolists would act in duopoly situations, in fact all of them ended up with attributing some quite unplausibly irrational behavior to their two duopolists. (For example, Cournot's duopolists persist in the same mistaken expectations about each other's behavior, even though their expectations are continually disappointed by the actual events. Moreover, they make no attempt to agree on a collusive solution, even though this would make both of them much better off.)

In retrospect, the basic reason why these distinguished economists did not succeed in their efforts was the fact that they did not have any general systematic theory of rational behavior in (what we now would call) game situations with strategical interdependence between two or more rational individuals. Their example seems to show that it is virtually impossible to develop a satisfactory theory of rational behavior for some specific game situation, such as duopoly, without relying on a more general theory of rational behavior covering a much wider range of game situations.

Yet, in actual fact, the first truly systematic attempt to analyze rational behavior over a broad class of game situations, Von Neumann and Morgenstern's theory of games (1944), has not yielded determinate solutions for the game situations occurring in economics. Their theory does provide a number of very important analytical tools for the analysis of any game situation (e.g., the concepts of expected-utility maximization, strategy, mixed strategy, coalition, characteristic function, dominance, etc.). It also furnishes a very satisfactory determinate solution for two-person constant-sum games, but fails to supply determinate solutions for two-person variable-sum games and for *n*-person games—though in fact virtually all empirical social situations, including those considered by economics, belong to these two game categories.

However, the present writer has shown [4] [5] [7] [8] [9] [10] that if we add a few very natural rationality postulates to those used by Von Neumann and Morgenstern, then we obtain determinate solutions for all classes of finite games (as well as for infinite games satisfying certain regularity requirements), both two-person and *n*-person, constant-sum and variable-sum, with and without transferable utility, cooperative and noncooperative, etc.[3] The solutions of all these games become special cases of the same general theory of rational behavior in game situations. As a result, our theory provides determinate predictions for duopoly, oligopoly, bilateral monopoly, bargaining, political power situations, etc.—once we make specific assumptions about the participants' utility functions, their strategical possibilities, and the information available to them. Thus it enables us to analyze all these situations in terms of the same general principles, without any need in the various particular cases for arbitrary *ad hoc* assumptions about people's behavior.

III

The basic difficulty in defining rational behavior in game situations is the fact that in general each player's strategy will depend on his expectations about the other players' strategies. Could we assume that his expectations were given, then his problem of strategy choice would become an ordinary maximization problem: he could simply choose a strategy maximizing his own payoff on the assumption that the other players would act in accordance with his given expectations. But the point is that game theory cannot regard the players' expectations about each other's behavior as given; rather, one of the most important problems for game theory is precisely to decide what expectations intelligent players can rationally entertain about other intelligent players' behavior. This may be called the problem of mutual "rational expectations."

Technically, a given player's expectations can be represented in terms of the subjective probabilities he assigns to various possibilities. Thus the problem of rational expectations can also be regarded as a problem of rationally chosen subjective probabilities; that is, as a

[3] Our theory is largely a generalization of earlier work by [13] [14] [15] [18] [20].

problem of deciding what subjective probabilities a given player can rationally assign to different possible strategy choices by the other players, when he knows that these other players are intelligent individuals just as he himself is.

On the fundamental level of analysis, the main novelty of our own approach to game theory is the new solution we propose for this crucial problem of mutual rational expectations (or of rationally chosen subjective probabilities).

Our theory makes use of two classes of rationality postulates in the analysis of game situations. One class consists of postulates of rational behavior in a narrower sense, which deal directly with a rational player's strategy choices in game situations. Intuitively they can be regarded as formalizations of the requirement that, other things being equal, a rational player will always give preference to strategies yielding him a higher payoff, but will be indifferent (and will choose at random) between strategies yielding him the same payoff.

The other class consists of postulates of rational expectations, which deal with rational players' expectations about each other's strategies. These postulates require a rational player not to act on the expectation that another rational player will choose a strategy inconsistent with our rationality postulates. More generally, they require him not to act on the expectation that another rational player will choose a strategy which the first player himself would regard as an irrational strategy (for any reason whatever), and which he himself would therefore never use in a similar case. (In particular, in a bargaining situation a rational player cannot expect a concession from a rational opponent if he himself would refuse such a concession were their objective positions and their utility functions exactly interchanged.)

IV

For lack of space we cannot here describe our rationality postulates in greater detail, nor can we show how these postulates actually allow derivation of determinate solutions for various games. (The interested reader is referred to [3] [4] [5] [7] [8] [9] [10].) Instead, we shall only indicate some of our main results in an informal way.

We need the following definitions. Neglecting intermediate cases, we shall speak of a vocal game if the players are free to communicate with each other, and shall speak of a tacit game if no communication is allowed. A game will be called "cooperative" if the players are free to make enforceable binding agreements as well as other binding commitments; e.g., irrevocable threats. In the opposite case a game will be called "noncooperative." (Our definitions differ from the more usual ones in making the distinctions vocal versus tacit and cooperative versus noncooperative mutually independent, thus permitting consideration of vocal games not allowing binding agreements, and of tacit games allowing binding agreements based on tacit understanding.)

We call a given strategy s_i of player i a best reply to the other $(n - 1)$ players' strategies $s_1, \ldots, s_{i-1}, s_{i+1}, \ldots, s_n$ if s_i maximizes player i's payoff if all other players' strategies are kept constant. We call a joint strategy $(s_1, \ldots, s_n)$ of the n players an equilibrium point if every player's strategy in it is a best reply to the other players' strategies.

We call a joint strategy stable if an agreement by the players to adopt this joint strategy would be self-enforcing, or at least would be enforced and made binding by the rules of the game. In a cooperative game every possible joint strategy will be stable (because all agreements by the players would have full binding force). In a noncooperative game only an equilibrium point can be stable (because agreements will be kept only so long as no player has an incentive to default).[4]

V

In any particular game the players usually have to solve the following problems:

1. The stability problem; i.e., the problem of identifying the set S of all stable joint strategies available to them.

2. The efficiency problem; i.e., the problem of finding the set E of efficient stable joint strategies, defined as those stable joint strategies which could not be replaced by other stable joint strategies to all players' common advantage. Any payoff vector $u = (u_1, \ldots, u_n)$ corresponding to some efficient stable joint strategy will be called an "eligible" payoff vector.

3. The bargaining problem. Different players will have opposite preferences among the various eligible payoff vectors of the game. The bargaining problem is the problem of agreeing on one unique eligible payoff vector u out of the set E^* of all eligible payoff vectors.

4. The strategy-coordination problem; i.e., the problem of agreeing on one unique joint strategy for achieving the payoff vector u already agreed upon. (This is a real problem only in tacit games.)

In cooperative games each player can strengthen his bargaining position by committing himself to use certain damaging strategies, called

---

[4] In actual fact, being an equilibrium point is only a necessary condition for stability but is in itself not a sufficient condition. If a joint strategy is an equilibrium point, then no player will have a positive incentive to switch over to a different strategy, but he may not have a positive incentive not to do so, either. Therefore, only equilibrium points satisfying certain additional stability conditions will be really stable [8] [9].

"threat strategies," against the other players if no agreement were reached on the payoffs of the game and a conflict situation arose. In an *n*-person cooperative game he can strengthen his bargaining position also by joining coalitions; i.e., by agreeing to cooperate with some players against some other players in such conflict situations. Therefore, in these games the bargaining problem gives rise to one or both of two further auxiliary problems for each player; viz., the problem of optimal threat strategies and that of optimal coalitions.

In some games there is only one stable joint strategy (e.g., in a non-cooperative game containing only one stable equilibrium point). In other games, even though there may be several stable joint strategies, only one of them is efficient, or at least all efficient joint strategies yield the same unique eligible payoff vector. In such games there is no bargaining problem. In all other games the solution of the game depends primarily on the solution of the bargaining problem.

VI

The bargaining problem can be approached from two rather different standpoints. One can ask the ethical question of what particular outcome would represent a "fair" solution (in terms of some moral criteria) [1] [16]. Or, one can ask the specifically game-theoretical question of what outcome will emerge if all parties follow their own interests in a rational manner. Our own analysis tries to answer this second, specifically game-theoretical, question.

Accordingly we shall assume that one player will make concessions to another, not because he feels some moral commitment to do so, but rather because he thinks it would be too risky, from his own point of view, to refuse these concessions. (We do not necessarily assume that the players pay no attention to moral considerations. But we assume that each player's utility function will already take account of any utility he may assign to moral values of any kind.)

Our analysis of the bargaining problem primarily tries to decide under what conditions a given player can or cannot rationally expect another intelligent player to make him a concession. As an answer to this question, our rationality postulates yield a decision rule identical to a decision rule for bargaining behavior first proposed by Zeuthen [20], which we call "Zeuthen's principle." Roughly speaking, the principle asserts that the answer depends on the highest risk (i.e., the highest probability of a conflict) each player would be willing to face rather than accept his opponent's terms. (This highest risk a given player is willing to face can itself be computed on the basis of the expected-utility maximization postulate.)

More particularly, of two players the one more willing to risk a conflict (the one willing to face a higher probability of a conflict) can reasonably expect a concession from the other player, while the one less willing to risk a conflict cannot expect a concession from his opponent and has to make himself a concession if a conflict is to be avoided.

In the case of two-person cooperative games, it can be shown that Zeuthen's principle leads to the Nash solution [3] [13] [15]. As Nash has pointed out, once we have a solution for the bargaining problem, the solution for the problem of optimal threat strategies is quite immediate. Intuitively speaking, Nash's definition for optimal threat strategies represents the best compromise between trying to maximize the costs of a conflict to the opponent and trying to minimize the costs of a conflict to oneself.

As has been mentioned, classical economic theory cannot specify the variables determining the outcome of a bargaining situation. In contrast, the Nash solution predicts that the solution will depend: (1) on each player's attitudes toward risk, as expressed by his cardinal utility function, and in particular on his willingness to risk a conflict rather than accept less favorable terms; and (2) on each player's ability to cause damages to the opponent in case of a conflict, and on the costs to him of causing these damages.

The Nash-Zeuthen theory enables us to avoid various common fallacies in the analysis of bargaining situations. One is the assumption that our opponent will accept any deal so long as this deal would still be better for him than facing a conflict would be.[5] (This would mean that we could reasonably expect all concessions to come from our opponent—as if he were the only one of the two of us who had an interest in avoiding a conflict.)

Another is the assumption that a rational bargainer will never make a threat which would commit him to a conflict strategy damaging not only to the opponent but also to him himself—even though such a threat can greatly improve the terms he can extract from his opponent. (For instance, it has been argued that a union can never rationally commit itself to a strike likely to result in a net loss to the union and its members.[6])

Both fallacies represent misapplications of the utility-maximization principle, whose precise interpretation involves many pitfalls in bargaining situations.

---

[5] This assumption I have called the "blackmailer's fallacy" [6, p. 74].
[6] For instance [12, Chap. VII].

VII

In the case of n-person cooperative games, our theory leads to different solution concepts, depending on the communication facilities open to the players.

If the communication facilities among the players have no bias in favor of any particular group of players, then according to our theory all possible $(2^n - 1)$ coalitions will be operative simultaneously in the game; that is, the members of every possible coalition will cooperate in protecting their common interests against the rest of the players. Hence each player will be a member of a large number of mutually intersecting coalitions and will tend to side with different coalitions on different issues. Thus, our model resembles what political scientists call the "pluralistic" model of society.

Under this assumption of unbiased communication facilities, our theory leads to a solution concept which is at the same time an n-person generalization of the two-person Nash solution, and also a generalization of a modified form of the Shapley value [7] [15] [18].

In contrast, the Von Neumann-Morgenstern theory and many other game-theoretical approaches lead to solution concepts based on the assumption that the players will form two or more disjoint coalitions (each of which may itself again possibly consist of two or more disjoint subcoalitions, etc.). This means that only a small subset of all possible coalitions will be operative in any particular game. Under our theory, such coalition structures can arise only if the communication facilities among the players are biased—in particular, if some players have an opportunity to negotiate a coalition agreement before the other players could make counteroffers to them.

For instance, in a symmetric three-person game with unbiased communication facilities, all three players will obtain the same payoff. Only if these facilities are biased and permit two players to reach an agreement before the third player could intervene will the solution be based on two of the players forming a two-person coalition against the third player and obtaining a payoff advantage over him. This follows from the general principle that any asymmetry among the players in the outcome must be explained by some asymmetry in the antecedent conditions—in this case in the communication facilities open to the players.

Finally, in the case of noncooperative games, the task of the players is to agree by bargaining on one particular equilibrium point satisfying the appropriate stability and efficiency requirements. Here (even if the game is an n-person one) the coalition problem does not arise, and so the bargaining problem can be analyzed simply in terms of Zeuthen's principle [8] [10].

VIII

We now have to say a few words about the analysis of conflict situations under our theory. In everyday language the term "conflict" may mean one of two things. It may mean a simple absence of cooperation (even in cases where no profitable cooperation is possible between the players at all): in this sense any two-person constant-sum game always represents a conflict situation.

More interesting is the other meaning. Here "conflict" refers to a situation where the players make no use, or make no full use, of some known and mutually profitable opportunities for cooperation. In this sense a conflict exists whenever the players' actual strategies represent an inefficient joint strategy (even though they know they would have some more efficient strategies).

Under our theory, a conflict in this second sense among rational players can arise only in the following cases:

1. In a cooperative game it can arise only if the players insist on mutually incompatible demands as a price of their cooperation—this again can happen only if they do not know one another's utility functions and strategical possibilities (since otherwise they could always avoid making mutually incompatible demands simply by asking for no more than the payoff the solution of the game assigns to each of them).

2. In a noncooperative game the players may have to forego the use of efficient joint strategies also because these strategies may be unstable; in other words, because they may have good reasons not to trust one another to abide by any agreement involving the use of these strategies. This is often called the "Prisoner's Dilemma" case.

3. The players may use what an observer considers to be an inefficient joint strategy; yet from the players' own point of view this may not be an inefficient strategy at all, because their real payoff targets may be different from what the observer thinks them to be. For instance, in a two-person game the observer may think that both players want to maximize their money gains while in actual fact each of them may want to maximize the difference between his own gain and that of his opponent. Thus what may look like inefficient strategies in a non-zero-sum game may be in fact very efficient strategies in the zero-sum game which the players are actually playing.[7]

---

[7] Though in this case the players' strategies will not represent a conflict in the second sense of the word, they will correspond to a conflict in the first sense. I owe the example to Professor Lawrence Fouraker.

REFERENCES

1. F. J. Anscombe and R. J. Aumann, "A Definition of Subjective Probability," *Annals of Math. Statis.*, 1963, pp. 199-205.
2. R. B. Braithwaite, *Theory of Games as a Tool for the Moral Philosopher* (Cambridge Univ. Press, 1955).
3. John C. Harsanyi, "Approaches to the Bargaining Problem Before and After the Theory of Games," *Econometrica*, 1956, pp. 144-57.
4. ———, "On the Rationality Postulates Underlying the Theory of Cooperative Games," *J. of Conflict Resolution*, 1961, pp. 179-96.
5. ———, "Rationality Postulates for Bargaining Solutions in Cooperative and in Non-Cooperative Games," *Management Sci.*, 1962, pp. 141-53.
6. ———, "Measurement of Social Power, Opportunity Costs, and the Theory of Two-Person Bargaining Games," *Behavioral Sci.*, 1962, pp. 67-80.
7. ———, "A Simplified Bargaining Model for the n-Person Cooperative Game," *Int. Econ. Rev.*, 1963, pp. 194-220.
8. ———, *Rational Behavior and Bargaining Equilibrium in Games and Social Situations* (book manuscript, to be published).
9. ———, "A General Theory of Rational Behavior in Game Situations," *Working Paper* No. 87 (1964, U.C. Center for Research in Management Science, to be published).
10. ———, "A General Solution for Finite Non-Cooperative Games, Based on Risk-Dominance," Chap. 29 in M. Dresher, L. S. Shapley, and A. W. Tucker (editors), *Advances in Game Theory* (Princeton Univ. Press, 1964).
11. I. N. Herstein and J. W. Milnor, "An Axiomatic Approach to Measurable Utility," *Econometrica*, 1953, pp. 291-97.
12. J. R. Hicks, *The Theory of Wages* (London: Macmillan, 1932).
13. John F. Nash, "The Bargaining Problem," *Econometrica*, 1950, pp. 155-62.
14. ———, "Non-Cooperative Games," *Annals of Mathematics*, 1951, pp. 286-95.
15. ———, "Two-Person Cooperative Games," *Econometrica*, 1953, pp. 128-40.
16. Howard Raiffa, "Arbitration Schemes for Generalized Two-Person Games," Chap. 21 in H. W. Kuhn and A. W. Tucker (editors), *Contributions to the Theory of Games*, Vol. II (Princeton Univ. Press, 1953).
17. L. J. Savage, *The Foundations of Statistics* (Wiley, 1954).
18. L. S. Shapley, "A Value for n-Person Games," Chap. 17 in H. W. Kuhn and A. W. Tucker (editors), *Contributions to the Theory of Games*, Vol. II (Princeton Univ. Press, 1953).
19. John von Neumann and Oskar Morgenstern, *Theory of Games and Economic Behavior* (Princeton Univ. Press, 1944).
20. Frederik Zeuthen, *Problems of Monopoly and Economic Warfare* (London: Routledge, 1930).

GAME-THEORETIC ANALYSES OF BARGAINING

Robert L. Bishop

In recent years game theorists have produced an interesting collection of bargaining theories, applicable to such basic economic problems as bilateral monopoly, duopoly, and the like. Because of its technical character, much of this literature is imperfectly accessible to many economists with a natural interest in the relevant applications. In addition, the theories themselves stand in some need of critical evaluation. Accordingly, it is the dual purpose of this paper to present both a comparatively nontechnical exposition and a critique of those theories.

I. CHARACTERISTICS OF THE GAME-THEORETIC APPROACH

Bargaining situations are of two basic types. The simpler one is illustrated by any of the standard instances of bilateral monopoly, where nonagreement has the unique consequence of no trade. When each bargainer can threaten that outcome but nothing worse, the parties may be said to be engaged in "fixed-threat" bargaining. The second and more general case of "variable-threat" bargaining implies that, in the absence of some mutually advantageous agreement, the parties have options as to the actions that they may unilaterally adopt; so their threats and counterthreats as to the damages that they may inflict on one another are inherently variable. Duopoly and other forms of oligopoly always involve variable threats; and so may the more complex forms of bilateral monopoly, for example when disagreements may be accompanied by violence or other harassments.

Although bargaining, whether fixed-threat or variable-threat, may readily involve more than two (natural or organizational) persons, discussion will be limited for the time being to the case where there are just two (as in most of the literature to be reviewed). The bargaining relationship may be either nonrecurrent or, in varying degrees, recurrent. Usually some form of explicit negotiation is visualized, with a binding agreement possible between the parties; but sometimes bargaining may be only tacit, provided that there is still some sound basis for an efficient agreement if the parties are willing to make one. An agreement is said to be "efficient" (or "Pareto-optimal," at least as far as the bargainers themselves are concerned) if it places the parties at some point on their "utility frontier," which is defined as the locus where, for any given attainable utility for one person, the other's utility is a maximum.[1] In general, then, the essence of a bargaining situation is that, although the parties have conflicting preferences as among the various eligible points on their utility frontier, they will both be better off if they can agree on some one such point, as compared with the consequences of nonagreement.

As in most of orthodox game theory, the bargaining theories of that species are based on the assumption that both bargainers know (and are known to know) all relevant data, including each participant's von Neumann-Morgenstern utility function. This means that the bargaining problem can be analyzed with reference to a known utility frontier.

Briefly, the utility theory of von Neumann and Morgenstern [2] holds that a person's preference between a given "sure thing" and a given "lottery" (or between a pair of lotteries) is always consistent with the assumption that he is maximizing the mathematical expectation of his utility. In principle, then, such a person's utility u can be experimentally determined as a function of his wealth w, though with an arbitrary scale factor of utility and an arbitrary point of zero utility. In the technical phrase, his utility function is determinate "up to an order-preserving linear transformation."

---

1. As emphasized by Fellner, "Prices and Wages under Bilateral Monopoly," this *Journal*, LXI (Aug. 1947), 503–32, an efficient agreement between bilateral monopolists typically requires an all-or-none deal, in which both price and quantity are specified; for, if the parties merely agree on a price and then let the quantity be determined by demand or supply (whichever is less), they will fail to reach their contract curve (and hence their utility frontier) except when demand and supply happen to be equal. This is often the case, notably in labor-management bargaining; for unions are typically unable to deliver a labor quantity in excess of what their constituents are willing to supply, and employers usually succeed in maintaining an analogous freedom on their side. Except for the further uncertainty as to what unions may seek to maximize (J. T. Dunlop, *Wage Determination under Trade Unions* (New York: A. M. Kelley, 1950), pp. 32–44), such cases involve no special analytical difficulty: it is merely necessary to substitute the relevant "pseudo" utility frontier for the "true" one. Similarly, in duopoly, the relevant utility frontier usually depends on whether or not side payments are permitted.

2. J. von Neumann and O. Morgenstern, *Theory of Games and Economic Behavior* (3d ed., Princeton: Princeton University Press, 1953).

This means that, if a certain utility function $u = u(w)$ is consistent with his risk-choices, so also is any linear transformation of that function, $u^* = au(w) + b$, where a is any positive constant (the order-preserving scale factor) and b is any constant (such that $-b/a$ determines the zero-utility point).

In particular, then, if a person has a consistently "neutral" attitude toward risks, such that he is always indifferent between (1) any (positive or negative) increment of wealth $\triangle w$ to be obtained with probability p and (2) the increment $p\triangle w$ to be received with certainty, his utility is a linear function of w and his marginal utility is a constant. On the other hand, if he consistently prefers the second alternative to the first or the first to the second, his utility function is concave from below (reflecting diminishing marginal utility) or concave from above (reflecting increasing marginal utility), respectively.

The other ingredient on which the utility frontier of a pair of bargainers depends is their objective-payoff frontier. For example, if a pair of isolated individuals possess given stocks of apples and nuts such that some mutually advantageous trade is possible, their objective-payoff frontier is defined by the paired quantities that might be traded in order to put the bargainers on their contract curve, somewhere within the relevant range where neither bargainer is worse off than in the absence of any trade. Alternatively, if the bilateral monopolists are, respectively, producer-seller and buyer-user of an intermediate product, their objective-payoff frontier is then a straight line with slope of -1, reflecting the various ways in which they might divide their maximized joint profit. Similarly, if the bargainers are duopolists, their profit frontier will again reflect the paired profits along their contract curve — except that, if side payments are permitted, the profit frontier will again be a straight line with slope of -1, passing through the one or more points where the joint profit is a maximum.

Given an objective-payoff frontier (say in dollars) and both bargainers' utility functions (with some arbitrary assignment of the utility scales and zero points), a utility frontier consists of the paired utilities of the various paired profits on the objective frontier.[3] This is the relevant utility frontier, at least in all of the usual

3. Except where otherwise indicated, it will be assumed that each person's utility depends only on his own objective payoff. There is no difficulty in principle, however, if a bargainer's utility also depends on the objective payoff of the other bargainer or on that of third parties who may also be affected by the bargaining. On the other hand, if the dependence of either bargainer's utility on the other's objective payoff is subject to change in the course of

cases where it is either linear or concave from below; but if it has any portions that are concave from above, or if it is initially discontinuous (for example consisting of just certain isolated points, as when the objects to be exchanged are indivisible), the orthodox prescription is to bridge those gaps with straight lines, reflecting the expected utilities implied by various probability deals.[4] Technically, this implies that the set of attainable utility points, as bounded on the critical side by the utility frontier, is a "convex set" — that is, an area such that any straight line between any two points within the area would also lie wholly within it.

To illustrate, if two bargainers have a linear profit frontier and each has a linear utility function, their utility frontier will also be linear (though still with arbitrary utility scales and origin). On the other hand, the same profit frontier will correspond to a utility frontier that is concave from below if either party has diminishing marginal utility while the other's is either diminishing, constant, or not too sharply increasing.

As treated by von Neumann and Morgenstern themselves, even the two-person bargaining problem lacks a unique solution; for its "solution" in their sense merely calls for an outcome somewhere on the relevant range of the utility frontier. At best, this represented no progress whatever; for Edgeworth had adopted the same view years before. Actually, however, the conclusion is logically objectionable; for, if bargainers cannot agree as to a particular point on their utility frontier, they are not going to reach it at all.

The theories to be considered here, on the other hand, are those that undertake to identify a solution worthy of the name — that is, a unique one. As dictated essentially by the nature of the problem, the simple case of fixed-threat bargaining will be considered first, to be followed later by the more general case of bargaining with variable threats.

---

negotiation, that would be a fatal complication, at least for the theories to be considered.

4. For example, if the utility frontier is initially either nonexistent or concave from below between the two points (u_{11}, u_{21}) and (u_{12}, u_{22}) (where u_{ij} is the ith person's utility at the jth point), an agreement to move to one point or the other, each with probability $\frac{1}{2}$, would yield expected utilities equal to those at the midpoint of the straight line joining the two points, namely $(\frac{1}{2})$ $(u_{11} + u_{12})$ for the first person and $(\frac{1}{2})$ $(u_{21} + u_{22})$ for the second; and similarly for other such probabilities and other such points on the same straight line. The validity of this operation rests on the basic properties of von Neumann-Morgenstern utilities. When the bargaining is recurrent, furthermore, an equivalent rectification may sometimes be achieved by an agreement to occupy the two points with stipulated frequencies. (In some practical applications such as duopoly, however, neither type of rectification may be feasible, both for legal reasons and for such economic ones as the existence of fixed costs.)

II. Theories of Fixed-Threat Bargaining

The leading entrant among bargaining theories of the more orthodox game-theoretic type is unquestionably the one proposed by John Nash. This will be considered first, and then it will be compared with its rivals.

Nash's Theory

When a pair of fixed-threat bargainers are fated to remain at their no-trade or status-quo threat point unless they can make some mutually advantageous agreement to move to some point on their (known and appropriately shaped) utility frontier, Nash concludes that the appropriate bargain is the one that maximizes the product of their utility increments from the threat point.[5] This conclusion follows from certain "axioms," which Nash regards as "fair" and "reasonable" conditions to be fulfilled when the bargainers are sufficiently knowledgeable and "rational." He first adopts, as a part of his conception of "rationality," one set of axioms that establish the relevance of von Neumann-Morgenstern utilities. Another axiom, that of "Pareto optimality," merely asserts that the bargainers shall move to some point on their utility frontier, rather than stop somewhere short of it. In view of the knowledge assumptions and as a part of what is essentially a recommended solution (rather than a descriptive or predictive theory under realistic knowledge conditions), this is hardly a controversial axiom. The specific solution point is then justified by three critical axioms.

(1) Since the solution is concerned with the increments of utility from the fixed threat point, it is convenient to set each person's utility equal to zero at that point, so that u_1 and u_2 as measured from the threat point reflect the utility increments of the two parties. The first critical axiom, which is a matter of *symmetry*, then asserts that, if the set of attainable points indicative of u_1 and u_2 (or the utility frontier in the relevant range) is symmetrical with respect to the line $u_1 = u_2$, the solution point lies on that line.[6] Thus, if it could somehow be known that the utility frontier of a certain pair of bargainers was a straight line with a slope of -1,

5. John Nash, "The Bargaining Problem," *Econometrica*, Vol. 18 (Apr. 1950), pp. 155–62. *Idem*, "Two-Person Cooperative Games," *Econometrica*, Vol. 21 (Jan. 1953), pp. 128–40.

6. In contrast to that initial formulation (Nash, "The Bargaining Problem," *op. cit.*, p. 159), Nash later stated his symmetry axiom in this more noncommittal form ("Two-Person Cooperative Games," *op. cit.*, p. 137): "The solution does not depend on which player is called player one." The first version seems preferable, because it is essential to include somewhere the assumption that the solution depends only on the attainable utility increments.

as in Figure Ia, this axiom (in conjunction with the Pareto-optimal axiom) would be sufficient to determine the Nash-solution point N at the midpoint of that line, such that the two parties would receive "equal" increments of utility in moving from the threat point T.

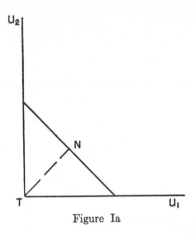

Figure Ia

(2) Actually, however, the fact that von Neumann-Morgenstern utilities are determinate only up to an order-preserving linear transformation implies that any other linear utility frontier would be no less acceptable. For example, suppose that the same scale is kept for u_2 as in Figure Ia, but each magnitude of u_1 is doubled. This linear transformation of the first person's utility function then yields a new utility frontier, which is again linear but with a slope of $-\frac{1}{2}$, as in Figure Ib. Nash's second critical axiom is now invoked: "Order preserving linear transformations of the utilities . . . do not change the solution." [7] Accordingly, since the midpoint of the new utility frontier is objectively the same as the old one's (giving twice the numerical utility but the same "real" utility to the person whose utility scale was arbitrarily stretched), this *transformation-invariance* axiom establishes that, if the midpoint of a linear utility frontier with a slope of -1 is the acceptable solution, so is the midpoint of any linear utility frontier, such as N in Figure Ib.

(3) A third axiom, asserting what has come to be called the *independence of irrelevant alternatives,* is needed to cover the transition from linear to nonlinear utility frontiers (of appropriately re-

7. "Two-Person Cooperative Games," *op. cit.,* p. 137. Oddly enough, this axiom was only implicit in Nash's initial paper, "The Bargaining Problem," *op. cit.,* p. 159.

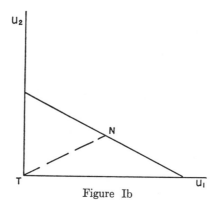

Figure Ib

stricted shape). It may be stated thus: if a linear utility frontier is unfavorably altered anywhere except at its midpoint (with the threat point still at the origin), the solution is not changed.[8] Consider, for example, the curvilinear utility frontier in Figure Ic, as

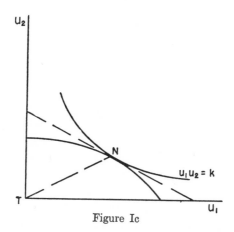

Figure Ic

compared with the linear frontier that is reproduced from Figure Ib. The new frontier lies everywhere inside the old one, except at the latter's solution point. In other words, the new frontier denies to the bargainers only certain points that were rejected alternatives

8. This axiom was stated in much the same way in both of Nash's papers: for example ("Two-Person Cooperative Games," *op. cit.,* p. 137), "If a game is changed by restricting the set *B* of attainable pairs of utilities and the new set *B'* still contains the solution point of the original game, then this point will also be the solution point of the new game." This is defective in that it does not specify that *B'* must also still contain the relevant threat point of the original game (which cannot be so easily taken for granted in variable-threat games — which Nash was then discussing — as it can be in the present fixed-threat context).

as compared with the preferred point N at the midpoint of the linear frontier. Accordingly, the third critical axiom establishes that N is still the solution point.[9]

These axioms are sufficient to establish that the solution point N always occurs where u_1u_2 is a maximum. Thus, anywhere on the linear utility frontier $u_2 = b - au_1$ (where a and b are both positive constants), the product of the utility increments from the origin is $u_1u_2 = bu_1 - au_1{}^2$; and this is found to be a maximum where $u_1 = b/2a$ and $u_2 = b/2$, which are respectively equal to half of the axis-intercept magnitudes, $u_1 = b/a$ and $u_2 = b$. Accordingly, u_1u_2 is a maximum at the midpoint of any linear frontier, or at the point on any appropriately curvilinear frontier that would similarly lie midway between the axis-intercepts of a line tangent to the curve at that point. Equivalently, the N point also occurs where the frontier is tangent to a curve of the form $u_1u_2 = k$, as illustrated in Figure Ic, or at the point where the frontier is unit-elastic.[1] Finally, if the slope of the utility frontier at N is $-a$, the slope of the line TN is a, since it equals $u_2 = b/2$ divided by $u_1 = b/2a$.[2]

An evaluation of Nash's rather elegant procedure will be given later, when it can be compared with some alternatives.

The Zeuthen-Harsanyi Theory

Especially as interpreted by Harsanyi,[3] Zeuthen's bargaining theory [4] yields the same result as Nash's, though it rests on a quite different rationalization, involving the patterns of concession when two bargainers have confronted one another with mutually incompatible initial demands. Zeuthen visualized a group of employers bargaining with a union over the wage rate; but, in his initially simplified example, he also assumed the amount of employment to be independent of the wage rate (as it might well be under efficient all-or-none bargaining, although that was not Zeuthen's rationale).

9. This axiom might better be referred to as implying "the independence (or irrelevance) of rejected alternatives," since that better expresses the grounds for their alleged irrelevance; but the other name is too well established to be worth changing now.

1. On the other hand, if the utility frontier has a discontinuity of slope at N, the tangency is just of the "general" kind, and N is merely the dividing point between the relatively elastic and relatively inelastic portions of the frontier.

2. Again, however, if the frontier's slope is discontinuous at N, the slope of the line TN is (except for sign) merely intermediate between the slopes of the two segments of the frontier in the immediate vicinity of N.

3. J. C. Harsanyi, "Approaches to the Bargaining Problem Before and After the Theory of Games," *Econometrica*, Vol. 24 (Apr. 1956), pp. 144–57.

4. F. Zeuthen, *Problems of Monopoly and Economic Warfare* (London: G. Routledge, 1930), Chap. 4.

Hence the parties would also be bargaining about the total wage bill, between a fixed maximum that the employers might conceivably pay and a fixed minimum that the union might conceivably accept. On the other hand, the rest of Zeuthen's discussion, including his side remarks and qualifications, suggests that he was really concerned with the "utilities" of various possible outcomes to the participants,[5] though in a sense antedating that of von Neumann and Morgenstern. This, it seems to me, goes a long way toward justifying Harsanyi's translation of Zeuthen's discussion into utility terms.[6]

So translated, the analysis begins with a situation in which each bargainer demands a highly favorable outcome for himself, as at the points labeled 1 and 2, respectively, on the utility frontier in Figure II (where u_{ij} is the utility of the ith person as proposed by the jth).

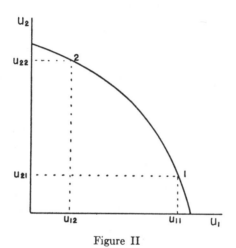

Figure II

5. *Ibid.*, p. 113.
6. On the other hand, Pen (who also has derived a large measure of inspiration from Zeuthen) feels that Harsanyi greatly underestimates the substantive differences between Zeuthen and Nash, despite the "identity of the solutions" that Harsanyi has demonstrated, but which Pen dismisses as merely an "affinity of form." J. Pen, *The Wage Rate Under Collective Bargaining*, trans. T. S. Preston (Cambridge: Harvard University Press, 1959), pp. xii–xiii. Pen's main objection is that, in contrast to the abstract and impersonal character of Nash's solution, "in which [the assumptions] of rational behavior and . . . perfect knowledge occupy a leading position" and in which "uncertainty plays no part," Zeuthen's theory as a whole gives much weight to the realistic uncertainties that are typically involved. This is true to at least a considerable extent (in part because Zeuthen was not wholly self-consistent, but mainly because of the ways in which he went on to qualify his initial model); but it still remains that Zeuthen and Nash do come to the same conclusion whe⌐ they make the same, admittedly idealized assumptions as to the knowledge of the bargainers.

Zeuthen then supposes each bargainer to deliberate between accepting the other's offer and holding out for his own in the hope that the other will accept it. From the first bargainer's point of view, for example, immediate capitulation would yield him the utility u_{12}, while stubbornness would yield him the greater utility u_{11} if the other surrenders or zero utility if the other proves equally adamant. Zeuthen then asks: what is the maximum subjective probability of conflict (c_1) that the first bargainer can rationally stand, in holding out for his own demand? The answer is: that value of c_1 that will make it a matter of indifference to him, as a matter of expected utilities, whether he capitulates or holds out indefinitely — that is, the value of c_1 that satisfies the equation, $u_{12} = (1 - c_1)u_{11}$. Hence the desired value of c_1 and the corresponding value of c_2 for the second bargainer are:

$$c_1 = \frac{u_{11} - u_{12}}{u_{11}}, \qquad c_2 = \frac{u_{22} - u_{21}}{u_{22}}.$$

Zeuthen now specifies (and this is the critical part of his theory) that the first bargainer will make at least some concession, and the second will not, if $c_1 < c_2$ (that is, if the first cannot stand as great a probability of conflict as the second); or the second bargainer will be the one to make a concession if $c_1 > c_2$; or they will both make simultaneous concessions if $c_1 = c_2 > 0$. Typically, however, neither makes a complete concession to the other's current demand, but rather concedes only enough to make it the other bargainer's turn to concede at least a little, whether unilaterally or simultaneously with a corresponding further concession by the first bargainer. In other words, the first bargainer makes a concession when $c_1 \leqslant c_2$, or when (with reference to the above two equations):

$$u_{11}u_{21} \leqslant u_{22}u_{12}.$$

Hence each concession by the first bargainer raises the utility product that he proposes ($u_{11}u_{21}$); and similarly, each concession by the second raises $u_{22}u_{12}$. Accordingly, these utility products are maximized and equated to one another when an agreement is finally reached, with $u_{11} = u_{12}$ and $u_{22} = u_{21}$ at a single point on the utility frontier, and with $c_1 = c_2 = 0$.[7]

7. For an axiomatizing of this theory, see Harsanyi, "On the Rationality Postulates Underlying the Theory of Cooperative Games," *Journal of Conflict Resolution*, Vol. 5 (June 1961), pp. 179–96; and, for a brief critique, see Bishop, "A Zeuthen-Hicks Theory of Bargaining," forthcoming in *Econometrica*. The latter paper also contains a brief exposition and evaluation of Hicks's bargaining theory (which antedates game theory and has little in common with it), as well as a novel Zeuthen-Hicks synthesis that makes the outcome depend on the comparative durations of strike that the parties can stand, in a Zeuthen-like

Raiffa's Theories

Under the frank label of "arbitration schemes," Raiffa has suggested a variety of possible ways in which bargainers might settle for some one point on their utility frontier. Though independently devised, one of these yields the Nash solution; but it will not be considered here because Raiffa himself considers that its rationalization is inferior to Nash's.[8] The other three, together with their differences from one another and from the Nash-Zeuthen solution, will be illustrated in the two bargaining situations shown in Figure IIIa and IIIb.

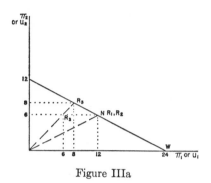

Figure IIIa

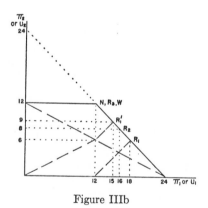

Figure IIIb

In both cases it is assumed that both bargainers have linear utility functions, so that the objective payoff frontier (relating π_1 and π_2 in dollars) will also serve as an acceptable utility frontier

sense (and which implies a different outcome from the Nash-Zeuthen one when the parties have unequal subjective rates of time-discount).

8. R. D. Luce and H. Raiffa, *Games and Decisions* (New York: Wiley, 1957), p. 143.

even when the utilities u_1 and u_2 are considered not comparable interpersonally. The first case (Figure IIIa) reflects the opportunity of two persons to receive positive payoffs if they can agree, without the possibility of any side payment, on amounts satisfying the relationship:

$$\pi_1 + \pi_2 \leqslant 24.$$

Otherwise neither receives anything. The second case (Figure IIIb) reflects a similar opportunity subject to the relationships:

$$\pi_1 + \pi_2 \leqslant 24 \qquad\qquad \text{and } \pi_2 \leqslant 12.$$

A payoff frontier might be of this type, for example, if there is (for an optimally constant amount of employment) a fixed surplus that may be divided in any proportion between a firm and its organized employees (that is, a surplus over and above the revenue that the firm must receive to stay in business and the wages that the work force could receive elsewhere), except that, in this firm's community (though not elsewhere), there is a governmentally decreed minimum wage that would require this firm to pay total wages of $\pi_1 \geqslant 12$ if it hires the optimal amount of labor.

(1) The solution points designated R_1 refer to outcomes based on a technique of successively "splitting the difference" between the maximum feasible demands that the two parties might make at each stage of a negotiation process.[9] Starting from the origin of Figure IIIb, for example, the parties initially demand utilities (or dollar payoffs) corresponding to the axis-intercept values of $u_1 = 24$ and $u_2 = 12$. The first man thus demands a solution at (24.0), while the second's demand could be satisfied at any point on the horizontal line between (0, 12) and (12, 12). Since (12, 12) is the only such point that is Pareto-optimal and thus on the utility frontier, Raiffa would presumably consider it to be the relevant one. On that basis, the two bargainers split the difference between (24, 0) and (12, 12), and thus end up at (18, 6), the point labeled R_1.

On the other hand, if the horizontal boundary at $\pi_2 = 12$ were replaced by a line that sloped ever so slightly downward from the π_2-axis to (12, 12), the second player's initial demand would be at that axis-intercept; and the first splitting of the difference would bring the players to a point slightly above (12, 6), at the midpoint of the straight line joining the axis-intercepts. As the process is then repeated from that point, the first player demands a solution

9. H. Raiffa, "Arbitration Schemes for Generalized Two-Person Games," H. W. Kuhn and A. W. Tucker (eds.), *Contributions to the Theory of Games* (Princeton: Princeton University Press, 1953), II, 361–87. Luce and Raiffa, *op. cit.*, pp. 136–37.

at a point on the utility frontier slightly above and to the left of (18, 6), while the second demands (12, 12) ; and, when the difference is split between those two demands, the solution is reached at a point on the utility frontier slightly above and to the left of (15, 9), labeled R_1'.[1]

(2) A second scheme, with outcomes designated by R_2, involves "equal" increments of utility from the threat point, as based on an interpersonal utility comparison of a purely *ad hoc* type.[2] Specifically, Raiffa suggests, the maximum attainable utilities of the two men may be taken as "equal" to another, simply for the purpose of arbitrating the one game. In Figure IIIb, then, the solution R_2 is at (16, 8), where each man receives two-thirds of his maximum conceivable payoff (24 and 12, respectively).[3]

Although R_1 and R_2 coincide with the Nash-Zeuthen point N in Figure IIIa, they differ from that point and from one another in Figure IIIb. As this reflects, both Raiffa schemes satisfy the Nash axioms of symmetry and transformation invariance, but not the independence-of-irrelevant-alternatives axiom. Indeed, all three points will coincide whenever (with the threat point at the origin) the utility frontier is symmetrical with respect to the line $u_1 = u_2$, or whenever it can be made symmetrical in that sense by a linear transformation of one player's utility scale. Otherwise, however, they will typically differ. In particular, they will differ if an otherwise symmetrical utility frontier is modified in the immediate vicinity of either axis, thereby illustrating the significant influence of those allegedly "irrelevant alternatives" in the two Raiffa schemes.

(3) The third of Raiffa's suggestions also calls for "equal" increments of utility from the threat point, but as based on a substantive interpersonal utility comparison, which would not depend

1. In other cases, of course, more than just one or two steps may be needed to reach the solution point; and, indeed, if the utility frontier is concave from below in the vicinity of the solution point, that point will only be approached as the number of steps becomes indefinitely large. Raiffa also suggests a "smoothed" version of the same process, which gives weight to every point on the utility frontier. Except when the utility frontier is linear, as in Figure IIIa, the result is a nonlinear path whose slope at any given point is the same (except for sign) as the slope of the straight line joining the two corresponding points currently demanded on the utility frontier. In Figures IIIa and IIIb, however, the smoothed version (involving the paths to R_1 and R_1', shown as broken lines) yields the same solution as the discrete version.
2. Raiffa, *op. cit.*; Luce and Raiffa, *op. cit.*, pp. 146–48.
3. Another scheme of the same *ad hoc* type has been suggested by R. B. Braithwaite, *Theory of Games as a Tool for the Moral Philosopher* (Cambridge, England: Cambridge University Press, 1955); but it will be considered only later, because it is inapplicable in fixed-threat bargaining.

in the *ad hoc* fashion on the payoffs in each given game.[4] For example, for the entire class of games in which the objective payoffs are in money, the convention might be adopted that equal monetary increments represent equal increments of utility, provided at least that both players have linear utility functions (or provided that neither of those functions is known to be other than linear). Or more generally, "it may be possible to determine a common unit by choosing two stimuli to serve as reference points for equating tastes."[5] Thus, on the assumption that the utilities in Figures IIIa and IIIb are interpersonally comparable, equal increments of utility from the threat point imply solutions at the points labelled R_3: (8, 8) in one case and (12, 12) in the other.[6] This scheme conforms to the axioms of symmetry and independence of irrelevant alternatives; but, because it rests on a substantive (rather than *ad hoc*) interpersonal comparison of utilities, it involves a deliberate rejection of the transformation-invariance axiom.

A Welfare Theory

Continuing with the assumption that some substantive interpersonal comparison is adopted, even if only by convention, we might substitute for the criterion of equal utility increments the rule that the sum of the utility increments be maximized, with the supplementary condition that they shall be as nearly equal as possible whenever their sum is a maximum at more than one point. Since this is essentially a welfare-economics rule, the points illustrating this solution are designated by W in figures IIIa and IIIb: (24, 0) and (12, 12), respectively. Like the third Raiffa scheme, this formula conforms to the axioms of symmetry and independence of irrelevant alternatives, but not to the transformation-invariance axiom.

Since this scheme may readily leave one of the parties with a zero utility increment, as in Figure IIIa, it is subject to the obvious difficulty of gaining that party's acceptance in any given, single

4. Raiffa, *op. cit.*; Luce and Raiffa, *op. cit.*, pp. 143–45.
5. Luce and Raiffa, *op. cit.*, p. 145.
6. Notice, however, that if the frontier in Figure IIIa were truncated at $u_2 = 6$ (in the same way that the frontier in Figure IIIb is truncated at $u_2 = 12$), a mechanical application of this rule would imply a solution at R_3' or (6, 6), which is not a Pareto-optimal point. Hence the rule might be modified to yield utility increments that are as nearly equal as possible, consistent with Pareto optimality. This would shift R_3' to N or (12, 6). On the other hand, if the truncation were made with a line that sloped ever so slightly downward from a point just barely above (0, 6) to (12, 6), R_3' would again be very close to (6, 6).

case.[7] Indeed, this solution could be spontaneously adopted only on the principle of brotherly love, when both players are willing to maximize $u_1 + u_2$.

On the other hand, this scheme, though not considered by Luce and Raiffa, would deserve serious consideration under a principle that they propose.[8] Thus, they first point out the apparent hopelessness of choosing among multiple arbitration schemes whose rankings would be strictly opposed as far as the preferences of two players of any given game are concerned. Instead, they suggest, it might be better to ask the same pair of people to evaluate the various alternative arbitration schemes with respect to a wide class of possible games, before they are confronted with the need to arbitrate any specific game. Then, for example, if two players are to play the game depicted in Figure IIIa and they are required to pick an arbitration scheme before they know who is to be player one, they will both choose the present scheme yielding W as the solution. In other words, if that solution could somehow be compelled in all individual cases by some social sanction (for example, a man refusing to accept W is no "gentleman," and as such is socially ostracized), its universal adoption might make everyone better off in the long run. In short, subject to the relevance and accuracy of the interpersonal utility comparison that is used to make the utilities of different persons additive, this is the only arbitration scheme among those considered that is systematically Pareto-optimal over a succession of different games — a strangely overlooked *desideratum.* At the same time, the Utopian character of this solution is its

---

7. It is also subject to what some commentators — e.g., Luce and Raiffa, *op. cit.,* pp. 151–52 — consider the drawback of "instability." Thus, as the slope of a linear utility frontier is conceived to vary from barely less than -1 to barely more than that magnitude, the solution point W shifts from one axis-intercept to the other, pausing momentarily at the midpoint of the frontier when its slope is exactly -1. This is considered a drawback mainly because, as Luce and Raiffa put it, "the utilities used must be determined by experimental techniques" and will, therefore, be subject to error; "so it would be most unfortunate if small perturbations in the utilities could produce drastic changes in the arbitrated solution." On the other hand, if maximizing the sum of utilities is what really matters, the division of that joint utility among the various eligible recipients matters very little (as Schelling has pointed out to me in private discussion). The instability in question concerns, of course, only that utility division.

The same instability also applies to the situation mentioned in the preceding footnote, where it is perhaps more serious, and also to the sudden shift between R_1 and R_1' in Figure IIIb, as discussed on pp. 570–71. Furthermore, as Luce and Raiffa point out, it is also involved in limiting cases where the set of attainable utilities approaches, in different possible ways, a line of finite length coinciding with the utility axis of one of the players (in all cases where the criterion of maximizing the sum of utilities is *not* used).

8. *Op. cit.,* pp. 122–23.

obvious and presumably fatal drawback. As Robertson has reminded us, what economists economize is "love." [9]

Further Critique

For convenient reference, the theories that have been reviewed are listed in Table I, together with an indication as to whether or not they conform to certain properties, of which the first three are the three critical axioms of Nash's theory. Since that theory has been deservedly admired as the most ingenious and plausible among those of the orthodox game-theoretic type, it may appropriately serve as the main focus of interest for a further critical evaluation.

(a) *Positive or normative?* It is a somewhat vexed question whether, or to what extent, bargaining theories such as Nash's are positive (that is, descriptive and predictive) or normative. Nash, taking his lead from the way in which von Neumann and Morgenstern handled the more tractable class of two-person constant-sum games, is primarily concerned with establishing the "value" of the two-person bargaining game to each participant. He thus says that it is his purpose "to obtain a definite 'solution' — making, of course, certain idealizations in order to do so. A 'solution' here means a determination of the amount of satisfaction each individual should expect to get from the situation, or, rather, a determination of how much it should be worth to each of these individuals to have this opportunity to bargain." [1]

It is a commonplace that even the well-established theory of the zero-sum (or, equivalently, constant-sum) game does not necessarily provide a reliable description or prediction as to how ordinary, fallible mortals will actually play that type of game; and this applies *a fortiori* to any one of the various rival theories that have been advanced about the class of variable-sum games. On the other hand, one can at least say what *minimum* value a constant-sum game will have to a participant, provided that he chooses a recommended strategy, irrespective of what strategy his opponent may adopt. This cannot be said, however, with respect to anything approaching a Pareto-optimal outcome of a bargaining game; for what either bargainer gets depends ineluctably on what the other bargainer will let him have.[2] Accordingly, since the value of any

9. D. H. Robertson, "What Does the Economist Economize," R. Lekachman (ed.), *National Policy for Economic Welfare at Home and Abroad* (Garden City, N.Y.: Doubleday, 1955), pp. 1–6.
1. "The Bargaining Problem," *op. cit.*, p. 155.
2. In general, the *minimum* value of *any* two-person game to one player is that implied when he plays his "maximin" strategy (maximizing his own

TABLE I

	Symmetry	Transformation Invariance	Independence of Irrelevant Alternatives	Pareto-Optimality over Succession of Games
Nash and Zeuthen (maximize product of utility increments)	Yes	Yes	Yes	No
Raiffa 1 (successively "split the difference")	Yes	Yes	No	No
Raiffa 2 (equate *ad hoc* utilities)	Yes	Yes	No	No
Raiffa 3 (equate substantive utilities)	Yes	No	Yes	No
Welfare (maximize sum of substantive utilities)	Yes	No	Yes	Yes

bargaining game to either player depends on *both* players' behaving in accordance with the *same* theory, one group of commentators (including, for example, Luce and Raiffa [3] and Wagner [4]) regard all such theories as "arbitration" (better, "mediation") formulas, any one of which may be normatively suggested as a "fair," "reasonable," or "equitable" way of resolving the conflicting aspirations of the bargainers and avoiding any actual conflict, in their own best interest. A further justification of this view is that ordinary bargainers, even under the most favorable conditions, would very likely need to have the merits of any one formula pointed out to them in a persuasive manner before there would be much chance of their both accepting it. If that type of agreement was once achieved, however, the personal services of an arbitrator or mediator would then be superfluous.

This interpretation is not necessarily unpalatable to Nash

payoff on the assumption that his fellow player plays his "minimax" strategy, which minimizes the first player's payoff on the assumption that he is seeking to maximize it). In a constant-sum game, in which all possible outcomes are Pareto-optimal, any maximin strategy of one player is also a minimax strategy (and, if he has more than one such strategy, they all have the same value). In fixed-threat bargaining, by contrast, the outcome is simply at the no-trade threat point if either player adopts his minimax strategy.

3. *Op. cit.*, pp. 121 ff.

4. H. M. Wagner, "A Unified Treatment of Bargaining Theory," *Southern Economic Journal*, XXIII (Apr. 1957), 380–97.

himself; for he seeks to justify his formula explicitly as a "fair"[5] and "reasonable" one,[6] specifically from the point of view of the bargainers themselves. At the same time, he can also be interpreted as subscribing to the alternative view, that his theory predicts how bargainers will actually behave if they are both sufficiently informed and "rational."[7] The rub here, of course, is that "rationality" has a varying content from one theory to another; so any experiment, provided that the necessary knowledge conditions are satisfied, would be testing not the theory but just the "rationality" of the subjects, in the individual theorist's preferred meaning. This stricture applies especially to Harsanyi, who is most emphatic in drawing a contrast between *"bargaining theories,* which try to predict the outcome of actual bargaining behavior" (though the predictions that he has in mind apply only to "perfectly rational" bargainers) and *"arbitration theories,* which try to supply criteria for defining a 'fair' solution for a bargaining situation."[8] Theories of the latter type, in his opinion, belong to welfare economics and therefore "will have to rely on interpersonal comparisons of utility." While this is one possible interpretation, it is certainly not an obligatory one. Rather, there is also a type of arbitration or mediation formula (closer to the philosophy of most professional arbitrators and mediators, even when third-party interests are indirectly involved) that may be recommended, not because it would maximize social welfare in the opinion of the intermediary, but solely because it is thought to have the best chance of being acceptable to the bargainers themselves, as a means of dissolving their threatened stalemate in their own best interest and in a way that will hopefully seem "fair" and "reasonable" to them.[9] This would seem to be the more generous interpretation of the theories in question; for the available observational and experimental evidence shows them to have, at best, dubious predictive value.

Whether descriptive or normative, however, Nash's solution is represented as "fair" and "reasonable" only with due regard to considerations of relative "power" and not at all to less worldly considerations of "social justice." For example, a necessitous bargainer with sharply decreasing marginal utility (to whom a failure

---

5. "The Bargaining Problem," *op. cit.,* p. 158.
6. "Two-Person Cooperative Games," *op. cit.,* p. 136.
7. Thus, the twice-used word "should" in the above quotation from Nash is not necessarily normative, since it may refer only to such conditions as knowledge and rationality.
8. "Notes on the Bargaining Problem, *"Southern Economic Journal,* XXIV (Apr. 1958), 471–73.
9. *Cf.* also Wagner's rejoinder to Harsanyi, "Rejoinder on the Bargaining Problem," *Southern Economic Journal,* XXIV (Apr. 1958), 477.

to make at least a small dollar gain would be inordinately painful as compared with a failure to make a still greater gain) will fare badly against an affluent man with constant or gently decreasing marginal utility, and even worse against a pathological gambler with increasing marginal utility.[1] Similarly, if one man suffers an envious decline of utility as his fellow player's payoff rises (or even if he is just successful in simulating that attitude), while the latter has a neutral reaction to the first player's payoff, the envious man gets the greater objective payoff in any otherwise symmetrical situation.[2]

1. Suppose, for instance, that one man's marginal utility is linearly de- creasing while the other's is constant, such that their increments of utility from the fixed-threat point are $u_1 = a\pi_1 - b\pi_1^2$ and $u_2 = c\pi_2$; and assume that their dollar-payoff frontier is $\pi_1 + h\pi_2 = k$. Then, since $u_2 = (c/h)(k - \pi_1)$, it can be shown that
$$u_1u_2 = (c/h)(a\pi_1 - b\pi_1^2)(k - \pi_1)$$
is maximized when
$$\pi_1 = \frac{a + bk - \sqrt{a^2 - abk + b^2k^2}}{3b}.$$
This result, which is already independent of c and h, is also independent of the absolute values of a and b. That is, by dividing both numerator and denominator through by b and then substituting $r = a/b$, we see that:
$$\pi_1 = \frac{r + k - \sqrt{r^2 - kr + k^2}}{3}.$$
Furthermore, if we divide through by k, we see that the first player's share of his maximum conceivable dollar payoff (π_1/k) depends only on r/k. Then, as r takes various possible values from zero to infinity (or as b, reflecting the steepness with which average and marginal utility decline, varies from in- finity to zero), π_1/k varies from 0 to ½. In other words, when b and r are both positive and finite, the Nash solution always gives the player with decreasing marginal utility less than he would receive if his marginal utility were constant (with $b = 0$) — and less than the player with constant marginal utility receives, except when h is sufficiently greater than unity. Furthermore, the more sharply does the first player's marginal utility decline (more precisely, the larger is b relative to a, or the smaller is r) the smaller is his payoff.

2. For convenience, assume that both utility functions are linear (from the threat point as origin): $u_1 = \pi_1 + a\pi_2$ and $u_2 = \pi_2 + b\pi_1$, where a and b are "sympathy" or "envy" coefficients according as they are positive or nega- tive. Assume also that the objective payoff frontier is given by $\pi_1 + \pi_2 = k$. We may then calculate that
$$\pi_1 = \frac{u_1 - au_2}{1 - ab} \text{ and } \pi_2 = \frac{u_2 - bu_1}{1 - ab},$$
so that the utility frontier is:
$$(1 - b)u_1 + (1 - a)u_2 = (1 - ab)k.$$
Hence, if a and b are both negative, it is essential that $ab < 1$, lest the com- bined envies move the utility frontier out of the first quadrant and thus destroy altogether the possibility for any mutually advantageous deal; and, if positive, it is essential that $a < 1$ and $b < 1$ if each player is to retain at least some positive interest in increasing his own dollar payoff at the other's expense. The Nash solution then calls for utility and dollar payoffs of:
$$u_1 = \frac{(1 - ab)k}{2(1 - b)}, \qquad u_2 = \frac{(1 - ab)k}{2(1 - a)}$$
$$\pi_1 = \frac{k(1 + ab - 2a)}{2(1 - a)(1 - b)}, \qquad \pi_2 = \frac{k(1 + ab - 2b)}{2(1 - a)(1 - b)}. \qquad \text{(cont.)}$$

(b) *Symmetry*. As to the content of Nash's theory, his symmetry axiom would appear at first glance to be the least vulnerable of any that he adopts; but this is not necessarily so.[3] Such an axiom has independent force only in situations that are deemed symmetrical in all relevant respects. Nash dismisses, however, all aspects of a bargaining situation except the von Neumann-Morgenstern utilities that are attainable. For one thing, this means that the symmetry axiom cannot have any independent force; for, even when the objective-payoff frontier is linear with slope of -1 and the utilities of both participants are linear, it is fundamentally gratuitous to regard objectively equal payoffs as yielding "equal" utility increments, as it would not be if a substantive interpersonal comparison of utilities were involved. Similarly, the stipulation that the solution should not depend on which player is called player one might be accepted in all situations in which both bargainers are natural persons of like characteristics in certain specified respects, but not necessarily otherwise, especially when either or both of the parties is a multiperson organization.

To illustrate the cogency of these objections, it may first be observed that Nash's theory of fixed-threat bargaining is extended without difficulty to the case of n persons. Thus, as long as any one player can hold the utilities of all at a fixed threat point, the only effective coalition is the one that embraces all participants; and, as far as that one coalition is concerned, the Nash axioms then dictate the solution that maximizes the product of all players' utilities, irrespective of n. As we know, furthermore, when an employer

Subject to the above restrictions on the values of a and b, these utilities are always positive; but both dollar payoffs will be positive only if $a < 1/(2 - b)$ and $b < 1/(2 - a)$, as one or the other may not be if a and b differ in sign. Then, if one of these inequalities is not fulfilled, the sympathetic saint not only lets the envious sinner have the entire bargaining payoff k, but may even grant him a further charitable donation.

When $a = b = 0$, of course, the utility and dollar payoffs of each player are both equal to $k/2$. If $a = 0$ and $0 < b < 1$, however, $\pi_1 = u_1 > k/2$ and $\pi_2 < u_2 = k/2$ (unilateral sympathy benefits only its object, but neither benefits nor hurts the sympathetic person in a utility sense). Alternatively, if $a = 0$ and $b < 0$, it follows that $\pi_1 = u_1 < k/2$ and $\pi_2 > u_2 = k/2$ (unilateral envy hurts only the victim, without benefiting or hurting the envier in a utility sense). When $0 < a = b < 1$, on the other hand, $\pi_1 = \pi_2 = k/2$ and $u_1 = u_2 > k/2$ (symmetrical sympathy does not affect the dollar payoffs, but it increases each person's utility); and, if $-1 < a = b < 0$, it is implied that $\pi_1 = \pi_2 = k/2$ and $u_1 = u_2 < k/2$ (the canker of symmetrical envy leaves dollar payoffs unchanged, but it depresses both utilities).

3. See also Schelling's argument, which is different from those presented here, that "symmetry in the solution of bargaining games cannot be supported on the notion of 'rational expectations'." *The Strategy of Conflict* (Cambridge: Harvard University Press, 1960), pp. 267 and 278–90. For a rebuttal in which symmetry is represented as a tautological necessity, see Harsanyi, "On the Rationality Postulates Underlying the Theory of Cooperative Games," *op. cit.*, pp. 188–89.

bargains with a single union over the division of a fixed surplus (as in the example mentioned above, p. 570) and when both parties have linear utility functions, the Nash solution calls for an equal division. On the other hand, if the single industrial union now divides itself into n craft unions, any one of which can halt all activity, the Nashian arbitrator thereupon awards the fraction $1/(n+1)$ of the available surplus to the employer and to the membership of each union. This would not follow, however, if the award in either case were based on either a maximizing of the sum of utilities or an equal sharing of utilities when they are deemed to be substantively comparable among natural persons (provided only that the individual utilities are independent of the various ways in which the workers might partition themselves into unions).

As a quite different point, bearing on the prediction of rational behavior rather than the recommendation of an outcome, consider the asymmetrical effect in an otherwise symmetrical individual bargaining game if, subject to the public gaze, one of the parties plays the same game either simultaneously or successively with many fellow players.[4] Provided only that a coalition among any appreciable number of those other players may be ruled out as impractical, the one player has the obvious advantage in any one of his games of being the only one able to make a persuasive "commitment" (of the kind that Schelling has discussed),[5] and he is thereby able to achieve an appreciably greater payoff than any rule of symmetry would give him.[6] Indeed, when he is selling a product to the many other

---

4. Cf. Schelling, *op. cit.*, pp. 29–30.

5. *Ibid.*, pp. 22 ff.

6. This involves another fundamental difference between variable-sum and constant-sum games. Indeed, if one man plays the same two-person constant-sum game either simultaneously or successively with many opponents and in the view of all, this would (if anything) improve the predictive value of the minimax theorem as far as his strategy is concerned, since there is that much more danger that any departure from his minimax strategy will be "found out" — just as there is when he plays the same game repeatedly with just one other person. As Schelling has emphasized, it is a privilege and a pleasure to be "found out" in a bargaining game (*op. cit.*, p. 160); for this justifies the maximum demand that the other player will grant rather than suffer a zero payoff himself.

As these observations imply, any multiplicity of games with at least one overlapping participant from one game to another is technically a single "supergame," with as many players as are involved in at least one of the "subgames." This does not matter if each subgame is of the two-person constant-sum type; for the solution of the supergame is then merely the collection of independent solutions of every subgame (the supergame is of the type called "inessential," in which coalitions make no difference). This is not so, however, if two or more of the subgames are of the variable-sum type. This is exceedingly destructive of the practical application of game theory to real life: the entire human condition is a single supergame, and none of its subgames can be "solved" except as a part of the supergame's solution.

persons, this is merely the case of simple monopoly if the customers can readily resell to one another; or it is the case in which the monopolist can practice near-perfect discrimination if the customers cannot resell and the requisite conditions of perfect knowledge are fulfilled.[7]

(c) *Independence of irrelevant alternatives.* This axiom is widely regarded as the most controversial one in Nash's theory, partly because he himself says: "It is probably harder to give a good plausibility argument for [this axiom] than for any of the others."[8] He speaks of it as a "localization" axiom, ruling out "action at a distance," and he adds that "it is as if a proposed deal is to compete with small modifications of itself and that ultimately the negotiation will be understood to be restricted to a narrow range of alternative deals and to be unconcerned with more remote alternatives." This merely seems to invite the skeptical rejoinder that the bargaining might better be concerned with all of the alternatives.

A different and probably stronger rationalization, as suggested by the distinctive exposition already given (pp. 564–66), is by analogy with an entirely plausible property of a maximizing decision by a single individual. Thus, if the curve of the form $u_1u_2 = k$ in Figure Ic is interpreted as an individual consumer's indifference curve, and if a straight budget line tangent to that curve is replaced by one that is concave from below, but still with the same tangency, it is a matter of elementary rationality that the consumer's equilibrium will not be changed. Hence, if a two-mind problem of the bargaining type can be treated in the same way as a one-mind maximizing problem, the plausibility of the axiom is definitively established. This argument is less persuasive as applied to Nash's theory, however, than it would be with respect to a welfare-economics formula based on a maximizing of some concept of social utility.

As it is, the harshest test of Nash's theory, as far as the independence of irrelevant alternatives is concerned, relates to the implication that the solution is not changed when utility frontiers

---

7. It is perhaps inadequately appreciated that the situation of a monopolist dealing with a single small customer is, technically, a case of bilateral monopoly. Both for the reason already given and others of a practical kind, the monopolist typically quotes a single price to most, if not all, of his potential customers, rather than engage in any undignified and time-consuming "bargaining;" and, when he does adopt a uniform-price policy, his profit-maximizing price is merely the Bowley or Stackelberg price, with the group of all customers regarded as the equivalent of a naively maximizing "person" in a two-person game. Especially when the customers are interested in buying markedly different quantities, however, the monopolist may indeed consent to bargain with some of them, with discrimination as the consequence.

8. "Two-Person Cooperative Games," *op. cit.*, p. 138.

are truncated as in Figure IIIb. Thus, consider again the application to the case of a union bargaining with an employer as indicated above (p. 570). If, in the absence of a minimum-wage law, the union accepts a wage exactly half-way between the maximum and the minimum that the employer might conceivably pay, Nash's theory requires that the union accept the same wage even after it has been made the minimum one by governmental decree. On the other hand, if the union now argues for a wage half-way between the maximum and the new minimum, it is merely seeking Raiffa's splitting-the-difference solution at R_1 in Figure IIIb.[9]

(d) *Transformation invariance.* This axiom, though widely regarded as eminently defensible, is actually one of the weakest components of Nash's theory. For one thing, in conjunction with the symmetry axiom, it actually involves an *ad hoc* interpersonal comparison of utilities of the same general type as that explicitly incorporated in the Raiffa solution at R_2 in Figures IIIa and IIIb. For another, it involves the logically objectionable procedure of deriving knowledge from ignorance, since it is only through a denial of any substantively valid interpersonal comparison that Nash feels free to establish, by an implicit appeal to the dubious "principle of insufficient reason," whatever *ad hoc* interpersonal comparison is needed to bring his symmetry axiom into play.

Thus, given any utility frontier of appropriate shape with the threat point at the origin, Nash specifies[1] that both players' utility scales be transformed in such a way that the frontier becomes tangent at the point (1, 1) to the line $u_1 + u_2 = 2$ (this being only a generalized tangency in some cases and a coincidence of the fron-

9. Especially in view of Raiffa's authorship of this and other alternative arbitration formulas, it is interesting that Luce and Raiffa, after considering the same sort of frontier truncation, end up with this affirmation of faith in Nash's axiom: "We feel at this time — the implication being that we have changed our minds in the past — that this argument against assuming independence of irrelevant alternatives loses its appeal when applied to bargaining problems; the reason is that the naturally distinguished trade [i.e., at the midpoint of the original frontier] serves to point out that certain aspirations are merely empty dreams." (Luce and Raiffa, *op. cit.*, p. 133.) At least in the example of the union's interest in something more than the legal minimum wage, it is not clear why that aspiration is necessarily an "empty dream."

Nor can an orthodox game theorist relevantly plead (as Nash himself once did privately) that the minimum wage has altered the relative "utilities"; for it is a basic principle of such theory that the players' utility functions and the attainable objective payoffs in any given game are wholly independent data. As an interesting example of Zeuthen's ambivalence (not shared, of course, by Harsanyi), his comment on the present point may be cited: "If there exists a legal minimum wage, it will raise the workers' expectations in the event of conflict and increase their demands accordingly, diminishing the fighting spirit of the employers." Zeuthen, *op. cit.*, p. 109.

1. "The Bargaining Problem," *op. cit.*, pp. 159–60.

tier with the constructed line in others). Hence, at that solution point, the bargainers receive "equal" utility increments of $u_1 = u_2 = 1$. Naturally, it is arbitrary and only as a matter of convenience that the point in question is $(1, 1)$ — any other point (a, a) on the line $u_1 + u_2 = 2a$ would do just as well; but it is *essential* that the point be one that implies "equal" increments of utility from the threat point, in order that the symmetry axiom may be relevantly invoked. For example, with a linear objective payoff frontier as in Figure IIIa and linear utilities for both players, the solution point $(12, 6)$ yields "equal" utility increments only when two dollars of π_1 are interpreted to yield the "same" utility as one dollar of π_2; but, if a side payment were allowed in that game (such that the payoff frontier became $\pi_1 + \pi_2 = 24$), the solution would be at $(12, 12)$, on the interpretation that equal values of π_1 and π_2 would then yield "equal" utilities. This is obviously an *ad hoc* interpersonal comparison in the sense that it changes for the same two players from one game to another; and it involves the principle of insufficient reason in that, if one dollar of π_2 might just as well imply the same utility as either one or two (or any other number of) dollars of π_1, that equation might just as well be established in such a way as to make the situation "symmetrical" in the sense relevant for the theory.[2]

III. Theories of Variable-Threat Bargaining

Since duopoly exemplifies variable-threat bargaining in much the same way that bilateral monopoly exemplifies fixed-threat bargaining, it is convenient to proceed immediately to a specific illustration.

2. Luce and Raiffa are among the eminent authorities who disagree with this interpretation, for they say: "Nash's solution has been falsely accused of establishing an implicit interpersonal comparison of utility." *Op. cit.*, p. 130. They have in mind, of course, Nash's fundamental agnosticism about any justifiably *substantive* interpersonal utility comparison (of the type that would remain valid from one game to another). With respect to the frankly *ad hoc* Raiffa procedure that yields solutions at R_2, however, they say "it yields an arbitrated solution which is *invariant with respect to origins and units of utility measurement* — even though as a technical device a specific pair of scales were singled out as an integral part of the analysis" (their italics). *Op. cit.*, p. 147. Precisely the same statement also applies to Nash's procedure. Indeed, this Raiffa solution and the Nash solution are always identical whenever, after the Nash transformation that makes the utility frontier tangent to a line with slope of -1 at the latter's midpoint, the maximum attainable u_1 equals the maximum attainable u_2.

An Illustrative Duopoly Situation

The selected case is one in which a pair of duopolists face a linear demand for a homogeneous product, which they can produce at constant but unequal average costs. Designating price as p, aggregate quantity as q, the respective individual quantities as q_1 and q_2, the respective average costs as c_1 and c_2, and some non-negative constant as h, let us specify that:

$$p = h + 20 - q = h + 20 - q_1 - q_2, \qquad c_1 = h, \qquad c_2 = h + 4.$$

If the duopolists are quantity-setters, their profit functions in the range where $h + 20 \geqslant p \geqslant 0$, or where $0 \leqslant q_1 + q_2 \leqslant h + 20$, are then:

$$\pi_1 = (p - c_1)\,q_1 = (20 - q_1 - q_2)\,q_1,$$
$$\pi_2 = (p - c_2)\,q_2 = (16 - q_1 - q_2)\,q_2.$$

Figure IV depicts certain loci and points that are implied by these profit functions. Thus, $\pi_1 = 0$ where $q_1 = 0$ or $q_1 + q_2 = 20$, and $\pi_2 = 0$ where $q_2 = 0$ or $q_1 + q_2 = 16$. Similarly, the Cournot-

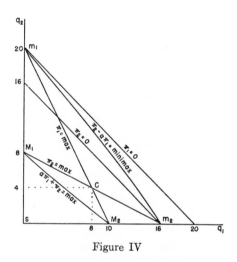

Figure IV

reaction schedules of the duopolists are designated by "$\pi_1 = \text{max}$" and "$\pi_2 = \text{max}$," respectively, since any point on either of those loci corresponds to the one duopolist's quantity (q_i) at which his profit is a maximum for the stipulated quantity (q_j) of the other duopolist. These Cournot-reaction functions, found by differentiating π_i partially with respect to q_i and then setting that partial derivative equal to zero, are:

$$q_1 = 10 - \tfrac{1}{2}q_2, \qquad\qquad q_2 = 8 - \tfrac{1}{2}q_1.$$

The Cournot equilibrium is then at point C, where those two reaction schedules intersect (with $q_1 = 8$, $q_2 = 4$, $\pi_1 = 64$, and $\pi_2 = 16$). If the duopolists' isoprofit curves were drawn in Figure IV, the ith duopolist's Cournot-reaction schedule would be seen to be the locus where his isoprofit curves would be momentarily parallel to the q_i-axis.[3]

There are two separate loci in Figure IV where the duopolists' isoprofit curves would be tangent to one another. One of these is the familiar "contract curve," where (in the absence of any side payments) one man's profit (π_i) is a maximum for any given attainable profit of the other man (π_j). This is designated by "$a\pi_1 + \pi_2 = $ max," since that magnitude is simultaneously maximized with respect to both q_1 and q_2 at any given point on the contract curve, for some appropriate positive value of a.[4] The other such tangency locus, which will subsequently be of interest as a "threat curve," is similarly designated as "$\pi_2 - a\pi_1 = $ minimax," since that magnitude is simultaneously minimized with respect to q_1 and maximized with respect to q_2 anywhere on that locus, again for some positive value of a.[5] In particular, the threat curve is the locus where the

3. Each of the first duopolist's isoprofit curves (for $0 < \pi_1 < 100$) rises from an intercept on the q_1-axis (where $0 < q_1 < 10$) to a maximum on his Cournot-reaction schedule, and it then falls to another intercept on the q_1-axis (where $10 < q_1 < 20$). As $\pi_1 \to 0$, these isoprofit curves approach the locus where $\pi_1 = 0$ (one branch of which is the q_2-axis, while the other is the line $q_1 + q_2 = 20$); and, as $\pi_1 \to 100$, they shrink toward the monopoly point $(10, 0)$. As long as $q_1 + q_2 < h + 20$, the isoprofit curves where $\pi_1 < 0$ are all negatively-sloped curves, asymptotic to the q_2-axis but intersecting the q_1-axis at points where $q_1 > 20$. The second duopolist's isoprofit curves might be described analogously.

4. Thus, for some constant value of a, the magnitude $a\pi_1 + \pi_2$ has a stationary value where:
$$\frac{\partial\pi_2/\partial q_1}{\partial\pi_1/\partial q_1} = \frac{\partial\pi_2/\partial q_2}{\partial\pi_1/\partial q_2} = -a.$$
Similarly, with respect to isoprofit curves of the form $\pi_1 = \pi_1(q_1, q_2)$ and $\pi_2 = \pi_2(q_1, q_2)$, their respective slopes are:
$$\left(\frac{dq_2}{dq_1}\right)_{\pi_1} = -\frac{\partial\pi_1/\partial q_1}{\partial\pi_1/\partial q_2}, \qquad \left(\frac{dq_2}{dq_1}\right)_{\pi_2} = -\frac{\partial\pi_2/\partial q_1}{\partial\pi_2/\partial q_2}.$$
Clearly, when those slopes are equated (as the condition of tangency of the isoprofit curves), that condition is equivalent to the one above.

5. To illustrate the determination of the contract and threat curves in the present example, the relevant partial derivatives are:
$$\partial\pi_1/\partial q_1 = 20 - 2q_1 - q_2, \qquad \partial\pi_1/\partial q_2 = -q_1,$$
$$\partial\pi_2/\partial q_1 = -q_2, \qquad \partial\pi_2/\partial q_2 = 16 - q_1 - 2q_2.$$
Then, combining those partial derivatives in the manner indicated in the preceding footnote, we obtain the condition for the tangency of the isoprofit curves:
$$(20 - 2q_1 - q_2)(16 - q_1 - 2q_2) = q_1q_2,$$
$$q_1^2 + q_2^2 + 2q_1q_2 - 26q_1 - 28q_2 + 160 = 0.$$
Furthermore, solving explicitly for q_1 and q_2, we find that:
$$q_1 = 13 - q_2 \pm \sqrt{9 + 2q_2},$$
$$q_2 = 14 - q_1 \pm \sqrt{36 - 2q_1}.$$ (cont.)

isoprofit curves are tangent and negatively sloped, while the contract curve is the similar tangency locus where the isoprofit curves are positively sloped.

The q_1-axis intercept of both the contract curve and the first duopolist's Cournot-reaction schedule is his monopoly point M_1, where π_1 is maximized with $q_2 = 0$; and similarly for the second duopolist's monopoly point M_2. Also identified in Figure IV are certain respective "maximin" points of the two men, m_1 and m_2. Thus, m_1 is the (least extreme) outcome if the first man undertakes to maximize π_1 at the same time that the second undertakes to minimize it, since the first man must then set $q_1 = 0$ (insuring $\pi_1 = 0$) lest the hypothetically malevolent second man set $q_2 \geqslant 20$ (in which event, provided that $h > 0$, any positive q_1 would cause π_1 to be negative).[6] In the same fashion, m_2 is the (least extreme) outcome if the second man maximizes π_2 while the first minimizes it.[7] Finally, if both men seek their "security levels" by simultaneously adopting their respective maximin strategies (as if each were needlessly afraid of encountering a maximally malevolent response from the other), the outcome is at the security-level point s, where $q_1 = q_2 = 0$ and $\pi_1 = \pi_2 = 0$.[8]

For convenient reference, the output and profit implications of the points already identified in Figure I (C, M_1, M_2, m_1, m_2, and s) are summarized in Table II (along with certain other entries whose significance will be developed in the course of the discussion).

Figure V shows two types of profit frontier. Thus, the linear locus where $\pi_1 + \pi_2 = 100$ is the relevant profit frontier if a side payment is permitted as a part of a collusive agreement. In that event, the first duopolist would produce his monopoly output of $q_1 = 10$ and the second would produce nothing; and the resulting jointly maximized profit could then be redistributed in any agreed

In each instance, the equation corresponds to the contract or threat curve according as the last term is negative or positive. As may be noticed in Figure IV, both of these curves are very nearly linear. They would be exactly linear if the duopolists' average costs were equal, as well as constant.

6. The point m_1 is the "least extreme" one in that $q_2 = 20$ is the smallest such magnitude consistent with this maximin outcome. Thus, at all of the other such maximin points (where $q_1 = 0$ and $q_2 > 20$), $\pi_1 = 0$ but π_2 is progressively smaller, the higher is q_2.

7. It is no accident that m_1 and m_2 occur at the axis intercepts of the threat curve. Thus, when $\pi_2 - a\pi_1$ is "minimaxed," the outcome approaches m_2 as $a \to 0$, or m_1 as $a \to \infty$. By the same token, m_1 and m_2 also occur at axis-intercepts of the Cournot-reaction schedules. For example, since m_1 is the point where q_2 is at least large enough to make $\pi_1 < 0$ if $q_1 > 0$, it is a point where π_1 is maximized at the zero level with $q_1 = 0$.

8. The situation would be the same if the duopolists had fixed costs, except that their security-level profits would then be losses equal to their respective fixed costs.

TABLE II

	q_1	q_2	q	$p-h$	π_1	π_2
C	8	4	12	8	64	16
M_1	10	0	10	10	100	0
M_2	0	8	8	12	0	64
m_1	0	20	20	0	0	−80
m_2	16	0	16	4	64	0
s	0	0	0	20	0	0
n_s	10	8	18	2	20	−16
N_s	10	0	10	10	68 *	32 *
n_n	11.66	5.90	17.56	2.44	28.44	−9.21
N_n†	7.14	2.29	9.43	10.57	71.42	18.29
S_s	10	0	10	10	50 *	50 *
S_n†	5	4	9	11	50	32
R_n†	6.10	3.12	9.22	10.78	60.98	24.98
R_s	10	0	10	10	77.69 *	22.31 *
b	9.09	9.14	18.22	1.78	16.15	−20.30
B_s	10	0	10	10	62.44 *	37.56 *
B_n†	5.53	3.58	9.11	10.89	55.29	28.62
N_s'	10	0	10	10	74 *	26 *
N_n'†	6.95	2.44	9.39	10.61	69.5	19.52
R_n'†	6.83	2.54	9.37	10.63	68.29	20.29
R_s'	10	0	10	10	76.20 *	23.80 *

* The profits so marked represent net profits after side payments.
† The magnitudes in these non-side-payment cases represent averages per period when q is either 10 or 8 (and $p-h$ is either 10 or 12) in each individual period.

fashion, by means of a side payment to the second duopolist (as a bribe for his not producing). On the other hand, if such a side payment is effectively prohibited but the duopolists can still make an agreement whereby only one of them produces at any given time, the frontier showing their mutually attainable average profits per period is the line where $.64\pi_1 + \pi_2 = 64$. In other words, in any given period it is possible for profits to be either (100, 0) or (0, 64); so, depending on the comparative numbers of such periods, average profits per period would correspond to those at various points on the indicated line. Alternatively, if the duopolists are willing to settle for a certain mathematical expectation of profit in each individual period, those mutually attainable expected profits could again be those at any point on the same line, depending on the agreed probabilities that either one duopolist or the other would be the sole active producer in that period. This would be equivalent to the other procedure, however, only if both duopolists have linear utility functions (such that each has a constant marginal utility);

and it would be inferior if either duopolist's marginal utility is diminishing while the other's is diminishing, constant, or not too sharply increasing.

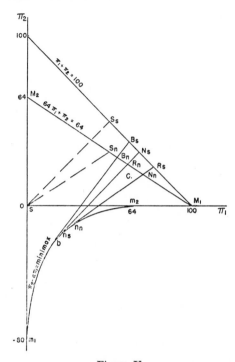

Figure V

Still a third type of profit frontier may be relevant, as an alternative to either of the two that are shown in Figure V. This would reflect the attainable profits if both duopolists are active producers at the same time, at any one of the eligible points on the contract curve of Figure IV. This frontier also has its axis-intercepts at $\pi_1 = 100$ and $\pi_2 = 64$, and it is actually very close to the linear $.64\pi_1 + \pi_2 = 64$; but it is very slightly concave from above, so that it lies "inside" that line when q_1 and q_2 are both positive.[9] Even though this curvilinear frontier is thus very slightly inferior to its linear approximation, it is nonetheless the relevant one when (1) side payments are effectively prohibited and (2) it is not

9. This frontier is so close to the corresponding linear one that it cannot conveniently be shown in Figure V. For example, one profit point on the curvilinear frontier is (60.5, 24.5) — when $q_1 = 5.5$ and $q_2 = 3.5$. By comparison, the point where $\pi_1 - \pi_2 = 36$ on the linear frontier is (60.98, 24.98).

feasible or otherwise desirable for only one duopolist to produce at a time.[1]

Also shown in Figure V is the locus reflecting the associated profits on the threat curve of Figure IV. Consistent with the fact that the threat curve in the output diagram lies between the respective zero-profit loci, the corresponding curve in the profit diagram implies that $\pi_1 \geqslant 0$ and $\pi_2 \leqslant 0$.[2]

The associated profits on the contract and threat curves are most conveniently expressed as functions of the parameter a. Thus, when $a\pi_1 + \pi_2$ has a stationary (maximum) value (on the contract curve and the corresponding profit frontier, when $3/5 \leqslant a \leqslant 2/3$), it may be calculated that:

$$q_1 = \frac{8(2-3a)}{(1-a)^2}, \qquad\qquad q_2 = \frac{4a(5a-3)}{(1-a)^2},$$

$$\pi_1 = \frac{32(2-3a)}{(1-a)^3}, \qquad\qquad \pi_2 = \frac{16a^2(5a-3)}{(1-a)^3}.$$

Similarly, when $\pi_2 - a\pi_1$ has a stationary (saddle-point) value (on the threat curves of Figures IV and V, when $0 \leqslant a \leqslant \infty$), it may be calculated that:

$$q_1 = \frac{8(2+3a)}{(1+a)^2}, \qquad\qquad q_2 = \frac{4a(5a+3)}{(1+a)^2},$$

$$\pi_1 = \frac{32(2+3a)}{(1+a)^3}, \qquad\qquad \pi_2 = -\frac{16a^2(5a+3)}{(1+a)^3}.$$

1. This may be so for many possible reasons. Even when a probability determination of the active producer is permitted in a "game" that is played only once, such a solution is undesirable when either duopolist has more than very slightly diminishing marginal utility, insufficiently counteracted by a possibly increasing marginal utility of the other. In that event, the corresponding *utility* frontiers are both concave from below. In the more relevant economic context of recurrent production, on the other hand, the persistence of fixed costs during a shutdown (and the special costs of resuming production) would effectively rule out any alternation of the role of active producer, irrespective of the duopolists' utility functions; and, even in the absence of fixed costs, such an alternation would undoubtedly be deemed illegal under antitrust laws.

2. Over the entire relevant range of the threat curve, the parameter a takes all positive values from 0 (at m_2) to infinity (at m_1). At any given point on the threat curve in the profit diagram, moreover, its slope is $d\pi_2/d\pi_1 = a$. Similarly, at any given point on the curvilinear profit frontier that is so very close to $.64\pi_1 + \pi_2 = 64$, its slope is $d\pi_2/d\pi_1 = -a$, though a then takes only the very limited range of values from 3/5 (at M_1) to 2/3 (at M_2).

Just as the contract and threat curves in Figure IV are the loci where the duopolists' isoprofit curves (if drawn) would be tangent to one another, so are the corresponding curves in figure V the loci of tangent points of "isoquants" — that is, curves that would show the related magnitudes of π_1 and π_2 when one of the outputs (q_i) is varied and the other (q_j) is held constant — cf. Nash, "Two-Person Cooperative Games," *op. cit.* Furthermore (*cf.* footnote 4, p. 584), the slopes of these isoquants are equal to $-a$ on the contract curve and to a on the threat curve; so, when they are tangent to one another, they are also tangent to the relevant tangency locus.

Also of subsequent interest is the fact that, anywhere on the threat curves:

$$\pi_2 - a\pi_1 = -\frac{16a(4 + 5a)}{(1 + a)^2}$$

Included among the points shown in Figure V are those corresponding to the ones previously identified in Figure IV; the other points in Figure V will be discussed later.

As based on this illustrative duopoly situation, the various extant theories of variable-threat bargaining may now be described. For simplicity, it will be assumed throughout this discussion that each duopolist's utility is a linear function of his profit. This means that each man's profit can serve as an acceptable index of his utility.

Nash's Theory

Nash represents his theory of variable-threat bargaining [3] as an extension and generalization of his theory of fixed-threat bargaining. Accordingly, his central problem is to identify and justify a relevant threat point. Once that is done, he naturally specifies the same type of movement from threat point to solution point as in the case of fixed-threat bargaining — that is, one that maximizes the product of utility increments between the two points. In turn, when that culminating movement is confidently anticipated by both participants, this provides the necessary clue for the determination of optimal threat strategies and a uniquely relevant threat point.

Although Nash provides an axiomatic justification of his procedure, the nature and plausibility of the two additional axioms involved in the transition from fixed threats to variable ones are rather obscure. On the other hand, the logic of his procedure is amply clear with reference to what he calls a "negotiation model."

This is a game consisting of two critical moves — a "threat" move and a "demand" move, in that order. The first has the purpose of determining a threat point, while the second allows the movement to the recommended solution point, on the relevant utility frontier. In the context of quantity-setting duopoly, for example, the threat move calls for each player to specify a quantity to which he would be irrevocably committed if no agreement were achieved on the demand move. These threat quantities are chosen independently and without any prior communication. Once chosen, however, each is revealed to the other player, so that both may know what the consequences would be if the threats had to be executed. On the

3. "Two-Person Cooperative Games," *op. cit.*

demand move, the players make their respective payoff demands, again independently and without any further communication. Those demands are then granted provided that they are compatible; otherwise the outcome would remain at the previously determined threat point.

Clearly, if the outcome of this game is to be Pareto-optimal, the players must have a high degree of mutual confidence in the compatibility of their demands; so we must assume, with Nash, that both participants instinctively accept the type of movement from threat point to solution point that he prescribes. Then, in the light of that anticipated movement on the demand move, each player's optimal strategy on the threat move may be determined.

This problem is comparatively simple when the utility frontier is linear, as it is with reference to either of the two linear profit frontiers in Figure V when both duopolists' utilities are linear functions of their profits. In general, then, if the profit frontier is given by $a\pi_1 + \pi_2 = k$, the utility frontier can be represented by $au_1 + u_2 = k$, as in Figure VI. We also know that, wherever the relevant

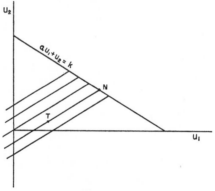

Figure VI

threat point (T) may be determined, it will be connected with the Nash-solution point (N) by a straight line of the form $u_2 = b + au_1$; for, as an implication of maximizing the product of the utility increments between T and N, the slope (a) of the line TN must be the same, except for sign, as the slope $(-a)$ of the utility frontier at N.[4] A variety of such lines are shown in Figure VI, any one of which might be the relevant one pending the actual determination of T.

4. Cf. p. 566.

The equation for each such line may be written, equivalently, as

$$u_2 - au_1 = b,$$

where a is the constant slope and b is a parameter corresponding to each line's intercept with the u_2-axis (since $u_2 = b$ when $u_1 = 0$). Furthermore, in the light of the mutually anticipated movement from T to N, the two players have squarely opposed interests as to the magnitude of b: the first player would like it to be as low as possible and the second would like it to be as high as possible. Accordingly, on the threat move, the first player seeks to minimize $u_2 - au_1$ while the second seeks to maximize that magnitude. In short, as our earlier discussion has foreshadowed, the threat move corresponds to a zero-sum game, with a uniquely valued "minimax" solution as far as the value of $u_2 - au_1$ is concerned.[5] Then, of course, the final solution is determined on the demand move at the point (N) where the line $u_2 - au_1 = b$ intersects the utility frontier.[6]

To illustrate, with reference to either of the linear profit (and utility) frontiers in Figure V, the duopolists' interests on the threat move are, respectively, to minimize and maximize:

$$\pi_2 - a\pi_1 = 16q_2 - q_2{}^2 - 20aq_1 + aq_1{}^2 - (1-a)q_1q_2,$$

where $a = 1$ when a side payment is permitted or $a = .64$ when it is not. As may readily be seen, this expression is minimized with respect to q_1 and maximized with respect to q_2 when, respectively:

5. Moreover, when certain continuity assumptions are satisfied (as in our duopoly illustration), Nash has shown that the optimal threat strategies (outputs) are necessarily "pure" rather than "mixed" (unique outputs, rather than probability mixtures of two or more different outputs). "Two-Person Cooperative Games," *op. cit.*, p. 135.

6. The situation is little different if the utility frontier is concave from below, rather than linear. (This might be illustrated, for example, if the profit frontier is linear but one duopolist has diminishing marginal utility and the other has diminishing, constant, or not too sharply increasing marginal utility. Alternatively, if both duopolists have linear utility functions, their non-side-payment profit and utility frontiers will both be concave from below if one of them has marginal cost that increases at a sufficient rate and the other has increasing, constant, or not too sharply decreasing marginal cost. For an example based on u-shaped costs, but with increasing costs in the relevant range, see J. P. Mayberry, J. F. Nash, and M. Shubik, "A Comparison of Treatments of a Duopoly Situation," *Econometrica*, Vol. 21 (Jan. 1953), pp. 141–54. Then the initially eligible lines connecting T and N are no longer parallel. Rather, they tend to converge as they approach the utility frontier. Nevertheless, even though a is no longer a constant, its value is uniquely related to that of b. Accordingly, if a is expressed as a function of b, the threat move can still be interpreted as a game of squarely opposed interests as to the value of b. Hence, locally, it is still the equivalent of a zero-sum game, just as if the utility frontier were a straight line tangent to the actual frontier at the point N.

$$q_1 = 10 + \frac{1-a}{2a} q_2,$$

$$q_2 = 8 - \frac{1-a}{2a} q_1.$$

Hence the threat outputs are determined where these "threat-reaction schedules" intersect. Those outputs and the associated threat profits, as functions of a, are then seen to be as indicated above, page 588. Similarly, the equation given on page 589 for $\pi_2 - a\pi_1$ corresponds to the line connecting the threat point with the desired solution point.

In the side-payment case, when $a = 1$, the optimal threat outputs are actually independent of one another, namely $q_1 = 10$ and $q_2 = 8$.[7] In turn, these outputs yield threat profits of $\pi_1 = 20$ and $\pi_2 = -16$, at the threat point in Figure V that is labeled n_s (where n stands for "Nash" and the subscript s stands for "side payment"). Similarly, the related side-payment solution point is identified as N_s, where $\pi_1 = 68$ and $\pi_2 = 32$ (each greater by 48 units than the corresponding threat profits). These output and profit implications at the points n_s and N_s are also shown in Table II.

In the non-side-payment case, when $a = .64$, the threat outputs are calculated as (11.66, 5.90), yielding threat profits of (28.44, -9.21). The movement to the profit frontier then yields (expected or average) profits of (71.42, 18.29).[8] The respective threat and solution points in this non-side-payment case are designated in Figure V and in Table II as n_n and N_n.[9]

7. These are, moreover, the respective monopoly outputs. That is always the result (for $a = 1$) whenever demand is a linear function of $q_1 + q_2$ and each duopolist's cost depends only on his own output; for the cross-product terms (involving $q_1 q_2$) in the individual profit functions then drop out of the expression for $\pi_2 - \pi_1$.

8. That is to say, these are the mathematical expectations of profits if the players agree that the first man will receive $\pi_1 = 100$ with a probability of .7142 and the second will receive $\pi_2 = 64$ with a probability of .2858. Alternatively, if the duopoly "game" is played 10,000 times, the players can receive these profits on the average per play if the first man makes his monopoly profit 7,142 times while the second makes his monopoly profit 2,858 times.

9. With reference to the very slightly concave profit frontier that is applicable if the duopolists produce on their contract curve, the calculation of the threat and solution points is more complex. Again, however, it is just a matter of finding a pair of points on the threat curve and profit frontier such that the line connecting them has the same slope (except for sign) as the frontier at the relevant point. Thus, designating profits at the threat and solution points with the superscripts t and s, respectively, we wish to find the value of a where:

$$\frac{\pi_2{}^s - \pi_2{}^t}{\pi_1{}^s - \pi_1{}^t} = a.$$

This can be done by substituting the values of each of these profits as a function of a (see abope, p. 588). That equation then reduces to $6a^2 + a - 3 = 0$, such that the relevant value is:

As to the validity of this theory, it obviously depends first of all on the validity of Nash's fixed-threat theory. Then, if that is granted, it further depends on the relevance of the negotiation model even when the duopolists are not constrained to "negotiate" in precisely that way. If Nash's negotiation model is indeed accepted as relevant, however, his solution thereby acquires strong credentials. Thus, if a Nashian movement from threat point to solution point is indeed foreordained, and if the duopolists must indeed commit themselves to threat strategies before making their ultimate profit (or utility) demands, the optimality of the specified threat strategies is readily defended; for if either duopolist adopts his Nash threat, the other must do so too in order to avoid receiving a lower ultimate profit after the demand move. The critical issue of the actual relevance of Nash's negotiation model will be discussed later.

A Shapley Theory

This theory is so named because, as Luce and Raiffa say, "it is a slight generalization of a very special case of the Shapley value of an n-person game." [1] It differs from Nash's theory in replacing the latter's threat point with a reference point corresponding to the security levels of the players. From that point, however, the movement to the relevant utility frontier is of the same type as that presented by Nash.

The security-level profits in our duopoly example are $(0, 0)$, at the point s in Figure V, since either duopolist would expose himself to a possible loss if he produced any positive output. Hence the implied Shapley solution occurs at the midpoint of the relevant linear frontier — that is to say, at S_s $(50, 50)$ when side payments are permitted or at S_n $(50, 32)$ when they are not. Either of these

$$a = \frac{-1 + \sqrt{73}}{12} = .628,667.$$

In turn, this implies the following values at the threat and solution points:

$$q_1{}^t = \frac{8(2 + 3a)}{(1 + a)^2} = 11.72, \qquad \pi_1{}^t = \frac{32(2 + 3a)}{(1 + a)^2} = 28.78,$$

$$q_2{}^t = \frac{4a(5a + 3)}{(1 + a)^2} = 5.82. \qquad \pi_2{}^t = -\frac{16a^2(5a + 3)}{(1 + a)^3} = -8.99,$$

$$q_1{}^s = \frac{8(2 - 3a)}{(1 - a)^2} = 6.61, \qquad \pi_1{}^s = \frac{32(2 - 3a)}{(1 - a)^3} = 71.25,$$

$$q_2{}^s = \frac{4a(5a - 3)}{(1 - a)^2} = 2.61, \qquad \pi_2{}^s = \frac{16a^2(5a - 3)}{(1 - a)^3} = 17.70.$$

The profits at this solution point, it may be noticed, are only very slightly smaller than those on the similar linear frontier.

1. *Op. cit.*, p. 137.

solutions is clearly more favorable to the high cost duopolist than the corresponding Nash solution — cf. Table II.

As the present examples illustrate (and as Luce and Raiffa also remark, with reference to a similar illustration), the Shapley solution is altogether insensitive to the differences in the participants' threat potentialities, as based on their cost differences in the duopoly application. When duopolists cannot agree as to a mutually profitable, collusive outcome, the only alternative is some form of non-cooperative behavior, if not warfare; and a simultaneous adoption of the maximin strategies of producing zero output hardly qualifies as among those plausible alternatives to collusion. "Shapley warfare," if it may be called that, consists of the engaging spectacle of a pair of rabbits who are both afraid to emerge from their holes, each in the mistaken fear that the other is a lion.

Raiffa's Theories

Raiffa specifies a generalization of his fixed-threat theories to the case of variable-threat bargaining in the Nash manner. That is to say, the bargainers are again supposed to determine their optimal threats with a view toward some confidently anticipated movement from threat point to solution point. The exact character of that movement varies, of course, from one theory to another.

Thus, when equal increments of profit are deemed to yield equal increments of utility (as in the fixed-threat solutions at R_3 in Figures IIIa and IIIb), the line connecting the threat and solution points in Figure V has unitary slope.[2] Hence the relevant threat point is the same as in the Nash side-payment case (n_s). Accordingly, when side payments are permitted, the solution point is also the same as in Nash's theory (N_s). Even when side payments are prohibited, however, this particular Raiffa theory still calls for the same threat point and the same direction of movement to a solution point, namely the one identified in Figure V and Table II as R_n. The profits at that point (60.98, 24.98), like those at n_s and N_s, differ by 36.[3]

Alternatively, when the participants' maximum possible objective payoffs (100, 64) are deemed to yield "equal" increments of utility (on the same *ad hoc* basis that yielded fixed-threat solutions

2. This type of solution was also singled out for special attention in Bishop, "Duopoly: Collusion or Warfare?" *American Economic Review*, L (Dec. 1960), 933–61.

3. For the corresponding solution on the curvilinear profit frontier corresponding to the contract curve, see footnote 9, p. 587.

at R_2 in Figures IIIa and IIIb), the slope of the line connecting the threat and solution points in Figure V is .64. Accordingly, this is the same line that connects n_n and N_n; so those points are also the relevant threat point and non-side-payment solution point in this Raiffa case. When side payments are permitted, however, the solution occurs at the point labelled R_s, where the implied profits are (77.69, 22.31).

Raiffa himself does not seem to contemplate applying his split-the-difference theory (which yields the fixed-threat solutions at R_1 in Figures IIIa and IIIb) to variable-threat bargaining. When it is so applied in the present context, however, it yields the same solutions as the Shapley procedure — S_s when, with a side payment allowed, the difference is split between profit demands of (100, 0) and (0, 100), or S_n when, with side payments prohibited, the difference is split between (100, 0) and (0, 64). On the other hand, the threat strategies underlying those outcomes are not unique; for any threats that cause threat profits to be $\pi_1 \leqslant 0$ and $\pi_2 \leqslant 0$ would justify each man's receiving exactly half of his maximum attainable profit. The critical threat in this case is that of the high cost duopolist, who must adopt a minimax strategy of $q_2 \geqslant 20$, with the implication that $\pi_1 \leqslant 0$ and $\pi_2 \leqslant -80$ (irrespective of the magnitude of q_1). This, incidentally, throws considerable doubt on the plausibility of a split-the-difference solution with variable threats; for it implies a solution wholly unaffected by the fact that the (negative) threat profits are, relatively, very unfavorable to the high-cost producer.[4]

Braithwaite's Theory

Braithwaite also specifies a threat-point determination in the Nash manner and a subsequent linear movement to the utility frontier.[5] The distinctive feature of his theory is that it is based on the "equating" of utility increments in accordance with an *ad hoc* formula, as in the corresponding Raiffa theory. Specifically, Braithwaite proposes, each participant's utility unit is taken to be the net change in his utility (whether positive or negative) when he shifts between his maximin and minimax strategies while the other person holds to his maximin strategy.[6]

4. In the side-payment case, on the other hand, if the side-payment frontier is regarded as extended into the range of negative values of π_2 (reflecting a possible side payment by the high cost man), the solution would be the same as in the Nash side-payment case — that is, with a threat point at n_s and a solution point at N_s.

5. *Op cit.*

6. Braithwaite calls a maximin strategy "prudential," since it guarantees

Braithwaite developed his theory in connection with a 2 x 2 matrix game in which each player's maximin and minimax strategies were unique. This need not always be so; and in that event the payoffs in question may be ambiguous. Furthermore, even when the indicated strategies are unique, there may be other troubles. For one thing, it is possible for a player's maximin and minimax strategies to be the same; or, even when they are different, they still might yield him the same payoff when the other person plays his maximin strategy. In each of these cases, Braithwaite's procedure is inapplicable. It is also inapplicable in any instance of fixed-threat bargaining. In that context, the adoption by either party of the minimax strategy of refusing any trade beneficial to the other results in zero payoffs for both; so maximin strategies are wholly indeterminate.

In our duopoly illustration, Braithwaite's procedure is imperfectly applicable at best, since the strategies of $q_1 \geqslant 16$ and $q_2 \geqslant 20$ all have the minimax property of preventing the other duopolist from exceeding his zero-profit security level. On the other hand, if this indeterminacy of minimax strategies is resolved by the selection of $q_1 = 16$ and $q_2 = 20$ as the relevant ones, the Braithwaite theory can be illustrated on that basis.[7] Specifically, since the respective maximin strategies of $q_1 = q_2 = 0$ yield security-level profits of $\pi_1 = \pi_2 = 0$, while a unilateral shift to a minimax strategy would yield $\pi_1 = 64$ or $\pi_2 = -80$, Braithwaite's formula decrees that $\pi_1 = 64$ and $\pi_2 = 80$ yield "equal" utilities to the two participants. In turn, this means that the slope of the line between threat point and solution point is $80/64 = 1.25$. Accordingly, when $a = 1.25$ is inserted in the relevant equations (see above, p. 588), the Braithwaite threat point is seen to imply $q_1 = 9.09$, $q_2 = 9.14$, $\pi_1 = 16.15$, and $\pi_2 = -20.30$. The threat point is labeled b in Figure V and Table II. Then the Braithwaite solution points may be calculated: with a side payment permitted, the solution at B_s yields profits of $(62.44, 37.56)$; and, with no side payment, the solution at B_n yields $(55.29, 28.62)$.

that the player will attain at least his security level; and he calls a minimax strategy "counter-prudential," since it guarantees that the other player will not exceed his security level.

7. This might be justified on the grounds that these particular minimax strategies yield maximum profits of $\pi_1 = 64$ and $\pi_2 = -80$, respectively, subject to the condition that the other duopolist's profit cannot then exceed zero. These minimax strategies would also be unique if the duopolists were arbitrarily limited to outputs of $q_1 \leqslant 16$ and $q_2 \leqslant 20$. By the same token, however, if narrower restrictions were placed on the outputs (as might be done in a matrix-game version of this duopoly situation), the minimax outputs would then be smaller, and the Braithwaite "solution" would thereby be changed.

Like the Raiffa theory that is also based on an *ad hoc* utility comparison, Braithwaite's satisfies the symmetry and transformation-invariance axioms, but not the independence of irrelevant alternatives. Unlike Raiffa, however, Braithwaite gives to those "irrelevant alternatives" a peculiarly implausible role, in that an unmistakable weakening of a player's position is capable of increasing his payoff. This is already apparent in our duopoly illustration to the extent that $s = 1.25$ is as large as it is, and therefore relatively favorable to the high-cost duopolist, only because his loss at the point m_1 is greater than the low-cost duopolist's profit at the point m_2.[8] This feature makes Braithwaite's theory vulnerable to a *reductio ad absurdum.* Suppose, for example, that the high-cost duopolist's average-cost schedule, while unchanged up to $q_2 = 19$, thereafter rises very steeply up to $q_2 = 20$. This makes his loss greater than 80 at the point m_1, and it therefore qualifies him for a greater profit than before, whether a side payment is permitted or not. If, in the limit, this duopolist's average cost becomes indefinitely high as $q_2 \to 20$, his profit approaches a maximum and the low-cost duopolist's profit falls toward zero. If only in the light of such cases, Braithwaite's theory hardly deserves the respectful attention that it has so far consistently received.

Other Theories

Especially in the comparatively rich context of our duopoly illustration, it would be hard to set a limit on the alternative "theories" that might be manufactured. Thus, on the analogy of the security level point (s), other reference points might be used, such as the Cournot point (C) or points reflecting the profits or utilities implied at the points of Stackelberg equilibrium, where one duopolist's profit is maximized on the Cournot-reaction schedule of the other.[9] Similarly, if the alternative institutional practice of price-quoting is considered, a further set of corresponding reference points can also be adduced. Furthermore, in connection with each reference point that might have some appeal, various types of movements to the relevant utility frontier can be specified.

8. Braithwaite's own basic illustration was not subject to this anomaly; for, when either player was assumed to shift unilaterally from maximin strategy to minimax (while the other held to maximin), the result was to increase his utility. Later, however, Braithwaite gave another illustration involving decreased utility in that transition, and he specifically adopted the view that the direction of change of utility should not matter.

9. For example, Stackelberg payoffs are involved in different ways in the proposals of A. M. Henderson, "The Theory of Duopoly," this *Journal,* LXVIII (Nov. 1954), 565–84 and Wagner, *op. cit.*

The only class of such alternative theories that will be singled out for specific comment is one suggested by Schelling's argument that "the perfectly 'moveless' or 'move-symmetrical' cooperative game . . . may degenerate into an ordinary tacit game."[1]   Thus, especially when a variable-threat bargaining game is played only once, and when the bargaining is subject to a deadline, at which the parties must then make their decisions unilaterally, Schelling points out that either party has it within his power to convert the initial bargaining or cooperative game into its tacit or noncooperative counterpart, simply by letting the time for negotiation expire without a cooperative agreement.   Under such circumstances, accordingly, that action becomes a relevant "threat" for either party.

In practice, duopoly always involves a recurrent relationship; and an indefinitely repeated "noncooperative" game is really the equivalent of a "cooperative" one to the extent that, with sufficiently perceptive players, tacit collusion is then a feasible outcome.[2]   Suppose, however, that this abstract "game" is to be played just once, as based on our duopoly illustration: at a specified deadline, each player must independently set his output (q_i), unless they can both agree before that time as to some outcome on their utility frontier. From Nash's point of view, it may be noticed, this game would be essentially equivalent to his negotiation model, but with the demand move preceding the threat move.

Now, it so happens that quantity-setting duopoly as a noncooperative game has only one really eligible "solution" — the Cournot point.   For one thing, that is the game's only "equilibrium point," since the Cournot strategies of $q_1 = 8$ and $q_2 = 4$ represent the only outputs such that, if each player correctly anticipates the other's choice, he cannot increase (and in our case would actually reduce) his own payoff by a unilateral shift to any other output.[3] For another, if the game is successively reduced by the elimination of "dominated" strategies, the game is "completely reduced" (in the limit) to just the Cournot outputs, which therefore constitute the

---

1. *Op. cit.*, p. 277.
2. Cf. Bishop, "Duopoly: Collusion or Warfare?" *op. cit.*
3. This means that the game has a unique solution "in the sense of Nash." Nash, "Non-Cooperative Games," *Annals of Mathematics*, Vol. 54 (Sept. 1951), pp. 286–95.   Luce and Raiffa, *op. cit.*, p. 106.   Except for some games with infinite sets of pure strategies, Nash has shown that every n-person noncooperative game has at least one equilibrium point (involving, in general, mixed strategies — of which the pure strategies in our example are a special case). Thus, not all non-cooperative games are "Nash-solvable," let alone uniquely so; ours, however, is.   Furthermore, since the Cournot point involves only pure strategies, it is the solution irrespective of utility patterns (provided only that each player's utility depends only on his own profit).

game's solution in what Luce and Raiffa[4] call "the complete weak sense." [5] Nor is there any approved "sense" in which this non-cooperative game has any other solution.

Accordingly, if the players meet the game-theoretic standard of "rationality," the Cournot solution, with its implied profits of (64, 16), would be the predictable outcome if the time for negotiation were allowed to expire — or if the players' demands were incompatible on the demand move of Nash's "reversed" negotiation model. This means that the relevant threat point in the present game is the Cournot point. That being so, a new set of "solutions" on the relevant utility frontier can be generated, depending on which fixed-threat bargaining theory is invoked to determine the movement from the Cournot threat point. The implied outcomes are shown in Table II for selected cases — where $N_s{'}$ corresponds to N_s except for the changed threat point, and so on.

Critical Evaluation

Naturally, all variable-threat bargaining theories are subject to the same misgivings that have been expressed earlier as to their fixed-threat counterparts. Even if some one fixed-threat theory is wholly accepted, however, its extension to the general case involving variable threats may or may not be regarded as valid. As before, Nash's theory is selected as the main focus for this further evaluation.

As earlier discussion has indicated, the validity of Nash's own generalization of his fixed-threat theory stands or falls on the relevance of his negotiation model. On the other hand, it has just been shown in the preceding section that this model may not be relevant in some circumstances. The question remains an open one, however, in contexts where neither the Nash model nor its "reversed" counterpart is inherently relevant.

For the sake of definiteness, let us suppose that the duopolists in our illustration have a recurrent relationship and are free to negotiate a collusive outcome, with side payments permitted; but,

---

4. *Op. cit.,* p. 109.

5. The first reduction limits the relevant strategies to $0 \leqslant q_1 \leqslant 10$ and $0 \leqslant q_2 \leqslant 8$; for, irrespective of the other player's output, each player's monopoly output ($q_1 = 10$ or $q_2 = 8$) yields him a greater payoff than would any larger output. Then the second reduction limits the relevant strategies to $6 \leqslant q_1 \leqslant 10$ and $3 \leqslant q_2 \leqslant 8$; for in the light of the maximum outputs in the first reduced game, the outputs of $q_1 = 6$ and $q_2 = 3$ similarly dominate all lower outputs. And so on. Since the Cournot-reaction schedules govern all of the successive game reductions, it is clear that in the limit only the Cournot-outputs are left.

unless and until they do so agree, of course, each must set his own output unilaterally. Even if both were disposed to accept the Nash solution in a fixed-threat situation, it may now be argued, the duopolists still might differ as to whether Nash's theory of optimal threats should be accepted when they are not inherently fixed.

Contemplating the implied profits of (68, 32) at N_s, for example, the low-cost duopolist might consider his share inadequate for several reasons. For one thing, he is actually worse off in that situation than he would be at the Nash solution point if side payments were prohibited, since the profits at N_n are (71.42, 18.29). After all, even when permitted, side payments need not actually be made except when they are mutually beneficial. Nash's counter-argument[6] is that the mere permissibility of side payments increases the high-cost duopolist's potentiality for "blackmail," and the low-cost duopolist had simply better pay it.

Alternatively, the low-cost man might argue that the potential benefits of collusion should be reckoned from the Cournot point as a base, since the Cournot profits of (64, 16) result when quantity-setting duopolists behave in a neutrally noncooperative fashion (maximizing their profits independently and without the vindictive or warlike motive of deliberately accepting a lower profit for oneself in order to inflict some simultaneous profit reduction on the other person).[7] Here, of course, Nash's reply would be that duopolists who cannot agree spontaneously on some division of the fruits of collusion need not (and typically do not) content themselves with just passive resistance or pacifistic noncooperation. Instead, they not only may but do adopt strategies of a distinctly punitive nature in an effort to coerce the acceptance of their (implicit or explicit) demands.[8]

At this point, the argument comes full circle. If warfare profits are indeed then used as the base from which a Nashian treaty of peace is negotiated, this implies an acceptance of his theory as to optimal warfare strategies. On the other hand, if either duopolist is content to hold out for his own profit demand by being just war-like enough to keep the other's profit some distance below what it

6. Mayberry, Nash, and Shubik, *op. cit.*, p. 153.

7. Or, if the duopolists were price-setters, the low cost man might urge as the relevant base the comparable Bertrand point, which would imply profits in the vicinity of (64, 0) — π_1 being slightly less than 64 when p_1 is set just below $h + 4$, so that π_2 would be negative if the high-cost man were to produce at all.

8. Furthermore, if only one duopolist is a passive profit-maximizer, the other could exploit that attitude by pushing the pacifist to a Stackelberg equilibrium — where profits would be (49, 18) or (72, 4), according as the first or second duopolist was the pacifist.

would be under the collusion proposed by the first, there is no inherent necessity for his warfare strategy to conform to Nash's specification. Accordingly, the issue does not seem to lend itself to a clear-cut resolution.

Furthermore, even if the relevance of Nashian threats survives the foregoing arguments, the wholly static character of his theory raises other questions of a dynamic nature precisely when the duopoly relationship is recurrent. In particular, may it not make a critical difference in the present example that π_2 is negative while π_1 is positive at a Nash threat point such as n_s? To be sure, as long as we hold to the simplifying assumption that both duopolists' utilities are everywhere linear functions of their profits, there is indeed no qualitative difference between positive and negative profits. Suppose, however, that the high cost duopolist can eventually be pushed into a range of diminishing marginal utility if he is forced to withstand a sufficiently prolonged period of negative profits. Nash's static theory does not then supply any obvious or satisfactory answer to the question of how the variable time-dimension of the warfare that may be threatened should be taken into account. The same problem is all the more acute, of course, when both duopolists have diminishing marginal utilities and different subjective rates of time-discount.[9]

Lastly, it is at least an implicit weakness of Nash's theory that it is not generalizable (at least without supplementary conditions) to the case of variable-threat bargaining among three or more persons (that is, to the case of oligopoly as distinct from just duopoly).[1] The reason is essentially the same as in the problem of generalizing the von Neumann-Morgenstern solution of the two-person zero-sum game to the n-person case, since Nash's theory of optimal threats involves the equivalent of a zero-sum game. With just two persons, there are no alternative coalitions that may be formed by various subsets of players. With three or more persons, however, the problems raised by the multiplicity of possible coalitions typically frustrate a unique solution, whether in a zero-sum game proper or in the threat portion of Nash's negotiation model of variable-threat bargaining. On the other hand, if that coalition

9. The latter consideration also represents the burden of my own attack on the Nash-Zeuthen theory in the context of fixed-threat bargaining between union and employer, specifically when (1) the relevant threat (though statically fixed) also involves the duration of a strike or lockout and (2) the contending parties have different subjective rates of time-discount. Cf. Bishop, "A Zeuthen-Hicks Theory of Bargaining," forthcoming in *Econometrica.*

1. In this respect, of course, the variable-threat theory differs from the fixed-threat theory — see above, p. 578.

problem were somehow solved or circumvented, it would only give rise to other problems relating to deliberately contrived changes in the number of players, as for example by mergers or the opposite among oligopolists. These further problems would be analogous to those previously discussed in the context of fixed-threat bargaining (see above, pp. 578–79).

IV. CONCLUSION

Various bargaining theories have been reviewed, first in the comparatively simple context of fixed-threat bargaining and then in the more general context of variable-threat bargaining. Even under the presumably favorable circumstances when von Neumann-Morgenstern utilities are accepted as relevant and the bargainers are assumed to possess all relevant knowledge as to the underlying situation, it has been argued that no one theory stands out as clearly superior to all of its rivals, even though Nash's theory is probably still the outstanding contender for that honor. This conclusion applies whether the theories in question are regarded as positive or, in one aspect or another, normative.

As positive theories, they would be difficult to test, both because of the unrealistic character of the knowledge assumptions and also because of the explicit (and question-begging) limitation of the theories' applicability to "rational" bargainers. Whether experimentally or just observationally, however, the theories do have some potentially interesting, testable features; and they are therefore deserving of more attention than they have received from empirical investigators, not only in various applied fields of economics but also in other social sciences. With reference to the theories' normative aspects, the assessment of their worth obviously depends on criteria of a more subjective character.

PART TWO
Economic Models of Bargaining

INTRODUCTION

Although game theory is undoubtedly the best-known approach to the analysis of interdependent decision making, there are several models in the field of economics which are highly relevant to the analysis of bargaining as a method of achieving negotiated settlements under conditions of strategic interaction. All these models are formulated primarily in terms of the well-known economic problem of bilateral monopoly.[1] In fact, most of them have grown out of even more specific substantive interests in such problems as wage determination in labor-management negotiations and price setting in various situations that resemble "isolated exchange." Consequently, the economic models of bargaining are, for the most part, relatively specific in substantive terms, in contrast to the theory of games which aims at the development of a remarkably general theory of interdependent decision making.

The economic models of bargaining also differ from the models of game theory in several other ways. To begin with, the economic models deal only with certain nonzero-sum or mixed-motive situations. Thus, they focus on inter-actions in which there is a distinct range of possible outcomes (the contract zone) within which each of the participants would prefer to reach an agreement than to accept an outcome of no agreement, even though they have conflicting interests concerning the precise terms of the agreement.[2] This means that situations involving pure conflict and pure cooperation are outside the scope of these models. Next, the economic models treat bargaining as a process of convergence over time involving a sequence of offers and counteroffers on the part of the participants. Consequently, the economic models are dynamic models which focus on the bargaining process as well as on the ultimate outcome of bargaining, whereas the game-theoretic models are predominantly static models which concentrate on the ultimate distribution of payoffs among the participants.[3] Finally, the economic models tend to emphasize the forma-tion of expectations about the behavior of the relevant other(s) in contrast to the models of game theory which stress either conditions that allow each player to make accurate predictions concerning the behavior of the relevant other(s) or characteristics of a permissible solution which are sufficient to yield determinate outcomes. Although the results are somewhat similar with respect to the problem of coping with strategic interaction and specifying the ultimate distribution of payoffs, the emphasis on the formation of expectations

[1] The concept "bilateral monopoly" refers to any situation involving a single seller and a single buyer who must either agree on specific terms of exchange between them-selves or fail to exchange their goods at all. For a discussion of the extent to which real-world cases of bargaining conform to these conditions see Jan Pen, *The Wage Rate under Collective Bargaining* (Cambridge, 1959), Chapter 2.

[2] In this sense, at least, the economic models focus on situations that are similar to those described as "bargaining games" within the theory of games.

[3] For a discussion that emphasizes this distinction see John G. Cross, *The Economics of Bargaining* (New York, 1969), Chapters 1 and 2.

in the economic models leads to an interest in dynamic adjustment processes which fits well with the underlying conception of bargaining as a process of convergence over time.

All this means that the conception of bargaining incorporated in the economic models differs substantially from the game-theoretic perspective on bargaining. Like the models of game theory, however, the economic models share among themselves a number of important features. First, they are heavily oriented toward interactions involving only two distinguishable actors.[4] This restriction follows directly from the origin of the economic models in the problem of bilateral monopoly. Similarly, they do not allow for the participation of collective or corporate entities in negotiations. Hence, insofar as business firms, labor unions, nation states, and so forth are involved, they are generally regarded either as monolithic entities or simply as potential influences on their delegates (or representatives) who are the actual bargainers.[5] Second, the economic models assume that the utility functions of the participants remain stable over time[6] and that there is a clearly identifiable "payoff possibility set" for any given interaction. Also, these models are based on the premises that a contract zone exists, that it can be identified with some precision, and that it remains more or less stable over time.[7] Where there is no contract zone, the parties are not likely to enter into negotiations at all. Third, the economic models deal almost exclusively with negotiations involving a single issue in contrast to a set of distinguishable issues.[8] Moreover, they usually focus on bargaining concerning an issue (or a good) that is homogeneous and continuously divisible, such as money.[9] This means that they are

[4] The principal exception is a brief appendix to Cross's work (Cross, *Economics of Bargaining,* Appendix E), and this effort is only a preliminary one which does not attempt to come to grips with a number of factors that would become relevant in N-person bargaining situations.

[5] For useful comments on this point see Pen, *Wage Rate under Collective Bargaining,* pp. 47–60, and Alan Coddington, *Theories of the Bargaining Process* (London, 1968), pp. 6–10. Cross (*Economics of Bargaining,* p. 68) argues that this limitation is not particularly important, however, since "the most important characteristic of groups —the difficulty of formulating consistent preference functions—does not in itself impede the operation of our model." But this apparent solution to the problems associated with collective entities is surely too simple. Among other things, it does not take into account the problems groups face in formulating any coherent preference ordering at all, let alone a transitive and consistent preference ordering.

[6] These utility functions need not be linear. However, it makes things simpler for the analyst if they are linear. Consequently, there is a strong tendency to focus on cases involving linear utility functions for illustrative purposes, leaving the problems of nonlinear utility functions for later scholars.

[7] These premises sometimes seem to conflict with other points emphasized by the formulators of the economic models. They are necessary, however, for the formulation of determinate solutions for the bargaining problem. Accordingly, when other elements in the models actually do contradict these premises, the models tend to become indeterminate. For an example see the discussion of Pen's work on pp. 136–137.

[8] For a helpful discussion of this point see Jan Pen, "A General Theory of Bargaining," pp. 41–42, reprinted herein.

[9] For some comments on the problems posed by this restriction see Cross, *Economics of Bargaining,* pp. 113–114 and Appendix D.

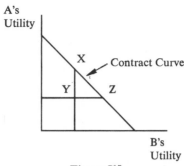

Figure I[15]

oriented primarily toward the analysis of issues like wage rates and prices in contrast to issues that are defined in terms of indivisible or lumpy goods.[10] Fourth, these models abstract away most contextual factors affecting bargaining by encapsulating them in parameters.[11] For example, such factors as the degree of organization of the participants, the resources of the players, and the prevailing rules of the game are subsumed in the cost functions and learning parameters of the two sides.[12] Accordingly, they are not subject to any detailed analysis on the basis of these models. Fifth, the economic models assume that the outcome of bargaining will be Pareto optimal with respect to the initial payoff possibility set, though some of them also emphasize costs associated with the passage of time in the course of bargaining.[13]

As indicated above, the economic models of bargaining are fundamentally convergence models. This means that they always start from the premise that the initial demands of the parties are incompatible, perhaps even falling outside the contract zone (for example, triangle XYZ in Figure I).[14] Given these initial conditions, the models proceed to analyze the processes through which

[10] This limitation is a relatively severe one. Especially in affluent societies and in noneconomic negotiations, bargaining concerning indivisible or lumpy goods appears to be prominent.

[11] Though each of the economic models employs parameters for this purpose, the specific parameters vary from one model to another. Hence, some of the differences among them can be clarified through an examination of the parameters they employ.

[12] For an argument to the effect that the whole concept of bargaining becomes fuzzy in the face of restrictions of this kind see Charles E. Lindblom, " 'Bargaining Power' in Price and Wage Determination," *Quarterly Journal of Economics,* LXII (1948), 396–417.

[13] It is important to emphasize the proviso "with respect to the initial payoff possibility set." As Coddington has argued, a settlement that is Pareto optimal in this sense may not be Pareto optimal as a *final* settlement, given the costs associated with the lapse of time. See Coddington, *Theories of the Bargaining Process,* pp. 9–10.

[14] This can happen when one or both of the bargainers are unaware of the utility function of the other. It can also occur when the "limits of the bargaining range" are not clearly defined, though this case is more difficult to deal with in the framework of the economic models of bargaining. For comments on these issues see Cross, *Economics of Bargaining,* pp. 81–82 and 117.

[15] In this simple example, the utility functions of the players (X and Y) are portrayed as linear for the sake of convenience.

the demands (that is, the offers and counteroffers) of the participants converge over time toward some specific point on the contract curve.[16] Therefore, the key element in each of these models is the development of a specific concession mechanism that permits the positions of the parties to converge in the course of a series of offers and counteroffers. Also, this is the point at which it is ultimately necessary to come to grips with any remaining elements of strategic interaction. And it is here that the economic models diverge from each other in crucial ways. Consequently, in commenting on the principal groups of these models, the following discussion emphasizes the nature of the concession mechanisms they employ.

The oldest and perhaps best known of the economic models of bargaining are those associated with Zeuthen's pioneering work on economic warfare under conditions of bilateral monopoly.[17] Zeuthen argues that each bargainer will assess the gains and losses associated with his bargaining strategies at any given point in a negotiation on an expected-utility basis. This leads to a two-stage model of the bargaining process. First, the individual always compares the certain value he can obtain by accepting the other side's current offer with the expected value of holding out for his own most favored outcome (that is, the expected value of settlement at his preferred outcome together with the expected value of a conflict or breakdown in the negotiations).[18] Given specific values for the other side's offer, his own most favored outcome, and the results of conflict, he then calculates the maximum probability of conflict he would be willing to accept in preference to acquiescing in the current offer of the other side.[19]

Second, at this point Zeuthen makes the explicit assumption that the next concession will always be made by the side willing to accept the *smaller* risk of conflict at any given moment in time.[20] But in making a concession the bargainer need not cave in entirely; he need only reduce his own demand (that is, alter his current offer) to the point where he is willing to accept a greater risk of conflict than the other bargainer. Accordingly, a situation arises in

[16] It can also happen that bargaining leads to a conflict or a breakdown in the negotiations without an agreement being reached. Because the economic models are ultimately based on a form of equilibrium analysis, they can also be used to determine the conditions of breakdown in bargaining situations.

[17] The basic presentation appears in Frederik Zeuthen, *Problems of Monopoly and Economic Warfare* (London, 1930), pp. 104–150 (partially reprinted herein).

[18] For a particularly clear and straightforward formulation of these calculations see Robert L. Bishop, "A Zeuthen-Hicks Theory of Bargaining," pp. 411–412, reprinted herein.

[19] The results of a conflict are generally determined by a variety of factors. And the players' evaluation of conflict is apt to vary depending upon whether they employ a short-term or a long-term perspective. Nevertheless, conflict was regarded as a costly outcome by Zeuthen. For the sake of convenience in employing models of this type, the utility functions of the players are often transformed so that the outcome of conflict can be presented as the zero point on the utility scale of each party.

[20] This is an assumption which Zeuthen never really defends in substantive terms, and it has been repeatedly criticized by those who have commented on Zeuthen's model. To take one example, Bishop's essay, "A Zeuthen-Hicks Theory of Bargaining," is based precisely on this point.

which each bargainer must continue to concede until he is willing to accept a larger risk of conflict than his opponent (partner), at which point the relationship is reversed. Under suitable conditions, this interaction process leads to a determinate solution at the point where the product of the utilities of the two sides reaches its maximum value.[21] Thus, the outcome of Zeuthen's bargaining process is similar to the Nash solution in game theory, even though the basic features of his model differ substantially from those of Nash's model.[22]

Since Zeuthen's model is capable of producing determinate results, it is apparent that it is not affected by the "outguessing" regress characteristic of situations involving strategic interaction. But what has become of strategic interaction in this model? In fact, the problems of interdependent decision making are absorbed in the assumptions of Zeuthen's model. Above all, it is assumed that each individual is able to attach a precise and meaningful value to the risk of conflict that the other side is willing to accept, though (as Zeuthen himself sometimes admits) this is an arbitrary procedure since the two sides would have every incentive to manipulate each other's information on this point.[23] Much the same thing can be said about the incentives of the parties to inflate their most favored outcomes, to deflate their understanding of the other side's offer, and to minimize the expected cost of conflict since the willingness of the bargainer to risk conflict is a function of these factors. Among other things, this means that "outguessing" activities may focus on utility functions as well as on approaches to the presence of strategic interaction itself whenever it is not explicitly assumed that the utility functions of the participants are fixed *and* known at the outset. Similarly, there is nothing intrinsically necessary about the assumption that the next concession will come from the side willing to withstand the smaller risk of conflict. If this relationship were not fixed by assumption and buttressed by additional assumptions affording the parties confident knowledge of each other's willingness to accept risk, the question of priority in the making of concessions would become a natural focus of strategic interaction. Finally, the same conclusion applies to the question of the size of the concession to be made at specific points in the bargaining process. There is nothing inherently necessary about the procedure of making the minimum concession necessary to push one's risk willingness above that of the other side, and in the absence of Zeuthen's specific assumptions this question also would be affected by strategic interaction. All this means that Zeuthen's restrictive assumptions have the effect of giving the parties perfect information (or if this formulation is more congenial, the

[21] For a particularly clear statement of the conditions necessary for the model to produce this outcome see Coddington, *Theories of the Bargaining Process,* pp. 29–35.

[22] This similarity between the solutions of the two models became apparent with Harsanyi's reformulation of the Zeuthen model—see John C. Harsanyi, "Approaches to the Bargaining Problem before and after the Theory of Games," reprinted herein. Harsanyi's argument that this permits a unification of the two models is commented upon at greater length in the Introduction to Part Three of this book.

[23] See especially Zeuthen, *Problems of Monopoly and Economic Warfare,* pp. 135–142.

ability to arrive at confident expectations about each other's probable behavior), with the result that each can treat his decision-making environment
at any given moment in time as if it were fixed. Therefore, Zeuthen eliminates
strategic interaction in a fashion that is reminiscent of the procedures employed in some game-theoretic models, even though his model of bargaining
allows for an interaction process involving offers and counteroffers.[24]

A second group of economic models of bargaining are characterized by
the fact that they ultimately fail to produce determinate results for the bargaining process even though they place great emphasis on the calculations of
the bargainers and concern themselves with the problem of developing a concession mechanism. Although his work derives in large measure from Zeuthen's the bargaining model formulated by Pen exemplifies this type of
model.[25] Pen's bargainer also calculates the gains and losses associated with
his alternative strategies on an expected-utility basis. Given specific values
for his own most favored outcome,[26] for the other side's current offer, and for
the results of conflict, he calculates the maximum risk of conflict at which it
is still worthwhile for him to hold out for his preferred outcome, just as
Zeuthen's bargainer calculates the maximum risk of conflict he can accept.
Pen labels this maximum acceptable risk of conflict the bargainer's risk
willingness or propensity to fight. At this point, however, the bargainer compares his propensity to fight with his estimation of the actual risk of conflict.[27]
In this connection, each party will continue to negotiate so long as his
propensity to fight exceeds his estimate of the actual risk of conflict. And
each will reach a personal equilibrium, at which he will be willing to stop
negotiating and enter into a contract, at the price or wage rate which gives him
a propensity to fight that just equals his estimate of the actual risk of conflict.

As Pen recognizes, there is no reason (other than sheer accident) to suppose that the same value for the price or wage rate will satisfy the personal
equilibrium conditions of both sides, at least at the outset. It is therefore
necessary to introduce some mechanism through which the equilibrium con-

[24] This is no doubt one reason why there is some confusion about the extent to which
Zeuthen's model should be grouped with the game-theoretic models of bargaining or the
economic models of bargaining. It is placed with the economic models in this book because (1) Zeuthen's substantive interests were similar to those of the formulators of the
economic models, (2) the model represents a shift from the game-theoretic conception
of perfect information toward the notion of developing confident expectations, and (3)
it is a process model allowing for a sequence of offers and counteroffers over time.

[25] Pen's extended analysis can be found in Pen, *The Wage Rate under Collective
Bargaining*. All the main features of his model, however, are well summarized in Pen,
"A General Theory of Bargaining," reprinted herein.

[26] Pen argues here that there is a difference between his model and Zeuthen's because the utility function of his bargainer "is not, as Zeuthen's, linear, but shows a
maximum. Therefore, the price that the bargainer strives for is not" arbitrary but is
well defined (Pen, "A General Theory of Bargaining," p. 34). But this difference has
no effect on the workings of the two models.

[27] Pen, "A General Theory of Bargaining," pp. 35–36. Note, however, that estimating the actual risk of conflict presents a problem since it is a natural focus for the
impact of strategic interaction.

ditions of one or both of the parties can be transformed to allow the same price or wage rate to satisfy both of them. Faced with this problem, Pen argues that "the function of the bargaining process is to transform the relevant magnitudes and relations in such a way that the equilibrium conditions are no longer in conflict. At the moment when both equations, which originally give different values for w [the wage rate or price], are transformed to such an extent that the solutions of w display the same value, equilibrium has been reached and the contract is concluded at this value of w."[28] Bargaining, therefore, refers to all those factors and processes that determine the extent to which the specific values of the terms in the individual equilibrium conditions of the parties can or will be transformed in the course of negotiations. But Pen offers no model of this transformation process.[29] That is, while he delineates the *dependent* variables involved in bargaining and specifies one *possible* outcome of the bargaining process (that is, agreement on a unique price or wage rate), Pen ultimately fails to produce a determinate model of bargaining.[30]

Despite his final failure, however, it is worth emphasizing that Pen succeeds in conceptualizing some major features of bargaining, as the term is commonly understood, more clearly than the game theorists and the formulators of the other economic models of bargaining. And he has some suggestive things to say about the use of various bargaining tactics in labor-management negotiations.[31] In essence, both his failure and his success stem from the fact that Pen does not, in the final analysis, exclude the impact of strategic interaction. Whereas the other models of bargaining are somewhat mechanistic and artificial, therefore, Pen's analysis leaves room for a wide variety of manipulative activities involving such devices as threats, promises, commitments, and so forth. It is undoubtedly true that indeterminateness is a high price to pay for these virtues, but it is also worth bearing in mind that artificiality and deficiencies in realism constitute a high price to pay for the derivation of determinate solutions in the logical sense.

Recently, a third distinct group of economic models of bargaining have received increasing attention. These models emphasize the role of time as a

[28] Pen, *The Wage Rate under Collective Bargaining* p. 137.

[29] For another discussion of this point consult Coddington, *Theories of the Bargaining Process,* pp. 38–40.

[30] It should be mentioned in passing that Pen's model exhibits several other features which set it apart from the other economic models of bargaining as well as the models of game theory. First, he introduces a "risk valuation function" to deal with attitudes toward risk. This function serves to modify the "neutral risk valuation" of the usual expected-utility calculations. Second, he formulates a "correspection function" to take into account the problem of imperfect information in the bargainers' estimates of the actual risk of conflict. This function suggests one possible technique for dealing with incomplete information in decision-making situations. However, both these functions amount to parameters whose values would be difficult to ascertain in empirical situations. In this sense, they constitute an additional limitation on the applicability of Pen's analysis. For Pen's own formulation of these functions see Pen, "A General Theory of Bargaining," pp. 34–36.

[31] See Pen, *The Wage Rate under Collective Bargaining,* pp. 136–147, and Pen, "A General Theory of Bargaining," pp. 39–42.

factor in bargaining and conceptualize the process of making concessions in terms of the adjustment of expectations through learning. The most important work along these lines is that of Cross, though the efforts of such scholars as Coddington and Nicholson are also relevant at this juncture.[32] In Cross's model, the individual bargainer starts his calculations with: (1) a specification of his own preference ordering for the outcomes in the payoff possibility set, (2) a schedule of costs arising from the time that elapses before a specific contract is agreed upon,[33] and (3) a precise estimate of the other side's concession rate over time.[34] Given this information, each bargainer proceeds to calculate the optimal level for his own initial demand on the assumption that "the other players will make all of the concessions."[35] This he does by taking into account the trade-offs between improvements in the final settlement terms associated with higher initial demands and the increased costs which higher demands produce as they extend the time required to reach a specific contract.

Having established the initial demands of the two sides, Cross then turns to the construction of a concession mechanism to allow the demands of the parties to converge over time. After stating his initial demand, each bargainer observes the behavior of the other side. If the other side acts in the expected fashion, the bargainer concludes that his estimate of the other's concession rate was correct and retains his initial bargaining plan in the next phase or round of the interaction. If the other party fails to respond in the expected fashion, on the other hand, the bargainer adjusts his expectations concerning the other's concession rate and formulates a new demand on the basis of his revised expectations. In general, if the other side concedes more slowly than he initially expected, the bargainer makes a concession whereas he revises his demand upward if the other concedes more rapidly than he expected.[36] The precise shifts in demands flowing from this process of adjustment, however, depend upon the exact values of parameters dealing with such things as the bargainer's learning skill (that is, sensitivity), learning speed, and discount rate for elapsed time in bargaining. The dynamism of the Cross model, there-

[32] Cross's full analysis appears in his *Economics of Bargaining*. The basic elements of his model can be found, however, in John G. Cross, "A Theory of the Bargaining Process," reprinted herein. For the work of Coddington and Nicholson see Coddington, *Theories of the Bargaining Process;* also M. B. Nicholson, "The Resolution of Conflict," reprinted herein.

[33] Cross includes several general types of cost. As he himself puts it, "The costs which time imposes on the negotiators can assume three different forms: (1) future agreements may be discounted to the present, (2) the value of the agreement may (primarily for technological reasons) change over time, and (3) there may be a fixed cost which recurs in each time period and which can be associated with the bargaining process itself" (Cross, *Economics of Bargaining*, p. 45).

[34] The present discussion focuses on Cross's basic model, what he describes as the "pure intransigence case." His discussions of bluffing and preagreement costs will be commented upon later in this book (see the Introduction to Part Four and the General Conclusion).

[35] Cross, *Economics of Bargaining*, p. 42.

[36] In some situations, externally imposed rules of the game make it impossible to revise demands upward. In his basic model, however, Cross deals with the general case in which demands can be revised either upward or downward (see *ibid.*, p. 50).

fore, arises from a relatively simple kind of learning theory that serves to activate the concession mechanism in the interactions between the two sides.[37]

Both bargainers engage in a similar sequence of expectations-demand-adjustment-expectations-demand, although the values of the parameters governing the formation of their expectations and their adjustment processes need not be symmetrical.[38] As a result, the interaction process generated by the model consists of "a repetition of these cycles until such time (if any) as agreement is reached.[39] Cross has shown that this process will produce determinate solutions given proper values for the parameters governing the behavior of the participants together with certain initial conditions.[40] As might be expected, for example, it yields the same result as the Nash solution "in the special case of identical players."[41] And Coddington has emphasized that the Cross model constitutes a relatively general framework within which it is possible to elaborate a variety of more specific models depending upon the form and the content of the various parameters.[42]

The concession mechanism of these learning models differs sharply from that of Zeuthen's model. Thus, Cross places his main emphasis on the costs of elapsed time to the bargainers[43] and on the phenomenon of learning, factors which do not appear in Zeuthen's model. Nevertheless, there is a distinct similarity in the manner in which the two types of model eliminate the effects of strategic interaction. For his part, Cross simply assumes that the players do not expect their own behavior to influence the behavior of the other player.[44] Thus, to take a specific example, he assumes that "player 1 does not think of r_2 [his estimate of player 2's concession rate] as a function of his own behavior."[45] This means that, at any given moment in time, each bargainer has a set of expectations about the other which: (1) he can rely on as certain, (2) can be stated in precise terms, (3) are not affected by strategic interaction, and (4) are not susceptible to manipulation by the other party. Similarly, it

[37] For a discussion of this part of the Cross model, which raises some critical points, see Coddington, *Theories of the Bargaining Process,* pp. 60–70.

[38] Cross himself begins with the symmetrical case (see Cross, *Economics of Bargaining,* pp. 57–63) but he goes on to consider some of the possibilities for asymmetries along these lines (Chapter 4).

[39] Coddington, *Theories of the Bargaining Process,* p. 15.

[40] If these conditions are not met, the model will lead to the breakdown of negotiations without arriving at a settlement. This will occur, for example, if the concession functions of the players are such that they always increase their demands after concessions on the part of the other. For comments on some of the ways in which instability can occur in this model see Cross, *Economics of Bargaining,* pp. 74–77.

[41] *Ibid.,* p. 59.

[42] Note especially that some of the parameters can take on different forms as well as specific values. For an exchange of views which touches on this question see Alan Coddington, "A Theory of the Bargaining Process: Comment" and Cross's "Reply," both reprinted herein.

[43] In this sense, the work of Cross exhibits a link to the earlier work of Hicks rather than Zeuthen (see Cross, *Economics of Bargaining,* p. 33).

[44] For an interesting discussion of the consequences of this assumption see Coddington, *Theories of the Bargaining Process,* pp. 49ff.

[45] Cross, *Economics of Bargaining,* p. 46.

means that the learning behavior of the parties during the course of the negotiations (in addition to the basic structure of their relationship) is exempt from
the manipulative activities often associated with strategic interaction. In support of this position, Cross points out that a consideration of strategic interaction would introduce "a variety of new problems, some of which would take
us far afield from our main topic and others of which are not subject to
satisfactory resolution at all."[46]

Several interesting conclusions flow from this discussion. In the first
instance, bargaining in the Cross model is essentially a routinized discovery
process. That is, a Cross-type bargainer starts out with a set of expectations
about the other party which are generally inaccurate (even though he initially
believes they are accurate) and which he learns to correct on the basis of
experience.[47] And given the structure of the model, the course of this discovery
process is fixed once specific values are attached to the various parameters. The
resultant interaction differs considerably from the interactions generated by
the Zeuthen model in which there are no costs arising from the elapse of time
and the parties enjoy what amounts to perfect information on a *de facto*
basis. But it contrasts even more sharply with Pen's model in which the
parties not only lack perfect information or certain expectations about the
behavior of the other side, but also devote a good deal of their attention to the
prospects of manipulating the other side's understanding of the underlying
nature of the situation. In short, the manipulative activities that many people
associate with bargaining in informal discussions are ruled out by initial
assumption in the Cross model and in the Zeuthen model, just as they are in
the models of game theory.[48]

Beyond this, there is one sense in which the Cross model yields what is
almost an embarrassment of riches. Thus, the model is based on a number of
parameters concerning such things as: the learning skill and learning speed
of the parties, each side's expectation of the other's concession rate, the fixed
costs of bargaining, and the discount rates in terms of which the players
calculate the present value of agreements reached in the future. These
parameters may display a variety of forms as well as specific values. There is
no reason to suppose that bargainers will ordinarily be symmetrical in these
terms. And some of these parameters would be difficult to deal with in
empirical terms. Under the circumstances, Cross's model is actually a general
framework within which numerous models of a more specific sort could be
developed.[49] Moreover, while it is easy to sympathize with his inclusion of this

---

[46] *Ibid.*, p. 129.

[47] At least one of the parties must have expectations that are inaccurate. In the
limiting case, only one player need be misinformed, but it is safe to assume that the
expectations of both sides will generally be inaccurate.

[48] This is why both these sets of models are grouped under the same heading in the
discussion of techniques for dealing with the problem of interdependent decision making in the General Introduction of this book. See Introduction, pp. 16–17.

[49] This appears to be one of the central points of Coddington's discussion of the
Cross model.

set of parameters, it is undoubtedly true that this characteristic of the model would produce a number of severe problems for efforts to apply it to empirical cases.

There are several other economic models of bargaining.[50] Bishop, for example, has combined one of the major insights of Hicks with the basic structure of the Zeuthen model.[51] Thus, he substitutes the concept of strike duration for Zeuthen's notion of conflict and calculates the maximum strike duration the parties can accept at any point in the bargaining process as a way of activating the concession mechanism.[52] Nevertheless, the preceding discussion of the principal groups of economic models of bargaining is sufficient to justify a number of conclusions about this conception of bargaining as an approach to the problem of interdependent decision making. The economic models are characterized by a welcome emphasis on processes and the dynamics of interaction sequences. And the most interesting of them involve a highly significant effort to combine some of the basic features of rational-choice models with at least elementary learning behavior.[53] But they still convey an image of bargaining that is somewhat mechanistic. In essence, this is due to the fact that the workings of the concession mechanisms as well as the basic structural features of the bargaining situation are specified at the outset in these models.[54] Consequently, the manipulative activities that are often associated with bargaining are abstracted away in analyses based on the economic models. Even though bargaining is now viewed as a process, therefore, it is still a somewhat mechanical process that does not offer any scope for something that could be labeled bargaining skill.[55]

[50] See especially Lucien Foldes, "A Determinate Model of Bilateral Monopoly," *Economica,* XXXI (1964), 117–131, and Bishop, "A Zeuthen-Hicks Theory of Bargaining," reprinted herein.

[51] Bishop, *ibid.* For the relevant section of Hicks's work see J. R. Hicks, *The Theory of Wages* (London, 1932), pp. 140–145.

[52] Calculating the appropriate figures for the costs of a strike per unit of elapsed time, however, would almost always turn out to be difficult. The costs arising from a strike involve a variety of factors, some of which often become apparent only in the subsequent course of events.

[53] The Cross model, together with Coddington's analysis of it, is the outstanding example.

[54] Pen's model constitutes an exception, but then it does not produce a determinate solution for the bargaining problem.

[55] Perhaps this is an appropriate place to point out that the economic models of bargaining also adopt an ambivalent attitude toward the concept of force. Unilateral imposition of solutions by sheer physical force is of course ruled out in such models because they deal with interaction processes. Nevertheless, those who have worked on these models have shown a persistent tendency to introduce the notions of force and power into their discussions of bargaining. Zeuthen hints that the ability to withstand a large risk of conflict can be regarded as a measure of force or power even though he sometimes seems to equate force with the intervention of outside actors, such as government, in the bargaining process. Pen has a lengthy discussion of economic power which he identifies with the propensity to fight in his model. And Cross argues that the concept "bargaining power" must "describe a player's ability to shift the costs of pre-agreement in such a way as to alter the outcome of the bargaining process" (Cross, *Economics of Bargaining,* p. 145). For Zeuthen and Pen, therefore, power is simply a description of certain features of their models of bargaining. But for Cross power operates outside the

It also seems worth commenting on the attitudes the economic models adopt toward rationality and information, concepts which occupy the center of attention in the models of game theory. Although all of these models assume rationality in the general sense of efforts to match means and ends purposively, there is a persistent air of ambiguity surrounding the notion of rationality in the economic models. Zeuthen adopted a highly ambivalent view on the question of rationality both conceptually and in the presentation of his specific model, a fact that has repeatedly led to confusion in discussions of his work over the years. Pen explicitly denies that his model is based on an assumption of rationality.[56] And given his emphasis on the possibilities of transforming basic features of the bargaining relationship (including the utility function of the bargainers),[57] it would seem that his denial of rationality has some real basis, though he continues to assume (at least tacitly) a basic form of means-ends rationality on the part of the bargainers. In addition, in in the Cross model rationality is strongly modified by the phenomenon of learning. Thus, while Cross's bargainers evidently adhere to the standards of rational choice in the formation of their utility functions and in the calculation of their optimum demand at any given point in the bargaining process, the key information upon which their decisions are based is governed by the learning model.

Similar remarks are pertinent with respect to the role of information in the economic models of bargaining. Zeuthen remained verbally hazy on this question, perhaps because he chose to lace his derivation of a determinate solution for the bargaining problem with periodic remarks about techniques through which the parties might be able to manipulate basic features of their relationship.[58] Zeuthen's ambiguity on this point has led to two distinct responses. Pen openly denies the presence of perfect information (or anything like it) in his model, and he therefore fails in the final analysis to produce a determinate solution for the bargaining problem.[59] Harsanyi, on the other hand, has reformulated the Zeuthen model in such a way as to emphasize its determinate aspects. This he accomplishes by cutting out Zeuthen's repeated comments on the prospects for manipulative activities and formalizing the capacity of the parties to develop confident expectations that allow each bargainer to make

---

basic model of bargaining so that it is necessary to construct a complementary model to assess the role of power. As a result, there is an interesting similarity between this aspect of Cross's work and the two-stage model of Nash in which the first stage (a zero-sum, threat game) operates to establish the base point of the bargaining game *per se*.

[56] Pen, "A General Theory of Bargaining," p. 269, reprinted herein.

[57] Among other things, this means that Pen's bargainer would tend to violate the requirement for consistency or stability of utility functions over time.

[58] See, for example, Zeuthen, *Problems of Monopoly and Economic Warfare*, pp. 106–108, herein.

[59] Pen, "A General Theory of Bargaining," p. 269, herein. In a footnote, Pen describes Zeuthen's model as involving perfect information and he puts forward the curious argument that determinate solutions for the bargaining problem can only be obtained by avoiding the assumption of perfect information and retaining uncertainty.

projections of the probable behavior of the other side.[60] Cross goes even further in substituting the development of confident expectations about the behavior of the other side for the introduction of perfect information in the traditional sense.[61] In his model, for example, the parties need not possess complete knowledge of each other's utility functions. Nevertheless, it should be stressed that insofar as expectations allow the bargainers to make confident predictions of each other's future behavior at any given point in the bargaining process, they serve the same function as the introduction of perfect information does in other models of bargaining. That is, they make it possible to derive determinate solutions for the bargaining problem by excluding the impact of strategic interaction.

Beyond this, several more specific conclusions are in order. First, the economic models are heavily restricted by their initial conditions and assumptions so that they are applicable only to a limited range of cases in the real world. This should not be taken as a severe criticism of the models since it is necessary to start somewhere in the development of theory, and the problem of interdependent decision making is widely recognized as a difficult one. But it does restrict the present usefulness of these models for descriptive purposes. Second, prospects for the empirical corroboration of the economic models of bargaining do not seem particularly bright at this time. Pen's model is largely untestable because it does not yield determinate results. In the other cases, little systematic work has yet been done that could have much impact on the validation problem. This is no doubt due in part to the problems of acquiring sound empirical data on many situations involving bargaining. But it is also due to the facts that the models are applicable only to highly restricted situations and that they include complicated parameters whose values would have to be known in order to derive specific predictions from them about bargaining in real-world situations. In any case, none of these models has yet passed any critical tests which would give it a presumptive empirical validity. Third, unlike the models of game theory, the economic models of bargaining are generally regarded as descriptive rather than prescriptive (or normative) models. Hence, it is difficult to interpret the *results* of the economic models as having any significance as prescriptive guidelines even though it is true, as Cross has demonstrated, that these models may lead to the conclusion that

[60] Harsanyi, "Approaches to the Bargaining Problem before and after the Theory of Games," reprinted herein. Harsanyi uses the concept of perfect information explicitly in describing his reformulation of the Zeuthen model. Given the fact that he is a game theorist, it is not surprising that Harsanyi was attracted to this phraseology in his reformulation, though Zeuthen himself did not explicitly refer to the concept of perfect information.

[61] In the models of game theory, the players are often able to acquire information that permits them to make accurate predictions of the behavior of the relevant other(s). In the economic models (especially that of Cross), however, the participants tend to form estimates of the behavior of the relevant other(s) and these estimates sometimes turn out to be incorrect. The use of the term "confident expectations" in this introductory discussion is meant to emphasize the difference between these two techniques for eliminating the effects of strategic interaction.

there is a substantial role for arbitration in many bargaining situations.[62] In this connection, it seems curious that the economic models of bargaining have not led to a substantial stream of experimental studies, as has been the case with the models of game theory.[63] But in any case, the predominantly descriptive orientation of the economic models means that the correspondence between the predictions of the models and actual outcomes in analogous real-world situations becomes all the more important in evaluating them.

[62] Cross, *The Economics of Bargaining,* Chapter 5.

[63] There are few experimental studies of bargaining dealing with the types of situation envisoned in the economic models. The best known is Sidney Siegal and Lawrence Fouraker, *Bargaining and Group Decision Making* (New York, 1960), which was undertaken in the hope of raising interesting hypotheses rather than testing propositions stemming from deductive models of bargaining.

ECONOMIC WARFARE

Frederik Zeuthen

1. ON "INDETERMINATE" WAGE PROBLEMS

It is generally maintained in cases where organizations of employers and workers are opposed to each other that it is possible to fix definite economic limits within which agreements may be obtained, but that the question as to at what point within these limits the settlement will be made is indeterminate from an economic point of view. To many people it will seem that the efforts to find a more definite economic solution to this problem are hopeless and futile. At negotiations between employers' and workers' organizations, purely personal elements, the skill of the negotiators, misunderstanding, bluff, and so on, undoubtedly play a considerable part. There is no need for us to describe in detail the whole of this recognized technique and psychology of negotiations, which is so important to the result. As mentioned at the end of the previous chapter, we shall deal mainly with the most extreme cases, in which both the employers and the workers of a trade are fully organized, and in which the possibility of variations in the volume of trade has no effect at all on the height of wage rates, which is determined exclusively by fighting or by threats.

In a mathematical appendix to his book, *Methods of Industrial Peace,* Professor Pigou has tried to fix the limits of a more definite range within which the verdict of arbitration is tenable or, what amounts to the same thing, the rates about which it is possible to come to an agreement. Let us, with Professor Pigou, call it the *range of practicable bargains.*

The establishment of any rate within these limits—by agreement or by arbitration—will be more advantageous than a conflict to either party; any rate outside these limits will be less advantageous than a conflict to one party, at the same time giving the other greater advantages than it would be possible for it to obtain within the limits.

The limits of the fighting sphere are determined by the expected result of a fight plus or minus the expected fighting costs. The workers will not be content with less than the result they expect to obtain through a fight, minus a reduction in the rate of wages, which means the same to them as the losses they expect the fight to involve; correspondingly with regard to the employers. The parties may possibly each expect a different result from the fight. It is of greater interest, however, that they may make quite different estimates of the cost of fighting, so that the limits of the fighting sphere need not be sought at the same distance on either side of the expected result. If now, we have a market with an elastic demand (otherwise we do not pay any regard to elasticity to begin with), the extent of the sales at different rates of wages will exert a certain influence on the comparison of the parties between different rates, and thereby on the differences in wages which correspond to the fighting costs, and on the limits of the fighting sphere (see section 5).

So far, we can trace the measurable quantities that enter into the considerations of the parties, including the estimated cost of conflict, but within the limits just discussed everything seems to be indefinite and economically indeterminate. If in a certain trade, for instance, wages fall below 63s., the employers' association will prefer any wage to conflict, and if they exceed 45s., the same will be true with regard to the trade union. It is within these limits that the wage problem is considered *indeterminate,* since in this case the settlement will depend on skill at negotiation, changing sentiments among the rank and file, accidental circumstances, bluff, and so on.

2. DETERMINING FORCES

Doubtless these factors considerably influence the result but, nevertheless, the economic forces that are at work outside the *range* are—as will be seen —not quite suspended within. Every solution is not equally probable, and if you take a large number of cases, you may expect the economic forces to express themselves in a certain tendency. This means that the question is not economically indeterminate, and that the problem is not insoluble if, like in other economic problems, one is content with a solution that amounts to only a definite tendency, a determinant, which together with other determinants of quite a different and less invariable nature, brings about the result in the particular case.

If, really, an ultimatum were always binding for the party that delivered it, the essential thing, when isolating the individual case, would be the fact, who first put forth the greatest possible claim within the "indeterminate" range. Here, of course, it would always be to the interest of the opposite side to avoid the conflict, but this is not the case, even though a tactical advantage may be gained by binding oneself to a claim one would prefer not to fight on.

An ultimatum may be withdrawn, however; if one has been delivered, and if neither of the parties are unconditionally in favor of a conflict, the main question will be, both for the party that has delivered the ultimatum and for its opponent, as to whether it should yield before the time of expiry or whether it should hope for the other party to do so. The more a claim does not harmonize with the actual conditions of power, the more vigorously will considerations of prestige and of fear of setting a dangerous example arise.

Even when, theoretically, there exists at least one possibility of peaceful settlement to the interest of both parties—when the lowest conceivable claim of the workers falls below the highest possible offer of the employers—the negotiations are often of such a nature that a fight within the *range of practicable bargains* is the result. It is to the interest of the respective parties to simulate a readiness to fight greater than they actually possess, and in case they should fail in this purpose, really to be as ready for conflict as they wish the other party to imagine. Agitation among the common members is generally the main method, though unreliable in its effects. The mobile heads of the organizations try to the best of their ability to place their heavy and less dirigible sections in a position which is neither too bold nor too modest. The individual party may then, by its more or less obstinate attitude, to a greater or smaller extent run the risk of a fight.

After having thus recognized the great uncertainty actually prevailing, as to where the settlement will be made within the range of practicable bargains and that, in spite of the existence of a number of possibilities of peaceful settlement, a conflict may easily ensue, we shall try to ascertain whether there is not, after all, a tendency in the direction of agreement at a definite rate. If the parties are directed by a definite and rational policy based on objective economic conditions and the conditions of power, these circumstances will determine the result.

The first question is: what values and what quantities should be the determining factors for the parties? The second: in what manner should the parties be guided by these quantities? Taking actual negotiations concerning wage problems, we are certain that the parties are guided by facts that may be expressed in figures, but how the calculation is actually made, it is not easy to see. Normally, the decision will be the result of an estimate of all the conditions at hand, that is, the real calculation is left to the subconscious and to one's instinct.

The quantities considered are the rates of wages in various instances together with the loss, cost, and unpleasantness of stoppage.

The higher the wage, the greater the sum of economic advantages for the workers during the period in which the agreement is in force, and the smaller the sum of advantages obtained by the employers. At any rate of wages that comes up for consideration, a comparison will take place between these expected values of settlement and the expected values of conflict at this very rate. In case of settlement, the expected values are, for the trade union, the value of the achieved rate multiplied by the number of employed workers, and for the employers, the value of the products less other costs, less wages. As will be evident from what follows, it is the difference between the expected advantages of settlement at different rates that is decisive for the action of the parties. The decisive factor will, consequently, be a difference between two rates or, if preferable, a corresponding difference per worker. The expected value of a conflict for either party will consist in a sum of the possible results of warfare, each of which is calculated according to its probability, less a corresponding sum for the possible costs of conflict.

If it is known with certainty, or if the parties think they know what will be the result of the fight, and how long it will last, the quantity is fairly simple, being the result of the fight less its costs. If there is any uncertainty with regard to the result of the fight, however, the expected value will become more complicated; it will then, as mentioned, depend on a series of possible settlements, possible costs, as well as the respective probabilities. If there exists a legal minimum wage, it will raise the workers' expectations in the event of conflict and increase their demands accordingly, diminishing the fighting spirit of the employers. The opposite is the case with regard to the general conditions limiting the possible rates. How to determine in practice the expected value in case of settlement and conflict (A and B in the figure and the equations below) is a problem in itself; see the points of view set forth in sections 5 and 6. Here, we shall have to deal mainly with the second part of the question: how are the parties to proceed rationally, when they have certain conceptions as to the value of settlement and conflict in a given situation? How are they to proceed when they are only able to estimate the difference between the expected value of settlement at two different rates and the difference in the expected value between a settlement and a conflict arising from the claim of the same rate, or when they are only able approximately to measure the proportion between two such differences?

If a very low rate is at issue, the expected gain of the workers from a conflict will be greater than that from a settlement and, consequently, they will be unconditionally in favor of a conflict. At the lower limit of the range of possible bargains the two expectations are equal. If the rate were to rise further, the workers would prefer to avoid conflict, but if they openly told the employers so, they would expect, normally, not to get a farthing more. Surely they would be willing to risk something in order to raise the rate beyond the point at which a settlement was worth no more to them than a conflict, and they would sacrifice something if they could thereby further reduce the claim of the employers. The sacrifice—as we shall see—may be measured in terms of the *probability* of *conflict to which they are willing to expose themselves by maintaining an ultimatum*. It is in fairly good accordance with the actual facts to assert that it is this standard of measurement that determines whether the trade union puts forward a claim beyond the utmost limit of its willingness to take up an unavoidable conflict, in the hope that the opposite party may be afraid to fight and therefore be willing to yield. The question arises as to how much they will risk. Since, however, the employers are in quite a similar situation, and are willing to incur a certain risk in order thereby to obtain a further reduction of wages below their own utmost limit, have we not then come into a sphere of pure chance?

3. CALCULATION OF THE PROBABILITY

As the question is rather complicated, and since we must be very accurate in our statement thereof, we shall examine it, at first, in a somewhat simplified form.

We presuppose, for the present, that the parties only reckon with the actual expected values to them of settlement and conflict, disregarding the unpleasantness or maybe, the attractiveness, of the element of uncertainty, that is, the cost of risk taking.

In the figure below (Figure 28), we have indicated the conditions on which the deliberations of the workers are based; at each rate of wages (L) their expectation of a settlement at that rate is A, and in case of conflict—B. The expected value of settlement is, for the present, assumed to be proportional to

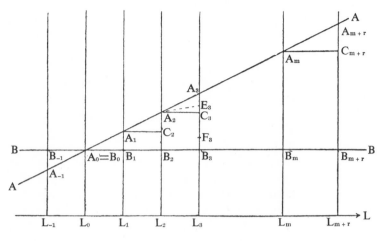

Figure 28

the rise in the rate of wages while the expected value of conflict is assumed to be constant, that is, A—A and B—B are straight lines, B—B being horizontal. As we shall see in sections 5 and 6, the suppositions are far from exact, and are in no way necessary for the achievement of our final result. We begin with a simplified case merely to give a clear outline of the essentials, that is, increasing advantage to the workers the higher the rate, and the existence of certain expectations in case of conflict, reserving the more doubtful questions as to the proportion in which the expectation of the workers rises at higher rates, and how the expectations in case of conflict vary in relation to the height of the wage in dispute.

The minimum demand of the workers is, in Figure 28, at the rate L_0, where $A_0 = B_0$; in this instance it is just the same to them whether settlement or conflict is the result, whereas at the lower rates, $B > A$, they prefer conflict, and at the higher rates, $A > B$, they prefer settlement.

The trade union will only find it to its advantage to maintain a claim for L_1 (practically the smallest possible increase over their minimum claim L_0) provided that the expectation of the profit that may be obtained by claiming L_1, L_0 being certain, is equal to the expectation of the loss that may be incurred thereby, that is, $(A_1 - B_1) (1 - c_1) = (A_0 - B_0)c_1$, where c_1 is the greatest probability of conflict to which they can advantageously expose themselves. As there is nothing to be lost through a conflict at the starting point when $A_0 = B_0$, c_1 will be equal to 1. It will then be most profitable to claim a wage which—practically speaking—lies just above their minimum demand, even if a conflict were then certain. This means that the range of practicable bargains is somewhat restricted by reckoning with intervals between the possibilities of negotiation.

If the trade union, thinking that a settlement may be obtained at L_1, nevertheless claims L_2, the corresponding probability of conflict that they dare to risk at the utmost, will be found from the equation: $(A_2 - C_2) (1 - c_2) = (A_1 - B_1)c_2$. As we presupposed, A—A is a straight line, and the rate intervals of $(L_1 - L_0)$ and $(L_2 - L_1)$ are equal, c_2 thus being equal to ½. Put into everyday language, this means that the leaders of the workers reasoned as follows: "The employers are willing to give 3s. a week beyond 45s. say, a rate which to us is no more advantageous than conflict. If we now demand a further 3s., that is, 51s. a week, we may expect a profit of 3s. per worker, but also a loss of 3s. per worker as compared with the 48s. of which we may be sure if we submit no further claim. Consequently, we only forward the claim if we think it most likely that the employers will agree to it, that is, we think that by demanding the 51s. we risk a probability of a conflict of 50 percent at the most. (If now, the increase from 45s. to 48s. has a greater utility to the workers than that from 48s. to 51s., they will not even risk a 50 percent probability, but only forward the claim for instance, if they think that the employers will reject it in but one case out of every three, that is, if the probability is 33⅓ percent at the most. This modification we shall, however, leave for the present.

In the same way we can find the highest probability the trade union leaders are willing to risk by going one step further, when it is supposed that a settlement may be obtained at A_2, A_3, and A_{n-1} respectively; it will, consequently, be ⅓, ¼, and $1/n$. The latter will also hold good when it is a question of infinitely small intervals, the varying size of the intervals not being decisive.

If it is certain that the employers will give a wage that is m above the minimum demanded by the workers, the latter will only find it advantageous to risk a probability of conflict corresponding to c in the following equation, by demanding a further increase of r (see the figure):

$$c(A_m - B_m) = (1 - c) (A_{m+r} - C_{m+r}) ;$$
$$c = (A_{m+r} - C_{m+r}) : ((A_{m+r} - C_{m+r}) + (A_m - B_m))$$
$$= (A_{m+r} - C_{m+r}) : (A_{r+m} - B_{m+r}).$$

This formula, which is true irrespective of the shape of the lines A—A and B—B, in so far as the fluctuations of the latter are relatively unimportant, says that the probability is the difference between the expectations of settlement at the two rates at issue divided by the difference between the expectations of settlement and conflict at the more favorable rate. The probability is, in other words, the *increase in wages divided by the fighting costs.*

If it be now supposed, as we have done hitherto, that A—A and B—B are straight lines, and that B is constant, we shall find that the various fully drawn triangles in the figure are similar, and that consequently, if the dispute is about L_m or L_{m+r}, $c = r: (m + r)$. At each wage interval the probability is found to be the same as the *proportion of the length of the wage interval to the distance from the minimum demand to the wage desired.*

The series of probabilities which we have found in that way are only marginal values concerning a possible step forward from a point at which a settlement can be obtained. As was seen, the probabilities mentioned decrease in a rapidly declining progression—gradually as they advance beyond the utmost point for unconditional conflict. The absolute magnitude of the probabilities is dependent on the length of the intervals, and if there is a choice between demanding much or nothing, they will risk a greater probability of conflict than where it is only the question of a small step forward.

4. Interplay between the Two Parties

The calculation of how great a probability of conflict one party, the trade union for example, will find it to its account to expose itself to at different rates affords, however, only one basis of how to act to the greatest advantage. The other set of conditions applies to the conjecture of the same party as to how the other party, the employers' association, say, will act to its advantage on its own presuppositions. In order that the parties can form a basis for a decision as to whether they ought to maintain a certain claim, it is necessary to have quantities that may be balanced against one another with regard to their action in the same wage interval. We must here have quantities of an equal dimension for either party at each rate of wages, besides the rate itself. Neither the expected values in money nor in utility can be compared for the two parties, because a basis of recalculation is lacking. In addition, how one is getting on is of little importance to the other. The threat to fight the matter out is the only thing that counts—and the variable element is the probability of conflict which the opposite party dare risk.

Either party will continue to increase its claims so long as the utmost probability of conflict to which it can find its advantage to expose itself is greater than the maximum probability which it thinks the other will risk, by opposing it within the same wage interval. As has been seen, the workers showed a willingness to risk constantly decreasing probabilities of conflict as the higher wage rates came up for deliberation, beginning with 100 percent at the lowest end of the range of practicable bargains. Similarly, they will imagine the employers to have a series of probabilities beginning with 100 percent at the top end of the range of practicable bargains which decreases gradually as the rate falls.

If we consider the position of the parties at a possible negotiation concerning various wage intervals of 3s., we may imagine the scales of probabilities to be as indicated in the table below. The scales are here supposed to correspond to quite similar views entertained by the leaders of both organizations. Now, if both parties had a perfectly accurate perception of each other's circumstances, and the risk which the other party was actually willing to run, that is, were aware of the other party's economic and psychological presuppositions, but not of their tactics in the particular instance, it would seem that the settlement were bound to fall at a definite point. In Section A of the table above, how great a risk of stoppage either party will be willing to run for each step of 3s. is stated, but as a matter of fact the negotiations will only

	Wage interval, shillings.					
	45–48	48–51	51–54	54–57	57–60	60–63
A. (Intervals 3s.)						
Trade union's readiness to risk a fight (percent)	100	50	33⅓	25	20	16⅔
Employers' readiness to risk a fight (percent)	16⅔	20	25	33⅓	50	100
B. (Different intervals)						

1. Situation	Employers' offer 45s.; Trade union's offer 66s. Employers' probability 100 percent; Trade union's probability 100 percent. Both interested in concessions.
2. Situation	Employers' offer 45s.; Trade union's offer 60s. Employers' probability 83⅓ percent; Trade union's probability 100 percent. Employers have to yield.
3. Situation	Employers' offer 51s.; Trade union's offer 60s. Employers' probability 75 percent; Trade union's probability 60 percent. Workers have to yield.
4. Situation	Employers' offer 51s.; Trade union's offer 57s. Employers' probability 50 percent; Trade union's probability 50 percent. Both interested in concessions.
5. Situation	Employers' offer 54s.; Trade union's offer 57s. Employers' probability 33⅓ percent; Trade union's probability 25 percent. Workers have to yield.
6. Situation	× Employers' offer 54s.; Trade union's offer 54s. Employers' probability 0 percent; Trade union's probability 0 percent. Agreement: 54s.

touch on a limited number of possibilities. Corresponding to the definite figures of the table we shall, in practice, have a less precise tendency, to a certain extent, because each of the parties is not directed by the unchangeable will of a single person.

Either party will try to achieve the most advantageous arrangement. Only in so far as both parties knew all of each other's presuppositions, and were convinced that the other would follow the wisest possible policy, would it be possible for either of them to calculate the result in advance. The result, however, is only brought about by mutual influences, a special form of the higgling of the market, not by competition, but by threats; and each will try to convince its opponent that its own threats are better founded and more irrevocable than those of the other. Consequently, the point is not merely to know one's own presuppositions and those of the opposite party, for A will only yield gradually as it becomes convinced that B is thinking that it (B) dares run a risk of conflict greater than that which A is prepared to face at the same stage of the negotiations.

In the imaginary labor-market mentioned in the table, both parties knew their own presuppositions as well as those of their opponents in case of settlement and of conflict at each rate of wages. On the basis thereof, they have calculated the same probabilities which workers and employers, respectively, dare risk within each of the intervals. We shall now be able to see what the result will be when the negotiations are concerned with the wage intervals of the smallest practicable size—3s.; if they start with larger intervals, it will be in the interest of the party that dares risk the smallest probability of conflict to shorten the interval by a concession. In the above examples equilibrium can only be established at 54s.

In reality, the parties will be greatly removed from one another to begin with; we may, for instance, imagine them to be proceeding in the manner indicated in the example in Section B of the table. The employers begin by demanding a reduction of the rate to 45s., and the workers, by demanding 66s., that is, a claim beyond the utmost point the employers can afford (situation 1 of the table). Both parties will here prefer unconditional conflict to submission (100 percent probability). However, both parties, as presupposed, prefer any rate above 45s. and below 63s. to a conflict; the workers for instance, will reduce their claim to 60s. (situation 2). They themselves constantly prefer unconditional conflict to the 45s. which the employers have offered them, but by yielding they succeed in forcing the employers into a situation where the latter must yield, because they are only willing to risk 83⅓ percent ((60–45) : (63–45)) probability on a claim of 45s. when they can have a settlement at 60s., whereas the workers will risk 100 percent. If now the employers offer 51s. (situation 3), it is the workers who only dare risk 60 percent, and consequently will prefer to make a concession to the employers, who dare risk 75 percent. As long as it is necessary, the parties will constantly try to undermine each other's desire of opposition by making greater concessions than they have done, but as far as possible they will not yield more than what is strictly necessary, if there is only a slight possibility of striking a good bargain. If, during the negotiations, the parties get into a position where they run an equal risk (for instance 50 percent each as in the interval from 51s. to 57s. in situation 4), they will both be interested in making concessions, as a conflict in that case will be the greater evil to each. Wherever they begin, and whichever method they follow, the negotiations must—under the imaginary circumstances which we assumed—end at one single point—settlement at 54s. (situation 6).

If, however, any other rate of wages is being discussed, either one or other of the parties will find it advantageous to make its opponent withdraw a step, by threatening it, and it will be to the advantage of the latter to yield as soon as the danger of war reaches a point beyond that which it itself dares risk, but denoting a probability less than that which the other dares to incur.

This concrete example will probably best show how the deliberations and actions of one party will make the other change its deliberations and actions. The result, however, will not be indeterminate or consist of indeterminable fluctuations to and fro, for in the case of both it is constantly a tendency in the same direction; generally, there is no going back upon an offer that has once been made, and concessions on the part of one party will force the other to do likewise. If they act rationally, the movement will continue until a point is reached at which there are no conditions for any further movement.

In the example of the table, it is clearly seen that the parties will meet midway. If it were a question of very small intervals, as for instance a farthing per week, the same fact would appear still more clearly. The two equally great probabilities at the point of meeting would be the small wage interval divided by the equally great distance from either of the outer points. That the parties will meet midway will also be evident from the general formula mentioned as to the probability of conflict. The workers will, in a given wage interval, risk a probability of $c = r : (m + r)$, that is, the proportion between the length of the interval and the distance to their utmost limit. The employers have a similar formula applying to the same wage interval of $c_1 = r : (p + r)$; and the distance between the outer points $r + m + p$ is given (p being the distance between the fighting point of the employers and the furthest limit of the fighting sphere, corresponding to the m of the workers in Figure 28). The workers will now have to yield, so long as m is greater than p, and vice versa; so long as r is greater than O, one or both of the parties will be interested in avoiding a conflict by making concessions. Consequently, in the given circumstances the result must be: $m = p$ and $r = o$.

5. ECONOMIC WARFARE AND THE VOLUME OF EMPLOYMENT
(WITH TWO ABERRATIONS)

Hitherto, in this chapter, we have only dealt with those cases in which for a short period in the future the volume of production was absolutely independent of the height of the rate of wages, at least within certain limits. The rate,

in these cases, could, neither wholly nor partly, be determined by an adjustment between the quantities supplied and demanded. . . . In real life, however, we shall more often have cases which, to a certain extent (that is, to an
extent insufficient to bring about a peaceful settlement satisfactory to either
party), show an adjustment of the sales to the height of the rate. . . . The
extent of the sales influences the attitude of the parties in the discussion of
each higher or lower rate. A series of characteristic points is here of importance, that is, the point of equilibrium at free competition and at bilateral
monopoly . . . or, if the latter equilibrium is impossible, the limits of the
sphere within which rates cannot be determined by variation in sales. . . .
In this way the limits of the striking range are also influenced as well as the
equilibrium within these points. But since the losses of the party through a
stoppage at the same time influence the determination of the latter set of
points, they will deviate from the former in one direction or other.

In cases where it is probable that a higher wage within the range of practicable bargains will involve diminished employment both of workers and of
machinery, the expectations in case of settlement will, as far as both parties
are concerned, be somewhat lower at the higher rates, and this will weaken the
workers' eagerness to fight for too high a wage, and strengthen that of the
employers, expressed in terms of the above-mentioned probabilities. Where
such a bending of the curves has a strong influence, it may, in so far as it gets
above the middle of the range of practicable bargains, probably be able to
shift the point of equilibrium to a point somewhat below the middle.

It is, however, not only too high a rate, but also too low a rate, which may
entail a decrease in employment. If the rate decreases, the volume of employment will increase in accordance with the demand curve until its intersection with the supply curve, after which it will decrease in accordance
with the latter. This fact is essentially of greater importance to the workers
when they cannot get employment elsewhere than when they have access to
other employment, even if not quite so well paid. Where a reduction of the rate
causes an increasing number of workers to leave the trade, the advantages to
the employers of a reduction in wages may be reduced thereby.

The reaction of the sales on the prices of the commodities may have an
effect which goes in the opposite direction to the one here mentioned. In so far
as production increases, the eagerness of the employers to fight for a reduction
in wages will be relatively diminished if the change entails a strong decline in
the prices of the commodities, whereas the opposite is the case when the
workers are driven out of the trade, and the quantity sold is reduced thereby.

Furthermore, the effects of a change in wages on the volume of employment
will very often be quite different in the long run from what they were within
the first period of the agreement. It may, for instance, be possible in the beginning, to force a great increase in wages because of the existence of buildings
and machinery, which are worth nothing if not used. The consequence, however, may be that the enterprises are not extended or kept in repair, and that
at a given opportunity the high-priced labor will be substituted by an increase

of machinery.[1] The monopolistic price policy is momentarily victorious, but in the long run, nevertheless, competitive equilibrium will assert itself—even though the result may be an absolutely different equilibrium from the one we should have experienced had the monopolistic interference not taken place. In a corresponding way it is conceivable that a monopolistic policy on the part of the employers may put a stop to the ingress of labor, and gradually drive the workers (especially the best of them) out of the trade. Of especial practical importance is a third case: a monopolistic price policy on the part of organized workers and employers, seen in the building trades, for instance, which increases the profits for both parties and at the same time reduces the employment to a certain extent. It must in this case be possible to prevent unorganized competitors from intruding into the trade.

First Aberration: A Monopolistic Increase in Wages and Total Wages

If the possibilities of employment are restricted in certain parts of the labor market, the result will be an increased supply of labor in other spheres; but it is wrong to conclude that the gain in wages in one market—according to a kind of wage-fund theory—will equal exactly what is lost elsewhere. The amount of labor may, however, be regulated by means of unemployment benefits and reduction of working hours.

The curves in Figures 29, 1 to 6, indicate the amount of labor in three pairs of labor markets. The amount of labor in each market is first A_1, and wages L_1. If, now, wages are increased in one market (the figures to the left) to L_2, the amount of labor will be reduced to A_2, and a workers will disappear. Thus in the second market there will be $A_1 + a = A_3$ workers, whereby the wages will decrease to L_3. The increase in wages for the number of workers remaining in the market with the high rate, is illustrated by the hatched area in the figures to the left. The loss in wages to the original number of workers employed in markets 2, 4, and 6 is here the hatched area, and the loss to the workers driven out of markets 1, 3, and 5 and over to markets 2, 4, and 6, the dark area.

The proportion between gain and loss is now determined by the shapes of the curves. In figures 1 and 2 an unequal distribution between the two uniform labor markets entails a decline in the total sum of wages, therefore in the average wage. In figures 3 and 4 (where the curve is shaped like a rectangular hyperbola), the total wages will in each separate market be constant, irrespective of the supply of labor (or of the height of the rate). This involves that the total amount of wages in the two markets together will be constant, irrespective of the distribution of the labor. A transference of labor from market 5, where the demand curve is steep, even at relatively large sales, to market 6, where the opposite is the case will, on the other hand, involve an increase in the total

[1] Gustaf Åkermann, *Realkapital und Kapitalzins*, and *Den industrielle arbetslönnens utvekling och återverkningar* (1927); Bertil Ohlin, *Saet Produktionen i Gang*, and his criticism of my book on the distribution of wealth in *Nationaløkonmisk Tidsskrift* (1929).

amount of wages, whereas a shifting in the opposite direction will have the contrary effect.

As, now, it is in those spheres in which a relatively large increase in wages can be obtained through a small efflux of labor when compared with the number of workers in the trade that we find the strongest tendencies toward adopting a monopolistic trade union policy, there is reason to suppose that the total wages of the country, in spite of the reduction in the quantity of production, will in many cases be increased as a consequence of the division of the market effected by the trade unions. On the other hand, a hindrance in the movements between several uniform rural districts will probably lower the total wages.[2] As a monopolistic wage policy, owing to the hindrance of the mobility of labor and the unemployment it entails, may reduce the total production, the gain for the working classes of all countries will, at any rate, be smaller than one would have supposed beforehand. On the other hand, a rate which, to begin with, is screwed up a little above the momentary point of economic equilibrium, may gradually become economically justified on account of increased efficiency.

Second Aberration: Higher Wages and Increased Consumption of the Workers

We shall now tackle another, though somewhat more remote, problem. Will the increase in consumption due to increase in wages lead to a greater volume of employment?

In the first place, will this be possible at full capacity in the long run?

In the following imaginary instance we shall try to find the conditions necessary for an increase in wages to involve an increase in consumption by the workers of their own products so that the demand for the said products will remain constant. Thereby we shall also, if we proceed one step further, obtain the conditions for an increase in the total sales.

An enterprise produces 1,000 pieces in the course of a certain period; the wages are 100 per piece, and the price 200. If the rate of wages is now increased by 20 percent to 120, and the price to 220, the labor income rises from 100,000 to 120,000. If we suppose 55 percent of the rise in income to be spent on buying the products of the enterprise, the workers can obtain fifty pieces thereby, and consequently, it will be possible to keep the quantity of production unchanged in case the former consumption (of which the workers may possibly themselves participate) at the 10 percent increase in wages is only reduced by 5 percent, that is, in case the elasticity of the previous consumption is only ½. The proportion between the decline in the previous consumption on one hand, and the rise in prices on the other, that is, the greatest elasticity for the old consumption which may give equilibrium, is ½. If the elasticity is smaller, the rise in wages will entail an increase in consumption.

---

[2] See Bowley's article "Wages and the Mobility of Labor," *Economic Journal* (1912).

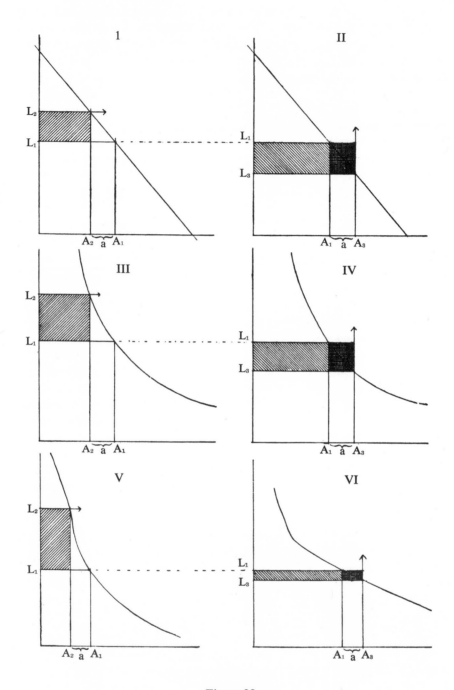

Figure 29

To express it generally as a function of the decisive variables, the greatest elasticity (the proportion between the relative change in the opposite direction in sales and price) for the old consumption which will not reduce the demand for the article is f.p : (p + s), where f is the part of the wage increase spent by the workers to purchase the article they produce themselves (in the above, 55 percent), p is the proportion between price and wages (in the above, 2), and s the increase in the rate of wages (in the above, 20 percent). f is to be found between 1 and 0, normally comparatively close to 0. p is greater than 1 (and generally essentially greater); p : (p + s) is smaller than 1—and in so far as it is only a question of tendencies toward a rise in the price, equal to 1. The formula, therefore, will normally give a result which is essentially less than 1; f, especially, as a rule is small if it is a question of a limited sphere of wages. This means that only where the old consumption is very inelastic, will there be any increase at all in the total demand. The articles in question must, consequently, be firmly demanded by the old consumers, and on the other hand, there must at the same time be a greatly increased demand on the part of the workers, who must spend a very great proportion of their extra wages on the purchase of their own product. This seems, beforehand, improbable, but it may form an exceptional case with an enterprise such as the Ford factories (before the competition became too heavy), in which one may expect a very great proportion of the wages beyond a certain limit to be spent on the purchase of Ford cars.

For much larger spheres, for instance, all labor in one or several countries, these conditions, however, cannot possibly be complied with. The conditions which we have found necessary for the exceptional case themselves show that they will not be present in large spheres, because the expenses cannot at the same time be raised on all sides without involving a corresponding rise in prices.

Now, if we leave the assumption of "the long run" and consider cases with unused capacity, p will decrease at an extension of production. Under such circumstances it is more probable that a rise will in special cases counteract unemployment.

We have, in this section, touched upon a number of important practical problems which are closely connected with the interests of workers and employers in changes in the rate of wages, as for instance, the effects of the elasticity of demand on the volume of employment and thereby its influence on prices. As a less important digression we have dealt with the possibility of increasing employment through increased consumption (which is absurdly exaggerated in popular discussions, but which perhaps is too easily ignored by some economists). Finally, we have pointed out the fact that the results obtained by fighting will often be of a very limited duration. It follows also, that the immediate liberty of action of the parties will be restricted, since they will, as a rule, be interested in the future development, and since it may be to the detriment of both to force a rate of wages that will not hold in the long run.

Now let us return to the symbolism we applied previously in this chapter: increasing possibilities of employment at certain changes in the rates of wages enhance the expected values of these, and thereby the corresponding eagerness to fight; but as soon as the point of greatest possibility of employment has been passed—the economic equilibrium under free competition—the expectations decrease, and the eagerness to fight is influenced correspondingly. The stronger the effects of the rate on employment, the smaller the deviation from the "economic point of equilibrium" (that is, the competitive equilibrium, here not very different from that of the bilateral monopoly). The more equal the estimate of the parties concerning the sacrifices of warfare, the smaller will be the deviations of the point of equilibrium (that is, equilibrium in the organized market) from the probable issue of a fight. The probable result of a fight as well as its deviation from the latter point of equilibrium is influenced by the ability of the parties to wait, that is, by their subjective rate of interest or, at any rate, the conditions determining it (see the first point in the next paragraph). Only in case this ability is unlimited will there be no point of equilibrium; otherwise there exists an economic equilibrium also when both parties are organized, but an equilibrium of which the subjective rates of interest of the parties form a part.

6. Other Deviations from the Simple Solution

In section 4, Interplay between the two Parties, we showed that under certain simplified assumptions the parties would meet at the point midway between their utmost concessions. In the preceding paragraph we dealt with the most important circumstances influencing the expectations of both employers and workers at each rate of wages, and thereby, their eagerness to fight, as well as the point of equilibrium. On the whole, deviations from the middle take place, when the expected values in case of settlement do not—as we have hitherto assumed in the formulas above—move proportionately with the changes of the wage, and when the expectations in case of conflict are not independent of the wage. None of these assumptions are quite applicable, even though the deviations may not be very great. Especially as far as the workers are concerned one may conclude that the expectations in case of settlement will not move proportionately with the change in the wage, because here, too, a great loss is felt relatively more than a small loss or a small gain. The bending of the line A—A in Figure 28 (for instance a lowering of A_3 to E_3) and the corresponding curve for the employers, will cause the progressions of probabilities to decrease more strongly. The parties become more peaceable, and in so far as it is mainly the workers who become more peaceable, the point of equilibrium—on account of what is usually the workers' smaller ability to wait—will fall to a rate somewhat below the middle. The large sum of money is valued relatively less than the small one, and the future income less than the present one, which in the sphere here dealt with will often be a condition of life. These are the same points of view which are applied elsewhere to the question of the rate of interest. (Whereas the bendings of the curves mentioned above will shift the point of equilibrium, the greater or smaller slope of the curves, that is, the proportion between the values of settlement and of conflict at the particular rates, is unimportant, as will be evident from the above formulas, and from the fact that the proportion A : B in the figure is a straight line.)

A conflict will probably be most protracted if it is occasioned by an extreme claim, which will be in accordance with the circumstance that the curve B—B in Figure 28 is actually somewhat arched (for instance B_3 raised to F_3). This fact, however, will scarcely involve any considerable shifting of the point of equilibrium, and in any case scarcely increase the probability of conflict, generally speaking.

Furthermore there are certain rates at which the eagerness to fight is suddenly and relatively strongly increased for psychological and practical reasons, that is, the money wage hitherto paid to the workers, or the wage calculated according to a generally accepted index, or the profit hitherto obtained by the employers for instance.

Finally, there is a fifth condition that may be imagined to involve a shifting of the point of equilibrium. We have, up to now, paid no regard to risk taking, that is, the unpleasantness of uncertainty, and have reckoned exclusively with the expected values as they would be accounted for by an organization that was so rich that one-tenth probability of settlement, which involved for instance 10 million units of utility, was of the same value to it as one-half probability of gaining 2 millions, the same being the case with regard to the costs of war. As the great gain is generally of comparatively light weight, and the great loss of comparatively heavy weight, the probabilities which the parties are willing to risk will be calculated somewhat more cautiously than they would according to the mathematical expectations. This will surely tend to make the prospects of peace noticeably greater, and may shift the point of equilibrium in a manner somewhat to the detriment of the most cautious and, so far, the weaker party. This may well be the workers who are the poorer party, but it may also be the employers if they are most strongly tied to the trade.

As the probabilities expressing the eagerness of the parties to fight at various rates of wages, according to the preliminary, theoretical solution, were decreasing in the, to begin with, steep progression of ½, ⅓, ¼ . . . it will (even with the later modifications) be highly improbable that the settlement will be made near any of the striking points. If nothing else is known about the modifying elements, there is a reasonable presumption that the middle of the range of practicable bargains will be the surest meeting place of the parties.

If there is a range of practicable bargains at all, that is, if the striking point of the workers falls at a lower rate than that of the employers, the two series of probabilities are bound to meet. Both of them begin at 100 percent, decrease as they approach each other, and will at an "unreasonably" far-reaching claim fall to 0.

Intersection in the middle does not mean that the unequal eagerness of the parties to fight will not influence the result: it is fully effective in the determination of the striking points, which again determine the middle. It is only increasing or decreasing strength within the range of agreement, however (an arched or sunken bending of A—A divided by B—B in Figure 28) that causes the point of intersection to fall after, or before, the middle.

Consequently, at mediations, which are not intended to shift the balance of power, it would seem a correct method to find out which rates are equally unfavorable to either of the parties as a conflict, for instance 63s. for the employers and 45s. for the workers, and then split the difference. If, however, the only certain information to be obtained is that the employers may be supposed to agree to 48s. and the workers to 57s. for instance, the uncertainty is considerably greater, because it is difficult to know whether there is an equal distance from those two points to the point of intersection, that is, if there is any possibility at all of a settlement. In so far as it is not a question of technical details in a proposal of settlement, it may perhaps be taken as the best sign that the parties are "equally dissatisfied"—that is, that neither of them can threaten the other effectively because they are willing to risk the same probability of conflict. Without knowing the outer points, a direct attempt may also be made to ascertain whether the probabilities seem to be equal by calculating for each party the proportion between the gain and—if a settlement is not reached—the loss, by a small change of the rate near the possible point of settlement. If one takes a point between the greatest concessions it is possible to force the parties to make (for instance employers 48s. and workers 60s.; see above), it would also be useful by means of the same method to find out if the parties were at the same distance from the point of settlement. We do not venture to say how far these methods may be applied to real life but, in any case, they are the consequence of the theory laid down in the present chapter.

7. APPLICATION OF THE IDEA OF PROBABILITY

We have here examined the cases where the parties were fully aware of the objective basis of each other's deliberations. The factor determining the course of the negotiations is the readiness of the respective parties to fight, calculated in terms of the probability of conflict to which they will expose themselves at each of the wage intervals under discussion during the negotiations. Just as in the market of a certain commodity, we shall, where the parties have a correct conception of each other's readiness to fight, have a demand curve and a supply curve in which to each price there corresponds another quantity (probability), which at the point of intersection will be equally great for both parties. The estimated gains and costs of the parties in terms of money or utility, are, on the other hand, only middle terms in the train of thought leading up to what is the decisive factor in relation to the opposite side: the magnitude of the probability of conflict to which they will expose themselves at a particular wage.

Of course, speaking of probabilities is a theoretical construction, when elsewhere it is assumed that everything is definite and clear to the two parties concerned. However, if both parties knew all objective circumstances and the train of each other's thought up to the moment when the decision was to be made, the result of their knowledge would even find expression in the amount of risk of conflict they were willing to run.

A GENERAL THEORY OF BARGAINING

Jan Pen

I. *The Present State of the Theory*

Until recently, economic science did not include a theory of bargaining. This unsatisfactory state of affairs is brought home to us by the fact that, beginning with Edgeworth, the price, under conditions of bilateral monopoly, is designated as "indeterminate" by authoritative economists (Böhm-Bawerk, Bowley, A. M. Henderson, Marshall, Nichol, Pigou, Stackelberg, Stigler, Tintner). This indeterminateness is not a characteristic of the price in itself (as is conceded by some of the aforesaid economists), but is a consequence of the inadequate theories of bilateral monopoly that miss their mark, *i.e.*, the determination of the final price resulting from the bargaining. If we accept the theory that this price is indeterminate, we submit to agnosticism. But the agnostic attitude is sometimes defended, by pointing out that the problem is not economic, but one that belongs in the realm of psychology. However, this argument cannot be accepted, because one of the tasks of economics is to elucidate the relation between the price and the psychological factors (the latter being known as *data*). Neither is it allowable to neglect the problem with the argument that the element of power plays a decisive rôle at the bargaining table; as will be shown below: power (as far as it is of an economic nature), can be analyzed by economic theory. The present state of the theory is all the more unsatisfactory because wage determination under trade unions, being a case of bilateral monopoly, is also left in the dark. Thus, this agnosticism would mean bankruptcy of the theory of wages.

In the meantime some rather isolated attempts have been made to tackle the problem. Dismissing such solutions as that by Cournot,[1] who supposes that one of the bargainers dictates the price and the other reacts by quantity manipulations, we must start out from an active attitude of both bargainers with respect to the price. *A fortiori* Schumpeter's peculiar theory, indicating the intersection of supply and demand as the final point of equilibrium, is not taken into consideration. This the-

* The author is an economist with the Dutch Ministry of Economic Affairs, The Hague, Holland.

[1] A. Cournot, *Recherches sur les Principes Mathématiques de la Théorie des Richesses* (1838), ed. 1938, p. 72.

ory implies a passive attitude with respect to price on both sides of the market, which is an altogether improbable supposition.[2]

Of minor importance are those theories that attempt to make the situation determinate by introducing special premises with respect to the behavior of the bargainers.[3] Fellner's[4] starting point (maximum collective gain) is interesting but too narrow to contribute to a *general* theory of bargaining. Even the Neumann-Morgenstern approach starts out from a set of too-specific premises, *e.g.*, rational conduct, neutral risk valuation, perfect insights[5]; the last supposition is very dangerous in this connection, as will be shown below. In the following sections we will try to construct a theory which is not based upon simplifying or inhibiting premises with respect to the conduct and the knowledge of the parties; in other words, a general theory.

At the beginning of the nineteen 'thirties, two attempts were made to determine the bargaining equilibrium between employers and trade union, *viz.*, by Zeuthen[6] and by Hicks.[7] The reasoning by Zeuthen will be outlined in Section IV. Hicks' theory runs as follows:[8] the central factor in the bargaining is the mutual threatening with a strike (or a lock-out). Both parties will have in mind some extreme wage rate, which they will accept rather than strike. This wage rate is a function of the expected length of the strike; the longer the strike the bargainer expects, the more unfavorable (to himself) will be his extreme wage rate. For the employer the said function—the concession function—is monotonously rising; for the worker the function—called resistance function—is monotonously falling. According to Hicks, the intersection of both curves indicates the bargaining equilibrium, provided that rational conduct and a certain amount of knowledge on the part of the bargainers are assumed.

However, the present author fails to see why the intersection determines anything. Hicks' reasoning is all about the limits of the contract zone, and explains nothing of what happens between these limits. At the intersection of the curves the contract zone is a single point, so there is

---

[2] J. Schumpeter, "Zur Einführung der folgenden Arbeit Knut Wicksells," *Archiv für Sozialwissenschaften* (1927), p. 238.

[3] For instance, Bilimovič ("Der Preis bei beiderseitigem Monopol," *Weltwirtschaftliches Archiv* [1943], p. 352) follows Jannacone in considering the case that both bargainers choose as their goal "equal negative deviations from the maximal collective gain." This hardly seems practicable.

[4] *Competition among the Few* (New York, 1949).

[5] Compare J. F. Nash, "The Bargaining Problem," *Econometrica* (1950), p. 155. This author also presupposes equal bargaining skill, whereby interesting aspects of the problem are left out of the picture.

[6] F. Zeuthen, *Problems of Monopoly and Economic Warfare* (1930), "Du Monopole Bilatéral," *Revue d'Economique Politique* (1933), and *Il Monopolio del Lavoro* (1936). Zeuthen's ideas have been further developed by H. Denis, *Le Monopole Bilatéral* (1943).

[7] J. R. Hicks, *The Theory of Wages* (1932).

[8] *Ibid.*, p. 141 ff.

no problem at all; but this situation will be realized only by the merest chance. There are no forces compelling the bargainers to the Hicksian point. In all situations where the limits of the contract zone do not coincide, this theory does not help us much further.

A more fruitful attempt is made by Shackle,[9] who has investigated the choices of the bargaining subject on the basis of some new ideas on the notion of probability. The different bargaining strategies offer different prospects of gains and losses. These prospects are in relation to certain probabilities as seen by the bargainer; these probabilities are called "potential surprise." The possible outcomes of a bargaining plan and the related values of the potential surprise are compared by means of indifference maps; so a rational choice can be made between the strategies.

In my opinion, the theory of Shackle is to be seen as a valuable theory of the bargaining *plans*. It offers, however, no answer to the important question as to which final price will result from the clash of the conflicting plans. Therefore it cannot be maintained that Shackle determines the outcome of the bargaining, and in this respect his theory remains unsatisfactory.

On the problems of bargaining and of economic power (bargaining power), some remarks are made by Dunlop, Slichter and Shister. These comments will be referred to below. They do not aim at a complete theory of bargaining, and, moreover, they do not elucidate the bargaining equilibrium.

The bargaining situation is, of course, dealt with by a great number of "labor economists." Their approach is in most cases of a preponderantly institutionalist character, and the central problem is hardly ever reached, let alone solved.[10] Even Ross,[11] who directs his attention to the "pressures" to which the trade union leader is exposed, neglects the problem of the bargain equilibrium, and the reader of this in other respects very illuminating book, cannot escape the impression that this equilibrium remains indeterminate.

As a final example of the deceptive character of the theory, Haley's contribution to the American Economic Association *Survey of Contemporary Economics*[12] may be cited. Haley answers the question as to what a bargainer will do if he has the power to dictate the conditions of the bargain to his adversary. In all cases outside this very exceptional one, contemporary theory leaves us in darkness.

[9] G. L. S. Shackle, *Expectation in Economics* (1949), p. 101 ff.

[10] For example, H. A. Millis and R. E. Montgomery, *Organized Labor* (1945); E. E. Cummings and F. D. Devijver, *The Labor Problem in the United States* (1947); H. A. Millis *et al.*, *How Collective Bargaining Works* (1945).

[11] A. M. Ross, *Trade Union Wage Policy* (1948).

[12] "Value and Distribution," *A Survey of Contemporary Economics* (Philadelphia, 1948), p. 34.

II. *The Problem and Its Data*

In the foregoing section the problem has been indicated: What are the factors that determine the result[13] of the bargaining? The answer to this question should not be a bare summing up of these factors, but the interplay between the factors and the way they influence the final result should also be made clear. The factors should be systematized in a scheme of reference that can serve as a tool in analyzing concrete bargaining processes.

Because all social phenomena are to a certain degree interdependent, all phenomena are, intrinsically, determining factors in the outcome of the bargaining process. Somewhere in the causal chain, we have to place a limit to our investigation. The first factor at the other side of this limit is called a datum.

The choice of this limit is arbitrary. We will draw the circle very closely, and start out from given preferences of the bargaining parties with respect to different possible outcomes of the bargaining process. Each bargainer will derive a certain satisfaction, which we call *ophelimity*, from the attainment of a certain price. The seller's ophelimity is denoted by S, the buyer's ophelimity by B. If we call the price p, we can designate the ophelimities as $S(p)$ and $B(p)$. These *ophelimity functions* are the primary data for our problem.

Although these functions are considered as data, this does not say that we will abstain from looking to see what is behind them. We will not attempt to construct a *theory* about the factors determining the ophelimities, but some remarks about these factors are necessary to avoid misunderstanding.

The determining factors of the ophelimity functions may be very complicated. The simplest case is that of two coldly calculating businessmen, say a monopolistic seller and a monopolistic buyer of a half-finished product. The ophelimities are in this case identical with (or parallel to) the profits. Instead of an ophelimity function we can speak of a profit function. These functions are not, as one might at first expect, monotonously rising (for the seller), or falling (for the buyer); at a higher price the buyer will decrease the quantity he is buying and this will depress the seller's profit.[14] So the seller's profit function will be represented by a curve that shows, somewhere, a maximum. The price at this maximum we call the seller's optimum price; it is denoted by p_s. In the same way the buyer's profit function shows a maximum at the price p_b. Now there is a bargaining problem if

$$p_s > p_b.$$

---

[13] We will speak mainly of price or wage bargains, so "the result" means "the final price." See, however, Section VII.

[14] We do not consider the case of simultaneous price- and quantity bargaining.

Apart from the sober profit figures there may, even in the case of bargaining businessmen, be psychological factors behind the functions. The attaining of a certain result may have a certain value in itself, just as the hunter who shoots a rabbit will derive a certain satisfaction from it, quite apart from the expected pleasure of his dinner. This we call the "ludic"[15] element behind the ophelimity. Sometimes it becomes apparent in a negative sense, especially when the bargainer is forced away from a price he has heavily insisted upon, and he fears to "lose face." In this case the ophelimity function may show a sharp peak at the price that was claimed before.

New complications arise when the bargaining businessman does not only represent his own firm but has to defend the interests of a combination of firms. If the profits of members of the group are affected by the outcome of the bargain in different degrees, the representative has to weigh the different interests. This weighing process may be very important in determining the shape of the ophelimity function. Furthermore, the bargainer may have been given certain instructions that make it very desirable for him to come home with a certain result. It is, of course, not our intention to treat here all the difficult problems connected with such situations.

A few comments ought to be made on the ophelimity function of the trade union or, rather, of the trade union's representative at the bargaining table. Just as with the businessman the relation between price and profit may be an important, but not the only, determining factor of the ophelimity, the relation between the wage rate and the wage bill may influence the trade union leaders' shape of the ophelimity function, without playing the only rôle. The elasticity of the demand for labor is only one of the determining factors of the ophelimity function. (It is to be remembered that the relevant factor in this connection is not the elasticity in fact, but the idea about the elasticity in the mind of the bargainer; this quantity lies somewhere between high negative values and considerable positive values, and may be governed by rather strange economic theories as well as by advanced econometric methods.) Differing with earlier views, Ross has pointed out that factors other than the said elasticity are much more important in shaping the ideas of the trade union's leader. If, for instance, the members of the union have for some reason or other a strong preference for a certain wage rate, and the leader believes he will lose the confidence of the members if he does not succeed in realizing the claimed wage rate, it is very improbable that the elasticity will influence his preference at all. In this case the ophelimity function will show a very high peak at the critical wage rate. Similarly, other preferences of the trade union's leader that were, from the viewpoint of the earlier theory, strange deviations can, in Ross's view, easily be accounted for. It is not necessary that they be dealt with here.

[15] From Latin *ludere:* to play a game.

The preceding remarks show that the ophelimity functions embrace all factors that determine the bargainer's preference for a certain outcome of the bargaining. No separation is made between "rational" and "irrational" factors.[16]

Thus stated, and starting from given conflicting preferences, the bargaining problem is seen as a power problem, because the ophelimity functions express the *will* of the subject. Power is defined as the capacity of one subject to carry through its will against the will of another subject. (According to these definitions the power of the trade union is not reduced by a high elasticity of the demand for labor. This factor may reduce the will to raise the wage rate; it is a volitional factor.) Now our problem can be formulated anew: what determines bargaining power?[17]

III. *The Fundamental Elements of Economic Power*

The concept of power as defined above is too wide for economic analysis; not all power is economic power. The general concept of power can be narrowed by considering the consequences, or by considering the roots, of the exercise of power. The former does not seem very practicable; the acceptance of this criterion would lead to the use of the term economic power in the case of employment of brute force for the purpose of extorting money, for instance. Such a concept of power would include numberless heterogenous elements, and might rightly be described as amorphous. Thus for analytical purposes the latter criterion is preferable. Economic power has economic causes, but may have non-economic, *e.g.*, political, aims. The acceptance of this fact will do much to clear away the confusion in regard to the determinateness of the price under bilateral monopoly. The problem is sometimes seen as non-economic in character,[18] but this is true only if the power is of a non-economic nature. If the state fixes a wage rate, the power behind the decision is of a political nature and cannot be analyzed by economic science. If the wage rate arises out of bargaining between businessmen and trade unions, the power may be of a purely economic character, and economic theory has a hold on it.

[16] This differs with the viewpoint of Zeuthen and Hicks, who presume that a conflict between the limits of the contract zone is possible (see below). This implies that the subject can choose in divergence from his own "preference," which is only possible if some kind of separation is made in the preference factors, for instance between "real" and "false" preferences, between "rational" and "irrational" preferences or between "fundamental" preferences and "whims."

[17] The notion of bargaining power is denied by Charles Lindblom, "Bargaining Power in Price and Wage Determination," *Quart. Jour. Econ.* (1948), p. 408, because, among other reasons, it is impossible to conceive of it apart from "the strength and the desire to use it." As will be shown below, the desire to use power is indeed a very relevant factor, but we deny that the conception of power thereby becomes superfluous. Our problem, however, is to find a means of escape from the difficulties indicated by Lindblom.

[18] *Cf.* G. Tintner, "A Note of the Problem of Bilateral Monopoly," *Jour. Pol. Econ.* (1939), p. 270.

Now we come to the question: when are the foundations of power economic in character? The answer is simple. Economics is the science of scarcity; scarcity gives rise to the dependence of the subject on certain quantities of goods. If these goods are in the hands of a seller who cannot be perfectly substituted by another seller, the buyer becomes dependent on the seller. The seller can exercise economic power by threatening to withhold the goods, that is to say, he is able to make the subject do things he would not have done otherwise. So economic power is controlled by two conditions: first, the dependence of the buyer who is to be subordinated to the seller; and second, a possibility for the supplier to withhold his offer or, more precisely, the buyer's belief, right or wrong, that this possibility exists.

The first condition implies imperfect possibility of substitution of sellers. Here lies the link between the theory of power and the theory of the market. It is possible (but it will not be attempted here) to integrate the following theory of bargaining with theories like Triffin's that focus attention on the elasticities of substitution.

The second condition—the possibility to withhold—is satisfied only if the sacrifice connected with the withholding of the supplies is not prohibitive for the supplier. The sacrifice consists in being deprived of the sum that the buyer is to pay. We see here that the powerful party must be, to a certain extent, independent of the party that is to be subordinate. This is the symmetrical, bilateral element in the situation. The fundamental element of economic power is the mutual dependence of the bargainers.

This concept of mutual dependence must now be specified as to quantity. This can be done by using the ophelimities. The buyer's loss in case of the withholding of the goods by the seller, equals $B(p)$, at least when the situation wherein no contract is made with the seller under consideration, yields for him an ophelimity$=0$. Usually this situation, which we will indicate by the term conflict,[19] yields a positive or a negative ophelimity. We call it the conflict ophelimity; it is denoted by B_c for the buyer and S_c for the seller. This ophelimity is not influenced by the price that is bargained for, and is not put down as its function.

The conflict ophelimity is, of course, a very strategic factor in our problem. The elements behind it are similar to those behind the ophelimity function. First, there is the amount of profit that may, in case of conflict, still be made; this quantity may be negative. Secondly, there are the ludic elements: the satisfaction which a bargainer who bears a grudge against his adversary, will derive from the conflict. Thirdly, on the labor market, the ophelimity may be influenced by political factors (like public opinion) and by the attitude amongst the rank and

---

[19] The conflict may be temporary or not; it may or may not be accompanied by some substitution of partners.

file of the trade union. All these factors have their counterpart in the factors behind the ophelimity function (the ophelimity of the contract). There is one factor, however, that has no such counterpart. It is the bargainer's estimate of the outcome of the conflict, especially when the conflict is of a temporary nature. A conflict that is considered beforehand as lost, will impart negative ophelimity. If the bargainer has confidence in the outcome of the conflict, it will yield him a high ophelimity at its very beginning. Generally, the ophelimity will be influenced decisively by the bargainer's expectation of the future. In the case of a temporary conflict the latter implies the bargaining constellation *vis à vis* the same adversary; in the case of a final conflict the possibility and profitability of finding a new partner is taken into account.

As it is not our intention to outline a theory of the conflict ophelimity, this quantity will be treated as given. We can now indicate the dependence of the buyer upon the seller as $B(p) - B_c$. This may be called *net contract ophelimity*. It is of course a function of the price p.

The bargainer can be subordinated only if he is dependent, that is if his net contract ophelimity is positive. The price at which

$$B(p) - B_c = 0$$

is the extreme price that can be imposed on the buyer. We call it the (upper) limit of the contract zone. In the same way, the seller's zero net contract ophelimity gives us the lower limit of the contract zone.[20] Between these limits lies a range of prices, at which the bargainers are "attached" to each other. (This does not mean, as is sometimes supposed, that within the contract zone, the quantity sold is not influenced by the price.) As long as the price lies within the contract zone, the situation is called bilateral monopoly; conversely, we define bilateral monopoly as any relation between a seller and a buyer that is characterized by a contract zone. The "conflict" may imply partner substitution; in that case bilateral monopoly is delimited by competition, which makes itself felt at the limits of the contract zone. Following this line of thought, the bargaining situation, bilateral monopoly, and economic power are not absolute concepts that have nothing in common with competition; on the contrary, they are supplementary to the notion of competition. They represent the element of "play" in a régime of competition.

The relation of the bargainers' net contract ophelimities is the fundamental factor in the notion of power. Both quantities are a function of the price. This is an indication that the functions determine among

[20] These limits differ from those indicated by Edgeworth (*Cf. Mathematical Psychics,* 1881.) The latter are relevant only if the powerful subject can impose an "all-or-none" clause on his adversary. *Cf.* W. Fellner, "Prices and Wages under Bilateral Monopoly," *Quart. Jour. Econ.* (1947), p. 524.

themselves the outcome of the bargaining. The higher the price which at a given moment is bargained for, the greater is the seller's net contract ophelimity, and the smaller is his power. The reverse holds for the buyer. Because economic power determines the outcome and is itself a function of the price, there exists a scissor-like movement essential to our problem.

However, this statement in itself does not solve the problem. The net contract ophelimities are fundamental, but they are not the only factors behind the notion of economic power. Other factors, *viz.*, those that determine the effectiveness of the threatening, are also relevant. These factors must now be found and examined.

IV. *Zeuthen's Theory of Economic Warfare*

Our investigation will be based on the work of F. Zeuthen, which may be considered a milestone in the history of the bargaining problem. Zeuthen was the first who went in search of the "values and quantities" that determine the bargainer's conduct. We shall not try to give a complete picture of his theory; only the more important aspects will be dealt with. Following Zeuthen, we shall discuss the labor market.

Zeuthen reasons as follows:[21]

At each step in the bargaining process the bargainer must compare the possible advantages and disadvantages. The advantages consist in the attainment of a more favorable price. The disadvantages consist in the possibilities of a conflict. The decisive factors in a bargainer's choice are not only the magnitude of these advantages and disadtages, but also the bargainer's estimation of their possibility. The latter expectation, designated as the *risk*[22] of a conflict, is the central factor in Zeuthen's theory.

Let us suppose, as Zeuthen does, that the trade union measures its ophelimity by only one criterion, the wage bill; and that the elasticity of the demand for labor is zero.[23] If we call the wage rate that is at stake at a given moment p, the wage rate the union hopes to reach p_n, and the amount of employment tg α (so that α is the ascent of the linear ophelimity function),[24] the possible advantage of a certain step for the trade union is expressed by

$$p_n \text{ tg } \alpha - p \text{ tg } \alpha.$$

[21] Derived from the last chapter "Economic Warfare" of *Problems of Monopoly and Economic Warfare* (1930).

[22] In this paper the word risk is used in a non-Knightian sense; risk is not distinguished from uncertainty. As a matter of fact, the risk of a conflict is uncertain in the Knightian sense; it cannot be computed in a statistical or actuarial way.

[23] These premises are, in the present author's opinion, not necessary. They will be omitted in the next section.

[24] The concept of the ophelimity function is not found in Zeuthen.

If we call the union's conflict ophelimity S_c, the possible loss connected with this step is

$$p \text{ tg } \alpha - S_c.$$

Now call the risk of a conflict connected with the step under consideration r. Then the actuarial value[25] of the gain is

$$(1 - r)(p_n \text{ tg } \alpha - p \text{ tg } \alpha)$$

and the actuarial value of the possible loss

$$r(p \text{ tg } \alpha - S_c).$$

The value of the behavior of the bargainer is[26]

$$(1 - r)(p_n \text{ tg } \alpha - p \text{ tg } \alpha) > r(p \text{ tg } \alpha - S_c)$$

out of which the maximum value of r can be solved

$$r_{max} = \frac{p_n \text{ tg } \alpha - p \text{ tg } \alpha}{p_n \text{ tg } \alpha - S_c}.$$

If r is smaller than this quantity, the trade union will press for a higher wage rate. As soon as r equals r_{max}, the bargainer is ready to enter into a contract. But this last line of thought is not followed by Zeuthen; we will pick it up again in the next section. Instead Zeuthen concentrates his attention on the function

$$r_{max} = r_{max}(p)$$

which has, for the union, a decreasing shape. In a similar manner, r_{max} can be determined for the businessman; here we find an increasing function. Now Zeuthen's theory culminates in the conclusion that, provided the fulfillment of certain conditions with respect to the rationality of the behavior and the perfectness of the bargainer's knowledge of each other's position, the bargaining equilibrium will be indicated by the intersection of both risk functions. To sum up: the outcome of the bargaining is, according to Zeuthen, determined by the equality of the mutual risk of a conflict that the parties dare to accept, and the maximum risk of a conflict that the bargainer will accept equals the quotient of his possible gain and his possible loss.

It is evident that this conclusion is very elegant. However, it cannot be accepted. There is a fatal missing link in Zeuthen's reasoning. The conclusion that the bargainers will stop bargaining and enter into a contract at precisely the point where their maximum risks are equal, is

[25] The term "actuarial value" means simply the product of risk and value. It does not imply that the risk can be ascertained by actuarial calculation.

[26] This, of course, presupposes neutral (actuarial) risk valuation. See below, Section V.

perfectly unwarranted. Even the supposition that the parties behave rationally and know quite a lot about each other brings no logic into the theory. Why should a bargainer submit at the moment his adversary accepts the same maximum risk as he does?

We must conclude that the intersection of the Zeuthenian curves is as meaningless as the intersection of the Hicksian curves.[27] But in other respects Zeuthen's theory has much more merit than that of Hicks. By emphasizing the rôle of the risk factor, Zeuthen elucidates the very essence of the bargaining process. The effectiveness of the threat depends upon the adversary's estimate of the risk of such a withholding. In the following sections we shall attempt to outline a theory of bargaining, using some of Zeuthen's ideas.

V. *The Equilibrium of One Bargainer*

In this section we shall try to throw light upon the factors that determine the equilibrium position of one bargainer, let us say the seller; that is, we will investigate at what price he will abstain from further bargaining and be willing to contract. The interplay between the bargainer and the bargainer equilibrium will be treated in the next section.

The first divergence from Zeuthen's system concerns the motivation of the bargainer. In our ophelimities all aims and preferences are presupposed. As a first consequence of this difference we need no distinction between rational and irrational behavior. Secondly, our ophelimity function is not, as Zeuthen's, linear, but shows a maximum. Therefore, the price that the bargainer strives for, is not a rather arbitrary p_n, but is well defined as p_s. The basic relation now takes the form

$$(1 - r)[S(p_s) - S(p)] > r[S(p) - S_c].$$

The most important difference from Zeuthen's formula is that this relation describes the choice of the bargainer as independent of the "rationality" of the choice. There remains only one Zeuthenian premise, *viz.*, the "actuarial mentality," or neutral risk valuation, which will be removed below. But apart from this, the bargainer simply cannot escape the "law" as expressed by our relation.[28]

Just as Zeuthen does, we derive[29]

---

[27] *Cf. supra*, Section I.

[28] Not any more than a subject can escape the "law" that he prefers an orange to an apple, if we observe that he chooses the former. Zeuthen's theory does not run in terms of revealed preference; he wants to know which results of the bargaining are more "probable" than others. His theory has a somewhat normative quality, for Zeuthen wants to tell the bargainer what to do. Our theory accepts the bargainer's conduct and tries to determine his decision *post facto*.

[29] The procedure followed is admitted only if the ophelimity is seen as a cardinal notion. The bargaining problem cannot be solved if we start from the Hicksian notion of preference alone. As is pointed out by Armstrong, "Uncertainty and Utility Function," *Econ. Jour.* (1948), the same holds for all problems in which uncertainty plays a rôle. The old controversy

$$r_{\max} = \frac{S(p_s) - S(p)}{S(p_s) - S_c} .$$

The seller is caved in when

$$\frac{S(p_s) - S(p)}{S(p_s) - S_c} - r_s^{\cdot\cdot} = 0.$$

We will now try to get rid of the premise of the neutral risk valuation. We define actuarial mentality as the propensity of the subject to value the expectation of an uncertain event, which is worth A and has a probability x, with xA. A subject with a non-actuarial mentality will value the expectation with another value, say Z. Now call $Z/A = y$; then the function $y = \Phi(x)$ expresses the risk valuation, this being the satisfaction (or dissatisfaction) the subject derives from the risk-taking as a fact in itself. We call Φ the *risk valuation function;* it is clearly a datum for economic science.

Now we can drop our last premise. The equilibrium of the seller is written

$$\Phi_s \left[\frac{S(p_s) - S(p)}{S(p_s) - S_c} \right] - r_s = 0.$$

Both terms at the left of the equation are fractions between 0 and 1. The first is the maximum risk of a conflict the subject will accept; this we call *propensity to fight.* The second is the factual risk of a conflict the subject expects. We must now investigate how this last quantity is determined.

For that purpose we remind the reader that the limit of the contract zone with which the seller is confronted is indicated by

$$B(p) - B_c = 0.$$

If the seller knew this limit, he would assign to r_s the value 0 for the whole range of the contract zone; at the limit, r_s would suddenly rise to 1. As a matter of fact, however, the bargainer will not know precisely his adversary's position, and he must rely on guesswork. The state of his knowledge is expressed by the function

$$r_s = F_s[B(p) - B_c].$$

This *correspection function*[30] F_s expresses the relation between the

---

about the good sense of a quantitative notion of utility cannot be discussed here. It is re- markable that recently the cardinal notion of utility is recommended by using the factor of uncertainty; *cf.* Morgenstern and Neumann, *Theory of Games and Economic Behavior* Chap. I and W. Vickrey, "Measuring Marginal Utility by Reaction to Risk," *Econometrica* (1945), p. 391.

[30] The word "correspection" is from Schumpeter, *op. cit.*

factual net contract ophelimity of the buyer and the risk of a conflict, as estimated by the seller. If the bargainer has a perfect insight of his adversary's position, his F coincides with the x and the y-axis. Generally the insight is imperfect, and F is a negatively inclined curve. If the bargainer underrates his partner's net ophelimity, that is, if he over-rates the risk of a conflict, his correspection function lies in the first quadrant. In the reverse case, it lies in the second quadrant. The shifts in the correspection function are often the main tactical factor in bargaining.

We can now sum up our reasoning in the following relation indicating the price at which the seller will stop bargaining and be amenable to contract.

$$\Phi_s \left[\frac{S(p_s) - S(p)}{S(p_s) - S_c} \right] - F_s[B(p) - B_c] = 0.$$

The relation contains six elements that are all given, *viz.*, the two ophelimity functions, the two conflict ophelimities, the seller's risk valuation function and the seller's correspection function. The former four elements are data for our problem; the latter two are data for economic science.

VI. *The Bargaining Equilibrium*

The equilibrium position of one bargainer is, of course, not a sufficient condition for the bargaining equilibrium. If the seller is, at a given price, ready to enter into a contract, but the buyer is not, the negotiations must continue. Therefore, the final price must satisfy two equations at the same time

$$\Phi_s \left[\frac{S(p_s) - S(p)}{S(p_s) - S_c} \right] - F_s[B(p) - B_c] = 0$$

$$\Phi_b \left[\frac{B(p_b) - B(p)}{B(p_b) - B_c} \right] - F_b[S(p) - S_c] = 0.$$

During the bargaining the two equations are conflicting. It is the task of the bargaining process to eliminate this conflicting character. This being established, the way to the analysis of the bargaining process is open; each maneuvre of the parties is reflected by the elements of the equations. The analysis of the bargaining process is the analysis of the shifts in these elements.[31]

Let us now try to outline some of these shifts. They will take place in the interplay between the parties; a number of steps in the bargaining

---

[31] Zeuthen's theory rests upon one equation—equality of the mutual propensity to fight— and therefore lacks the possibility to discern the *necessity* of the equilibrating shifts.

process have no other intention than to shift the adversary's position.

The first element of our equations, the risk valuation function, is a too deeply rooted characteristic of the subject's psychical structure to be affected by the bargaining. It may change but it is not adaptable to strategical manipulation.

The second element is the ophelimity function. Even when the ophelimity is completely determined by money profit, it may be influenced by the bargaining process. The bargainer may succeed in attempting to convince his partner that the latter entertains a wrong conception of the relation between the price and profit. But, of course, this line of attack is usually rather futile. On the labor market it often seems more fruitful than between businessmen; the union may point out that a higher wage will have a favorable influence on the worker's morale and on profits; and the employer may hold that profits are already so small that they do not admit of higher wages, so that employment will suffer much more from an increase in the wage rate than the union believes. In answer to this, the union may call attention to the beneficial effects of the raising of the worker's purchasing power and profits. Similar discussions between bargainers are to be considered as a mutual pushing and pulling of each other's ophelimity functions.

Furthermore, the bargainer can influence his partner's ophelimity function by preventing ludic shifts of it. He must, for instance, create a friendly atmosphere which facilitates his partner's retreat from too ambitious claims.

The shifts in the partner's ophelimity function which the bargainer attempts to bring about, can be distinguished as horizontal and vertical shifts. With horizontal shifts, the tops of the functions come closer to each other; the seller tries to pull the buyer's function to the right, the buyer tries to pull the seller's function to the left. The vertical downward shifts leave the optimum price unaffected but lessen the intensity with which the bargainer strives for a certain outcome. The buyer tries to diminish p_s as well as $S(p_s)$ at a given p_s. Both shifts give a more favorable bargaining equilibrium to the buyer.

The interest of the parties in the shifts of each other's ophelimity functions is of a twofold nature. This is easily deduced from the equations. The seller's ophelimity function does not only, among other functions, determine the seller's propensity to fight, but also the buyer's expectation of the risk of a conflict. If the seller's ophelimity function shifts to the left and the buyer does not perceive it, he will still profit by it because the seller's propensity to fight will *ceteris paribus* decrease; but if the buyer does perceive the shift, he will profit more, because of the then apparent decrease in r_b.

The shifts that are dealt with above are peaceful in character. They consist in influencing the adversary's will, and depend in a certain sense on his cooperation. This is not the case with the influence exerted by the third element of the equation, the conflict ophelimity. The opponent's conflict ophelimity must be made as small or as negative as possible, and this is done by outright threatening. The conflict must be depicted as long and bitter, which may give the bargaining a warlike character. This strategy is, like the manipulation of the ophelimity function, a two-edged sword: it decreases the other party's propensity to fight as well as the first party's idea of the risk of a conflict.

We come now to the fourth and last element of the equations, the correspection function. It is clearly capable of wide shifts, which are, in many cases, the main equilibrating factor in the bargaining process. The parties will try to shift the opponent's function upwards and to the right, and in the meantime try to fit the own correspection function as closely as possible to the X- and the Y-axis. When F coincides with the X- and the Y-axis, the bargainer knows his adversary's extreme price and he can, without risking a conflict, stick to a price that is somewhat less unfavorable to the opponent than the extreme price. It is to be remembered that as a consequence of our definition of the ophelimities, the possibility of a conflict within the contract zone is excluded. If a bargainer who is seen through, changes his ideas under heavy pressure of his adversary, the latter's correspection remains perfect only if he is fully aware of the change of the former's ophelimities. Therefore a theoretical setup that is based on the hypothesis of full insight is a very dangerous one.

It is dangerous in still another respect. A subject that possesses full insight into his adversary's position cannot effectively be threatened within the contract zone. If we suppose perfect insight at both sides of the bargaining table, all threatening must necessarily be in vain, the execution of economic power is impossible, and the outcome is indeterminate.[32]

The influencing of the other party's correspection function can be attempted by two methods. The first is the direct one: the belittling of the *own* contract ophelimity by pointing out, on the one hand, that a certain price is very unsatisfactory, and, on the other hand, that a conflict is regarded with indifference or even with confidence. The second method is the indirect one. It consists in starting out with high claims that are only compatible with a high propensity to fight. Now, generally, a high propensity to fight means a low net contract ophelimity.[33] The risk of a conflict is inflated by one of the parties with no other

[32] We must therefore conclude that all theories that assume perfect knowledge of the adversary's position (Nash, Zeuthen, and particularly Denis, *op. cit.*, p. 60) are on a wrong track. By eliminating uncertainty, the essence of the problem is lost. This is a case in which the economist's cherished hypothesis of a perfect knowledge does not make things determinate but indeterminate.

[33] The relation between the two is explained below, Section VII.

intention than the shifting of the opponent's correspection function. This is a dangerous strategy, for if the bluffing partner is seen through he must reiterate. If he fears loss of face or if other reasons make him stick to his claims, this implies a shift in the ophelimity function which will show a sudden peak at the claimed price. If this peak lies outside the contract zone, a conflict will arise.

The foregoing remarks do not pretend to give a complete picture of bargaining tactics. They merely indicate some of the main possibilities. However, all other possible tactics can be dealt with in an analogous manner, using the equations as a starting point of the analysis.

Furthermore, our reasoning makes it possible to outline the somewhat hazy notion of "bargaining skill" that is used by some authors,[34] as the personal capacity of the bargainer to shift the elements of the bargaining situation, as set forth above, in his favor. This concept may be seen as a last rudiment of the notion of "rationality" in the bargainer's conduct. All other concepts of "rationality" seem to me superfluous and harmful when used in connection with the bargaining process.

VII. *The Significance of the Foregoing Theory*

A first superficial glance at the equations that constitute the essence of our theory might give rise to the too optimistic view that the theory gives the result of the bargaining in an exact, predictable way. Of course this is not so. The formulas are exact indeed, but prediction is not. There are two reasons for this. In the first place, ophelimities are not (yet) adaptable to direct measurement, and neither the risk valuation nor the correspection function can be ascertained exactly. Secondly, if some measuring technique could be made to apply to the elements of the bargaining situation (which, in the author's opinion, is by no means impossible), the shifting character of the elements would still be a serious obstacle to prediction.

If this be true, can we still legitimately stick to our thesis that our equations determine the outcome of the bargaining? We can. For the theory indicates the factors that determine the outcome. Although the equations do not primarily aim at quantitative goals, they make the result of the bargaining determinate, in the sense that they give a condensed theory of the determination of the result. They guarantee that our theory is a closed system; no factor is overlooked.[35] The determining factors are not only enumerated, but their interplay is also exposed.

The significance of the theory lies mainly in the elucidation of the

---

[34] J. T. Dunlop, *Wage Determination under Trade Unions* (1944), p. 119, calls it "pure bargaining power."

[35] This is true only as far as the data of our problem are considered. Behind the data, and in particular behind the ophelimities, lies a host of factors that are only hinted at in the foregoing. This point comes up for discussion below, when Dunlop's analysis is dealt with.

notion of bargaining power. Given the ophelimity functions (expressing the opposed wills of the bargainers), economic bargaining power depends on the conflict ophelimities, the risk valuation functions, and on the capacity of the parties to shift these determinants. The net contract ophelimities, being the most fundamental elements of economic power, turn out to play a twofold rôle. On the one hand, the opponent's dependence on the bargain (defined as his net contract ophelimity) determines, together with the correspection function, the bargainer's estimate of the risk of a conflict. On the other hand, the bargainer's own dependence on the bargain is one of the factors determining his propensity to fight, which equals in equilibrium the estimated risk of a conflict. The relation between the propensity to fight and the net contract ophelimity is as follows: the difference between the denominator and the numerator of the quotient that determines, together with the risk valuation function, the propensity to fight, equals the net contract ophelimity.[36]

The usefulness of our scheme of reference can be shown by applying it to a number of special cases. This will not be done here. However, the usefulness can be illustrated to some extent by comparing the scheme of reference with existing views. As an object for comparison we choose Dunlop's view on the matter, because it includes one of the very rare attempts to elucidate the concept of bargaining power (with respect to the labor market).

Dunlop classifies the factors determining bargaining power as follows:[37]

1. Tastes of workers and employers, with respect to wages and man-hours bought and sold—the indifference maps. Institutional factors, such as property rights and wage-hour legislation, which influence conditions of demand and supply, should also be included.
2. Market conditions, specially the type of competition in the labor market, the product market, the market for complementary factors of production, and the market for competitive factors of production. In the last two markets, elasticities of substitution are important factors.
3. Pure bargaining power: ability to get favorable bargains, apart from market conditions.

[36] If this latter quantity equals zero, the quotient equals unity. In that case the propensity to fight also equals unity, whatever the shape of the risk valuation may be, and the bargainer has reached the limit of the contract zone. The irrelevance of the shape of Φ in this limiting case is the outcome of the fact that there is no uncertainty when the bargainer himself decides to break off the bargaining; the risk of a conflict is 100 per cent. There is another limiting case in which Φ is irrelevant, viz., when the bargainer reaches his optimum price. The aforementioned quotient is then zero, and the propensity to fight is also zero. The bargainer can reach this extreme position only if his estimate of the risk of a conflict is zero too. These limiting cases are interesting in a theory of oligopolistic price determination, that can be generalized from our theory of bargaining. Limited space forbids dealing with this point here.

[37] Dunlop, op. cit., p. 77, ff.

Some objections to this enumeration may be raised. First, it seems rather incomplete. It especially lacks the conflict ophelimity, or the factors behind it, such as the degree of unionization. Perhaps the missing factors are to a certain extent included in the "market conditions." This brings us, however, to a second objection: the enumeration is lacking in clarity. It is not clear whether factors are omitted because they are, in Dunlop's opinion, of no importance, or because they are already included in some of the enumerated factors. In other words: the enumeration lacks a definite structure.[38] Now both objections have a deeper root in what is the real criticism of Dunlop's classification, namely, that the enumeration of the factors is nothing but an enumeration. There is no analysis of the interplay *between* the factors, there is no theory.[39] Therefore, we cannot be sure that the enumeration is complete, and for the same reason, the classification is more or less hazy.[40]

A comparison between Dunlop's classification and our equations shows clearly the difference between the two forms of reasoning. The equations indicate the interplay and the structure of the determining factors. It is to be remembered, however, that they do so only in regard to the elements that are given for our problem, *viz.*, the ophelimities, the risk valuation functions, and the correspection functions. Behind these factors lie more determining factors; some of them are mentioned in the foregoing sections, but we have not endeavored to construct a *theory* about these deeper-seated factors. This is the reason for the choice of our data.

The question arises in how far our theory is general. It was pointed out above that, in principle, all possible lines of conduct of the bargainers can be analyzed within the framework of the equations. There is, however, one type of strategy which is formally covered by the analysis, but on which the theory does not shed much light. It is the simultaneous manipulation of two variables which are both at stake. For instance, the bargaining on the labor market may be about the wage rate and, let us say, a pension scheme. The union may open the negotiations with a high claim in respect to the pension scheme, only with the intention to lessen this claim in favor of the wage-outcome. Formally, tactics of this kind can be dealt with by considering the pension claim as one of

---

[38] For instance, it does not seem impossible that the elasticities of substitution are, in some way or other, affecting the shape of the indifference maps.

[39] This is not to say that Dunlop's book contains no theory about wage determination. Of course it does. But the theory runs in terms of supply and demand curves (or revenue and cost curves) and, therefore, it does not determine the equilibrium of bargaining. For Dunlop's treatment of the situation of bilateral monopoly, *cf. op. cit.*, p. 88.

[40] Another example of an incomplete enumeration is Shister's analysis, "The Theory of Union Wage Rigidity," *Quart. Jour. Econ.* (1943), p. 530. Shister divides the notion of bargaining power into three elements, *viz.*, the elasticity of the demand for labor, the skill of the bargainer, and the ability to strike successfully. This, too, is a partial enumeration that throws a spotlight on certain factors and leaves others in the dark.

the determinants of the shape of the ophelimity function. This procedure leaves the pension-outcome unanalyzed. Therefore it would be necessary to consider the ophelimity function of the pension-outcome (p not symbolizing the wage rate, but some criterion of the pension scheme), and to put side by side two equations for the bargain equilibrium with respect to the pension-outcome. Then we have two sets of equations. Formally, the wage-pension combination is determined by the four equations but it may be doubted if this method is still feasible. It does not furnish a comprehensive scheme of reference for all the steps in the bargaining process, and in particular, no light is shed upon the interrelationship of the two sets of equations. We must conclude that this kind of double-criterion bargaining is not dealt with in a satisfactory way in our theory.

Multiple-criterion bargaining excluded, the theory covers the whole field of the bargaining process. The theory is general in another respect. A number of constellations that are not commonly seen as bargaining situations, or as cases of bilateral monopoly, can still be treated as such, if we are willing to give a somewhat formalistic extension to the limiting cases of bargaining, *viz.*, to the one-sided power relation. The situation in which the seller fixes his price, that is, dictates his will to the buyer, can be seen as a limiting case of bilateral monopoly; the latter concept being defined as a situation in which a contract zone exists. This possible extension of the theory of bargaining cannot be attempted here; in the writer's opinion, it can contribute to our insight into oligopolistic problems.[41]

Finally, the equations can be applied to some non-economic, *e.g.*, political bargains. It is to be remembered that in this case the threatening, too, has a non-economic character. The greatest difficulty here seems to be the ascertaining of the precise criterion that is at stake; most political bargains are about multiple-criterion outcomes, that are very difficult to condense into a single criterion. As pointed out above, this is a serious obstacle to the applicability of our theory. As the application to non-economic bargains lies outside the scope of economic theory, the multiple-criterion character of these bargains calls for no discussion here.

[41] Even perfect competition can formally be treated as a limiting case of the bargaining situation. The ophelimity functions are represented by coinciding verticals. The conflict ophelimity equals, for both parties, the contract.ophelimity: there is no net contract ophelimity, and no mutual dependence of the bargainers. The propensity to fight is zero for the market price, and unity for all deviations from it. The correspection is perfect. The risk of a conflict is zero for the market price, and unity for all deviations from it. The exercise of economic power is impossible.

A ZEUTHEN-HICKS THEORY OF BARGAINING
Robert L. Bishop

Harsanyi [1], after translating Zeuthen's bargaining theory [5, Ch. 4] into modern utility terms, has shown that it implies the same outcome as Nash's theory [4], namely a settlement that maximizes the product of the utility increments of the two parties. In the same paper, Harsanyi also reviewed Hicks's comparable theory [2, pp. 140–45] and found it, understandably, distinctly inferior to Zeuthen's. The context that both Zeuthen and Hicks had in mind was labor-management bargaining, where agreements and conflicts have time dimensions. Specifically in such situations, it will be suggested, it is possible to combine the central conceptions of both Zeuthen and Hicks in a composite theory that is superior to either of the separate ones. To prepare the way for the composite theory's presentation, its components will be briefly summarized.

1. ZEUTHEN'S THEORY (HARSANYI'S VERSION)

NEITHER ZEUTHEN nor Harsanyi pay any attention to the time aspects of either the bargained agreement or the possible conflict (strike) that is implied in the absence of an agreement. Rather, especially as interpreted by Harsanyi in the manner of modern game theory, the parties are assumed to contemplate a static utility frontier in an effort to find some one point on it that will be mutually acceptable. Suppose, for example, that the relevant utility frontier is the one pictured in Figure 1, where u_1 and u_2 represent the von Neumann-Morgenstern utilities of the respec-

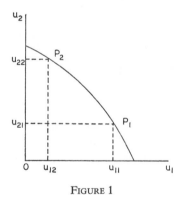

FIGURE 1

tive parties and the origin is the point at which they are fated to remain if they cannot conclude some mutually advantageous agreement. (Consistent with the fact that such utilities are determinate only up to order-preserving linear transformations, a property of the proposed solution is that it is independent of such transformations.) The bargainers are also visualized as confronting one another with some initially rather extreme demands, as at points P_1 and P_2, respectively. The utilities at those points are designated by two subscripts, such that u_{ij} is the utility of the ith person as proposed by the jth.

Zeuthen's theory is then concerned with the process by which the bargainers may be expected to make certain suitable concessions, until their respective demands have become compatible at some single point on the frontier. The concessions are visualized as being made in the light of certain comparative subjective probabilities of the conflict that would ensue if suitable concessions were not made.

Specifically, if the two parties are currently demanding outcomes at points P_1 and P_2, respectively, Zeuthen would ask: what is the maximum subjective probability of conflict (c_1) that the first bargainer can rationally stand, in holding out for his preferred point P_1, rather than give in to the other's demand for P_2; and similarly for the second bargainer's maximum such probability (c_2)? The answers are that:

$$c_1 = \frac{u_{11}-u_{12}}{u_{11}}, \quad c_2 = \frac{u_{22}-u_{21}}{u_{22}}.$$

This follows in the case of the first bargainer, for example, because he is assumed to weigh (1) the utility that he can achieve with certainty by giving in completely to the other's demand (u_{12}) and (2) the expected utility implied if he holds out for his own demand and thus runs the risk of an irreconcilable conflict (this expected utility being equal to 0 with respect to the chance that the conflict will materialize plus $(1-c_1)u_{11}$ with respect to the chance that the other will give in to him). He is then indifferent between these two alternative courses of action when

$$u_{12}=(1-c_1)u_{11} .$$

The first of the above equations is then justified because it is deducible from this one; and similarly for the second.

The critical step in the Zeuthen-Harsanyi prescription of "rational" bargaining behavior is now at hand. The first bargainer will make at least some concession, and the second will not, if $c_1 < c_2$ (that is, if the first cannot stand as great a probability of conflict as the second); or the second bargainer will be the one to make a concession if $c_1 > c_2$; or they will both make simultaneous concessions if $c_1 = c_2 > 0$. Typically, however, neither makes a complete concession to the other's current demand, but rather concedes only enough to make it the other bargainer's turn to make a concession too, whether unilaterally or simultaneously with a corresponding further concession by the first bargainer. In other words, the first bargainer makes a concession when $c_1 \leqslant c_2$, or when (with reference to the above two equations)

$$u_{11}u_{21} \leqslant u_{12}u_{22} .$$

Hence each concession by the first bargainer raises $u_{11}u_{21}$, the utility product that he proposes; and similarly, each concession by the second raises $u_{12}u_{22}$. Accordingly, these utility products are maximized and equated to one another when an agreement is finally reached, with $u_{11} = u_{12}$ and $u_{21} = u_{22}$ at a single point on the utility frontier, and with $c_1 = c_2 = 0$.

This is not the place for a full critique of the merits and defects of this theory, which would also require an evaluation of Nash's quite different but parallel rationalization of the same end result. It is well to indicate, however, that I do not share Harsanyi's insistence (which is even more emphatic than Zeuthen's) that bargaining behavior must be in accordance with this model if it is to escape the charge of being "irrational." Even when the bargaining situation is essentially static and nonrecurrent, and even when the conditions of requisite knowledge are fulfilled (unlikely as this may be in practice), there still seem to me to be ample grounds for resisting the Zeuthen-Harsanyi prescription.

For one thing, it should be noticed that the question of who concedes a little is answered with reference to the expected utilities involved in either making or not making a different and typically much larger concession, all of the way to the other bargainer's current demand. On the other hand, that large hypothetical concession is really not seriously considered at all, except as a means of determining some smaller actual concession. Furthermore, the subjective probabilities of conflict, which motivate the concessions, are mechanical ones that the bargainers must arrive at in a uniquely specified way, rather than truly subjective estimates that they might make in any way that they happened to see fit. Thus, even though the theory is ostensibly rooted in a process of successive concessions, as in many instances of realistic bargaining, it really implies a fore-ordained outcome that the bargainers might just as well establish without any play-acting. These aspects of the theory are merely the more obvious ones upon which skepticism may appropriately be focussed.

2. HICKS'S THEORY

In Hicks's view, the most eligible outcome of a union-management bargaining negotiation is at a point where the two parties would be willing to run the risk of a strike of the same duration, rather than make any further concessions. Specifically, each bargainer is assumed to have a subjective function showing, for any given wage rate, the maximum duration of strike that he is willing to risk rather than to concede more. Illustrative curves are shown in Figure 2, where the wage rate w is measured on the vertical axis and strike duration s is on the horizontal. What Hicks calls the employer's "concession curve" is E, and the union's "resistance curve" is U. Since the curves have appropriately contrasting slopes and intercepts on the wage-rate axis, they have a unique point of intersection. That point reflects, accordingly, the terms on which the threatened conflict might best be avoided.

In Hicks's exposition, however, the intersection point is not represented as the

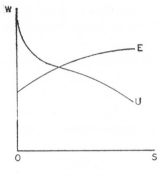

FIGURE 2

central tendency of the bargaining outcome, as it might be if there were some symmetrical degree of uncertainty on each bargainer's part as to the true position of the other bargainer's curve. Instead, Hicks's theory embodies a rather surprising asymmetry in that the intersection point corresponds to "the highest wage which skilful negotiation can extract from the employer," [2, p. 144]. In turn, this result rests on two underlying asymmetries. First, Hicks apparently assumes implicitly that the employer somehow knows the position of the union's curve, while the union does not have similar knowledge of the employer's. Second, Hicks seems to visualize that wage rate proposals are made exclusively by the union, while the employer never makes counteroffers, but merely rejects or accepts any proposed wage rate according as it does or does not exceed the level where the two curves intersect (knowledge of that intersection point being thus imputed to the employer). Accordingly, as Hicks concludes, the wage rate that the union may persuade the employer to accept can be at or below the intersection point, but never above it (though it would always be at that point if its position were also known to the union).

Even if these unexplained asymmetries could somehow be defended, the theory would still suffer from the critical defect that it does not undertake to explain how the curves in question are determined. All that Hicks says about the employer's concession curve [2, p. 142] is that it leaves the wage rate axis at "the wage which the employer would have paid if unconstrained by Trade Union pressure" and then rises to (or perhaps approaches asymptotically) "some wage beyond which no Trade Union can compel an employer to go." On the other hand, the union's resistance curve is depicted as leaving the wage rate axis well above the maximum wage that the employer might conceivably accept (again reflecting, presumably, the union officials' ignorance of that maximum), and nothing very definite is said as to its rate of decline. If the union's curve declines slowly enough, however, it will intersect the employer's curve at (or indefinitely close to) the maximum feasible wage. Furthermore, Hicks does not face up to the conceptual difficulties implied by the inescapable interdependence of the two curves, if only in the sense that either party's willingness to endure a strike of any specified duration would surely depend on its estimate of the other's similar willingness. In addition, either party's willingness to endure a strike surely depends also on (1) the alternative outcome that it could obtain without a strike and (2) its estimates of the likelihood of various possible outcomes following a strike of various possible durations.

Nevertheless, despite these very serious defects, Hicks's theory does have the merit of at least calling attention to the obviously relevant consideration of estimated strike duration as a part of the negotiators' deliberations. It is that element, lacking in Zeuthen's theory, that may be fruitfully incorporated in a composite Zeuthen-Hicks theory.[1]

3. THE COMPOSITE THEORY

Instead of relating the maximum tolerable duration of strike to a particular, single outcome (as Hicks does), let us specify (in close analogy to Zeuthen's formulation) that this duration depends on both the outcome that the one bargainer currently proposes and also the outcome that the other bargainer is currently willing to accept. Let us suppose that the parties are negotiating a contract that will run for t units of time provided that they come to an immediate agreement, but which will run for only $t-s$ units of time if a strike of s units' duration takes place. For convenience, it is assumed that the data underlying the parties' utility frontier are expected to remain unchanged through time. Hence the utility frontier in Figure 1 may again be assumed to apply, depicting the attainable utilities per unit of time. As before, naturally, both utilities remain at the origin for the duration of any strike that might take place.

Initially, for simplicity, let us suppose that both parties have zero rates of time discount. Then, if they are currently offering one another agreements at points P_1 and P_2, respectively, the first bargainer can gain either tu_{12} by accepting the other's offer forthwith or $(t-s_1)u_{11}$ by winning his own demand after a strike lasting s_1 units of time. Hence, equating these magnitudes, we find the maximum duration of strike that he might be willing to endure for a complete victory, and similarly the corresponding figure for the second bargainer:[2]

$$s_1 = \frac{t(u_{11}-u_{12})}{u_{11}}, \quad s_2 = \frac{t(u_{22}-u_{21})}{u_{22}}.$$

[1] Interestingly enough, Hicks once said of Zeuthen's theory and his own [3, p. 18]: "The two methods appear to be complementary." The remark stands without explanation, however; so it is not clear whether he had in mind the kind of complementarity to be suggested here.

[2] Naturally, if a strike were actually to take place, neither bargainer could rationally count on winning his own demand fully when the strike was over. With reference to the *maximum* duration of strike that each might rationally stand, however, the calculation is appropriately based on that maximally optimistic possibility.

On the other hand, the strike duration s_i is not visualized here as the maximum that may be *threatened* by the ith party. If a strike actually takes place, no definite limit can be placed on its

From this point on, the argument is strictly analogous to Zeuthen's. The first bargainer makes a concession when $s_1 \leqslant s_2$ (that is, when he is not willing to risk a longer strike than the other), or when $u_{11} u_{12} \leqslant u_{21} u_{22}$; and so on until an agreement is reached at the point where $s_1 = s_2 = 0$, $u_{11} = u_{12}$, $u_{21} = u_{22}$, and $u_{11} u_{21} = u_{12} u_{22}$ is a maximum.[3]

The same result, identical with Zeuthen's, may also be demonstrated when both parties discount future utilities at the same positive rate. When they have different rates of time discount, however, the bargainer with the lower rate fares better.

To see this, consider the tractable case where the contract is to be a perpetual one, and where the parties' utilities are discounted at the constant, instantaneously compounded rates of r_1 and r_2, respectively. The present value of immediate surrender is thus u_{12}/r_1 to the first bargainer; and the corresponding present value of winning his current demand after a strike of duration s_1 is $u_{11}/r_1 e^{r_1 s_1}$. Hence, setting these present values equal to one another, we find his maximum tolerable duration of strike (again on the most optimistic possible expectation of complete victory), and similarly for the second bargainer:

$$s_1 = \frac{\log u_{11} - \log u_{12}}{r_1}, \quad s_2 = \frac{\log u_{22} - \log u_{21}}{r_2}.$$

The first bargainer is again assumed to make a concession when $s_1 \leqslant s_2$, or when

$$u_{11} u_{21}^{r_1/r_2} \leqslant u_{12} u_{22}^{r_1/r_2}.$$

Hence his concessions raise the lefthand side of this expression, and the second bargainer's concessions similarly raise the righthand side, until $u_{11} = u_{12} = u_1$ and

---

duration; so each party is implicitly threatening an indefinitely long one, subject to a capitulation or substantial concession being made sooner or later by the other party. As is about to be indicated in the text, the strike duration s_i figures in the theory as merely an index governing "rational" concessions, just as Zeuthen's conflict probability c_i does. It should be appreciated that neither Zeuthen's theory nor this one involves a prediction of the frequency or duration of conflicts; each is really concerned only with the terms on which conflicts may be "rationally" avoided. (The comments in this paragraph are prompted by some informal pre-publication reactions, including some by Harsanyi along the lines of his criticisms of Hicks's theory [1, pp. 154–55].)

[3] This formulation, especially when future satisfactions are undiscounted, is perhaps reminiscent of a familiar type of disapproving comment sometimes made about strikes. Especially when employer and union are not very far apart in their demands, the union is often reproached for its intransigence (notably in conservative newspaper editorials) with the calculation that, even if the workers were to win their full demands after a comparatively short strike of x weeks' duration, it would require the lengthy subsequent interval of y weeks for the workers to make up for their income lost during the strike. On the other hand, if the same type of computation is also made with respect to the employer's profits, he too would be found to need some interval of y' weeks to make up for his x weeks of strike losses, even if he were to win his full demands. Then, if it is specified that concessions be made in accordance with the comparative magnitudes of y and y', the consequences turn out to be the same as in the text (at least in the corresponding stationary situation). The demonstration is similar to that in the text.

$u_{21}=u_{22}=u_2$, whereupon $u_1 u_2^{r_1/r_2}$ is a maximum. At this point the utility frontier is tangent to a curve of the form $u_1 u_2^{r_1/r_2} = k$; and that may be recognized as the point where the elasticity of u_1 with respect to u_2 is $(du_1/du_2)(u_2/u_1) = -r_1/r_2$. Clearly, when $r_1 = r_2$, it is again implied that $u_1 u_2$ is a maximum. Otherwise, however, the higher r_1 is relative to r_2, the smaller is u_1 and the greater is u_2. On the other hand, as the contract duration $t \to 0$, the solution approaches the point at which the utility frontier is tangent to a curve of the form $u_1 u_2 = k$, since the magnitudes of r_1 and r_2 then have a vanishing effect. Hence, in general, the solution will lie between the two indicated points when $0 < t < \infty$.

It is worth a moment's digression to emphasize the substantive difference between this theory and the Nash-Zeuthen one. Although the latter theory abstracts from the time element, the natural way to apply it in the present context would be in terms of the present values of the attainable future utilities. On that basis, however, it would still yield a different result from the present theory whenever $r_1 \neq r_2$. In the case of a perpetual contract in a stationary situation, for example, the present values of any specified agreement would be u_1/r_1 and u_2/r_2; and, if the product of those present values is maximized, the result is the same as the maximizing of $u_1 u_2$. In other words, because the Nash-Zeuthen solution is independent of the utility scales of u_1 and u_2, and hence of u_1/r_1 and u_2/r_2, the result is independent of the magnitudes of r_1 and r_2.

Realistically, because the future is neither stationary nor certain, union-management contracts are typically of rather short duration. At the same time, however, relations between the parties are expected to continue indefinitely, in the form of successively negotiated contracts. Accordingly, if the present theory were to be applied merely in the context of a current contract period (as it would properly be if relations between the parties were expected to cease altogether at the contract's termination), the outcome would be sensitive to the contract duration; and this would make the contract period itself a matter of crucial dispute. Specifically, the party with the lower r would have a special stake in lengthening the contract period, while the other would prefer a succession of contracts of indefinitely short duration.

To avoid this anomalous dependence of an outcome on mere contract duration, it would seem to be far more logical to adopt as the relevant context for the theory the actually expected time span of relations between the parties. In the ordinary case, of course, this is indefinitely long. Several considerations favor this interpretation. For one, especially with reference to an abnormally short contract period, the duration of strike that may be threatened is not inherently limited to such a time span; indeed, the ultimate threat is always a perpetual strike or lockout. For another, it is frequently observed that the motivations underlying a strike may well involve considerations stretching well beyond a current contract period, since future negotiations are widely appreciated to be influenced by the memory of previous bargaining behavior. Furthermore, even the utilities of a given agreement are often affected by the net change that it involves from the preceding agreement; so, in general, a current agreement may regularly be assumed to have implications for the ones that follow. Finally, it would indeed be inappropriate to let the mere duration of an agreement have the substantive influence on its content that the alternative interpretation would imply. In a world of uncertain change, the appropriate determinants of contract duration, and hence of the frequency of contract negotiations, are the costs of the negotiation process itself (if only in terms of the time and nervous energy of the negotiators) as balanced against the advantages of being able to revise existing terms in the light of imperfectly foreseen changes of circumstance.

In short, as long as the relations between the bargaining parties are expected to continue indefinitely, it is here suggested that the present theory be applied as if any current contract were a perpetual one, irrespective of its actual duration. For example, a two-year contract may be looked upon, just for the purpose of applying the present theory, as if the anticipated conditions during that period were then to be repeated in every subsequent two-year period.

The task of further generalizing the present theory will not be attempted here; but the implications—and difficulties—of such generalization may be briefly indicated. For one thing, the parties' time-discount rates are not likely to be constants in reality, but variables depending on both the dating and magnitudes of the future utilities to be discounted. In addition, the difficulties occasioned by the uncertainty of the future utilities are all too obvious. Moreover, even if each party's own utilities and discount rates were somehow confidently known to itself, distinctive difficulties would still attach to the problem of knowing the same things about the other party (since each has an incentive to misrepresent in a way favorable to itself).

Finally, and quite apart from the foregoing difficulties, the basic validity of the Zeuthen-Hicks theory is also subject to the same sorts of misgivings as those already expressed above about Zeuthen's, even though it is superior on the one score of facing up to the time element of bargaining agreements and possible conflicts.

Massachusetts Institute of Technology

REFERENCES

[1] HARSANYI, J. C.: "Approaches to the Bargaining Problem Before and After the Theory of Games," *Econometrica*, 24, 144–57, 1956.

[2] HICKS, J. R.: *The Theory of Wages*, London: Macmillan and Co., 1932.

[3] ———: "Annual Survey of Economic Theory: The Theory of Monopoly," *Econometrica*, 3, 1–20, 1935.

[4] NASH, JOHN: "The Bargaining Problem," *Econometrica*, 18, 155–62, 1950.

[5] ZEUTHEN, F.: *Problems of Monopoly and Economic Warfare*, London: G. Routledge and Sons, 1930.

A THEORY OF THE BARGAINING PROCESS
John G. Cross

Economists traditionally have had very little to say about pure bargaining situations in which the outcome is clearly dependent upon interactions among only a few individuals. Except for a few models which have been based upon strong institutional assumptions, we have had to fall back on Edgeworth's model of bilateral monopoly in which only a "trading area" is delimited with no further restriction of the outcome. Within this area, the solution is said to depend upon the "bargaining abilities" of the individuals, a thoroughly vague concept which is primarily intended to give the whole problem to the psychologists, thus absolving economics of the guilt of leaving the issue up in the air.[1] It is not obvious, however, that the economist's techniques are inadequate for a solution, although the few attempts that have been made have not been met with appreciable success. It is the purpose of this paper to offer a precise analysis of bargaining by means of a positive theory based upon familiar economic concepts. It is hoped that this work will prove to be operational in the sense that the independent and dependent variables may be related to familiar quantities which are already commonly accepted as relevant in the context of bargaining.

It would not be useful for us to enter into any analyses of the extensive literature which relates to this subject; nevertheless there is need for some consideration of the Nash theory and the recent empirical work of Siegel and Fouraker, since an explicit attempt is made to relate our model to their conclusions.

* The author, a member of the staff of the Institute for Defense Analysis, would like to thank William J. Baumol and Harold W. Kuhn for their valuable advice and comments on this paper.

1 The literature abounds, however, with quasi-bargaining theories introduced in various attempts to fill the gaps in our understanding of oligopolistic markets. There are, moreover, several models which address themselves directly to the bargaining problem (i.e., bilateral monopoly). Besides those mentioned in the text, the most notable are those of F. Zeuthen [19] [20], J. Harsanyi [5], J. Pen [10] [11], J. R. Hicks [6], L. Foldes [4] (this is an outgrowth of the Hicks model), and R. L. Bishop [forthcoming in *Econometrica*]. It would not be fruitful to go into these models here, however, both because extensive criticisms already exist elsewhere (especially see Bishop [1]) and because they have little direct bearing on what is to follow. It should be observed, however, that the contribution of this paper stems from the explicit introduction of expectations into a model similar to Hicks's.

I. *The Nash Theory*

The most precise (but not descriptive) of previous theories is certainly that of J. Nash [9]. Nash conceived of the bargaining problem purely in terms of the increments in utility which each negotiator receives from each point of agreement. Thus "zero" utility for each negotiator relates to the point of total disagreement. Nash then assumed that it is reasonable to expect the outcome of a bargaining process to satisfy the following three conditions:

1. Pareto optimality—the outcome will lie on the northeast boundary of the utility-possibility set (this boundary necessarily has a negative slope).

2. Independence of irrelevant alternatives—consider two different bargaining situations with the same origin (i.e., the same disagreement point), and in which all the possible outcomes of one are included in the other; then, if the actual outcome of the larger game is also a possible outcome in the smaller, it will be the final outcome for the smaller game as well.

3. Symmetry—if the set of possible utility outcomes happens to be symmetric (that is, if for every point $U_1=a$, $U_2=b$ in the outcome set, the point $U_1=b$, $U_2=a$ is also in the set), then the outcome of the bargaining will give $U_1=U_2$. (Again, we are taking U_1 and U_2 as utility increments, assuming $U_1=0$, $U_2=0$ at the point of disagreement.)

Nash chose to formulate a model in which interpersonal comparisons were not a factor. Thus, the predicted agreement point must be independent of any interpersonal utility comparisons whether valid or not. This assumption required the model to obey a fourth rule.

4. The model must predict the same actual outcome despite any linear transformations of the players' utility functions.[2]

On the basis of these four conditions, Nash came to the remarkable conclusion that the only function which can consistently describe the outcome of the bargaining process as he conceived it is the one that maximizes the product of the players' utilities (the utilities being measured as increments from the point of disagreement).[3] Nash originally

---

[2] Note that this assumption also strengthens condition (3) to state that whenever there exists any linear utility transformation which can make the outcome set symmetric, we must have $U_1=U_2$ with the utilities expressed in terms of the same utility transformation.

[3] The foregoing description of the Nash theory is a very slight modification of the material in Luce and Raiffa [8].

We may sketch a simple proof of the theorem as follows: consider a utility-payoff set bounded by the straight line $U_1+U_2=k$. The symmetry assumption requires the outcome U_1^*, U_2^* to obey the condition $U_1^*=U_2^*=k/2$. Thus the point of agreement must be at the midpoint of the (straight) boundary line of the set. Through shifts in the units in which one or both players' utilities are measured (holding the origins constant), *any* straight boundary line in $U_1 \times U_2$ space can be given the form $U_1+U_2=k$. Moreover, the midpoints of straight lines always refer to the same actual outcomes under linear transformations. Thus the independence of linear

took the position that this function constitutes a positive theory in that it describes actual bargaining outcomes, but more commonly the analysis has been given a normative interpretation, and the Nash solution has been taken as a "desirable" outcome of the bargaining process. Finally, for the sake of future reference, it is useful to point out that in the case of a continuous utility-possibility set, for which the first-order derivatives on the northeast boundary of the set are always defined, the Nash point is the point for which $U_1/U_2 = -dU_1/dU_2$, where dU_1/dU_2 is the slope of the boundary.[4]

Since extended discussions of this model exist in both Luce and Raiffa [8] and Bishop [1], we will restrict ourselves to pointing out two important reasons for attempting to improve upon the Nash model as a general description of the bargaining process. First, it offers no analysis of the dynamic process of disagreement-concession-agreement that constitutes the very essence of the bargaining process. We are given only a solution criterion with no insight into its *raison d'être*. Thus it does not even partially answer the question that often is most interesting to us: under what conditions will the solution *deviate* from an idealized condition, and how will the variation take place? Second, acceptance of the descriptive interpretation of the Nash model would imply acceptance of the conclusion that all the information which is necessary for the analysis is contained in the set of possible utility-payoff combinations. All other variables (time, prices, relative intelligence of the bargainers, the arguments of the utility functions, etc.) must not enter in any essential way because their introduction would necessarily violate one or more of the Nash assumptions.[5]

---

transformations of utility assumption implies that all utility sets bounded by straight lines have the midpoints of those lines as expected outcomes. Furthermore, the congruence of triangles ABC, BEO, and BDE in the diagram guarantees that such outcomes will always satisfy the condition $U_1/U_2 = -dU_1/dU_2$, where dU_1/dU_2 is the slope of the straight line, and it is easy to show that this condition in turn assures us that the product U_1U_2 has been maximized (see footnote 4). Now consider any convex outcome set bounded by $U_1 = f(U_2)$. In our continuous example, we can always find a straight line which is tangent to $U_1 = f(U_2)$ such that a point of tangency, U_1', U_2', includes the midpoint of the straight line (rotate the tangent line around the boundary—at some point our condition must be satisfied). Independence of irrelevant alternatives now ensures that U_1', U_2' is the outcome of the smaller game, and it is obvious that if this point maximizes the product U_1U_2 on the straight line, U_1', U_2' must also maximize the possible utility product of the game bounded by $U_1 = f(U_2)$.

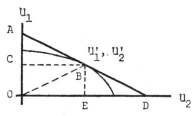

[4] The boundary is defined as $U_1 = f(U_2)$; we want to maximize P where $P = U_1U_2$; $dP/dU_2 = U_1 + U_2(dU_1/dU_2)$; so for a maximum: $U_1/U_2 = -dU_1/dU_2$.

[5] For example, the easiest assumption to violate through the introduction of new variables is symmetry: if the solution depends upon *anything* besides utilities, then even in the case of a symmetric outcome set, we have no reason to expect $U_1 = U_2$ at the point of agreement.

II. *The Empirical Conclusions of Siegel and Fouraker*

Some excellent experimental work on bargaining has been conducted recently by S. Siegel and L. Fouraker [16]. They have performed a series of two-person bargaining experiments set in the context of bilateral monopoly. Besides studying the actual point of agreement, Siegel and Fouraker compared bargaining outcomes under various controlled conditions, studying the effects of complete vs. incomplete information,[6] and variations in the structure of the payoffs.

Below, we have simply listed those conclusions of the Siegel-Fouraker study which seem to be the most relevant to the discussions in this paper:

1. There is a tendency for bargainers to negotiate contracts that are Pareto optimal [16, p. 41].[7]

2. "Increasing the amount of information available to the bargainers tends to lead to a more equal division of the joint payoff" [16, p. 70].

3. Supplementing the higher payoffs to only one player so as to increase the utility to him of these outcomes tends to increase his payoff at agreement [16, pp. 62–70].

4. "Occasionally an opponent would offer an unexpectedly generous bid (this might be unintentional—the opponent would be maintaining a constant payoff plateau or concession rate, but moving toward the Paretian optima in his bids). The subject's usual reaction was to raise his own payoff request—make his next bid one which would yield a higher profit to him than would have been yielded by his own previous bid" [16, p. 81]. In other words, his usual reaction was to raise his expected payoff.

5. There is some evidence that increasing the information to one player alone tends to decrease his payoff at agreement [16, pp. 57–58].

III. *The Components of Bargaining Processes*

We may characterize the bargaining process in terms of two limiting cases: (1) the Pure Bluffing case—each participant plans to give in as the other does, expecting ultimately to achieve agreement at some intermediate point which may even go beyond the point to which the other

---

[6] Experimentally, this was done by permitting one player to see the other's profit table in cases in which he was to have complete information.

[7] Unfortunately, Siegel and Fouraker's use of a bilateral monopoly model leads to payoff tables in which all the Pareto optimal points also represent the joint maximum; so that from their experiments it is impossible to tell whether the tendencies are specifically toward the joint maximum, or just toward Pareto optima. Siegel and Fouraker tend to use these expressions interchangeably; we have substituted "Pareto optimal" simply because it seems more plausible to us that this is the correct interpretation. It may be, however, that conclusions (1) could be put much more strongly.

expects to concede;[8] (2) the Pure Intransigence or Asymmetrical case—each expects to obtain agreement at his initial demand, anticipating that the other player will make all of the concessions.

The case of pure bluffing alone would be a relatively uninteresting one in which no real disagreement existed at all. That such a case often does exist, however, is clear from certain labor-management disputes in which, just before strike-time, each party sends behind-the-scenes envoys to the other in hopes of discovering its real expectations and finding agreement staring them in the face.[9] It is the asymmetrical case (2) that fosters disagreement in the bargaining problem as we usually think of it. Most bargaining situations, of course, are best represented as a mixture of our two components—that is, the players demand more than they expect to obtain (bluffing), but the expectations themselves are not initially compatible (asymmetry). Because of the importance of the asymmetrical (intransigence) component and shortage of space, we must base our simple model upon this aspect alone, leaving an adequate discussion of bluffing to later studies.

IV. *Notation*

Formal analyses of the bargaining process often have been conducted in terms of utility units rather than physical "payoff" units. In general, however, people do not bargain over utilities—"you take two utiles, and I'll take three"—they bargain in terms of more objective quantities: states of their mutual environment or the division of goods. Depending upon the circumstances, we must measure the players' outcome demands by means of one of two alternative types of variable. In cases in which a fixed quantity of a homogeneous good i is being divided into smaller quantities, we can indicate player j's demand by means of a quantity variable q_{ij}. In this case, we shall have disagreement whenever

---

[8] The term "bluffing" is commonly used in several distinct ways. The meaning which we have in mind here refers to a player's deliberate misrepresentation of his outcome expectations in order to influence his opponent; that is, he demands x while he expects (or would otherwise expect) to receive y ultimately.

Bluffing can also refer to misrepresentation of other (we would say less basic) aspects of a bargaining situation, especially with respect to a player's own utility function ("We can't possibly offer a higher wage—we would go out of business"). This kind of bluffing does not alter the specific positions of the bargainers; it is simply an aspect of the verbal waffle which accompanies any bargaining process (although, of course, it may have some significant effects).

Finally, bluffing may be meant to refer to specific strategic opportunities which may come up in individual bargaining situations, such as the chance to conceal the existence of certain possible outcomes, misrepresent the actual consequences of disagreement, etc., but as these do not appear to be fundamental to the bargaining process in general, we shall not consider them.

[9] A case in which management clearly harbored such hopes appears in A. H. Raskin's description of the 1962–63 New York newspaper strike [13].

the sum of the players' demands exceeds the total amount available: i.e., whenever

$$\sum_j q_{ij} > M_i$$

where M_i is the total quantity of the ith good. If we are simply dividing a sum of money, this notation would be appropriate. In other cases in which the available amount of the good is variable, unknown, or perhaps not even defined, it is more appropriate to consider an ordered index P which ranges over the various outcome alternatives, and to indicate the outcome demand of player j by means of a variable P_j. Labor-management wage negotiations are the best examples of this case—here we would simply associate P with the wage rate. In a two-person negotiation of this type, we would have disagreement whenever $P_1 > P_2$ (if we associate P_1 with the union demand). The only formal difference between the two notations lies in a reversal of sign between the players in some of our expressions using the P-notation (player II prefers *higher* q_2, but *lower* P_2, as our examples were formulated). Simply to avoid possible sign confusion, therefore, we shall adhere to the quantity notation.

We shall consider the simplest case of a bargaining process—two persons bargaining over the division of a fixed quantity, M, of a single good which is continuously divisible. Following Nash, we may write utility functions for players I and II in terms of the utility increments that they may receive, $U_1 = f(q_1)$ and $U_2 = g(q_2)$, by adjusting the origins of our functions so that $f(0) = 0$, and $g(0) = 0$. So we have (assuming that the first two derivatives of the utility functions always exist):

(1)
$$f(0) = 0 \qquad f'(q_1) > 0 \qquad f''(q_1) < 0$$
$$g(0) = 0 \qquad g'(q_2) > 0 \qquad g''(q_2) < 0$$

V. *The Dynamic Nature of the Bargaining Process*

As any economist knows, time has a cost, both in money and in utility terms; it is our position that it is precisely this cost which motivates the bargaining process. If it did not matter when people agreed, it would not matter whether or not they agreed at all. The influence of time upon bargaining may assume three different forms. First, it appears naturally in a discounting function if the players discount future benefits (an agreement must offer a benefit, even if, as in the case of prestrike labor bargaining, the players are not at a point of physical disagreement; otherwise, there would be no bargaining). Second, the utility of agreement itself may change with the calendar date (the cake gets moldy before we agree on how to cut it, etc.). Finally, there is a fixed cost of bargaining which recurs in each time period. This last cost may vary from the simple personal inconvenience of having to spend time in this rather than other occupations, to the immense cost in terms of loss of profit and fixed cost of a temporarily unproductive plant which is faced by a strike-bound firm. These costs are all unaffected by the point of agreement, and therefore they have not been included in our "utility" functions.

Since the present value of any anticipated outcome is affected by the time at which it would be reached, it is necessary for each player to estimate the time required for agreement. This time is obviously a function of a player's own demand. For example, player I estimates the amount of time necessary to obtain a payoff quantity q_1 by observing the current demand of player II, q_2, and considering the amount of time that it will take II to concede over the difference $(q_1 + q_2 - M)$. Player I, however, has no specific knowledge of player II's utility function, and hence he can make no precise estimate of II's relative rates of concession over various payoff demands.[10] In such a case, player I is forced to make some general estimate of II's rate of concession, and in fact it appears to be reasonable for our purposes to assume that player I initially expects some positive concession rate. We shall call this rate r_2. By restricting our simple model to bargaining situations in which bluffing does not occur, we have already assumed that player I does not think of r_2 as a function of his own behavior. The expected time necessary to reach agreement such that player I receives a quantity q_1 is then given by the expression $(q_1 + q_2 - M)/r_2$, which we shall represent by w.

We shall introduce our time dependence by assuming that the utility functions express utilities at the time of agreement and then appropriately adjusting them back to the present. First, we shall assume the existence of an exponential discounting function[11] such that, with other factors neglected, the present value of a demand for a quantity q_1 is given by the expression $f(q_1)e^{-aw}$. Second, suppose that player I faces a fixed-cost rate C_1, where C_1 is expressed as a utility value per time period. The total expected cost of bargaining, Z, may be expressed in present-value terms as the sum of a stream of costs C_1 appropriately discounted; that is, $Z = C_1 e^{-a} + C_1 e^{-2a} + \cdots + C_1 e^{-aw}$, or in continuous terms:[12]

----

[10] Player II may greatly prefer an outcome q' over q'' and be nearly indifferent between q'' and the inferior quantity q''', even where $q' - q'' = q'' - q'''$. In this case, if we knew his utility function, we would expect II to concede more slowly from q' to q'' than he does from q'' to q'''.

[11] A theorem of Robert H. Strotz [18], when applied to the following model, demonstrates rather forcefully that this is a desirable assumption.

[12] This may be thought of as an infinite stream of costs originating at the present time minus an infinite stream of costs originating at the time of agreement. In present-value terms, this is $C_1/a - (C_1/a)e^{-aw}$.

$$Z = C_1 \int_0^w e^{-ax}dx = \frac{C_1}{a}(1 - e^{-aw}).$$

For the purposes of this simple model, we shall postpone any dependence upon calendar date.

Now the total value to player I of insisting on a return q_1 is:[13]

$$U_1' = f(q_1)e^{-aw} + \frac{C_1}{a}e^{-aw} - \frac{C_1}{a}.$$

To decide what outcome to demand, player I chooses the quantity which satisfies his preferences—that is, the q_1 which maximizes the present value of his utility U_1', remembering that w, the time required to reach agreement, is a function of q_1. Differentiating U_1' with respect to q_1 and noting that $\partial w/\partial q_1 = 1/r_2$, we obtain the first- and second-order conditions:[14]

(2)
$$\left[f(q_1) + \frac{C_1}{a}\right]\frac{a}{r_2} = f'(q_1)$$

and $f'(q_1) - a/r_2 + f''(q_1) < 0$, or since $f'(q_1) > 0$, and $r_2 > 0$:

(3)
$$\frac{f''(q_1)}{f'(q_1)} r_2 - a < 0.$$

VI. Learning

Player I demands a payoff quantity, q_1, on the basis of an *expected* rate of concession from the other player, r_2; if player II in fact does not concede at that rate, then clearly I's expectations will alter—that is, r_2

---

[13] Note that an increase in costs, C, *increases* U_1; that is, increases the utility of agreement. One must bear in mind the fact that U_1' measures the *gain* in utility which player I obtains through agreement over permanent disagreement. This gain is certainly increased as the costs of disagreement are increased.

[14] We observed that any delay in the date of agreement will impose a cost on player I which is given by the discount rate, a. That is, he will lose a per cent of his total expected return for every time-period delay. Thus, since an increase in his demand, Δq_1, will put off agreement by $\Delta q_1/r_2$ units of time, such an increased demand will cost him $\Delta q_1 a/r_2$ per cent of his return or $\Delta q_1 a/r_2 U_1$ "utils," where U_1 is the undiscounted utility which player I expects to receive from his current demand. On the other hand, his return is increased by $\Delta U_1 = \Delta q_1 f'(q_1)$. Since $U_1 = f(q_1) + C_1/a$, it follows that so long as $f'(q_1) > a/r_2[f(q_1) + C_1/a]$; that is, so long as the marginal return from an increase in his demand is greater than its marginal cost, player I will be better off if he increases his demand. He will have maximized his return when equality holds. This is essentially the meaning of condition (2). Condition (3) simply requires that for condition (2) to represent a maximum, the expression $f'(q_1)$ must be decreasing relative to $a/r_2[f(q_1) + C_1/a]$ as q_1 is increased. Conditions (1) are obviously sufficient for this to be the case. We might add here that Siegel and Fouraker tended to favor a satisfying type of model of their bargainers' behavior. It is easy to demonstrate, however (see Section VI), that their results are perfectly compatible with utility-maximizing models.

will change, and, as a consequence, he will demand a different q_1. At this point we are naturally led to examine a process of *learning.* Most generally, a learning model is a time-dependent relation which must satisfy at least the following conditions:

$$\frac{dr_2}{dt} > 0, \quad \text{if} \quad -\frac{dq_2}{dt} > r_2;$$

(4)
$$\frac{dr_2}{dt} = 0, \quad \text{if} \quad -\frac{dq_2}{dt} = r_2;$$

$$\frac{dr_2}{dt} < 0, \quad \text{if} \quad -\frac{dq_2}{dt} < r_2.$$

That is, if player II concedes faster than is expected, player I will increase his estimate of II's concession rate; if player II concedes just as rapidly as is expected, player I will retain his original estimate, r_2, and so on.

Furthermore, it is reasonable to assume that the magnitude of dr_2/dt varies positively with the discrepancy between $-dq_2/dt$ and the expected rate of concession; that is, the greater the error in player I's expectations, the faster his expectations will change. Thus we will assume:

(5)
$$\frac{d\dot{r}_2}{d(-r_2 - \dot{q}_2)} > 0$$

where $\dot{r}_2$ is defined as dr_2/dt, and $\dot{q}_2$ as dq_2/dt.

Later, a more specific characterization of learning behavior will be used, but for the present, we shall be content with just the conditions (4) and (5).[15]

VII. *The Process of Concession*

We may observe from equation (2) that player I's outcome demand, q_1, is a function of time owing to its dependence upon r_2. We can find

---

[15] Expressions (4) and (5) do seem to correspond to a very general characterization of most existing learning theory. Although work attempting to define mathematically the time path of learning is decidedly in the minority in the otherwise extensive psychology literature on learning, some useful models do exist, notably those of Hull (see E. Hilgard [7, pp. 1–115), and K. Spence [17]), and Bush and Mosteller [3]. Also see A. T. Poffenberger, ed. [12]. It may be argued that even our generalized learning model should follow Bush and Mosteller in making use of statistical variations. We do have some doubts, however, as to the appropriateness of probabilistic elements in a behavioral theory.

his concession rate, $-\dot{q}_1$, simply by differentiating (2) with respect to t and solving for dq_1/dt, which yields:[16]

(6)
$$\dot{q}_1 = -\frac{1}{\dfrac{f''(q_1)}{f'(q_1)}r_2 - a}\frac{dr_2}{dt}.$$

In the light of (3), expression (6) requires that q_1 should vary in the same direction as r_2. In other words, if player I discovers that player II is yielding more rapidly than he expected, he will increase his demands. Conversely, he will reduce his demands if he discovers that player II is not giving in as fast as he formerly thought. Thus expressions (3) and (6), in conjunction with our learning theory, would already lead us to expect Siegel and Fouraker's conclusion #4 (see Section I) to the effect that sudden large concessions from one player tend to encourage increased demands on the part of the other. This conclusion also has the advantage of strongly supporting one's intuitive notions as to the consequence of unexpected concessions.

All the previous analysis may be applied to player II just as it was to player I, with similar results. In the case of player II, the expressions corresponding to (2)–(6) may be obtained simply by reversing the subscripts (and substituting b, player II's discount rate, for a). Notice that we have imposed no restriction on the possible signs of the $\dot{q}$'s. If $\dot{q}_1$ is positive, player I is increasing his demands. Often, retraction of an offer during negotiation is thought to be either unethical or at least undesirable because of the unfavorable utility shifts which such behavior may induce in the other player. In fact, Siegel and Fouraker, in their empirical study, deliberately formulated their rules so as to eliminate this possibility (they stipulated that any price-quantity bid, once made, was always good). Nevertheless, such retractions sometimes occur in practice. We will, therefore, retain the possibility of their occurrence, recognizing that forces probably exist which discourage increases in demands during the course of negotiations.

VIII. *Bargaining*

The essential nature of the bargaining process may now be described. We should start with r_1 and r_2 positive (if r_1, for example, were less than or equal to zero, that is, if player I were expected to hold out forever, player II would give in immediately). It is impossible that neither bar-

---

[16] That is, if r_2 changes by some amount Δr_2, the cost, $a/r_2[f'(q_1)+C_1/a]$, of a unit increase in player I's demand is changed, and he will adjust q_1 until the marginal return $f'(q_1)$ is equal to the new marginal cost $a/r_2+\Delta r_2[f'(q_1)+C_1/a]$. Expression (6) simply represents Δr_2 and the resulting change in q_1 in terms of time.

gainer will shift: if player I is not conceding, for example, player II will learn that his estimate of $-\dot{q}_1$ is too high, r_1 will fall, and player II's demand, q_2, will decrease along with it. If $-\dot{q}_2 = r_2$, then player II will make the entire concession himself. If player II gives in at a rate less than that which player I expects, then r_2 will fall as well, and player I will reduce his own demand, q_1. Thus we have the general case of a convergent bargaining process—whenever both actual concession rates are less than the expected rates.

We should also be aware at this point of a potential instability in this bargaining model: suppose that player II, for example, is a very sensitive learner, and he finds that player I is conceding at a rate significantly below his expectations. If he responds very strongly to this information, he may be found to be giving in at a rate greater than player I expects. Player I will naturally increase his demands in response, the extent of the increase depending upon expression (6) and his learning capacity. Now, if this increase in demands is sufficiently strong, r_1 will again fall strongly (depending upon II's capacity to learn), and II may give in even more rapidly.[17] This sequence may still converge so long as player II concedes faster than player I retracts his position, in which case, the conditions characterizing the point of agreement (to be formulated in a later section) are no different from those of the previous case. It may be, however, that either the sequence does not converge or that it does not converge soon enough, so that the point of "agreement" will simply be at or arbitrarily close to the best possible outcome for player I.

We can observe from expression (6) that the rate of concession varies inversely with the value of the expression $f''(q_1)/f'(q_1)r_2 - a$ or, in the special case of linear utility functions, with the value of the discount rate itself. Thus high learning rates and low discount rates will tend to induce instability in our model. The stringency of the resulting stability condition cannot be evaluated without some information as to the actual form of the learning functions in bargaining situations. One might infer from most of the recent widely publicized negotiations that learning rates are quite low. It is probably true also that the process of bluffing makes a considerable contribution toward stability through its impedance of the learning process.

IX. *The Convergence of Expectations*

Suppose we have two players who are relatively similar in that their abilities to learn and their discount rates are nearly equivalent. Further, suppose that r_2, player I's expectation of II's rate of concession, is

---

[17] It is not sufficient for instability to have $-\dot{q}_2 > r_2$; we must also have a strong response to this condition on the part of player I; otherwise, player II, not observing much of a change in $\dot{q}_1$, may fail to repeat the cycle, and we will have $-\dot{q}_2 < r_2$.

greater than r_1, and finally, consider the situation at the start of the bargaining process, when neither is giving in. According to our assumption that large errors in expectations bring about more rapid changes in expectations [see expression (5), Section VI], r_2 will fall faster than r_1. Thus we observe the two expected concession rates approaching one another.

This conclusion may be obtained more rigorously by means of a graphical analysis. Let us assume that the utility functions of the two players are linear, their discount rates are equal, and that their learning functions are identical. Suppose further that player II is conceding, but at a rate below that expected by player I. From our discussion in the last section, we concluded that player I will reduce his demand, q_1, at a rate which depends upon r_2 and upon the discrepancy between r_2 and player II's actual concession rate, $-\dot{q}_2$; the larger this discrepancy, the more q_1 is reduced. Thus the greater is the concession rate of player II, $-\dot{q}_2$, for example, the smaller will be the resulting concession rate of player I. When $-\dot{q}_2 = r_2$, the expectations of player I are realized, and he retains his previous demand (i.e., $-\dot{q}_1 = 0$). This information appears on Figure 1. Placing $-\dot{q}_1$ and $-\dot{q}_2$ on the axes, we have drawn a line (F) with negative slope which intersects the $-\dot{q}_2$ axis at the point $-\dot{q}_2 = r_2$. This line represents player I's reaction to any concession rate $-\dot{q}_2$, given his expectation, r_2, and may be put in the notational form $-\dot{q}_1 = F(-\dot{q}_2, r_2)$. In exactly the same fashion, we construct the line $-\dot{q}_2 = G(-\dot{q}_1, r_1)$ relating player II's rate of concession to his expecta-

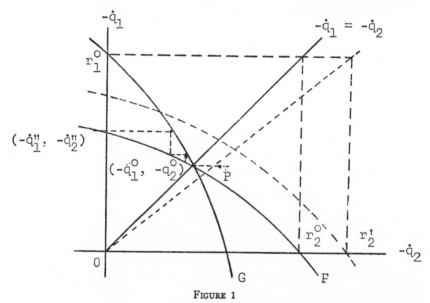

FIGURE 1

tion, r_1, and his opponent's concession rate $-\dot{q}_1$. As the graph is drawn, we have deliberately constructed the special case $r_1 = r_2$ $(r_1^o = r_2^o)$ in order to show the symmetrical (and, as it will turn out, the final-equilibrium) state.

It is evident that under these circumstances, the two instantaneous rates of concession will be given by the point $(-\dot{q}_1^o, -\dot{q}_2^o)$, the point of intersection of the functions F and G (by symmetry of the situation, $\dot{q}_1^o = \dot{q}_2^o$); that is, if we consider the situation from the point of view of a period analysis, we shall move from any point $(-\dot{q}_1'', -\dot{q}_2'')$ to the point of intersection, as in the case of the dotted example on the diagram. Now suppose r_2 is increased, *ceteris paribus*, to r_2'. This will *shift* the line $-\dot{q}_1 = F(-\dot{q}_2, r_2)$ to the right to a position such as that shown on the dashed line on the graph. The effect of this shift is to increase $-\dot{q}_1$ immediately, and to move the point of intersection of F and G up to the left. We may now expect to obtain the relationship $-\dot{q}_1 > -\dot{q}_2$, which, in our symmetrical example, implies the condition $-\dot{r}_2 > -\dot{r}_1$; that is, r_2 is falling faster than r_1, tending to *shift* the function F down faster than the function G, restoring equality.[18]

Furthermore, it is important to show that the ratio r_1/r_2 will tend toward a value of unity.[19] Let us arbitrarily retain r_1 at a value of r_1^o and increase r_2 from r_2^o to r_2', and attempt to preserve the new value of the ratio $r_1/r_2(=r_1^o/r_2')$ over time. One way to accomplish this would be to retain $\dot{r}_1$ at its previous value and increase $\dot{r}_2$ in the same proportion as r_2 was increased in going from r_2^o to r_2'. This condition would be satisfied by some point P (see Figure 1) at which $-\dot{q}_1 = -\dot{q}_1^o$ and $-\dot{q}_2 > -\dot{q}_2^o$. However, no point above and to the left of P could possibly satisfy this condition since at any such point we would have $-\dot{q}_1 > -\dot{q}_1^o$ and $-\dot{q}_2 < -\dot{q}_2'$. Since the new intersection of our response functions F' and G is above and to the left of P, we must have r_2 falling too rapidly relative to r_1 to prevent the ratio r_1/r_2 from increasing. This process will continue until we reach a point at which $r_1/r_2 = 1$, and where, as a consequence, $\dot{r}_2 = \dot{r}_1$.

It should be observed that we are assuming here that, as r_2 rises, the slope of the function F does not flatten so rapidly as to permit an intersection below and to the left of P. It is sufficient for this condition that every point of F moves upward and to the right as r_2 is increased; that is, that the new function F nowhere intersects the original function F

---

[18] This analysis oversimplifies the problem somewhat by neglecting the fact that the curves F and G are also shifting as the concession rates $-\dot{q}_1$ and $-\dot{q}_2$ approach their intersection. For the purposes of this paper, we shall generally assume that the convergence to point $(-\dot{q}_1^o, -\dot{q}_2^o)$ is instantaneous. A period analysis can be constructed, however, containing both phases of the problem, and such a model gives substantially the same results as the one given above.

[19] If r_1/r_2 does not converge toward unity, it is essentially trivial to point out that r_1 and r_2 approach one another as they both approach zero.

in the positive quadrant. We must require, therefore, that the response functions F and G always satisfy the conditions $\partial F/\partial r_2 \geq 0$; $\partial G/\partial r_1 \geq 0$ (in the positive quadrant); that is, for example, that a *ceteris paribus* increase in r_2 induces a higher concession rate from player I. It may be observed that our second learning condition (5), $d\dot{r}/d(-\dot{q}-r) > 0$, virtually guarantees that this restriction will be satisfied so long as the second-order terms [e.g., $f''(q_1)/f'(q_1)$ in the denominator of (6)] do not increase rapidly as r_2 or r_1 are increased.[20] In our special case in which the utility functions are linear, of course, this condition must be satisfied.

Two other points should be noted here. First, our demonstration of the equilibrium behavior in our model does not depend on any linearity assumptions, although, of course, in a case in which the utility functions are not linear, we cannot expect the equilibrium point to be identical to that of a linear model. Second, it is not likely that our conditions $\partial F/\partial r_2 > 0$; $\partial G/\partial r_1 > 0$ are violated at *all* points on the functions F and G. There may be at worst a limited number of values of r_2, r_1 for which the ratio r_1/r_2 may be expected to display equilibrium properties [$r_1/r_2 = $ const.]. Thus the conditions of the previous paragraph may be taken to be uniqueness conditions; if they are violated over only limited ranges, our equilibrium analysis is valid, and we are only prevented from pointing to one single expected outcome.

If it happens that the players are not identical (in learning abilities, discount rates, etc.), these differences are easily introduced into our model. For example, if player I is a more able learner than player II, he will concede more rapidly for every value of $-\dot{q}_2$ (if $-\dot{q}_2$ is less than r_2) than in the previous case. Thus the slope of F, $d\dot{q}_1/d\dot{q}_2$, will be greater than before, and our diagram now has the form (for $r_1 = r_2$) which is drawn in Figure 2. When $r_1 = r_2$, we expect to find player I conceding more rapidly than player II. It follows that r_2 will tend to fall faster than r_1, and thus the equilibrium state must have r_2 smaller than r_1. On the other hand, if player I has a higher discount rate than player II, the function $-\dot{q}_1 = F(-\dot{q}_2, r_2)$ has a form similar to the dotted example in Figure 2. Through reasoning similar to that used above, we may conclude that, in this case, r_2 will tend to be larger than r_1.

We have drawn the graph in such a manner that the response of each player to a discrepancy between his expectations and reality is not too great: this represents the case of a stable bargaining process. In fact, we can see from the graph that whenever the function G intersects the function F from lower right to above left, the negotiation will be stable. If we define the slope of the function F, $\partial F/\partial(-\dot{q}_1)$, as $-A$ and the

[20] That is, we are asking that a change in r_2 not be accompanied by a second-order shift in the denominator of (6) which is sufficient to nullify the effect of the change on $\dot{q}_1$.

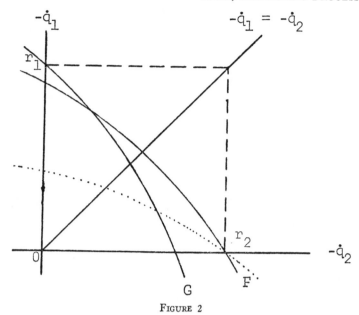

FIGURE 2

slope of the function G, $\partial G/\partial(-\dot{q}_1)$, as $-B$, then our stability condition is $1/B > A$, or $AB < 1$.

If the two lines had intersected one another in the opposite fashion, we would have had instability on two counts: we would not expect to find the actual rates of concession at the point of intersection of F and G (a period analysis now takes us away from that point, as one can readily observe from the dotted time path in Figure 3), and the condition $r_2 > r_1$ tends to make r_1 fall faster than r_2. In this case, we are unable to make any prediction concerning the outcome of the negotiation.

X. *The Point of Agreement and the Nash Solution*

It is now useful to characterize the point of agreement formally. Agreement is defined by the situation in which the sum of the players' demands is equal to the available supply, that is: $\bar{q}_1 + \bar{q}_2 = M$. Let us divide equation (2), the utility-maximization expression for player I, by the similar utility-maximization expression for player II as follows:

(7)
$$\frac{f'(\bar{q}_1)}{g'(M - \bar{q}_1)} = + \frac{f(\bar{q}_1) + \dfrac{C_1}{a}}{g(M - \bar{q}_1) + \dfrac{C_2}{a}} \cdot \frac{a}{b} \cdot \frac{r_1}{r_2}.$$

If we follow Nash's example and shift the origins of our utility func-

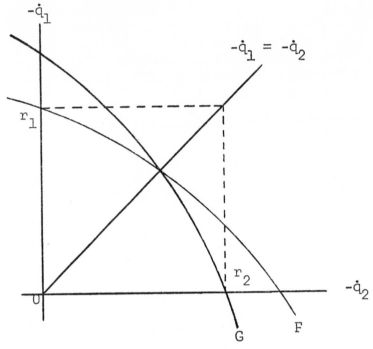

FIGURE 3

tions U_1' and U_2' so that the point of disagreement is at the origin,[21] and if we consider the utilities at the *time of agreement* (i.e., neglect the time-discounting factors), we obtain the following utility functions:

(8)
$$U_1 = f(\bar{q}_1) + \frac{C_1}{a}$$

$$U_2 = g(M - \bar{q}_1) + \frac{C_2}{a}.$$

That is, the utility of agreement to each player is equal to the utility of his payoff [e.g., $f(q_1)$] *plus* the cost saving which results from the existence of a state of agreement rather than a state of disagreement (e.g., C_1/a). If we transform expression (7) into utility terms according to this definition of the utility functions, we obtain:

(9)
$$\frac{dU_1}{dU_2} = - \frac{U_1}{U_2} \frac{a}{b} \frac{r_1}{r_2}$$

where dU_1/dU_2 is the slope of the Pareto optimum curve in $U_1 \times U_2$ space, at the point determined by $\bar{q}_1$.

[21] The functions U_1' and U_2' were formulated without taking into account the bargaining (disagreement) costs C_1/a and C_1/b.

Now we apply the conclusions of the previous sections to the special linear and symmetric situation. In the case of similar players (players with equal discount rates, so that $a=b$, and equivalent learning abilities), we concluded that we had an equilibrium relationship between expectations when $r_1=r_2$. In this case, expression (9) becomes simply

$$\frac{dU_1}{dU_2} = -\frac{U_1}{U_2},$$

the expression which characterizes the Nash solution to the bargaining problem (see Section I). Thus we obtain the rather satisfying result from our model that in the special case of identical players, the bargaining outcome can be expected to be the Nash solution.

We need not rely on linear utility functions for this conclusion. Suppose we impose the Nash condition of "symmetry" upon the bargaining situation in a slightly less general form. Assume that if $q_1=q_2$, then there exists some linear utility transformation such that:[22]

$$f(q_1) = g(q_2).$$

It follows by differentiation that for q_1 always to equal q_2:

$$f'(q_1) = g'(q_2),$$
$$f''(q_1) = g''(q_2).$$

We may conclude, therefore, that at the point where $q_1+q_2=M$ (and of course $q_1=q_2=M/2$):

$$\frac{f''(q_1)}{f'(q_1)} = \frac{g''(q_2)}{g'(q_2)}.$$

Making our assumption of "similarity" between the players ($a=b$, and the learning abilities are identical), then the preceding relations ensure that equation (6) becomes perfectly symmetrical for the two, and we clearly have an equilibrium state at $r_1=r_2$. That is, by equation (9), we have the Nash Point as the solution, and since $dU_1/dU_2=-1$ at q_1, $U_1=U_2$.[23]

However, even given our "similarity" assumption, the solution to our model as given by (10) is generally *not* the Nash solution. The dependence of our results on second-order derivatives as well as first is

[22] The Nash assumption is weaker than this because it only requires that for any q_1 there exists some q_2 (not necessarily equal to q_1), such that $f(q_1)=g(q_2)$ and $q_1+q_2\leq M$.

[23] It must be remembered at this point that the condition $r_1=r_2$ is only achieved if the bargaining process takes enough time for the initial discrepancies to be eliminated. Otherwise, the solution which is derived from our model will differ from the actual results. In fact, as we shall show later, some error is almost always to be expected, although our solution will always serve as the focus toward which a stable bargaining process will tend.

sufficient to show that the two solutions will be different in all but fortuitous cases. This difference is due to the introduction of physical payoffs as important variables in the model.[24]

XI. *Further Conclusions on the Equilibrium Point*

Several other conclusions follow at once from the analysis. We concluded earlier that if player I is a more sensitive learner, the bargaining process will tend to yield the condition $r_2 < r_1$ (i.e., player II expects player I to concede more rapidly than player I expects player II to concede). Referring to equation (9), it is clear that a decrease in r_2 relative to r_1 at agreement results in a smaller value of U_1 relative to U_2 (and a larger dU_1/dU_2) than before. Hence the better a learner he is, the more the outcome will go against a player! It does not follow that such a player is made worse off by his superior ability—it may be that the saving in time which results from his more rapid concession outweighs the loss in undiscounted utility of the outcome. Naturally, the other player gains, and he probably gains more than the faster learner.[25] One cannot help noticing a striking resemblance between this conclusion and Siegel and Fouraker's observation (#5, Section II) to the effect that increasing the information available to a player tends to reduce his payoff. We may suggest that in their experiments, increasing one player's information concerning the other player's payoff utilities sharpened the first player's awareness of the other's rate of concession and simply increased his learning rate.[26]

We also concluded earlier that if player I used a higher discount rate (*a*) than player II, the bargaining process would tend to yield the condition $r_2 > r_1$. Referring to equation (9), we find this to have ambiguous consequences. Compared to the symmetrical case, as we have just

[24] That is, nonlinear utility functions are relevant in the bargaining process, and hence (referring to Section I) we do not satisfy either symmetry (in its general sense—our special case is not sufficient for the Nash theorem) or Independence of Irrelevant Alternatives even in the case of "similar" players. This model does satisfy Pareto optimality (in this simple model, there are no alternatives which are not optimal) and independence of linear transformations of the utility functions.

[25] The potential gain of a more rapid learner is only offered as a possibility—in general, he probably will not gain on balance. Note that this conclusion applies only to a player's learning *rate*. If one player has additional insight into the *nature* of the other player's learning process (e.g., its functional form or some relevant parameters), and this type of knowledge is not symmetrically held by the other, then the first player can almost certainly gain. The players' relative insights into one another's learning behavior is another important parameter which, unfortunately, has had to be neglected in our simple model.

[26] Perhaps it should be emphasized that the Siegel-Fouraker game was two-dimensional, and that in such a case, it is practically impossible for a player to tell whether an opponent's movement from a point (x, y) to a point (x', y'), where $x > x'$ and $y < y'$, constitutes a concession or not. Hence possession of information about the utilities associated with these points would greatly increase one's ability to estimate a rate of concession.

shown, a higher value of a tends to decrease the ratio r_1/r_2 by reducing player I's concession rate, and this alone would increase player I's outcome utility. However, a high discount rate also leads player I to sacrifice some payoff units at the start of the negotiation in order to hasten agreement [see equation (2)]. The net effect of these two forces is uncertain, however, and so we should have to use specific examples in order to obtain definite results.[27]

An inspection of equation (2) coupled with conditions (1) supports the intuitively reasonable hypothesis that high values of the bargaining costs, C_1 and C_2, will induce the players to make relatively lower payoff demands throughout the negotiation. This initial reduction in demands is certain to reduce the time required for the bargaining process, simply because agreement is reached with higher values of r_1 and r_2 than before. Intuitively, this conclusion is quite plausible; it may be taken, for example, as a major explanation for the vastly different amounts of time which are taken by different kinds of negotiations. A housewife normally spends only a few minutes bargaining over the price of a household item (on the rare occasions when she bargains over them at all) simply because the inconvenience which would accompany such a bargaining process is so large relative to the value of the good, while a labor dispute may last for months, and international negotiations in which the physical costs of bargaining are virtually nil (relative to the importance of the outcome) may last for years (e.g., test-ban talks, talks over Berlin, trade negotiations, etc.).[28] We can also observe that *rising* costs during negotiations will bring about additional concessions. For example, in prestrike labor-management negotiations, the costs are very low compared to costs during the strike. Thus so long as the expected date of agreement comes before the strike deadline date, a bargainer will make relatively large demands, but he will make significant concessions before he will permit the expected time of agreement to extend beyond the strike date. If the strike comes, nevertheless, his rate of concession will be reduced because he is no longer faced by a deadline beyond which bargaining costs are again made higher (unless there is a

[27] Bishop [1] has concluded that higher discount rates always tend to reduce a player's payoff, primarily because his model does not consider the dynamics of concession and hence misses part of the influence of the discount rate. Assuming a linear learning model [see equations (10), Sec. XII] and assuming *equal* learning rates, it is not hard to show that our model also yields this result. We might expect the opposite conclusion if the opponent's learning ability is relatively high.

[28] Of course, these second two examples depend upon negotiations between two groups rather than two individuals, and the reader may wish to make some qualifications here. The significance of a shift from individual to group negotiations is probably vastly overrated, however. It is perhaps conceivable that groups should have lower learning rates than individuals, but the most important characteristic of groups—the difficulty of formulating consistent preference functions—is irrelevant from the point of view of our model.

threat of government intervention or some similar event which imposes additional utility costs on him). Thus we would expect labor negotiations to follow a pattern of relatively stable (and low) concession rates at first, rapid concession as the strike deadline approaches, and lower concession rates afterward—a sequence which in fact is commonly observed.[29]

It should be observed that rising costs can bring about a semblance of negotiation without any changes in expectations (i.e., without any equilibrating process) taking place.[30] Thus, for example, as public officials bring increasing pressure upon striking unions and their employers, concessions—the symbols of "responsible collective bargaining"—come about, even to the point of agreement. In the extreme case, the outcome depends only upon the initial conditions and the relative pressures imposed on the two sides, and hence it is essentially arbitrary, having no relationship to the Nash Point or any other theoretical solution. A more appropriate analysis would probably treat this case as a three-way bargaining process—a problem which is beyond the scope of this paper.

We must also point out one rather awkward point in our theory—that is, that our "Nash Point" before a strike is by no means equivalent to the "Nash Point" after a strike. Only if the discounted stream of bargaining costs which appear after the strike are the same for both parties [i.e., $C_1/a = C_2/b$ so that in equation (8), U_1 will equal U_2 whenever $f(\bar{q}_1) = g(M - \bar{q}_2)$] will the Nash solution be the same in both cases. This is really a consequence of our procedure which classifies any state in which agreement does not prevail as a disagreement point. Nash certainly meant his solution to be constant over time, and for this reason, it might be desirable to add this further condition (that the discounted cost streams must be equal) to our earlier set of conditions under which our model yields the Nash Point as its solution. On the other hand, such a procedure would obscure the fact that the bargaining process is heavily influenced by current conditions, and that the costs of such possibilities as strikes or lockouts may never even be relevant in arriving at agreement; to evaluate the agreement in terms of the worst possible form of conflict would not seem to be realistic.

At this point, we may indicate how our model may help us to understand two more of Siegel and Fouraker's observations. Their conclusion (#2, Section II) that increasing (utility) information to both players tends to increase the equality of the payoffs may be taken as an indication that such information (again simply that of having a table of the

[29] For example, see Reynolds [14, p. 182]. We may infer from Raskin's description of the recent New York newspaper strike [13] that this phenomenon appeared in that case as well.

[30] Thus increasing costs (or decreasing value of the payoff over time) are used by both Bishop and Foldes to obtain determinate bargaining models.

opponent's monetary returns as well as one's own) tended to make expectations more realistic as well as more symmetric (when presented with a relatively symmetric bargaining situation, one would tend to expect a symmetric outcome). Furthermore, both players were now in possession of an important common source of information—we would expect this to make their learning abilities relatively more equal. Since we have no reason for believing the players' discount rates to be very different, and since the monetary payoff functions were fairly symmetric, this would all tend to favor the Nash Point where $U_1 = U_2$.

Siegel and Fouraker's conclusion (#3, Section II) that adding to the utility of higher payoffs for one player tended to increase his physical payoff at agreement is easy to treat. Their method was to supplement the return to one player of any payoff above some q' by a fixed increment. Thus the utility function for player I (if he is the favored player) could be written:

$$U_1 = f(q_1 + \xi)e^{-aw}$$

where

$$\xi(q_1, q') \text{ is defined as } \begin{cases} k & \text{if} \quad q_1 > q' \\ 0 & \text{if} \quad q_1 < q' \end{cases}.$$

We may expect a player in these circumstances to behave just as we described in our previous model, except when his payoff approaches q', at which point he will refuse to concede for a considerable time. A concession from q' to $q'-1$ would involve the utility loss associated with $k+1$ payoff units, while saving only as much time as is associated with one payoff unit. This reluctance can be expected to lower his opponent's estimate of his concession rate and cause player II to concede instead (which in turn reduce the usual decline in r_2). Thus even if player I does eventually go below q', the outcome may be expected to favor him. The fact that in several of Siegel and Fouraker's cases, the payoffs to the favored players were significantly above q' would indicate that there was some bluffing taking place as well, causing a player to balk at an inflated demand and forcing the other player to concede much more sharply than before.

We do not mean to imply that we have explained Siegel and Fouraker's results—no empirically untested model could do so—but it is significant that results so similar to theirs can be obtained from our model.

XII. *A Linear Model*

The conclusions of the foregoing model were very qualitative in nature; in fact, we were able to describe a definite solution (the Nash solution) only in a very special case in which the players, for all intents and purposes, were identical. In this section we will make use of a simple linear example of our general model with the principal intent of obtaining a more detailed analysis than we have been able to make heretofore. The results which we derive here, of course, will not be those of a general model, but they should serve nevertheless as useful aids in the estimation of magnitudes which are involved in less restricted bargaining processes.

We shall simplify our learning model by assuming that the players modify their expectations according to a constant proportion of the *error* in their expectations:

$$\dot{r}_2 = \alpha\left[-\dot{q}_2 - r_2\right]$$
$$\text{(10)} \qquad\qquad \dot{r}_1 = \beta\left[-\dot{q}_1 - r_1\right]$$

where α and β are characteristics related to the rates at which players I and II are able to learn.[31] Expressions (10) do satisfy both of the conditions for learning which are set out in expressions (4) and (5) in Section VI.[32]

We have already made limited use of a linearity assumption on the players' utility functions as one means of deriving the Nash solution to the bargaining process (in the case of similar players). For the purposes of this model, we assume that player I has the utility function $U_1 = \xi_1 q_1$ where q_1 is his share of the benefits of agreement (this function is deliberately chosen so that $U_1 = 0$ when $q_1 = 0$). Substituting this function into equation (2), we may solve for player I's demand:

---

[31] These really represent an exponential theory of learning: if $\dot{q}_2$ were constant over time, equations (10) would imply:

$$r_2(t) = \lfloor - q_2 + (r_2)_{t=0} \rfloor e^{-\alpha t}.$$

Exponential forms do appear in the psychology literature: see for example, Poffenberger [12, pp. 296–300].

[32] This assumption also permits us to solve for the slopes of the response functions F and G which we defined as $-A$ and $-B$ respectively (see Section IX). Thus $-A$ may now be written

$$-A \equiv \frac{\partial \dot{q}_1}{\partial \dot{r}_2} \cdot \frac{\partial \dot{r}_2}{\partial \dot{q}_2} = \frac{\alpha}{\dfrac{f''(q_1)}{f'(q_1)} r_2 - a}$$

with a similar expression for $-B$. We noted (in Section IX) that when the condition $AB > 1$ holds, our model of the bargaining process is unstable. Thus it is sufficient for stability to have $A < 1$, $B < 1$, for which, in turn, sufficient conditions are $\alpha < a$, $\beta < b$. In other words, we are assured of stability if each individual's rate of learning is less than his rate of discounting. This conclusion corresponds to our intuitive discussion of instability in Section VIII. If the players' learning rates are high (α, β large) and if they tend to respond markedly to changes in their expectations (a and b small), then an increase in one player's demand (or a reluctance to concede) will give rise to a relatively large concession from the other which, in turn, will reinforce the first player's demands for a larger share of the outcome.

(11)
$$q_1 = \frac{r_2}{a} - \frac{C_1}{\xi_1}\frac{1}{a}.$$

Putting this and our linear learning model into our general model, we may solve for the players' outcome demands as functions of time:

(12)
$$q_1(t) = \frac{1}{a}\left[k_1 d^{x_1 t} + k_2 e^{x_2 t}\right] - \frac{1}{a}\frac{C_1}{\xi_1}$$

$$q_2(t) = \frac{1}{b}\left[m_1 e^{x_1 t} + m_2 e^{x_2 t}\right] - \frac{1}{b}\frac{C_2}{\xi_2}$$

where $k_1 > 0$, $k_2 \gtrless 0$, $m_1 > 0$, $m_2 \gtrless 0$, $x_1 < 0$, and $x_2 < 0$ are various dynamic parameters.[33]

By making use of this model, we may, of course, derive all of the general conclusions which we obtained earlier. It should be emphasized here that although r_1 and r_2 approach their equilibrium relationship only asymptotically, equations (12) indicate that a state of agreement is approached more directly. This fact may be more clear from the example of equations (12) which is plotted on the graph in Figure 4. Here we have graphed player I's outcome demand (q_1) and the residual which player II's demand implicitly leaves to player I, ($M - q_2$), against time. Agreement occurs when $q_1 = M - q_2$.

For certain values of t, equations (12) may yield values for q_1 and q_2 which are beyond the resources of the bargaining situation (the dashed lines in Figure 4). In these cases, a player simply demands the maximum payoff which is possible. Notice, though, that the mechanism of our model does not operate under such circumstances, since the rate of change of such a player's demand is zero even when his expectations are changing. It is not until both players are within the boundaries of the bargaining situation that our analysis will hold.

$$x_1 \equiv \frac{-\alpha - \beta + \sigma}{2(1 - AB)}$$

$$x_2 \equiv \frac{-\alpha - \beta - \sigma}{2(1 - AB)}$$

$$k_1 \equiv \frac{1}{\sigma}\left[\beta A r_2' + \tfrac{1}{2}(\alpha - \beta + \sigma)r_1'\right]$$

$$m_1 \equiv \frac{1}{\sigma}\left[\alpha B r_1' + \tfrac{1}{2}(-\alpha + \beta - \sigma)r_2'\right]$$

$$k_1 + k_2 = r_1'$$

$$m_1 + m_2 = r_2'$$

$$\sigma = \left|\,[(\alpha - \beta)^2 + 4\alpha\beta A B]^{1/2}\,\right|$$

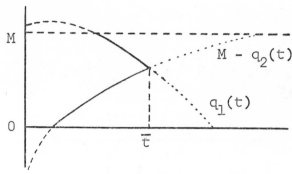

FIGURE 4

We can determine the amount of time necessary for agreement, $\bar{t}$, by solving the agreement condition:

$$q_1(\bar{t}) + q_2(\bar{t}) = M$$

for $\bar{t}$. If we substitute equations (12) into this expression, we could, in principle, obtain $\bar{t}$. The resulting expression is too complicated for direct solution, however, and so we will simplify our example further by applying the "similarity" conditions ($a=b$, $\alpha=\beta$) to the model. We may then solve the above equation for $\bar{t}$:

$$(13) \qquad \bar{t} = -\left[\frac{1}{\alpha} + \frac{1}{a}\right] \ln \left[\frac{\dfrac{C_1}{a\xi_1} + \dfrac{C_2}{a\xi_2} + M}{\dfrac{r_1'}{a} + \dfrac{r_2'}{a}}\right].$$

From equation (11), and the essential bargaining condition that $q_1 + q_2 > M$ at time $t=0$, we may conclude that the expression in the brackets of equation (13) must be positive but less than 1, and therefore that the logarithm of that quantity must be negative.

From expression (13), we may again deduce the conclusion that higher values of C (higher bargaining costs) decrease the necessary amount of bargaining time. It should be remembered that higher bargaining costs hasten agreement only by reducing the player's demands at any given level of expectations. Bargaining costs in this model have no influence over the players' expectations (of one another's concession rates) or their rates of change. Thus the level of costs (if it remains fixed) does not affect the rate at which concession takes place.

Expression (13) also indicates that higher rates of learning (for both players) reduce the time required by the bargaining process, as will higher rates of discounting. We note, however, that although an increase in player I's discount rate, a, reduces $\bar{t}$, it need not reduce the product

$a\bar{t}$; if it does reduce this expression, too, then the higher discount rate is advantageous to the two players because it increases the expected value to each of them of the whole bargaining process—that is, the discount factor $e^{-a\bar{t}}$ is nearer unity.

Knowing the total bargaining time, $\bar{t}$, it is possible to determine the actual point of agreement by substituting the value for $\bar{t}$ [equation (13)] into equation (12) in order to obtain $q_1(\bar{t})$ and/or $q_2(\bar{t})$:

$$(14) \quad q_1(\bar{t}) = \frac{M}{2} - \frac{1}{2}\frac{C_1}{a\xi_1} + \frac{1}{2}\frac{C_2}{a\xi_2} + \frac{r_1' - r_2'}{2a}\left[\frac{\dfrac{C_1}{a\xi_1} + \dfrac{C_2}{a\xi_2} + M}{\dfrac{r_1'}{a} + \dfrac{r_2'}{a}}\right]^{a+\alpha/a-\alpha}$$

where r_1' and r_2' are the expected concession rates at the start of the bargaining process. We observe that the first three terms on the right of equation (14) correspond to the solution for the symmetric case which we derived in Section X.[34] Thus, equation (14) is significant in that the far right-hand term gives us the *deviation* of the actual bargaining outcome from the "ideal" solution which would appear if bargaining took an infinite amount of time. The fact that the condition $r_1/r_2 = 1$ is only approached asymptotically implies that since agreement in this model takes a finite time, the outcome will not correspond to the "predicted" solution if the initial expected concession rates (r_1' and r_2') are not equal. Besides the obvious conclusion that greater discrepancies between the two initially expected concession rates result in a greater error in our model in predicting the actual outcome, we observe from equation (14) that small values of C_1 and C_2 (the bargaining costs) will tend to decrease the deviation as well. This last conclusion is simply a consequence of the fact that high costs tend to reduce the time taken by the bargaining process and thus give the ratio r_1/r_2 less time to adjust to its stable value. Higher rates of learning will decrease the error in spite of their tendency to accelerate bargaining, because they bring about more

---

[34] That is, equation (7) becomes

$$\frac{\xi_1}{\xi_2} = +\frac{\xi_1 q_1 + \dfrac{C_1}{a}}{\xi_2(M - q_1) + \dfrac{C_2}{a}}$$

which reduces to

$$q_1 = \frac{1}{2}\left[M - \frac{C_1}{a\xi_1} + \frac{C_2}{a\xi_2}\right].$$

This is simply the symmetric Nash outcome which we mention in footnote 3.

rapid adjustments of r_1 and r_2 as well. The impact of changes in the discount rate, a, is ambiguous, although in most reasonable cases increases in the discount rate can be shown to increase the error.[35] This is because increases in the discount rate tend to decrease bargaining time by reducing initial demands [see equation (3)] as well as by increasing the adjustment rates of r_1 and r_2 (the first of these tends to increase the error, the second to decrease it—hence the ambiguity).

Finally, it must be remembered that the error term here is really only approximate. Even if the players' learning behavior and the utility functions actually are linear as we have assumed, our results depend upon the instantaneous learning model which was chosen for our example. We are actually studying only the behavior of the intersection of the functions F and G (see Section IX) without regard to any time lags which may appear in arriving at that intersection. Lagged models would naturally alter our error term somewhat.

XIII. *A Numerical Example*

In conclusion, it may prove to be interesting to put some numbers which correspond roughly to our own experience into this model in order to get some indications of the magnitudes of the quantities which are involved. For the sake of variety, we will assume that the total amount of the payoff commodity which is to be divided is variable or unknown, in which case the P-index measure of the players' outcome demands is more appropriate than our quantity notation (see Section IV). Such a model is obtained simply by substituting P_1 for q_1, and $M - P_2$ for q_2 in all our equations, where M is now to be interpreted as the maximum value to which the P-index can attain (M is constant in this interpretation, even if the total quantity whose division is indicated by P is not). As we have already pointed out, except for a few changes in sign (which are necessary to preserve the meaning of our expressions), the model is unchanged, and as it happens, equations (13) and (14) retain their forms completely (with P_1 substituted for q_1).

Imagine a labor-management negotiation in which the wage may range between 0 and 100 (at 100, the firm goes out of business—the total surplus which is being divided implicitly by the wage becomes zero).[36] We have a complete solution only for the symmetrical case; so we must assume the same discount and learning rates for both parties. Suppose the discount rate (a) is .25, and the learning rate (α) is .20,

---

[35] Take logs and compare the expressions d/da (ln a) with d/da $[(a-\alpha)/(a+\alpha)]$.

[36] This, of course, makes linear utility functions impossible over the whole range of P—we shall only assume that the functions are linear in the relatively small range over which the bargaining takes place.

both on a yearly basis. Neither bargainer in a union-management dispute has any illusions about being able to obtain either the entire surplus or a substantially larger portion of it for himself, nor does either expect to be able to obtain large rapid concessions from the other—experience has shown that this is unlikely (and analysis of a model in which the players expect rapid concessions would suffice to show how such experience may come about). Thus let us assume initial expected concession rates of $r_1' = 12.5$ and $r_2' = 17.5$ where these are also on a yearly basis.

Consider first a case with no bargaining costs. In this case, expression (13) gives us a $\bar{t} = 1.67$; that is, it takes over a year and a half to reach agreement. On the other hand, the deviation from the "predicted" solution is only -1.87; that is, the wage turns out to be 48.13 instead of 50 as is predicted by the simple model. This is not a large deviation considering the large discrepancy between r_1' and r_2' (i.e., the initial demands—given by equation (11)—are given by a union demand of 50, and a management offer of only 30).

Now let us add bargaining costs to the situation. Suppose the costs to the union are fairly high, and $C_1/\xi_1 = 3$, while the costs to the management are lower: $C_1/\xi_1 = 1$. These are sufficient to shorten the bargaining time to about .3 years, or four months (bargaining costs which summed to five or more would bring about immediate agreement[37]). In this case, however, the deviation from the predicted outcome is -7.33; that is, the union gets a wage 7.33 less than would be predicted. It should be noticed also that the disproportionate costs have shifted the expected (Nash) solution. The predicted solution is now 46, having moved in management's favor because of the higher bargaining costs to the union. In view of these results, it is not hard to surmise why international negotiations, where learning and discount rates are probably lower than in the above example, expectations may be more optimistic, and bargaining costs are practically zero, can last for years, although for that same reason we would expect that the outcomes will be fairly near to the Nash solution.

The above results are fairly sensitive to changes in the data. For example, a decrease in the learning rate from .20 to .15 in the case of zero bargaining costs has the consequence of increasing the length of the bargaining time to 1.95 and of increasing the error in the general prediction to -4.83. On the other hand, more similar values r_1' and r_2' would bring about a considerable reduction in the deviation (i.e., if

---

[37] We have not put down the costs C_1 or C_2 explicitly; we are simply assuming the costs to be such that when they are appropriately adjusted by the utility factors ξ_1 and ξ_2, they may be compared to a change in 3 and 1 units of P (in one year) respectively.

the difference $r_1' - r_2'$ were reduced to 2.5, the deviation would be halved).

REFERENCES

1. R. L. BISHOP, "Game-Theoretic Analyses of Bargaining," *Quart. Jour. Econ.*, Nov. 1963, *77*, 559–602.
2. ———, "A Zeuthen-Hicks Model of the Bargaining Process," forthcoming in *Econometrica*.
3. R. R. BUSH AND F. MOSTELLER, *Stochastic Models for Learning*. New York 1955.
4. L. FOLDES, "A Determinante Model of Bilateral Monopoly," *Economica*, May 1964, *31*, 117–31.
5. J. C. HARSANYI, "Approaches to the Bargaining Problem Before and After the Theory of Games: A Critical Discussion of Zeuthen's, Hicks', and Nash's Theories," *Econometrica*, April 1956, *24*, 144–57.
6. J. R. HICKS, *The Theory of Wages*. London 1935.
7. E. R. HILGARD, *Theories of Learning*. New York 1956.
8. R. D. LUCE AND H. RAIFFA, *Games and Decisions*. New York 1957.
9. J. P. NASH, "The Bargaining Problem," *Econometrica*, April 1950, *18*, 155–62.
10. J. PEN, "A General Theory of Bargaining," *Am. Econ. Rev.*, March 1952, *42*, 24–42.
11. ———, *The Wage Rate Under Collective Bargaining*. Cambridge, Mass. 1959.
12. A. T. POFFENBERGER, ed., *Modern Learning Theory*. New York 1954.
13. A. H. RASKIN, "The New York Newspaper Strike," *New York Times*, April 1, 1963.
14. L. G. REYNOLDS, *Labor Economics and Labor Relations*. Englewood Cliffs 1959.
15. T. C. SCHELLING, *The Strategy of Conflict*. Cambridge 1960.
16. S. SIEGEL AND L. E. FOURAKER, *Bargaining and Group Decision Making*. New York 1960.
17. K. W. SPENSE, *Behavior Theory and Learning*. Englewood Cliffs 1960.
18. R. H. STROTZ, "Myopia and Inconsistency in Dynamic Utility Maximization," *Rev. Econ. Stud.*, 1956 (3), *23*, 165–80.
19. F. ZEUTHEN, "Du Monopole Bilateral," *Revue d'Economie Politique*, 1933, *47*, 1651–70.
20. ———, *Problems of Monopoly and Economic Warfare*. London 1930.

A THEORY OF THE BARGAINING PROCESS

COMMENT: *Alan Coddington*
REPLY: *John G. Cross*

J. G. Cross's theory of the bargaining process is composed of three elements: a theory of decision-making, a theory of expectations, and a theory of learning. The theory of decision-making consists of the maximization of the present value of an expected payoff, in utility terms, and this aspect of Cross's work will not be questioned in the present paper. The theory of expectations, however, will be examined from the point of view of both empirical plausibility and theoretical fruitfulness, and as a result of this analysis a reinterpretation will be suggested. This will be shown to have repercussions not only within the learning part of the model, but also for the predictions of the theory as a whole. It will be argued that the revised model has some relevance to a bargaining situation of considerable theoretical interest and practical importance, which could not otherwise have been treated within the framework of the Cross theory. This is a bargaining situation involving "brinkmanship."

I. *Bargainer's Expectations*

The particular aspect of the theory of expectations which I would like to examine is that concerning each bargainer's expectations of the other's concession rate. Obviously, relatively simple assumptions must be made about the behavior of such rates if an analytically manageable model is to be built. However, by making the particular assumption that he does, Cross automatically excludes from his theory a particularly interesting case—that of bargaining involving brinkmanship. What I mean here by a brinkmanship situation is one in which a bargainer expects his opponent to make a concession at some point in the future and, in the light of this expectation, is prepared to wait, making no concession himself. Casual observation seems to suggest that this brinkmanship type of situation is one that typically occurs in bargaining processes.

Let us confine our attention, as Cross does, to the pure intransigence case of bargaining, i.e., the case where each bargainer always expects to obtain agreement at his own current demand. Using the Cross notation, we have utility functions $f(q_1)$, $g(q_2)$ defined over the quantity variables q_1, q_2 where q_1 is I's share of Q, q_2 is II's share, and the total amount of Q is M. Disagreement occurs when the demands $q_1 + q_2 > M$, and the amount of disagreement (i.e., the total concessions which must be made before agreement is possible) is $(q_1 + q_2 - M)$. In his paper Cross supposes that each bargainer expects the other to concede at a certain rate, i.e., he expects the other to make a continuous series of demands with no discrete jumps. Thus, if I expects II to concede at the rate r_2, he is expecting that $-(dq_2/dt)=r_2$. However, each expects the other to start conceding, but neither intends making any concession himself. According to Cross, each bargainer immediately begins to modify his expectations of the other's concession rate, since in general

$$-\left(\frac{dq_1}{dt}\right)_{t=0} \neq r_1$$

$$-\left(\frac{dq_2}{dt}\right)_{t=0} \neq r_2;$$

and hence the expectations r_1, r_2 must change. These new expectations due to learning feed back into the equation by which each made his original optimal choice of q_j, and a new optimal q_j can be found in each case. And what looks like a new optimum to the bargainer who made it, looks like a concession (or retraction) to the other. Hence the r_j are further modified, and so it goes on.

Let us focus our attention on the form of expectations the bargainers are assumed to have. According to Cross's assumptions each bargainer expects the other to concede at a constant rate over future time (although this rate which is constant over future time may in fact change as present time elapses). It is my contention that bargainers are typically faced with a different form of expectation from this one, the difference being one which materially affects the workings of Cross's model.

In practice, each bargainer typically expects any concession to occur in a sudden discrete lump.[1] Thus, in the pure intransigence case where each bargainer expects the other to agree to his own demand, I may expect II to make the whole concession suddenly from q_2 to $M-q_1$ at or before some point in the future, t_2, and II may expect I to make the whole concession suddenly from q_1 to $M-q_2$ at or before some point in the future, t_1. Thus if neither bargainer has made any concession up to some point in time which is less than both t_1 and t_2, the situation is quite consistent with the expectations of each bargainer. Hence, neither bargainer will modify his expectations as a result of the other's failure to concede during this period, as they would under Cross's assumptions. In fact no learning can occur in this case until the time $t=\min(t_1, t_2)$, at which point one of the bargainers must modify his original expectations.

It is here that an interesting asymmetry, which was absent in Cross's theory, arises. Whereas with Cross's theory the bargainers could learn that their estimates of the concession rate were correct or too large or too small, learning in the present theory is confined to discovering that the estimate of the time before the other bargainer concedes completely is too small.

---

[1] What I am arguing against here is not the assumption of continuity by the use of differential equations rather than difference equations, which is a legitimate analytical approximation, but rather the assumption that the expected rates of concession r_j are independent of future time.

Whereas Cross's estimated concession rates r_j can increase or decrease as a result of learning, the times t_1, t_2 in the brinkmanship theory can only increase as a result of learning.

Bargainers whose expectations run along brinkmanship rather than constant-concession-rate lines are not in a position to engage in the kind of learning process which is basic to the Cross theory. We will perhaps understand this better if we consider both kinds of expectation as special cases of the general case: the expected concession rate of bargainer II is a function of future time, $R_2(t)$. The expected time elapsing before agreement occurs, w, is then given implicitly by

(1)
$$\int_0^w R_2(t)dt = -(q_1 + q_2 - M).$$

Following R. H. Strotz [2] and Cross [1], the optimal choice of q_1 is given by the condition that the present value of I's expected payoff, $f(q_1)e^{-aw}$, is a maximum with respect to the choice of q_1 (neglecting any fixed costs of bargaining per period, since these add nothing new in principle to the discussion).

$$\frac{d}{dq_1} f(q_1)e^{-aw} = 0$$

i.e.,
$$f'(q_1) - af(q_1)\frac{dw}{dq_1} = 0$$

(2)
$$f'(q_1) + a\frac{f(q_1)}{R_2(w)} = 0$$

since
$$\frac{dw}{dq_1} = \frac{-1}{R_2(w)}.$$

Now $R_2(t)$ is bargainer I's guess at the value of $-(dq_2/dt)$ at time t after the start of the bargaining. After time t_0 has elapsed, I knows the value of $-(dq_2/dt)$ for all $t \leq t_0$, and hence I can learn about the function $R_2(t)$ in the interval $0 \leq t \leq t_0$. However, in order to solve equation (1) for w, for any given q_1, I will in general have to estimate $R_2(t)$ for $t > t_0$. It may be possible for a bargainer to use the learning about $R_2(t)$ for $t \leq t_0$ to modify his expectation of $R_2(t)$ for $t > t_0$, but it is here that the two special cases arise. These, together with the general case, are shown in Figure 1. This figure displays various assumptions which could be made about the expectations which each bargainer has of the other's concession behavior. The most general assumption would be that bargainer I, say, expects II's demand to be some (well-behaved) function of future time which, in the above notation, will be given by

$$q_2(t) = \overset{0}{q_2} + \int_0^t R_2(z)dz$$

(where the ith demand of the jth bargainer is q_j^i). Such an assumption is not very fruitful, since it is devoid of any implication regarding the workings of the model. A more restrictive assumption is shown as the Cross case. This involves expecting that the other bargainer's demand will decrease linearly with future time or, in other words, that he will concede at a constant rate. The brinkmanship assumption, on the other hand, restricts the form of expectation in another way. What is expected here is that a time

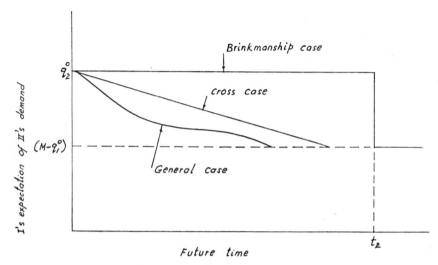

FIGURE 1. EXPECTATIONS OF CONCESSION BEHAVIOR

will come (t_2) at which the other bargainer will give in to the demand which is being made of him.

Let us examine the effect of learning in the circumstances characterized by the three different forms of expectations represented in Figure 1.

1. In the case of the Cross assumption, any learning about II's concession rate, $-(dq_2/dt)$, for $t>0$ will, at that particular instant, modify the slope of the line for all future time in an unambiguous way (i.e., the slope is correct or too big or too small at that particular instant).

2. In the general case, any learning about $-(dq_2/dt)$ for $t \le t_0$ modifies $R_2(t)$ for $t \le t_0$ and could conceivably be used to make modifications of $R_2(t)$ for $t > t_0$, but not in an unambiguous way. However, if one could develop a reasonable learning model for this general case, then, with any well-behaved R-function, this modification of the Cross theory would presumably yield a determinate solution through the process of utility maximization by each bargainer. (We note that the R-function in the pure brinkmanship case is not well behaved in that it is not differentiable at $t=t_2$.

3. In the brinkmanship case any learning about q_2 for $t \leq t_0$ does not modify the curve at all if $t_0 < t_2$ and $t = t_2$ is the only point at which it can be modified. A learning model to account for this case would differ from Cross's in an essential way.

We see that as we examine different forms of expectations regarding concessions from the other bargainer, Cross's learning-concession process works in the special case of expected concession rates constant over future time, runs into difficulties in the general case of expected concession rates a function of future time, and breaks down in the brinksmanship case. (That is to say, it breaks down in the sense that it would not yield a solution in the absence of a considerably modified learning model.) Thus, bargaining processes in which expectations of brinkmanship are an essential component would require a development of Cross's theory to describe them adequately. We here outline a possible development in this direction.

II. *A Brinkmanship Model*

In the brinkmanship case, I expects II to give in completely to his own demand, q_1, after holding out for a time t_2. Thus, if we apply the principle of utility maximization to predict I's choice of the value of q_1, we find no limit imposed. With the theory as it stands, utility maximization would require that I demands the largest q_1 which is possible, i.e., $q_1 = M$. Similarly, this principle would require II to demand $q_2 = M$. This rather barren position can be avoided by reasoning as follows: I knows that, if q_2^i is II's demand, he can have $q_1 = (M - q_2^i)$ immediately, but demands for $q_1 > (M - q_2^i)$ will take longer to obtain (and similarly for II). We suppose, then, that each bargainer expects the time which the other will hold out before giving in completely to be a function of his own demand. I expects $t_2 = F(q_1)$, II expects $t_1 = G(q_2)$. Following Cross in making a linear assumption, we have:[2]

$$(3) \qquad\qquad t_2 = U(q_1 + \overset{0}{q_2} - M)$$

[2] It could be argued that the linear expectations used here and in Cross's theory are not economically plausible since each bargainer knows that no bargain will ever be concluded outside the contract zone, i.e., there should be no finite t_2 corresponding to $q_1 > M$ and no finite t_1 corresponding to $q_2 > M$. (In practice, things are a bit fuzzier than this because neither bargainer knows the size of M exactly.) The linear functions, however, yield a finite t_j for any q_k, however large.

Plausible nonlinear functions expressing the expectations within the contract zone would be, for example:

$$t_2 = \frac{S_1(q_1 + \overset{0}{q_2} - M)}{(M - q_1)}, \qquad q_1 \leq M$$

$$t_1 = \frac{S_2(\overset{0}{q_1} + q_2 - M)}{(M - q_2)}, \qquad q_2 \leq M.$$

Here the times become infinite as the ends of the contract zone are reached. Such refinements are not considered here since they raise many issues which are not directly relevant to the argument of this paper.

(4) $$t_1 = V(\overset{0}{q_1} + q_2 - M)$$

where U, V can, for the moment, be thought of as parameters.

If we assume discounting functions e^{-at} for I and e^{-bt} for II, then the present value to I of the demand q_1 is $f(q_1)e^{-at_2}$ where t_2 is given by (3). The condition that q_1 maximizes this expression is

(5) $$f'(q_1) - aUf(q_1) = 0.$$

And similarly for II,

(6) $$g'(q_2) - bVg(q_2) = 0.$$

These are the conditions that each bargainer makes, in the light of his own expectations, an optimal demand.

Suppose the original q_1, q_2 at $t=0$ are such that

$$t_2 = \overset{0}{t_2} < t_1 = \overset{0}{t_1}.^3$$

I cannot do any learning until $t=\overset{0}{t_2}$ and II cannot do any until $t=\overset{0}{t_1}$. Thus, in our case of $\overset{0}{t_2}<\overset{0}{t_1}$, I is the first to do any learning. At time $t=\overset{0}{t_2}$ I observes that II does not give in and realizes that his expectation of t_2 was wrong. Thus he wishes to revise his estimate, and we may suppose that he comes to the conclusion that he has been associating too low a value of t_2 with each value of q_1. I's learning will therefore lead to an upward shift in his t_2-function, although we still must have $t_2=0$ when $q_1=(M-q_2^0)$. The t_2-function pivots upwards about $q_1=(M-q_2^0)$ as a result of learning. This result follows from supposing that

$$U = U_0 \qquad \text{when } t \leq \overset{0}{t_2}$$

$$U = U_1 > U_0 \quad \text{when } \overset{0}{t_2} < t \leq \overset{1}{t_2}$$

or, in general,

(7) $$U = U_{i+1} > U_i \quad \text{when } \overset{i}{t_2} < t \leq \overset{i+1}{t_2}.$$

Similarly, for II we would have

(8) $$V = V_{i+1} > V_i \quad \text{when } \overset{i}{t_1} < t \leq \overset{i+1}{t_1}.$$

This then is the basis of a modified learning theory applicable to the brinkmanship case.

---

3 If I makes the first demand he will have to use an estimate of q_2^0, $q_2=q_2$, say, this being the demand he expects II to make. This yields an expected delay time $t_2=t_2^*$. However, as soon as II's actual demand q_2^0 becomes known (still at $t=0$) q_2^* is replaced by q_2^0 and t_2^* is modified to $t_2^0=U(q_1^0+q_2^0-M)$.

Let us examine the workings of this model. After a time $t < t_2$ has elapsed, the present value of I's expected payoff is $f(q_1)e^{-a(t_2-t)}$, and the q_1 which maximizes this is given by

$$f'(q_1) - a\frac{dt_2}{dq_1}f(q_1) = 0,$$

which is identical with (5) above since $dt_2/dq_1 = U$. Hence, although the present value of I's expected payoff is increasing as time passes, the value of q_1 which maximizes it is invariant with respect to time, so long, of course, as the parameters remain unchanged.

The q_1 which satisfies (5) can be thought of as the solution of the pair of simultaneous equations

(9) $$y = f'(q_1)$$

(10) $$y = aUf(q_1).$$

Consider now what happens when I learns at time t_2^0 and increases the value of U. As shown in Figure 2, the function OS will shift upwards to OT, giving a new value for the optimal q_1, OB. This will be less than the previous value, OA. Thus I makes a concession AB. Here we are faced with a similar

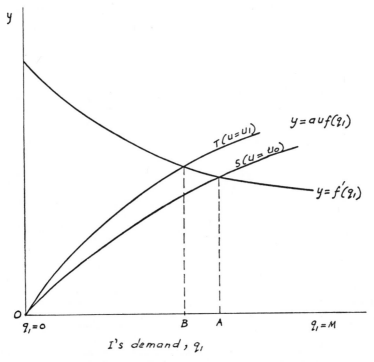

FIGURE 2. THE OPTIMAL-DEMAND DECISION

paradox to that which Cross observed in connection with the intransigence aspect of the theory. Each bargainer expects the other to make complete concessions $q_1 \to (M - q_2)$ and $q_2 \to (M - q_1)$, but each himself only makes what are in general partial concessions (like AB). Any change in q_1 could be a complete concession if U increases enough to bring the intersection above or to the left of $q_1 = (M - q_2)$.

When II observes I make a partial concession at a time t_2^0, he does not regard this as inconsistent with his expectation that I will give in completely at or before $t = t_1^0 (> t_2^0)$. Hence II does not do any learning until $t = t^0_1$, in which case V increases, giving a new value for $t_1 (t_1^1 > t_1^0)$,[4] and a new optimal q_2 less than the previous one.

Thus, since each change of demand by one or the other bargainer represents a partial concession and not a retraction, the learning-concession process should lead eventually to an agreement. A learning theory consistent with (7) and (8) but giving the actual changes in U, V, and hence in t_1, t_2, would enable a solution to be derived.

Whereas in Cross's original version changes in demands could be concessions or retractions, in this brinkmanship version of the theory, all the changes in demands are concessions. The reason for this is that when a bargainer gets to the time at which he expects a complete concession, he can learn that his estimate of the time was correct (if the other gives in) or that it was too small (if the other does not give in). Thus, learning in the brinkmanship model always consists in increasing the expectation of the time t_1 (or t_2), i.e., in increasing U or V. (In Cross's theory the rates r_1, r_2 could increase or decrease as a result of learning.) Thus, the function $y = aUf(q_1)$ can shift upwards but not downwards. Since $y = f'(q_1)$ is a strictly decreasing function of q_1, by the assumption of diminishing marginal utility, we can see that if $y = aUf(q_1)$ (which is a strictly increasing function of q_1) shifts upwards, it must always intersect $y = f'(q_1)$ at a smaller value of q_1, i.e., the change of q_1, being a decrease, represents a concession and not a retraction.

This analysis may cast some light on one of Cross's comments. He says [1, p. 76]:

> Often, retraction of an offer during negotiation is thought to be either unethical or at least undesirable because of the unfavorable utility shifts which such behavior may induce in the other player. . . . Nevertheless, such retractions sometimes occur in practice. We will, therefore, retain the possibility of their occurrence, recognizing that forces probably exist which discourage increases in demands during the course of negotiations.

It seems that the model here developed displays the forces which discourage increases in demands during the course of the negotiations by taking into account the brinkmanship aspects of the bargaining process.

---

[4] In order for $t_1^i > t_1^{i-1}$ we require that $dt_1/dq_2 < 0$, since q_2 cannot increase over time. It can be shown that a sufficient condition for this is $t_2 > 1/a$. (In fact this is a rather strong condition and, in general, t_2 does not have to be as large as this for the condition to hold.) Similarly, we require $t_1 > 1/b$. To simplify the analysis we assume that these conditions are satisfied.

In summary, it seems that one aspect of Cross's model which is over-restrictive, in the sense that it appears openly inconsistent with casual observation, is the assumption of the expectation of a rate of concession independent of future time. However, it would appear that, with the type of modifications suggested above, the essence of Cross's argument would remain. It would still be possible, as has been indicated, to construct a determinate, descriptive theory of the bargaining process based on the utility-maximizing behavior of individuals.

ALAN CODDINGTON*

* The author is the Ellis Hunter Memorial Fellow in Economics at the University of York. He would like to thank John H. Williamson for his valuable advice and comments on earlier versions of this paper.

REFERENCES

1. J. G. CROSS, "A Theory of the Bargaining Process," *Am. Econ. Rev.*, March 1965, *55*, 67–94.
2. R. H. STROTZ, "Myopia and Inconsistency in Dynamic Utility Maximization," *Rev. Econ. Stud.*, 1956, *23*(3), 165–80.

REPLY: *John G. Cross*

There is little doubt that concessions during the bargaining process are composed of discrete lumps. The presence of indivisible components of the payoff is by itself sufficient for this conclusion and furthermore there is substantial evidence that bluffing behavior tends to bring about discontinuous changes in explicit demands as well. Alan Coddington's primary objection to my model is not that assuming a constant concession rate makes for a poor approximation to discrete reality, however, but rather that even "casual observation"(!) suggests that negotiators expect no concessions at all until a time of utter capitulation is reached. Since expectations themselves are generally not observable under any but the most carefully controlled experimental circumstances, I conclude that Coddington is inferring his hypothesis from observations of bargaining *behavior*. This, then, is in part an empirical question. Of course one can find many examples of negotiations in which initial demands are preserved over considerable periods before any concessions are made. These circumstances, however, need not be associated with discontinuous expectations, for they are easily attributable to the presence of bluffing behavior and to the absence of any substantial disagreement costs as well (e.g., the strike date may still be six weeks away and, although initial positions have been outlined, serious negotiations have not yet even begun). Furthermore, both logical and empirical considerations lead me to be skeptical about Coddington's hypothesis:

1. Coddington's own model predicts that the negotiators will concede continuously after some point in time. Logically, it is hard to see why experienced negotiators would not come eventually to *expect* such behavior.

We are asked to accept a model in which an individual's expectations lead to outcomes which are fundamentally different from those anticipated, and yet in which subsequent negotiations are approached with expectations which are unchanged from their original form! Coddington attempts to avoid this dilemma by assuming that each player simply disregards any of his opponent's concessions which fall short of utter capitulation, but again one must be nagged by the realization that each player knows that his own concessions *do* reflect his own preferences and expectations, and hence that they should not be disregarded.

2. Experimental evidence does not support Coddington's suggestion that a substantial period will pass without serious concessions. For example, Figure 1 contains a plot of a typical case from Siegel and Fouraker's [2] bargaining experiments.[1] Concessions here take place immediately and, in fact, they are virtually continuous.

3. Empirical studies place so much significance upon the *sequence* of concessions that it is hard to believe that they would not be taken seriously by the negotiators themselves. For example, in a recent study, R. W. Walton and R. B. McKersie specifically state that "the alternation of concessions is not a mechanical process. *Each side is alert to the meaning of the other's concession*" [3, p. 88, italics added]. That is, not only are concessions *expected*, but they are deliberately analyzed for new information.

A related point deals with Coddington's suggestion that even very large concessions coming long before the expected capitulation date will not influence the behavior of a negotiator. This position also appears to be implausible on empirical grounds. For example, Walton and McKersie devote some time to the dangers of "signalling weakness" to an opponent through one's own concession behavior [3, pp. 89–90]. Furthermore, as Coddington realizes, his hypothesis would preclude the retraction of bids during negotiations—a phenomenon which is far from uncommon in experience. I am afraid that Coddington has misinterpreted those statements which I made regarding the retraction of bids, and which he has quoted in his *Comment*. I was by no means searching for economic forces which could prevent "undesirable" demand retractions. In fact, it should be emphasized that my statements were meant to reflect my decision to reject just such a model as Coddington has proposed. The point is that any mechanistic model of behavior must either introduce psychological variables relevant to the environment in which the operation takes place or it must not be construed to cover situations in which that environment is likely to be altered drastically. Retractions can generate resentment, and the resulting change in psychological atmosphere can alter the whole course of the bargaining process. (Indeed, in many historical cases, it has.) Thus I was not seeking a device to *prevent* retractions, but rather was expressing doubt that their extent and frequency could be described adequately without a more psychologically-oriented model.

---

[1] Figure 1 is reproduced from Figure 5.2, page 78, S. Siegel and L. E. Fouraker, *Bargaining and Group Decision Making* (New York, McGraw-Hill Book Company, 1960) with permission from the publisher.

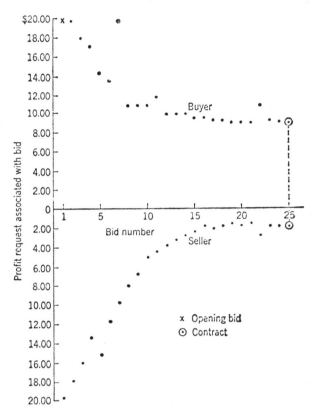

FIGURE 1

Source: From *Bargaining and Group Decision-Making* by S. Siegel and L. Fouraker. Copyright 1960 by McGraw-Hill Book Company. Used by permission.

Coddington states that his modifications do not affect the determinacy of the model. This is not strictly true. Although his model does have a determinate solution, his refusal to permit intermediate concessions to influence the learning process has eliminated a crucial interdependence which was present in my original formulation. Suppose that we consider one bargainer in Coddington's model. This individual makes a bid, say q_1^0, which he maintains over a period t_0; after t_0, if his opponent has not already capitulated, he begins to concede regardless of what his opponent may be doing. If the other never concedes at all, the first player will eventually give in all the way to $q_1 = M - q_2^0$. The important point is that, under Coddington's formulation, *until agreement is reached, each player's time path of concessions is completely independent of the other's behavior,* and, in fact, each player's concessions are determined solely by his own initial expectations and by the nature of his own learning process. The outcome, of course, is dependent upon the same variables. A major aspect of my own model was the demonstration of the existence of an equilibrium process during negotiation, such that within the limits imposed by the finite time dimension of bargaining, the outcome is *independent of initial expectations* (and hence of the initial demands). Of course, neat dynamic properties of economic models cannot be taken as indicators of their empirical validity, and for this reason, it would be unfair to cite these properties as a criticism of Coddington's comment. Nevertheless, I think this distinction between the workings of the two models is extremely important; if the equilibrium process does not hold, we must conclude that random variations in initial expectations are directly reflected in bargaining outcomes, and our hopes of constructing a model, capable of reasonably accurate prediction, must be greatly dimmed.

Finally, the generalized expected-concessions function, $R(t)$, is a useful addition to the theory. As Coddington points out, it is not difficult in principle to deal with this function. The learning model can be simpler than he supposes, however. For the simple model, we needed only the learning condition that the expected concession rate was increased whenever actual concessions were found to exceed expectations, and vice versa. In the general case, when the expected rates are found to underestimate reality, we would have the value of

$$\int_0^{q_1+q_2-m} \frac{1}{R(t)} \, dq,$$

decreasing for all values of (q_1+q_2-M). (Although Coddington does not mention it, it is likely that the function $R(t)$ is dependent upon M as well as upon time and the learning process.) The model can then be carried through just as before, with the forms of the $R(t)$ functions becoming important additional parameters in the determination of negotiation outcomes. For example, it can be shown (if it is not already obvious) that, even if the two parties expect the bargaining process to take the same total amount of time, the outcome, *ceteris paribus*, will be biased against the party who expects his opponent to concede at the higher initial rate.

JOHN G. CROSS*

* The author is assistant professor of economics at the University of Michigan.

REFERENCES

1. J. CROSS, "A Theory of the Bargaining Process," *Am. Econ. Rev.*, March 1965, *55*, 67–94.
2. S. SIEGEL AND L. E. FOURAKER, *Bargaining and Group Decision Making.* New York 1960.
3. R. E. WALTON AND R. B. MCKERSIE, *A Behavioral Theory of Labor Negotiations.* New York 1965.

THE RESOLUTION OF CONFLICT

M. B. Nicholson

SUMMARY

The paper deals with the resolution of conflict by bargaining, a term which is defined broadly. It is more concerned with the actual results of bargains than "fair" results, and discusses some conditions under which one party concedes to another in a bargaining situation. The difficult and ambiguous role of information in bargaining is also discussed.

THIS paper makes no pretence to be an endeavour to provide a simple or even a complex set of rules whose application will enable all conflicts to be resolved in socially harmless ways. I wish I could do this, but I cannot, nor do I imagine anyone will be able to do so for very many years to come. Instead I shall be analysing the features of one form of conflict, an analysis which I hope will throw light on what sorts of factors conflict resolution must take into account. It is a prolegomenon to the resolution of conflict rather than a discussion of conflict resolution as such.

Though this a lecture which is in part under the auspices of the Royal Statistical Society, it is only indirectly connected with any form of analysis which could be properly called statistical.

The pioneer of the statistical analysis of conflict was, of course, Dr Lewis Fry Richardson, the bulk of whose work is contained in the two posthumously published books *Arms and Insecurity* and *Statistics of Deadly Quarrels* (Richardson, 1960a, b). He spent a large part of his life classifying, counting and relating variables in the hope of gaining insight into the conflict behaviour of societies. This paper, though, does not attempt to fall into that style of work. Its connections with statistical analysis are tortuous. A little of what I shall say impinges on topics discussed under the general rubric of the "Theory of games" which, in the hands of scholars such as Savage, is closely intertwined with "statistical decision theory". Similarly, approaches to the theory of bargaining by, for example, Professor Nash (1950) and Professor Braithwaite (1955) have been made under this same rubric. I shall be discussing bargaining later in my paper, though in a somewhat different sense from these discussions. This interconnection between the subject-matter of my paper and matter falling under the general heading of statistical analysis might with justice be thought a little weak and I do not wish to stress them.

Conflict is ubiquitous in the social life of all animals including mankind. It is, of course, the latter species of animal which most closely concerns us. In order to get to grips with the problem, we must define the term "conflict" more closely.

A conflict arises when two or more people or groups endeavour to pursue goals which are mutually inconsistent. "Conflict resolution" is the process by which two

† Organized by the Royal Statistical Society in conjunction with the Eugenics Society and the Master of Pembroke College, Cambridge.

parties reconcile their goals to the extent that they are mutually consistent. The conflict is resolved when the two parties are willing to accept some position as a *status quo*, either because the costs of inducing further conflict would outweigh the benefits of any improved settlement which may result, or because, on some criterion or other, they are willing to accept the settlement as "fair". It might be argued that this last category of settlements is non-existent. Man is a purely self-seeking animal who derives no satisfaction whatever from the contentment of others. This may conceivably be true in international relations. In ordinary individual human contact and intercourse it seems less justifiable. Certainly the work of people like Nash and Braithwaite operates and even defines concepts of fairness which are not purely self-oriented—the former implicitly and the latter explicitly.

The process of conflict resolution covers the range of activities which include at one end the talking between the contesting parties to the other extreme of violent warfare. This definition identifies warfare as a device for the resolution of conflict which, from one point of view, seems a natural usage, though it also does violence to a perfectly conventional usage of the term which takes warfare as the conflict, not the means for resolving the conflict. I shall return to this apparent dilemma later.

First, however, I want to stress a point which is frequently made, notably by Kenneth Boulding. Conflict resolution does not mean conflict elimination. The process of conflict resolution can involve costs but also it can involve benefits either to the conflicting parties or to some other groups. It is a proposition widely accepted by economists that competition between firms or indeed between any forms of organizations makes for efficiency. If this is true, we do not want to eliminate this form of conflict. Indeed it is commonly asserted that British industry should become more competitive, which is to say, become more not less involved in conflict. Resolution of conflicts between industrial firms is regarded as socially harmful when it takes such forms as price-fixing. Even conflicts which do not by themselves involve social benefits nevertheless need not be regarded as necessarily socially deleterious, providing they are solved in ways involving little cost. I am not suggesting that countries should cease to have conflict between themselves, even if such an eventuality were remotely possible. I am suggesting only that we should improve the means for conflict resolution so that they do not involve such serious social costs as war. In arguing this way we are not arguing that conflict is harmful by itself, but just that certain forms of conflict resolution are harmful. We want to keep the conflicts, but replace gun-fights by law courts, revolutions by elections, and international wars by international conciliation, mediation and law.

Now let us return to the slightly embarrassing terminological point we became involved in, which classified war as a means of resolving conflict. Suppose two countries are in disagreement over who should control some third country. They might try and solve this problem by attempting to formulate a treaty and the process of trying to construct this treaty is bargaining, a term which we shall come back to. If they fail to achieve a mutually satisfactory treaty they might do a variety of things, but let us assume that they are going to war. In my terminology they are embarking on a process of conflict resolution. However, this form of conflict resolution is itself another conflict in its own right. Within the context of the war itself the two parties have inconsistent aims and are, in a perhaps rather extended usage of the term, trying to reconcile them. In effect they are using this second conflict to improve their bargaining position in the first, for the winner, if this is an identifiable party in the conflict, will be able to bargain in the original situation from a stronger position than he would have been able to do had the war not been fought. In effect there is an over-all bargain or conflict here which is resolved by a mutually acceptable treaty. However, encompassed within the general conflict, there are second-level conflicts which are conflicts designed to improve bargaining positions rather than actually achieve the final solution itself. There is, of course, a limiting case of this where one party so completely subjugates the other in war that it is able to dictate terms, though it is arguable that complete dictation, even in such instances as the defeat of Germany in 1945, is a myth. There can, however, be little doubt that there can be an improvement in a bargaining situation owing to the successful prosecution of a war.

There are many methods of conflict resolution, that is, the selection of acts which will result in the achievement of mutually consistent goals.

I want to discuss one very broad category of resolution procedures, namely bargaining, which I shall define rather widely in a manner which includes a wider class of activities than would be normally placed under this heading. On the basis of this analysis, I shall make some suggestions, albeit modest ones, for the improvement of conflict resolution.

I shall define bargaining as any process by which two (or more) parties come to some arrangement whereby their acts become consistent, where this arrangement is brought about by the parties involved in the conflict alone, and where the parties do not follow some procedure which by itself will determine the results of the bargain. I can perhaps explain this most clearly by explaining what, under this definition, is not regarded as bargaining. The settlement of a dispute by legal means in a law court is not bargaining. The procedure for the settlement of conflicts by this means is laid down and the solution of the conflict determined by the court must then be accepted by the participants. Similarly, the settlement of a dispute by an arbitrator when the parties bind themselves to accept the settlement is not bargaining even though of course the disputants plead their cases before the arbitrator. Resolution by chance methods such as tossing a coin is similarly not bargaining.

There may be bargaining about what procedure to adopt. In the case of a chance device as a means of solving a conflict, there may be bargaining about what probabilities to assign to the favourable outcome for each party. However, once the procedure is agreed upon, the activity of tossing a coin or of going through the law court is not bargaining. This might be illustrated by an example somewhat removed from the international sphere. If a married couple separate they may bargain with each other as to how to divide their assets. This, under my definition, is bargaining. However, if a law court decides on the alimony which the wife receives then this is not bargaining but is, as far as the disputants are concerned, simply the application of a procedure which will give some result.

The definition of bargaining does not exclude using the services of a mediator to help in the process of bargaining, as this does not set into motion an actual conflict resolution procedure. That is, anything which happened with a mediator could in principle happen without the mediator. He acts as a catalyst, not as an inherent part of the bargaining procedure. This is not the case when there is an arbitrator who determines the solution.

Before embarking on this discussion I should make it clear that although I am discussing something which could be appropriately regarded as the theory of bargaining, it is not quite the same problem as that which has been discussed under this heading in the game theory, which is sometimes also referred to as the theory of co-operative games. These theories, and I refer particularly to those of Braithwaite and Nash, are more interested in prescribing what they regard as the conditions which give a fair or equitable bargain. In the case of Nash, for instance, he prescribes four rules which he thinks would characterize a fair bargain and goes on to discuss what the characteristics of the result would be. However, we are not interested in fair bargains as such but in the actual bargaining procedure. Above all we are interested in knowing the conditions under which the participants will accept a resolution of the conflict, and which conditions will make them hold out for something better.

Let us look at the activity of bargaining more closely. In Fig. 1 the pay-offs to the party α are represented by points on the vertical axis, whereas pay-offs to β are

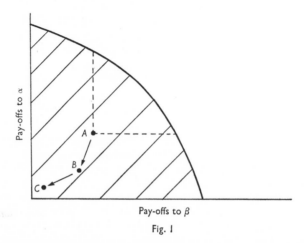

Fig. 1

represented by pay-offs along the horizontal axis. These pay-offs should be interpreted as a rate of benefit with respect to time, not the over-all benefit accruing from some particular policy. Any points within the area circumscribed by the axes and the curved line are ones which are attainable and are normally referred to as the "bargaining set". This diagram, or at least something akin to it, is familiar in other analyses of bargaining.

In applying this sort of model to an international bargaining situation, or indeed any other bargaining situation, there is an acute problem of measurement. Along the axes we must put some numbers which purport to be operational measures of utility or something of the sort. In most analyses of bargaining they are assumed to be utilities of the type defined by von Neumann and Morgenstern (1953). For individuals, this procedure is at least in principle operational. It is less clear what sort of measure could appropriately be used in discussing bargaining between national states. Even if a von Neumann–Morgenstern measure were in principle operational, it certainly would not be a practicable procedure to actually measure it. There is, I think, an interesting problem awaiting solution of defining operationally some appropriate measure of "national interest".

Fortunately, the usefulness of the argument does not rest completely on being able to define an operational cardinal measure of national interest. An ordinal measure is quite sufficient to preserve the essential characteristics of the situation. For example, the property that A is north-east of B is invariant with respect to any order-preserving scheme of measurement, and this, basically, is all we need.

From any point within the area such as *A* it is possible to come to some agreement which will be to the benefit of both parties if they move north-east to the boundary. If they are at some point on the boundary then it is only possible for one party to get some improvement in his position at the expense of the other. Suppose that the bargainers are at point *A*. Their goals are inconsistent, as α would like to move as far upwards as possible, while β would like to move as far to the right as possible. Thus we have a conflict situation in the sense in which we earlier defined it. Both can benefit by moving to some point within the dotted lines. Let us call the process of discussion between the parties as to which point on the north-east boundary (or indeed any other point) they should agree to end up at as a process of *negotiation*. Negotiation is clearly one form of conflict resolution and it is commonly conceived of as being the most civilized form. While negotiation is going on, both parties are losing in that they are not on the boundary.

It is not infrequent in conflicts for one (or both) parties deliberately to worsen his own position in order to worsen the rival's position in the hope of improving his bargaining positions. In other words, this move is perceived as making it possible to arrive at a better ending point even though the intermediate costs of this are greater. This activity can be defined as the *escalation* of a conflict. In Fig. 1 this is illustrated by a move on the part of β to point *B* and a counter-escalation on the part of α to point *C*. We subsume the whole of this activity, both negotiation and escalation, and indeed any moves or projected moves within the bargaining set, under the general heading of bargaining.

Let us interpret this type of model in international contexts. The interpretation is, of course, an extremely stylized one indeed and pretends to be nothing else. One of the more modest assumptions is that it is restricted to two parties.

Two countries, α and β, are in conflict over the degree of control which they should have over some third piece of territory. This is an extremely common form of international conflict, both currently and historically. Vietnam is a topical example, as is the Indo–Pakistan dispute over Kashmir. A past example is the dispute over Alsace–Lorraine which has been intermittently regarded as either French or German. Fishing-rights disputes could be regarded as a special case of this class of dispute. For convenience, suppose that α has a high degree of control over the territory which β disputes, and that the consequence of this is a great deal of tension between the two countries. This is perceived as a cost by both parties as it disrupts diplomatic and economic relations, and may involve both of them in an expensive programme of armament and inconvenient deployment of armed forces. There are some situations which could be regarded by both parties as better for each. A solution might be for β to recognize the control of α over some other territory in exchange for acquiescence in the present situation. Both would gain from the consequent reduction in tension. Alternatively, α might relinquish some of its control and again benefit from the reduction in tension. The situation is rendered interesting by the possibility of some agreement which would bring about mutual benefit. The current situation involves costs to both in the sense of opportunity costs, that is, the existence of something better which is being forgone through continuing in the present situation.

The situation is not, however, stuck at its present form. The conflict can be escalated by one or both parties increasing the tension and perhaps moving further into warfare or into a near-warfare situation. War, in this framework, becomes a secondary conflict which is used to force a result in the primary conflict. We can adapt Clausewitz's dictum and say that "War is bargaining by other means".

Let us first consider a situation where neither side, for means not for the moment analysed, considers escalation from the current position, C. To further simplify the problem, let us also assume that both parties have made a "final offer" of a treaty (see Fig. 2) where α's offer is illustrated by A' and β's "final offer" is illustrated by B'. Under what conditions does one party (say α) give in to β's offer? The "final offer" made by β is better for α than is the current situation though not of course better than its own offer. This also applies to α.

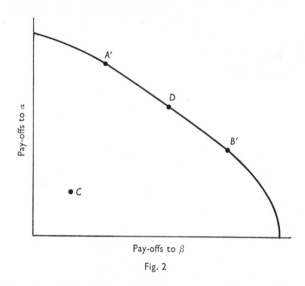

Fig. 2

Intuitively it is clear that whether it pays α to give in to β's demand rather than hang on for his own demand to be satisfied depends on how long α expects β to hang on before conceding. The longer it takes β to give in, the less worth while it is for α to wait until his own demand is satisfied. The choice becomes for α: whether to take immediately β's offer and gain something or delay a little until β gives in, getting a higher pay-off in the future, but nevertheless doing without some immediate gains. Obviously if α is ever going to give in, the sooner he does it the better. The problem is complicated a bit if agreements when made are asssumed to be of indefinite duration. It would appear that in this case it was always worth while waiting for the better outcome. However, a country's valuation of an agreement at some future date, say five years' time, is lower than its valuation of the same agreement in the current period, partly because the situation in the world is likely to have changed, making the agreement less relevant, and partly because there is always some danger of the rival breaking the agreement. Thus it is appropriate to discount the future pay-offs of the agreement, making its value period by period diminish. Let us represent this on Fig. 3. The base line, the x-axis, represents the situation of remaining at the current conflict position and we want to analyse deviations in the pay-offs from that position. The total value through time of giving in immediately to β's demand is represented by the area under the downward-sloping line starting at P. The value to α of β giving in to him at time t_b is given by the area under the downward-sloping line starting at Q. If β had given in immediately, then the value to α would have been the area under the line from P and also that area under the dotted continuation of that line back to the y-axis.

Whether the first area is greater or less than the second depends on where t_b is. The further to the left it is (i.e. the quicker β gives in) then the more likely is α to hang on and not give in, whereas the further to the right it is the more likely is α to concede to β's demand. Immediately t_b is not actual time of concession but α's prediction of it, and all depends on his prediction.

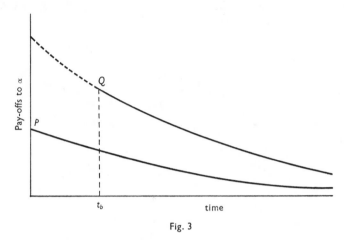

Fig. 3

This can be represented more formally as follows. Let us denote the pay-offs to α by lower-case letter a's subscripted; so, for example, a_c denotes the pay-off at point C. The over-all advantage to α of conceding to β immediately is thus going to be $(a_b - a_c)$ discounted by the "fall-off" factor which we denote by f to emphasize that, while it is a formal concept similar to an economist's discount rate, there the connection ends.

This expression is

$$\int_0^\infty (a_b - a_c)\, e^{-ft}\, dt = (a_b - a_c)/f. \tag{1}$$

The advantage to α of hanging on at the present conflict position providing β concedes at point t_b will similarly be

$$\int_{t_b}^\infty (a_a - a_c)\, e^{-ft}\, dt = (a_a - a_c)/f\, e^{-ft}. \tag{2}$$

α will thus concede immediately to β if the first expression exceeds the second, that is if

$$(a_b - a_c) > (a_a - a_c)\, e^{-ft}. \tag{3}$$

A similar sort of analysis can be carried out for β.

Now if one party is ever going to give in to the other the sooner he does it the better, because at least his limited gains start immediately and not later. It is worth while hanging on in the inferior position only if the later gains exceed the gains of immediate submission. Superficially this model seems to imply that bargains will be immediately settled, for one of the parties should realize that he will have to give in ultimately so the sooner it is done the better. This interpretation, however, neglects the fact that α's estimate of β's surrender date is only an estimate which is based on perhaps virtually no evidence. As time progresses he will adjust his estimate of the surrender date and of course β will do likewise with regard to his own estimates of α's surrender date. As experience of the conflict is gained, at least one of the parties will have to adjust his estimate, and as it recedes further into the distance he will sometimes have to conclude reluctantly that he had made a mistake and belatedly give in. It is not at all inconceivable that his surrender will have come so late that even his rival has failed to benefit by it, which of course implies that the rival also made a miscalculation concerning the surrender date.

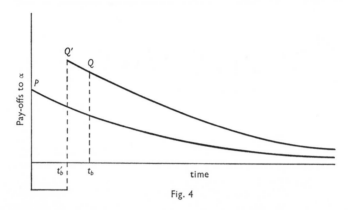

Fig. 4

The posing of the model in terms of just two final offers requires the surrender of one party and the victory of the other. This of course is unrealistic in many contexts. Compromise agreements are common enough in life. Suppose that when it is clear that neither party is going to surrender immediately, β suggests a compromise solution at D. Will α accept it or not? What considerations would induce β to make this offer, and what considerations would induce α to accept it? The analysis is, of course, a simple application of the rule already developed. β will make the offer if it was a point to which, if it had been put initially in the bargaining situation, he would have surrendered. This means that the following condition holds:

$$(b_d - b_c) > (b_b - b_c)\,e^{-ft_a}. \tag{4}$$

Similarly, α will accept the bargain if it was a condition to which he would surrender which is, of course, that :

$$(a_d - a_c) > (a_a - a_c)\,e^{-ft_a}. \tag{5}$$

The extension of the model to include compromise possibilities is therefore not at all difficult. Unfortunately, there is no guarantee that such a compromise agreement is always possible. If each side is convinced that the rival is going to concede the original demands at an early date, then there is no compromise which either will be willing to offer, so conflict goes on as before.

The model is basically the same if we introduce escalation into it. The effect of an escalation is to impose a cost on both parties. However, this additional cost will shorten the concession time, so one party might deliberately escalate to do this, hoping that the shortening of the concession time will more than compensate for the additional costs of the escalation. The contrasting alternatives to α of immediate concessions, waiting at the existing level when β's concession time is estimated at t_b, and escalating such that the concession time is reduced to t_b' are shown in Fig. 4.

The interesting thing about this model is that it implies that if a conflict persists then it is due to one or both of the parties being under some misapprehension about the behaviour of the other person. This is, of course, in line with general observation. If the final settlement of a strike were known to the participants in it at the beginning of the strike, then there would be no point in going through with it. Instead it would be sensible to move directly to the solution point. The same is true of wars. This suggests that the approach to conflict resolution in this sort of framework is through the provision of further information. The problem unfortunately is of what information, for, as might be guessed, there are some problems involved in this issue.

Before going on to them, I would like to bring in one further issue which is relevant to the information question. An escalation is not usually a one-sided affair. If one party escalates then the other party will normally escalate in response and the end point is that the conflict is carried out at a more intense and costly level. It is common for a participant who finds his rival escalating to assume that it is in his interests to escalate in response and the quicker the better. Now in order to be prepared to respond to an escalation quickly it is necessary to make some preparations which will be observed by the rival. These might be interpreted by the rival for what they are, essentially defensive preparations, unfortunately they can also be interpreted as preparations to initiate the escalation. It is very difficult to distinguish, between actions which are intended to convey the message "I am able to do something" and those conveying the message "I am going to do something". The confusion is likely to be aggravated in tense conflict situations where the evaluations of subjective probabilities of acts might get erratic and subject to pessimism. That is, it is at least a possible hypothesis that people's judgements of subjective probabilities incline to increasing the probabilities of unfavourable outcomes in situations where there is some tension between the parties. It is clear, of course, that if one party thinks that the other party is about to act aggressively then he himself will prepare to act aggressively and perhaps do so even though the whole business started from a misperception of the initial situation.

Once we have introduced the notion of misperceptions, or even of probabilities, we are back in the land where the provision of information becomes a more important issue. The problems here are formidable but at least there is one saving grace. Information is something which might really be a factor in a situation which is variable and susceptible to manipulation. One can often suggest ways of ending conflicts, but these depend on being able to alter things which are not in practice alterable. At the extreme, we can recommend a moral improvement in man as the way of ending war. It would seem that we would have to stop at the recommending stage. We can, however, recommend improving (or possibly restricting) the supply of information, knowing it is something which is actually alterable.

We have suggested that the fact that conflicts are resolved by costly methods is due to misperceptions and the implication would seem to be that the provision of further information would correct this problem. Unfortunately this is a trickier question than it may appear at first sight.

Let us reason this out in terms of the non-escalation model. There are two strategies available to each participant: concede immediately or fight. If both parties concede, we assume that the pay-off to α is somewhere in between what it would have been if he had made the unilateral concession and what it would have been if β had made the unilateral concession. If he is fighting then he must presume that he will come out better in a fight with β than if he had made a unilateral concession himself.

That is, in the joint pay-off matrix below, where the subscripted entries denote the overall pay-offs resulting from the policies, the bottom row dominates the top from α's point of view.

β's choices

		Concede	Fight
α's choices	Concede	α_{cc}, β_{cc}	α_{cf}, β_{cf}
	Fight	α_{fc}, β_{fc}	α_{ff}, β_{ff}

$$\alpha_{fc} > \alpha_{ff} > \alpha_{cc} > \alpha_{cf}.$$

If the fight continues between the two parties then β must believe that the pay-offs in his pay-off matrix are similarly ordered. However, one of these must be wrong, as one of them is going to have to concede and lose if a fight takes place. The elements of the true matrix of (say) α would be ordered as follows:

$$\alpha_{fc} > \alpha_{cc} > \alpha_{cf} > \alpha_{ff}.$$

Now let us assume that we have an "omniscient mediator" who knows in fact how the conflict will end if it is fought out. That is, he knows what in fact should be put in the bottom right-hand box. There are two possibilities: the predictions of one of the parties are wrong or the predictions of both of them are wrong. Suppose that α is right but β is wrong the elements of the matrix might be ordered as follows:

Orderings for α: $\alpha_{fc} > \alpha_{ff} > \alpha_{cc} > \alpha_{cf}.$

Orderings for β: $\beta_{cf} > \beta_{cc} > \beta_{fc} > \beta_{ff}.$

If both were wrong and while α wins in the conflict nevertheless it is only after doing worse than he would have done by conceding, then the matrix might be:

Orderings for α: $\alpha_{fc} > \alpha_{cc} > \alpha_{cf} > \alpha_{ff}.$

Orderings for β: $\beta_{cf} > \beta_{cc} > \beta_{fc} > \beta_{ff}.$

In this situation what is the onmiscient mediator going to do? Both sides, after all, have the strong incentive to try to convince the opponent that they themselves are going to hang on for longer. It is even in their interests to argue that they are irrational, and will pursue the conflict even though it is more harmful to do so. The information that the omniscient mediator has to try to convey is that he really knows what the end result of the conflict will be and can predict the outcome better than the participants. Even if a losing party agrees, it is not in his interests to admit it. However, the mediator's problem is perhaps not quite so severe. What he has to do is convince the parties that he really does know the opponent's concession time and then try to solve the problem of settling the division of the over-all outcome in the mutual concession box. This places it back into the area of more orthodox bargaining theory though even here the problems of sorting out an equitable agreement are by no means trivial. Those familiar with treatments of the bargaining problem will recognize some difficulties in interpreting such mathematically sophisticated ideas in more down-to-earth terms. The problem of information in this sort of situation is the problem of the mediator convincing everyone that he really knows the outcome of the conflict if it goes on. Unfortunately few of us could claim to have such confidence in our analyses of actual conflicts, but it is in this area that the quantity of work done is beginning to pick up momentum. When this is better known we can start on the difficulties inherent in the problem I have outlined.

One final issue I should like to raise, though unfortunately not answer. The type of analysis we have performed depends on the behaviour of the participants being in some sense "rational".

Rationality is of course an awkward word which is used to mean a wide variety of things, so it requires defining here in a manner suitable for our purposes. We shall approach it from the rear and define instead three individually sufficient characteristics of irrational conduct. First, we regard it as irrational to have a utility of winning as such. The only elements which should enter into any utility function are the actual elements which are being bargained about. Second, there should be no utility attached to the opponent's discomfort as such. A loss to the opponent is not of itself desirable to a rational bargainer. (On this definition of rationality it is of course irrational to seek retributive punishment.) Finally, it is irrational to evaluate information inappropriately. Any act can, of course, only be treated as rational in the context of the information available and different information might make different acts rational, given the objectives of the act. It is then necessary to use information to modify the probabilities of outcomes in some appropriate way. This, of course, leaves wide open the question of what the appropriate use of information is; so all this last point does is to identify a problem area, not solve it.

This is very clearly not the only way of defining rationality even within a context of a bargaining theory. Its justification is almost entirely that it simplifies the problem for the purposes of initial analysis.

The element of irrationality which has entered into the analysis is in the concession that in times of conflict the assessment of the probabilities of a rival's hostile actions might be exaggerated and also that the perception of the rival's weaknesses may be exaggerated. These are not factual points which have been established, but observation would seem to bear them out. The frequency of ongoing conflicts alone supports the second point at least. However, in violent conflicts there are other non-rational elements which enter into the picture which can be subsumed under my definition or even something broader. Man is often alleged to be a particularly aggressive form of animal. This statement as it stands tells us either too much or too little. Certainly there is very little we can do about it. However, we can be aware that when violence becomes an instrument of policy, people's attitudes become much more rigid and it is hard to avoid the feeling that there is some fascination with the whole ethos of violence. This, of course, aggravates the problem of conflict resolution. This was very clear in such socially pathological cases as Nazi Germany but even today one cannot avoid the feeling that military force is glamourized. If this is correct, then the application of our rational models is inhibited though perhaps not completely destroyed. The hardening of objectives means, in terms of the models, that far from seeking a compromise solution, the "final offers" diverge, making the solution point recede. This clearly happened in the two world wars of this century. The framework of the analysis still remains the same. This might be cold comfort if resolution becomes harder. I have no clear recommendation to make on this point other than that which anyone would have made. The glamorization of violence is wrong; it might lead to actual violence. People in power and who make or influence decisions should be self-aware on this point and should endeavour to make decisions not in the pursuit of power and honour and glory but in the pursuit of the common good.

REFERENCES

BRAITHWAITE, R. B. (1955). *The Theory of Games as a Tool for the Moral Philosopher*. Cambridge: University Press.

NASH, J. F. (1950). The bargaining problem. *Econometrica*, **18**, 155–162.

NEUMANN, J. VON and MORGENSTERN, O. (1953). *The Theory of Games and Economic Behavior* (3rd ed.). Princeton: University Press.

RICHARDSON, L. F. (1960a). *Arms and Insecurity*. London: Stevens.

—— (1960b). *Statistics of Deadly Quarrels*. London: Stevens.

PART THREE
Prospects for a Unified Theory

INTRODUCTION

Given the existence of a number of different models of bargaining, it is hardly surprising that some scholars should turn their attention to the links among them and the prospects for constructing a unified theory of bargaining. As Pen, for example, was already saying in 1956, "There are two groups of solutions, those which go back to Zeuthen and those which are inspired by Morgenstern and Neumann. The connection between these two lines of thought forms a challenging problem. Do they supplement one another? Do they exclude one another? Can they be united into one theory."[1]

Undoubtedly, the single most important contribution to the development of a unified theory of bargaining is Harsanyi's effort "to show that Nash's and Zeuthen's bargaining theories are mathematically equivalent (except that Nash's theory covers a wider range of situations than Zeuthen's theory does in its original form)."[2] In essence, what Harsanyi has done is to recast Zeuthen's model in such a way as to accentuate its determinate elements and to strip away its ambiguous features.[3] First he assumes that Zeuthen's bargainers are "perfectly rational." This means that they make error-free calculations, exhibit no differences at all with respect to bargaining skill, and, according to Harsanyi, can always preclude the use of manipulative tactics such as commitments against themselves by making prior commitments to disregard commitments on the part of the other player.[4] Second, Harsanyi assumes that the players in Zeuthen's model always possess perfect information.[5] Sometimes this means only that each bargainer always has precise and accurate knowledge of the other player's "risk willingness." At other times, however, he goes even further and implies that the two parties must be assumed to know each other's cardinal utility function,[6] as is the case in the

---

[1] Jan Pen, *The Wage Rate under Collective Bargaining* (Cambridge, 1959), p. xii.

[2] John C. Harsanyi, "Notes on the Bargaining Problem," p. 474, reprinted herein. Nash's model is applicable to a wider range of cases since it covers asymmetric as well as symmetric bargaining situations while Zeuthen's original model envisions symmetric bargaining.

[3] For Harsanyi's basic argument see John C. Harsanyi, "Approaches to the Bargaining Problem before and after the Theory of Games," reprinted herein. In interpreting Harsanyi's reformulation of Zeuthen, it may help to bear in mind that the bulk of Harsanyi's work falls under the heading of the theory of games.

[4] On these points see especially Harsanyi, "Notes on the Bargaining Problem," reprinted herein.

[5] Harsanyi, "Approaches to the Bargaining Problem before and after the Theory of Games," pp. 149 and 155, reprinted herein.

[6] It is not clear what Zeuthen's position is on this issue. Harsanyi often implies that knowledge of this kind must be assumed and Wagner also seems to adopt this interpretation—Harvey M. Wagner, "A Unified Treatment of Bargaining Theory," p. 388, reprinted herein. On the other hand, the crucial point in Zeuthen's argument is that the bargainers know each other's risk willingness at each stage in the negotiations. And although it is true that a party's risk willingness is dependent upon various aspects of his utility function, Zeuthen generally tends simply to assume that the players are aware of each other's risk willingness without discussing how they acquire this information.

models of game theory. Third, Harsanyi equates the threat point in Nash's model of bargaining with the notion of a conflict situation in Zeuthen's model.[7] Zeuthen was always somewhat vague on the precise nature of the outcome of conflict and, in any case, the payoffs to the players associated with conflict will always be difficult to calculate since they will be affected by a number of interacting variables. Moreover, it is possible to argue that Zeuthen's conflict situation should be equated with specific reference points other than Nash's threat point.[8] It is therefore important to be clear about the connection Harsanyi makes between the Nash and Zeuthen models on this issue. Given this articulation and reformulation of the Zeuthen model of bargaining, Harsanyi is able to demonstrate that it produces the same solution as Nash's model. That is, Zeuthen's bargainers will now reach an equilibrium at the point where the product of their utility gains is maximized.

Harsanyi's efforts to unify the Nash and Zeuthen models have elicited several critical reactions that are worth noting. In the first instance, Pen, who tends to emphasize the less determinate features of Zeuthen's original presentation, denies that Harsanyi has actually achieved a unification of the two models and claims that he "overestimates the importance of an affinity of form."[9] Pen argues that "in Zeuthen's theory, risk and uncertainty determine the atmosphere of the bargaining process . . . while in Nash the equilibrium of bargaining is determined by the maximum of a function in which this uncertainty plays no part."[10] Thus, he concludes that Harsanyi's reformulation actually changes Zeuthen's model rather than demonstrating that it is equivalent to Nash's model. In addition, Pen objects to Harsanyi's clear-cut emphasis on perfect rationality and perfect information in his reformulation of Zeuthen's model. According to Pen, this not only does violence to Zeuthen's conception of bargaining, it also causes "the real content of the bargaining problem to vanish into thin air."[11] And he concludes by saying that he does "not believe that we shall get any nearer to the solution of the problem by reducing the bargainers to computing machines."[12]

Wagner, on the other hand, criticizes Harsanyi's analysis not so much because it diverges from Zeuthen's original presentation as because he is dubious about several important features of the reformulation itself. First, he

[7] For a clear statement of Harsanyi's position on this issue see Harsanyi, "Notes on the Bargaining Problem," reprinted herein.

[8] For a clear discussion of the principal alternatives see Robert L. Bishop, "Game-Theoretic Analyses of Bargaining," pp. 582–602, reprinted herein.

[9] Pen, *Wage Rate under Collective Bargaining*, p. xii.

[10] *Ibid.* Pen also cites a survey article written by Zeuthen himself in 1955 in support of his interpretation of Zeuthen's position on these questions.

[11] *Ibid.*, p. xiii.

[12] *Ibid.* Similar criticisms have been directed at most of the models of bargaining which produce determinate results. Such criticisms are not very satisfying, however, since any model that produces determinate results must, *ipso facto*, be characterized by logical closure. It is more to the point to argue that a given deductive model is not realistic with reference to the empirical world, and this may be what Pen actually has in mind in his criticism of Harsanyi's reformulation of the Zeuthen model.

points out that Harsanyi is ambivalent on the question of commitments, ultimatums, and so forth, since he completely rejects their relevance in his general effort to equate the Nash and Zeuthen models but explicitly praises Nash's inclusion in his own model of "threats," which are analytically similar to commitments and ultimatums.[13] In view of the fact that threats play a crucial role in Nash's two-stage model of bargaining, he argues that this ambivalence amounts to an inconsistency in Harsanyi's reasoning. Second, Wagner criticizes Harsanyi's procedure of equating "Zeuthen's 'conflict situation' with the situation in Nash's model where no agreement is reached and where both parties have to carry out their threats."[14] Whereas Harsanyi claims that this procedure is "natural,"[15] Wagner points out that there are actually several other plausible interpretations of Zeuthen's conflict situation.[16] It would be possible, for example, to identify the outcome of a conflict for the players with the payoffs they would receive if they treated the situation as a noncooperative game and employed their minimax (or maximin) strategies. Under these conditions, conflict would yield the players their security level rather than the Nash outcome of no agreement, with the result that the ultimate solution generated by the Zeuthen model would not coincide with the solution of the Nash model.[17] For these reasons, Wagner concludes that Harsanyi has demonstrated the equivalence of the Nash and Zeuthen models only for a well-defined special case and not for the general case.

It should be emphasized that if one accepts all the details of Harsanyi's reformulation of Zeuthen's model, the Zeuthen and Nash models are in fact "mathematically equivalent" in the sense that they yield the same solution. In this sense, then, Harsanyi can claim justification for his position. The difficulty is that his reformulation is open to serious objections both with respect to the specific elements he includes and with respect to things he leaves out. Pen, for example, is quite right in saying that Harsanyi has chosen to cut out the less determinate elements that are certainly evident in Zeuthen's own presentation of his work.[18] Although it is possible to understand Pen's objections, therefore, this line of thinking also raises serious problems. Thus, in his own efforts to revise and extend Zeuthen's approach to the bargaining problem, Pen fails to achieve determinate results even though he does have some

---

[13] For Wagner's own discussion of this criticism see Harvey M. Wagner, "Rejoinder on the Bargaining Problem," pp. 478–479, reprinted herein. As Wagner points out, Nash defines a threat in the following terms: "A threatens B by convincing B that if B does not act in compliance with A's demands, then A will follow a certain policy T"—John F. Nash, "Two-Person Cooperative Games," p. 130, reprinted herein.

[14] The quote is from Harsanyi, "Notes on the Bargaining Problem," p. 475, herein.

[15] For Harsanyi's description of his procedure in these terms see *ibid.*

[16] Wagner, "Rejoinder on the Bargaining Problem," pp. 480–482, reprinted herein. And for a somewhat clearer discussion of the same point see Bishop, "Game Theoretic Analyses of Bargaining," pp. 582–602.

[17] On the derivation of the Shapley value see R. Duncan Luce and Howard Raiffa, *Games and Decisions* (New York, 1957), pp. 137–140.

[18] For Zeuthen's own presentation see Frederik Zeuthen, *Problems of Monopoly and Economic Warfare,* partially reprinted herein.

interesting things to say about bargaining.[19] The objections raised by Wagner, on the other hand, are more serious than those of Pen. Even accepting the definition of rationality incorporated in game theory (which is presumably what Harsanyi has in mind), it is clear that rationality and efforts to employ threats, commitments, and so forth, are not always mutually exclusive. Schelling has commented on the uses of such bargaining tactics by rational individuals in a wide range of situations,[20] and Ellsberg has demonstrated that they may be relevant even in two-person, zero-sum situations unless additional restrictive assumptions are added to the von Neumann-Morgenstern solution.[21] Similarly, Wagner is basically right about the connection between Nash's threat point and Zeuthen's notion of a conflict situation. Although Zeuthen himself was always vague on the exact meaning of a conflict situation, it is not logically necessary (or even "natural") to identify such a situation with Nash's threat point under all circumstances.

Beyond this, it is important to emphasize that Zeuthen's model of bargaining is a dynamic one in the sense that it seeks to predict the path that the offers and counteroffers of the bargainers will take as they converge toward a solution over time. That is, Zeuthen's model is a process model, even though it does not emphasize the time factor, as do later models such as that of Cross,[22] whereas Nash's model deals only with the results or outcome of bargaining. Harsanyi himself uses the word "complementary" rather than "equivalent" in describing this aspect of the relationship between the two approaches.[23] And as these terms imply, the models are in fact considerably different even though they yield the same solution if one accepts Harsanyi's reformulation of Zeuthen's model.

There is also some question about the wider significance of Harsanyi's efforts to link these two theories of bargaining. It is of course always a matter of substantial interest, at least in mathematical terms, when it can be demonstrated that the same results can be derived from two different sets of axioms or assumptions. But the extent to which this has in fact happened in the present case is open to serious doubts because Harsanyi's reformulation of Zeuthen's model involves some changes in (or questionable interpretations of) Zeuthen's original argument which are of crucial importance in demonstrating the mathematical equivalence of the two models. Even more important, however, it is necessary to emphasize that there are severe limitations on the

---

[19] Pen makes the interesting claim that it is precisely the presence of uncertainty which makes the bargaining problem soluble rather than insoluble. But he fails to sustain this argument by developing a determinate model of bargaining. For a more detailed assessment of Pen's analysis of bargaining see the Introduction to Part Two of this book.

[20] Thomas C. Schelling, *The Strategy of Conflict* (Cambridge, 1960), esp. Chapter 5.

[21] Daniel Ellsberg, "Theory of the Reluctant Duelist," reprinted herein.

[22] On this point see John G. Cross, *The Economics of Bargaining* (New York, 1969), pp. 23-28. It should be noted, however, that Cross occasionally overemphasizes this argument in his effort to clarify the new features incorporated in his own model.

[23] Harsanyi, "Approaches to the Bargaining Problem before and after the Theory of Games," pp. 151-152, reprinted herein.

practical significance of Harsanyi's conclusion. Thus, both the Zeuthen model and the Nash model are special cases that have no decisive claim to superiority over other existing models of bargaining. Raiffa, Shapley, and Braithwaite, for example, have constructed models to deal with "bargaining games" which yield solutions that differ from the Nash solution.[24] And Bishop has achieved similar results in his effort to combine some of the insights of Hicks with the basic features of Zeuthen's model.[25] Even if one accepts Harsanyi's argument about the mathematical equivalence of the Zeuthen and Nash models, therefore, his tendency to suggest that this demonstrates the superiority of the Nash-Zeuthen model over other models of bargaining would seem to be without justification.[26]

Harsanyi's work constitutes the most important effort to construct a unified theory of bargaining, but there are other links among the models of bargaining which should be mentioned in this discussion. As noted in the Introduction to Part Two of this book, Pen's analysis of bargaining is largely derivative from Zeuthen's earlier work.[27] Thus, Pen initially defines the bargaining problem in the same way as Zeuthen, and his bargainers calculate their propensity to fight in much the same way as Zeuthen's bargainers determine their risk willingness. But Pen departs from Zeuthen's analysis when it comes to specifying a concession mechanism, and it is this divergence that leads to Pen's ultimate failure to derive determinate solutions from his analysis of bargaining. Whereas Zeuthen simply assumes that the player with the lower risk willingness will always make the next concession, Pen's bargainer compares his propensity to fight with his estimate of the actual risk of conflict and reaches a personal equilibrium where these two factors just balance each other.[28] Under the circumstances, Zeuthen's model produces a distinct convergence process while Pen's analysis leads only to two individual equilibrium conditions that are unlikely to be compatible with each other, at least at the outset. And Pen is ultimately unable to construct a determinate model to explain the transformation of the individual equilibrium conditions in such a way as to make them compatible. The striking similarities between Zeuthen's and Pen's analyses of the bargaining problem, therefore, do not lead to a unified theory but to two separate analyses, one of which at least implies a determinate solution and the other of which leads only to a suggestive commentary on the uses of different bargaining tactics.

[24] Harsanyi, in particular, attempts to accentuate the differences between these models and the Nash model by labeling them "arbitration theories" rather than "bargaining theories." For a discussion of the reasons why this distinction is not persuasive see the Introduction to Part One of this book.

[25] Robert L. Bishop, "A Zeuthen-Hicks Theory of Bargaining," reprinted herein.

[26] Harsanyi has voiced his views on this subject on a number of occasions. For a good statement on his position, however, see Harsanyi, "Approaches to the Bargaining Problem before and after the Theory of Games," reprinted herein.

[27] Pen himself characterizes his work in this manner—Pen, *Wage Rate under Collective Bargaining,* pp. xi and xiii.

[28] For the details see J. Pen, "A General Theory of Bargaining," pp. 34–36, reprinted herein.

Bishop, on the other hand, has combined certain features of Hicks's analysis of bargaining with the basic structure of the Zeuthen model to produce a composite model which he describes as a Zeuthen-Hicks theory of bargaining. In essence, Bishop discards Zeuthen's notion of risk willingness as the engine of the concession mechanism and replaces it with Hicks's notion of strike duration.[29] The result is an analysis of bargaining which retains the basic structure of the Zeuthen model but which makes it more dynamic and sensitive to the importance of the time factor in bargaining.[30] But this modification of the Zeuthen model is by no means free from objections. In order for a player to calculate the expected utility associated with a strike at any given point in the bargaining process he must know the probability of a strike occurring, the likely duration of a strike, and the cost to him of a strike per unit of elapsed time. And these factors are all difficult ones to come to grips with not only because they will be functions of a variety of antecedent variables, but also because they will generally be affected by the impact of strategic interaction. Moreover, Bishop's composite model yields different solutions for the bargaining problem than the Zeuthen model even though it has many features in common with Zeuthen's model.[31] This result actually indicates a movement away from rather than toward a unified theory of bargaining. That is, it suggests that even models characterized by a great many similarities, let alone models that are more fundamentally divergent, will often yield incompatible solutions for the bargaining problem.

Finally, the bargaining model developed by Cross exhibits several interesting links to earlier models even though it diverges quite sharply from previous theories in other respects. To begin with, Cross acknowledges a link between his own perspective and the early work of Hicks. As Cross himself puts it, Hicks was the first to (1) recognize "the importance of a relationship between the amount of time which a negotiator *expects* to lapse before agreement is reached, and the magnitude of his payoff demand," and (2) suggest "that a strike reflects a *mistake*."[32] But these links between Cross and Hicks are more conceptual than analytic since Hicks never developed his ideas along these lines into a sophisticated model and since Cross's own model contains a number of crucial features that Hicks never introduced.[33]

There are also two points at which Cross's work exhibits interesting links to the Nash model. First, even though the two models have radically different structures, the Cross model yields the Nash solution in the special case of identical players.[34] More specifically, the Cross model yields this result when the two players have "identical learning abilities, identical discount rates, and symmetric utility functions," and the impact of bluffing is the same on both

---

[29] Bishop, "A Zeuthen-Hicks Theory of Bargaining," reprinted herein.
[30] On this point see Cross, *Economics of Bargaining*, p. 34.
[31] Bishop, "A Zeuthen-Hicks Theory of Bargaining," pp. 416–417, reprinted herein.
[32] Cross, *Economics of Bargaining*, p. 33 (italics in original).
[33] On this point see especially *ibid.*, pp. 45–48.
[34] *Ibid.*, pp. 57–60.

players.[35] As Cross says, this is a "rather satisfying result,"[36] but its importance should not be overestimated since Cross-type bargainers will be identical in the relevant respects only by sheer coincidence, and in real-world situations it must be expected that these conditions will be extremely rare. Second, there is a distinct connection between Nash's analysis of threats and Cross's analysis of pre-agreement costs.[37] In both cases, the result is a kind of two-stage model. Nash envisions a preliminary, zero-sum-type game in which the threats of the players set the base points of their utility functions in the bargaining phase of the interaction, thereby determining the ultimate distribution of values between the two sides.[38] Cross, on the other hand, speaks of costs that the players can impose on one another at specific points during the course of negotiations. But this also leads to a type of two-stage model since the primary effect of these imposed costs is to reduce the demand of any party upon whom such costs are imposed in the next phase of the negotiations.[39] Although this link is an important and interesting one, Cross is no doubt justified in warning that its significance should not be overemphasized.[40] His analysis focuses on pre-agreement costs in contrast to Nash's disagreement costs; he incorporates his pre-agreement costs into the dynamics of his process model, and the models he constructs to calculate the effects of pre-agreement costs are different from Nash's analysis of threats in terms of zero-sum games.

Despite these important links between the work of Cross and his predecessors, there is a general sense in which Cross's analysis of bargaining suggests growing divergences in this field rather than movement toward a unified theory. Thus, Cross attaches crucial importance to several factors such as learning, concession rates, and the lapse of time which either do not appear in other theories of bargaining or have only been introduced on a casual basis. The basic structure of the Cross model, therefore, is radically different from the game-theoretic models of bargaining and it represents a substantial shift from the other economic models of bargaining as well. Beyond this, the solutions generated by the Cross model for the bargaining problem are not compatible with previous solutions except in the highly restricted case of identical bargainers mentioned above. This development is important enough in itself. But it looms as an even more serious problem when it is added to the fact that there were already a number of divergent "solutions" for the bargaining problem prior to the construction of the Cross model.

[35] *Ibid.,* p. 175.

[36] *Ibid.,* p. 58.

[37] For Nash's analysis of threats see Nash, "Two-Person Cooperative Games," reprinted herein, and for Cross's analysis of pre-agreement costs see Cross, *Economics of Bargaining,* Chapters 6 and 7.

[38] As Wagner points out, a curious feature of Nash's analysis of threats is that the players choose their threats on the assumption that they will not actually have to execute them even though the threat point will determine the outcome of the bargaining phase of the interaction—Wagner, "Rejoinder on the Bargaining Problem," reprinted herein.

[39] On this point see Cross, *Economics of Bargaining,* pp. 153–154.

[40] For Cross's own argument on this point see *ibid.,* pp. 123–124.

The conclusion to be drawn from this discussion is simple enough, although it has far-reaching implications. There are important links among some of the existing models of bargaining. Nevertheless it is perfectly clear that there exists no unified theory of bargaining at this time. If anything, the divergences among the models are becoming greater rather than smaller. This is the case despite the fact that there are distinct similarities between the game-theoretic and the economic models of bargaining with respect to their techniques for handling the problems introduced by the phenomenon of strategic interaction. When we extend our scope to consider manipulative models of bargaining, which do not exclude the impact of strategic interaction altogether through the introduction of initial assumptions of a restrictive nature, it is to be expected that the prospects for a unified theory of bargaining in the immediate future will decline even further.[41] This should not, of course, be read as an expression of pessimism concerning the prospects of constructing deductive theories of bargaining in general. But it does pose an important and stimulating challenge for the future to those whose work lies in this field.

[41] For an extended discussion of the manipulative models of bargaining see the Introduction to Part Four of this book.

APPROACHES TO THE BARGAINING PROBLEM BEFORE AND AFTER THE THEORY OF GAMES

John C. Harsanyi

IT IS PROPOSED to show that Professor Zeuthen's solution of the bargaining problem[2] (antedating the von Neumann-Morgenstern theory of games[3] by more than a decade) is mathematically equivalent to Mr. Nash's solution[4] (based on the theory of games), except that Zeuthen regards the two parties' mutual bargaining threats as given while Nash furnishes a solution also for the problem of selecting optimal threats. At the same time, it will be submitted that Zeuthen's approach in turn supplements Nash's more abstract treatment in an important way by supplying a plausible psychological model for the actual bargaining process. However, certain minor changes in the basic postulates of Zeuthen's theory and a simplification of Nash's method for finding the optimal threats will be suggested. Comparing Nash's theory with Professor Hicks' theory of collective bargaining[5] (published shortly after Professor Zeuthen's), it will be argued that the former rests on assumptions both more realistic and more consistent with the postulate of rational behaviour. Finally, the economic significance of the Zeuthen-Nash theory of bargaining will be discussed.

1. THE INDETERMINACY OF THE BARGAINING PROBLEM IN ORTHODOX ECONOMICS

As is well known, ordinary economic theory is unable to predict the terms on which agreements tend to be reached in cases of oligopoly, of bilateral monopoly, and in general in situations where settlements must be arrived at by means of explicit or implicit bargaining. Still less is current economic theory (even with the help of current political theory) able to predict on what terms agreements tend to be reached in situations where one or both of two bargaining parties use political pressure as one of the bargaining weapons.

All that orthodox economic theory can say in these cases is that any agreement tends to fall within a certain range, called by Professor Pigou the "range of practicable bargains," defined by the following two properties: (1) It is on the (Edgeworth) contract curve, i.e., the locus of situations where neither party's position can be improved without at the same time worsening the position of the other party. (2) It is on this curve between two limits, which may be called

---

[1] The author would like to thank Professor H. W. Arndt, of Canberra University College, and Mr. W. R. Lane, of the University of Queensland, for reading the manuscript of this paper and for making helpful comments.

[2] F. Zeuthen, *Problems of Monopoly and Economic Warfare*, London, 1930, Chap. IV.

[3] The first edition of the *Theory of Games and Economic Behavior* was published in 1944, the second in 1947.

[4] J. F. Nash, Jr., "The Bargaining Problem," *Econometrica*, Vol. 18 (1950), pp. 115–162, and "Two-Person Co-operative Games," *ibid.*, Vol. 21 (1953), pp. 128–140.

[5] J. R. Hicks, *The Theory of Wages*, London, 1932, Chap. VII.

the "maximum-concession points" of each party, and which are determined by the fact that neither party would accept an agreement that put him in a worse position than the conflict situation (not reaching an agreement). In other words, each party's maximum-concession point is that point at which all the net gain resulting from the agreement and the co-operation agreed upon would go wholly to the other party. But current economic theory does not explain how the position of the actual agreement point is determined *within* this range of practicable bargains, that is, how the division of the net gain is determined between the two bargaining parties.

At the same time, the theory of games itself, as developed originally by von Neumann and Morgenstern, is no more able than is orthodox theory to determine the exact position of the agreement point within the range of practicable bargains. Only on the basis of *additional* assumptions[6] does the theory of games furnish a determinate solution, as we shall see.

The unpredictability of the outcome of bargaining is, however, by no means a law of nature, but is only a gap in current economic and political theories. In practical life experienced businessmen, politicians, diplomats, etc., seem to be often quite able to predict the terms of different agreements with reasonable accuracy when they have sufficient information on the bargaining situation. Of course, information on the two parties' general economic and political strength alone may not suffice: the outcome may depend significantly on such "accidental" factors as the bargaining skill of the two parties' actual representatives.[7] But it is a perfectly legitimate question (and one to which we are entitled to an answer from economics and political science) to ask what sort of agreement tends to result from a given objective economic and political balance of power between two parties (as well as from given subjective attitudes on their part) if all disturbing forces are assumed away[8] (e.g., by postulating perfect rationality and perfect knowledge). In the absence of a theory yielding determinate predictions as to the outcome of bargaining, even the mere *description* of many social situations in a satisfactory way becomes impossible.[9] Thus a determinate

----

[6] Besides Nash's approach to be discussed, an alternative method for finding determinate solutions has been proposed by Mr. Raiffa, but his solutions involve arbitration, not bargaining. See H. Raiffa, "Arbitration Schemes for Generalized Two-Person Games," University of Michigan, Report No. M720–1, R 30, June, 1951; reprinted (in a shortened form) in *Contributions to the Theory of Games*, ed. by H. W. Kuhn and A. W. Tucker, Vol. II, Princeton, 1953, pp. 361–387.

[7] Often the bargaining skill of these representatives is not really an accidental factor because the ability to hire more skilled negotiators itself depends on greater economic or political strength.

[8] Abstraction from disturbing forces in constructing theoretical models is no more objectionable in the theory of bargaining than it is in other parts of social science, and only requires the same sorts of precautions in applying conclusions to the real world.

[9] For example, such descriptive terms as the "balance of power" between two parties (or even the term economic or political "power" itself), the degree of a bargaining party's "determination" or "toughness," the strength of the economic or political "pressure" one party can exert against the other, etc., can be given a definite meaning only on the basis of such a theory.

solution for the bargaining problem—as attempted by the three theories to be discussed—would fill a significant gap in both economics and political science.

2. BARGAINING WITH, AND WITHOUT, A CHOICE AMONG ALTERNATIVE THREATS

An important advance over earlier authors has been the clear distinction in Nash's theory between bargaining situations that do and those that do not allow each party a choice among alternative threats by which to bring pressure to bear upon the other party.

Bargaining situations with one possible threat by each party arise either when the two parties can achieve a certain gain by co-operation but when each of them can threaten to withhold his co-operation unless a profit-sharing agreement satisfactory to him is reached, or when one or both parties are able to inflict one particular sort of positive damage on the other party and use this possibility as a threat. It is, however, often a matter of definition what we regard as mere non-co-operation and what we regard as positive damage, and so it is desirable to bring both cases under the same terminology by concentrating on the fact that in either case an agreement will mean at least a *relative* gain to both parties over the conflict situation resulting from the absence of agreement. In both cases agreement means saving the costs of a conflict and this saving can be divided between the two parties.

But in more general situations the bargaining parties will have a choice among several possible threats, each involving different degrees of non-cooperative or positively damaging behaviour. Of course, if there is no obligation to carry out threats in the absence of agreement, the choice among alternative threats may become trivial since each party may then use the most formidable threat against his opponent as a matter of mere bluffing. To exclude this possibility, we may assume that each party is forced to carry out this threat if agreement fails.[10] Or alternatively we may assume—in accordance with the postulate of perfect knowledge—that each party can distinguish mere bluffs from serious threats (say, on the basis of Nash's theory of optimal threats). We may even admit the possibility that explicit threats are not used at all during the negotiations, for it suffices if both parties can form a reasonably accurate *estimate* of what retaliation would result in the event of a conflict. In any case, if bluffing is made impossible or useless, the choice among alternative threats becomes a very real problem since, in general, the more effective a certain non-co-operative or positively damaging policy is against the opponent the more expensive it tends to be also to the party using it.

We begin, however, with the simpler problem of bargaining with *given* threats, assuming that each party's threat is uniquely given either because he has only one possible threat or because the problem of choosing among several possible threats has already been solved. Accordingly, both parties will be assumed to know what kind of conflict situation will result if no agreement is reached.

[10] In an abstract model we may imagine, as Nash does, that the carrying-out of threats is enforced by some kind of special authority. In the real world, of course, the enforcing agency might simply be the fear of discrediting oneself and spoiling the efficacy of one's threats in the future.

3. NASH'S UTILITY-PRODUCT MAXIMIZATION RULE

The bargaining problem has an obvious determinate solution in at least one special case: viz., in situations that are completely symmetric with respect to the two bargaining parties. In this case it is natural to assume that the two parties will tend to share the net gain equally since neither would be prepared to grant the other better terms than the latter would grant him. For instance, everybody will expect that two duopolists with the same cost functions, size, market conditions, capital resources, personalities, etc., will reach an agreement giving equal profits to each of them.

Nash's theory of bargaining (with given threats) is fundamentally a generalization of this principle[11] for the more general case of asymmetric situations. This generalization is achieved by postulating that the general solution should have desirable mathematical properties.[12] Nash's conclusion is that, if both parties' utilities are measured by von Neumann-Morgenstern cardinal-utility indices, they will reach an agreement at that point of the range of practicable bargains at which the *product* of the utilities each party ascribes to his net gain (over the conflict situation) is *maximized*.

It is worth noting that this solution does not presuppose the interpersonal comparability of utilities since the index for each party's utility can be chosen independently of the other's (because the solution is invariant with respect to changes in the zero point or the unit of either party's utility index; in effect this invariance property is one of the postulates actually used by Nash in deriving his solution).

Moreover, it is easy to see that in the symmetric case this solution gives equal shares to both parties,[13] so that it is a generalization of the solution suggested above for this special case.

4. THE MATHEMATICAL EQUIVALENCE OF ZEUTHEN'S AND NASH'S THEORIES

We now show that Zeuthen's solution is equivalent to Nash's.

Zeuthen's approach is based on a direct analysis of the process of collective bargaining on the labour market, but it has general validity for any sort of bargaining situation.

Suppose that Party 1 would like to achieve the terms A_1, but has been offered only the less favourable terms A_2 by Party 2. Will he accept A_2 or will he insist on obtaining A_1? This will obviously depend on Party 1's view of the probability that Party 2 would definitely reject the terms A_1, and that his own insistence on them would lead to a conflict.

Let $U_1(A_1)$ and $U_1(A_2)$ be the net utility gains over the conflict situation that Party 1 would derive from A_1 and A_2, respectively. By assumption, $U_1(A_1) > U_1(A_2)$. Moreover, let p_2 be the probability that Party 2 would finally reject the

---

[11] The present writer feels that this aspect of Nash's approach deserves greater emphasis than it received in Nash's original exposition.

[12] Nash's second paper also gives an alternative derivation. See his "Two-Person Cooperative Games," *loc. cit.*, esp. pp. 131–134.

[13] This applies, of course, only if both parties' cardinal utility functions (i.e., their attitudes towards risk-taking) are also similar (symmetric).

terms A_1. Then, if Party 1 accepts A_2 he will obtain $U_1(A_2)$ with certainty, while if he rejects A_2 and insists on the better terms A_1 he will have the probability $(1 - p_2)$ of obtaining the higher utility $U_1(A_1)$ and the probability p_2 of obtaining nothing. Therefore, on the assumption that Party 1 tries to maximize his expected utility,[14] he will accept the terms A_2 if $U_1(A_2) > (1 - p_2) \cdot U_1(A_1)$, that is, if $[U_1(A_1) - U_1(A_2)]/U_1(A_1) < p_2$, and will reject A_2 and insist on the better terms A_1 in the opposite case. Consequently, the utility quotient $[U_1(A_1) - U_1(A_2)]/U_1(A_1)$, which may be written briefly as $\Delta U_1/U_1$, expresses the maximum risk (maximum probability of conflict) that Party 1 is prepared to face in order to secure the better terms A_1 instead of the less favourable terms A_2.

On the other hand, denoting the net utility gains Party 2 would derive from the two situations by $U_2(A_1)$ and $U_2(A_2)$ (where $U_2(A_1) < U_2(A_2)$), it can similarly be shown that the maximum risk Party 2 would take in order to achieve the terms A_2 more favourable to him is equal to the utility quotient $\Delta U_2/U_2 = [U_2(A_2) - U_2(A_1)]/U_2(A_2)$. Thus the two utility quotients $\Delta U_1/U_1$ and $\Delta U_2/U_2$—which in a sense measure the relative advantage of A_1 over A_2 to Party 1 and the relative advantage of A_2 over A_1 to Party 2, respectively—decide the strength of each party's "determination" to insist on the alternative more favourable to himself.

At this point Professor Zeuthen introduces the further assumption[15] that each party will make a concession to his opponent once he finds that the latter's determination is firmer (i.e., the latter's readiness to risk a conflict is greater) than is his own. Thus Party 1 will always make a further concession if

(1) $$[U_1(A_1) - U_1(A_2)]/U_1(A_1) < [U_2(A_2) - U_2(A_1)]/U_2(A_2)$$

while Party 2 will always make a concession in the opposite case. A concession need not be the complete acceptance of the other party's last offer, but it must be large enough to reverse the inequality sign in (1) if the utilities corresponding to the new offer are substituted. (Zeuthen also assumes that if both parties' utility quotients happen to be exactly equal, *both* of them will make some concession in order to avoid a deadlock.) This process will continue until the two parties meet somewhere in the middle. It will end after a finite number of steps because the indivisibility of the smallest monetary unit (and other technical or psychological indivisibilities) sets a lower limit to the size of admissible concessions.

Zeuthen has also shown that this process will actually lead, in the essentially symmetric case assumed by him, to an equal division of the net gain. This is, of course, in agreement with Nash's theory. It is easy to see, however, that Zeuthen's

[14] That is, the actuarial value of his (cardinal) utility. Actually, Zeuthen measures the values of A_1 and A_2 to each party, not in terms of utility, but in terms of money, and assumes that each party tries to maximize the actuarial value of his net money gain. This assumption, however, is valid only in the special case when the marginal utility of money is constant to both parties. In the more general case we must measure all values in terms of von Neumann-Morgenstern cardinal utility.

[15] The intuitive plausibility of this assumption has been questioned (see J. Pen, "A General Theory of Bargaining," *American Economic Review,* Vol. XLII, No. 1 (March, 1952), esp. 33–34). We shall, however, see that this assumption can be dispensed with as an independent postulate (see Section 5 below).

model leads to the same solution as Nash's theory in the general case as well. In effect, inequality (1) can also be written in the form:

$$(2) \qquad U_1(A_1) \cdot U_2(A_1) < U_1(A_2) \cdot U_2(A_2)$$

so that we can restate Zeuthen's assumption by saying that the party whose last offer is associated with a lower value of the utility product, $U_1 \cdot U_2$, than is his opponent's last offer will always make a further concession and put forward a new offer associated with an even higher value of the product $U_1 \cdot U_2$ than was his opponent's last offer. (If both parties' last offers gave the same value for $U_1 \cdot U_2$, both will make concessions and put forward offers giving higher values of $U_1 \cdot U_2$.) Thus, each new offer made during the negotiations is bound to increase the value of the product $U_1 \cdot U_2$ and in the end the two parties will arrive[16] at terms that maximize[17] the value of $U_1 \cdot U_2$—which is exactly Nash's solution.

5. DERIVATION OF ZEUTHEN'S BASIC ASSUMPTION FROM MORE GENERAL POSTULATES

We propose to derive now, from a few simpler and more general postulates, Zeuthen's assumption that each bargaining party will be prepared to make a concession to his opponent whenever he finds that the latter's readiness to risk a conflict is at least as great as his own.

For this purpose we need the following postulates:

I. *Symmetry.* The bargaining parties follow identical (symmetric) rules of behaviour (whether because they follow the same principles of rational behaviour or because they are subject to the same psychological laws).[18]

II. *Perfect knowledge.* Each party can estimate correctly the probability that the other party will definitely reject a certain offer.

III. *Monotonity.* Suppose that Party 1 has received the offer A_2 from Party 2. Then, the probability p_1 of Party 1's rejecting A_2 and insisting on the more favourable terms A_1 is a monotone nondecreasing function[19] of the difference $U_1(A_1) - U_1(A_2)$ if all other independent variables are kept constant.

[16] Actually, they arrive at slightly different terms if at the end of the negotiations one party "overshoots the mark" by an over-generous concession. Strictly speaking, we have to assume that each party always makes the smallest concession which suffices to reverse the inequality (2). This assumption is permissible since the sizes of concessions are assumed to have a lower bound.

[17] If the upper-right boundary of the set of the pairs of real numbers (U_1, U_2) (which represent the possible values of the two parties' net utility gains) is a smooth curve without an angular point, the same argument can also be put in the following way. At the equilibrium point the inequality (2) must be replaced by an equality for small displacements and so we must have $d(U_1 \cdot U_2)/dU_1 = d(U_1 \cdot U_2)/dU_2 = 0$. But this means that the product $U_1 \cdot U_2$ must have a maximum at this point since the set of the pairs (U_1, U_2) is a convex set.

[18] This postulate is here equivalent to the assumption which we would express on the common-sense level by saying that each party will make a concession at a given stage of the negotiations if and only if he thinks he has at least as much "reason" as his opponent has to yield ground at that point.

[19] We cannot make p_1 a monotone strictly increasing function of this difference since p_1 cannot increase further once it has reached unity, however much this difference further increases.

IV. *Expected-utility maximization.* Unless both parties agree to make simultaneous concessions, each party will make a concession if and only if his making this concession will give him a prospect with higher expected utility than his refusing the concession would.

IV'. *Efficiency.* However, the two parties will agree to make simultaneous concessions if this policy gives both of them higher expected utilities than they would obtain otherwise.

We shall first assume that Postulate IV applies without the qualifications expressed in the qualifying clause ("Unless . . .) and in Postulate IV', and shall later consider what modifications are needed in our conclusions in view of these qualifications.

We have seen above (p. 148) that Party 1 will or will not insist on the more favourable terms A_1 according as the utility quotient $\Delta U_1/U_1$ is larger or smaller than p_2. To derive this result we used only the utility maximization postulate (corresponding to Postulate IV). This result can also be expressed as follows:

$$(3) \quad p_1 = 0 \text{ if } p_2 > \Delta U_1/U_1, \quad \text{and} \quad p_1 = 1 \text{ if } p_2 < \Delta U_1/U_1,$$

where p_1 denotes the probability that Party 1 will reject the terms A_2.

By the same token the analysis of Party 2's behaviour gives us:

$$(4) \quad p_2 = 0 \text{ if } p_1 > \Delta U_2/U_2, \quad \text{and} \quad p_2 = 1 \text{ if } p_1 < \Delta U_2/U_2.$$

On the other hand, it is easy to see that (3) and (4) together require that one of the following three possibilities should be true:

(a) Either $p_1 = 0$ and $p_2 = 1$, or

(5)   (b) $p_1 = 1$ and $p_2 = 0$, or

(c) $p_1 = \Delta U_2/U_2$ and $p_2 = \Delta U_1/U_1$.

But we have still to find out when each of these three cases applies. Now, (3) makes p_1 a function of p_2 and $\Delta U_1/U_1$. We can therefore write:

$$(6) \qquad\qquad p_1 = F(p_2, \Delta U_1/U_1).$$

Similarly, on the basis of (4) as well as the Symmetry Postulate (I), we have:

$$(7) \qquad\qquad p_2 = F(p_1, \Delta U_2/U_2).$$

(6) and (7) are two simultaneous equations in the two unknowns, p_1 and p_2. Since they are symmetric with respect to these unknowns their solution must be of the form:

$$(8) \quad p_1 = G(\Delta U_1/U_1, \Delta U_2/U_2) \quad \text{and} \quad p_2 = G(\Delta U_2/U_2, \Delta U_1/U_1).$$

But the function G is uniquely determined by Postulate III and property (5), so that we have:

$$(9.1) \qquad\qquad p_1 = 0 \text{ and } p_2 = 1, \qquad \text{if } \Delta U_1/U_1 < \Delta U_2/U_2,$$

(9.2) $p_1 = p_2 = \Delta U_1/U_1,$ if $\Delta U_1/U_1 = \Delta U_2/U_2,$

(9.3) $p_1 = 1$ and $p_2 = 0,$ if $\Delta U_1/U_1 > \Delta U_2/U_2.$

(9.2) is, however, inconsistent with Postulate IV' since it will result in wasteful conflicts with probability $(\Delta U_1/U_1)^2$, which can be avoided if the two parties agreed to make concessions simultaneously, i.e., adopt the rule of behaviour:

(9.2') $p_1 = p_2 = 0$ if $\Delta U_1/U_1 = \Delta U_2/U_2.$

Thus we obtain the result that:
Party 1 will make a concession if $\Delta U_1/U_1 < \Delta U_2/U_2$;
Party 2 will make a concession if $\Delta U_1/U_1 > \Delta U_2/U_2$; and
Both will make concessions if $\Delta U_1/U_1 = \Delta U_2/U_2$, as desired.

6. PSYCHOLOGICAL MODELS AND THE AXIOMATIC METHOD

The somewhat unexpected identity of the solutions yielded by Nash and by Zeuthen is a most encouraging sign because on the surface their approaches appear rather different. Many economists as well as other empirical social scientists will probably find Zeuthen's reasoning more convincing as it is based on a fairly plausible psychological model of the bargaining process, and, at the same time, they may look somewhat askance at Nash's game-theoretical method, which relies on abstract mathematical postulates whose empirical relevance may be less obvious. But, in actual fact, the two approaches are complementary.

The abstract axiomatic method should primarily be regarded as a heuristic device. If it can be shown that there is, consistent with peoples' behaviour in a certain situation, one and only one hypothesis satisfying certain attractive general postulates (whether formal postulates based on considerations of mathematical simplicity, continuity, symmetry, determinateness, etc.,[20] or "material" postulates suggested by observation or introspection), this is a strong argument[21] *for* this particular hypothesis—or at least *against* any alternative ones—even if no convincing psychological model is known which would explain the behaviour predicted by this hypothesis. Of course, if a satisfactory psychological model is also found, this will further increase our confidence in the hypothesis. But the converse is equally true. Our confidence in a given psychological model will certainly increase if the pattern of behaviour predicted by it is found to be one and the only one compatible with certain general postulates that are otherwise attractive to us.

Thus Zeuthen's and Nash's theories corroborate each other. At the same time,

---

[20] The history of the natural sciences—especially in the last few decades—has forcibly attested to the heuristic value of the axiomatic method and, in particular, of formal mathematical simplicity, etc., requirements in the selection of scientific hypotheses.

[21] But, obviously enough, it is never a conclusive argument. However plausible a certain postulate seems to be at first sight, there is always the possibility that it will have to be dropped if further empirical research finds it inconsistent with the actual facts—or even if further theoretical analysis finds it inconsistent with some other logical or mathematical postulates of a more fundamental nature.

Zeuthen's approach supplements Nash's in at least two important respects. It furnishes a more detailed analysis of the actual bargaining process. Moreover, it explains how the result of the bargaining process depends on the two parties' cardinal utility functions in the von Neumann-Morgenstern sense, i.e., on their attitudes towards risk-taking—a dependence which in Nash's theory must be assumed (in order to obtain a determinate solution) without the possibility of being explained.

On the other hand, owing to its higher level of abstraction and its mathematical rigour, Nash's theory has the important advantage of complete generality, which assures us that no particular case falling within the scope of the theory will possibly be overlooked. While Zeuthen's argument in its original form is restricted to symmetric bargaining situations, Nash's theory automatically covers the asymmetric case also and even lends itself naturally to extension to the still more general case of bargaining with a choice among several alternative threats. Moreover, whereas Zeuthen's argument as it stands is limited to collective bargaining, Nash's theory at once covers all of bilateral monopoly, duopoly, and bargaining by means of political pressure, etc., without restriction.[22]

7. NASH'S THEORY OF OPTIMAL THREATS

Nash's theory of the selection of "optimal" threats by each bargaining party naturally follows from his theory of bargaining with given threats.

He has shown that both parties always have optimal threats with maximin and minimax properties: i.e., if a given party uses an optimal threat, he will be assured of obtaining the best terms that can be exacted at all in the given situation from a rational opponent.[23] Nash also gives a geometric method by means of which both parties' optimal threats in this sense can be determined.[24] A simpler method can, however, be found on the basis of the following consideration.

Any threat aims at increasing the cost of a conflict to one's opponent without "unduly" increasing the cost of a conflict to oneself. Nash's concept of optimal threats makes possible an exact definition of what "unduly" means here. It can be shown that it is always profitable to increase the cost of a conflict to one's opponent if the cost to oneself either fails to increase at all or increases only in a smaller *proportion*;[25] and it is always profitable to allow the cost of a conflict to

---

[22] No economic theory relying on the concepts of orthodox economics alone could possibly cover such prima-facie different phenomena as duopoly, bilateral monopoly, etc., by the same argument; this is possible only on the higher level of abstraction adopted by the theory of games.

[23] It is, of course, assumed throughout that, after the choice of threats by each party, the outcome of bargaining is determined according to Nash's utility-product maximization rule.

[24] See his "Two-Person Co-operative Games," *loc. cit.*, esp. pp. 134–136.

[25] This can be shown as follows:

Suppose that in the original position each party's net gain connected with the equilibrium agreement point (as above the conflict situation) is $\bar{U}_1$ and $\bar{U}_2$ respectively. Obviously $\bar{U}_1$ and $\bar{U}_2$ will also express the cost of a conflict to each party. Moreover, we know that

one's opponent even to decrease if the cost to oneself decreases in a still higher proportion. On this basis each party's optimal threat is easily found.

Not only will both parties follow the rule of behaviour expressed in this conclusion, but they will also expect each other to follow it. If either party attempted to put forward a threat that in the event of a conflict implied a policy disproportionately burdensome to himself in relation to its damaging effect on his opponent, the opponent would regard it as a mere bluff.

(a) $$\bar{U}_1 \cdot \bar{U}_2 > U_1 \cdot U_2$$

where U_1 and U_2 are utility gains connected with any alternative terms. Now let the cost of a conflict to Party 1 and Party 2 increase by $a \cdot \bar{U}_1$ and $b \cdot \bar{U}_2$ respectively, where

(b) $$a < b.$$

Then the net utility gains connected with any terms will also increase by $a \cdot \bar{U}_1$ and $b \cdot \bar{U}_2$ for each party. Suppose the net utility gains connected with the new equilibrium agreement point (as above the new conflict situation) are $(\bar{U}'_1 + a \cdot \bar{U}_1)$ and $(\bar{U}'_2 + b \cdot \bar{U}_2)$, while the net utility gains connected with the same point in the original position (as above the original conflict situation) were $\bar{U}'_1$ and $\bar{U}'_2$. According to the utility maximization rule, in the new position the utility product *now* connected with the *new* equilibrium point must be larger than the utility product now connected with the *old* equilibrium point, so that

(c) $$(\bar{U}'_1 + a \cdot \bar{U}_1) \cdot (\bar{U}'_2 + b \cdot \bar{U}_2) > (\bar{U}_1 + a \cdot \bar{U}_1) \cdot (\bar{U}_2 + b \cdot \bar{U}_2).$$

On the other hand, (a) implies that

(d) $$\bar{U}'_1 \cdot \bar{U}'_2 < \bar{U}_1 \cdot \bar{U}_2.$$

(c), (d) and (b) taken in conjunction give us:

(e) $$\bar{U}_1 \cdot (\bar{U}'_2 - \bar{U}_2) > \bar{U}_2 \cdot (\bar{U}_1 - \bar{U}'_1).$$

It will be shown that (e) entails that

(f) $$\bar{U}'_1 > \bar{U}_1 \quad \text{and} \quad \bar{U}'_2 < \bar{U}_2.$$

For, suppose that $\bar{U}'_1 < \bar{U}_1$, so that $\bar{U}'_2 > \bar{U}_2$, then (e) could be written as

(g) $$(\bar{U}'_2 - \bar{U}_2)/(\bar{U}_1 - \bar{U}'_1) > (\bar{U}_2/\bar{U}_1).$$

Let us denote the upper-right boundary curve of the set of all possible pay-off points (U_1, U_2) by C. (The curve C represents, of course, the contract curve between the two parties, and both the point (U_1, U_2) and the point (U'_1, U'_2) will lie on C.) Then two cases may be distinguished.

(1) If the curve C has no angular point at $(\bar{U}_1, \bar{U}_2)$, then the tangent drawn to C at $(\bar{U}_1, \bar{U}_2)$ will have the backward slope $\bar{U}_2/\bar{U}_1$ because $(\bar{U}_1, \bar{U}_2)$ is the point at which the product $U_1 \cdot U_2$ takes its maximum value. Therefore, in view of (g), the point $(\bar{U}'_1, \bar{U}'_2)$ would lie above and to the right of this tangent, which is impossible since the set of the points (U_1, U_2) is a convex set.

(2) If the curve C does have an angular point at $(\bar{U}_1, \bar{U}_2)$, two tangents can be drawn to it at this point. The tangent, however, that is drawn from the side nearer to the point $(\bar{U}'_1, \bar{U}'_2)$ will, in general, have a slope even smaller than $\bar{U}_2/\bar{U}_1$ so that the point $(\bar{U}'_1, \bar{U}'_2)$ will all the more lie above and to the right of this tangent, which is once more impossible because of the convexity of the set of points (U_1, U_2).

Consequently, (f) must be true, and the new equilibrium agreement point $(\bar{U}'_1, \bar{U}'_2)$ must be more favourable than (or at worst as favourable as) the old equilibrium agreement point $(\bar{U}_1, \bar{U}_2)$ was to Party 1—which is what we have wanted to show.

8. COMPARISON OF HICKS' THEORY OF BARGAINING WITH THE NASH-ZEUTHEN THEORY

It is instructive to compare Nash's above theory of optimal threats with Hicks' theory of collective bargaining on the labour market (1932).[26]

Hicks' theory can be summarized as follows. Each bargaining party will make a concession if, in his view, the strike resulting from his refusing this concession would cost him more than the concession would. (Of course, costs must be reckoned at their present values to make significant comparison possible.) The higher a given wage rate the more its acceptance will cost the employer and the longer the strike he will be prepared to endure rather than to accept this wage rate. Thus each wage rate will be associated in the employer's mind with a strike of a given length (with one which would be just as expensive as accepting this wage rate), higher wage rates being associated with longer strikes. On the other hand, the lower a given wage rate the more its acceptance will cost the trade union (in terms of disutility) and the longer the strike they will be prepared to undertake rather than to accept this wage rate. Thus each wage rate will be connected in the trade unionists' minds with a strike of a given length (one which would be just as bad as accepting the wage rate), but in this case lower wage rates will be connected with longer strikes. There will be a unique wage rate that both parties associate with a strike of the same length: this is the highest wage rate that the union can exact from the employer. The latter in effect will not accept a wage rate higher than this one since he knows that his refusal can at worst result only in a strike short enough to cost him less than accepting this wage rate would. On the other hand, for opposite reasons he will certainly be prepared to accept this particular wage rate or, of course, any lower one.

As is easy to see, the primary difference between Hicks' theory and Nash's is Hicks' assumption that either party will choose, or threaten to choose, a strike in preference to a concession only if this strike is expected to cost him less than the concession.[27] By contrast, in Nash's theory each party is ready to exert pressure on the other party by the threat of a strike whose actual occurrence, if agreement failed, would cost the threatening party *more* than a concession would, provided the threat is likely to exact better terms from the other party if agreement succeeds.[28]

I think it must be admitted that Nash's assumption is the more realistic one. Trade unions, employers, and bargaining parties in other fields, do use threats of retaliation that would, if carried out, entail losses for themselves no less than for

---

[26] *Op. cit.* (See footnote 5 above).

[27] Professor Hicks admits that a union may occasionally embark upon strikes not profitable in terms of immediate results and costs in order to keep the employer aware of the union's power (*op. cit.*, p. 146). But he does not discuss the use of threats of such "unprofitable" strikes as bargaining weapons.

[28] Thus in Nash's theory it is not required that this strike should itself be a profitable venture, but only that its cost to this party should not be out of proportion to the losses this strike would cause to the other party.

their opponents—and it is rational for them to do so since they can thereby achieve better terms.[29]

9. ON THE ECONOMIC MEANING OF THE NASH-ZEUTHEN THEORY

What is the economic meaning of the Nash-Zeuthen theory of bargaining?

We have seen that this theory goes beyond orthodox economic theory in that it not only states that the agreement point will lie somewhere within the range of practicable bargains, but also predicts the actual position of this point within this range. Moreover, it predicts the two parties' behaviour even in the more general case where the limits of the range of practicable bargains themselves depend on the two parties' behaviour (viz., on the threats they use against each other).

According to this theory the most important factors determining the position of the agreement point within the range of practicable bargains are the two parties' attitudes towards risk-taking as expressed by their cardinal utility functions. A bargaining party will reach better terms the greater his risk preference, and the smaller the risk preference of his opponent. Thus orthodox economic theory is right in taking the view that, on the basis of the variables considered by the orthodox theory, the position of the agreement point is indeterminate within the range of practicable bargains: for it to become determinate it is necessary, though not yet sufficient, that the two parties' cardinal utility functions are also included among the variables of the theory.

The two parties' cardinal utility functions, however, are not the only variables influencing the position of the agreement point within the range of practicable bargains. This position will also depend on the conditions under which economic values (especially money) can be transferred from one party to the other: in particular, on whether, in the event of one party's making a concession to the other, the former's net loss will exceed, equal, or fall short of the latter's net gain. An obvious case where the net loss and the net gain will not be equal is a situation in which transfers are subject to transport costs. But the same will apply also if the two parties are subject to income taxation at different marginal rates. Again, in duopoly situations where direct side payments between the duopolists are not possible for one reason or another, but where concessions can take only the form of reducing output or allowing the opponent's output to rise, the loss in profits to one party will generally differ from the gain in profits accruing to the other party.[30] The conditions of transfer in this sense will obviously influence the readiness of both parties to make concessions and, therefore, the final outcome of the bargaining. We cannot here go into the details (which the reader can

---

[29] Professor Hicks' theory yields a determinate solution only because this special assumption just discussed reduces the range of practicable bargains to one unique point. If this assumption is dropped, indeterminacy returns and recourse must be made to some other theory of bargaining to obtain a determinate solution.

[30] For an analysis of a duopoly situation on the basis of Nash's theory and a comparison of the results with other theories of duopoly, see J. P. Mayberry, J. F. Nash, and M. Shubik, "A Comparison of Treatments of a Duopoly Situation," *Econometrica*, Vol. 21 (1953), pp. 141-154.

easily work out for himself), but it can be shown, for example, that each party's willingness to make concessions will be greater the more progressive the income tax to which he is subject[31]—a fact not unfamiliar to observers of wage determination by collective bargaining.

Another important corollary of the Zeuthen-Nash theory is the possibility of determining the exact economic value (nuisance value) of the ability to exert economic, political, or other pressure. Take the following simple example. Suppose that Party 1 tries to blackmail Party 2 by the threat of causing him a damage of $1000 unless Party 2 pays a certain amount. What is the amount they will tend to agree upon?

Some people would probably argue that this figure would be just a little below $1000 since Party 2 would be prepared to pay anything short of the full $1000 in order to avert Party 1's damaging action. But this would be no more valid than to argue that Party 1 would be ready to accept any amount, however small, since, if no agreement could be reached, he would receive nothing at all. In actual fact, these two arguments prove only that any figure between $0 and $1000 would be within the range of practicable bargains, but they tell us nothing about which figure will in fact be agreed upon. To determine this figure one must know the two parties' attitudes towards risk-taking as expressed by their cardinal utility functions.

The conclusion reached has general validity. The value of the ability to exert pressure on people by economic, political, or other threats is in general less than the value of the loss which the victim would suffer if these threats were carried out. The exact ratio between these two values, on the other hand, is primarily determined by the two parties' attitudes towards risk (and, of course, by the extent to which the threatened party can use effective counter-threats).

It may be noted that the bargaining theory considered here can be rendered more dynamic by allowing for the fact that, in deciding on their policies, the bargaining parties may also consider the effects of their present behaviour on their future bargaining positions. A tough policy followed in the present may increase the chance of a conflict in the present transaction, but may at the same time help to gain the reputation of toughness and thereby help to obtain better terms in other transactions. Taking account of this fact increases the relative desirability of obtaining better terms in the present deal and has the same effect on a bargainer's behaviour as an increase in his risk preference. The final terms reached will be most affected when this consideration has a much different importance for the two parties, e.g., if one of them is a large economic or political unit expecting to have to settle many similar transactions by bargaining in the future, while the other party is a small unit expecting to be involved in few or no similar transactions. In this case, the greater the difference between the sizes and transaction volumes of the two units, the tougher the policy that the larger unit

[31] The reason is that, other things being equal, a progressive income tax tends to decrease the value of the utility quotient $\Delta U/U$ because it raises the marginal rate of taxation relative to its average rate, and this is the case all the more, the more progressive this income tax is.

will find it profitable to follow; and if this difference is considerable, the smaller unit may be forced back virtually to its maximum-concession point—which means, of course, the disappearance of actual bargaining in the usual sense. Markets with one large monopolist (or monopsonist) on one side and a great number of small atomistic competitors on the other and oligopolistic markets with one large price leader and a greater number of followers are both instances of such a situation.[32]

The main applications of the Zeuthen-Nash theory of bargaining are obviously in the fields of duopoly, of bilateral monopoly (including the problem of collective bargaining on the labour market), and of bargaining with the help of political pressure. (Another of its applications is in the analysis of political equilibrium between two political units, but this is beyond the scope of this paper.) But in no other field, perhaps, has its superiority over earlier theories been more conspicuous than in the field of duopoly, which has so notoriously defied so many of the great names of economic science.[33]

On the other hand, the most important limitation[34] of the Zeuthen-Nash theory lies in the fact that it is restricted to two-party bargaining situations ("two-person games"), so that it is, for instance, inapplicable to oligopoly situations with more than two oligopolists. The removal of this restriction depends on finding a satisfactory determinate solution for the general n-person game;[35] and a solution to this problem will do much more than make a general theory of oligopoly possible; it will open the way for a general theory of the distribution of income and of power within society.

University of Queensland

[32] The last part of our argument, of course, has carried us over from the field of two-person games to the field of n-person games (with a large value for n), a field we are not qualified to enter in strict logic (but see footnote 35).

[33] See footnote 30.

[34] Another important limitation is the restrictive assumption of perfect knowledge, in particular the assumption that each bargaining party perfectly well knows the other party's subjective preferences (including his attitude towards risk-taking) as well as his objective damaging power. This assumption excludes the use of secrecy, deception and bargaining skill, so important in the real world. But it can be shown that this restrictive assumption might be dropped without essentially affecting the validity of the theory. Only, the position of the agreement point must now be made dependent not only on the two parties' *actual* cardinal utility functions but also on each party's *estimate* of the other party's utility function, and even on each party's estimate of what the other party's estimate is of his own (the first party's) utility function, etc. (which is the traditional problem of "conjectural variation"). But the discussion of this problem must be left for another occasion.

[35] For a solution of this problem in relation to a certain important but restricted class of n-person games, see L. S. Shapley, "A Value for n-Person Games," in *Contributions to the Theory of Games*, ed. by H. W. Kuhn and A. W. Tucker, Vol. II, Princeton, 1953, pp. 307–317. (It may be mentioned that the same value for this class of n-person games was found independently by the present writer before Mr. Shapley's paper became available in Australia.) A more general solution, extending the Zeuthen-Nash concept of bargaining equilibrium to the n-person co-operative game, will be described in a forthcoming paper of the present writer.

COMMENT ON THE BARGAINING PROBLEM

Jan Pen

The solution of this problem goes back essentially to F. Zeuthen of Copenhagen, who in his *Problems of Monopoly and Economic Warfare,* published in 1930, was the first writer to give a theory of bilateral monopoly in which the process of pressure and counterpressure between employers and labor was closely followed. This was an important step forward, for previously (since Edgeworth) such a process had always been held to be intangible. Another attempt was later made by Hicks (1932), but, as will be explained below, this must be regarded as a failure. A more recent solution by Shackle (1949) is also discussed later; he follows a line of reasoning which is not inspired by Zeuthen, but displays a certain affinity with the latter's views.

The important solution of Zeuthen has so far met with little response in literature. When I wrote this study in 1950 (published in Dutch under the title: *De Loonvorming in de Moderne Volkshuishouding* [Leiden]) the only continuation of his work known to me was a book by H. Denis, *Le Monopole Bilatéral* (1943). But in my opinion Denis has added little to the fundamental ideas of Zeuthen. Zeuthen himself, when giving a survey of the state of the problem in the journal *Economie Appliquée* in 1955, does not mention any other contributions either. An exception to this is an article written by me, reprinted herein, "A General Theory of Bargaining," in which attention is drawn to the possible extension of Zeuthen's theory. As will be seen below, these fundamental ideas seemed to me in some respects to be capable of amplification and extension. Zeuthen's analysis can be widened into a bargaining theory which comprises psychological elements and can thus be integrated with the analysis of human relations. At the same time, this wider approach could contain elements from economic theory—the classification of the forms of the market. A number of pages (which will doubtless prove the most tiresome to many readers) are devoted to an attempt to localize the bargaining situation in the midst of other forms of the market. This book therefore comprises both economic and psychological elements. It consequently tries in a certain sense to be a synthesis.

As mentioned above, there is little to report since 1950 with regard to a further development of the line of thought initiated by Zeuthen. But in recent years there has come to the fore an entirely different approach to the same and related problems: the theory of games. In their *Theory of Games and Economic Behavior,* Neumann and Morgenstern have given the strategy of freely acting man just as central a place as it received in Zeuthen's theory. The reader will note that in the following chapters wage determination under a bilateral monopoly is repeatedly dealt with, perhaps not as a "game of strategy," but certainly as a relation between men in which the "ludic" (from the Latin *ludere:* to play a game) element plays an important part. The theory of games and the theory of bargaining are therefore related. Whereas Morgenstern and Neumann did not devote detailed attention in their famous book to the solution of the bargaining situation, this was done by J. F. Nash, who develops their ideas ("The Bargaining Problem" and "Two-Persons Co-operative Games," both reprinted herein).

This is not the most suitable place to go into the development of the theory by Nash. Apart from his conclusion—agreement will be reached at the point where the product of net contract ophelimities is maximized—his work contains an important analysis of what he calls the optimal threats. A discussion of these interesting points cannot be fitted into a short preface.

We shall merely mention the fact that now there are two groups of solutions, those which go back to Zeuthen and those which are inspired by Morgenstern and Neumann. The connection between these two lines of thought forms a challenging problem. Do they supplement one another? Do they exclude one another? Can they be united into one theory?

J. C. Harsanyi has tried to answer these questions, with particular reference to the last one ("Approaches to the Bargaining Problem before and after the Theory of Games: A Critical Discussion of Zeuthen's, Hicks's and Nash's Theories," reprinted herein). His point of view is simple: the results of Zeuthen and Nash are "mathematically equivalent." He describes this "identity of the solutions" as "somewhat unexpected," which is certainly an understatement. The mathematical properties of the two results may be reducible to a common denominator, but the essence of the two trains of thought is certainly not. Harsanyi overestimates the importance of an affinity of form. The fundamental difference between the two approaches lies in the fact that in Zeuthen's theory, risk and uncertainty determine the atmosphere of the bargaining process, by which his analysis can be generalized into a chapter in the doctrine of human relations, while in Nash the equilibrium of bargaining is determined by the maximum of a function in which this uncertainty plays no part. The somewhat paradoxical situation occurs that in Nash's theory of games, the psychological factors have disappeared. The fact that this must be so emerges from the article by Nash, where it is explicitly assumed that the bargainers possess "equality of bargaining skill" and behave "rationally." It is true that Zeuthen, too, originally introduced similar hypotheses, but they are at variance with the essence of his theory, as he later clearly explained in his article in *Economie Appliquée*, p. 333, mentioned above. Harsanyi has derived the formal similarity of the solutions of Zeuthen and Nash from a system of assumptions, in which that of rational behavior and that of perfect knowledge occupy a leading position. By doing this he has caused the real content of the bargaining problem to vanish into thin air. This is all the more so when Harsanyi postulates perfect knowledge, and explains this as follows: "Each party can estimate correctly the probability that the other party will definitely reject a certain offer"; now the real bargaining problem has become insoluble. As I shall explain hereafter, this means that the threat of a conflict no longer has any effect, and that the wielding of economic power is out of the question. The conclusion must be that Harsanyi has been unable to bridge the two approaches—that of

Zeuthen and myself on the one hand and that of the theory of games on the other. I am in the dark about the real importance of his contribution. I really do not believe that we shall get any nearer to the solution of the problem by reducing the bargainers to computing machines. What we need is a rational theory of possibly irrational processes.

For all that, the question still remains of the relation between the two approaches; that of the "propensity to fight" and the theory of games of strategy. It seems to me that in the views of Nash the concept of "optimal threats" in particular may be rewarding. The threats reveal a crucial point. This idea, which is typical of the theory of games, has not yet been used by Zeuthen or myself. A synthesis of the various elements in Zeuthen, Nash, and myself is now being attempted by W. van der Ster (University of Uppsala). Some of his ideas are to be found in "Conflit et correspection en tant que facteurs décisifs dans le monopole bilatéral," *Economie Appliquée,* no. 1 (1957). His work was not yet completed at the time this preface was written. Perhaps he, or others, will give the answer to a number of questions posed here. As can be seen from the above, I regard my theory as a step (after the work of Zeuthen, a small one) along a road which may yet prove to be a long one: that of the integration of the bargaining situation into the complex field of human relations.

A UNIFIED TREATMENT OF BARGAINING THEORY
Harvey M. Wagner

Just as economic analysis historically has progressed from considerations of supply and demand conditions starting at the economy as a whole, then narrowing to the industry and finally to the individual firm, theories of wages have run a parallel course. Wage theory on the micro level, at least in modern times, has been termed the "theory of bargaining." Three outstanding approaches warrant our attention, viz., bilateral monopoly, risk evaluation, and the theory of games.[1] The purpose of this paper is to synthesize the interesting and valid conclusions from these separate approaches, and to present a unified picture of the pure theory of bargaining to date.

The typical framework for the analysis of conflicts assumes (1) both the buyer of labor services, viz. management, and the seller of labor services, viz. the union, are able to exercise a certain degree of monopoly power in setting the wage rate, (2) only a single bargaining situation is to be considered, and this contract is to be effective over a stated period of time, (3) the wage contract is negotiated at a micro level, i.e., between one firm and one union, or possibly one industry and one union, (4) other wages and external influences in the economy are given, and (5) each of the parties to the contract has a specified pattern of tastes which may be represented by means of an ordinal utility function.

Although we might have been more ambitious in considering the possibility of the bargaining situation modifying the negotiators' utility functions, we have decided to explore the essence of the bargaining problem with as few complicating factors as appear permissible, and we shall not elaborate in detail on the important topic of how each party arrives at its own utility function. Furthermore, the reader is of course aware that union-management contracts in real life situations ordinarily cover a wide range of employment stipulations and considerations (conditions of employment, fringe benefits, overtime pay, intra-firm wage structure, etc.). Again in order to make the analysis tractable we shall restrict ourselves to considering the determination of only two variables, viz. the wage bill and the amount of employment in the firm (or industry).[2] Needless to say, the universality of our conclusions must be tempered by the restrictive nature of our assumptions.

It is generally recognized that the solution to the wage contract problem given the above framework is practically always indeterminate. This is not to infer that we have no information as to the range of possibilities for a settlement

* The author is indebted to Professors Charles A. Myers, Abraham Siegel, and Robert Solow for their criticisms of an earlier draft of this paper. Any shortcomings of the analysis are of course the author's responsibility.

[1] Since we shall utilize *marginal product* considerations in our analyses of the above three approaches, we shall not consider it here as a separate theory.

[2] Or equivalently, the wage rate and the amount of employment.

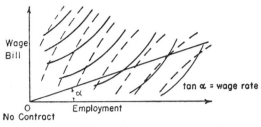

Fig. 1

nor under certain additional assumptions that we have no answer to the key questions: (a) what will be the wage resulting in the buyer-seller contract?, (b) how will the wage be arrived at?, and (c) what will be the factors influencing both the contract established and the manner in which it is established?

I. BILATERAL MONOPOLY

We employ as the basic tool of our theory a direct adaptation of the Edgeworth box diagram. Figure 1 illustrates both management's and the union's indifference curves (given their ordinal utility functions), each curve representing one party's preferences between total wages (wage bill) and the total amount of employment.[3]

The solid and segmented contours are the union's and management's indifference curves, respectively. The north-west direction indicates higher levels of satisfaction for the union and the south-east direction indicates higher levels of satisfaction for management. The origin represents the no contract point.

A uniform wage rate is represented by the tangent of an upward sloping line starting at the origin; the steeper the slope, the higher the wage rate. We have somewhat arbitrarily drawn the shape of the union's curves. Their appearance in Figure 1 is the usual shape found in consumer demand theory, i.e., the union has a diminishing marginal rate of substitution as between the wage bill and the "negative" of employment, i.e., leisure.[4] If the union were interested only in maximizing the wage rate, its indifference curves would coincide with the wage lines through the origin. If the contours are concave from below or if they are parallel upward sloping straight lines, then the union prefers to make no contract for employment below a certain wage, and above that wage is willing to contract for an unlimited amount of labor.[5]

---

[3] Note we assume that both a "unit of employment" as well as its associated wage rate are well defined terms; the wage bill = total amount of employment × wage rate.

[4] A case can clearly be made for differently shaped and sloping union indifference curves; there is of course no irrefutable reason to suppose that a union's curves will in general be identically patterned after an individual laborer's curves. We have drawn the union's contours as in Figure 1 mainly for the purpose of ease in exposition. See, e.g., J. R. Hicks, *The Theory of Wages* (London: Macmillan Co., 1935), p. 247; J. T. Dunlop, *Wage Determination Under Trade Unions* (New York: Macmillan Co., 1944), p. 231.

[5] It may help the reader to construct the analogy in consumer demand theory for the two good cases: assume the consumer has concave to the origin indifference curves and a given amount of one commodity. Depending upon the relative barter rate between the two com-

Similarly, there are several possible shapes for management's indifference curves, depending upon both monetary and non-monetary considerations. We shall find it most convenient to suppose that the sole factor determining the shape is the firm's marginal value product (MVP) function for labor services. For example, a horizontal MVP function implies management's willingness to hire an unlimited amount of labor up to a certain wage $w = MVP = $ constant, and above that wage to hire a zero amount; hence management's indifference curves in Figure 1 would be a set of parallel straight lines, all of whose slopes equal the critical wage rate. Management's indifference curves as they appear in the figure imply a monotonically downward sloping MVP curve for labor services.[6] We can define a mathematical function of the MVP relation for labor services which will represent management's indifference function passing through the origin.[7] The remaining indifference curves for management are vertical shifts of the curve passing through the origin, an upward movement yielding a less and a downward movement implying a more preferred position. Given any wage line, we then determine the point of tangency to some management indifference curve; we may interpret the tangency condition as an equality between the wage rate and the value of the MVP at that level of employment.[8]

We call the locus of tangency points of the wage rate lines and management's indifference curves the management-consumption curve. Similarly we call the locus of tangency points of the wage rate lines and the union's indifference curves the union-offer curve. Finally we denote the locus of tangency points of management's and the union's indifference curves as the contract curve; given a particular management (union) indifference curve, we can find a point on it representing a tangency condition between this curve and the highest of the union's (management's) indifference curves which touch management's (union's) contour.[9] Figure 2 illustrates all the relationships just defined.

Given a point on the union's offer curve, the angle of the tangent at that point represents the amount by which total wages must be increased to induce an additional amount of employment to be forthcoming; equivalently the angle is the marginal value of the supply curve of the trade union. Hence if management

---

modities, the consumer chooses either to keep all of the amount of his original commodity or to trade all of it.

[6] Although we could consider a more general MVP curve as in W. Fellner, "Prices and Wages under Bilateral Monopoly," *Quarterly Journal of Economics*, 1947, LXI, pp. 503–532, we would only be unnecessarily complicating the analysis for our purpose. The reader might construct management's indifference curves when the firm's MVP curve appears as in Fellner, p. 508.

[7] The ordinate of management's indifference curve through the origin at employment E_1 is the definite integral of the MVP curve from 0 employment to E_1; in other words, it is the total value product (TVP) of E_1 labor services.

[8] This conclusion follows directly from the fact that at each E any management indifference curve is TVP plus a constant k, and hence the tangency condition implies an equating of the wage rate to the derivative of ($TVP + k$), viz., MVP.

[9] See T. Scitovsky, *Welfare and Competition* (Chicago: R. D. Irwin, 1951), p. 417; W. Leontief, "The Pure Theory of the Guaranteed Annual Wage Contract," *The Journal of Political Economy*, 1946, LIV, pp. 76–79.

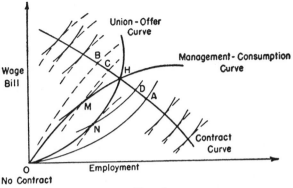

FIG. 2

were able to set the wage, it would select w_N (the wage associated with a line from the origin going through point N), since at that point the union's offer curve is tangential to the best of management's indifference curves touching the offer curve.

Similarly if the union were able to set the wage rate, it would pick w_M (the wage associated with a line from the origin going through the point M), since at that point the union would be equating the increment of total wages received from the marginal unit of employment given and the marginal rate of substitution between employment and wages; equivalently, M represents the point on management's consumption curve which maximizes the union's utility.[10]

Given a wage line which intersects both the offer and the consumption curves, the smaller amount of labor will be employed. We might note that for any specified level of employment (except at H), there are two levels of wages which will cause the same amount of employment to be utilized, one being favorable to management and one to labor. At point H, the price line is tangent to a management indifference curve and a labor indifference curve, which in turn, are tangent to each other. As is well known, given any point off the contract curve, there exists a point on the contract curve such that both parties are better off; on the other hand, given any point on the contract curve, it is not possible to make one party better off without making the other party worse off. H is the only point such that both parties are offering and consuming the amount of labor services and total wages they wish and such that it is not possible to find another solution in which both parties are better off. If either w_M or w_N initially prevailed, it would still be possible to make both parties better off by another contract settling on a point which is on the contract curve. How may such a "better point" be achieved?

Scitovsky[11] suggests that if, say, the wage rate first became w_M, at that point a second contract would be made for an additional amount of labor, and the process would continue until finally some point on the contract curve is reached.

[10] Points M and N are sometimes referred to as Stackelberg equilibrium solutions.
[11] *Ibid*, p. 418.

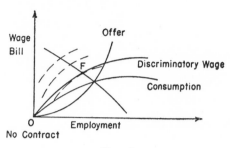

Fig. 3

Fellner[12] proposes the possibility of the original contract containing an "all-or-nothing" clause, i.e., a specification of both the wage rate and the amount of employment; assuming that the dominating party is acting optimally, we can again conclude that the final Fellner-type agreement is on the contract curve. A third approach, which is offered by Leontief,[13] suggests an alternative way of looking at the same problem. Consider the union's making a discriminatory wage offer. In other words, instead of the union offering a single wage rate for each unit of employment, it suggests a rate which varies at different employment levels (Figure 3).

The slope of the tangent at each point on the discriminatory wage curve yields the wage rate for that "unit" of employment. One can clearly see that the union should suggest the adoption of a contract in which prevailed very high wage rates for the first few units of employment and monotonically lower rates for additional units.[14] If management accepts the union's wage structure proposal, the firm will arrive at a contract at point F. No Scitovsky-type recontracting need take place nor does the union need an all-or-nothing clause, because F is the equilibrium point for management facing the discriminatory wage structure illustrated.

Previous theoretical analyses have recognized a basic indeterminateness in the uniform wage rate contract, which, it is usually suggested, would lie between the upper and lower limits w_M and w_N ; Fellner and Leontief have postulated even wider limits if an all-or-nothing or discriminatory wage clause is added, but their limits depend on a very strong implicit assumption, viz., a neutral valuation of the "no contract" possibility for both parties. Under this assumption, management prefers any contract yielding a positive amount of profits, no matter how small, to a contract yielding a zero or negative level of profits. Similarly the union prefers a contract which is strictly to the left of its indifference curve through the origin even though the outcome may be arbitrarily close to this curve. A contract will not take place at any points on each party's indifference curves through the origin or to the right of the union's or to the left of management's curves; these regions we call the Unwilling Zones. Thus the range of po-

---

[12] Fellner, op. cit., p. 512.

[13] Leontief, op. cit., p. 77.

[14] The discriminatory curve must lie entirely above management's indifference curve through F, except at F where it is tangent.

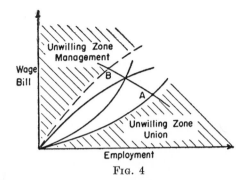

Fig. 4

tential contracts under a neutral no contract evaluation is bounded by the indifference curves passing through the origin, as is illustrated in Figure 4.[15] The optimal all-or-nothing or discriminatory wage contract for labor would be on the contract curve close to *B*, and for management on the contract curve close to *A*.[16]

There is evidently a direct relation between the Unwilling Zones determined by the indifference curves and the range of wage rates such that a contract will not take place. Provided that the "tangent" line (taken from the left) of the union's indifference curve through the origin at that point is not horizontal, there will be a finite range of relatively low wages such that the union will prefer no contract at all rather than one at a wage rate within this finite interval. Similarly, provided that the tangent line of management's indifference curve through the origin at that point is not vertical, there will be a finite range of relatively high wages such that management will prefer no contract to one at a wage rate within this finite range. The latter conditions are analogous to "corner tangencies" occurring in ordinary consumer indifference maps.

It is interesting to note two conclusions which are evident from Figure 2. First it is obviously to both parties' advantage to settle on a contract, for the no contract point (i.e., the origin) is not on the contract curve. Secondly, in the

[15] Because of the particular shape of the indifference contours in Figures 1 and 2, there exist regions in which contracts will not take place. If the indifference curves were differently shaped there might not be an *area* of unwillingness. For example, if the union's indifference curves indicated only a preference to maximize a uniform wage rate, then the horizontal axis (a *line*), where $w = 0$, contains the entire locus of points at which the union would be unwilling to make a contract.

[16] There is a semantic difficulty which we face in using the term "contract curve." The contract curve is defined simply as a locus of tangencies. This definition does not carry with it the implication that every point on the contract curve is an *a priori* candidate for an actual contract. Indeed as Figure 4 demonstrates, there may be whole zones encompassing segments of the contract curve which represent situations that in actuality would never take place. Since the points *A* and *B* in Figure 4 are contained in these zones, the relevant segment of the contract curve is "open" at both ends. Thus there does not exist a *best* all-or-nothing or discriminatory wage contract point for either labor or management. One may of course eliminate the formal mathematical difficulty of no unique optimum for each party by altering our neutral valuation assumption to include a desire to make contracts on as well as within the boundaries of the indifference curves passing through the origin. See Leontief, op. cit., p. 77.

process of bargaining, management, say, may initially offer a very low wage, which if accepted would result in a contract below N; as negotiations ensue, management, in a purported effort to "compromise," may suggest a higher wage $\leq w_N$, resulting in both the union's and management's being better off. Analogously, the union has the same possible strategy using an initial wage rate offer above w_M.

We shall now drop the assumption of neutral valuation of a no contract situation. Suppose management, say, considers a strike or lockout position as resulting in a specific net monetary loss.[17] In this case, under purely static assumptions, management would be willing to pay a wage bill resulting in a direct loss up to an amount equal to the expected loss resulting from a lockout. Such a valuation enlarges the contract possibilities, because management's selection of the no contract indifference curve is above the one passing through the origin by a vertical distance equal to the expected loss from a lockout. Management would make a contract for any wage short of an infinite one, although if the wage were very high, it would find it advantageous to purchase as few labor services as possible.

Similarly if the union viewed a strike as a net loss, it would be willing to accept a contract within a finite range to the right of its indifference curve passing through the origin. The union would be willing to settle on a contract at any strictly positive wage rate, no matter how low, although if the wage were very low, the union would find it to its advantage to supply an arbitrarily small amount of labor. In any event a no contract situation would be non optimal.

Negative valuations have little effect on the range of the final uniform wage contract since rates between w_M and w_N still seem optimal; such valuations seem to take on importance mainly when all-or-nothing ultimatums are possible, since the potential points on the contract curve increase in an unfavorable direction for each party placing a negative valuation on a no contract point. One effect of a negative valuation, which will be discussed below in our treatment of the theory of games, may be its influence upon the wage actually determined within the range w_M to w_N.

We may define a positive valuation of a no contract situation as the estimation on the part of the union that the wage if a dispute arises will finally be settled not below some given wage, or on the part of management that if a dispute arises the wage will finally be settled not above some given wage. Each party then has a point on his own offer or consumption curve below which he believes he need never go. We call the indifference curve through each of these points the critical or minimal indifference curves. The area in which a contract may be made is determined by the critical indifference curves for each party. Clearly it is optimal for a strike or lockout to occur only if each party's critical indifference curve does not touch or intersect the other party's corresponding critical curve. Strictly speaking, we should realize that when a strike or lockout appears optimal, neither party is "at fault" for presumably either one could have selected a

---

[17] That is, a net loss which, if it occurs, is a fixed "cost" over the period during which the contract is to extend.

lower minimal indifference contour. If one wishes to introduce ethical standards in establishing the cause of a no contract result, one might presumably be interested in which party (or parties) has a positive or negative valuation of the no contract situation.

Up to now we have discussed the conditions under which a contract will take place, the indeterminacy of the actual contract in the area of potential settlements, the relevant range of wage rates within which the contract will be made, and the determination of the most favorable contract from each party's point of view. We should be aware that our analysis has been based on the assumption that each party has full knowledge of the other party's reaction to any given wage rate. This assumption is truly basic in a theory of bargaining; for when each party is ignorant of his opponent's reaction to a given wage, he cannot estimate a best course of action to take, even if he alone has sole power to set the wage.[18] We can readily appreciate the necessity for assuming some information about the opponent's reaction by referring to Figure 2, where w_M and w_N are determinable only if both parties have a knowledge of the other's reaction curve. When risk evaluation considerations are introduced by an assumption of "imperfect knowledge," we do *not* mean that each party no longer is able to estimate with some degree of accuracy the offer or consumption curves. It is the imperfect knowledge of not knowing what strategy one's opponent will adopt which is at the heart of the uncertainty problem.

II. RISK EVALUATION

The risk evaluation approach to a "solution" of the bargaining problem has been been most notably expounded by Zeuthen, Pen, and recently Harsanyi.[19] We shall find it useful to develop our own risk evaluation notation before examining the analyses of the above authors. We let U^L and U^M denote the union's and management's utility functions, respectively. We extend the notion of a U function, as defined in section I, to now include randomized events as well as certainty events. For example, $U(X, Y; 1 - p, p)$ is defined as the ordinal value of the utility function for the composite event of X occurring with probability $1 - p$, and Y occurring with probability p, where X and Y are mutually exclusive and completely exhaustive events. Our further assumptions about U are (a)

---

[18] At best we can say that if each party is perfectly ignorant of the other party's reaction curve (i.e., offer or consumption curve), contracts will be proposed, discussed, but not accepted until at least one of the following occurs: (a) each party discovers his opponent's reaction curve and realizes the inherent *ex ante* indeterminacy of the situation, (b) the point H is reached and each party is willing to keep the contract, feeling that since at the prevailing wage the total amount of labor supplied is the same as the total amount of labor demanded, this "should" be the solution, or (c) the negotiators get tired of bargaining and settle on some arbitrary wage rate.

[19] F. Zeuthen, *Problems of Monopoly and Economic Warfare* (London: Routledge & Sons, 1930); J. Pen, "A General Theory of Bargaining," *American Economic Review,* 1952, LXII, pp. 24–42; J. C. Harsanyi, "Approaches to the Bargaining Problem Before and After the Theory of Games: A Critical Discussion of Zeuthen's, Hicks', and Nash's Theories," *Econometrica,* XXIV, 1956, pp. 144–157.

given two composite events E_1 and E_2, either $U(E_1) > U(E_2)$, $U(E_1) = U(E_2)$, $U(E_1) < U(E_2)$, implying preference, indifference, or dislike between E_1 versus E_2, (b) U is transitive, (c) given any composite events E_1, E_2, and E_3, such that $U(E_2) \leqq U(E_1) \leqq U(E_3)$, then there exists a probability p^* such that $U(E_1) = U(E_2, E_3; 1 - p^*, p^*)$.[20]

We know from our previous analysis that there exists a wage w_i such that $U^L(w; 1) = U^L(C; 1)$ for all wages $w \leqq w_i$, where C stands for the outcome of a conflict (no contract). Similarly, there exists a wage w_j such that $U^M(w; 1) = U^M(C; 1)$ for all wages $w \geqq w_j$. We are assuming that the values for U for certainty events are based on the utility of the final outcome—the amount of employment and wage bill—resulting from the establishment of a particular wage w. Then we know that U^L reaches a constrained maximum at w_M and U^M reaches a constrained maximum at w_N, provided that $U^L(w_M; 1) > U^L(C; 1)$ and $U^M(w_N; 1) > U^M(C; 1)$. Finally we know that $U^L(w; 1) = U^L(C; 1)$ for $w \geqq w_j$, and $U^M(w; 1) = U^M(C; 1)$ for $w \leqq w_i$, since wage rates within these ranges result in a conflict.[21]

Although the theory of games approach usually contains sufficient assumptions to permit linear operations on the utility functions,[22] we need not postulate the extra restriction at this stage of our analysis.

Consider the state in the bargaining process where management has made an offer $w^* \leqq w_M$ and the union has made a counter offer $w^{**} \geqq w_N$. Zeuthen has suggested in effect the following: management determines p^* such that $U^M(w^{**}; 1) = U^M(w^*, C; 1 - p^*, p^*)$, and similarly the union determines p^{**} such that $U^L(w^*; 1) = U^L(w^{**}, C; 1 - p^{**}, p^{**})$. Thus it is proposed that each party, contemplating a composite event which combines the possibility of obtaining its offer versus the possibility of a no contract situation, determines the probability mixture in the composite event which results in its being indifferent as between that event and the certainty alternative of accepting the opponent's offer.

Assuming each party has full information about the other party's utility function, Zeuthen reasons that since each p indicates the "willingness of a conflict," the party with the lowest p has more to lose from a conflict and should back down from his offer; if $p^* = p^{**}$, but $w^* \neq w^{**}$, then either one or both parties should back down, for otherwise a conflict results which is harmful to both parties.

We shall criticize Zeuthen's analysis by an exposition of the economic "game"

---

[20] When we come to the theory of games approach, we also need to make use of a further assumption (d) if for two composite events E_1 and E_2, $U(E_1) = U(E_2)$, then given some composite event E_3 and any probability p, $U(E_1, E_3; 1 - p, p) = U(E_2, E_3; 1 - p, p)$, (the strong independence property). See P. A. Samuelson, "Probability, Utility, and the Independence Axiom," *Econometrica*, XX, 1952, pp. 670–678.

[21] The reader may have noted that we are now considering utility functions in which the wage rate appears explicitly as an argument. But as before, the utility function inherently depends upon the *outcome* of a wage rate w which is either insisted upon or agreed to.

[22] See footnote 20.

Union		Management		
		Accept w^{**} I	Wait for union to move II	Make new offer III
Accept w^*	I	X	w^*	X
Wait for management to move	II	w^{**}	C	$w^* < w_2 \leqq w^{**}$
Make new offer	III	X	$w^* \leqq w_1 < w^{**}$	$w^* < w_3 < w^{**}$

Fig. 5

X: We postulate that it is impossible for management (union) to declare strategy I and the union (management) to simultaneously declare strategies I or III; if management (union) declares strategy I, the union (management) announces strategy II, and a contract is made at wage w^{**} (w^*).

which both parties are assumed as playing, and by a discussion of what their optimal strategies should be. Figure 5 portrays each party's evaluation of the situation at a particular stage in the bargaining, where each party is considering the outcomes after it declares its intentions.[23]

A wage w_j represents the outcome at the end of the bargaining and presumably depends on the path of negotiations which is taken. The outcome C occurs if both parties decide not to make another offer or to accept a previous one.

It is clear from an examination of management's (labor's) utility function that if $w^* < w^{**}$, management (labor) III is always at least as good as management (labor) I and usually is better. Therefore it does not seem pertinent for each party to consider either the acceptance of the opponent's offer, or a composite event in which the opponent is supposed to be randomizing between the party's own offer and a conflict. It is true that if the union (management) were to play strategy I with probability $1 - p^* (1 - p^{**})$ and strategy II with probability $p^* (p^{**})$, then management (union) would be indifferent as between choosing its own strategy I or II. But as we have indicated, the union (management) will not consider strategy I. Thus the only justification for a calculation and comparison of p^* and p^{**} is that such a procedure leads to a sensible selection of a strategy.

Zeuthen's reasoning is that if, for example, the union plays its strategy II with a probability $p' < p^*$, management should choose its own strategy II; but the conclusion is not generally valid. If the union has made a firm commitment as to the strategy it will use, and w_1 is sufficiently high, then it is possible

[23] The reader should distinguish between our version of Zeuthen's game situation and a game as we shall define it in the next section. Here we do not assume *both* players first make their choice of strategies, and then simultaneously announce them. Also we presently allow a party to change its initially announced strategy after hearing its opponent's but before the final outcome has occurred.

Zeuthen in his formulation further considers the situation where there is a lack of complete knowledge about the opponent's utility function. Also he makes use of a cardinal utility function, which at this point we find is not necessary to assume. We return to a discussion of the latter assumption below in our analysis of Harsanyi's contribution.

for $U^M (w^{**}; 1) > U^M(w_1, C; 1 - p', p')$. In other words, if the union randomizes between its strategies II and III, playing II with probability p', management II may turn out *not* to be a good strategy. On the other hand, if management has the opportunity of influencing the union's plans by the selection of its own strategy, then although $p' > p^*$ before management announces its intentions, management might benefit by selecting strategy II, attempting to convince the union that the offer is an ultimatum, and finding that the union pays heed to its immediate self-interest by switching to strategy III. What is more, if either party can be convincing that it will choose strategy II for the remainder of the negotiations, the defensive party would be better off in the immediate situation to submit rather than incur a conflict.[24] Thus we see that a comparison of p' and p^* is not meaningful without further postulating about the finality of a declared strategy; the party first declaring an ultimatum is assured of being better off, *provided that* he can rely on his opponent bowing to present self-interest. The last qualifying phrase gives us the key to why priority per se in making an ultimatum does not yield *the* solution to the bargaining problem: an opponent may refuse to accept an ultimatum, even though in so doing he hurts himself, because concomitantly he is able to penalize his opponent for being stubborn. In the long run of bargaining situations, such a short run self-penalizing strategy may be optimal.

In concluding our criticism of Zeuthen's argument, we note that just as p^* does not reflect management's willingness to choose strategy II, p^{**} does not yield information about p'. Hence a comparison of p^* and p^{**} seems irrelevant for the purpose of selecting a good strategy.

It might occur to us to make calculations with composite events containing strategies II and III with a view toward revising Zeuthen's approach. But unless additional assumptions are made as to the entire bargaining process, we see immediately that the quantities w_j are unknowable until the end, and although we have certain bounds for w_j, this information is not sufficient to calculate composite indifference relations.

Pen, elaborating on Zeuthen's analysis, not only considers the parties' making irrelevant probability calculations, but also postulates that they consider the composite events containing w_M and C for the union, and w_N and C for management, rather than w^{**} and C, and w^* and C, respectively. For reasons analogous to those offered in criticism of Zeuthen's thesis, we believe that these calculations are truly not pertinent.

III. THEORY OF GAMES

We are now at the point in our analysis where we realize we can place certain limits on the contracts possible and that we suspect there may be some bargaining strategies for each party which will necessarily result in a determinate solution. We shall make use of the theory of games to sharpen our notions as to the contract zone as well as to the possible equilibrium contracts. Finally we shall

---

[24] Our argument parallels that of T. C. Schelling, "An Essay on Bargaining," *American Economic Review*, 1956, XLVI, pp. 281–306.

Table of Outcomes

Union		Management	
		Accept N or conflict I	Accept any offer II
Accept M or conflict	I	C	M
Accept any offer	II	N	H

Fig. 6

discuss the possibility of deriving a unique "fair" solution to the bargaining problem by utilizing the theory of games approach.

Let us examine the notion of the non-cooperative game which was developed by Nash.[25] Formally a non-cooperative game assumes a conflict situation in which both opponents have no means of direct communication, collaboration, or coalition. Although on the surface such a game appears to be irrelevant for union-management bargaining situations, its application is valuable in that the non-cooperative game yields what each party can at least be assured of regardless of his opponent's strategy.

The wage negotiation game in mathematical language is "non-zero sum," since under any contract the loss which accrues to management, say, is not necessarily equal to the gain accruing to the union. We now assume that the property in footnote 20 holds in addition to those we have previously postulated. Although the model which we have been considering (Figure 2) allows for a continuum of possible wage contracts and strategies, we can obtain the results we desire from considering a non-cooperative game in which each player (management and the union) has only two strategies (Figure 6).

We conceive of the non-cooperative game as each party's deciding upon a strategy, then informing an "umpire" (an arbitrator or an enforcement agent) of the choice, and the umpire in turn informing each player of the outcome, pictured in Figure 6; although we generally admit composite strategies (i.e., probability mixtures of "pure" strategies), in the examples to follow a consideration of randomizing is not necessary. We have arbitrarily decided that for our analysis when both parties choose their strategy II, H will be the outcome. Let us first study the game in which each party has either a neutral or a negative valuation of the no contract outcome C. Then the payoff tables for each party might appear as in Figure 7. The actual numbers in Figure 7 are arbitrary.

Consider the following pairs of strategies: union I—management II, or union II—management I. We say that each of these strategies represents an equilibrium pair, for in the first pair, had the union been informed that management was going to choose strategy II, the union would have still chosen strategy I, and vice versa; a similar stability phenomenon holds for the second pair. On the other hand, any other pair of pure strategies does not exhibit stability. Consider

[25] J. Nash, "Non-Cooperative Games," *Annals of Mathematics*, 1951, 54, pp. 286–295.

Payoff to Union

U	M	
	I	II
I	0	3
II	1	2

Payoff to Management

U	M	
	I	II
I	0	1
II	3	2

FIG. 7

Payoff to Union

U	M	
	I	II
I	0	3
II	1	2

Payoff to Management

U	M	
	I	II
I	−10	1
II	3	2

FIG. 8

union I—management I; as soon as either party has knowledge of the other's choice, he is induced to change his strategy. Nash has proven that there always exists at least one pair of equilibrium strategies,[26] and we have seen that there may be more than one pair.[27] Furthermore, some equilibrium pairs are better than others for a given player, and some pairs may be strictly worse than others for both players.[28]

An important result of the non-cooperative game situation (i.e., one for which there is no agreement as to the level of employment, but only as to the wage rate) is that the union can always guarantee itself $U^L(N)$ and management can always guarantee itself $U^M(M)$ by the choice of strategy II. In other words, either party can give in to his opponent's best overall wage rate. Hence for this situation we can further narrow the range of possible contracts to those in the area bounded by union's indifference curve through N and management's indifference curve through M.

If, say, management has a large negative valuation of a lockout (because of a resultant substantial real economic loss), whereas the union does not (Figure 8), then we gain some insight into the factors deciding which equilibrium pair of strategies might result. It seems likely that the pair union I—management II will be chosen, for the union by a threat to choose strategy I appears to be able

[26] In general situations, an equilibrium strategy might involve a randomizing between several pure strategies.

[27] The reader may wonder why the outcome H is not an equilibrium point. This is so because of the particularly simple game we have set up; if, for example, we had given to each player an additional strategy III "Accept H or conflict," then union III-management III would also turn out to be an equilibrium pair.

[28] See A. Henderson, "The Theory of Duopoly," *Quarterly Journal of Economics*, 1954, LXVIII, pp. 565–584.

Payoff to Union		
	M	
U	I	II
I	2	3
II	0	1

Payoff to Management		
	M	
U	I	II
I	2	0
II	3	1

FIG. 9

to force management to select strategy II. Whereas the union can afford the selection of I if management chooses I, management has relatively more to lose in this situation.

We recall that a strike or lockout may seem desirable if both parties have a positive valuation of a non contract situation (Figure 9). We easily determine that the only equilibrium pair of strategies is union I—management I, resulting in no contract. Even if the ordinal utilities along the main diagonal are interchanged, a no contract situation arises. Were an agreement possible between management and the union in this latter case, such that they both would choose strategy II, then each party would be better off. We are thus led to the consideration of cooperative games.

In a cooperative game we allow both the union and management to attempt an agreement on what appears to be a mutually beneficial contract. From our analysis above, we know that the cooperative contract should guarantee that each player does at least as well as when no cooperation takes place. The mere permission to coalesce is still not strong enough to determine a unique solution in the mutual bargaining situation, but we can attempt to find a unique solution if we consider an umpire or arbitrator making a decision according to a set of presumably reasonable and fair rules. Nash, Raiffa, and Braithwaite[29] have each advanced sets of rules, and we should realize that there does not exist a unique collection of "reasonable and fair" rules; hence different theorists have come to different conclusions as to the particular solution of a bargaining problem. For an understanding of the techniques such theorists use, we merely need to expound Nash's reasoning and postulates:

We desire that our solution not only should be unique, but also should have the following properties: (a) there exists no alternative contract such that one party can be better off *without* making his opponent worse off, (b) the solution does not change if we apply positive linear transformations to either or both of the utility functions, where we define such a transformation on $U(X)$ to be $U'(X) = aU(X) + b$, $a > 0$ (X may be a composite event), (c) if we are given

[29] J. Nash, "Two-Person Cooperative Games," *Econometrica*, 1953, 21, pp. 128–140; H. Raiffa, "Arbitration Schemes for Generalized Two-Person Games," *Contributions to the Theory of Games, II*, Annals of Mathematics Study No. 28 (Princeton: Princeton University Press, 1953), pp. 361–387; R. B. Braithwaite, *Theory of Games as a Tool for the Moral Philosopher* (Cambridge: Cambridge University Press, 1955).

a certain set of possible contracts from which we determine a solution, then any subset of these possible contracts containing the original solution must also have this contract as its solution, and finally, (d) if for each possible contract X, where $U^L(X) = a$ and $U^M(X) = b$, there exists a contract Y where $U^L(Y) = b$ and $U^M(Y) = a$, then our solution Z must satisfy $U^L(Z) = U^M(Z) = k$. The first requirement seems natural from our usual discussion of Pareto optimum points; our second requirement seems minimal since we are only postulating an ordinal utility function. The last two assumptions are far from trivial. One implies that the removal of "irrelevant" contracts should not change the previous solution,[30] and the other introduces a notion of fairness, or equivalently, the removing of any personal biases in the result of arbitration other than those which are inherent in the utility functions.[31]

To construct the Nash solution, we determine a two dimensional figure representing each party's utility for every possible contract. We ascertain the range of possible contracts by a consideration of the non-cooperative game. Specifically, as we concluded in the case of the neutral no contract valuations, the range of possible contracts falls between labor's indifference curve through N and management's indifference curve through M, which intersect the contract curve at points D and C, respectively (Figure 2). The two dimensional utility figure appears in Figure 10, where we have made a transformation of each utility function such that $U^L(N) = U^M(M) = 0$, and where the point C and D correspond to the same lettered points in Figure 2. The possible contracts of interest are on the upper outer boundary of the utility figure, and, provided the boundary does not contain any composite events,[32] there is a one-to-one correspondence of points on this locus and the points on the old contract curve between C and D; we shall therefore also call this locus the contract curve. Our solution is that point S on the contract curve which is tangent to the highest curve in the set of rectangular hyperbolas intersecting the contract curve; or

[30] On the surface this postulate seems reasonable. We shall consider an illustration which is intended to throw some doubt on the "fairness" of the assumption: Suppose two parties, appealing to an arbitrator, are arguing over a settlement in the range \$50 to \$100. The arbitrator, acting fairly and having the knowledge of both parties' utility functions, makes an \$80 judgement. Suppose that the arbitrator is later faced with the identically same situation, with the only exception that the range for settlement has changed to \$50 to \$80. Would or should he in fairness make the identical \$80 judgement, as the postulate requires? This whole question is related to the theory of games problem of finding an "optimal" strategy which while satisfying other nice properties is not affected by the introduction or disappearance of inadmissible strategies. See, e.g., H. Chernoff, "Rational Selection of Decision Functions," *Econometrica*, 1954, 22, pp. 422–443.

[31] Nash includes two other axioms in his system, but we shall not state them here since they tend to be of a strictly mathematical nature and do not have a direct influence upon our analysis.

[32] It is possible that the contract curve from Figure 2 might produce a contract curve which is non convex from above in Figure 10. But we have permitted an assumption which definitely establishes convexity, viz., that we include in the range of possible contracts those which can be formed by a randomization of any two contracts in Figure 2.

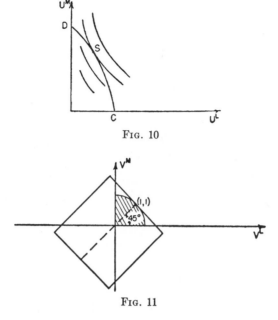

FIG. 10

FIG. 11

equivalently, S is that point which maximizes $U^L(X)U^M(X)$.[33] The reader can verify that properties (a) and (b) above are satisfied by a point constructed in this manner. To prove that this point is indeed the solution, we make positive linear transformations on U^L an U^M such that at the tangency point S, $V^L(S) = V^M(S) = 1$, where V^L and V^M are the transformed utility functions. Using the utility figure defined by the V functions, we draw a square which completely encloses the utility figure and whose upper right hand side is tangent to the contract curve at S and is bisected at the point S (Figure 11). This large square represents a hypothetical range of possible situations, and by conditions (a) and (d) above, the point S is the solution to this set.[34] Hence by condition (c), S is also the solution to the original range of contracts.

We should recognize that the actual solution which we derive depends upon two important factors: first, we know each party's ordinal utility function; hence, secondly, we can determine each party's minimal level of utility that it can assure itself. In some cases this minimum may be determined by a positive valuation of the no contract situation for either or both of the parties, rather than by a consideration of the offer and consumption curves alone.

We argued in section II that without further assumptions, each party may not

[33] H in Figure 2 will correspond to S only in the unlikely case that $U^L(X)U^M(X)$ is maximized exactly at H. Otherwise, H will lie to the left or right of S on the contract curve depending upon whether $U^M(H) > U^M(S)$ or $U^L(H) > U^L(S)$, respectively.

[34] The reader might note the artificiality of this construction. What we are contemplating is the solution to some purely hypothetical situation which might or might not occur in reality. We then use the solution of this conjectured situation in our analysis of the problem at hand. See footnote 30.

find Zeuthen's strategy either reasonable or optimal. In this section we found that a unique solution to the bargaining problem in game theoretic terms can only be realized by our imposing a certain set of "fair rules." Harsanyi[35] has attempted to show that if we assume in the risk evaluation approach that each party's utility function obeys those postulates presumed in the theory of games, and furthermore if *we* require the parties obey Zeuthen's strategies as *rules*, then these rules, if carefully defined, would also lead to Nash's solution.

Harsanyi's analysis is not strictly correct. He follows Zeuthen in assuming that p* and p** (defined in section II) are computed with C in the utility functions. He then states that $U(C) = 0$ for both parties and goes on to show an equivalence between both sets of rules. But the Nash solution does not necessarily assume that $U(C) = 0$ for both parties, and in fact, as we have reasoned under a neutral valuation of the no contract situation, $U^L(N) = U^M(M) = 0$ in the Nash construction. The equivalence proof rests on the proviso that $p*$ and p** are computed in a composite event comparing the possibility of the party's own proposal being accepted and the possibility of an event yielding a zero value for the utility function.

Reflection will convince one that the latter proviso is not trivial, and indeed we are doubtful whether Zeuthen-type reasoning is logically consistent with Nash-type reasoning. The Nash solution is fundamentally based on what either party can secure for itself without mutual cooperation. If a non-cooperative situation occurs, we have shown that the minimal utility each party can expect is taken on at his opponent's Stackelberg equilibrium point (see footnote 10). We find it difficult to pay heed to the spirit of Zeuthen's reasoning and at the same time insert this point for C in Zeuthen's formula. In a "step by step" negotiation game, such as Zeuthen depicts, the utility which each party can at least assure itself is better than that for either C or the Stackelberg point, viz., it is the utility for the opponent's last offer. Substituting this wage in the Zeuthen composite event formulas results trivially in $p = 1$, implying that both parties will always give in until they converge upon the same wage. Unless we can justify the Nash non-cooperative point substitution, the manipulations below do not support a proof of general equivalence between the two sets of rules.[36]

In any event, although Harsanyi is encouraged that both sets of *rules* can potentially lead to the same solution, we wish to stress that caution must be taken not to confuse the distinction between what an individual party would be inclined to do in his own self-interest, and what *we* might feel both parties should do in the light of fairness.

[35] Harsanyi, op. cit., pp. 147–149.

[36] The proof is as follows: the theory of games axioms allow us to write Zeuthen's formulas as $U^M(w^{**}) = (1 - p^*)U^M(w^*) + p^*U^M(X)$ and $U^L(w^*) = (1 - p^{**})U^L(w^{**}) + p^{**}U^L(Y)$, where $U^M(X) = U^L(Y) = 0$. We can then express the first and second relations as functions of p^* and p^{**}, respectively. If $p^* < p^{**}$, algebraic manipulation will yield $U^M(w^{**})U^L(w^{**}) > U^M(w^*)U^L(w^*)$. By the Nash rule, w^* is not the solution. By the Zeuthen rule, management should make a new offer $w > w^*$ so as to eliminate the inequality. Parallel reasoning follows for $p^* > p^{**}$. If $p^* = p^{**}$, but $w^* \neq w^{**}$, then by the Nash rule it can be shown that there exists a w such that $U^M(w)U^L(w)$ is greater than $U^M(w^{**})U^L(w^{**}) = U^M(w^*)U^L(w^*)$, and by the Zeuthen rule, both parties should yield.

IV. SUMMARY

In retrospect, we have investigated a number of properties existing in a bargaining situation not only by drawing upon the usual analysis of bilateral monopoly, but also by relating the approaches of risk evaluation and theory of games. We have affirmed that the bargaining contract remains indeterminate unless we introduce some sort of arbitration or behavioral procedure based upon a given set of rules. If the contract is to be determined by bargaining alone, we have noticed that the range of possible contracts is restricted to those yielding at least each party's non-cooperative attainable utility. Lastly we have illustrated that there will be a certain set of strategies that lead to a termination of bargaining and have given some indication as to which of these possible equilibrium situations may actually result. Although we have made many simplifying assumptions, we are still able to exhibit the main problems existing in a bargaining situation. We are not inclined to believe that the introduction of more realistic assumptions will remove the *ex ante* indeterminacy.

THE BARGAINING PROBLEM

NOTES: *John C. Harsanyi*
REJOINDER: *Harvey M. Wagner*

I

In a recent paper[1] H. M. Wagner has argued that the only way of deriving a determinate solution for a bargaining situation is by means of introducing "fairness" considerations or similar moral criteria. In the case of Nash's theory of bargaining in particular, Wagner claims that two of Nash's axioms (presumably axioms 7 and 8 of Nash's 1950 paper, or equivalently axioms V and IV of his 1953 paper)[2] have the nature of moral postulates, rather than the nature of assumptions about the actual behaviour of rational bargainers. As similar views were earlier expressed by other authors,[3] and as the issue is crucial for the theory of bargaining, I should like to use this opportunity, first of all, to make some comments on this problem. Then, I propose to deal with Wagner's criticism of Zeuthen's bargaining model, and with his objections to my proof of the mathematical equivalence of Zeuthen's and Nash's theories.[4]

I now propose to show that there is no need for invoking moral considerations in connection with Nash's axioms. The first of the two axioms in question in fact expresses an important structural property of the *actual* bargaining process: as has been pointed out by Nash, it expresses the fact that in bargaining the range of the possible alternative deals considered by the two bargaining parties is continually narrowed down more and more so, that in the end any proposed deal has to compete only with close alternatives but not with the more remote alternatives already rejected by the bargaining parties at earlier stages.[5]

Nash's other axiom is a symmetry postulate. It expresses the idea that in a perfectly symmetric bargaining situation involving two rational players neither player will be prepared to give his opponent better terms than he is given himself by the latter. This mechanism will tend to give rise to a symmetric solution

---

[1] "A Unified Treatment of Bargaining Theory," in this Journal, April 1957, Vol. XXIII, pp. 380–397.

[2] See J. Nash, "The Bargaining Problem," *Econometrica*, 1950, Vol. 18, pp. 155–162; idem, "Two-Person Cooperative Games," *Econometrica*, 1953, Vol. 21, pp. 128–140.

[3] Cf. H. Raiffa, "Arbitration Schemes for Generalized Two-Person Games," in *Contributions to the Theory of Games*, Vol. II, ed. by H. W. Kuhn and A. W. Tucker, Princeton, 1953, pp. 361–387; and R. B. Braithwaite, *The Theory of Games as a Tool for the Moral Philosopher*, Cambridge, 1955.

[4] See J. C. Harsanyi, "Approaches to the Bargaining Problem Before and After the Theory of Games: A Critical Discussion of Zeuthen's, Hicks', and Nash's Theories," *Econometrica*, April 1956, Vol. 24, pp. 144–157.

[5] See Nash, 1953, p. 138. Actually, I have shown in my earlier paper (see previous footnote) that by means of Zeuthen's model the Zeuthen-Nash solution can be derived without the use of this axiom, merely by the use of the usual rationality postulates and a symmetry postulate.

in any symmetric bargaining game between two rational individuals, quite irrespective of the moral standards (if any) of the two bargaining parties.[6]

We have to distinguish between *bargaining theories*, which try to predict the outcome of actual bargaining behaviour, and *arbitration theories*, which try to supply criteria for defining a "fair" solution for a bargaining situation. The former belong to positive economics, the latter to welfare economics. The Nash-Zeuthen theory of bargaining falls into the former category: it deals with rational bargainers each of whom considers only what his own interests are[7] and what may be acceptable to the other party in terms of the latter's own interests.

Of course, anybody may define, if he wishes to, his own standard of "fairness" in terms of the Nash solution. In that case for him this solution may have the nature of both a "bargaining theory" and an "arbitration theory." But I agree with Professor Braithwaite that as an arbitration theory the Nash solution is not particularly attractive: in many cases it yields a payoff distribution that most of us would regard as inconsistent with the standards of fairness we entertain.

This is of course not surprising. In the case of a symmetric game, where the two parties are equally "strong," both bargaining theories and arbitration theories will furnish a solution that gives equal payoffs to both parties. But in the general case a good bargaining theory will realistically predict that the "stronger" party will obtain a larger payoff—while an arbitration theory expressing common standards of "fairness" will still tend to recommend an equal, or at least a less unequal, payoff distribution. Therefore it is impossible for the same theory to be both a good bargaining theory and a good arbitration theory.

A point closely related is this. As I have argued elsewhere,[8] the moral standards of most of us require—whether we are aware of this fact or not—judgement of income distributions (payoff distributions) in terms of interpersonal utility comparisons. For this reason *arbitration theories* will have to rely on interpersonal comparisons of utility. On the other hand, *bargaining theories* that predict actual bargaining behaviour can be reasonably expected, like other parts of positive economics, to be independent of interpersonal utility comparisons, and therefore to yield solutions invariant with respect to order-preserving linear

[6] Though the Nash-Zeuthen theory of bargaining does not depend on the influence of moral considerations upon the bargaining process, it does not necessarily exclude the possibility of such influence. Clearly, all moral attitudes that the two parties may have must be incorporated into their utility functions. The Nash-Zeuthen theory has to be applied to the two parties' utility functions when all of their attitudes and preferences—selfish or unselfish, moral or non-moral—which may influence their bargaining behaviour, have been fully allowed for.

[7] In the sense of considering only his own utility function. But this utility function may possibly attach utility to altruistic, cultural, etc. interests the bargainer concerned has appreciation for (cf. previous footnote).

[8] See my "Cardinal Welfare, Individualistic Ethics, and Interpersonal Comparisons of Utility," *Journal of Political Economy*, 1955, Vol. LXIII, pp. 309–321.

transformations of either player's utility function—an invariance property that the Nash solution does possess (this property is actually one of Nash's axioms).

II

I am now going over to discussing Wagner's criticism of Zeuthen's bargaining model. Zeuthen makes the following assumption.[9] Suppose that at a certain stage of the negotiations the first bargaining party makes a certain offer A_1 while the second party makes a certain offer A_2. Let p^* be the maximum risk (i.e., the highest probability of conflict) that the first party would be prepared to face in order to obtain the terms A_1 rather than the terms A_2 less favourable to him. Let p^{**} be the maximum risk that the second party would be ready to face in order to obtain, conversely, A_2 rather than A_1. Then if $p^* < p^{**}$ it will always be the first party who will make the next concession while if $p^* > p^{**}$, the opposite will be true.

Wagner finds this assumption unsatisfactory on the ground that either party can improve his bargaining position by committing himself in advance to an uncompromising attitude. For instance, even if $p^* < p^{**}$ (which means that according to Zeuthen's theory the first player ought to make the next concession)—if the first player declares that he will make no further concession at all, and if he can convince the second player that he really means what he says, it will be rational for the second player to yield ground because he knows that this is now the only way of reaching an agreement. Thus the player who commits himself in advance to an unflexible policy may be able to achieve better terms than predicted by Zeuthen's theory.[10]

Now Wagner is no doubt right that committing oneself in advance to an uncompromising attitude is a very strong bargaining weapon. But it is a bargaining weapon that cannot be used against a really proficient player, let alone against the perfectly rational players envisaged by Zeuthen's (and Nash's) theory.[11]

A player can preclude the use of this bargaining weapon against himself if he makes a prior commitment at the beginning of the game that he will always resist and disregard any attempt by his opponent to make use of this weapon. This is what must actually happen if both players are rational. For, committing himself in advance to making no further concessions cannot be used by *both* players at the same time as an effective bargaining weapon, as the use of this strategy by both players would necessarily result in a conflict. (In contrast, both players can simultaneously use the strategy of committing themselves to *resisting* the application of that bargaining weapon.) On the other

---

[9] F. Zeuthen, *Problems of Monopoly and Economic Warfare*, London, 1930, Chap. IV.

[10] Cf. also T. C. Schelling, "An Essay on Bargaining," *American Economic Review*, 1956, Vol. XLVI, pp. 281–306.

[11] Nash in his 1950 paper assumed "equal bargaining skill" on the part of both parties. In his 1953 paper he has realized that the assumption of perfect rationality is sufficient. Cf. Nash, 1953, pp. 137–138.

hand, neither player can rationally tolerate that the other player *alone* should use this bargaining weapon.

In general, no strategy can be regarded as admissible between two rational players which would inevitably lead to a conflict if both players were to make use of it. The strength of the Zeuthen-Nash bargaining theory lies precisely in the fact that it suggests strategies that both of two rational players can use without thereby setting off a conflict. By this means the theory brings in clear relief the fundamental *symmetry* of the bargaining situation with respect to two rational bargainers.

III

In my earlier paper[12] I have tried to show that Nash's and Zeuthen's bargaining theories are mathematically equivalent (except that Nash's theory covers a wider range of situations than Zeuthen's theory does in its original form). Wagner in his paper takes issue with this conclusion.

In Nash's model the two parties are assumed to start negotiations by making a *threat*, i.e., stating the strategies that each of them would follow in case no agreement could be reached.[13] Let t_1 and t_2 be the two parties' threats and let $V_1(t_1, t_2)$ and $V_2(t_1, t_2)$ be the utility levels that the two parties assign to the situation where no agreement would be reached and where both parties would have to implement their threats. Moreover let $V_1(A)$ and $V_2(A)$ denote the utility levels that the two parties assign to a proposed agreement A. (For the sake of clarity I am using different notations from Wagner.) Then, according to Nash's theory the two parties will come to accept an agreement A such that maximizes the product

(1) $$\pi = [V_1(A) - V_1(t_1, t_2)] \cdot [V_2(A) - V_2(t_1, t_2)].$$

The application of this conclusion to particular cases is simple enough. For instance, in the case of collective bargaining $V_1(A)$ and $V_2(A)$ would represent the utilities that the management and the trade union, respectively, would associate with some proposed wage rate—while $V_1(t_1, t_2)$ and $V_2(t_1, t_2)$ would represent the utilities that each of them would associate with a strike or lockout situation (as in this case the threats of the two parties would normally refer to a strike and/or lockout).

Wagner's interpretation of Nash's theory is different. He apparently argues that the product to be maximized in Nash's theory is

(2) $$\pi' = [V_1(A) - V_1(S_2)] \cdot [V_2(A) - V_2(S_1)]$$

where $V_1(S_2)$ is the utility that the first party assigns to the second party's Stackelberg equilibrium point while $V_2(S_1)$ is the utility that the second party assigns to the first party's Stackelberg equilibrium point. This would mean, for instance, in the case of collective bargaining that $V_1(S_2)$ [or $U^L(N)$ in

[12] See footnote 4.
[13] Nash, 1953, p. 130.

Wagner's notation] is the utility that the union would attach to the wage rate most preferred by the management, and that $V_2(S_1)$ [or $U^M(M)$ in Wagner's notation] is the utility that the management would attach to the wage rate most preferred by the union.

However, it is hard to see how this interpretation of Nash's theory can be maintained—for it would mean essentially that the threat that the union uses against the management as its main bargaining weapon is the "threat" of accepting the wage rate most favourable to the management, whereas the threat that the management uses against the union is the "threat" of accepting the wage rate most favourable to the union—a very peculiar interpretation of what a threat is.

My proof of the mathematical equivalence between Nash's and Zeuthen's theories is based on showing that Zeuthen's model also leads to maximizing the product defined above under (1). Zeuthen's model, of course, does not involve threats by the bargaining parties. But it seems natural to identify Zeuthen's "conflict situation" with the situation in Nash's model where no agreement is reached and where both parties have to carry out their threats. For example, in the case of collective bargaining both Zeuthen's conflict situation and Nash's threat-implementation situation would correspond to a strike and/or lockout.

In my original paper, I have analysed a situation where the first party's last offer has been A_1 while the second party's last offer has been A_2, with $V_1(A_1) > V_1(A_2)$ but $V_2(A_1) < V_2(A_2)$. However, instead of the utility functions V_1 and V_2 I have used the functions U_1 and U_2 defined as the "net utility gains *over* the conflict situation"[14] that the two parties would derive from a given situation. That is, in my present notation

$$U_1(A_1) = V_1(A_1) - V_1(C) \qquad\qquad U_1(A_2) = V_1(A_2) - V_1(C)$$

$$U_2(A_1) = V_2(A_1) - V_2(C) \qquad\qquad U_2(A_2) = V_2(A_2) - V_2(C)$$

Of course

$$U_1(C) = V_1(C) - V_1(C) = 0 \qquad\qquad U_2(C) = V_2(C) - V_2(C) = 0$$

i.e., in the conflict situation itself the "net utility gain *over* the conflict situation" is zero for both parties. Wagner has apparently overlooked my definition of these quantities as he objects to my making $U_1(C) = U_2(C) = 0$.[15]

Zeuthen's argument is based on the fact that if both parties try to maximize their expected utilities then the maximum risk (i.e., the highest probability of a conflict) that the first party will be prepared to face in order to obtain the terms A_1 rather than the terms A_2 less favourable to him will be[16]

$$p^* = \frac{U_1(A_1) - U_1(A_2)}{U_1(A_1)} = \frac{V_1(A_1) - V_1(A_2)}{V_1(A_1) - V_1(C)}$$

[14] My paper, *loc. cit.*, p. 147. (Italics added.)
[15] Wagner, p. 396.
[16] For derivation of this formula, see F. Zeuthen, *op. cit.*; or my own paper, p. 148.

while the maximum risk that the second party will be prepared to face in order to achieve, conversely, A_2 rather than A_1 will be

$$p^{**} = \frac{U_2(A_2) - U_2(A_1)}{U_2(A_2)} = \frac{V_2(A_2) - V_2(A_1)}{V_2(A_2) - V_2(C)}.$$

(Cf. our argument in Section II above.)

Wagner surprisingly claims[17] that this formula always trivially yields $p^* = p^{**} = 1$, which is clearly not the case. He also claims that if $p^* = p^{**} = 1$ this would mean that both parties would "always give in until they converge upon the same wage rate" (i.e., upon the same terms). Actually $p^* = p^{**} = 1$ would mean exactly the opposite, viz., that the two parties would never make any concession at all, as they would face *any* risk, including the certainty of a conflict, rather than make a concession. Wagner here has obviously forgotten his own definition of the p's.

IV

To sum up, I have argued that the Zeuthen-Nash theory is not an "arbitration theory," giving criteria for a "fair" payoff distribution, but is a "bargaining theory" proper, predicting the actual bargaining behaviour of rational individuals. I have also submitted that Wagner's criticism of Zeuthen's bargaining model is inconsistent with the assumption that both bargainers are perfectly rational. Finally, I have tried to show that Wagner's objections to my proof of the mathematical equivalence of Nash's and Zeuthen's theories are based on a misunderstanding of Nash's theory and on other oversights.

JOHN C. HARSANYI

REJOINDER: *Harvey M. Wagner*

Although it is ordinarily a privilege as well as a compliment to be able to express one's own thoughts on a serious subject, especially when challenged by a formidable opponent, I confess that in this case I have a certain misgiving, since the arguments of my colleague Mr. J. C. Harsanyi are seemingly based on a cursory reading of my previous article and on undiscerning interpretation of Nash's papers.[1] Consequently, I am obliged to devote a disturbingly large portion of this note to patiently guiding Harsanyi through my article; the remainder of the paper will be directed toward the more crucial aspects in the game theory approach.

Previously, (p. 380) I stated that my purpose was "to synthesize the interesting and valid conclusions from (the) separate approaches and to present a unified picture of the pure theory of bargining to date." The exponents of

[17] Ibid.

[1] Needless to say, the present debate can only alert the reader to the points of contention; the serious student must refer to the original sources in the literature to resolve the issues for himself. Page numbers appearing in parentheses will refer to my original article and Nash's papers; the complete citations are given in Harsanyi's note. I recently had the opportunity to read R. D. Luce and H. Raiffa's excellent survey, *Games and Decisions,* Wiley, New York, 1957. Luce and Raiffa give a detailed critique of bargaining theory, Chapter 5 and 6, and take an intermediate stand between Harsanyi and myself.

the game theory technique, Nash, Raiffa, and Braithwaite, each present different motivations and rationale; Nash himself makes three tries at offering arguments for a solution. Lest the reader think that I was seriously misrepresenting the *common* themes in these authors' writings by my use of the adjectives "fair" and "reasonable," he may verify that *all three* game theorists employ these very words.[2] In the summary of my paper, (p. 397) I concluded that "the bargining contract remains indeterminate unless we introduce some sort of arbitration *or* behavioral procedure based upon a given set of rules." This view is hardly that which Harsanyi attributes to me in the opening sentence of his note; if anything, it parallels his own dichotomous characterization of solutions to a conflict problem.

Harsanyi is evidently confused in his understanding of my discussion of Nash's axiom 7 (1950, p. 159) or equivalently V (1953, p. 137). I interpreted the axiom's implication as (p. 394) "the removal of 'irrelevant' contracts should not change the previous solution," and continued by saying that "on the surface this postulate seems reasonable"; such statements appear to be in general accord with Harsanyi's interpretation expressed in his note. But then in footnote 30, I suggested that in an arbitration scheme the implication of the axiom might produce a result which appears *un*fair; this conclusion also seems to be in general accord with Harsanyi's expressed opinion. The question remaining is whether this and the other postulates seem reasonable for a behavioristic theory, and we shall elaborate our opinion on this matter presently. (The criticisms, which already have appeared in footnotes 30 and 34, are easily formulated in behavioristic terms, and, consequently, will not be repeated here.)

Harsanyi and I have a substantive disagreement over the implication of Nash's axiom 8 (1950, p. 159) or equivalently IV (1953, p. 137). Somehow Harsanyi has mystic faith in being able to contemplate the existence of a "perfectly symmetric bargaining situation." Nash's postulate requires that when a two dimensional figure (p. 359) is drawn representing the set of utilities of the two players for the various outcomes and when by a linear transformation of the utility functions a symmetrical (with respect to a 45° line through the origin) geometrical figure results, then the outcome is at the intersection of the 45° line and the contract curve. First, note that the geometrical symmetry is easily destroyed by a linear transformation of either of the utility functions.[3]

---

[2] Nash, 1950, p. 158; 1953, p. 136, p. 138. Raiffa, p. 361. Braithwaite, pp. 5–6, p. 36, p. 40. (See Harsanyi's note for complete citations.)

[3] The reader, unfamiliar with the fine points of game theory, might wonder why we concentrate on *linear* transformations of the utility function. Present day ordinal utility doctrines hold that in Edgeworth box type diagrams (Figure 1, p. 381) it is the shape of the indifference curves which is important and not the numbering system; therefore, any strictly monotonic increasing transformation of the numbering system is permissible, since the indifference loci are left unaffected. But the von Neumann-Morgenstern utility axioms are stronger than the ordinalist's axioms, and game theorists' assumptions produce a utility function which is unique up to origin and scale, in other words, unique up to a *linear* transformation only. Hence, economists who feel that the numbering system in the Edgeworth diagram should be irrelevant in the analysis of a conflict situation are in essence stating that they reject the game theorists' utility function, and, a fortiori, the various game theory solutions to the conflict problem.

Second, note that Harsanyi wants a bargaining theory to avoid interpersonal utility comparisons. What magical property is then to be associated with the symmetry point? Nash's rationale is obscure (if not question begging). Harsanyi, disclaiming a need for evoking moral considerations, chooses to argue that when geometrical symmetry can be produced, "neither player will be prepared to give his opponent better terms than he is given himself by the latter." But what are *terms*? How does one player weigh the *terms* he is offering against the *terms* he is being offered without making interpersonal utility comparisons? If both players realize that the geometrical symmetry is a fluke of the selection of the origins and scales for each of their utility functions, why should they think that this fluke should yield the reasonable solution to their problem?[4]

By the same token, what is the meaning of Harsanyi's notion "equally strong"? Harsanyi would have us believe that the Nash theory predicts the "stronger party will obtain a larger payoff"; I find this phrase difficult to interpret without succumbing to some sort of interpersonal utility comparison. By guising his arguments in connotative expressions, Harsanyi overlooks the anomaly in his own reasoning. Because the mathematics of Nash's approach implies that the solution is determined by "local" properties of the contract curve, a host of different utility configurations can be drawn, all having the same solution. Therefore, Harsanyi's conception of strength must have effect with reference to "local" properties. But how will one player manifest his "strength" when "ultimately the negotiation will be understood to be restricted to a narrow range of alternative deals and to be unconcerned with more remote alternatives"?[5]

Harsanyi has even miscomprehended the central thesis of my critique of Zeuthen's theory. Here I must draw the line in reprinting my own article because of space limitations, and I simply refer the reader to the original section for the detailed presentation (especially pp. 389–390). In brief, I argued that Zeuthen's probability calculations and comparisons are irrelevant to a player for the purpose of his selecting a good strategy, a conclusion which follows whether or not ultimatums are admissible courses of action. I was quite explicit (p. 370) in pointing out the strategic difficulties associated with the use

[4] Today when it has become fashionable to apply high powered mathematical methods to economic problems, often times with a view to removing restrictive assumptions in previous models, it is not uncommon for the analyst to overshoot the mark and make other assumptions which are equally as restrictive, although possibly in a more subtle vein. For example, *part* of the controversy between ordinal utility and revealed preference theory arose over one faction postulating the actual existence of indifference and the other side postulating the opposite. It is my feeling (and probably that of some of the other revealed preference exponents) that the truly unrestrictive approach should be eclecticism (i.e., not rejecting either one situation or the other). A similar case is suggested by the "symmetry" axiom, where symmetry is defined according to some mathematical convention. As economists we may be reluctant to espouse a theory which inevitably produces mathematically unsymmetric solutions under mathematically symmetric conditions; however, such caution is not equivalent to a justification for a postulate that a symmetric solution should always result under mathematically symmetric conditions.

[5] Nash (1953), p. 138.

of ultimatums, and why they may not produce the desired effect (contrast this and the analysis in my previous paper with the conclusion that Harsanyi attributes to me in the second paragraph of his Section II).

Paradoxically, Harsanyi completely rejects the notion of an ultimatum as an admissible strategy in a bargaining theory, especially "against the perfectly rational players envisaged by Zeuthen's (and Nash's) theory"; but at the same time he extols Nash's inclusion of a "threat" in his bargaining theory, where Nash defines (1953, p. 130) a threat as "A threatens B by convincing B that if B does not act in compliance with A's demands, then A will follow a certain policy T." Nash was very careful to protect himself against such anomalies (1953, pp. 130–131, p. 136). We shall attempt to resolve below Harsanyi's puzzling ambivalence toward threats, demands, and ultimatums.

Harsanyi's misdirected argument concerning the employment of ultimatums forces us to take notice of his uncautious application of the term "perfectly rational." An economist typically attaches one of two meanings to the term: (first sense) the possession of a revealed wisdom, (second sense) the capacity for logically deriving correct conclusions from a set of premises or axioms. It is vacuous to attempt to dismiss—as Harsanyi does with respect to the employment of ultimatums—a type of action as irrational in the second sense, i.e., when it does not conform to a set of axioms, if the very axiom system is under question as being irrational in the first sense. It is my own feeling, and I imagine some other economists agree, that the utmost sapience on the part of each player is the revelation of the inherent indeterminacy of the conflict problem. Since, say, Nash's and Braithwaite's approaches in general lead to different points on the contract curve, why sagacity would dictate to *both* parties that one author's rationale is more reasonable than the other's seems hard to imagine.

I am amazed that Harsanyi was not able to read correctly my remark on the substitution of the opponent's last offer for the conflict point C in Zeuthen's formula (p. 396). Contrary to Harsanyi's allegation, I neither symbolically nor verbally stated that $p^* = p^{**} = 1$. I claimed that trivially $p = 1$ is the only value which satisfies U (opponent's last offer; 1) $= U$ (own last offer, opponent's last offer; $1 - p$, p) in each player's utility function; I concluded that an extension of *Zeuthen's* rule for breaking tied values for p would result in both parties yielding.

I have left for the last contention the vital and subtle issue between Harsanyi and me, concerning the disputed proof of the mathematical equivalence of Nash's and Zeuthen's theories. We must be very careful here, because we are in danger of having the debate take a course observed in similar discussions in the literature in which each participant addresses himself to an essentially different question. I confess that in the first instance I am to blame for "muddling up" in my paper the notion of the solution of the non-cooperative game, the conflict point, and the threat point in the cooperative game (pp. 395–396). I fear from Harsanyi's note that he is still befuddled.

The difference of opinion between Harsanyi and me results from our failing heretofore to distinguish—believe it or not—three structurally different models. In Nash's 1953 paper he first presents what he calls the Negotiation Model (1953, pp. 130–136) in which the notion of a threat point is prevalent; he then gives an Axiomatic Approach (1953, pp. 136–140), about which he says "the axioms ... lead to the same solution that the negotiation model gave us; yet the concepts of demand or threat do not appear in them."[6] It is a version of Nash's axiomatic approach that appears in my paper. Consequently, Harsanyi is in error in attaching (or suggesting that I attached) a "threat" interpretation to the normalizing of the utility functions at the values of the Stackelberg solutions.[7] Why I suggested this normalization will be repeated in a moment.

Harsanyi has failed to realize that my criticism of his making the conflict point the origin for the utility functions was directed at *why* and not *how* he did this (actually I used the same type construction myself).[8] Even the tyro mathematical economist can deduce from Nash's 1953 paper the all-importance to the solution of where the origin for the utilities are located, and further what a mathematically complicated analytical question is generally involved. Harsanyi's only assurance is that "it seems natural (or 'normal') to identify Zeuthen's 'conflict situation' with the situation in Nash's model where no agreement is reached." Nash appeals to the celebrated Kakutani topological fixed point theorem (as generalized by Harsanyi's and my colleague Karlin) to prove the existence of his result (1953. p. 135); we might at least expect more from Harsanyi than an "it seems natural" to suffice for a proof of his conjectured equivalence.

Nash demonstrates that the solution to the axiomatic approach is identical to that of the negotiation game, and, therefore, being a sophisticated mathematician, he substitutes the rigor of his previous arguments for plausible reasoning concerning the zero point for the utility functions in his handling of the axiomatic model. Accepting Nash's lead, we are required to demonstrate whether or not the Zeuthen conflict point is indeed the threat point in the negotiation model between union and management. Before we can attempt such a demonstration, it is obvious that the definition of a threat must be clarified.[9]

[6] The above quotation may answer the paradox in Harsanyi's paper and note in which he rejects the idea of an ultimatum but accepts the concept of a threat, which Nash defines with reference to a demand in the negotiation model. Despite Nash's avowal that his two models are conceptually different, Harsanyi has found it to his liking to discard the demand notion, but to retain the term "threat" and continue to use it in the axiomatic approach (without alerting his readers to this practice).

[7] I am somewhat puzzled by Harsanyi's peculiar verbal rendition of a Stackelberg point "the utility that the union (management) would attach to the wage rate most preferred by the management (union)"; at best, such wording is misleading.

[8] In case the reader is still wondering about the legitimacy of Harsanyi's manipulations yielding "net utility gains," we point out that all Harsanyi has done (which he himself could have stated directly and simply) is to make an admissible linear transformation on the utility function $aU + b$, where $a = 1$ and $b = -U(C)$.

[9] The phrase "threat point" is unfortunate terminology for the student trying to fathom the meaning of Nash's construction, since for the cursory reader the term evokes the impression that each player pays attention to the harmful effects resulting if the threat were

Mayberry, Nash, and Shubik[10] are quite clear in their treatment of a duopoly game as to what they mean by a threat, viz., the quantity of output which each firm would produce if the negotiation model demands are incompatible. What is the nature of a threat in a labor-management game? One thing is clear, a threat must be a course of action which can be taken in a non-cooperative situation, i.e., an action which is possible regardless of what the opponent does (of course the *utility* of the final outcome is a joint function of the two players' strategies). Nash circumvents any detailed discussion of the outline of a non-cooperative situation by saying (1953, p. 129) "by beginning with a space of mixed strategies instead of talking about a sequence of moves, etc., we presuppose a reduction of the strategic potentialities of each player to the normal form." In other words, the Nash utility diagram represents all possible outcomes from any conceivable sequence of moves in the game. In my paper, I used an idealized delineation (Figure 6, p. 391) of the courses of action open to each party in one possible version of a non-cooperative situation. By the very nature of the normal form construction, playing of this non-cooperative game must be imbedded in the complete list of possible strategies defining the two dimensional utility diagram; similarly, if instead, Harsanyi's implicit version of the non-cooperative game were truly applicable, it would be included in the normal form strategies.

In my non-cooperative model, it can be seen that a conflict can only arise if *both* parties select a particular strategy; thus, as I visualized the situation, "it takes two to conflict." Under this model, we can easily construct examples where the two strategies leading to a conflict do not represent the threat point in Nash's negotiation game; such examples are based on the fact that Nash's solution depends on local properties of the contract curve.[11] If, on the other hand, the non-cooperative game is such that each player can effect a conflict solely by his own action, then, as we shall indicate, the conflict point is the threat point. The practical distinction between the two non-cooperative games is of more than minor significance, as relatively recent legislative developments in United States labor law indicate. Today it is legally obligatory for management

---

carried out. Actually each Nash player at most gives only transient consideration to the utilities of the threat point; what are important to him are the utilities of the *final* outcome on the contract curve. Since the latter utilities are determined by the location of the threat point, each player chooses his threat—in full knowledge that he will never (except in degenerate cases) end up at this point—with a primary view toward the ultimate outcome. In short, each "perfectly rational" opponent in deciding his threat plays a game of "let's pretend."

[10] "A Comparison of Treatments of a Duopoly Situation," *Econometrica*, Vol. 21 (1953), pp. 141–154.

[11] For example, suppose the contract curve is represented by the equation $4(U^M)^2 + (U^L)^2 = 16$ in the non-negative quadrant, where the conflict point is the origin of the axes, $M = (2, 1.6)$, $N = (1, 1.9)$, and $H = (1.74, 1.8)$ (the first coordinate refers to the union's utility, and the second coordinate to management's utility). Using the conflict point C for the Nash construction, the solution yields $U^L = 2.8^+$, $U^M = 1.4^+$. But management can assure itself at least 1.6 by playing its strategy II in the non-cooperative game; hence, the conflict point is not the Nash threat point in this case.

and the union to bargain collectively; neither party has unilateral power to cause a conflict by a refusal to bargain. Consequently, each participant must make an offer, and the opponent always has the option of accepting the offer. Therefore, I criticized Harsanyi on his unquestioning identification of Zeuthen's no contract point and Nash's threat point; depending on the particular underlying non-cooperative game, or more precisely, on the specific range of possible threats, these two points simply need not be the same.

Now suppose that each player does have the threat of unilaterally causing a conflict. Since for *any* pair of threats, the corresponding final solution (by the Nash axiom system) is on the contract curve, each Nash player can assure himself the utility on this locus associated with a normalization at the conflict point. In general, any other threat, i.e., some point off the contract curve, would imply that the final solution on the contract curve would make *one* of the parties worse off than if he threatened to conflict, and, hence, would not constitute an optimal threat point for *both* parties.[12]

When I suggested that the origin for the Nash solution be at the Stackelberg utility levels, I gave the erroneous impression that my suggestion was equivalent to Nash's model. What I should have made clear was that I was presenting the Nash construction *after* the origin for the utility functions had been determined. On the basis of the particular non-cooperative game in my paper, I recommended the Stackelberg utility levels normalization, since they were equivalent to the maximin utilities in my non-cooperative game, and a fortiori, were maximal utilities each player could gurantee himself regardless of his opponent's action and whether or not they played according to Nash rules.[13]

As a final comment—and maybe now I too am deceived by connotative phrases—I find it hard to believe that a model which seems unfair to *us* as an arbitration theory can serve as a framework for bargaining theory, which purportedly reflects a mode of behavior acceptable to *both* players. Evidently Harsanyi does not share my dubiety.

HARVEY M. WAGNER

[12] The exceptions to this statement lie on a line through the conflict point and the Nash solution point.

[13] My suggestion follows that of Shapley; see Luce and Raiffa, *op. cit.,* pp. 137–140, for a discussion of the procedure.

PART FOUR
Manipulative Models of Bargaining

INTRODUCTION

The game-theoretic conception of bargaining has yielded a number of elegant models, but it abstracts away all the dynamic aspects of bargaining and severely limits the applicability of the concept even in the analysis of static relationships. By contrast, the economic conception of bargaining as an interaction process involving offers and counteroffers permits the introduction of dynamic elements into the analysis of bargaining. But the models that have so far been derived from this conception are heavily restricted in terms of applicability and they exhibit a mechanistic quality which stems from the fact that they abstract away all the manipulative activities commonly associated with bargaining. Moreover, neither of these conceptions has yielded predictions about bargaining which correspond at all well with the actual processes and outcomes of bargaining in analogous real-world situations.

Recognizing these limitations of the game-theoretic and economic models of bargaining, a number of scholars have turned to an alternative approach to the analysis of situations involving interdependent decision making in their efforts to come to grips with the bargaining problem.[1] The resultant conception of bargaining rests on the following basic premises. To begin with, bargaining is closely associated with the presence of both strategic interaction and imperfect information. That is, strategic interaction and imperfect information are necessary conditions for the occurrence of bargaining even though these conditions need not remain in force until the end of the interaction between the parties involved. Next, bargaining focuses on the possibilities for manipulating the expectations of other players concerning such things as the structure of the situation at hand and the probable behavior of the party doing the manipulating. By contrast with the game-theoretic conception of bargaining, this means that bargainers will attempt to manipulate the understanding of the other side both about their approach to the presence of strategic interaction and about the content of the payoff matrix itself. And by contrast with the economic models, it means that bargainers will try to manipulate each other's perceptions of such thngs as their "risk-willingness," utility functions, and learning behavior. Finally, bargaining, according to this conception, requires the possibility of extensive communication among the players involved.[2] Thus, it is not sufficient to limit communication among bargainers to exchanges that can be incorporated at the outset in a fixed game matrix or in the parameters of an economic model of bargaining.[3] In fact, it is the combination of opportunities for communication with the presence of strategic interaction which paves the way for the manipulative activities that constitute the core of bargaining.

[1] For a general discussion of this approach to interdependent decision making see Thomas C. Schelling, *The Strategy of Conflict* (Cambridge, 1960), Chapter 1.

[2] The term "communication" is employed here in the broad sense to include the transmission of information through actions as well as words.

[3] On this point see, *inter alia,* Schelling, *Strategy of Conflict,* pp. 146–150.

These premises lead to a definition of bargaining in the following terms: bargaining is the manipulation of the information of others in the interests of improving the outcome for one's self under conditions of strategic interaction.[4] This simple definition, however, has a number of far-reaching implications. And a brief consideration of the most important of them will help to clarify the fundamental divergences between this perspective on the bargaining problem and the conceptions dealt with in earlier parts of this book.

First, the presence of strategic interaction is a necessary though not a sufficient condition for the occurrence of bargaining. The fact that strategic interaction is a necessary condition for bargaining flows directly from the definition set forth above. Note, however, that rational individuals need not attempt to bargain whenever they become involved in situations affected by strategic interaction. On the contrary, situations of this kind may occur in which rational individuals decide that the expected costs outweigh the expected benefits of bargaining. In the context of this conception of bargaining, therefore, it is important to consider the question of when to bargain as well as the question of how to bargain.[5]

Second, bargaining cannot occur in situations where the parties possess perfect information along all dimensions or are able to formulate confident expectations of the behavior of the relevant others. In the first instance, this follows because these conditions are incompatible with the presence of strategic interaction.[6] In addition, however, it is clear that the information conditions of individuals possessing perfect information or confident expectations would be immune from manipulation so there would be no scope for bargaining activities. As a result, the condition of perfect information (or confident expectations) can be thought of as the limiting case in which there is no room

---

[4] Those who have contributed to the development of this conception of bargaining have moved toward it from very different backgrounds. A few illustrations will serve to clarify this point. First, the most important contributions have been made by Schelling and Ellsberg, who started from criticisms of orthodox game theory: Thomas C. Schelling, "An Essay on Bargaining," and Daniel Ellsberg, "The Theory and Practice of Blackmail," both essays reprinted herein. Second, Pen ultimately arrives at a conception of bargaining that is quite similar to the manipulative conception even though he confuses this development with his earlier equilibrium analysis and fails to carry it very far: J. Pen, "A General Theory of Bargaining," reprinted herein. Third, Stevens appears to have a somewhat similar notion of bargaining even though he has not developed his ideas on bargaining *per se* in any formal fashion: Carl M. Stevens, "On the Theory of Negotiation," *Quarterly Journal of Economics,* LXXII (1958), 77–97. Fourth, the empirical studies of labor-management negotiations conducted by Walton and McKersie reflect a related conception of bargaining in highly informal terms, perhaps because they owe a major intellectual debt to the earlier work of Schelling—R. E. Walton and R. B. McKersie, *A Behavioral Theory of Labor Negotiations* (New York, 1965). Fifth, Cross's idea of "bluffing" is of some relevance to the manipulative conception of bargaining even though it taps only one limited aspect of the bargaining problem—John G. Cross, *The Economics of Bargaining* (New York, 1969), Chapter 8.

[5] The question of when to bargain is explored in some detail in Oran R. Young, "The Bargainer's Calculus," published for the first time in this book, pp. 364–387.

[6] For a detailed examination of this point see the General Introduction to this book.

for bargaining at all.[7] And any procedure that leads to the achievement of perfect information in an interaction process will, *ipso facto,* serve as a device for the termination of bargaining.

Third, bargaining as defined here is not relevant to situations in which individuals attempt to cooperate or compete without any ability to communicate whatsoever. In such cases, there is no way in which the players can manipulate each other's information conditions even though their decision-making problems may well be affected by strategic interaction.[8] As a result, their choices become a function of their own contemplations unsupported by manipulative efforts despite the fact that these contemplations may involve the formation of expectations about the probable behavior of the other party and activities that amount to "outguessing" behavior. The outcomes in such cases, therefore, will be determined by the initial characteristics of the players and will not be affected by bargaining.[9]

Fourth, though bargaining ultimately depends on success in manipulating the perceptions and expectations of others, there is an important link between these manipulative activities and reality. Thus, as Schelling has often emphasized, it is easier to persuade others that you are angry if you are in fact angry or to communicate an ironclad commitment if you have taken concrete steps to make your commitment inescapable.[10] Nevertheless, this link is sometimes a tenuous and indirect one, and success in bargaining ultimately goes to the player who can manipulate the information conditions of others regardless of the techniques he employs to accomplish this objective.[11] Under the circumstances, this connection between manipulative activities and reality has become an important focus of analysis for students of bargaining.

Fifth, it is evident that bargaining will always involve efforts to supply information to others. This is so whether the information in question concerns matters previously unknown to the target or the inaccuracy of information previously assumed to be correct by the target. It does not follow from this, however, that the information supplied by a bargainer must be true or accurate in any sense of those terms. In fact, the bargainer has a range of options along these lines. He may supply information that is true and complete or information that is correct as far as it goes but carefully selected to create a desired impression. By the same token, he may supply information

[7] Note also that this means that bargaining will not occur in situations in which the individual's decision-making environment is fixed or can be treated as if it were fixed.

[8] For an interesting discussion of the problems of coordination in such situations see Schelling, *The Strategy of Conflict*, pp. 53–67.

[9] It should be noted, however, that bargaining can occur in situations characterized by various asymmetries with respect to communication or even in the limiting case in which only one-way communication is possible.

[10] See, for example, Schelling, "An Essay on Bargaining," pp. 282–283, reprinted herein.

[11] On this point see Ellsberg, "Theory and Practice of Blackmail," esp. pp. 345–346. reprinted herein. Ellsberg also points out that the link between the manipulation of expectations and reality is apt to be influenced by the payoff structure of the target. An individual with a great deal to lose, for example, will normally take a bargainer's threat of punishment more seriously than an individual who has little to lose in any case.

that is partially or selectively false or information that is totally false.[12] Even more important, bargainers often supply information whose truth or falsity is deliberately left indeterminate. A bargainer may communicate a contingent threat to another individual, for example, in the hope that the other will capitulate to his demand without forcing him to decide whether or not to carry through on his threat. In general, bargainers will make their decisions concerning the type(s) of information to supply on the basis of a cost-benefit calculation dealing with the specific situation at hand.[13]

Sixth, manipulative bargaining can occur in situations that range all along the spectrum from purely cooperative to purely competitive interactions. Accordingly, there is no reason why this conception of bargaining should be associated exclusively, or even predominantly, with the analysis of conflict.[14] Consider first those cases in which the structural features of the relationship are fixed and known at the outset. Even when interactions of this type are characterized by pure cooperation,[15] there may be some scope (and need) for the players to manipulate each other's information concerning mechanisms for the coordination of their actions.[16] Similarly, as Ellsberg has shown in his critique of the von Neumann-Morgenstern solution for two-person, zero-sum games, it is possible to imagine a role for bargaining under conditions of pure competition.[17] It follows that there will be room for bargaining in any interaction exhibiting both cooperative elements and competitive elements. Consider now cases in which the structural features of the relationship are not fixed and known at the outset. Here the scope for bargaining is simply extended all along the spectrum from pure cooperation to pure competition. Whereas bargaining is restricted in the first set of cases to efforts to manipulate the expectations of others concerning specified choices, in the second set it

[12] Cross emphasizes this possibility almost exclusively in his analysis of bluffing. Thus, he defines bluffing as "a player's deliberate misrepresentation of his outcome expectations in order to influence his opponent"—Cross, *Economics of Bargaining*, p. 64. This is one of the principal reasons why Cross's analysis of bluffing does not belong in the mainstream of the manipulative conception of bargaining.

[13] Those who have contributed most of the manipulative conception of bargaining have tended to place primary emphasis on the communication of contingent actions. Nevertheless, it seems reasonable to conclude that rational bargainers will pay close attention to the specific features of the situation at hand in deciding what type(s) of information to supply.

[14] A number of writers have made complaints about the manipulative conception of bargaining along these lines. For a prominent example see Anatol Rapoport, "Strategic and Non-Strategic Approaches to Problems of Peace and Security," Kathleen Archibald, ed., *Strategic Interaction and Conflict* (Berkeley: Institute of International Studies, 1966), pp. 88–102.

[15] On games of pure cooperation see Schelling, *Strategy of Conflict*, pp. 89–99.

[16] Consider the following example: two individuals will receive $100 each if they give the same number when asked by a third party to name a positive number. If the players are allowed to communicate, it will not take them long to agree on a specific number in this situation of pure cooperation. Nevertheless, if they do not manipulate each other's information to settle on a common response, they may be unable to realize their common interest in receiving $100 apiece.

[17] Daniel Ellsberg, "Theory of the Reluctant Duelist," reprinted herein.

can also extend to the manipulation of the content and basic dimensions of the relationship itself.[18]

Seventh, bargaining is often casually conceptualized as a phenomenon involving roughly symmetrical activities on the part of two or more purposive actors. However, situations involving manipulative bargaining may vary greatly in these terms. Thus, perfectly symmetrical bargaining is the limiting case in which the players engage in equal or identical efforts to manipulate the information conditions of each other.[19] And perfectly asymmetrical bargaining is the other limiting case in which only one of the players makes any effort at all to manipulate the information conditions of the other(s).[20] It seems reasonable to conclude on *a priori* grounds that perfectly symmetrical bargaining will seldom occur in the real world, if only because the resources and personal attributes of the players are unlikely to be identical. Situations that approximate perfectly asymmetrical bargaining, on the other hand, are probably more likely to occur in reality. The activities of advertisers and propagandists, for example, sometimes approach the pole of perfectly asymmetrical bargaining, even though it is true that some targets of these activities make deliberate efforts to conceal or distort their decision-making situations.[21]

Given this general conception of bargaining, what are the possibilities for constructing models dealing with the relevant manipulative activities? As it happens, this perspective has led to the analysis of a wide range of "bargaining tactics," and it is not feasible to review them all here.[22] Nevertheless, it is possible to indicate the range of potential tactics and to give some flavor of the type of analysis that flows from this conception of bargaining. For convenience, let us begin with situations in which the scope for manipulative

[18] Note also that this conception of bargaining is defined in terms of personal gain in contrast to community or group interests. That is, bargaining is an activity engaged in by individuals for their own benefit, however this may be defined. It does not follow from this, however, that bargaining and the achievement of community interests (however defined) are necessarily incompatible.

[19] Note that the notion of equal or identical efforts to bargain would generally be difficult to pin down in empirical terms. In principle, this problem could be handled by defining some numeraire resource in terms of which all specific efforts to bargain could be measured. But the establishment of the necessary transformation functions would not be easy.

[20] Note that even in perfectly asymmetrical cases of bargaining, strategic interaction may remain prominent. Advertisers, for example, are heavily dependent upon the reactions of the consumers who, in turn, often rely extensively on information supplied through advertising. Similarly, the condition of imperfect information is frequently a leading feature of such asymmetrical interactions.

[21] Finally, this discussion of the implications of the manipulative conception of bargaining should include the fact that there are some interesting links between bargaining and the supply of collective goods. On this subject see Norman Frohlich, Joe A. Oppenheimer, and Oran R. Young, *Political Leadership and Collective Goods* (Princeton, 1971), esp. Chapter 5.

[22] For fuller discussions of bargaining tactics consult, *inter alia,* Schelling, *Strategy of Conflict;* Ellsberg, "The Theory and Practice of Blackmail," reprinted herein; Fred Iklè, *How Nations Negotiate* (New York, 1964); Herman Kahn, *On Escalation* (New York, 1965); Thomas C. Schelling, *Arms and Influence* (New Haven, 1966), and Oran R. Young, *The Politics of Force* (Princeton, 1968).

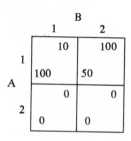

Figure I

bargaining is narrow and from these progress toward situations that generate wider prospects for bargaining.

Consider first the prospects for bargaining when the payoff matrix is fixed *and* known at the outset. Figure I can be taken as an illustration of this case so long as it is assumed that players have no ability to manipulate the figures in the cells of the matrix.[23] Here A would profit substantially if he could persuade B that a choice of strategy two on his (B's) part would lead to a choice of strategy two on his own part and, therefore, an outcome in the lower right corner.[24] Success in this effort would insure an outcome in the upper left corner, thereby raising A's payoff fifty "utiles" over his security level.[25] Note also that A would not have to make his commitment to strategy two in response to B's strategy two an absolute one if he could count on B's calculating his payoffs in terms of expected utility.[26] Given the specific numbers in Figure I, for example, B should be willing to agree to playing his strategy one if he calculated the probability that A would respond to his strategy two with his own strategy two as greater than 90 percent.[27]

In this situation, the problem for A is to persuade B that the chances of his going through with his commitment are $> .9$ even though he (A) would lose fifty utiles by doing so[28] and despite the fact that the payoff matrix itself cannot be manipulated as a technique for making the commitment credible.

[23] As Schelling has put it, this implies that the values in the cells of the matrix "are obvious in an obvious way to both persons." Schelling, "An Essay on Bargaining," p. 302, reprinted herein.

[24] For convenience, the discussion in this Introduction focuses on the tactical options of one player (A). It would be possible, however, to consider the tactics and counter-tactics available to B, and such an emphasis would lead more directly to various problems associated with the interaction itself, such as the danger of stalemate.

[25] Thus, by playing his strategy one A could guarantee himself a minimum payoff of fifty utiles regardless of B's choice.

[26] Ellsberg, in particular, has explored the significance of this point. See Ellsberg, "The Theory and Practice of Blackmail," reprinted herein.

[27] Ellsberg refers to this probability as B's "critical risk," *ibid.*, p. 348, reprinted herein. He is careful to discuss the critical-risk threshold in approximate rather than precise terms. This caution stems from the ambiguities of the notion of "subjective probabilities" and the information problems that commonly characterize interactions of this kind.

[28] On the importance of this point see Schelling, "An Essay on Bargaining," p. 293, reprinted herein.

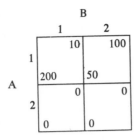

Figure II

There are several distinguishable tactics that A might employ for this purpose. He can attempt to convey an appearance of irrationality to persuade B that he is capable of deliberately choosing an inferior outcome.[29] Or he can try to generate and exploit uncertainties in B's thinking about the nature of the situation or introduce risks which he (A) is unable to control.[30] The scope for tactics of this kind is somewhat restricted, but it is not eliminated, by the assumption that the payoff matrix is truly known to everyone as well as fixed. In addition, it has been suggested that A can utilize factors outside the original game in his manipulative efforts by doing such things as betting on the outcome with a third party or staking his general bargaining reputation on the outcome of his interaction with B.[31] But tactics of this kind shade rapidly over the boundaries of the case under consideration here since they are apt to involve at least a *de facto* alteration of A's side of the payoff matrix for the original game.[32]

When the payoff matrix is both fixed and known, bargaining must focus squarely on the approaches of the players to the phenomenon of strategic interaction *per se*. In a sense, therefore, such situations lead to bargaining in its purest form. In addition, bargaining of this type offers a particularly clear contrast with the game-theoretic conception of bargaining. Thus, game theory relies on the introduction of initial assumptions such as those involved in the analysis of two-person, zero-sum games and in the Nash solution for nonzero-sum games, to eliminate all vestiges of strategic interaction. But the conception of bargaining under consideration here focuses precisely on the presence of strategic interaction in outlining the manipulative tactics available to the players.

[29] For additional material on this option see Ellsberg, "The Theory and Practice of Blackmail," pp. 361–363, reprinted herein; Schelling, *Arms and Influence,* pp. 36–43; and Kahn, *On Escalation,* esp. Chapter 1. Schelling has coined the phrase "the rationality of irrationality" to describe this tactic.

[30] See also Ellsberg, "The Theory and Practice of Blackmail," pp. 361–363, reprinted herein; Schelling, *The Strategy of Conflict,* pp. 187–203, and his *Arms and Influence,* Chapter 3. Schelling has often described such tactics in terms of the notion of "the threat that leaves something to chance."

[31] On these possibilities see Schelling, "An Essay on Bargaining," reprinted herein.

[32] Thus, outside bets or the involvement of reputation are generally influential to the extent that they increase or decrease the effective payoffs to the bargainer associated with specific cells in the initial payoff matrix.

Consider next the prospects for bargaining in the presence of a variable pay-off matrix. As Figure II suggests, the starting point here is much the same as in the previous case. Player A is still anxious to achieve an outcome in the upper left corner by persuading B that the result will be the lower right corner if he (B) insists on playing his strategy two.[33] But now the scope for bargaining is broader because A can consider tactics involving the content of the payoff matrix as well as the tactics outlined in the discussion of the preceding case.

The introduction of a variable payoff matrix opens up a wide range of new bargaining tactics, and it is here that such familiar notions as threats and promises become particularly prominent in the analysis of bargaining.[34] In the first instance, A may try to improve his situation by expanding or reducing his own range of strategies. Thus, he can win if he can convince B that a choice of strategy two on his (B's) part will effectively obliterate alternative one as far as he (A) is concerned. Notions of this kind lie behind Schelling's apparent paradoxes concerning the advantages of such moves as "bridge burning" and deliberately reducing one's freedom of choice.[35] Similarly, A can attempt to expand or reduce B's strategies in such a way as to improve his own (A's) situation. Tactics of this kind are widely regarded as more difficult to employ successfully than the previous type, although they are often discussed in the context of efforts to dislodge another player from a previous commitment in order to prevent the occurrence of a stalemate.[36] Beyond this, A can try to alter the payoffs (or perceptions of them) in specific cells of the matrix to his own advantage. There are numerous specific tactics that fall under this heading, but several simple examples related to Figure II will give some impression of the issues involved. Thus, A may deliberately try to persuade B that his own payoff in the upper right corner is lower than it appears in the initial matrix. If he can convince B that his (A's) payoff in this cell is actually minus one, for example, his threat to respond to B's strategy two with his own strategy two becomes clear and rational and he can win the outcome in the upper left corner. By the same token, A may try to persuade B that the upper left corner is not so bad for him (B) as it seems in the initial payoff matrix. He may, for example, offer B some compensation for playing strategy one, a move which has the effect of increasing B's payoff for the upper left corner.[37] In fact, A could offer B a "side payment" of anywhere from ninety-

---

[33] In fact, A will now be more anxious to achieve an outcome in the upper left corner since this will improve his payoff by 150 rather than fifty utiles. This leads to the concept of bargaining "stakes," a notion that has sometimes been used as a measure of an individual's incentives to bargain. Note that this conception of bargaining stakes does not involve interpersonal comparisons of utility.

[34] See, in particular, Schelling, "An Essay on Bargaining," reprinted herein, and his *The Strategy of Conflict*, Chapter 5.

[35] *Ibid.*

[36] On this possibility see, for example, Schelling, *Arms and Influence*, pp. 59–69.

[37] Note that the concept of compensation raises analytic problems, however, since it ordinarily implies the possibility of interpersonal comparisons of utility.

one to 149 utiles, with the result that both players would be better off with the solution in the upper left corner than with the solution in the upper right corner.[38] Note that this tactic would involve a promise to induce B to play his strategy one rather than a threat to compel him to forego playing his strategy two.

It should be noted that this rich range of potential bargaining tactics is ruled out by assumption in the models of game theory and in the economic models of bargaining. This is true of all game-theoretic models because they are based on the explicit assumption that the payoff matrix is both fixed and known at the outset. In the case of the economic models, on the other hand, the situation is a little more complicated. Some of these models rule out tactics of this kind through certain knowledge of risk willingness or utility functions while others do so through confident expectations of various learning parameters. In each case, however, the result is the same.

The tactics discussed in the preceding paragraphs also bring into focus several additional distinctions of some importance. In the first instance, there is the difference between positive and negative sanctions. Positive sanctions, such as promises, amount to rewards for compliance whereas negative sanctions, such as threats, involve the imposition of costs for failure to comply.[39] Although these two types of sanction are similar in analytic terms, the pragmatic problems they generate in actual bargaining situations sometimes differ considerably.[40] Next, Schelling has emphasized a distinction between deterrence and compellence in the use of negative sanctions.[41] Deterrent threats, for example, involve commitments to retaliate in the event that the other player carries out a specified action. Compellent threats, by contrast, are based on commitments to punish the other player in the event that he does *not* carry out a desired act. Here, too, it is useful to juxtapose the analytic similarity of these bargaining tactics with the fact, which Schelling illustrates quite clearly, that they are apt to pose somewhat different requirements for bargainers in real-world situations.[42] Finally there is an important distinction between present and future actions in the formulation of bargaining tactics. Many familiar tactics, such as threats and promises, are predicated on the notion of a contingent action that will be executed at some future date if the other side meets (or fails to meet) certain specific requirements. And it is the contingent nature of such tactics which gives rise to the well-known

[38] At this point, however, a new bargaining problem arises concerning the size of A's side payment to B.

[39] Critics of this conception of bargaining have sometimes argued that its developers have given disproportionate consideration to negative sanctions in contrast to positive sanctions.

[40] Schelling tends to emphasize the distinction between threats and promises very heavily. See his "An Essay on Bargaining," reprinted herein. It is not entirely clear, however, whether he believes there are important analytic as well as pragmatic differences between them.

[41] Schelling, *Arms and Influence,* pp. 69–78.

[42] *Ibid.,* pp. 78–86.

problem of credibility in manipulative bargaining.[43] It is possible, on the other hand, to make use of present actions in the interests of bargaining. Thus, current punishments or rewards may serve the purpose of a bargainer by inducing the other player to recalculate his position in a fashion favorable to the bargainer.[44] This is particularly true if the current punishment or reward can be portrayed as one of a distinct series of similar actions that will continue to occur in subsequent time periods unless the bargainer takes steps to stop them. In such cases, the advantages of both present and contingent actions can be combined in one set of bargaining tactics.[45]

Consider finally the prospects for bargaining about the nature of the payoff matrix itself. Here the parties can bargain not only about their approaches to strategic interaction and the specific content of the payoff matrix but also about the basic features of their relationship itself. This means that the players may attempt to manipulate each other's knowledge of the following matters, listed here in increasing order of generality. First, there is room for bargaining concerning the general preference structure of the parties. To put this possibility in concrete terms, efforts may be made to manipulate the way the other player interprets the various outcomes as well as the specific numbers he attaches to the cells of the payoff matrix. Second, bargaining may focus on the initial identification of the alternative strategies available to each side.[46] Here the issue in question concerns the dimensions of the payoff matrix rather than the content of the specific cells. Third, the bargainers may concentrate their efforts on controlling the definition or formulation of the fundamental issue (if any) at stake in their relationship. Here the problem is to determine the subject matter to be described by the payoff matrix, and it is worth bearing in mind that an ability to exercise control at this level may have far-reaching consequences for such things as the mix of competition and cooperation in the interactions of the players and the distribution of tactical advantages in the more detailed phases of the bargaining.[47]

These broader prospects for bargaining are clearly ruled out by assumption in the models of game theory and in the economic models of bargaining. All these models take up the bargaining problem after the issues under consideration here have been settled by one means or another. In addition, the possi-

[43] For Schelling's initial formulation of this problem see Schelling, "An Essay on Bargaining," pp. 282–287, reprinted herein. And for a more recent account that is richer in nuances see Schelling, *Arms and Influence*, Chapter 2.

[44] Cross's notion of pre-agreement costs can easily be interpreted in this light, Cross, *Economics of Bargaining*, Chapters 6 and 7. Note, however, that Cross considers only punishments in this connection. This position is necessitated by the specific features of Cross's learning model, but it may not always hold in real-world bargaining situations.

[45] For an initial discussion of this possibility see Schelling, "An Essay on Bargaining," pp. 297–298, reprinted herein. For a more detailed discussion relating to international bargaining see Young, *Politics of Force*, esp. Chapter 8.

[46] For an interesting comment on the problems of identifying the alternative strategies of the players see Anatol Rapoport, *Two-Person Game Theory* (Ann Arbor, 1966), pp. 201–202.

[47] For a discussion of these points see Young, *Politics of Force*, Chaper 15.

bilities of bargaining about the basic form and dimensions of the payoff matrix have not received any extended treatment in the analyses of manipulative bargaining associated with scholars such as Schelling and Ellsberg. Thus, students of manipulative bargaining have generally begun by assuming some initial formulation of a payoff matrix, even if it is subject to a certain amount of manipulation in the course of bargaining. As a result, the case in which the scope for bargaining is most extensive has so far received the least attention in efforts to construct systematic analyses of bargaining.

So far this discussion of manipulative tactics has focused on the efforts of one player to manipulate the first-order information of the other. That is, most of the options identified were cast in terms of efforts by A to alter B's understanding of his (B's) situation or of his (A's) own immediate choices. Nevertheless, the continued presence of strategic interaction in such situations insures that there are distinguishable levels at which bargaining activities can be pitched. This point can be illustrated in simple terms with reference to the concept of a commitment.[48] In the first instance, A may wish to manipulate B's first-order information about himself. Thus, he can try to persuade B that he (A) is committed to a given course of action. By the same token, however, A may concentrate on efforts to manipulate B's second-order information. As a result, he may attempt to persuade B that he (A) is committed to acting on the basis of a specific understanding of his (B's) probable behavior. And the same thing may happen with respect to B's third-order information. That is, A may wish to persuade B that he (A) is committed to acting on the basis of a specified understanding of B's understanding of his (A's) probable behavior. Under the circumstances, it is apparent that the problems associated with the "outguessing" regress are directly relevant to manipulative bargaining and that they cannot be eliminated unless some set of restrictive assumptions or premises is introduced to accomplish this objective.

This discussion of the relevance of the "outguessing" regress to manipulative bargaining makes it possible to clear up an ambiguous point raised by Harsanyi concerning "committal tactics."[49] Harsanyi argues that "perfectly rational" players can always preclude the use of effective commitments against each other because each player can make "a prior commitment at the beginning of the game that he will always resist and disregard any attempt by his opponent to make use of this weapon."[50] Consequently, Harsanyi concludes that the role of manipulative tactics has been considerably overemphasized. Unfortunately, however, the nature of the "outguessing" regress makes the problem more complicated than this. Thus, one player may commit himself to a policy of disregarding such a prior commitment on the part of the other

[48] For a discussion that deals with this point in similar terms see Schelling, *The Strategy of Conflict,* esp. Chapter 5.

[49] The clearest statement of Harsanyi's position on this point is John C. Harsanyi, "Notes on the Bargaining Problem," reprinted herein.

[50] *Ibid.,* p. 473, reprinted herein.

player, and this process may go on until the impact of strategic interaction is banished through the introduction of some set of restrictive assumptions. Moreover, there are two distinct ways of breaking this deadlock. One way is to lay down some set of criteria that a solution of the bargaining problem must meet, as in the case of the Nash solution.[51] Here the possibility of manipulative bargaining is effectively eliminated along with the impact of strategic interaction, in the initial formulation of the problem. But the price is high since this procedure leads to imposed solutions and a rather mechanistic conception of bargaining.[52] The other way of breaking the deadlock is to introduce some asymmetries between the players with respect to such things as the move structure of the interaction, initial resource endowments, bargaining skill, and so forth.[53] It is true of course that such a procedure does violence to the cherished game-theoretic assumption of perfect symmetry between the players, but it may well constitute a more realistic perspective on the bargaining problem than the assumption of perfect symmetry.[54]

The analysis of bargaining in terms of manipulative tactics has also given rise to some related insights that are well worth bearing in mind in any effort to come to grips with the bargaining problem. To begin with, scholars such as Schelling and Ellsberg have repeatedly emphasized the notions of "bargaining moves" and the move structure of any given interaction.[55] These notions flow naturally from a concern with bargaining tactics but they lead to an important criticism of the widespread focus on games in normal form since the dynamic aspects of bargaining cannot be meaningfully conceptualized within the timeless framework of games in normal form.[56] Similarly, the analysis of bargaining moves leads to a concern with the problem of the initiative which is lacking in other conceptions of bargaining. Thus, it can be shown that the locus of the initiative sometimes has far-reaching consequences in bargaining situations.[57] While it is never advantageous (and it may be disadvantageous) to possess the initiative in a two-person, zero-sum situation, for example, it is frequently a decisive advantage to control the initiative in a nonzero-sum situation. Next, an emphasis on manipulative tactics produces an analytic interest in the possibility of stalemate between bargainers who become committed to

[51] On the assumptions underlying the Nash solution see John F. Nash, "The Bargaining Problem," and "Two-Person Cooperative Games," both reprinted herein. And for an extended discussion of these assumptions consult Robert L. Bishop, "Game-Theoretic Analyses of Bargaining," reprinted herein.

[52] For a fuller discussion of these points see the Introduction to Part One of this book.

[53] For a discussion of this option see Schelling, *Strategy of Conflict*, Appendix B.

[54] For an exchange of views on this point see *ibid.*, and John C. Harsanyi, "On the Rationality Postulates Underlying the Theory of Cooperative Games," *Journal of Conflict Resolution*, V (1961), 179–196.

[55] For a particularly clear statement on this point see Schelling, *Strategy of Conflict*, pp. 267–278.

[56] *Ibid.*

[57] This question has been discussed by a number of scholars but see, *inter alia*, Ellsberg, "Theory of the Reluctant Duelist," reprinted herein; Schelling, *Arms and Influence*, pp. 43–49; and Young, *Politics of Force*, Chapter 14.

incompatible positions.[58] And this perspective leads to a concern with such matters as bargaining impediments and processes of "decommitment" as well as to an explanation of the fact that bargaining in real-world situations often results in outcomes that are not Pareto optimal for the participants.[59] In addition, the analysis of bargaining in terms of manipulative activities has led to a useful emphasis on the problems of credibility. Since bargaining tactics frequently involve efforts on the part of the bargainer to "commit himself in advance to an act that he would in fact prefer not to carry out in the event,"[60] a major concern in the analysis of manipulative bargaining is the various techniques whereby one player can persuade another of the credibility of his bargaining position. And the requirements of credibility sometimes have a substantial impact on the ultimate agreement reached by the players or even preclude the possibility of reaching a stable agreement at all.[61] Finally, this conception of bargaining makes it possible to consider the impact on bargaining of a variety of structural features of the relationship between the parties and of the setting in which their interaction occurs. Perhaps the most well-known work along these lines is Schelling's analysis of the role of salience or prominence in bargaining situations.[62] But Schelling and others have also given some consideration to the relevance of other structural factors such as constraints on communication, the presence of externally imposed rules of the game, the impact of third parties, the number of players, the enforceability of agreements, the possibility of compensation, the use of bargaining agents, the effects of introducing collective actors, the significance of intersecting negotiations, and so forth.[63]

It is apparent from this discussion that the manipulative conception of bargaining has a number of attractive features. The attractions of this conception can be summarized by saying that it introduces a distinct note of realism that is lacking in the other conceptions of bargaining by: (1) moving away from payoff matrixes, utility functions, and factors such as risk willingness which are fixed and known at the outset, (2) allowing strategic inter-

[58] For a discussion that places particular stress on this point see Thomas C. Schelling, "Game Theory and the Study of Ethical Systems," *Journal of Conflict Resolution,* XII (1968), 34–44.

[59] Among the many discussions of these problems, see Schelling, *Arms and Influence,* and Young, *Politics of Force,* Chapter 10. Problems of this kind also lead directly into the analysis of roles for third parties in bargaining situations. On this subject see Oran R. Young, *The Intermediaries* (Princeton, 1967).

[60] Schelling, "An Essay on Bargaining," p. 293, reprinted herein. As Schelling also emphasizes at this point, "more than communication is involved when one threatens an act that he would have no incentive to perform but that is designed to deter through its promise of mutual harm."

[61] If the players do not trust each other and they are unable to make ironclad promises, for example, they may end up without any agreement at all. On problems of this kind see *ibid.,* pp. 299–300, reprinted herein.

[62] Schelling, *Strategy of Conflict,* esp. pp. 99–118.

[63] For a useful outline of relevant structural factors see Schelling, "An Essay on Bargaining," reprinted herein. For more detailed discussions of a number of these factors consult Schelling, *Strategy of Conflict,* and Young, *Politics of Force.*

action to play some role beyond the initial statement of the problem, (3) introducing a variety of important concepts relating to bargaining tactics, and (4) reducing the mechanistic quality of the other models of bargaining. As a result, the manipulative conception permits the analysis of a variety of bargaining activities that do not seem to fit into the other conceptions of bargaining.

At this point, however, it is also necessary to come to grips with the shortcomings of the manipulative conception of bargaining. Above all, there is no escaping the fact that this conception has not led so far to the construction of determinate models of bargaining. Scholars such as Schelling and Ellsberg have brilliantly probed the repertoire of tactics available to bargainers in various situations. They have identified a range of factors that can be expected to play some role in determining the outcome of bargaining in various situations. And they have often posed provocative questions that simply were not raised at all in previous analyses of bargaining.[64] These are unquestionably important achievements, but they do not amount to determinate models capable of predicting when the rational individual will engage in bargaining activities,[65] specifying the tactics or combination of tactics which will be employed in various types of interaction, and identifying the outcomes that will flow from the utilization of these combinations of tactics. In fact, those who have developed this conception have tended to acquire conceptual flexibility by relaxing some of the restrictive assumptions of the other models of bargaining without introducing alternative assumptions. As a result, the achievement of determinate models based on the manipulative conception would require the formulation of new assumptions and/or parameters, a requirement the scholars who have employed this conception of bargaining generally have been unwilling to meet. In this sense, there is a remarkable similarity between the work of these scholars and that of Pen,[66] even though analysts such as Schelling and Ellsberg have carried the study of bargaining tactics much further than has Pen.

Once again, therefore, we arrive at the conclusion that it is impossible (in analytic terms) to achieve determinate solutions for problems involving interdependent decision making so long as there is any scope for strategic interaction. Although the manipulative conception of bargaining clearly indicates that strategic interaction need not be excluded at the outset and that major insights can be achieved by allowing for the presence of strategic interaction beyond the initial formulation of the bargaining problem, it does not alter the fact that strategic interaction must be eliminated at some point in the

[64] In addition to the references cited previously, see also Kathleen Archibald, ed., *Strategic Interaction and Conflict,* on this point.

[65] This raises another important distinction between the manipulative conception and the game-theoretic and economic conceptions of bargaining. In game-theoretic models, it is assumed that the players must make a choice among their available strategies. And in the economic models of bargaining, there is no way for the players to escape making some offers and counteroffers. By contrast it is not necessary for an individual to engage in efforts to manipulate the information conditions of others. As a result, the rational individual must decide when to bargain as well as how to bargain.

[66] For a good summary of Pen's perspective on the bargaining problem see his "A General Theory of Bargaining," reprinted herein.

analysis if determinate results are to be achieved. This point has sometimes been obscured by the widespread tendency to clothe the manipulative conception of bargaining in the language of game theory. But this verbal link does nothing to resolve the fundamental issue at stake.

So far there have been three distinct reactions to this important weakness in the manipulative conception. Some have taken this problem as conclusive evidence of the superiority of the game-theoretic or economic conception of bargaining. Those who have taken this position, such as Harsanyi, have generally tried to depreciate the significance of the insights stemming from the manipulative conception and to minimize the lack of realism which plagues the game-theoretic and economic models.[67] A second group of scholars has tended to content themselves with efforts to probe the range of possible bargaining tactics together with imaginative speculations concerning the application of this conception of bargaining to various real-world situations.[68] The work of Schelling often exemplifies this pattern.[69] A third reaction is to embark on the search for determinate models designed to deal with the activities of rational individuals with respect to manipulative bargaining. The recent work of Young, for example, is directed toward this problem of closing important gaps left by previous studies of manipulative bargaining.[70] This work suggests, however, that it will be necessary to make extensive use of restrictive assumptions and/or parameters to achieve this objective.

In closing, several lesser shortcomings of the manipulative conception of bargaining should be mentioned. First, as indicated earlier, this conception does not have much to say concerning the prospects for bargaining about the basic form and dimensions of the payoff matrix. Yet phenomena of this kind appear to be of considerable importance in many real-world bargaining situations. That is, the knowledge the players possess about each other at the outset is often extremely sketchy even by the somewhat relaxed standards of the manipulative conception of bargaining.[71] Second, there is a deep-seated ambivalence in this conception of bargaining between statics and dynamics. Thus, the emphasis on notions such as moves, threats, promises, and initiative suggests an active concern with processes of interaction. But a great deal of work within this framework remains closely tied to the game-theoretic focus on outcomes in contrast to processes. The result is a distinct tendency toward the development of a taxonomy of bargaining tactics from the point of view

[67] Harsanyi has developed this position in a number of essays. Consult, among others, "On the Rationality Postulates Underlying the Theory of Cooperative Games," and "A General Theory of Rational Behavior in Game Situations", *Econometrica,* XXXIV (1966), 613–634.

[68] It is remarkable how many of the scholars interested in the manipulative conception of bargaining have concentrated primarily on problems in the field of international relations in applying their ideas to real-world situations.

[69] Moreover, Schelling's recent work has generally been even more specifically applied in its orientation than his earlier work.

[70] See Young, "The Bargainer's Calculus," herein.

[71] For a discussion that raises a number of points which are relevant to this conclusion see Rapoport, *Two-Person Game Theory,* pp. 186–214.

of the individual player without an equal emphasis on the interaction processes that are likely to take place between two (or more) bargainers who attempt to use manipulative tactics simultaneously. Third, there is extensive confusion concerning a number of the principal features of the manipulative conception of bargaining arising from the fact that it has often been clothed in the language of game theory. As demonstrated earlier in this discussion, the manipulative conception runs directly counter to some of the major assumptions of game theory, tends to emphasize phenomena that are abstracted away in game-theoretic models, and evokes a conceptual atmosphere that diverges radically from the imagery surrounding the theory of games.[72] Under the circumstances, the verbal link between the manipulative conception and the theory of games has tended to obscure the fact that this approach to the bargaining problem represents a fundamental alternative to both the game-theoretic and the economic models of bargaining. Fourth, the manipulative conception has not yet yielded much in the way of deductively derived propositions that can be subjected to empirical validation. This shortcoming stems directly from the fact that this conception has so far produced an emphasis on taxonomic speculation in contrast to formal models of manipulative bargaining. And it represents a particularly severe problem for an analytic perspective that is overwhelmingly descriptive rather than prescriptive in its basic orientation.

[72] These are among the reasons why the manipulative conception is classified as a distinct approach to the problems of interdependent decision making in the General Introduction to this book.

AN ESSAY ON BARGAINING

Thomas C. Schelling

This chapter presents a tactical approach to the analysis of bargaining. The subject includes both explicit bargaining and the tacit kind in which adversaries watch and interpret each other's behavior, each aware that his own actions are being interpreted and anticipated, each acting with a view to the expectations that he creates. In economics the subject covers wage negotiations, tariff negotiations, competition where competitors are few, settlements out of court, and the real estate agent and his customer. Outside economics it ranges from the threat of massive retaliation to taking the right of way from a taxi.

Our concern will *not* be with the part of bargaining that consists of exploring for mutually profitable adjustments, and that might be called the "efficiency" aspect of bargaining. For example, can an insurance firm save money, and make a client happier, by offering a cash settlement rather than repairing the client's car; can an employer save money by granting a voluntary wage increase to employees who agree to take a substantial part of their wages in merchandise? Instead, we shall be concerned with what might be called the "distributional" aspect of bargaining: the situations in which a better bargain for one means less for the other. When the business is finally sold to the one interested buyer, what price does it go for? When two dynamite trucks meet on a road wide enough for one, who backs up?

These are situations that ultimately involve an element of pure bargaining— bargaining in which each party is guided mainly by his expectations of what the other will accept. But with each guided by expectations and knowing that the other is too, expectations become compounded. A bargain is struck when somebody makes a final, sufficient concession. Why does he concede? Because he thinks the other will not. "I must concede because he won't. He won't because he thinks I will. He thinks I will because he thinks I think he thinks so. . . ." There is some range of alternative outcomes in which any point is better for both sides than no agreement at all. To insist on any such point is pure bargaining, since one always *would* take less rather than reach no agreement at all, and since one always *can* recede if retreat proves necessary to agreement. Yet if both parties are aware of the limits to this range, *any* outcome is a point from which at least one party would have been willing to retreat and the other knows it! There is no resting place.

There is, however, an outcome; and if we cannot find it in the logic of the situation we may find it in the tactics employed. The purpose of this chapter is to call attention to an important class of tactics, of a kind that is peculiarly appropriate to the logic of indeterminate situations. The essence of these tactics is some voluntary but irreversible sacrifice of freedom of choice. They rest on the paradox that the power to constrain an adversary may depend on the power to bind oneself; that, in bargaining, weakness is often strength, freedom may be freedom to capitulate, and to burn bridges behind one may suffice to undo an opponent.

Bargaining Power: the Power to Bind Oneself

"Bargaining power," "bargaining strength," "bargaining skill" suggest that the advantage goes to the powerful, the strong, or the skillful. It does, of course, if those qualities are defined to mean only that negotiations are won by those who win. But, if the terms imply that it is an advantage to be more intelligent or more skilled in debate, or to have more financial resources, more physical strength, more military potency, or more ability to withstand losses, then the term does a disservice. These qualities are by no means universal advantages in bargaining situations; they often have a contrary value.

The sophisticated negotiator may find it difficult to seem as obstinate as a truly obstinate man. If a man knocks at a door and says that he will stab himself on the porch unless given $10, he is more likely to get the $10 if his eyes are bloodshot. The threat of mutual destruction cannot be used to deter an adversary who is too unintelligent to comprehend it or too weak to enforce his will on those he represents. The government that cannot control its balance of payments, or collect taxes, or muster the political unity to defend itself, may enjoy assistance that would be denied it if it could control its own resources. And, to cite an example familiar from economic theory, "price leadership" in oligopoly may be an unprofitable distinction evaded by the small firms and assumed perforce by the large one.

Bargaining power has also been described as the power to fool and bluff, "the ability to set the best price for yourself and fool the other man into thinking this was your maximum offer."[1] Fooling and bluffing are certainly involved; but there are two kinds of fooling. One is deceiving about the facts; a buyer may lie about his income or misrepresent the size of his family. The other is purely tactical. Suppose each knows everything about the other, and each knows what the other knows. What is there to fool about? The buyer may say that, though he'd really pay up to twenty and the seller knows it, he is firmly resolved as a tactical matter not to budge above sixteen. If the seller capitulates, was he fooled? Or was he convinced of the truth? Or did the buyer really not know what he would do next if the tactic failed? If the buyer really "feels" himself firmly resolved, and bases his resolve on the conviction that the seller will capitulate, and the seller does, the buyer may say afterwards that he was "not fooling." Whatever has occurred, it is not adequately conveyed by the notions of bluffing and fooling.

How does one person make another believe something? The answer depends importantly on the factual question, "Is it true?" It is easier to prove the truth of something that is true than of something false. To prove the truth about our health we can call on a reputable doctor; to prove the truth about

---

[1] J. N. Morgan, "Bilateral Monopoly and the Competitive Output," *Quarterly Journal of Economics,* 63:376n6 (August 1949).

our costs or income we may let the person look at books that have been audited by a reputable firm or the Bureau of Internal Revenue. But to persuade him of something false we may have no such convincing evidence.

When one wishes to persuade someone that he would not pay more than $16,000 for a house that is really worth $20,000 to him, what can he do to take advantage of the usually superior credibility of the truth over a false assertion? Answer: make it true. How can a buyer make it true? If he likes the house because it is near his business, he might move his business, persuading the seller that the house is really now worth only $16,000 to him. This would be unprofitable; he is no better off than if he had paid the higher price.

But suppose the buyer could make an irrevocable and enforceable bet with some third party, duly recorded and certified, according to which he would pay for the house no more than $16,000, or forfeit $5,000. The seller has lost; the buyer need simply present the truth. Unless the seller is enraged and withholds the house in sheer spite, the situation has been rigged against him; the "objective" situation—the buyer's true incentive—has been voluntarily, conspicuously, and irreversibly changed. The seller can take it or leave it. This example demonstrates that if the buyer can accept an irrevocable *commitment* in a way that is unambiguously visible to the seller, he can squeeze the range of indeterminacy down to the point most favorable to him. It also suggests, by its artificiality, that the tactic is one that may or may not be available; whether the buyer can find an effective device for committing himself may depend on who he is, who the seller is, where they live, and a number of legal and institutional arrangements (including, in our artificial example, whether bets are legally enforceable).

If both men live in a culture where "cross my heart" is universally accepted as potent, all the buyer has to do is allege that he will pay no more than $16,000, using this invocation of penalty, and he wins—or at least he wins if the seller does not beat him to it by shouting "19,000, cross my heart." If the buyer is an agent authorized by a board of directors to buy at $16,000 but not a cent more, and the directors cannot constitutionally meet again for several months and the buyer cannot exceed his authority, and if all this can be made known to the seller, then the buyer "wins"—if, again, the seller has not tied himself up with a commitment to $19,000. Or, if the buyer can assert that he will pay no more than $16,000 so firmly that he would suffer intolerable loss of personal prestige or bargaining reputation by paying more, and if the fact of his paying more would necessarily be known, and if the seller appreciates all this, then a loud declaration by itself may provide the commitment. The device, of course, is a needless surrender of flexibility unless it can be made fully evident and understandable to the seller.

Incidentally, some of the more contractual kinds of commitments are not as effective as they at first seem. In the example of the self-inflicted penalty through the bet, it remains possible for the seller to seek out the third party and offer a modest sum in consideration of the latter's releasing the buyer from the bet, threatening to sell the house for $16,000 if the release is not forthcoming. The effect of the bet—as of most such contractual commitments —is to shift the locus and personnel of the negotiation, in the hope that the third party will be less available for negotiation or less subject to an incentive to concede. To put it differently, a *contractual* commitment is usually the assumption of a contingent "transfer cost," not a "real cost"; and if all interested parties can be brought into the negotiation the range of indeterminacy remains as it was. But if the third party were available only at substantial transportation cost, to that extent a truly irrevocable commitment would have been assumed. (If bets were made with a number of people, the "real costs" of bringing them into the negotiation might be made prohibitive.)[2]

The most interesting parts of our topic concern whether and how commitments can be taken; but it is worth while to consider briefly a model in which practical problems are absent—a world in which absolute commitments are freely available. Consider a culture in which "cross my heart" is universally recognized as absolutely binding. Any offer accompanied by this invocation is a final offer, and is so recognized. If each party knows the other's true reservation price, the object is to be first with a firm offer. Complete responsibility for the outcome then rests with the other, who can take it or leave it as he chooses (and who chooses to take it). Bargaining is all over; the commitment (that is, the first offer) wins.

Interpose some communication difficulty. They must bargain by letter; the invocation becomes effective when signed but cannot be known to the other until its arrival. Now when one party writes such a letter the other may already have signed his own, or may yet do so before the letter of the first arrives. There is then no sale; both are bound to incompatible positions. Each must now recognize this possibility of stalemate and take into account the likelihood that the other already has, or will have, signed his own commitment.

An asymmetry in communication may well favor the one who is (and is known to be) unavailable for the receipt of messages, for he is the one who

---

[2] Perhaps the "ideal" solution to the bilateral monopoly problem is as follows. One member of the pair shifts his marginal cost curve so that joint profits are now zero at the output at which joint profits originally would have been maximized. He does this through an irrevocable sale-leaseback arrangement; he sells a royalty contract to some third party for a lump sum, the royalties so related to his output that joint costs exceed joint revenue at all other outputs. He cannot now afford to produce at any price or output except that price and output at which the entire original joint profits accrue to him; the other member of the bilateral monopoly sees the contract, appreciates the situation, and accepts his true minimum profits. The "winner" really gains the entire original profit via the lump sum for which he sold royalty rights; this profit does not affect his incentives because it is independent of what he produces. The third party pays the lump sum (minus a small discount for inducement) because he knows that the second party will have to capitulate and that therefore he will in fact get his contingent royalty. The hitch is that the royalty-rights buyer must not be available to the "losing member"; otherwise the latter can force him to renounce his royalty claim by threatening not to reach a bargain, thus restoring the original marginal cost situation. But we may imagine the development of institutions that specialize in royalty purchases, whose ultimate success depends on a reputation for never renegotiating, and whose incentives can thus not be appealed to in any single negotiation.

cannot be deterred from his own commitment by receipt of the other's. (On the other hand, if the one who cannot communicate can feign ignorance of his own inability, the other too may be deterred from his own commitment by fear of the first's unwitting commitment.) If the commitments depend not just on words but on special forms or ceremonies, ignorance of the other party's commitment ceremonies may be an advantage if the ignorance is fully appreciated, since it makes the other aware that only his own restraint can avert stalemate.

Suppose only part of the population belongs to the cult in which "cross my heart" is (or is believed to be) absolutely binding. If everyone knows (and is known to know) everyone else's affiliation, those belonging to this particular cult have the advantage. They can commit themselves, the others cannot. If the buyer says "$16,000 cross my heart" his offer is final; if the seller says "$19,000" he is (and is known to be) only "bargaining."

If each does not know the other's true reservation price there is an initial stage in which each tries to discover the other's and misrepresent his own, as in ordinary bargaining. But the process of discovery and revelation becomes quickly merged with the process of creating and discovering commitments; the commitments permanently change, for all practical purposes, the "true" reservation prices. If one party has, and the other has not, the belief in a binding ceremony, the latter pursues the "ordinary" bargaining technique of *asserting* his reservation price, while the former proceeds to *make* his.

The foregoing discussion has tried to suggest both the plausibility and the logic of self-commitment. Some examples may suggest the relevance of the tactic, although an observer can seldom distinguish with confidence the consciously logical, the intuitive, or the inadvertent use of a visible tactic. First, it has not been uncommon for union officials to stir up excitement and determination on the part of the membership during or prior to a wage negotiation. If the union is going to insist on $2 and expects the management to counter with $1.60, an effort is made to persuade the membership not only that the management could pay $2 but even perhaps that the negotiators themselves are incompetent if they fail to obtain close to $2. The purpose—or, rather, a plausible purpose suggested by our analysis—is to make clear to the management that the negotiators could not accept less than $2 *even if they wished to* because they no longer control the members or because they would lose their own positions if they tried. In other words, the negotiators reduce the scope of their own authority and confront the management with the threat of a strike that the union itself cannot avert, even though it was the union's own action that eliminated its power to prevent the strike.

Something similar occurs when the United States Government negotiates with other governments on, say, the uses to which foreign assistance will be put, or tariff reduction. If the executive branch is free to negotiate the best arrangement it can, it may be unable to make any position stick and may end by conceding controversial points because its partners know, or believe obstinately, that the United States would rather concede than terminate the negotiations. But, if the executive branch negotiates under legislative authority, with its position constrained by law, and it is evident that Congress will not be reconvened to change the law within the necessary time period, then the executive branch has a firm position that is visible to its negotiating partners.

When national representatives go to international negotiations knowing that there is a wide range of potential agreement within which the outcome will depend on bargaining, they seem often to create a bargaining position by public statements, statements calculated to arouse a public opinion that permits no concessions to be made. If a binding public opinion can be cultivated and made evident to the other side, the initial position can thereby be made visibly "final."

These examples have certain characteristics in common. First, they clearly depend not only on incurring a commitment but on communicating it persuasively to the other party. Second, it is by no means easy to establish the commitment, nor is it entirely clear to either of the parties concerned just how strong the commitment is. Third, similar activity may be available to the parties on both sides. Fourth, the possibility of commitment, though perhaps available to both sides, is by no means equally available; the ability of a democratic government to get itself tied by public opinion may be different from the ability of a totalitarian government to incur such a commitment. Fifth, they all run the risk of establishing an immovable position that goes beyond the ability of the other to concede, and thereby provoke the likelihood of stalemate or breakdown.

INSTITUTIONAL AND STRUCTURAL CHARACTERISTICS OF THE NEGOTIATION

Some institutional and structural characteristics of bargaining situations may make the commitment tactic easy or difficult to use, or make it more available to one party than the other, or affect the likelihood of simultaneous commitment or stalemate.

Use of a Bargaining Agent. The use of a bargaining agent affects the power of commitment in at least two ways. First, the agent may be given instructions that are difficult or impossible to change, such instructions (and their inflexibility) being visible to the opposite party. The principle applies in distinguishing the legislative from the executive branch, or the management from the board of directors, as well as to a messenger-carried offer when the bargaining process has a time limit and the principal has interposed sufficient distance between himself and his messenger to make further communication evidently impossible before the time runs out.

Second, an "agent" may be brought in as a principal in his own right, with an incentive structure of his own that differs from his principal's. This device is involved in automobile insurance; the private citizen, in settling out of court, cannot threaten suit as effectively as the insurance company since the latter is more conspicuously obliged to carry out such threats to maintain its own reputation for subsequent accidents.[3]

Secrecy vs. Publicity. A potent means of commitment, and sometimes the only means, is the pledge of one's reputation. If national representatives can arrange to be charged with appeasement for every small concession, they place concession visibly beyond their own reach. If a union with other plants to deal with can arrange to make any retreat dramatically visible, it places its bargaining reputation in jeopardy and thereby becomes visibly incapable of serious compromise. (The same convenient jeopardy is the basis for the universally exploited defense, "If I did it for you I'd have to do it for everyone else.") But to commit in this fashion publicity is required. Both the initial offer and the final outcome would have to be known; and if secrecy surrounds either point, or if the outcome is inherently not observable, the device is unavailable. If one party has a "public" and the other has not, the latter may try to neutralize his disadvantage by excluding the relevant public; or if both parties fear the potentialities for stalemate in the simultaneous use of this tactic, they may try to enforce an agreement on secrecy.

Intersecting Negotiations. If a union is simultaneously engaged, or will shortly be engaged, in many negotiations while the management has no other plants and deals with no other unions, the management cannot convincingly stake its bargaining reputation while the union can. The advantage goes to the party that can persuasively point to an array of other negotiations in which its own position would be prejudiced if it made a concession in this one. (The "reputation value" of the bargain may be less related to the outcome than to the firmness with which some initial bargaining position is adhered to.) Defense against this tactic may involve, among other things, both misinterpretation of the other party's position and an effort to make the eventual outcome incommensurable with the initial positions. If the subjects under negotiation can be enlarged in the process of negotiation, or the wage figure replaced by fringe benefits that cannot be reduced to a wage equivalent, an "out" is provided to the party that has committed itself; and the availability of this "out" weakens the commitment itself, to the disadvantage of the committed party.

Continuous Negotiations. A special case of interrelated negotiations occurs when the same two parties are to negotiate other topics, simultaneously or in the future. The logic of this case is more subtle; to persuade the other that one cannot afford to recede, one says in effect, "If I conceded to you here, you would revise your estimate of me in our other negotiations; to protect my reputation with you I must stand firm." The second party is simultaneously the

---

[3] The formal solution to the right-of-way problem in automobile traffic may be that the winner is the one who first becomes fully and visibly insured against all contingencies; since he then has no incentive to avoid accident, the other must yield and knows it. (The latter cannot counter in kind; no company will insure him now that the first is insured.) More seriously, the pooling of strike funds among unions reduces the visible incentive on each individual union to avoid a strike. As in the bilateral monopoly solution suggested earlier, there is a transfer of interest to a third party with a resulting visible shift in one's own incentive structure.

"third party" to whom one's bargaining reputation can be pledged. This situation occurs in the threat of local resistance to local aggression. The party threatening achieves its commitment, and hence the credibility of its threat, not by referring to what it would gain from carrying out the threat in this particular instance but by pointing to the long-run value of a fulfilled threat in enhancing the credibility of future threats.

The Restrictive Agenda. When there are two objects to negotiate, the decision to negotiate them simultaneously or in separate forums or at separate times is by no means neutral to the outcome, particularly when there is a latent extortionate threat that can be exploited only if it can be attached to some more ordinary, legitimate, bargaining situation. The protection against extortion depends on refusal, unavailability, or inability, to negotiate. But if the object of the extortionate threat can be brought onto the agenda with the other topic, the latent threat becomes effective.

Tariff bargaining is an example. If reciprocal tariffs on cheese and automobiles are to be negotiated, one party may alter the outcome by threatening a purely punitive change in some other tariff. But if the bargaining representatives of the threatened party are confined to the cheese-automobile agenda, and have no instructions that permit them even to take cognizance of other commodities, or if there are ground rules that forbid mention of other tariffs while cheese and automobiles remain unsettled, this extortionate weapon must await another opportunity. If the threat that would be brought to the conference table is one that cannot stand publicity, publicity itself may prevent its effective communication.

The Possibility of Compensation. As Fellner has pointed out, agreement may be dependent on some means of redistributing costs or gains.[4] If duopolists, for example, divide markets in a way that maximizes their combined profits, some initial accrual of profits is thereby determined; any other division of the profits requires that one firm be able to compensate the other. If the fact of compensation would be evidence of illegal collusion, or if the motive for compensation would be misunderstood by the stockholders, or if the two do not sufficiently trust each other, some less optimum level of *joint* profits may be required in order that the initial accrual of profits to the two firms be in closer accordance with an agreed division of gains between them.

When agreement must be reached on something that is inherently a one-man act, any division of the cost depends on compensation. The "agenda" assumes particular importance in these cases, since a principal means of compensation is a concession on some other object. If two simultaneous negotiations can be brought into a contingent relationship with each other, a means of compensation is available. If they are kept separate, each remains an indivisible object.

It may be to the advantage of one party to keep a bargain isolated, and

---

[4] W. Fellner, *Competition Among the Few* (New York, 1949), pp. 34–35, 191–97, 231–32, 234.

to the other to join it to some second bargain. If there are two projects, each with a cost of three, and each with a value of two to A and a value of four to B, and each is inherently a "one-man" project in its execution, and if compensation is institutionally impossible, B will be forced to pay the entire cost of each as long as the two projects are kept separate. He cannot usefully threaten nonperformance, since A has no incentive to carry out either project by himself. But if B can link the projects together, offering to carry out one while A carries out the other, and can effectively threaten to abandon both unless A carries out one of them, A is left an option with a gain of four and a cost of three, which he takes, and B cuts his cost in half.

An important limitation of economic problems, as prototypes of bargaining situations, is that they tend disproportionately to involve divisible objects and compensable activities. If a drainage ditch in the back of one house will protect both houses; and if it costs $1,000 and is worth $800 to each homeowner; neither would undertake it separately, but we nevertheless usually assume that they will get together and see that this project worth $1,600 to the two of them gets carried out. But if it costs 10 hours a week to be scoutmaster, and each considers it worth 8 hours of his time to have a scout troop but one man must do the whole job, it is far from certain that the neighbors will reach a deal according to which one puts 10 hours on the job and the other pays him cash or does 5 hours' gardening for him. When two cars meet on a narrow road, the ensuing deadlock is aggravated by the absence of a custom of bidding to pay for the right of way. Parliamentary deadlocks occur when logrolling is impracticable. Measures that require unanimous agreement can often be initiated only if several are bundled together.[5]

The Mechanics of Negotiation. A number of other characteristics deserve mention, although we shall not work out their implications. Is there a penalty on the conveyance of false information? Is there a penalty on called bluffs, that is, can one put forth an offer and withdraw it after it has been accepted? Is there a penalty on hiring an agent who pretends to be an interested party and makes insincere offers, simply to test the position of the other party? Can all interested parties be recognized? Is there a time limit on the bargaining? Does the bargaining take the particular structure of an auction, a Dutch auction, a sealed bid system, or some other formal arrangement? Is there *a status quo,* so that unavailability for negotiation can win the *status quo* for the party that prefers it? Is renegotiation possible in case of stalemate? What are the costs of stalemate? Can compliance with the agreement be observed? What, in general, are the means of communication, and are any of them susceptible of being put out of order by one party or the other? If there are several items to negotiate, are they negotiated in one comprehensive negotiation, separately in a particular order so that each piece is finished before the next is taken up, or simultaneously through different agents or under different rules.

---

[5] Inclusion of a provision on the Saar in the "Paris Agreements" that ended the occupation of Western Germany may have reflected either this principle or the one in the preceding paragraph.

The importance of many of these structural questions becomes evident when one reflects on parliamentary technique. Rules that permit a president to veto an appropriation bill only in its entirety, or that require each amendment to be voted before the original act is voted on, or a priority system accorded to different kinds of motions, substantially alter the incentives that are brought to bear on each action. One who might be pressured into choosing second best is relieved of his vulnerability if he can vote earlier to eliminate that possibility, thereby leaving only first and third choices about which his preference is known to be so strong that no threat will be made.

Principles and Precedents. To be convincing, commitments usually have to be qualitative rather than quantitative, and to rest on some rationale. It may be difficult to conceive of a really firm commitment to $2.07½; why not $2.02¼? The numerical scale is too continuous to provide good resting places, except at nice round numbers like $2.00. But a commitment to the *principle* of "profit sharing," "cost-of-living increases," or any other basis for a numerical calculation that comes out at $2.07½, may provide a foothold for a commitment. Furthermore, one may create something of a commitment by putting the principles and precedents themselves in jeopardy. If in the past one has successfully maintained the principle of, say, nonrecognition of governments imposed by force, and elects to nail his demands to that principle in the present negotiation, he not only adduces precedent behind his claim but risks the principle itself. Having pledged it, he may persuade his adversary that he would accept stalemate rather than capitulate and discredit the principle.

Casuistry. If one reaches the point where concession is advisable, he has to recognize two effects: it puts him closer to his opponent's position, and it affects his opponent's estimate of his firmness. Concession not only may be construed as capitulation, it may mark a prior commitment as a fraud, and make the adversary skeptical of any new pretense at commitment. One, therefore, needs an "excuse" for accommodating his opponent, preferably a rationalized reinterpretation of the original commitment, one that is persuasive to the adversary himself.

More interesting is the use of casuistry to release an opponent from a commitment. If one can demonstrate to an opponent that the latter is not committed, or that he has miscalculated his commitment, one may in fact undo or revise the opponent's commitment. Or if one can confuse the opponent's commitment, so that his constituents or principals or audience cannot exactly identify compliance with the commitment—show that "productivity" is ambiguous, or that "proportionate contributions" has several meanings—one may undo it or lower its value. In these cases it is to the opponent's disadvantage that this commitment be successfully refuted by argument. But when the opponent has resolved to make a moderate concession one may help him by proving that he *can* make a moderate concession consistent with his former position, and that if he does there are no grounds for believing it to reflect on his original principles. One must seek, in other words, a rationalization by which to deny oneself too great a reward from the opponent's concession, otherwise the concession will not be made.[6]

THE THREAT

When one threatens to fight if attacked or to cut his price if his competitor does, the threat is no more than a communication of one's own incentives, designed to impress on the other the automatic consequences of his act. And, incidentally, if it succeeds in deterring, it benefits both parties.

But more than communication is involved when one threatens an act that he would have no incentive to perform but that is designed to deter through its promise of mutual harm. To threaten massive retaliation against small encroachments is of this nature, as is the threat to bump a car that does not yield the right of way or to call a costly strike if the wage is not raised a few cents. The distinctive feature of this threat is that the threatener has no incentive to carry it out either before the event or after. He does have an incentive to bind himself to fulfill the threat, if he thinks the threat may be successful, because the threat and not its fulfillment gains the end; and fulfillment is not required if the threat succeeds. The more certain the contingent fulfillment is, the less likely is actual fulfillment. But the threat's efficacy depends on the credulity of the other party, and the threat is ineffectual unless the threatener can rearrange or display his own incentives so as to demonstrate that he would, *ex-post,* have an incentive to carry it out.[7]

[6] In many textbook problems, such as bilateral monopoly between firms, the ends of the bargaining range are points of zero profits for one or the other party; and to settle for one's minimum position is no better than no settlement at all. But, apart from certain buying and selling situations, there are commonly limits on the range of acceptable outcomes, and the least favorable outcome that one is free to accept may be substantially superior to stalemate. In these cases one's overriding purpose may be to forestall any misguided commitment by the other party. If the truth is more demonstrable than a false position, a conservative initial position is indicated, as it is if any withdrawal from an initial "advanced" position would discredit any subsequent attempt to convey the truth. Actually, though a person does not commonly invite penalties on his own behavior, the existence of an enforceable penalty on falsehood would be of assistance; if one can demonstrate, for example, his cost or income position by showing his income tax return, the penalties on fraud may enhance the value of this evidence.

Even the "pure" bilateral monopoly case becomes somewhat of this nature if the bargaining is conducted by agents or employees whose rewards are more dependent on *whether* agreement is reached than on how favorable the terms of the agreement are.

[7] Incidentally, the deterrent threat has some interesting quantitative characteristics, reflecting the general asymmetry between rewards and punishments. It is not necessary, for example, that the threat promise more damage to the party threatened than to the party carrying it out. The threat to smash an old car with a new one may succeed if believed, or to sue expensively for small damages, or to start a price war. Also, as far as the power to deter is concerned, there is no such thing as "too large" a threat; if it is large enough to succeed, it is not carried out anyway. A threat is only "too large" if its very size interferes with its credibility. Atomic destruction for small misdemeanors, like expensive incarceration for overtime parking, would be superfluous but not exorbitant unless the threatened person considered it too awful to be real and ignored it.

We are back again at the commitment. How can one commit himself in advance to an act that he would in fact prefer not to carry out in the event, in order that his commitment may deter the other party? One can of course bluff, to persuade the other falsely that the costs or damages to the threatener would be minor or negative. More interesting, the one making the threat may pretend that he himself erroneously believes his own costs to be small, and therefore would mistakenly go ahead and fulfill the threat. Or perhaps he can pretend a revenge motivation so strong as to overcome the prospect of self-damage; but this option is probably most readily available to the truly revengeful. Otherwise he must find a way to commit himself.

One may try to stake his reputation on fulfillment, in a manner that impresses the threatened person. One may even stake his reputation *with the threatened person himself,* on grounds that it would be worth the costs and pains to give a lesson to the latter if he fails to heed the threat. Or one may try to arrange a legal commitment, perhaps through contracting with a third party.[8] Or if one can turn the whole business over to an agent whose salary (or business reputation) depends on carrying out the threat but who is unalterably relieved of any responsibility for the further costs, one may shift the incentive.

The commitment problem is nicely illustrated by the legal doctrine of the "last clear chance" which recognizes that, in the events that led up to an accident, there was some point at which the accident became inevitable as a result of prior actions, and that the abilities of the two parties to prevent it may not have expired at the same time. In bargaining, the commitment is a device to leave the last clear chance to decide the outcome with the other party, in a manner that he fully appreciates; it is to relinquish further initiative, having rigged the incentives so that the other party must choose in one's favor. If one driver speeds up so that he cannot stop, and the other realizes it, the latter has to yield. A legislative rider at the end of a session leaves the President the last clear chance to pass the bill. This doctrine helps to understand some of those cases in which bargaining "strength" inheres in what is weakness by other standards. When a person—or a country—has lost the power to help himself, or the power to avert mutual damage, the other interested party has no choice but to assume the cost or responsibility. "Coercive deficiency" is the term Arthur Smithies uses to describe the tactic of deliberately exhausting one's annual budgetary allowance so early in the year that the need for more funds is irresistibly urgent.[9]

A related tactic is maneuvering into a *status quo* from which one can be dislodged only by an overt act, an act that precipitates mutual damage be-

---

[8] Mutual defense treaties among strong and weak nations might best be viewed in this light, that is, not as undertaken to reassure the small nations nor in exchange for a *quid pro quo,* but rather as a device for surrendering an embarrassing freedom of choice.

[9] A. Smithies, *The Budgetary Process in the United States* (New York, 1955), pp. 40, 56. One solution is the short tether of an apportionment process. See also T. C. Schelling, "American Foreign Assistance," *World Politics,* 7:609–625 (July 1955), regarding the same principle in foreign aid allocations.

cause the maneuvering party has relinquished the power to retreat. If one carries explosives visibly on his person, in a manner that makes destruction obviously inevitable for himself and for any assailant, he may deter assault much more than if he retained any control over the explosives. If one commits a token force of troops that would be unable to escape, the commitment to full resistance is increased. Walter Lippmann has used the analogy of the plate glass window that helps to protect a jewelry store: anyone can break it easily enough, but not without creating an uproar.

Similar techniques may be available to the one threatened. His best defense, of course, is to carry out the act before the threat is made; in that case there is neither incentive nor commitment for retaliation. If he cannot hasten the act itself, he may commit himself to it; if the person to be threatened is already committed, the one who would threaten cannot deter with his threat, he can only make certain the mutually disastrous consequences that he threatens.[10] If the person to be threatened can arrange before the threat is made to share the risk with others (as suggested by the insurance solution to the right-of-way problem mentioned earlier) he may become so visibly unsusceptible to the threat as to dissuade the threatener. Or if by any other means he can either change or misrepresent his own incentives, to make it appear that he would gain in spite of threat fulfillment (or perhaps only that he thinks he would), the threatener may have to give up the threat as costly and fruitless; or if one can misrepresent himself as either unable to comprehend a threat, or too obstinate to heed it, he may deter the threat itself. Best of all may be *genuine* ignorance, obstinacy, or simple disbelief, since it may be more convincing to the prospective threatener; but of course if it fails to persuade him and he commits himself to the threat, both sides lose. Finally, both the threat and the commitment have to be communicated; if the threatened person can be unavailable for messages, or can destroy the communication channels, even though he does so in an obvious effort to avert threat, he may deter the threat itself.[11] But the time to show disbelief or obstinacy is before the threat is made, that is, before the commitment is taken, not just before the threat is

[10] The system of supplying the police with traffic tickets that are numbered and incapable of erasures makes it possible for the officer, by writing in the license number of the car before speaking to the driver, to preclude the latter's threat. Some trucks carry signs that say, "Alarm and lock system not subject to the driver's control." The time lock on bank vaults serves much the same purpose, as does the mandatory secret ballot in elections. So does starting an invasion with a small advance force that, though too small and premature to win the objective, attaches too much "face" to the enterprise to permit withdrawal: the larger force can then be readied without fear of inviting a purely deterrent threat. At many universities the faculty is protected by a rule that denies instructors the power to change a course grade once it has been recorded.

[11] The racketeer cannot sell protection if he cannot find his customer at home; nor can the kidnapper expect any ransom if he cannot communicate with friends or relatives. Thus, as a perhaps impractical suggestion, a law that required the immediate confinement of all interested friends and relatives when a kidnapping occurred might make the prospects for ransom unprofitably dim. The rotation of watchmen and policemen, or their assignment in random pairs, not only limits their exploitation of bribes but protects them from threats.

fulfilled; it does no good to be incredulous, or out of town, when the messenger arrives with the committed threat.

In threat situations, as in ordinary bargaining, commitments are not altogether clear; each party cannot exactly estimate the costs and values to the other side of the two related actions involved in the threat; the process of commitment may be a progressive one, the commitments acquiring their firmness by a sequence of actions. Communication is often neither entirely impossible nor entirely reliable; while certain evidence of one's commitment can be communicated directly, other evidence must travel by newspaper or hearsay, or be demonstrated by actions. In these cases the unhappy possibility of both acts occurring, as a result of simultaneous commitment, is increased. Furthermore, the recognition of this possibility of simultaneous commitment becomes itself a deterrent to the taking of commitments.[12]

In case a threat is made and fails to deter, there is a second stage prior to fulfillment in which *both* parties have an interest in undoing the commitment. The purpose of the threat is gone, its deterrence value is zero, and only the commitment exists to motivate fulfillment. This feature has, of course an analogy with stalemate in ordinary bargaining, stalemate resulting from both parties' getting committed to incompatible positions, or one party's mistakenly committing himself to a position that the other truly would not accept. If there appears a possibility of undoing the commitment, *both* parties have an interest in doing so. How to undo it is a matter on which their interests diverge, since different ways of undoing it lead to different outcomes. Furthermore, "undoing" does not mean neglecting a commitment regardless of reputation; "undoing," if the commitment of reputation was real, means disconnecting the threat from one's reputation, perhaps one's own reputation with the threatened person himself. It is therefore a subtle and tenuous situation in which, though both have an interest in undoing the commitment, they may be quite unable to collaborate in undoing it.

Special care may be needed in defining the threat, both the act that is threatened against and the counter act that is threatened. The difficulty arises from the fact, just noted, that once the former has been done the incentive to perform the latter has disappeared. The credibility of the threat before the act depends on how visible to the threatened party is the inability of the threatening party to rationalize his way out of his commitment once it has failed its purpose. Any loopholes the threatening party leaves himself, if they are visible to the threatened party, weaken the visible commitment and hence reduce the credibility of the threat. (An example may be the ambiguous treatment of Quemoy in the Formosa Resolution and Treaty.)

---

[12] It is a remarkable institutional fact that there is no simple, universal way for persons or nations to assume commitments of the kind we have been discussing. There are numerous ways they can try, but most of them are quite ambiguous, unsure, or only occasionally available. In the "cross-my-heart" society adverted to earlier, bargaining theory would reduce itself to game strategy and the mechanics of communication; but in most of the contemporary world the topic is mainly an empirical and institutional one of who can commit, how, and with what assurance of appreciation by the other side.

It is essential, therefore, for maximum credibility, to leave as little room as possible for judgment or discretion in carrying out the threat. If one is committed to punish a certain type of behavior when it reaches certain limits, but the limits are not carefully and objectively defined, the party threatened will realize that when the time comes to decide whether the threat must be enforced or not, his interest and that of the threatening party will coincide in an attempt to avoid the mutually unpleasant consequences.

In order to make a threat precise, so that its terms are visible both to the threatened party and to any third parties whose reaction to the whole affair is of value to the adversaries, it may be necessary to introduce some arbitrary elements. The threat must involve overt acts rather than intentions; it must be attached to the visible deeds, not invisible ones; it may have to attach itself to certain ancillary actions that are of no consequence in themselves to the threatening party. It may, for example, have to put a penalty on the carrying of weapons rather than their use; on suspicious behavior rather than observed misdemeanors; on proximity to a crime rather than the crime itself. And, finally, the act of punishment must be one whose effect or influence is clearly discernible.[13]

In order that one be able to pledge his reputation behind a threat, there must be continuity between the present and subsequent issues that will arise. This need for continuity suggests a means of making the original threat more effective; if it can be decomposed into a series of consecutive smaller threats, there is an opportunity to demonstrate on the first few transgressions that the threat will be carried out on the rest. Even the first few become more plausible, since there is a more obvious incentive to fulfill them as a "lesson."

This principle is perhaps most relevant to acts that are inherently a matter of degree. In foreign aid programs the overt act of terminating assistance may be so obviously painful to both sides as not to be taken seriously by the recipient, but if each small misuse of funds is to be accompanied by a small reduction in assistance, never so large as to leave the recipient helpless nor to provoke a diplomatic breach, the willingness to carry it out will receive more credulity; or if it does not at first, a few lessons may be persuasive without too much damage.[14]

The threatening party may not, of course, be able to divide the act into

---

[13] During 1950, the Economic Cooperation Administration declared its intention to reward Marshall Plan countries that followed especially sound policies, and to penalize those that did not, through the device of larger or smaller aid allotments. But since the base figures had not been determined, and since their determination would ultimately involve judgment rather than formulas, there would be no way afterwards to see whether in fact the additions and subtractions were made, and the plan suffered from implausibility.

[14] Perhaps the common requirement for amortization of loans at frequent intervals, rather than in a lump sum at the end of the loan period, reflects an analogous principle, as does the custom of giving frequent examinations in a college course to avoid letting a student's failure hinge exclusively on a single grading decision after the course is finished.

steps. (Both the act to be deterred and the punishment must be divisible.) But the principle at least suggests the unwisdom of defining aggression, or transgression, in terms of some critical degree or amount that will be deemed intolerable. When the act to be deterred is inherently a sequence of steps whose cumulative effect is what matters, a threat geared to the increments may be more credible than one that must be carried out either all at once or not at all when some particular point has been reached. It may even be impossible to define a "critical point" with sufficient clarity to be persuasive.

To make the threatened acts divisible, the acts themselves may have to be modified. Parts of an act that cannot be decomposed may have to be left out; ancillary acts that go with the event, though of no interest in themselves, may be objects to which a threat can effectively be attached. For example, actions that are only preparatory to the main act, and by themselves do no damage, may be susceptible of chronological division and thus be effective objects of the threat. The man who would kick a dog should be threatened with modest punishment for each step toward the dog, even though his proximity is of no interest in itself.

Similar to decomposing a threat into a series is starting a threat with a punitive act that grows in severity with the passage of time. Where a threat of death by violence might not be credited, cutting off the food supply might bring submission. For moral or public relations purposes, this device may in fact leave the "last clear chance" to the other, whose demise is then blamed on his stubbornness if the threat fails. But in any case the threatener gets his overt act out of the way while it is still preliminary and minor, rather than letting it stand as a final, dreadful, and visible obstacle to his resolution. And if the suffering party is the only one in a position to know, from moment to moment, how near to catastrophe they have progressed, his is the last clear chance in a real sense. Furthermore, the threatener may be embarrassed by his adversary's collapse but not by his discomfort; and the device may therefore transform a dangerous once-for-all threat into a less costly continuous one. Tenants are less easily removed by threat of forcible eviction than by simply shutting off the utilities.[15]

A piecemeal approach may also be used by the threatened person. If he cannot obviate the threat by hastening the entire act, he may hasten some initial stage that clearly commits him to eventual completion. Or, if his act is divisible while the threatener's retaliation comes only in the large economy size, performing it as a series of increments may deny the threatener the dramatic overt act that would trigger his response.

---

[15] This seems to be the tactic that avoided an explosion and induced de Gaulle's forces to vacate a province they had occupied in Northern Italy in June 1945, after they had announced that any effort of their allies to dislodge them would be treated as a hostile act. See Harry S Truman, *Year of Decisions* (New York, 1955), pp. 239–42; and Winston S. Churchill, *Triumph and Tragedy,* vol. VI of *The Second World War* (Boston, 1953), pp. 566–68.

THE PROMISE

Among the legal privileges of corporations, two that are mentioned in textbooks are the right to sue and the "right" to be sued. Who wants to be sued! But the right to be sued is the power to make a promise: to borrow money, to enter a contract, to do business with someone who might be damaged. If suit does arise, the "right" seems a liability in retrospect; beforehand it was a prerequisite to doing business.

In brief, the right to be sued is the power to accept a commitment. In the commitments discussed up to this point, it was essential that one's adversary (or "partner," however we wish to describe him) not have the power to release one from the commitment; the commitment was, in effect, to some third party, real or fictitious. The promise is a commitment to the second party in the bargain and is required whenever the final action of one or of each is outside the other's control. It is required whenever an agreement leaves any incentive to cheat.[16]

This need for promises is more than incidental; it has an institutional importance of its own. It is not always easy to make a convincing, self-binding, promise. Both the kidnapper who would like to release his prisoner, and the prisoner, may search desperately for a way to commit the latter against informing on his captor, without finding one. If the victim has committed an act whose disclosure could lead to blackmail, he may confess it; if not, he might commit one in the presence of his captor, to create the bond that will ensure his silence. But these extreme possibilities illustrate how difficult, as well as important, it may be to assume a promise. If the law will not enforce price agreements; or if the union is unable to obligate itself to a no-strike pledge; or if a contractor has no assets to pay damages if he loses a suit, and the law will not imprison debtors; or if there is no "audience" to which one can pledge his reputation; it may not be possible to strike a bargain, or at least the same bargain that would otherwise be struck.

Bargaining may have to concern itself with an "incentive" system as well as the division of gains. Oligopolists may lobby for a "fair-trade" law; or exchange shares of stocks. An agreement to stay out of each other's market may require an agreement to redesign the products to be unsuitable in each other's area. Two countries that wish to agree not to make military use of an island may have to destroy the usefulness of the island itself. (In effect, a "third-party commitment" has to be assumed when an effective "second-party commitment" cannot be devised.)[17]

Fulfillment is not always observable. If one sells his vote in a secret election,

---

[16] The threat may seem to be a promise if the pledge behind it is only one's reputation with his adversary; but it is not a promise from which the second party can unilaterally release the threatener, since he cannot convincingly dissociate his own future estimate of the threatener from the latter's performance.

[17] In an earlier age, hostages were exchanged.

or a government agrees to recommend an act to its parliament, or an employee agrees not to steal from inventory, or a teacher agrees to keep his political opinions out of class, or a country agrees to stimulate exports "as much as possible," there is no reliable way to observe or measure compliance. The observable outcome is subject to a number of influences, only one of which is covered by the agreement. The bargain may therefore have to be expressed in terms of something observable, even though what is observable is not the intended object of the bargain. One may have to pay the bribed voter if the election is won, not on how he voted; to pay a salesman a commission on sales, rather than on skill and effort; to reward policemen according to statistics on crime rather than on attention to duty; or to punish all employees for the transgressions of one. And, where performance is a matter of degree, the bargain may have to define arbitrary limits distinguishing performance from nonperformance; a specified loss of inventory treated as evidence of theft; a specified increase in exports considered an "adequate" effort; specified samples of performance taken as representative of total performance.[18]

The tactic of decomposition applies to promises as well as to threats. What makes many agreements enforceable is only the recognition of future opportunities for agreement that will be eliminated if mutual trust is not created and maintained, and whose value outweighs the momentary gain from cheating in the present instance. Each party must be confident that the other will not jeopardize future opportunities by destroying trust at the outset. This confidence does not always exist; and one of the purposes of piecemeal bargains is to cultivate the necessary mutual expectations. Neither may be willing to trust the other's prudence (or the other's confidence in the first's prudence, and so forth) on a large issue. But, if a number of preparatory bargains can be struck on a small scale, each may be willing to risk a small investment to create a tradition of trust. The purpose is to let each party demonstrate that he appreciates the need for trust and that he knows the other does too. So, if a major issue has to be negotiated, it may be necessary to seek out and negotiate some minor items for "practice," to establish the necessary confidence in each other's awareness of the long-term value of good faith.

Even if the future will bring no recurrence, it may be possible to create the equivalence of continuity by dividing the bargaining issue into consecutive parts. If each party agrees to send a million dollars to the Red Cross on condition the other does, each may be tempted to cheat if the other contributes first, and each one's anticipation of the other's cheating will inhibit agreement. But if the contribution is divided into consecutive small contributions, each can try the other's good faith for a small price. Furthermore, since each can keep the other on short tether to the finish, no one ever need risk more than

---

[18] Inability to assume an enforceable promise, like inability to perform the activity demanded, may protect one from an extortionate threat. The mandatory secret ballot is a nuisance to the voter who would like to sell his vote, but protection to the one who would fear coercion.

one small contribution at a time. Finally, this change in the incentive structure itself takes most of the risk out of the initial contribution; the value of established trust is made obviously visible to both.

Preparatory bargains serve another purpose. Bargaining can only occur when at least one party takes initiative in proposing a bargain. A deterrent to initiative is the information it yields, or may seem to yield, about one's eagerness. But if each has visible reason to expect the other to meet him half way, because of a history of successful bargaining, that very history provides protection against the inference of overeagerness.[19]

An Illustrative Game

Various bargaining situations involving commitments, threats, promises, and communication problems, can be illustrated by variants of a game in which each of two persons has a pair of alternatives from which to choose. North chooses either A or α; East chooses either B or β. Each person's gain depends on the choices of both. Each of the four possible combined choices, AB, $A\beta$, αB, or $\alpha\beta$, yields a particular gain or loss for North and a particular gain or loss for East. No compensation is payable between North and East. In general, each person's preference may depend on the choice the other makes.

Each such game can be quantitatively represented in a two-dimensional graph, with North's gain measured vertically and East's horizontally, and the values of the four combined choices denoted by points labeled AB, $A\beta$, $\alpha\beta$, and αB. In spite of the simplicity of the game there is actually a large number of qualitatively different variants, depending not only on the relative positions of the four points in the plane but also on the "rules" about order of moves, possibility of communication, availability of means of commitment, enforceability of promises, and whether two or more games between two persons can be joined together. The variations can be multiplied almost without limit by selecting different hypotheses about what each player knows or guesses about the "values" of the four outcomes for the other player, and what he guesses the other party guesses about himself. For convenience we assume here that the eight "values" are obvious in an obvious way to both persons. And, just as we have ruled out compensation, we rule out also threats of actions that lie outside the game. A very small sample of such games is presented.

---

[19] Perhaps two adversaries who look forward to some large negotiated settlement would do well to keep avenues open for negotiation of minor issues. If, for example, the number of loose ends in dispute between East and West should narrow down so much that nothing remains to be negotiated but the "ultimate issue" (some final, permanent disposition of all territories and armaments) the possibility of even opening negotiations on the latter might be jeopardized. Or, if the minor issues are not disposed of, but become so attached to the "big" issue that willingness to negotiate on them would be construed as overeagerness on the whole settlement, the possibility of preparatory bargains might disappear.

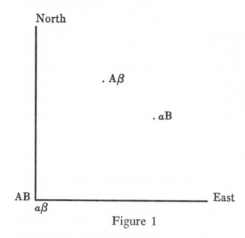

Figure 1

Figure 1 represents an "ordinary" bargaining situation if we adopt the rule that North and East must reach explicit agreement before they choose. $A\beta$ and αB can be thought of as alternative agreements that they may reach, while AB and $\alpha\beta$, with zero values for both persons, can be interpreted as the bargaining equivalent of "no sale." Whoever can first commit himself wins. If North can commit himself to A he will secure $A\beta$, since he leaves East a choice between $A\beta$ and AB and the former is obviously East's choice under the circumstances. If East could have committed himself first to B, however, North would have been restricted to a choice of αB or no agreement (that is, of αB or AB) and would have agreed to αB. As a matter of fact, first commitment is a kind of "first move"; and in a game with the same numbers but with moves in turn, first move would be an advantage. If, by mistake, both parties get committed, North to A and East to B, they lock themselves in stalemate at AB.

Figure 2 illustrates a deterrent threat if we interpret AB as the *status quo*, with North planning a shift to α (leading to αB) and East threatening a shift to β (resulting in $\alpha\beta$) if he does. If North moves first, East can only lose by moving to β, and similarly if North can commit himself to α before East can make his threat; but if East can effectively threaten the mutually undesirable $\alpha\beta$, he leaves North only a choice of $\alpha\beta$ or AB and North chooses the latter. Note that it is not sufficient for East to commit his *choice* in advance, as it was in Figure 1; he must commit himself to a *conditional* choice, B or β depending on whether North chooses A or α. If East committed his choice he would obtain only the advantage of "first move"; and in the present game, if moves were in turn, North would win at αB regardless of who moved first. (East would choose B rather than β, to leave North a choice of αB or AB rather than of $\alpha\beta$ or $A\beta$; and North would take αB. North, with first move, would choose α rather than A, leaving East $\alpha\beta$ or αB rather than $A\beta$ or AB; East would take αB.)

Figure 3 illustrates the promise. Whoever goes first, or even if moves are

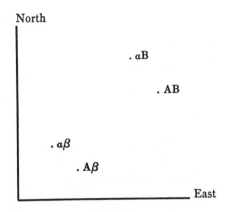

Figure 2

simultaneous, αB is a "minimax"; either can achieve it by himself, and neither can threaten the other with anything worse. Both would, however, prefer $A\beta$ to αB; but to reach $A\beta$ they must trust each other to be able to make enforceable promises. Whoever goes first, the other has an incentive to cheat; if North chooses A, East can take AB, and if East chooses β first, North can choose $\alpha\beta$. If moves are simultaneous each has an incentive to cheat, and each may expect the other to cheat; and either deliberate cheating, or self-protection against the other's incentive to cheat, indicates choices of α and B. At least one party must be able to commit himself to abstention; then the other can move first. If both must move simultaneously, both must be able to make enforceable promises.

Figure 4 is the same as Fig. 3 except that αB has been moved leftward. Here, in the absence of communication, North wins at $\alpha\beta$ regardless of whether he or East moves first or moves are simultaneous. If, however, East can communicate a *conditional* commitment, he can force North to choose A and an outcome of $A\beta$. But this commitment is something more than either a

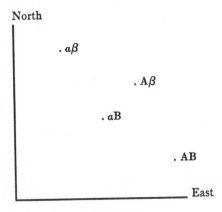

Figure 3

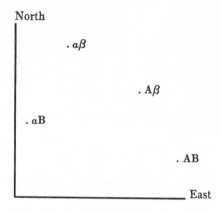

Figure 4

promise or a threat; it is both a promise and a threat. He must threaten αB if North chooses α; and he must promise "not AB" if North chooses A. The threat alone will not induce North to avoid α; αB is better than AB for North, and AB is what he gets with A if East is free to choose B. East must commit himself to do, for either α or A, the opposite of what he would do if he were not committed: abstention from AB or immolation at αB.

Finally, Figs. 5 and 6 show two games that separately contain nothing of interest but together make possible an extortionate threat. Figure 5 has a minimax solution at αB; either can achieve αB, neither can enforce anything better, no collaboration is possible, no threat can be made. Figure 6, though contrasting with Fig. 5 in the identity of interest between the two parties, is similarly devoid of any need for collaboration or communication or any possible threat to exploit. With or without communication, with or without an order of moves, the outcome is at AB.

But suppose the two games are simultaneously up for decision, and the same two parties are involved in both. If either party can commit himself to a

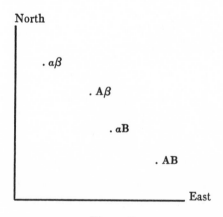

Figure 5

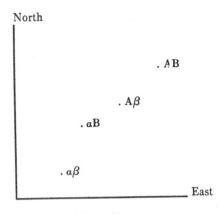

Figure 6

threat he may improve his position. East, for example, could threaten to choose β rather than B in game 6, unless North chose A rather than α in game 5; alternatively, North could threaten α in game 6 unless East chose β in game 5. Assuming the intervals large enough in game 6, and the threat persuasively committed and communicated, the threatener gains in game 5 at no cost in game 6. Because his threat succeeds he does not carry it out; so he gets AB in 6 as well as his preferred choice in game 5. To express this result differently, game 6 supplies what was ruled out earlier, namely, the threat of an act "outside the game." From the point of view of game 5, game 6 is an extraneous act, and East might as well threaten to burn North's house down if he does not choose A in 5. But such purely extortionate threats are not always easy to make; they often require an occasion, an object, and a means of communication, and additionally often suffer from illegality, immorality, or resistance out of sheer stubbornness. The joining of two negotiations on the same agenda may thus succeed where a purely gratuitous threat would be impracticable.

If North cannot commit himself to a threat, and consequently desires only to prevent a threat by East, it is in his interest that communication be impossible; or if communication occurs, it is in his interest that the two games not be placed on the same agenda; or if he cannot prevent their being discussed together by East, it is in his interest to turn each game over to a different agent whose compensation depends only on the outcome of his own game. If North can force game 6 to be played first, and is unable to commit himself in response to a threat, the threat is obviated. If he can commit his choice in game 5 before the threat is made, he is safe. But if he can commit himself in game 5, and game 6 is to be played first, East could threaten to choose β in game 6 unless North assumed a prior commitment to A in game 5; in this case North's ability to commit himself is a disadvantage, since it permits him to be forced into "playing" game 5 ahead of 6.

Incidentally, dropping AB vertically in Fig. 2 to below the level $\alpha\beta$ would illustrate an important principle, namely, that moving one point in a manner "unfavorable" to North may actually improve the outcome for him. The threat that kept him from winning in Fig. 2 depends on the comparative attractiveness of AB over αB for North; if AB is made worse for him than $\alpha\beta$ he becomes immune to the threat, which then is not made, and he wins at αB. This is an abstract example of the principle that, in bargaining, weakness may be strength.

THE THEORY AND PRACTICE
OF BLACKMAIL[1]

Daniel Ellsberg

PREFATORY NOTE, 1968

In March, 1959, while a member of the Society of Fellows, Harvard University, I delivered a series of public lectures in Boston, under the auspices of the Lowell Institute; these lectures were subsequently broadcast over WGBH, an educational FM station. The overall subject of the series was, "The Art of Coercion: A Study of Threats in Economic Conflict and War." The following essay was the opening lecture.

I have reprinted this lecture as it was delivered on March 10, 1959, almost ten years ago. It was before I came to RAND, before I worked on general war "bargaining," or worked on cold wars in the Pentagon, or took part in a hot war in Vietnam: much painful, but mostly relevant, experience. And a lot of relevant history has happened to the world since then—including successful United States coercion in the Cuban missile crisis and disastrous failure against North Vietnam. For these and still other reasons (I have thought more about the problem) I would write fairly differently on this subject as of today: and perhaps I will.

The reason for exhuming this paper as a P at this time is that it received fairly wide distribution in this form eight to ten years ago, resulting in a number of citations in the literature of bargaining theory, resulting in a backlog of requests for reprints. I am happy to fill them, but with the above *caveat:* and the additional one that the simple concepts presented here inevitably look much less novel now than they did in 1959, in particular, after the appearance of applications by Glenn Snyder and others, and much independent work by Tom Schelling. Schelling's "An Essay on Bargaining" [reprinted in this collection] was so stimulating to my work here, and his later work has become so widely familiar, that it seems worth explaining that at the time this was written Schelling had not presented any *formalization* of his pathbreaking notions on bargaining and threats, and it was a major aim of my lectures to accomplish this.

A last caution. At least one reader inferred, and published the inference, that I am not merely an analyst but a fan of blackmail, for individuals and governments. He was mistaken.

PREFATORY NOTE, 1974

I scarcely foresaw in 1959 that in the next fifteen years the government of my own country would be the major practitioner of violent blackmail, or

[1] Any views expressed in this paper are those of the author. They should not be interpreted as reflecting the views of the RAND Corporation or the official opinion or policy of any of its governmental or private research sponsors.

terrorism, in the world. I did not foresee that we would drop 7½ million tons of bombs—four times the total tonnage of World War II—on Indochina between 1965 and 1973, as threat after U.S. threat failed to induce Vietnamese "compliance" with U.S.-picked regimes or with U.S. policies opposing self-determination and social change. Illegitimate coercive violence by states—particularly the United States—continues as in Hitler's day to provide the bulk of illustrative material for the analyst of blackmail, though officials and media prefer to focus public attention on such relatively small-scale phenomena as bank robberies, hijackings, and political kidnapping by resistance groups, while ignoring the terrorism of states.

Needless to say, every aspect of my own thinking on these matters, conceptual and moral, has come up for reexamination during this period and has evolved greatly since the writing of this essay midway in the Cold War.

> Your generals talk of maintaining your position in Berlin with force. That is bluff. If you send in tanks, they will burn and make no mistake about it. If you want war, you can have it, but remember, it will be your war. Our rockets will fly automatically.
>
> NIKITA KHRUSHCHEV, June 23, 1959

> Q: What do you think of talk such as this?
>
> THE PRESIDENT: Well, I don't think anything about it at all. I don't believe that responsible people should indulge in anything that can be even remotely considered ultimatums or threats. That is not the way to reach peaceful solutions.
>
> PRESIDENT EISENHOWER, July 8, 1959

Like it or not, the language of threat and ultimatum is today—this month, this year—the language of diplomacy. It is, for many, an unfamiliar discourse. For them these lectures, whose subject is the logic and the rhetoric of threats, may provide some guide to current headlines.

A tone of some perplexity seems clear in the President's closing comments in a press conference in the spring of 1959, in which he had faced questions on Berlin that he had heard earlier over Lebanon, Iraq, and Quemoy: "We are living in a sort of a half world in so many things. We are not—we are not fighting a war, we are not killing each other, we are not going to the ultimate horror. On the other side of the picture, we are not living the kind of normal, what we'd like to call a normal life. . . . We just must not ever be indifferent to what is happening in the world today."[2]

And what *is* happening? It wants defining; how shall we name it? Call it blackmail; call it deterrence; call both—as we shall, in these lectures—*coercion:* the art of influencing the behavior of others by threats. Like those of any art, its techniques, goals, requirements impose certain patterns on the behavior of those pursuing it. Our objective will be to understand some aspects of these patterns in the behavior of people who are engaged in choosing threats, in supporting them, in making them credible and effective.

[2] *New York Times,* March 5, 1959.

In later lectures, we shall be interested in the operation of a political system in which some are making threats and others are ignoring them, resisting, obeying, or making counterthreats. The curious "half world" to which the President refers—in which we live—is such a system.

To understand the workings of this system is to understand, in some degree, many paradoxical aspects of present-day diplomacy. This includes the most perplexing, awful fact of all: though war has become an "ultimate horror," it has not become impossible.

Nuclear weapons have one, pre-eminent use in politics: to support threats. These threats recommend themselves, almost inescapably, as tools of policy not only to expansionist powers but also to status-quo nations seeking only to deter aggression and to preserve an orderly world society. It is perhaps unfortunate that the President's statement, cited at the head of this lecture, is not quite accurate; threats and ultimatums *can* lead to peaceful "solutions" (not, typically, mutually desirable ones), which is why they are used. Yet the gist of the President's remark is valid, and ominous. A mutual process of threat and counterthreat, commitment and countercommitment, can interlock to make all choices dangerous; and to increase the possibility of a war desired by none.

The ability to coerce is a form of power: perhaps the most important form underlying calculations of the "balance of power." Other modes of power important in the relationship of state to citizen—the abilities to educate, to inform, to propagandize, to inculcate habits of obedience or loyalty or respect for authority—are less significant in the relations of sovereign states. The power to *compel* by sheer, overmastering force ("naked power") remains; but its use is limited, practically, to war. It is the *threat* to compel or to punish—in short, coercion—which is the peacetime tool of diplomacy. And the ability effectively to threaten is by no means equivalent to the (related) ability actually to compel physically or to punish. In the remainder of this lecture, we shall examine abstractly conditions that bear upon the varying influence of threats.

Abstract patterns of threat-behavior can be identified in many concrete settings: economic bargaining, extortion, the use of lawsuits, the deterrence of crime, normal diplomacy, and conventional war. I shall be drawing most of my examples and applications from the field of national, military blackmail. The analysis I shall propose, nevertheless, derives initially from an interest in economic bargaining, and has its roots in the economic literature on that subject. Economists will recognize the strong influence throughout of game theory,[3] of Zeuthen's essay on economic warfare,[4] and of Thomas Schelling's recent brilliant article, "An Essay on Bargaining."[5] (My approach, however,

---

[3] The best overall reference on game theory is Duncan Luce and Howard Raiffa, *Games and Decisions* (New York, 1957), partially reprinted herein.

[4] Frederick Zeuthen, *Problems of Monopoly and Economic Warfare* (London, 1930).

[5] Thomas C. Schelling, "An Essay on Bargaining," reprinted in this collection.

differs in some fundamental ways from these.) In this lecture, we shall examine a situation in which a single threatener confronts a relatively passive subject. The questions we shall ask are very basic ones: what are the data that are relevant to this "blackmailer's" decisions; how are they measured and represented (this last is critical because these variables are subjective); how, fundamentally, do they hang together, how do they interact in their influence on decision.

Let us suppose that I am the coercer, or threatener, or as we shall say, "blackmailer"; you are my subject, or "victim." The goal of coercion is the goal of all power relationships; my problem is to influence your behavior in accordance with my desires: to make you do what I prefer that you should do. But unlike most modes of power, coercion is designed to influence not your behavior in general, but what the economist calls your "rational decisions": your choices among alternative actions, insofar as these choices are determined by your own subjective expectations and preferences.

The word "rational" here has a technical and fairly limited meaning. It does not mean "reasonable," in any overall sense. It means only that the choice is in some sense controlled by the actor's current expectations of the outcomes of his actions and by his preferences. Those expectations and preferences themselves may seem highly "unreasonable," or as crazy as they could be. A good deal of "insane" behavior, in other words, might be "rational" in this technical sense, whereas habitual or unreflective responses, though perfectly normal and reasonable, might be classed as "nonrational" behavior. None but "rational" behavior is subject to coercion; only the man rational in this sense can be blackmailed or deterred.

For coercion operates upon expectations: *your* expectations of *my* behavior. For this to be effective, your expectations must influence your behavior; but that is not enough. First of all, my choice must "make a difference" to you; my actions must affect the outcomes to your actions.

Suppose that I have to give—but also to withhold—something that you want: a job, services, goods, honor, authority. Or—and this turns out to be an equivalent condition—suppose that I can inflict some loss on you, relative to the status quo: by violence, by military action, by using my influence over others who have control over you.

Finally, suppose that I have some means of communicating with you and that I can *change* your expectations, to some extent, of my behavior. Given all these conditions, I can set out to *coerce* you: to influence you to choose the action *I* prefer you to take, by increasing your expectation that if you do not, I will choose some response leading to an outcome still worse for you than compliance.

Does this sound complicated? If we were to continue purely verbally, it would get more so. We can simplify the argument a great deal by referring to a diagram known as a payoff matrix, which shows the relationships of the variables we are considering: the strategies, and the evaluation of their outcomes.

	Comply	Resist
Accept	90	100
Punish		0

The game of "blackmail" is defined by the following rules. You, the "victim," will pick one of two possible strategies, represented here by the two columns of the matrix, labeled, "Comply" or "Resist." I, the "blackmailer," will pick a row *after* you have chosen; my two possible choices are labeled, "Accept" and "Punish." When we have both chosen strategies, our "payoffs" are shown as the numbers in the matrix at the intersection of that row and that column. *This diagram shows only your payoffs.* The payoff numbers indicate not the concrete, "objective" outcomes of the game—which may be various amounts of money, or exchanges of goods, or levels of violence—but your evaluation of these outcomes, your preferences among them. The numbers are intended to reflect not only your *order* of preference for the outcomes, but—in a sense we shall consider later—your *degree,* or *intensity* of preference among them.

Let us assume that you will choose "rationally." Clearly, in this game it "makes a difference" to you which action *I* will choose. If you were to choose the strategy, "Comply," you would be guaranteed an outcome to which you have assigned the payoff number, 90. If you pick the strategy, "Resist," you might get 100, or you might get 0, depending on which strategy I chose. (Incidentally, instead of using the phrase, "you might choose the strategy 'Comply' or 'Resist,'" let us just say from now on, "You might Comply," and so on.) Therefore, your expectations of my choice will influence your own choice. If you were *certain* that I would Accept, you would Resist; if you were certain that I would Punish you for Resisting, you would, with these payoffs, Comply.

But what if you are not certain what I will do? I suggest: if the risk of getting 0 is "small enough," you will choose to Resist; if it is "too large" you will prefer the certainty of 90 that you associate with Comply.

Suppose that, before we begin any interaction, or let us say, at a particular stage in our negotiations, I expect you to pick your second strategy, Resist. At that point, in other words, I would expect you to assign a very low likelihood to my choosing Punish: perhaps 0 likelihood. And finally, we will suppose that, for some reason, I would *prefer* that you choose your first strategy, Comply. Why? Let us defer that question for later.

My problem as a blackmailer is to convince you that I am "too likely" to respond with my second strategy, Punish, for you to accept the *risk* that *your* own second strategy, Resist, would entail. In other words, I must make you believe that 0 is so likely an outcome of Resist that Comply with its "safe" outcome of 90, looks better.

Concretely, these strategies might refer to one of many situations. In a bargaining situation, Resist might correspond to your insistence on your own "last offer," which, if I should Accept, will have the value 100 for you. I threaten that if you do not, instead, Comply with *my* "last offer" to you, which has the value 90 for you, there will be "no deal"; I will break off negotiations, leaving you with an outcome of 0. In labor negotiations, the threatened punishment for failing to Comply might be a strike or lockout. In the rackets, demolition or physical violence. Between firms, a price war, a lawsuit. In negotiations between states, the issue might be control over a piece of territory: the strategy Punish might cover sanctions from breaking off negotiations, through economic pressure and propaganda, to various levels of war. Obviously, the appropriate payoffs—if they can be estimated meaningfully at all—will be obscure in various degrees for these cases. To give our intuition something to work on in this example, however, let us start by assuming that these particular numbers correspond to *money* outcomes, dollar payoffs.

To consider the strategies abstractly once more, if I can persuade you that I am going to Punish you, my problem is solved; but this may be impossible. In any case, let us say, I cannot rely on doing it. Fortunately for me, it is not necessary. To be effective, my threatened punishment need not be certain, only "sufficiently likely."

How likely must it be? That is a question that I propose as a contribution to the discussion of bargaining and coercion. For it to be meaningful we must have an operational notion of "degrees of likelihood" in the mind of a player. Game theory, rejecting earlier notions of an "objective probability" assigned to choices by a rational opponent, has avoided the concept of "expectation" or "likelihood" altogether. But this ignores the fact that, typically, a player could tell us quite readily that he believes his opponent to be "more likely" to choose one particular strategy than some other. And this does not mean that he believes his opponent's choice to be "really" random: For example, chosen by flipping a coin. His statements about "likelihood" reflect merely his own uncertainty, his own "degrees of belief" in his predictions of his opponent's choice.

If we wish to measure these "likelihoods" on the basis of his observable behavior, not merely his statements, we can offer him various side bets on the choices his opponent will make. By the odds that he insists on before he will bet on various strategies—the odds that make him indifferent between betting on one strategy or another—we can infer, perhaps, that he regards one particular action by his opponent as a "long shot," another as "almost a sure thing" (that is, he will bet on the first only at very favorable odds; on the second perhaps he will "give" odds). Some experiments have suggested that a player's choices among these "gambles" may be so consistent that fairly precise estimates of the likelihoods he assigns to various events are possible. In any case, this sort of betting behavior will often give reliable *rough* indications of his different degrees of belief (and *I* would be willing to make use of the rough data we could get just by *asking* him).

For convenience, I will assume from now on that a player's state of uncertainty, his expectations, can be represented by a distribution of "subjective probabilities": numbers obeying the axioms of probabilities but which represent the player's own degrees of belief. Depending on what operation we choose to measure these, to say that he assigns a probability of .5, or 50 percent, to a particular event (such as an opponent's strategy) will mean either: (a) that he says, or feels, that this event is "as likely as not"; or (b) that we *observe* that he is indifferent between betting *on* this event or betting *against* it: that is, between wagering a fixed sum that the event *will* happen or that it will *not* happen. To say that he assigns more than 50 percent will mean that he regards it as "more likely than not"; or, that he would prefer to stake a fixed sum that it *will* happen than that it will not happen.

In these terms, the question, "How likely must it seem to you that I will carry it out, for my threat to influence you?" becomes: "What subjective probability, at a minimum, must you assign to my choosing Punish for you to prefer Comply to Resist?"

If we regard these payoffs as representing money, it seems plausible that there is some likelihood of $0 that would make you roughly *indifferent* between the certainty of $90 and a gamble that offered you $0 with that probability and $100 otherwise. Thus, if you assigned that probability to Punish, you would be indifferent between Resist and Comply. If you thought the risk that I would Punish were *greater* than that, you would Comply; if you assigned *less* than that likelihood to my carrying out my threat, you would Resist. That is, you would accept this (small) risk of getting $0, in hopes of getting $100 rather than the $90 you could get by complying. This hypothetical probability, whatever it is, then forms a threshhold: I will refer to it from now on as your *critical risk,* defined for these particular payoffs. Since it represents the maximum risk of punishment that you will accept, in choosing to Resist, we might term it your "willingness to resist": keeping in mind that it is measured by this hypothetical threshold probability—which in turn, as we shall see, depends on your payoffs.[6]

Now we can imagine you making your choice by comparing your actual expectation, in the end, with your critical risk; you Comply if you decide that the "actual risk" is higher than the critical level; otherwise you Resist my threats, refusing to comply. And my problem as a blackmailer is to ensure—by actions that either change your payoffs, hence your critical risk, or that increase your expectation of punishment—that your estimate of the actual risk is greater than the critical risk. How to do this is, of course, the heart of the blackmailer's art.

I do not mean to imply that either the blackmailer or his victim sees the problem in just this way, or that they make any such comparisons consciously. I propose merely to interpret, explain, their behavior in terms of these concepts. And even if I, as a blackmailer, did imagine that you have some threshold probability which I must surpass, neither I, nor any third party—or for that matter, even you—could estimate that threshold at all precisely.

[6] Frederik Zeuthen has an equivalent threshold concept in his essay, "Economic Warfare," reprinted herein. He applies it to a bilateral bargaining situation, a context we will consider in later lectures. I am indebted to Harvey Wagner for this important reference.

Still, let us see whether our intuition cannot provide some very rough hint as to where your critical risk might lie with the payoffs we have assumed.

Let us suppose, to begin, that the numbers in the matrix represent money payoffs. If the victim complies, he gets $90. If he resists, he may do $10 better; he can get $100 if I fail to carry out my threat. On the other hand, he may do $90 worse; he will get $0 if I do carry out my threat. "Resist" thus has the character of an "all-or-none" bet. He will resist if he is certain that I will not carry out my threat; but he will comply if he assigns more than some particular, roughly defined probability to my carrying out the threat. Before he will choose to comply, how sure does he have to be that I will do what I say? How sure would *you* have to be?

Is your answer like mine: *not very sure?* Then your "critical risk"—as mine would be—is *low* in this situation. If your intuition does not turn up an answer immediately, let us approach one more gradually. Would you decide to comply if you were 90 percent sure that I would punish you for resisting (that is, 90 percent sure that you would get 0)? If so, your critical risk is below 90 percent. Would you still take the sure $90 if you thought it merely "more likely than not" that I would carry out my threat? Then your critical risk is below 50 percent. (You will not "accept" even a .5 probability of punishment, when your alternative is a sure $90).

What would you choose if you assigned only a 5 percent chance to my punishing you? If you would then quickly choose Resist, accepting the chance of punishment in return for the hope of gain, we can infer that your threshhold probability, your critical risk, is greater than 5 percent, and so on. Before too long, no doubt, your answers would become halting and inconsistent; we would be left with a range of, say, 5 to 20 percent covering your elusive critical risk: that minimum probability of punishment that would shift you from Refuse to Comply. This critical risk represents the minimum "credibility" that a blackmailer must achieve for his threat to influence you. Facing this empirical data, a conservative blackmailer would aim at achieving at least a 20 percent likelihood in your mind that you would punish him for refusing.

Incidentally, if you happened to be the sort who followed the rule of thumb: choose that action with the highest "expectation" of money, that is, with the highest weighted average of money payoff, then I could compute your critical risk precisely. In this case it would be 10 percent. If you assigned 10 percent probability to $0 and 90 percent to $100, given your second strategy, you would be just indifferent between that strategy, which would then offer an expected payoff of $90, and your first strategy. If you assigned more than 10 percent, you would comply; if less, refuse. (There is a simple way to compute this result, which will be presented later.)

But (in all cases) such precise calculation is thoroughly unrealistic; the usefulness of this approach in no way hinges on achieving such spurious accuracy. At most, what we will hope to agree on is a judgment of the form: "The threshold is *low;* the victim does not need to be *very* sure of punishment before he will comply." Or an even cruder judgment can still be useful: "Low or not, the critical risk in this case is *lower* than in some other": That is, lower than in the following case:

	Comply	Resist
Accept	10	100
Punish		0

Here, in money terms, only my "offer" has changed: Comply now gives you 10. Refuse still offers, for you, a possible $100: a possible $0. Yet, the overall *structure* of the payoff matrix has changed. Has anything happened to your "willingness to resist": your critical risk? By complying now you accept the certainty of $10. If you refuse, you will sacrifice that $10, if I carry out my threat; but you could gain $90, if I should fail to do so. In the earlier case, let us say, you would have complied if you had assigned as much as one-fourth, even one-fifth, likelihood to my punishment. Would you still?

My own intuition gives me an answer. It seems to me that you will "need" to be more sure than before that I will carry out my threat before you will comply; that is, whatever your critical risk was before, I will guess that it is *higher* now. Now that I offer you less for compliance, *I must manage to make my threat more credible than it had to be before.*

In fact, with these payoffs, I would be willing to go further and guess not only that your critical risk now is higher, but also that it is fairly *high.* Not 87 percent, not 93 percent; just, *high.* My estimates, indeed, may never get more precise than that; but that may be just close enough.

In practice, of course, your choice will not depend only on the *money* outcomes; your willingness to take risks involving these outcomes will reflect many other considerations. For example, if you defined the messages I was sending you as "blackmail," you might find "submitting to blackmail" so distasteful that you would Refuse unless you were "almost certain" that I would carry out my punishment, or perhaps even if you were certain. In the analysis, your payoffs should reflect such feelings; they imply that the payoff to "compliance" would appear very low, perhaps even lower than that of "punishment." Again, even a small loss, or a small gain, may weigh heavily with you. For this analysis, we want payoff numbers that indicate to us just how you *would* gamble on these outcomes. The outcomes will typically not be money, or money alone; there may be no plausible "objective" index of the "size" of the outcome. But we are not interested in "size" in any objective sense; all we are interested in is the player's subjective, relative evaluation of the outcome: specifically, what bets he will take, what he will reject, in choosing among gambles that offer these outcomes with various probabilities. If we can actually observe his choices among such gambles—fine. As L. J. Savage has shown,[7] following the work of Frank Ramsey,[8] it may be possible to estimate both payoffs and probabilities from this pattern of choices. But I

[7] L. J. Savage, *The Foundations of Statistics* (New York, 1954).
[8] Frank Ramsey, "Truth and Probability" (1926) in *The Foundations of Mathematics* (London, 1931).

suspect that we may be able to make fairly reliable, though rough, guesses about a player's relative payoffs by inferring his "degree of preference" from many other types of evidence besides his betting behavior. An actual blackmailer, after all, must make such guesses; and he will; and at least in some, sufficiently "obvious" cases, I think we can predict roughly his answers.

What went through the mind of the bank teller in New York last December, as he read the note that a "little old lady" pushed through his window?[9] "I have acid in a glass," the note said, "and if you don't give me what I want I'll splash it on you." He looked up, saw about ninety customers in the bank, a grey-haired lady in a brown cloth coat before his window, and on his ledge, a six-ounce water glass with a colorless liquid in it. He returned to the note, and read: "I have two men in here. I'll throw the acid in your face and somebody will get shot. Hurry. Put all the fives, tens and twenties in this bag." He complied.[10]

Why? A matter of reflex? Try that on the reflexes of your own teller. Because he was quite certain that the glass contained acid, and that she would throw it at him? An unlikely estimate. (It turned out later that she had stolen the glass from a cafeteria and filled it with tapwater.) Did he obey because he hastily calculated that his critical risk was 14 percent, and the actual risk she presented was 23 percent? No, and yet it would not require much reflection on his part to conclude that there was *some* chance that she was telling the truth; and looking into his heart, he might well have concluded that he did not need to be *very* sure.

The little old lady had to face beforehand the problem of estimating these factors. As predictions go in the social sciences, hers were pretty good.

We have more data on the mental processes of the next teller to face the lady. This was in a bank one block north, the following month; the operation was virtually identical, the note in this case reading: "Put $5000 in $5, $10, and $20 bills in bag. There is acid in the glass. You wouldn't want it in your face. Don't try to warn anybody until I am out of here. Oh yes, I am being guarded by two guns. Let's not let your customers or co-workers get hurt."

The newspaper account continues: "Mr. ———'s first impulse when he read the note was to duck behind the counter and set off the alarm but he reconsidered when he looked up and saw the water glass. 'She tilted it just to show me that there was something in it,' he recalled later. He put his right hand up in front of his face and with his left began cramming bills into the paper bag."[11]

As it happened, the teller's caution led him to hand the paper bag over the glass partition instead of unlocking the grille; this lapse from normal procedure

---

[9] *New York Herald Tribune,* December 4, 1958.

[10] This robbery was accomplished at lunch hour on one of the busiest corners in the world: Seventh Avenue and 34th Street, across the street from Macy's. The lady walked out, with glass in hand, past an armed guard; she had not uttered a word. Her exit was followed closely by the entrance of two armed guards, two uniformed patrolmen with drawn weapons, and two FBI agents who happened to be on the corner.

[11] *New York Herald Tribune,* January 3, 1959.

was noticed by a vice-president standing nearby, who had also seen the note being passed. He shouted, "Grab that woman!" and the lady surrendered quietly.[12]

If we accept the notion that we can make some meaningful estimates of "critical risks" in different situations, we can ask: On what does the critical risk depend? What factors make it go up or down? This is of interest to the blackmailer, since, other things being equal, he will prefer a situation in which his threat does not "need" to be so credible. The general answer is that it is the whole structure of the victim's payoffs that determines the critical risk. In this simple case, as the possible gains from Resisting, relative to the outcomes to Complying, increase relative to the possible losses, then the critical risk, the "willingness to Resist," goes up. For example, I can reduce your critical risk by threatening a worse punishment than before. Or, as we have already suggested, your critical risk goes up the worse the "offer" I make to you: That is, the worse your outcome to Comply, relative to the payoffs to Resist.

This last point was illustrated in an interesting bargaining session in a Chemical Corn Exchange Bank eight blocks away from the first in which the little old lady scored. The note, typed on the back of a check, read: "Have a grenade in my hand and two more. I will use them. Didn't come here to get caught. Take a look. Toss in your and your neighbor's money. Put $5000 in bundled 20 and 10s in coin bag. Count it. Don't stuff it. Keep quiet until I'm out the door or this place will look like a battlefield."[13]

To this the man added verbally: "I'm not fooling." The teller told police the man was clutching "something" in his left hand and he "believed it was a grenade." The teller counted out $5,000 from a cash supply of $50,000 and put it in the bag. Then occurred a little exchange that suggests that, given the teller's actual expectation that the man was holding a grenade and would use it to blow up the teller (and himself), he regarded the actual risk as "too high" to argue with $5,000 at stake, but not high enough when the "offer" was very much worse.

Eying the remaining $45,000 in the pile, the robber asked: "What about the rest?" According to the newspaper account, "Mr. ———— told him: 'That's all you asked for, $5,000,' and handed over the bag containing $4,000 in $20 bills and the rest in $10 bills." The man departed without further argument, passing the guard and crossing Fifth Avenue in front of the Public Library.

A crucial element in the success of all these robberies was that, confronted by the threat of acid or grenade (combined with modest demands), the tellers'

---

[12] She was eventually convicted of the two robberies (when confronted by her first victim, she volunteered, "Oh yes, that's the boy I held up last time") without ever having given her address (or, some suspected, her correct name). As for the $3,420 from the first robbery, she informed police: "A few seconds after leaving the bank, the paper bag with the money was jostled from my hands and fell to the street. A man picked it up and tried to hand it to me but I was so nervous I said, 'It doesn't belong to me' and walked on."

Police described the story as "fantastic."

[13] *New York Herald Tribune,* November 4, 1958.

critical risks ("willingness to resist") were *low*. Now, any one of us might have predicted, as did the robbers, that this would be the case. This does not necessarily mean that you should give up a good, alternative means of liveli-hood to make your fortune with a glass of water and a paper bag. There is more to the blackmailer's art than estimating the victim's critical risk. How does he (or she) manage to ensure that his victim will estimate the "actual risk" as *higher* than his critical level? How does he do this with sufficiently high confidence that he is willing to gamble on his own success? What are the obstacles in his way, the limitations on his ability to influence his victim's expectations? These are the central problems in coercion.

They involve, primarily, influencing your expectations. Well, how do you form your expectations of my behavior in the first place? How would you arrive at them if I were doing nothing to influence you?

You can go by past experience, if you know any that seems relevant. How have I behaved in "games" with others? With you? Do I "tend" to carry out my threats, my predictions? Or do I bluff? How do people "like me" typically behave—on the basis of your experience, or what you read in the papers? If I know "the record" you are likely to be looking at, I can guess at your initial expectations. I may be able to fill in the record a bit for you, underline certain parts, lie about it; but on the whole there is little I can do to manipulate your expectations by changing the record.

With or without experience to go on, the victim has another basis for ex-pectations: his estimates of the *blackmailer's payoffs*. If you regard me as "rational," in our limited sense, then your question, "How is he likely to respond to my actions?" translates into: "What will he *want* to do? What will it pay him to do? Which will he see as the *best* choice for him to make, given my choice?" You may have no idea what my payoffs are, in which case these questions go unanswered. At best, your estimates will be rough and uncertain, perhaps even more than my estimates of your payoffs, since it is typical for the blackmailer to know a good deal more about his victim than the victim knows about him. Still, you usually will make some assumption, perhaps very well informed, about my payoffs; and when you do, it will influence your expecta-tions.

And this can be the blackmailer's primary obstacle, the crucial limitation on his ability to influence. The effect of his own payoffs on the victim's ex-pectations will often be the factor that he must change, or counteract, or sur-mount, if he is to succeed. For typically, if the victim should fail to "obey," it would be *costly* for the blackmailer to carry out his threatened punishment. It would not, in general, give him his best outcome under the circumstances: that is, given the victim's actual, rebellious choice. Which is to say, it would be *irrational* to carry out the threat. It would mean, for the blackmailer, de-liberately passing up an outcome that he preferred; he could, if he chose, do better. Why wouldn't he? That question is bound to occur to the victim; and the blackmailer knows it.

We can illustrate this problem with our payoff matrix by adding to the diagram the blackmailer's payoffs. These numbers will appear to the left of the victim's corresponding payoff; from now on, the first number in the box at the intersection of a row and column signifies the payoff to the "row" player (the blackmailer), the second the payoff to the "column" player (the victim). For example:

	Comply	Resist
Accept	100, 10	50, 100
Punish		0, 0

It is a while before this type of diagram begins to look as simple as it really is; the trick is to learn to look only at the left-hand payoff in each pair—by rows—when we are interested in the blackmailer's payoffs, and at the right-hand payoffs—by columns—when we are discussing the victim's payoffs. We will assume that there is no basis whatever for comparing the victim's payoffs directly to the blackmailer's payoffs, or vice versa. One might be expressed in dollars, the other in rubles, with no given exchange rate; or one might be dollars, the other "utilities" (measured by some psychological test). A given payoff for the victim, say, has meaning only in relation to the other payoffs *for the victim;* there is no basis for saying that it is "more" or "less" than any given payoff of the blackmailer.[14] Thus, if the blackmailer Accepts and the victim Resists, there is no basis in the numbers above for saying that the victim's payoff is better, in any sense, than that of the blackmailer (to make the point in familiar, though not quite conclusive, terms: the victim's payoff might be expressed in pennies, the blackmailer's in dollars).

In this example, if the victim Resists and the blackmailer carries out his threat to Punish, the victim gets 0, instead of the 10 he could have had with certainty if he had chosen Comply. But the punishment is costly also for the blackmailer; his payoff, from choosing Punish, is 0 instead of the 50 that he could have had (given the victim's prior choice; the blackmailer, remember, always moves second) by choosing Accept. Can he convince the victim that, if the occasion arose, he would pick 0 instead of 50?

The first point to make—following from all our earlier discussion—is that he need not make the victim *certain* that he would do this. The victim must believe merely that the likelihood of the threatened action is greater than his own "critical risk," a factor which depends only upon the structure of his own payoffs.[15] The question we now face is: how does the blackmailer make his

[14] I am underlining this point so much because this is a major distinction between the approach I am proposing in these lectures and many earlier treatments of threat-situations. For example, Luce and Raiffa, in their discussion of game-theoretical approaches, several times mention that it is possible to judge the effectiveness of threats only if comparisons may be made between the players' payoffs. In other words, they, and other writers, have stressed that it is necessary for the threatener to be able to say, "This would hurt you more than it would me." Many critics have doubted that it is possible to make such comparisons, on a meaningful, empirical basis; and my own approach convinces me that it is not *necessary* to do so. At any rate, we will not.

[15] I have not been drawing comparisons between the approach presented here and alternative, earlier approaches. This is a convenient place to remark that the above point is, so far as I am aware, a novelty of the present analysis.

threat appear even *slightly* likely, against the evidence of his own payoffs? For with the payoffs as given, it would clearly be irrational for the blackmailer to carry out the threatened punishment, if the victim, after all, failed to Comply. And this example is not peculiar. It is not the exception but the rule for a threat to have a certain built-in implausibility, being costly—or irrational— for the threatener to carry out. His efforts to overcome this barrier to belief account for the most characteristic, and paradoxical, features of threat-behavior. (I owe this conception of the central problem of threat-behavior to Thomas Schelling's pathbreaking article, "An Essay on Bargaining," reprinted herein.)

A good deal of our subsequent discussion will be devoted to illustrating and analyzing the techniques whereby a threatener (including a victim making counterthreats) attempts to make it sufficiently plausible that he will carry out a costly threatened action. There seem to be four main approaches, of which the first two, in particular, have been discussed exhaustively in Schelling's article, to which I refer the reader for extended treatment.

First, the blackmailer can voluntarily but irreversibly give up his freedom of choice;[16] he can make it impossible for himself not to carry out his threat. If he can in some way bind his own hands, destroy his alternatives, he may be able to "make it true" that he would carry out his threat, for the reason that he would have no choice. For example, he might irrevocably give control of the punishment strategy to a subordinate, an ally, an agent who would actually be more likely to carry it out (presumably because his payoffs have a different structure). United States relations with Chiang on the Quemoy issue might be pertinent here, or the proposal to give NATO nations independent control of nuclear weapons.

This might be represented in the matrix by deleting certain rows, or entries, symbolizing: (a) that these have been eliminated as feasible alternatives for the blackmailer; and (b) that his opponent recognizes this. Thus, in our example, the blackmailer might be able to "strike out" the first row, perhaps thus "compelling" the victim to believe that the consequence of Resist must be 0.

	Comply	Resist
Accept	100, 10	50, 100
Punish		0, 0

Here we find the blackmailer striving to achieve his goal by eliminating opportunities, contracting his set of alternatives, although discussions of bargaining often rule this out axiomatically. This was the type of possibility, emphasized by Schelling, that gave his article a paradoxical flavor for most readers. The resolution of the paradox is that the blackmailer, by his tactic of "tying one hand behind him,[17]" hopes for a favorable effect on his opponent's expectations.

---

[16] Schelling, "An Essay on Bargaining," reprinted herein.

[17] At this point we might look again at the wording of Khrushchev's statement to

The same flavor of paradox, and the same explanation, attaches to the next type of tactic. It may actually be rather rare that a blackmailer can tie his hands irrevocably, quite literally destroy alternatives. But even when he cannot make the actions in question (that is, failure to punish) impossible, he may be able to make them *costly*. Although Schelling does not emphasize the distinction in that article, most of the examples of "commitment" in his essay fall into this category. The player binds himself to incur certain costs or penalties or to forego certain advantages if he should fail to carry out a pledge. Thus he reduces his own payoff incentives to break the pledge—perhaps to the point where it would become irrational to break it—thereby hoping to make his pledged action seem more likely to his opponent.

We can represent this behavior neatly in our formal model by allowing the player the opportunity to *lower his own payoffs;* this "move" serves to formalize most of the behavior examined by Schelling, behavior which is ignored or excluded in most game-theoretical discussion and which tends to appear puzzling or perverse in actual experience.[18]

Thus, the blackmailer may seek to *change* his payoffs from those presumed in our example to the following:

	Comply	Resist
Accept	100, 10	−1, 100
Punish		0, 0

Here he has done nothing but *worsen* one of his own payoffs; yet he may have improved considerably his chances for winning a favorable outcome! He has made it plausible that he will carry out his threat by making it rational to do so.[19]

Concretely, the blackmailer may make a contractual agreement with a third party to choose Punish if the victim chooses Resist, making himself liable to forfeit or penalty or suit if he fails to carry out this action. Or he can stake his honor, his prestige, his reputation for honesty—if he has any of these—on carrying out this prediction. These new obligations are then symbolized in our model as subtractions from his previously determined payoff to choosing Accept when the victim chooses Resist (that is, the payoff for failure to punish). If he can actually lower that payoff below that for Punish (and even, to some extent, if he cannot go that far) he will have removed (or

---

Harriman, cited at the head of the lecture: "Our rockets will fly *automatically*." "And his colleagues around the table," Harriman continues, "chorused the word, 'Automatically.' " *Life,* July 13, 1959, p. 33.

[18] In Schelling's most recent publication on this subject, "The Strategy of Conflict: Prospectus for a Reorientation of Game Theory," *Journal of Conflict Resolution,* II, no. 3 (Sept., 1958), 240, he has proposed independently this same formalization of his earlier work.

[19] It might seem natural to infer from this that the victim is subsequently *certain* to Comply, since, it might be argued, he will assume that the blackmailer is now certain to carry out his threat. However, there are good reasons to be discussed for avoiding this assumption. The fact is that this tactic does have risks for the blackmailer; it does not guarantee him a win.

reduced) his evident incentive to back down from the threat, which presumably becomes more convincing to the opponent. Thus the importance of honor, reputation, prestige, to a blackmailer. They can be pawned. They can be wagered, risked, put up as security; they are something to lose, which can make more credible choices designed to preserve them.

Or the stakes can be more tangible. Chiang made a threatened defense of Quemoy against invasion far more credible, though this may not have been his direct intention, by stationing one-third of his troops on the island: thus "making it true" that he had a great deal to lose by accepting the loss of the island.

These two types of tactics are basic, but they have certain drawbacks in making credible what amount to *suicidal* threats. Whose honor, whose reputation for honesty is so great that to wager it would make it actually *rational* to carry out such a threat? And who, with such issues at stake, would really bind himself irrevocably to carry out a suicidal punishment?

The problem is not an academic one, for precisely these questions have been raised repeatedly about the use of the deterrent threat of massive retaliation. As Secretary of State Dulles described the policy,[20] "The basic decision was to depend primarily upon a great capacity to retaliate, instantly, by means and at places of our choosing." No one denied that we had this capacity; the doubt was that we could make an opponent believe that we would use it, on occasions when it would obviously not be the optimum move to make. And that—in a world in which the Russians also possessed atomic weapons and a long-range air force—seemed to cover just about every occasion short of an all-out attack on the United States.

In 1952 Dulles had stated: "The only way to stop prospective aggressors is to convince them in advance that if they commit aggression, they will be subjected to retaliatory blows so costly that their aggression will not be a profitable operation."[21] But *how* convince them, when it is evident that retaliation might be no less costly for *us?*

The point is obvious if we attempt to sketch a payoff matrix. First, say, the Soviet payoffs might have this character:

		SU	
		Status quo	Aggression
	Accept	0	10
US			
	Retaliate		−1000

Their two (column) strategies are labeled Status quo, and (limited) Aggression; the latter refers to some expansionist move which does not include an attack upon America. The United States strategy of Retaliate implies massive retaliation on Russia, using SAC and thermonuclear weapons.

Clearly, if the Soviet Union were certain that we would retaliate thus, they

[20] Department of State *Bulletin,* XXX (January 25, 1954), 107–110.

[21] *New York Herald Tribune,* May 16, 1952. In this formulation, the essential similarity shows up clearly between the "deterrent" threat and the "blackmail" we have been discussing till now.

would refrain from their limited aggression. But would they be certain? It is not enough, the critics of the massive retaliation strategy pointed out, for the United States simply to tell them we would retaliate; for consider the corresponding United States payoffs (which we show to the left of the Soviet Union payoffs):

	SU	
	Status quo	Aggression
Accept	0, 0	-10, 10
Retaliate		-1000, -1000

If the Soviet Union chose their limited aggression and we "accepted," we would be worse off than the status quo; we would have suffered a loss of -10. But if we carried out the threat of a nuclear attack on Russia, the loss would be immeasurably greater: -1000. Would the United States take that choice?

"I think the answer is clearly no," said Dean Acheson recently, after putting this question to himself.[22] "To invoke our 'great capacity to retaliate' is to insure an experience by us of the Soviet's 'great capacity to retaliate.' "

We have already seen that the general problem of credibility is by no means peculiar to threats of massive retaliation. On the other hand, the tactics considered so far—binding oneself irrevocably, or putting up forfeits—do not seem too helpful to the threatener in this case. Is it credible that we would be willing really to cross out the first row in that matrix? Is our honor (or anything else) really so valuable that, by pledging it against our threat to retaliate, we would reduce -10 (in the upper right-hand corner) to -1010 (thus making retaliation "rational")? "No," the critics of massive retaliation have generally answered; and there is valuable insight in their reaction.

Still, this is not the whole story. These critics have often weakened their case—from the point of view of this discussion—by appearing to assume that the threatened retaliation must be perfectly certain to be effective at all. In his book *Power and Diplomacy* (written a year before the 1958 Quemoy crisis), Acheson asked:[23] "Do any of us seriously believe that an American government would take the position that an attack on Quemoy would involve the destruction of Peiping or Moscow, or both, *and of New York?* "The answer is, of course, that the threat is not credible."

And it is "the essence of deterrence," he asserts earlier, "that the threat should be credible."[24]

These assertions suggest the existence of just two classes of threats: "credible" or "incredible." Now, we can make finer distinctions than that; and we must, for a real understanding of this problem. The essence of deterrence (as of blackmail) is that the threat should be credible *enough*. To put the problem that way is to suggest the question: just how credible must this particular

---

[22] Dean Acheson, "Wishing Won't Hold Berlin," *Saturday Evening Post,* March 7, 1959, p. 85.

[23] Dean Acheson, *Power and Diplomacy* (Cambridge, 1958), p. 51 (italics his).

[24] *Ibid.,* p. 47.

threat be? And a glance at plausible payoffs for the massive retaliation threat shows up another peculiarity of that situation; while the threat seems unlikely to be very credible, it would not appear that it *had* to be very credible.

Consider our hypothetical payoffs. Soviet aggression offers them a possible gain of 10 over the status quo (if the United States does not retaliate) but a possible loss of -1000 (if we do). Given the United States payoffs, it would clearly be hard for the United States to make its threat seem, say, "as likely as not." But given the Soviet Union payoffs, it is hard to believe that they would *need* to assign that much likelihood, for them to be deterred. With payoffs like these, in other words, it seems plausible (to me, at any rate) that the Soviet "critical risk" would be well under 50 percent.

This is not an argument in favor of relying on "low-likelihood" threats. Acheson's judgment that the threat of massive retaliation might not be credible *enough* (to rephrase his statement in our terms) in a particular case is undoubtedly sound. But unless we face the full complexities of the problem, we cannot understand the incentives that can lead reasonable men to commit themselves to relatively implausible threats (on the conceivably well-founded hope that they will prove plausible enough). Nor would we prepare ourselves for the possibility that we might have to *face* such threats from our opponents.

Given, then, that our threatener may not have to make his threat very credible (his victim's critical risk may be low), but that the tactics we discussed earlier may not suffice to make it credible at all: there remain two more classes of tactics that may be effective. First, as a blackmailer, I may create and exploit uncertainty in my opponent's mind as to my true payoffs: make him unsure in his predictions of the actions that would truly be rational for me. Finally, I can appear *irrational;* for which purpose, of course, it helps to *be* irrational. Irrational, perhaps, in being erratic, inconsistent, unpredictable; or again, in having abnormal, "unreasonable" expectations or preferences.

I shall discuss these methods later in detail in an examination of Hitler's diplomacy: "The Political Uses of Madness." Meanwhile, we might note that they seem highly relevant to the bank robbery examples mentioned earlier. In those cases, a low critical risk was a common element on the part of the victims; at the same time, an obviously "reasonable" threatener would have had trouble in making the threats in question seem plausible in the slightest. The teller might well reason: "If I were standing out there, I would *never* throw the acid, or drop the grenade, no matter what happened." But his next thought is bound to be: "*I* would never be standing out there with a grenade in the first place." The very presence of these people in the bank, pushing homicidal notes through the window in full presence of customers and guards, is very impressive warning to the teller not to rely on inferring their payoffs and behavior patterns from his own.

This sort of consideration will usually create only a small uncertainty in the victim's mind; but given a low critical risk, that may be enough. And critical risks can be very low. About the same period that the little old lady was operating on Seventh Avenue, a young electrical engineer held up two Chemical Corn Exchange Banks in succession (one in Penn Station; one on Broadway near 38th) *with a comb*. Each time he asked for $5,000; the note in the second case, on the back of a deposit slip, advised: "Look at the gun. Don't try to signal. Don't try to press alarm. Put $5,000 in 100s, 20s, and 10s in this envelope. Keep quiet till I'm out."[25] The instruction to look at the gun was a nice touch, since he did not have one. As the newspaper put it: "A comb stuck in ———'s belt, high across his chest, appeared to Mr. ——— to be the handle of a pistol. He immediately counted out $7,060 and thrust it into the brown manila envelope ——— pushed toward him." (In this case, the robber was caught after a chase; but, it turned out, his *three* earlier comb heists had been successful.)

Notice the recurrence of the $5,000 figure in the successful "offer"; interesting, too, that the man with the bag of grenades had selected a Chemical Corn Exchange Bank. Had the word gotten out about the critical risks of Chemical Corn Exchange tellers? "ask for $5,000 and you're in . . . point anything at them—cookies, milk bottles, rolled newspapers. . . ?"[26] Their "willingness to resist" seems on a par with that of an American POW described in a recent book on the POW's in Korea. Explaining why he had given information after thirty-five minutes of mild questioning, he said: "They said they had ways of making me talk, so I talked."

Incidentally, notice the rich array of possible explanations our discussion suggests for this man's behavior. His critical risk might have been very low; either because (a) torture had a very great negative payoff for him, or (b) the information requested represented to him a very small "demand." Or he might have regarded the actual risk of punishment as very high, because of clues in the environment, or shared experience, or conservative assumption. The Army's categorization of its POW's is less fine-grained; they decided he was a "coward."

It is a peculiarity of thermonuclear threats that they make cowards of practically everyone. Very few are the objectives that would seem worth— to anyone—a *high* probability of nuclear retaliation.

There may have been some tendency on the part of Western diplomats to rely rather heavily on this facet of the situation. "What protects Berlin," Raymond Aron wrote in 1957, "is not the Soviet conviction that the Western powers would prefer death to the abandonment of the capital, but the doubt which subsists in spite of everything in the minds of the Soviet leaders about

25 *New York Herald Tribune,* March 10, 1959. The earlier robbery is reported in *New York Herald Tribune,* February 20, 1959.

26 Two weeks after this hypothesis was advanced in public, the management of the Chemical Corn Exchange system, as though they had reached a similar conclusion, began the installation of a system that would photograph customers *automatically*. In the course of the installation, a customer obtained several thousand dollars from a teller with a note that simply began, "Give me . . ." and made no mention whatever of weapon or punishment. He walked out with the money past workmen installing the new apparatus. (On a subsequent attempt, he was unmasked as an accountant who had taken, each time, a short break from his officework.)

the Western reaction."[27] That doubt may still shield Berlin. It is hard, at this moment,[28] to see what else does.

Nevertheless, Acheson points out in his book, such a policy has risks. "To put forward as a policy a threat which is incredible may be to stay within the yet uncharted bounds of permissible fraud in politics, but it is highly dangerous for the country."[29] This is quite true, as far as it goes. It may, in other words, be dangerous to be a sheep in wolves' clothing. But the risks are more widespread than that. It can also be dangerous to commit oneself to the most highly credible threats: if there is a significant chance that they will not be credible enough. And that there always will be.

Our threats can fail for a great variety of reasons. For example: (a) if we underestimated the "required credibility" (the opponent's critical risk) for this threat, that is, if we misread the opponent's payoffs; (b) if the opponent did not find our commitment as credible as we expected, credible enough; (c) if he should be irrational, impulsive, careless; (d) if he should be committed, himself, to the action we are trying to deter.

Deterrence has been perhaps too often described in terms of "posing risks." When it involves commitment, it also means *taking* risks: the risks that it will fail, that the threat will have to be carried out because the threatener has left himself no choice. The risks must be calculated; but how will the results be checked? Not only are the estimates subjective; they are estimates, largely, of subjective variables. What are the opponent's payoffs; what outcomes does he expect from given strategies, how does he evaluate

[27] Raymond Aron, *On War* (New York, 1959), p. 113.

[28] March 10, 1959: the date that this Lowell Lecture was delivered. At the time of this editing, July, 1959, there seems little reason to change the remark.

The Presidential press conference next day, March 11, 1959, threw further insight into United States strategy at that point in the Berlin crisis. The President made the following comments: "We are certainly not going to fight a ground war in Europe. . . . You wouldn't start the kind of ground war that would win in that region if that were going to make the way you had to enforce your will. You have got to go to other means." He said further: "I don't know how you could free anything with nuclear weapons. . . . Destruction is not a good police force. You don't throw hand grenades around the streets to police the streets so that people won't be molested by thugs. Well, now, this is exactly the way that you have to look at nuclear war, or any other. . . . And, I must say, to use that kind of a nuclear war as a general thing looks to me a self-defeating thing for all of us, because after all, with that kind of release of nuclear explosions around this world, of the numbers of hundreds, I don't know what it would do to the world, and particularly the northern hemisphere; and I don't think anybody else does. But I know it would be quite serious."

These views seemed to some listeners to be contradictory. The question was raised, that if ground war were ruled out and nuclear war didn't free anyone, what threat did the President have in mind? The President's reply: "I didn't say that nuclear war is a complete impossibility."

In the context of his other remarks, it was clear that the threat being posed was that of a *possibility* (which, in fact, the President tended to minimize) of a nuclear response. As Aron had suggested, this could be effective, given a sufficiently low critical risk in the opponent. But it might also be pointed out that if such a threat works today in deterrence, it might work tomorrow in blackmail.

[29] Acheson, *Power and Diplomacy*, p. 47.

those outcomes? To what extent is he a gambler? What alternatives does he see? What does he expect me to do; how does he see my payoffs, my expectations? How will my tactics influence his expectations? How likely is he to have committed himself? To act carelessly, irrationally? What risks will he take, and what does he think the risks are?

Our analysis tells us the relevance of those questions; it suggests concepts for representing and comparing the answers, some hints for drawing implications from the answers; but it does not give the answers. To find those answers is not within the scope of our logic, nor, as yet, of any science: it is an art.

Our policy of deterrence has been described, and defended, in these apt terms, written after Korea, Indochina, and the first shelling of Quemoy: "You have to take chances for peace, just as you must take chances in war. Some say we were brought to the verge of war. Of course we were brought to the verge of war. The ability to get to the verge without getting into the war is the necessary art."[30]

But blackmailers too can calculate risks—and take them. They too can go to the verge of war; and this fact has an important bearing on the risks of deterrence.

In this abstract discussion, we have examined the anatomy of blackmail. In the next lecture, we shall hear the *sound* of blackmail; the words that Adolph Hitler spoke, and their echoes, that won him half of Europe before the firing of a shot. There is the artist to study, to learn what *can* be hoped for, what can be done with the threat of violence.

[30] John Foster Dulles, quoted in, "How Dulles Averted War," *Life,* Jan. 16, 1956, p. 78.

THE BARGAINER'S CALCULUS

Oran R. Young

This essay is concerned with bargaining defined as the manipulation of the information of others in the interests of improving the outcome for one's self under conditions of strategic interaction. Most scholars who have worked with this conception of bargaining have focused on the range of tactics available to the individual bargainer. Thus, they have concentrated on the examination of such devices as commitments, threats, and promises.[1] It is important to emphasize, however, that this manipulative conception, unlike the other major conceptions of bargaining, does not make bargaining mandatory for the individual. Game-theoretic models of bargaining, for example, are concerned primarily with criteria of selection for individuals who must make a choice among some specified set of strategies.[2] Similarly, the economic models of bargaining deal, for the most part, with the ways in which individuals who are actively engaged in bargaining formulate their offers and counteroffers.[3] By contrast, individuals facing problems of interdependent decision making are not compelled to engage in manipulative activities. On the contrary, they may decide to make their choices on the basis of some procedures that do not involve any bargaining at all. Within the framework of the manipulative conception of bargaining, therefore, it is important to come to grips with the problem of *when* to bargain as well as the problem of *how* to bargain.

The purpose of this essay is to examine the calculus of the rational individual as he decides whether or not to engage in manipulative activities under conditions of strategic interaction. To this end it deals, for the most part, with a highly simplified model of manipulative bargaining. In many ways this model is an unrealistic one. Thus, it leaves out a number of possibilities for bargaining as well as a variety of factors that will sometimes influence the bargainer's calculus in real-world situations. Nevertheless, the fact that the model is a simple one may help to reveal the principal problems that the rational individual must come to grips with in deciding when to bargain.

A. BASIC ASSUMPTIONS AND DEFINITIONS

The following assumptions are required for the construction of the model set forth in this essay. Above all, it is assumed that individuals behave rationally. Rationality involves the following conditions:[4] (1) the individual evaluates alternatives in his environment on the basis of his preferences among

---

[1] For an outstanding example see Thomas C. Schelling, *The Strategy of Conflict* (Cambridge, 1960).

[2] For a fuller discussion of this point see the Introduction to Part One of this book.

[3] The analytic perspective underlying these economic models is discussed in some detail in the Introduction to Part Two of this book.

[4] For a good introductory analysis of these conditions consult Ward Edwards, "The Theory of Decision Making," *Psychological Bulletin*, LI (1954), 388–417.

them, (2) his preference ordering is consistent and transitive, and (3) he always chooses the preferred alternative. In the first instance, this means that the individual perceives his decision-making environment in terms of differentiated alternatives, that he is able to identify a specified set of alternatives in any given situation, and that he can rank these alternatives on the basis of his preferences among them. In addition, rationality implies that the individual can specify his preferences among alternatives whose outcomes are risky rather than certain.

There are several subsidiary assumptions that should also be mentioned here. First, the concept "actor" refers to any behaving unit that makes choices among differentiated alternatives whether it is a single individual or a collective entity. Although most of the analysis in this essay is couched in terms of individuals as actors, the model is, in principle, applicable to the bargaining calculus of collective entities as well. Second, actors are assumed to evaluate their alternatives solely in terms of their own self-interests. This means that individuals do not place any value on the utility of others as an end in itself. Third, individuals employ expected-utility calculations whenever they are required to choose among risky alternatives.[5] In the body of this essay, it is assumed that individuals evaluate risk itself in a neutral fashion, although it would be easy enough to alter this assumption by introducing a "risk-evaluation" function.[6] Fourth, though the manipulative conception of bargaining is incompatible with interactions in which the players possess perfect information along all dimensions, it is assumed in this essay that individuals possess a good deal of information about their choice problems.[7] In the specific model set forth below, for example, each player has complete knowledge of the utility function of the relevant other as well as his own utility function.[8]

B. The Rationality of Bargaining

It seems correct, as an empirical generalization, to conclude that manipulative bargaining is a widespread activity in many sociopolitical systems. This is true even in various economic interactions, such as oligopolistic markets, where it is not unreasonable to define the payoff possibility set in terms of a common monetary unit and where some of the relevant probability distributions can be meaningfully calculated on the basis of empirical frequencies.[9]

[5] On the implications of this assumption see Milton Friedman and L. J. Savage, "The Expected-Utility Hypothesis and the Measurement of Utility," *Journal of Political Economy,* LX (1952), 463–474.

[6] In fact, such functions are seldom employed. For some interesting comments on this possibility, however, see J. Pen, "A General Theory of Bargaining," pp. 34–35, reprinted herein.

[7] For further comments on the incompatibility between perfect information and manipulative bargaining consult the Introduction to Part Four of this book.

[8] Note, however, that this is not the only assumption about information which could be employed in analyses of the bargainer's calculus.

[9] On this point see especially Thomas C. Schelling, "An Essay on Bargaining," reprinted herein.

And manipulative bargaining appears to be a major feature of many interactions among the members of family units, interest groups, political parties,
nation states, and so forth. But just when will the rational individual decide to
engage in bargaining activities of this kind in the interests of improving his
own situation?

To begin with, it is possible to derive several conditions that are necessary,
though not sufficient, for the occurrence of bargaining from the manipulative
conception itself.[10] First, it follows directly from the definition that bargaining
will occur only under conditions of strategic interaction. Note, however, that
strategic interaction is not a sufficient condition for the occurrence of bargaining. Second, bargaining requires the presence of imperfect information since
it is impossible to manipulate the information condition of any individual who
possesses perfect information along all dimensions. Third, bargaining will
occur only when communication (in the broadest sense) is possible, since the
manipulation of another individual's information condition depends upon
the supply of information to him.

These conditions place important limitations on the range of situations in
which bargaining can occur. They are sufficient, for example, to demonstrate
that bargaining will not occur in situations characterized by perfect competition.[11] This is so because perfect competition is defined in such a way that it
leaves no scope for strategic interaction and that it allows each participant to
act, for all practical purposes, as if he were facing a fixed decision-making environment. As a result, individuals will react to perfect competition as if they
possessed perfect information.[12] Even when the conditions outlined in the
preceding paragraph are taken into account, however, a wide range of situations remains in which the individual will have to decide whether efforts to
bargain will be profitable for him. Under the circumstances, the rational individual will approach the question of when to bargain on the basis of a cost-
benefit calculation. That is, he will weigh the probable gains to be had from
bargaining against the expected costs of bargaining in deciding what the extent
of his bargaining program should be.

To facilitate the examination of this calculus consider a highly simplified
bargaining situation exhibiting the following characteristics. First, there are
only two players. Second, each player has two strategies (or differentiated
alternatives) from which to choose, so that there are four possible outcomes

[10] These conditions are analyzed in greater detail in the Introduction to Part Four of
this book.

[11] The phrase "perfect competition" refers to any exchange relationship in which no
individual participant has any personal influence on the terms of exchange (for example,
the market price). For a discussion that alludes to the incompatibility of manipulative
bargaining and perfect competition without analyzing it in detail, see Charles E. Lindblom, " 'Bargaining Power' in Price and Wage Determination," *Quarterly Journal of
Economics*, LXII (1948), 396–417.

[12] Alternatively, the participant in such situations can be regarded as perfectly
ignorant rather than perfectly informed. The idea of a fixed market price, however,
permits the individual to make decisions under these conditions *as if* he had perfect
information.

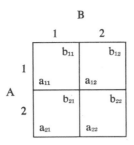

Figure I

for their interaction. Third, the utility function of each player is fixed and known at the outset. Consequently, the scope for manipulative bargaining is highly restricted, though it is not eliminated altogether.[13] Fourth, the relationship of the players is nonzero-sum in character. Fifth, the situation is "one-shot" in nature rather than being a single round in an iterative sequence. Sixth, the players are able to communicate freely with each other during the course of the interaction. Seventh, compensation and side payments are not permitted. Eighth, as in game theory, the interaction terminates with independent choices on the part of the two players. That is, each player ultimately chooses his own strategy in the absence of definitive evidence concerning the choice of the other player.[14]

The basic structure of this simplified bargaining situation is represented in matrix form in Figure I. In a situation of this kind, the conditions governing the bargaining calculus of the rational individual can be stated in the form of simple equations. To see this consider the following terms that enter the bargainer's calculus:

u_i = the ith possible differential payoff (that is, gain or loss) resulting from bargaining (see Figure II for examples),

p_i = the probability of receiving u_i, given a certain expenditure of resources on bargaining,

$U = \sum_{i=1}^{n} u_i p_i$ = the expected gains from bargaining, given a certain expenditure of resources on bargaining,

n = the number of possible outcomes that can result from bargaining,

du_i = the change in u_i which occurs as a result of expending resources on bargaining (given the assumptions of this essay, $du_i = 0$),

dp_i = the change in p_i which occurs as a result of expending resources on bargaining,

$dU = \sum_{i=1}^{n} du_i p_i + u_i dp_i$ = the change in the expected gains from bargaining which occurs as a result of expending resources on bargaining,

---

[13] For a discussion of the additional possibilities that arise when this assumption is relaxed see the Introduction to Part Four of this book.

[14] That is, neither player is able to make his own choice after the other player has already made and revealed his choice.

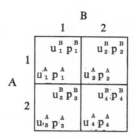

Figure II

C = the resources expended on bargaining,

π = the bargainer's expected-value payoff.

It is now possible to formulate the bargainer's calculus. Any individual, A,[15] will find it profitable to bargain when $\pi^A > 0$ in the equation[16]

$$U^A - C^A = \pi^A \text{ or } \sum_{i=1}^{n} u_i^A p_i^A - C^A = \pi^A \qquad (1).$$

Similarly, A will find it worthwhile to allocate resources to bargaining so long as[17]

$$\frac{d[(\sum_{i=1}^{n} u_i^A p_i^A) - C^A]}{dC^A} > 0 \text{ or } \frac{d(U^A - C^A)}{dC^A} > 0 \qquad (2).$$

This condition can be simplified as follows

$$\frac{dU^A}{dC^A} - \frac{dC^A}{dC^A} > 0 \text{ or } dU^A > dC^A \qquad (3).$$

And it follows that A will reach a personal equilibrium with respect to bargaining when

$$d(\sum_{i=1}^{n} u_i^A p_i^A) = dC^A \text{ or } dU^A = dC^A \qquad (4).$$

In general, these equations indicate that the rational individual will always wish to maximize the difference between U^A and C^A. That is, he will be interested in maximizing the expected gain associated with his bargaining activities. There are, however, some complications involved in the computation of values for the terms in these equations in specific situations. To see how these complications arise consider the simple bargaining situation portrayed in

---

[15] Later on in this essay player B's calculus will also be considered. In general, the calculations of any individual other than A can be examined simply by changing the superscripts in equations 1 to 4.

[16] In this analysis, it is assumed that opportunity costs do not affect the decisions of the rational individual concerning the desirability of bargaining in specific situations. This assumption can be relaxed, however, without any fundamental alterations in the argument developed in this essay.

[17] The treatment of the second-order maximum conditions has been omitted in this essay for the sake of simplicity of exposition.

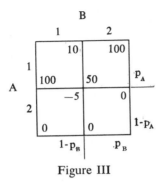

Figure III

Figure III. Here the figures in the cells are the payoffs associated with the players' strategies (as in game theory), and the probability terms at the margins represent the likelihood of the players choosing their first or second strategies at the termination of the interaction when they make their final choices.

The term $u_i\big]^n_{i=1}$ in the bargaining equations is a measure of the possible (not expected) gains or losses from bargaining or the outcomes that may occur as a consequence of bargaining.[18] It is formed by comparing the outcome a player would expect to receive in the absence of bargaining with the various outcomes that might occur as a result of bargaining. Accordingly, $u_i\big]^n_{i=1}$ will always take the form of a series of utility differentials. Now, consider A's possible gains or losses from bargaining in the simple case under discussion. If A decides not to bargain, he will play his dominant strategy A_1 and he will expect B to do likewise.[19] This will produce an outcome of A_1B_2 which yields a payoff of 50 to A. Since this is not the best possible outcome for A in the situation at hand, however, he may wish to consider the prospects of bargaining. If A does bargain, there are four possible outcomes. First, he may be able to achieve an outcome of A_1B_1 by committing himself to respond to B's strategy B_2 with his own strategy A_2 and promising to play A_1 in response to B_1.[20] Here his overall payoff would be 100, and the gains from bargaining, u^A_1, would be $100 - 50$ or 50. Second, A's bargaining activities may be ineffectual if B becomes committed to his strategy B_2 with the result that A finally gives in by playing his strategy A_1 and accepting an outcome of A_1B_2. In this case, u^A_2

---

[18] The expression $u_i\big]^n_{i=1}$ is an index of all the values of u from 1 to n. It does not indicate that any arithmetic operation is to be performed on these values.

[19] A must expect B to play his dominant strategy if he (A) refrains from bargaining since this choice will produce the best possible outcome for B in the situation at hand.

[20] Interest in the manipulative conception of bargaining was originally stimulated, to a considerable degree, by prospects of this kind. For early formulations see Schelling, "An Essay on Bargaining," reprinted herein, and Daniel Ellsberg, "The Theory and Practice of Blackmail," also reprinted herein.

would equal $50 - 50$ or 0. Third, various problems of misunderstanding or inaccurate communication could produce an outcome of A_2B_1 in which A insists on punishing B even though B ultimately submits to A's demands. Here u_3^A would be $0 - 50$ or -50. Finally, A's efforts to bargain might lead to a stalemate and an outcome of A_2B_2.[21] In this case, u_4^A would be -50 since A would lose the 50 he could have obtained in the absence of bargaining. This discussion can now be summarized in the statement that $u_i^A\big]_{i=1}^n = (+50, -50, -50, 0)$.

The possible gains and losses from bargaining for B are similar to those for A, although they are somewhat more complicated in form. If A refrains from bargaining, B can simply play his dominant strategy B_2 which will lead to an outcome of A_1B_2 and yield him an outcome of 100. Since this is the best possible outcome for B in the situation at hand, he would have no incentive to bargain (unless he derived some pleasure from the act of bargaining itself). In this case, therefore, we obtain $u_i^B \leqq 0$. For reasons touched on above, however, A might well make an effort to bargain rather than acquiescing in the outcome at A_1B_2. If A should follow this course, B's payoff from a policy of avoiding bargaining would shift from 100 to $100(p_A) + 0(1 - p_A) = 100(p_A)$, where p_A is the probability that A will choose his strategy A_1 at the termination of the interaction and $1 - p_A$ is the probability that A will choose his strategy A_2 in the end. Here B would have some incentive to bargain in order to obtain the benefit of a certain outcome at A_1B_2 by minimizing the chances of an outcome at A_2B_2 [in other words to gain $u_2^B = 100(1 - p_A)$ by taking steps to give p_A a value of 1].

B's attitude toward bargaining, therefore, would be influenced by his estimate of the value of p_A in the wake of A's bargaining activities (should A refrain from bargaining B can safely assume that he will play his dominant strategy with a probability of 1). Should B consider bargaining in response to A's bargaining activities, however, he will also face four possible outcomes. He may commit himself to his strategy B_2 and succeed in securing an outcome at A_1B_2. Here u_2^B would equal $100(1 - p_A)$ or 100 with certainty rather than $100(p_A)$. His bargaining activities may lead to stalemate and an outcome of A_2B_2. Here he would lose what he could have gained had he refrained from bargaining. That is, $u_4^B = 0 - 100(p_A)$ or $-100(p_A)$. He may end by submitting to A's demands and accepting an outcome at A_1B_1. In this case, u_1^B would equal $-100(p_A) + 10$ or the loss of his expected payoff in the absence of bargaining coupled with a gain of 10. Or B may ultimately capitulate to A's demands only to suffer the punishment of having A play his strategy A_2 due to some misunderstanding. Now the outcome would be A_2B_1, and $u_3^B = -100(p_A) - 5$ or the loss of the expected payoff in the absence of

---

[21] That is, both A and B may become irrevocably committed to playing their strategy 2 in the course of the bargaining. For some interesting comments on the notion of decommitment in the context of the problem of impending stalemate, see Thomas C. Schelling, *Arms and Influence* (New Haven, 1966), pp. 59–69.

bargaining together with an additional loss of 5. Accordingly, B's possible gains and losses from bargaining can be summarized as follows: $u_i^B\big]_{i=1}^n =$ $[100(1 - p_A), -100(p_A), -100(p_A) + 10, -100(p_A) - 5]$.

Several additional points relating to $u_i\big]_{i=1}^n$ in the bargaining equations deserve mention here. First, the situation portrayed in Figure III is one in which the several values of $u_i^A\big]_{i=1}^n$ and $u_i^B\big]_{i=1}^n$ are particularly easy to calculate. In other situations, the bargainer might have to come to grips with additional complications. In a situation involving more strategies and, therefore, a larger payoff matrix, $u_i^A\big]_{i=1}^n$ and $u_i^B\big]_{i=1}^n$ would involve a greater number of utility differentials.[22] Similarly, if the players did not have dominant strategies, the outcome in the absence of bargaining would have to be calculated on some other basis.[23] This arises from the fact that an individual contemplating the gains and losses from bargaining must have some base point with which to compare the possible results of bargaining.[24] Beyond this, there would of course be additional difficulties if the strategies and utility functions of the players were not fixed at the outset. Situations of this kind would require major changes in the procedures for calculating the possible gains and losses from bargaining.[25]

Second, the possible gains and losses from bargaining may vary from one situation to another and even among situations characterized by the same basic structure, such as the prisoner's dilemma or the game of chicken. The model under discussion in this essay, for example, places no limits at all on the range of variation in the values associated with $u_i\big]_{i=1}^n$. It is not surprising, therefore, that the values attached to $u_i\big]_{i=1}^n$ have sometimes been suggested as an indicator of the individual's incentives to bargain in any given situation. Thus, an individual for whom the possible outcomes of bargaining are large and uniformly positive may be disposed to engage in extensive bargaining activities. By contrast, an individual who might lose a great deal from an outcome of stalemate would tend to be hesitant about bargaining even if this were only one of the possible results of bargaining and the chances of it occurring were small.[26] In the context of the model under discussion here, however, the values attached to $u_i\big]_{i=1}^n$ constitute only a highly restricted indi-

---

[22] Beyond this, the introduction of additional players would necessitate the use of an n-dimensional payoff matrix.

[23] The specific situation under discussion in the text, therefore, is a special case. In the general case, additional assumptions concerning the specification of the base point for the calculation of the possible gains and losses from bargaining would have to be introduced. Although this would complicate the model, there is an ample supply of alternative assumptions that could be employed for this purpose.

[24] Without such a basis of comparison, the rational individual would have no way of calculating the possible gains and losses associated with manipulative bargaining.

[25] Under these conditions, bargaining might affect the basic form, dimensions, and content of the payoff matrix facing the players.

[26] On the importance of expected-utility calculations in this connection see Ellsberg, "The Theory and Practice of Blackmail," reprinted herein.

cator of the individual's incentives to bargain. This is so because the rational individual, in contemplating the profitability of bargaining, will always take into account the values associated with $p_i\big]_{i=1}^{n}$ and C as well as the values attached to $u_i\big]_{i=1}^{n}$, and he will be interested in maximizing the value of equation 1 rather than the values of $u_i\big]_{i=1}^{n}$ alone.

Third, efforts have occasionally been made to compare the incentives of the players to bargain by comparing the values attached to terms like $u_i^A\big]_{i=1}^{n}$ and $u_i^B\big]_{i=1}^{n}$. But this is a more complex problem than it seems at first glance. In the context of the present model, it is not possible to compare the values attached to $u_i^A\big]_{i=1}^{n}$ and $u_i^B\big]_{i=1}^{n}$ in any direct fashion since this would require interpersonal comparisons of utility.[27] Specifically, it is *not* assumed that the two expressions $u_i^A\big]_{i=1}^{n} = (+50, -50, -50, 0)$ and $u_i^B\big]_{i=1}^{n} = [100(1 - p_A), -100(p_A), -100(p_A) + 10, -100(p_A) - 5]$ are based on the same utility scales. Nevertheless, it may be possible to say something about the *relative* incentives of the players to bargain. To take an extremely simple situation, if one player may be able to improve his payoff 100 percent with no chance of losing more than 25 percent as a consequence of bargaining while the other player could gain no more than 25 percent and might lose up to 100 percent, it seems intuitively reasonable to say that the first player will experience, in relative terms, four times the incentive to bargain that the second player experiences.[28] But this is a highly restricted measure of the comparison between the incentives of the players to bargain both because $u_i^A\big]_{i=1}^{n}$ and $u_i^B\big]_{i=1}^{n}$ need not be based on the same utility scale and because it ignores the role of $p_i\big]_{i=1}^{n}$ and C in the bargainer's calculus.

The term $p_i\big]_{i=1}^{n}$ in the bargaining equations represents the probability of occurrence of the possible outcomes, $u_i\big]_{i=1}^{n}$, that may result from bargaining.[29] Thus, p_i^A is the probability of receiving u_i^A, given a certain expenditure of resources on bargaining by player A. If the players do not consider bargaining, $p_i\big]_{i=1}^{n}$ will be irrelevant since they will not be concerned with the possible consequences of bargaining $(u_i\big]_{i=1}^{n})$. Whenever the players do contemplate the prospects of bargaining, however, $p_i\big]_{i=1}^{n}$ will be relevant and it will always take

[27] For a general discussion of the problem of interpersonal comparisons of utility consult Kenneth J. Arrow, *Social Choice and Individual Values* (2nd ed., New York, 1963), Chapter 2.

[28] That is, since the first player can gain more and lose less in comparison with his own payoffs in the absence of bargaining than the second player in comparison with his own payoffs, the first player will experience a greater *relative* incentive to bargain.

[29] The expression $p_i\big]_{i=1}^{n}$ is an index of all the values of p from 1 to n. It does not indicate that any arithmetic operation is to be performed on these values.

the form of a set of probabilities such that there is one for each of the values of $u_i \big]_{i=1}^n$ and that taken together they sum to 1. Similarly, $dp_i \big]_{i=1}^n$ is a measure of the effect of expending resources on bargaining. That is, when an individual expends additional resources on bargaining, he will expect this action to have some effect on each of the values previously associated with $p_i \big]_{i=1}^n$.

It follows from this discussion that the impact of $p_i \big]_{i=1}^n$ on the bargainer's calculus will always be closely linked to the values of $u_i \big]_{i=1}^n$ and C. Consequently, the rational individual will be interested in the values associated with $p_i \big]_{i=1}^n$ in conjunction with the values of $u_i \big]_{i=1}^n$ and C and not in $p_i \big]_{i=1}^n$ as an isolated factor. Beyond this, it is worth noting that the values attached to $p_i \big]_{i=1}^n$ in a given situation may represent an aggregate of subsidiary factors. That is, an individual may well adopt a bargaining program that includes a number of distinguishable bargaining tactics, and $p_i \big]_{i=1}^n$ in equations 1 to 4 subsumes the impact of any given set of bargaining tactics taken as a whole.

Consider now the values of $p_i^A \big]_{i=1}^n$ for the situation portrayed in Figure III. It is of course true that the interaction between A and B will always terminate with certainty at one of the four possible outcomes: A_1B_1, A_1B_2, A_2B_2, or A_2B_1. On an *ex post facto* basis, therefore, it would be possible to assign values of $(1, 0, 0, 0)$ to $p_i^A \big]_{i=1}^n$ with the result that $\sum_{i=1}^n u_i^A p_i^A$ would equal $50(1) = 50$, or $0(1) = 0$, or $-50(1) = -50$, depending upon which of the four possible outcomes actually occurred. Nevertheless, A will not be able to predict the final outcome of the interaction with certainty ahead of time. Among other reasons, the impact of strategic interaction guarantees that this will be the case.[30] Accordingly, in calculating the profitability of bargaining on an *ex ante* basis, A must ultimately attach some "subjective probabilities" to the four possible outcomes and compute the value of $\sum_{i=1}^n u_i^A p_i^A$ in terms of expected utilities.[31] In this connection, note that the value of this expression will also be a function of the value of C^A. This is so because the values A attaches to $p_i^A \big]_{i=1}^n$ will vary as a function of the amount of resources he expends on bargaining. Assuming that A succeeds in attaching subjective probabilities to the four possible outcomes, $\sum_{i=1}^n u_i^A p_i^A$ will equal $50(p_1^A) + 0(p_2^A) + (-50)(p_3^A) + (-50)(p_4^A)$, where $p_1^A + p_2^A + p_3^A + p_4^A = 1$. Under the circumstances, A

[30] That is, A's decision will be dependent upon his estimate of B's choice which will, in turn, be a function of B's estimate of A's choice.

[31] For relevant discussions of the notion of subjective probabilities see Edwards, "Theory of Decision Making," and Ellsberg, "The Theory and Practice of Blackmail," reprinted herein.

may find it worthwhile to engage in bargaining so long as $\sum_{i=1}^{n} u_i^A p_i^A > 0$ or $U^A > 0$, but he will not make a final decision on this question until he takes into account the effect of C^A.

Unlike A, B would be perfectly content to refrain from bargaining and play his dominant strategy, if he could count on A to do likewise. If he expects A to bargain, however, B will also have some incentives to engage in bargaining. In the event that he does decide to bargain, B's calculations concerning the efficacy of bargaining will be much the same as those of A. Thus, $p_i^B \big]_{i=1}^{n}$ will involve four possible outcomes, and B will find it necessary to attach subjective probabilities to these outcomes on an *ex ante* basis. Having done so, he will arrive at the following conclusion: $\sum_{i=1}^{n} u_i^B p_i^B = 100(1 - p_A)(p_1^B) + [-100(p_A)](p_2^B) + [-100(p_A) + 10](p_3^B) + [-100(p_A) - 5](p_4^B)$, where p_1^B, p_2^B, p_3^B, and p_4^B are his estimates of the subjective probabilities and $p_1^B + p_2^B + p_3^B + p_4^B = 1$.

The only difference between the positions of A and B at this point arises from the fact that A may wish to initiate bargaining even if he does not expect B to take an active interest in bargaining whereas B would be happy to avoid bargaining if he could count on A to do likewise. In assessing the profitability of bargaining, therefore, B will estimate the probability that A will in fact make an effort to bargain.[32] If B estimates the probability of A's bargaining as p_e^B, he can evaluate his own options in the following terms. He can refrain from bargaining no matter what A does. This would yield B an expected pay-off of $100(1 - p_e^B) + [100(p_A)] (p_e^B)$. Alternatively, he can adjust his activities to those of A and consider bargaining whenever he expects A to bargain. This would yield him an expected payoff of $100(1 - p_e^B) + [100(p_A) + (\sum_{i=1}^{n} u_i^B p_i^B - C^B)] p_e^B$. Under the circumstances, B would find it profitable to bargain whenever the expected value of such a strategy was greater than the expected value of refraining from bargaining regardless of A's behavior: that is, whenever

$$[100(p_A) + (\sum_{i=1}^{n} u_i^B p_i^B - C^B)] p_e^B > [100(p_A)] (p_e^B).$$

The central problem in calculating values for $p_i^A \big]_{i=1}^{n}$ and $p_i^B \big]_{i=1}^{n}$ in any specific situation lies in attaching subjective probabilities to the possible outcomes of bargaining, given a certain expenditure of resources on bargaining. There can be no logically definitive technique for the accomplishment of this task since the presence of strategic interaction assures that the outcome of bargaining for each player will always be a function of the actions (or choices) of the other.[33]

---

[32] Before the interaction actually starts, B may experience some difficulty in estimating this probability. After the beginning of the interaction, however, he should be able to answer this question by inference from A's behavior. At this point, B's estimate of the probability that A will bargain is likely to take on a value of 1 or 0.

[33] For a more detailed discussion of this point see the general Introduction to this book.

Consequently, the rational individual will have no alternative to the use of some rules of thumb or decision rules in assigning the relevant subjective probabilities (more on these rules later).[34] This implies the introduction of a parameter governing the selection of rules of thumb by the individual and, therefore, the possibility of asymmetries in the bargaining behavior of two rational individuals facing a similar situation. Beyond this, it should perhaps be re-emphasized that the values an individual assigns to $p_i \Big]_{i=1}^{n}$ in any given situation will be a function of the resources he devotes to bargaining. Thus, the more an individual spends on his bargaining program, the more favorable the results are likely to be,[35] although this relationship will be affected by the behavior of the other player and need not be linear in form.

As indicated above, C represents the cost to the individual of achieving any given set of values for $p_i \Big]_{i=1}^{n}$. In general, it will be a complex term affected by a number of subsidiary factors. Specifically, the costs of bargaining can be separated into variables and parameters in the context of the model under discussion here.

To start with the variables, the most important resources required for many bargaining programs are the time and energy of the individual bargainer.[36] Nevertheless, bargaining sometimes involves the expenditure of other resources as well. A bargainer who wishes to make a credible commitment, for example, will often find it necessary to employ political capital, expend concrete physical resources, or undertake actions he would otherwise prefer to avoid in the interests of giving his commitment an ironclad appearance. In addition, real-world cases of bargaining often involve the use of resources in the form of side payments and efforts to build up bargaining reputations.[37] Note, however, that these latter costs are ruled out by assumption in the simplified model under consideration in this essay.

The rational individual will always experience difficulties in determining the effects of expending resources on bargaining on the values attached to $p_i \Big]_{i=1}^{n}$. Above all, this is a consequence of the now familiar problem of strategic interaction, which insures that the impact of A's investment in bargaining will be a function of B's bargaining program while the impact of B's investment will, in turn, be a function of A's program. Consequently, the rational individual will find it necessary to make use of rules of thumb in establishing a

[34] Moreover, the rational individual must somehow reckon with the fact that he might conceivably achieve favorable results in a situation involving strategic interaction by engaging in a silent "outguessing" contest with the other player while refraining from explicit bargaining activities altogether. On possibilities of this kind see Schelling, *The Strategy of Conflict,* pp. 58–67.

[35] This is why the rational individual will always attempt to maximize the difference between U and C.

[36] For a discussion that emphasizes the costs of bargaining see Gordon Tullock, *Private Wants, Public Means* (New York, 1970), pp. 55–70.

[37] For a discussion of manipulative bargaining which places these possibilities in perspective see Schelling, "An Essay on Bargaining," reprinted herein.

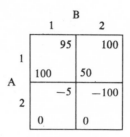

Figure IV

meaningful transformation function relating C to $p_i\big]_{i=1}^{n}$.

A related problem arises from the fact that A's transformation function relating C^A to $p_i^A\big]_{i=1}^{n}$ will be affected by B's payoff structure for the interaction and vice versa. To see this compare the bargaining situation portrayed in Figure IV with that of Figure III. In general, the more B has to gain from resisting, the harder and more costly it will be for A to induce him to accept his desired outcome (that is, A_1B_1 in both Figures III and IV). In the case portrayed in Figure III, B would lose 90 by accepting an outcome of A_1B_1 and he would lose 100 from an outcome of stalemate at A_2B_2. In the case of Figure IV, by contrast, he would lose only 5 by accepting A's desired outcome of A_1B_1 whereas he would lose 200 from an outcome of stalemate. Under the circumstances, it seems reasonable for A to conclude that the bargaining costs of achieving outcome A_1B_1 will be less in the case portrayed in Figure IV than in the case outlined in Figure III, even though the reduction in costs need not be a linear function of the utility differentials involved, and the rational individual will normally find it necessary to employ subjective estimates in calculating the consequences of this factor.[38]

Several additional factors affecting C must be accounted for in the context of the present model through the introduction of parameters. First, the transformation function relating C to $p_i\big]_{i=1}^{n}$ will be sensitive to such things as the intellectual abilities and bargaining skills of the players.[39] And the role of this factor is made more complex by the fact that the impact of abilities and skills will be a function of the relationship between the players in these terms rather than the absolute level of the abilities and skills of either player. The effects of this factor on the calculations of the individual bargainer, therefore, will vary from one bargaining situation to the next. Second, because bargaining is ordinarily a time-consuming process, it is necessary to take into account any costs accruing to the players from the passage of time associated with bargain-

[38] Note, however, that the argument of this paragraph does not require interpersonal comparisons of utility.

[39] The issue of intellectual skills and bargaining abilities has been the subject of considerable controversy among students of bargaining. For some comments on this controversy see the Introduction to Part Four of this book, pp. 313–314, and the references cited there.

ing. These costs might include such things as the deterioration of payoffs over time and any fixed costs of bargaining per unit of time spent in the bargaining process.[40] To specify the impact of this factor with precision it is necessary to compare the time required to reach an outcome through bargaining with the time needed to reach an outcome in the absence of bargaining.[41] Third, in the real world there appear to be numerous situations in which the act of bargaining itself is a source of pleasure or pain for the individual involved.[42] Consequently, the value an individual attaches to C in his calculations may be increased or decreased by his attitude toward bargaining *per se.*[43] This may lead an individual to avoid bargaining in most situations. But in extreme cases, it may also lead some individuals to embrace almost any opportunity to bargain for the sheer pleasure of bargaining itself.[44]

All this leads to two final comments on the role of C in the bargaining equations. The rational individual may encounter problems of aggregation with respect to this term over and above the difficulties involved in calculating the individual components of the term. That is, since the constituents of C are somewhat disparate in nature, it may not always be easy to decide how to aggregate them in such a way that the result can be plugged into the bargaining equations as a single term. In addition, the introduction of parameters into the analysis of the profitability of bargaining has several important consequences. Such parameters are a potential source of asymmetries among rational individuals facing similar bargaining problems. And some of these parameters may pose challenging problems of identification in real-world situations.[45]

This discussion of the principal terms in the bargainer's calculus suggests several general conclusions about manipulative bargaining. It will always be difficult for rational individuals to avoid a sense of ambiguity in making judgments about the profitability of bargaining in specific situations.[46] This is due,

[40] For a helpful discussion of bargaining costs of this kind see John R. Cross, *The Economics of Bargaining* (New York, 1969), esp. p. 45.

[41] Outcomes achieved in the absence of bargaining are sometimes conceptualized as occurring instantaneously. But this is more an artifact of the models of game theory than an accurate description of reality.

[42] This phenomenon is quite similar, in analytic terms, to the possibility of an individual deriving pleasure or pain from the act of gambling *per se* in contrast to the results of gambling.

[43] For the testimony of one who apparently places a negative value on bargaining *per se* see Tullock, *Private Wants, Public Means,* p. 55.

[44] Thus, it is possible to imagine cases in which the C term in the bargainer's calculus acquires a positive value.

[45] The introduction of parameters into logical models is a device for handling unanalyzed aspects of the problem without sacrificing logical closure. Where the values of the relevant parameters are difficult to ascertain with precision in empirical terms, however, serious obstacles arise in efforts to test or corroborate propositions derived from the models.

[46] Ambiguity arises when an individual lacks confidence in the values he attaches to one or more of the terms in his decision-making equations, even though the values he employs are numerically precise. For an outstanding analysis of ambiguity in this sense see Daniel Ellsberg, "Risk, Ambiguity, and the Savage Axioms," *Quarterly Journal of Economics,* LXXV (1961), 643–669.

above all, to the fact that several of the factors in the bargainer's calculus will be subject to the impact of strategic interaction. This means that individuals will find it necessary to employ rules of thumb in computing values for several factors in their bargaining equations. And it implies that judgments concerning the rationality of bargaining in specific situations will be dependent upon the efficacy of the rules of thumb employed in calculations about bargaining. Next, the preceding analysis suggests the likelihood of considerable asymmetries in the propensities of rational individuals to bargain in similar situations. Even in the highly simplified model under consideration here, the impact of various parameters may well lead individuals to vary a good deal in their evaluations of the costs and benefits associated with bargaining.[47] Beyond this, it seems worth emphasizing that manipulative bargaining may be directed toward the calculations of another player concerning the profitability of bargaining itself. That is, there will sometimes be cases of bargaining about bargaining as well as bargaining about specific substantive issues. In essence, this possibility arises from the fact that any individual's bargaining calculus will be affected by strategic interaction at several points.

Finally, it seems intuitively reasonable to conclude that the type of bargaining under analysis here will be a common enough response of rational individuals to the presence of strategic interaction.[48] Thus, individuals in such situations may attach high positive values to $u_i\big]_{i=1}^n$; it would sometimes be reasonable for rational individuals to assign favorable sets of values to $p_i\big]_{i=1}^n$; and there is no reason to conclude that the value of C will always be large even though it will ordinarily be made up of several components. At the same time, this analysis makes it clear that it is desirable to avoid the conclusion that strategic interaction will always or even generally produce efforts to bargain in a manipulative fashion. In fact, it is easy enough to imagine situations involving strategic interaction in which rational individuals would find it preferable to refrain from manipulative bargaining.

C. THE END OF BARGAINING

The argument of the preceding sections is sufficient to determine when manipulative bargaining will occur in the context of a simple model of the bargainer's calculus. Specifically, bargaining will occur when

$$U^A - C^A > 0 \text{ or}$$
$$U^B - C^B > 0.$$

This conclusion has several direct implications for bargaining under conditions of strategic interaction. First, manipulative bargaining may not occur

---

[47] This conclusion is particularly important since it raises questions about the symmetry assumptions that are explicit or implicit in many analyses of bargaining.

[48] If this conclusion is correct, it has far-reaching implications for the game-theoretic and economic models of bargaining, since all these models abstract away the possibility of manipulative bargaining entirely.

at all in situations characterized by the presence of strategic interaction. It is not difficult to imagine cases in which neither of the conditions stated above holds. Second, when bargaining does occur, it will cease only at the point where *both* of the following conditions hold[49]

$$\frac{d(U^A - C^A)}{dC^A} = 0 \text{ or } dU^A = dC^A \text{ and}$$

$$\frac{d(U^B - C^B)}{dC^B} = 0 \text{ or } dU^B = dC^B.$$

Third, there is ample room for asymmetries with respect to bargaining. Only A or B may find the payoffs associated with bargaining greater than 0, and even when both players do engage in bargaining, they need not stop at the same time.

The highly simplified model under discussion in this essay does yield definite results with respect to the occurrence of manipulative bargaining, therefore, even though the conditions stated above will be affected by a number of subsidiary variables and parameters in specific situations. Nevertheless, this is a somewhat limited result. In particular, there are two additional questions that arise in those cases where one or both of the players do engage in manipulative bargaining: (1) what tactics or bargaining programs will the player(s) employ? and (2) what will the outcome of the interaction be? The analysis of this essay does not yield any new conclusions concerning the selection of tactics. Though it is clear that the individual will select his bargaining tactics in such a way as to obtain the most favorable value of U at the least cost, the model does not deal with the relative advantages of specific tactics in achieving this result.[50]

The argument of the preceding section does suggest, on the other hand, several worthwhile comments about the outcome of the interaction between the players. Here there are three distinct cases. To clarify the differences among these cases consider again the bargaining situation portrayed in Figure III. First, there is the case in which neither player finds it profitable to engage in manipulative bargaining. Under these circumstances, the outcome will be A_1B_2 since both A and B will play their dominant strategies without attempting to manipulate each other's information condition. Note also that it is the prospect of this outcome in the case of A and a variation on it in the case of B which the two players employ as base points in calculating the possible gains and losses from bargaining.

Second, there is the case in which each player makes a final and independent choice at the time he stops bargaining. This case, in turn, yields four possible outcomes. If A succeeds in his efforts to commit himself credibly to a policy of responding to B's strategy B_2 with his own strategy A_2, the out-

[49] The treatment of the second-order maximum conditions has been omitted in this essay for the sake of simplicity of exposition.

[50] For studies focusing on the advantages and disadvantages of various tactics see Schelling, *The Strategy of Conflict,* and Ellsberg, "The Theory and Practice of Blackmail," reprinted herein.

come will be A_1B_1. If B is able to make a prior and persuasive commitment to his strategy B_2, on the other hand, the outcome will be A_1B_2. If a stalemate occurs, the outcome will be A_2B_2. And if a misunderstanding leads A to punish B even though B is ready to give in to A's demands, the outcome will be A_2B_1. The model under consideration in this essay does not enable prediction on an *ex ante* basis of which of these four possible outcomes will actually occur. Thus, the model focuses on the decisions of the players about the profitability of engaging in manipulative bargaining. It does not lay down criteria governing their final choices once they decide to stop bargaining.[51]

Third, there is the case in which an interval occurs between the time at which at least one of the players stops bargaining and the time at which the players make their final choices. Here a new possibility arises. One or both of the players may engage in silent "outguessing" activities even after they terminate their efforts at manipulative bargaining.[52] When this occurs, the ultimate outcome of the interaction will be affected by these post-bargaining, "outguessing" activities as well as by the prior employment of various bargaining tactics. And any effort to predict the outcome of the interaction would have to take this phenomenon into account.

D. BARGAINING VS. VOTING

It is interesting to compare the simple model of the bargainer's calculus set forth in the preceding sections with the models of rational voting constructed by Downs and Tullock.[53] The basic voting model has been cast into formal terms by Tullock in the following equation.[54] The individual will find it rational to vote when $P > 0$ in the expression[55]

$$BDA - C_V = P$$

where:

B = benefit expected to be derived from success of your party or candidate

D = likelihood that your vote will make a difference

A = your estimate of the accuracy of your judgment

[51] If a player were able to assign values of $(1, 0, 0, 0)$ to $p_i\big]_{i=1}^{n}$, his final choice would be clear-cut. For reasons spelled out previously, however, the rational individual will ordinarily find it impossible to do this (at least with any confidence) on an *ex ante* basis. Under the circumstances, he will have to devote serious attention to the development of criteria governing his final choice.

[52] For an analysis that is relevant to this possibility see Schelling, *The Strategy of Conflict*, pp. 58–67.

[53] Anthony Downs, *An Economic Theory of Democracy* (New York, 1957), Chapter 3, and Gordon Tullock, *Toward a Mathematics of Politics* (Ann Arbor, 1967), Chapters 7 and 8.

[54] Tullock, *Toward a Mathematics of Politics*, Chapter 7. The equation itself appears on p. 109. Note also that this equation does not include the effects of opportunity costs.

[55] The notation employed in this equation is Tullock's; it should not be confused with the notation used in the bargainer's calculus.

C_V = the cost of voting, and
P = payoff.

A comparison of this equation with the bargaining model summarized in equations 1 to 4 indicates several major differences between the bargaining problem and the voting problem. In the first instance, a large electorate and the operation of certain specific procedural rules (for example, one-man, one-vote) are necessary conditions for the argument propounded by Downs and Tullock to the effect that rational individuals will often find voting unprofitable. Otherwise, any given individual might discover that he had considerable voting power, and small groups might easily take steps to coordinate their behavior. By contrast, the analysis of the bargainer's calculus in this essay focuses on situations involving only two players. And intuitively it seems reasonable to conclude that there will be a tendency for manipulative bargaining to be more widespread in situations involving a relatively small number of actors than in situations involving a large number of actors. This is so because the presence of large numbers of participants will tend to generate difficulties in identifying and acquiring information about specific bargaining relationships as well as problems in communicating effectively with individual bargaining partners.[56]

Next, Downs and Tullock argue that the value of D will always be extremely small or even negligible since each individual must assume that his vote will be only one of a very large number of votes and that he will have little ability to heighten the impact of his voting behavior by coordinating his actions with those of other members of the electorate. In the bargaining equations, on the other hand, $p_i\big]_{i=1}^{n}$ may sometimes display a highly favorable distribution of values from the point of view of the individual bargainer. This may be due in part to the fact that bargaining need not involve a large number of actors. Even more important, however, it stems from the fact that there is no reason to assume that each bargainer will place a similar value on the efficacy of bargaining (that is, $\sum_{i=1}^{n} u_i p_i$), as is the case with the efficacy of voting in models of Downs and Tullock. This is perhaps the most important diff between the two models.

Beyond this, several of the factors in the bargaining equations w ject to the impact of strategic interaction, whereas strategic inter sumed to play either no role (Tullock) or only a very small r in the decisions of individuals concerning the rationality of exclusion of strategic interaction from the voting model is sc in terms of realism since it appears to rest on a highly qu

[56] That is, even though the individual may feel the impact o situations involving large numbers of players, he is apt to delineating specific possibilities for manipulative bargaining wi

[57] Tullock, *Toward a Mathematics of Politics,* p. 29, an *of Democracy,* Chapter 3.

between elections and markets characterized by perfect competition.[58] But it undoubtedly makes it easier to construct straightforward generalizations about the profitability of voting, at least as portrayed by Downs and Tullock, than about the rationality of engaging in manipulative bargaining. At the same time, this difference increases the likelihood that at least some individuals will characteristically evaluate bargaining in more favorable terms than voting.

Finally, it is interesting to note that the cost of bargaining, C, is a decision variable in the bargainer's calculus while the cost of voting, C_V, is a parameter in the voting model. This means that bargainers can control the amount of resources they expend on bargaining and that the values of C and $p_i\big]_{i=1}^{n}$ will be interdependent whereas the voter must treat C_V as a fixed cost. In most real-world situations, moreover, the cost of voting will be considerably less than the values of C under active consideration by the bargainer. Thus, it is apt to be the relative lack of benefits rather than the high cost of voting which may lead many individuals to conclude that voting is irrational. This suggests that the average individual is apt to regard voting as a peripheral and relatively unimportant matter. In the case of bargaining, on the other hand, the prospect of substantial rewards will induce some rational individuals to engage in bargaining activities even though the cost of bargaining may well be relatively high. Whether a given individual ultimately decides for or against bargaining, therefore, he is apt to regard his bargaining problem as a matter of considerable importance in contrast to his tendency to evaluate his voting problem as a peripheral issue.

E. SOME IMPORTANT PARAMETERS

The central argument of this essay is complete. Nevertheless, several important problems were shunted aside in previous sections by describing them as parameters. It is the purpose of this section to explore, if not to resolve, several of these problems.

1. *Rules of thumb.* The concept "rule of thumb" has been employed in this essay to refer to procedural devices that the rational individual can make use of in coming to grips with the problem of uncertainty (in the technical sense).[59] As such, the use of rules of thumb constitutes an alternative to a

---

[58] In perfect competition markets, for example, it is assumed that the individual participants have no ability to coordinate their actions. But this is an extremely restrictive assumption in the context of the voting problem as is demonstrated by the influential roles commonly played by individual leaders, interest groups, and political parties whose objectives are precisely to coordinate the actions of the voters.

[59] Uncertainty occurs when the individual has no sure basis for the assignment of values to one or more of the terms in his decision-making equation. In the case of probabilities, for example, uncertainty occurs when the relevant probabilities cannot be calculated in terms of mathematical ratios or empirical frequencies. As many scholars have pointed out, it is always possible to solve this problem analytically by introducing the notion of "subjective probabilities." But this is often only a technical solution, since the relevant subjective probabilities are apt to rest on nothing more than intangible and

policy of avoiding situations involving uncertainty on the grounds that they are unmanageable from the point of view of rational choice. In the model of the bargainer's calculus set forth in this essay, rules of thumb play a crucial role. Thus, it is through the utilization of such rules that the individual is enabled to break the dilemma of strategic interaction, a dilemma that amounts to an especially troublesome form of uncertainty from the point of view of the individual player. Specifically, rules of thumb play a key role in the computation of values for $p_i \big]_{i=1}^{n}$ and in establishing a transformation function relating $p_i \big]_{i=1}^{n}$ and C.

Where does the individual acquire rules of thumb?[60] As it happens, there are numerous techniques for the development of rules of thumb that may prove helpful to the rational individual in coming to grips with the bargainer's calculus. A few examples, however, may help to clarify the origins of such rules. Empirical generalizations may serve as rules of thumb, though their utilization may prove unusually hazardous under conditions of strategic interaction where the players have incentives to manipulate each other's information conditions and to engage in "outguessing" activities. It is sometimes possible to proceed by imitating the behavior of another individual who has a reputation for being especially successful in dealing with the bargainer's calculus. In some cases, there may be interesting prospects for the use of simulation in assigning values to factors that are affected by strategic interaction. A relatively common procedure is to appeal to some authority or set of authorities or, to describe this procedure in its contemporary guise, to employ a panel of "experts." And in general, the variety of possible sources for rules of thumb is limited only by the imagination of the players themselves. Under the circumstances, the criteria governing the selection of specific rules of thumb must be represented in the model of the bargainer's calculus in terms of a parameter. And it seems probable that the content of this parameter will vary among individuals, or at least among groups of individuals.[61]

There are also several points to be made concerning the evaluation of rules of thumb. Any rule of thumb may yield an erroneous answer in a given bargaining situation. This is so because rules of thumb are only procedural devices for coping with strategic interaction; they do not solve the resultant problems of uncertainty in any logical or analytic sense. Accordingly, the rational individual will find rules of thumb helpful only on the basis of some (at least rough) expected-utility calculation. In addition, the intrinsic qualities

---

imprecise feelings. For a helpful survey of efforts to deal with the problem of uncertainty see R. Duncan Luce and Howard Raiffa, *Games and Decisions* (New York, 1957), Chapter 13.

[60] For a discussion of rules of thumb which is helpful on this point see Armen A. Alchian, "Uncertainty, Evolution, and Economic Theory," *Journal of Political Economy,* LVIII (1950), 211–221.

[61] In a sense, this parameter can be conceptualized as a personality constant. Insofar as there are distinct personality types, therefore, it may be possible to identify groups of individuals who share the same value for this parameter.

of a rule of thumb are not of crucial importance in evaluating its usefulness. Again, this is the case because such rules do not solve the dilemma of strategic interaction in logical terms. What matters, therefore, is the extent to which the use of a given rule improves the individual's ability to deal with the bargainer's calculus in pragmatic terms. As a result, cases will almost certainly arise in which the rational individual will prefer rules of thumb that seem intuitive and, in a sense, "irrational" to rules that have an *appearance* of formal elegance and logical neatness.

It is also possible for the rational individual to expend resources on the improvement of existing rules of thumb or the development of new rules. This point has several interesting implications in the context of the bargaining problem. First, the individual will always have incentives to continue using rules of thumb that are already available and to select rules that are simple and inexpensive to develop. But in making final decisions on these matters he will also compare the costs of developing new rules with the expected value of any improvements in his efforts to deal with the bargainer's calculus which would flow from their application. Second, the costs of developing new rules of thumb can be viewed as a kind of fixed expense that can be amortized as a function of the number of times the rules are used. As a result, the rational individual may regard such costs as an investment which need not be charged entirely to any given effort to bargain. Third, other things being equal, any costs involved in the improvement or development of rules of thumb can be expected to operate as a restriction on the attractiveness of bargaining, even though expenditures along these lines may be profitable in specific cases.

2. *Ambiguity.* The discussion of uncertainty in the preceding paragraphs also suggests that the phenomenon sometimes described as ambiguity will often affect the bargainer's calculus.[62] Ambiguity occurs when a rational individual has doubts about the accuracy of the subjective estimates he ultimately makes in assigning values to various terms in his decision-making equations. In such cases, the individual ends up with precise values for the terms in his expected-value computations, but he is not confident of their accuracy. Since the rules of thumb that the individual employs to break the dilemma of strategic interaction in the bargainer's calculus must be based on some notion of pragmatic utility rather than logical necessity, it seems certain that feelings of ambiguity will be widespread among rational individuals attempting to calculate the profitability of bargaining.

There are two distinct ways of handling the problem of ambiguity within the model of the bargainer's calculus under consideration. The easiest procedure is to ignore ambiguity by assuming that rational individuals will always

[62] For a general discussion of the significance of ambiguity see Ellsberg, "Risk, Ambiguity, and the Savage Axioms." And for an exchange of views on several conceptual problems arising from this concept see Harry V. Roberts, "Risk, Ambiguity, and the Savage Axioms: Comment," *Quarterly Journal of Economics*, LXXVII (1963), 327–336, and Daniel Ellsberg, "Reply," *Quarterly Journal of Economics*, LXXVII (1963), 336–342.

adopt a neutral attitude toward it.[63] Any individual who follows this course will simply plug his subjective estimates into his bargaining equations and pay no attention to the fact that he may not feel confident of their accuracy. Alternatively, the individual may choose to include some indicator of his attitude toward ambiguity in his computations.[64] If he adopts a "conservative" attitude toward ambiguity, for example, he can modify his subjective estimates to make them less favorable toward a policy of engaging in bargaining activities. And if he wishes to give himself the benefit of the doubt in the face of ambiguity, he can follow the opposite course. In either case, however, when an individual does not adopt a neutral attitude toward ambiguity, his posture on this issue will have to be represented in the model of the bargainer's calculus through the introduction of a parameter.

3. *Adaptation.* In general, manipulative bargaining takes time. This is so even in "one-shot" interactions of the type described in the simple model of this essay. To begin with, it takes time to make the calculations involved in the bargainer's calculus. And beyond this, it takes time to select and execute specific bargaining tactics as well as to observe the results of bargaining. Even though it is possible to conceive of a player's final choice among strategies as a kind of instantaneous event, therefore, bargaining itself must be regarded as a time-consuming process.[65]

Under the circumstances, an individual may change the values he assigns to various terms in his bargaining equations during the course of bargaining. In fact, there are several distinct ways in which this can occur. First, the individual may acquire new information about the structure of the situation or about the behavior of the other player from the bargaining process itself. Second, the other player may successfully manipulate his information concerning one or more of the factors in his bargaining equations. Third, he may simply change his mind about such things as the appropriate rules of thumb to employ or his attitude toward ambiguity. Note, however, that the terms in the individual's bargaining calculus will not be equally sensitive to changes of this kind. In the illustrations used in previous sections, for example, the values of $u_i^A \big]_{i=1}^n$ can be computed with certainty and will therefore not be subject to change during the course of bargaining. The values of $p_i^A \big]_{i=1}^n$ and c^A, on the other hand, are likely to be quite sensitive to change in some interaction processes. This is especially true of $p_i^A \big]_{i=1}^n$, which is composed entirely of a set of subjective probabilities whose values will be heavily affected by the impact of strategic interaction.

[63] This is the position adopted by those whose conception of utility stems from the work of von Neumann and Morgenstern. For a clear-cut exposition of this conception of utility consult L. J. Savage, *The Foundations of Statistics* (New York, 1954).

[64] For some preliminary comments on this alternative see Ellsberg, "Risk, Ambiguity, and the Savage Axioms," and Pen, "A General Theory of Bargaining," pp. 35–36, reprinted herein.

[65] For a particularly clear-cut exposition of the points raised in this paragraph see Schelling, *The Strategy of Conflict,* pp. 267–268.

Evaluative changes during the course of bargaining are sometimes discussed in terms of the concept of learning.[66] Nevertheless, this concept does not seem entirely appropriate in describing the phenomenon under discussion here. Thus, changes of the type in question will not necessarily produce improvements in the accuracy, in any sense of that term, of the values assigned to the relevant terms in the bargainer's calculus. The fact that the kind of bargaining under analysis focuses directly on efforts to manipulate the information conditions of others makes this point particularly clear-cut. Accordingly, it seems more appropriate to employ the term "adaptation" rather than the term "learning" to describe such changes in the calculations of the individual during the course of bargaining.

F. CONCLUSION

The model set forth in this essay deals with the bargainer's calculus or the factors governing the decisions of the rational individual concerning *when* to bargain in contrast to *how* to bargain. In general terms, the principal conclusions of the argument can be stated as follows. Empirically speaking, it seems reasonable to conclude that manipulative bargaining will be a common enough activity in a wide variety of sociopolitical interactions. But there will also be numerous situations involving strategic interaction in which rational individuals will refrain from bargaining. Next, it is to be expected that there will be significant asymmetries among rational individuals with respect to their decisions about bargaining in similar situations. This is due, in large part, to the impact of various parameters affecting the bargainer's calculus. Finally, the rational individual is always likely to experience difficulties in making precise calculations about the profitability of bargaining. This is due, above all, to the intimate link between strategic interaction and bargaining.

At the same time, it is well to bear in mind that this model is a highly simplified one. Two sets of limitations, in particular, seem especially important for future analyses of the bargainer's calculus. First, the model restricts the scope for manipulative bargaining to a minimum through the assumption that the strategies (or alternatives) and the utility functions of the players are fixed and known at the outset.[67] This means that there is no room for bargaining about the content of the payoff matrix. And bargaining about such things as the basic form and dimensions of the payoff matrix is even further outside the boundaries of this model. Any relaxation of these restrictions might increase the attractiveness of bargaining in various sociopolitical interactions.[68] But it would certainly make it harder for the rational individual to calculate

[66] For a particularly important effort to analyze the process of bargaining in terms of the concept of learning consult Cross, *Economics of Bargaining,* esp. Chapter 3.

[67] For a discussion of the additional possibilities for bargaining which arise when these assumptions are relaxed see the Introduction to Part Four of this book.

[68] It should not be assumed, however, that it would *necessarily* increase the attractiveness of bargaining. Thus, the costs as well as the benefits associated with bargaining might increase with the relaxation of these restrictions.

with any precision the probable gains and losses from manipulative bargaining.

Second, the assumptions of this model make it impossible to deal with various structural factors that sometimes play a significant role in bargaining in real-world situations.[69] It is not difficult to enumerate a number of factors of this type. New questions would arise, for example, if there were more than two players or the players represented fundamentally different types of actor. The introduction of collective entities rather than individuals as actors would also raise additional problems. The possibility of negotiations that intersect both across issues at the same time and through time generates new issues involving such phenomena as reputation, precedent, analogic reasoning, and so forth, as well as a variety of new tactics for the players. And the profitability of manipulative bargaining may be affected by a number of contextual factors, such as the institutional or organizational setting of the interaction, the format of negotiations, and the prevailing rules of the game. The analysis of all these questions, however, must await further developments in the construction of models of the bargainer's calculus.

[69] For a brief survey of the significance of a number of these structural factors see Schelling, "An Essay on Bargaining," reprinted herein.

CONCLUSION

THE ANALYSIS OF BARGAINING:
PROBLEMS AND PROSPECTS

Oran R. Young

The principal purpose of this conclusion is to examine the problems that arise in moving from logical constructs to real-world applications in the analysis of bargaining. In this connection, it will readily become apparent that there is a considerable gap between the existing models of bargaining and reality in a wide range of situations. Accordingly, much of the following discussion deals with problems that remain to be overcome in the study of bargaining.[1] This should not, however, be read as a severe criticism of previous analyses of the bargaining problem. Rather, it is a clear indication of the stimulating challenges that still lie ahead in the study of bargaining.

Recent decades have witnessed impressive progress in the construction of deductive models of bargaining. Prior to the pioneering economic analyses of Zeuthen and the early work of the game theorists, the bargaining problem was generally written off as insoluble. That is, analyses of bargaining situations ordinarily ended with the identification of a contract zone and some statement to the effect that the specific outcome within this zone must be regarded as indeterminate. At the present time, by contrast, we have a number of distinct models that are relevant to the bargaining problem *per se*. And several of these models culminate in determinate solutions concerning the allocation of the value(s) at stake.

These recent models of bargaining constitute an outstanding source of insights and conceptual stimulation for future analyses of bargaining. Nevertheless, they are all subject to severe limitations, at least in their current form. Above all, none of these models produces good predictions or satisfactory explanations concerning bargaining in the great majority of real-world cases. Consequently, they fail to meet the most important of the traditional criteria for the evaluation of "descriptive" or "positive" theories.[2] In addition, the existing models of bargaining often emphasize different substantive problems and, in some cases, they lead to incompatible results. And the resultant lack of consensus among students of bargaining is currently increasing rather than decreasing.[3] Finally, all the existing models of bargaining abstract away various interesting phenomena that are commonly thought of as important features of bargaining. Though these restrictions are required for the achievement of logical closure in most cases, they constitute a distinct limitation of the usefulness of the existing theories of bargaining.

---

[1] For an account that deals with some of the same problems in an interesting fashion see Martin Shubik, "On the Study of Disarmament and Escalation," *Journal of Conflict Resolution*, XII (1968), 83–101.

[2] For a discussion of game theory which adopts a similar position see Anatol Rapoport, *Two-Person Game Theory* (Ann Arbor, 1966), Chapter 12.

[3] For a discussion of the growth of dissensus along these lines see the Introduction to Part Three of this book.

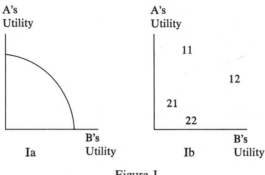

Figure I

A. SPECIFIC PROBLEMS OF APPLICATION

Even if we accept the basic analytic framework of the existing models of bargaining, a number of specific problems often stand in the way of applications to real-world situations. This is especially true of bargaining concerning noneconomic issues, which are frequently difficult to define with any precision. But similar problems also arise in a great many economic interactions. In this connection, consider the following sets of problems as they relate to the models of bargaining set forth in the preceding parts of this book.

First, it may be difficult to establish the initial conditions of an interaction involving bargaining. It is sometimes hard for the players to identify their bargaining partners with precision. This is especially true in large groups in which there are numerous relationships involving strategic interaction. The alternative strategies available to one or more of the players may be vague or undifferentiated so that it is difficult even to begin the process of constructing a utility function. And the range of alternatives available to any player may be subject to change during the course of the interaction rather than being fixed at the outset. That is, some of the initial alternatives may become irrelevant while new alternatives may be introduced during the course of bargaining.[4] If any of these conditions prevail, it will not be possible to portray the payoff possibility set for a bargaining situation as in Figures Ia and Ib, a fact that raises serious problems since the possibility of portraying the basic situation in this fashion is generally assumed in deductive analyses of bargaining.

Second, even if the alternative strategies available to the participants are fixed and known at the outset, the individual players may encounter difficulties in constructing clear and precise preference orderings or utility functions. It is sometimes hard to compare alternative strategies in such a way as to establish distinct preferences among them. Such problems are apt to arise when the outcomes associated with the alternatives are defined in terms of different payoff units and there is no convenient unit of exchange or numeraire

[4] On this point see, inter alia, Harold W. Kuhn, "Game Theory and Models of Negotiation," Journal of Conflict Resolution, VI (1962), 4.

resource that can be employed as a common denominator in evaluating the outcomes. And additional problems must be overcome when one or more of the alternatives available to a player represents a complex package (or lottery ticket) of uncertain outcomes.[5] Even if he has some clear basis for comparing his alternatives, moreover, the individual player may still experience problems with his utility function. His preference ordering may turn out to be intransitive.[6] Or his utility function may exhibit inconsistencies if he changes his evaluation of the various alternatives during the course of the interaction. Such inconsistencies are particularly apt to occur when the information possessed by the players is highly imperfect, and they may be a function of the bargaining process itself.[7] Note that the presence of any of the problems raised in this paragraph would make it impossible to attach meaningful and/or stable utility scales to the axes of Figures Ia and Ib.[8]

Third, individuals involved in strategic interaction will often experience severe problems in acquiring certain knowledge about the relevant other. It is difficult enough in many situations to pin down the identity of the other player and to establish that his behavior is fundamentally rational. But this is only the first requirement along these lines posed by the existing models of bargaining. Depending upon the particular model in question, the individual player needs detailed information about the utility function, the risk willingness, or the learning behavior of the other player. And as many writers have pointed out, any individual may experience incentives to conceal information about these matters or to manipulate the knowledge of them possessed by his bargaining partner.[9] Consequently, it is not surprising that these problems are dealt with in many models of bargaining simply by assuming at the outset that each player possesses the requisite information about his partner.[10]

Fourth, in real-world situations, bargaining often involves lumpy or indivisible goods. By contrast with bargaining about wage rates or price levels, bargaining over an indivisible good must lead to an outcome in which one side or the other gains sole possession of the good. The result is a bargaining problem that is difficult to conceptualize either in terms of the rules of division

[5] A succinct and straightforward analysis of the problems referred to in this sentence and the preceding one can be found in Rapoport, *Two-Person Game Theory,* Chapter 2.

[6] Note that intransitive preference orderings cannot be represented in terms of the interval utility scales frequently employed in analyses of interdependent decision making.

[7] See, for example, Kuhn, "Game Theory and Models of Negotiation," p. 3.

[8] Cross has argued that the presence of inconsistent utility functions "does not in itself impede the operation of our model"—John G. Cross, *The Economics of Bargaining* (New York, 1969), p. 68. But it is hard to see how this claim can be accepted. Thus, where there are inconsistencies of this kind the players will find it impossible to calculate their optimal demands in a stable fashion, and the graphic models employed by Cross cannot be constructed in a clear-cut fashion.

[9] See, for example, Rapoport, *Two-Person Game Theory,* pp. 201-202.

[10] For an analysis that attempts to deal with the problems raised by a lack of knowledge of the utility function of the other player see John C. Harsanyi, "Bargaining in Ignorance of the Opponent's Utility Function," *Journal of Conflict Resolution,* VI (1962), 28–38. Note, however, that Harsanyi is reduced to suggestions involving devices such as the introduction of "stereotype" utility functions.

associated with the game-theoretic models of bargaining or in terms of the convergence processes of the economic models of bargaining. There are two ways of solving this problem, but each technique generates additional difficulties of its own. In the first instance, the players may bargain over the allocation of a set of lottery tickets, each of which gives the possessor a certain probability of receiving the good in question.[11] But this system may prove quite unappealing to one or both of the players when the stakes are high or the interaction is non-iterative, and it raises additional questions concerning the attitude of the players toward risk. In addition, the problems of indivisible goods may be overcome by a system of side payments which allows the player who receives an indivisible good to compensate the other player.[12] There are many real-world situations, however, in which side payments are impermissible. And in any case, the calculation of side payments would necessitate the formulation of a subsidiary model since there may well be scope for bargaining about the nature and the size of the side payments themselves.

Fifth, while most of the existing models deal with bargaining about a single, well-defined issue, bargaining in real-world situations often involves several distinct issues at the same time. In principle, it is possible to collapse a multiplicity of issues into a single set of utility functions (that is, one for each of the players) by treating all possible combinations of outcomes for the issues as separate alternatives for the players and expressing the expected values associated with these alternatives in terms of some common unit of utility. In reality, however, this procedure is apt to prove well beyond the capabilities of the players.[13] Consequently, interactions involving several issues at the same time will often have to be represented in terms of a multidimensional payoff space. Moreover, it should be noted that individuals engaged in bargaining may experience incentives to manipulate this aspect of their interaction. Thus, they may attempt to gain advantages by linking together previously unrelated issues or by separating issues that the other players regard as forming a natural unit. Or they may try to determine the agenda for bargaining by influencing the order in which distinct issues are taken up in the negotiations.

Sixth, as indicated in the preceding parts of this book, many of the models of bargaining rely heavily on the introduction of parameters.[14] This practice is often unavoidable in dealing with analytic complexities that cannot be handled within the framework of a given model but it generates several distinct problems affecting applications to reality. To begin with, it is frequently difficult to obtain specific values for the parameters, and this problem is apt to become particularly severe in the case of parameters whose values can be

---

[11] Thus, the probabilities associated with all of the lottery tickets would sum to one.

[12] For a general discussion of side payments or compensation see R. Duncan Luce and Howard Raiffa, *Games and Decisions* (New York, 1957), pp. 180–181.

[13] On this issue see J. Pen, "A General Theory of Bargaining," pp. 41–42, reprinted herein, and Cross, *Economics of Bargaining*, pp. 113–114 and Appendix D.

[14] This is especially true of the economic models dealt with in Part Two of this book.

expected to vary from one player to the next. This problem has seldom been dealt with in anything but the most sketchy fashion in analyses of bargaining.[15] In addition, there is always the temptation to manipulate the values of parameters to make the proposition derived from a given model fit some preconceived pattern or match empirical observations. Consequently, unless the values of the parameters employed in such models can be established on some independent basis, the propositions derived from the models tend to become nonfalsifiable.

B. Strategic Interaction and Dynamics

The impact of strategic interaction must be eliminated in situations involving interdependent decision making in order to achieve determinate results. This is always true even though strategic interaction need not necessarily be excluded at the outset. Moreover, it is worth emphasizing that the elimination of strategic interaction requires the introduction of restrictive assumptions of one sort or another. This is so because strategic interaction produces a regress that cannot be solved directly in logical terms. Accordingly, a crucial question in the construction of bargaining models concerns the selection of specific assumptions designed to exorcise the impact of strategic interaction.

As it happens, there are several distinct types of assumption which can be employed to achieve this result. And divergences in these terms account for some of the most important differences among the existing models of bargaining. Since none of the resultant procedures for eliminating the impact of strategic interaction can be regarded as "right" or "wrong" in logical terms, any judgment concerning the relative usefulness of these procedures must rest on the extent to which they lead to models that generate propositions which correspond well with empirical realities. As mentioned previously, however, none of the existing models of bargaining produces good predictions or satisfactory explanations concerning the great majority of real-world cases. The question of the relative usefulness of the alternative procedures for dealing with strategic interaction in the analysis of bargaining, therefore, remains an open one.

Bargaining is ordinarily conceptualized as a time-consuming activity.[16] Consequently, successful analyses of bargaining must come to grips simultaneously with the dynamics of bargaining processes and the problem of strategic interaction. In practice, it has proved extremely difficult to fulfill satisfactorily this set of requirements. The game-theoretic models of bargaining simply exclude the dynamic aspects of bargaining, along with the impact of

[15] For an analysis that at least raises a number of the aspects of this problem see Alan Coddington, *Theories of the Bargaining Process* (London, 1968), esp. Chapters 4 and 6.

[16] It can be argued that bargaining is not visualized as a time-consuming activity in the game-theoretic conception. But even this is doubtful. See, for example, Thomas C. Schelling, *The Strategy of Conflict* (Cambridge, 1960), Appendix B.

strategic interaction, in their initial formulation by conceptualizing the bargaining problem in a static fashion. The result is a focus on outcomes which abstracts away many issues commonly included in the bargaining problem and generally fails to produce predictions about bargaining which are applicable to real-world situations. The economic models of bargaining, by contrast, leave room for dynamics even though they also eliminate strategic interaction in their initial formulation. In this context, one of the most encouraging developments in the study of bargaining is the effort embodied in some of the economic models to combine the basic ideas of rational choice with the concept of learning in order to analyze the dynamic aspects of bargaining in a systematic fashion.[17] But it must be added that even these models produce a highly mechanistic conception of bargaining processes which is hard to match with analogous real-world activities. Finally, the models associated with the manipulative conception of bargaining are sensitive both to the limits of excluding strategic interaction at the outset and to the restrictions of eliminating the dynamic aspects of bargaining. But this conception has not led to any resolution of these problems since the manipulative models characteristically fail to produce determinate solutions for the bargaining problem. In the final analysis, therefore, the need remains for satisfactory procedures to deal simultaneously with strategic interaction and the dynamic aspects of bargaining.

C. STRUCTURAL FACTORS

All the existing models of bargaining are highly simplified in structural terms. That is, they abstract away a number of structural factors that are often relevant to real-world situations through the introduction of initial assumptions of a restrictive nature. As it happens, however, these neglected structural factors sometimes have a substantial impact on the course of actual bargaining situations. The present section, therefore, offers a general outline of the relationship of the most important of these factors to bargaining.[18]

To begin with, all the deductive models of bargaining treat the players, for all practical purposes, as single individuals in contrast to collective or corporate entities.[19] In many real-world situations, however, the relevant actors are complex collective entities or even aggregates composed of several distinct collective entities.[20] This is true of international relations, many types of political interaction, and even a considerable portion of the situations involving

[17] The outstanding example is the Cross model. For the details see Cross, *Economics of Bargaining,* esp. Chapters 3 and 4.

[18] For a brief but helpful survey of the relevance of a number of structural factors see Thomas C. Schelling, "An Essay on Bargaining," reprinted herein.

[19] All formal models of choice treat individuals as well-coordinated entities. It is worth noting here, however, that from the point of view of psychology the individual himself may be regarded as a collective entity.

[20] International alliances, for example, can be thought of as aggregates composed of several distinct collective entities.

strategic interaction in the fields of economics and sociology. Under the circumstances, most students of bargaining have proceeded either by assuming that it is reasonable to treat collective entities as if they were single individuals in analyzing their bargaining activities or by arguing that the real bargainers are delegates or representatives of the collective entities so that the collective entities themselves are only external pressures on the bargainers.[21] Both of these procedures, nevertheless, have the effect of abstracting away the basic problems associated with collective entities rather than solving them.

The introduction of collective entities as players raises two distinct sets of issues affecting the analysis of bargaining. First, the external behavior of a collective entity is a function of internal interactions among its members, and most of these internal interactions will be affected to some degree by strategic interaction. Consequently, the problem of strategic interaction must be dealt with in determining the external behavior of any given collective entity, and there is room for the occurrence of lower levels of bargaining within the overall bargaining problem. Among other things, this means that the external behavior of a collective entity is apt to fluctuate as a function of changing fortunes in its internal bargaining processes.[22] Second, the members of collective entities often experience role conflicts that affect their participation in the decision-making processes of the collective entity and, therefore, the external behavior of the collective entity itself. That is, the members of such entities are ordinarily interested in maximizing the returns to several role premises simultaneously, and the requirements posed by these premises are sometimes contradictory. As a result, the determination of the external behavior of collective entities depends upon a subsidiary analysis of the consequences of these role conflicts. In terms of the bargaining problem, all this means that the utility functions of collective entities may be unspecifiable, intransitive,[23] or inconsistent over time. And as indicated in a previous section, each of these conditions is incompatible with the analytic requirements of the existing models of bargaining.

Next, even where the problems associated with collective actors are surmountable, there are other structural factors involving the actors or players which are generally neglected in the formal models of bargaining. In the first instance, while real-world bargaining sometimes involves more than two players with distinct role premises or utility functions,[24] many of the existing

[21] For an explicit argument along these lines see Jan Pen, *The Wage Rate under Collective Bargaining* (Cambridge, 1959).

[22] That is, the stakes of bargaining within collective entities can often be defined in terms of alternative external policies.

[23] For a lengthy analysis that is relevant to this point even though it formulates the issue in a somewhat different fashion see Kenneth J. Arrow, *Social Choice and Individual Values* (2nd ed., New York, 1963).

[24] It is sometimes argued that this is not so since it is usually possible to identify two distinct "sides" in most bargaining situations. But this view appears to be based on a serious oversimplification of reality in many cases. Many interactions in the international arena and in multiple-party political systems, for example, generate N-person bargaining.

models of bargaining focus primarily on the two-person case,[25] and have little to say about the problem of coalition formation which may become important whenever an interaction involves three or more players. On the contrary, students of bargaining have often devoted their efforts to reducing bargaining situations to two-person interactions through such devices as grouping several players into composite "sides" or limiting the relevant contract zone to a set of outcomes which is of interest to only two players.[26]

There are also extensive possibilities for the occurrence of influential asymmetries between the players. Despite the cherished game-theoretic assumption of essential symmetry between the players involved in strategic interactions,[27] important asymmetries along these lines appear to be common in real-world situations.[28] And it is possible to introduce at least some asymmetries between the players without necessarily sacrificing analytic rigor. In fact, steps in this direction have already been taken by those who have worked with the economic models of bargaining. The Cross model, for example, makes it possible to consider asymmetries affecting such things as the learning parameters, discount rates, and fixed costs of bargaining of the players.[29] Nevertheless, the scope for asymmetries between the players remains highly restricted even in these models. Thus, it would also be interesting to consider the consequences of various differences with respect to such matters as the information conditions of the players,[30] the resources available to them,[31] intellectual capabilities, psychological attributes other than learning,[32] and so forth. The introduction of asymmetries of this kind would undoubtedly complicate the resultant models and necessitate the introduction of additional parameters, but it would also make future analyses of bargaining more realistic.

If we turn our attention away from the players or actors, additional

[25] The exceptions, however, are important. Thus, many of the models of N-person game theory are relevant to the analysis of bargaining. And Cross has made a preliminary effort to extend his analysis of two-person bargaining to the N-person case (Cross, *Economics of Bargaining,* Appendix E).

[26] For an analysis that emphasizes this latter procedure see Pen, *The Wage Rate under Collective Bargaining.*

[27] Note, however, that even game theory allows for some asymmetries between the players. Thus, the players may have different numbers of strategies and different utility functions.

[28] Perhaps the most articulate proponent of the assumption of essential symmetry is John C. Harsanyi. See his "Notes on the Bargaining Problem," reprinted herein; "On the Rationality Postulates Underlying the Theory of Cooperative Games," *Journal of Conflict Resolution,* V (1961), 179–196; and "A General Theory of Rational Behavior in Game Situations," *Econometrica,* XXXIV (1966), 613–634.

[29] See Cross, *Economics of Bargaining,* esp. Chapter 4.

[30] Note that Hicks explicitly assumed asymmetries of this kind in his analysis of labor-management bargaining. On the role of these asymmetries in Hicks's model see Robert L. Bishop, "A Zeuthen-Hicks Theory of Bargaining," reprinted herein.

[31] In his pioneering analysis of bargaining, Zeuthen often comments on differences of this kind. See Frederik Zeuthen, *Problems of Monopoly and Economic Warfare,* partially reprinted herein.

[32] Rapoport has been particularly active in suggesting the relevance of these factors. For a brief example of his views on this issue see Rapoport, *Two-Person Game Theory,* pp. 206–209.

structural factors come into focus. The existing models of bargaining deal almost exclusively, for example, with "one-shot" interactions. That is, they focus on well-defined bargaining situations that occupy distinct tracts of time and do not overlap into other time periods. In many real-world situations, however, bargaining is an iterative activity that occurs repeatedly in successive time periods in such a way that there are significant interdependencies among distinct cases of bargaining.[33]

This iterative aspect of bargaining introduces a number of new questions involving such factors as reputation, precedent, and analogic reasoning.[34] These factors can be expected to have influential consequences for the activities of individual bargainers. First, the rational individual will take into account the past bargaining behavior of his partners in making his own choices in any given situation involving strategic interaction.[35] Second, each player will consider the probable impact of his activities on future cases of bargaining in deciding on his program in a current interaction. In extreme cases, an individual may even be willing to suffer a loss in a current situation in order to establish a bargaining reputation that is expected to produce compensatory gains in future situations. Third, the existence of interdependencies among distinct cases of bargaining generates new opportunities for the development of manipulative tactics. To improve his prospects in a given interaction, for example, a player may stake his overall bargaining reputation on the outcome or emphasize the relevance of past precedents that are favorable to his position.[36] Fourth, successive cases of bargaining are never perfectly iterative if only because the occurrence of any given case of bargaining becomes part of the background or "history" of each new case of bargaining. And the degree to which successive instances of bargaining are similar or dissimilar may vary greatly along a number of dimensions.[37] As a result, it is sometimes possible for individual players to gain advantages by deliberately propagating analogies between a current interaction and one or more carefully selected past cases of bargaining.

Finally, there are several interesting structural factors associated with the context or setting within which any given case of bargaining occurs. The existing models of bargaining generally deal with bargaining under conditions that can be described as "isolated exchange." This means that the interaction must be regarded as divorced from any broader setting or environment and that the analysis will focus on the activities of essentially symmetrical players.

[33] The iterative nature of many situations involving strategic interaction has been emphasized repeatedly by Rapoport. See, for example, Anatol Rapoport and Albert Chammah, *Prisoner's Dilemma* (Ann Arbor, 1966), Chapter 5.

[34] For a brief discussion that indicates the relevance of these factors see Schelling, "An Essay on Bargaining," pp. 292–301, reprinted herein.

[35] See, *inter alia,* Rapoport and Chammah, *Prisoner's Dilemma,* Chapter 6.

[36] On this point see Schelling, "An Essay on Bargaining," reprinted herein.

[37] The relevant dimensions include the identity, nature, and number of the players; the information conditions of the players; the nature of the issues at stake; the extent to which the situation is affected by interdependencies with other interactions; the nature of the context, and so forth.

In real-world situations, however, the assumption of isolated exchange tends to abstract away a variety of influential factors. In fact, informal discussions of bargaining often emphasize heavily factors of this kind, and some writers have gone so far as to argue that the concept of bargaining cannot be meaningfully defined without reference to these factors.[38]

A few examples drawn from the field of labor-management negotiations may help to clarify the nature and relevance of these contextual factors. First, there is the question of institutional or organizational structure. It is apt to make a difference, for example, whether the firm or the union is a monopolist capable of controlling all the resources on its side of the bargaining counter.[39] Second, there are the rules of the game under which the players engage in bargaining. Such rules often ban the use of certain potential instruments of bargaining.[40] And they may well be asymmetrical in form as, for example, when unions are made liable for any damage resulting from strikes or firms are not permitted to coordinate their activities in dealing with organized labor. Third, there is the general environment or atmosphere within which any specific bargaining interaction takes place. Thus it may make a difference what the level of unemployment is at the time bargaining occurs and whether the market for the firm's product(s) is a buyer's or a seller's market.[41] This is one of the reasons why an ability to determine the time at which bargaining will occur may have important tactical consequences. Fourth, there are sometimes links between a given case of bargaining and other negotiations occurring at the same time. A specific bargaining session, for example, may acquire symbolic value because it is expected to set the standard for other cases occurring at the same time or it may be regarded as unimportant if some other interaction is expected to play this symbolic role.[42] Fifth, the details of the negotiating format sometimes have an impact on the course of bargaining in the sense that they accommodate the strengths of one side or the other. This factor subsumes a number of distinct issues from the establishment of an agenda to the formulation of procedural rules governing such matters as the treatment of amendments and riders to general agreements.[43]

In closing this discussion of structural factors, it should also be noted that there are two distinct perspectives that can be adopted in the analysis of such

[38] This seems to be the position adopted, for example, by Charles E. Lindblom, " 'Bargaining Power' in Price and Wage Determination," *Quarterly Journal of Economics,* LXII (1948), 396–417.

[39] For some interesting comments on this point consult Zeuthen, *Problems of Monopoly and Economic Warfare,* reprinted herein.

[40] Governments, for example, often attempt to enforce rules banning the use of overt violence as an instrument of bargaining.

[41] See, for example, Zeuthen, *Problems of Monopoly and Economic Warfare,* pp. 121–130, partially reprinted herein.

[42] In the American automobile industry, for example, the unions frequently concentrate their bargaining activities on negotiations with one of the firms in the expectation that the resultant settlement will set the standard for agreements with the other firms.

[43] For a brief discussion of this point see Schelling, "An Essay on Bargaining," pp. 289–291, reprinted herein.

factors. In the first instance, it is possible to treat any given set of structural arrangements as fixed at the outset. This perspective leads to a form of comparative statics in which the differences among various fixed structural arrangements are examined. At the same time, however, it is important to notice that many of the structural factors can be altered or changed so that individual players may attempt to gain advantages by manipulating them. Thus, there are sometimes tactical advantages to be had from being a collective entity rather than a single individual,[44] and many asymmetries between the players have favorable consequences for one side or the other. Similarly, individuals may attempt to manipulate factors arising from the iterative nature of bargaining such as the roles of reputation and precedent. And most of the contextual factors can be subjected to various forms of manipulation. In general, activities of this kind will be governed by cost-benefit calculations on the part of the individual players even though these calculations may become relatively complicated in some specific situations.

D. INITIAL CONDITIONS

The existing models of bargaining ordinarily begin with the assumption that the payoff possibility set or the payoff matrix for the interaction at hand can be specified at the outset. This means that the basic issues at stake and the overall dimensions of the resultant interaction are fixed by initial assumption. In real-world situations, however, it is sometimes unclear just who the players are, what the basic issues are, or what the specific alternatives available to each player are. This possibility raises three issues that deserve comment at this point.

If the basic issues at stake are not fixed by assumption, it becomes possible to analyze the ways in which issues come into existence and crystallize among specific individuals. In fact, there is usually nothing inexorable about the definition of issues that lead to bargaining or the timing of their emergence as subjects of active interest. Consequently, the arts of creating issues at propitious moments in time and regulating their detailed formulation can be regarded as important antecedents to the bargaining problem *per se.* And it is even possible to approach the analysis of many activities of this kind from the perspective of the manipulative conception of bargaining.[45]

Next, so long as the basic issues at stake under conditions of strategic interaction are not treated as fixed and unchangeable, there may be prospects for reconceptualization on the part of the players. That is, whenever the initial conditions of an interaction are regarded as fluid, the players may alter their

[44] To mention only one well-known example, a collective entity may gain tactical advantages by dispatching a representative who cannot alter his negotiating instructions without a lengthy process of consultation with headquarters.

[45] For an analysis of international bargaining along these lines see Oran R. Young, *The Politics of Force* (Princeton, 1968), Chapter 15. Note, however, that it is difficult to construct formal models that deal with these activities. For some comments on this point see the Introduction to Part Four of this book, esp. pp. 311–312.

perceptions of the issues at stake, the available alternatives, and so forth. Prospects of this kind have aroused considerable interest, especially among psychologists and social psychologists, as an approach to the problem of conflict "resolution" in interpersonal and intergroup relations.[46] At the present time, however, there are no deductive models that are explicitly relevant to this phenomenon.

In addition, this is a convenient place to refer to the notion of nonstrategic modes of thought. A number of scholars, who are critical of what they regard as "strategic" reasoning, have argued that it would be desirable to devote greater attention to nonstrategic modes of thought.[47] Although arguments of this kind tend to be a little vague, it is possible to identify several distinct meanings that can be associated with the notion of nonstrategic modes of thought. First, the concept may refer to the idea that it is preferable to handle situations involving strategic interaction through procedures such as third-party adjudication rather than through bargaining. Several techniques for dealing with strategic interaction in the absence of bargaining were identified in the general introduction to this book, and some of them have received considerable analytic attention from time to time.[48] Second, the notion of non-strategic modes of thought may be employed to indicate the desirability of relaxing the self-interest assumption included in all the existing models that are relevant to the problem of strategic interaction. This would lead to a study of empathy and altruism in contrast to the allocation of values among separable individuals, and it would produce renewed emphasis on the idea of reconceptualization. Note, however, that this idea introduces the problem of interacting utilities, a problem that has yet to be solved in any formal model of choice.[49] Third, strategic modes of thought are sometimes contrasted with systemic modes of thought. Rapoport, for example, has argued that strategic analysis is "dominated by a theory of rational decision extended to situations involving conflict,"[50] whereas systemic analysis "searches not to discover ploys which confer advantage on seekers of power, but to discover laws which govern large-scale historical events."[51] It is not clear exactly what this distinction amounts to in analytic terms since most studies of the problem of strategic

---

[46] For general discussions of this perspective on conflict "resolution" see Kenneth Boulding, *Conflict and Defense* (New York, 1962), Chapter 15, and Jack Sawyer and Harold Guetzkow, "Bargaining and Negotiation in International Relations," in Herbert C. Kelman, ed., *International Behavior* (New York, 1965), pp. 466–520.

[47] Most of these arguments are based explicitly on normative or prescriptive grounds rather than descriptive considerations.

[48] For a useful analysis of arbitration from this perspective see Cross, *Economics of Bargaining,* Chapter 5.

[49] The problem of interacting utilities is treated in an interesting fashion in Stefan Valavanis, "The Resolution of Conflict when Utilities Interact," *Journal of Conflict Resolution,* II (1958), 156–169.

[50] Anatol Rapoport, "Strategic and Non-Strategic Approaches to Problems of Security and Peace," in Kathleen Archibald, ed., *Strategic Interaction and Conflict* (Berkeley: Institute of International Studies, 1966), p. 88.

[51] *Ibid.,* p. 101.

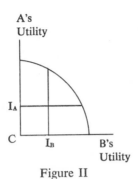

A's
Utility

I_A

C I_B B's
Utility

Figure II

interaction can be regarded as special cases of systemic analysis and any successful theory is apt to be usable for manipulative as well as contemplative purposes.[52] It is possible, however, that Rapoport's position constitutes a plea for less emphasis on the role of the actors in systemic models and more emphasis on such things as the structural features and the contextual properties of the relevant systems *per se.*

E. THE PERTINENCE OF BARGAINING

Once the initial conditions of a situation involving strategic interaction are established, what is the scope for bargaining? Although the various models differ somewhat on this point, perhaps the most prominent indicator of the scope for bargaining is the size of the contract zone or the range of outcomes yielding gains for both sides.[53] An examination of Figure II will clarify this point.[54] Here I_A represents settlement at a point where player S would just prefer reaching an agreement with B to accepting an outcome of no agreement or conflict. That is, unless an agreement with B yields him a payoff of $C + I_A$ or more, A will prefer an outcome of no agreement. And I_B is the analogous point for player B. Under the circumstances, there are three distinct cases concerning the size of the contract zone in the relationship between S and B. If the utility vectors originating at I_A and I_B intersect beyond the social welfare frontier, bargaining cannot lead to an agreement, and negotiations between the players will either never occur or be broken off without yielding an agree-

[52] For a discussion of this point see Oran R. Young, "The Intellectual Bases of 'Conflict Management,'" paper delivered at the 12th S. H. Bailey Conference, London, January 2, 1970, esp. pp. 15–18.

[53] It should be emphasized that this is not the only indicator of the scope for bargaining. Thus, the existence of a contract zone implies that the relationship between the players is a competitive-cooperative one. Under some conceptions of bargaining, however, there may be scope for bargaining even under conditions of pure cooperation and pure conflict.

[54] The discussion of this figure follows the formulation of Pen. See Pen, *The Wage Rate under Collective Bargaining,* Chapter 4.

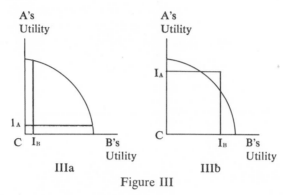

Figure III

ment.[55] If the utility vectors meet on the social welfare frontier, there is a unique settlement point producing a gain for both sides and agreement can be reached without extensive bargaining. But this outcome will occur only by coincidence. Finally, if the utility vectors intersect at a point inside the social welfare frontier, there will be a set of possible agreements yielding gains for both sides. This is the situation actually portrayed in Figure II. In such cases, the vast majority of the mutually beneficial points of settlement will yield differential payoffs for the players, and bargaining will often be prominent. It is the establishment of a specific point of agreement within this range which Schelling describes as "pure bargaining."[56]

In general, the pertinence of bargaining can be said to increase as the size of the contract zone becomes larger and the availability of alternative techniques of handling the problem of strategic interaction declines. Consequently, it is interesting to note that these factors tend to vary greatly in real-world situations. Several illustrations will help to clarify this point. Many international interactions in the nuclear age, for example, are thought to exhibit the characteristics displayed in Figure IIIa. Here the contract zone is extremely large since both players would prefer almost any agreement to an outcome of conflict.[57] And if this idea is coupled with the proposition that the international arena produces few alternatives to bargaining in handling the problem of strategic interaction, we need not be surprised by the fact that the concept of bargaining has become a major topic of interest among students of international relations in recent years.[58] Racial conflicts in some societies, on the other hand, may approach the situation portrayed in Figure IIIb. Here there is

[55] Situations of this kind would be analogous to zero-sum relationships in game theory. For an analysis of the argument that there may still be some scope for bargaining under these conditions see the Introduction to Part One of this book, pp. 26–27.

[56] Schelling, "An Essay on Bargaining," pp. 281–282, reprinted herein.

[57] This preference ordering is a function of the potential destructiveness of war in the nuclear age. In this connection, some observers would argue that the boundaries of the contract zone in Figure IIIa should fall right on the axes rather than inside them.

[58] In this connection, it is quite remarkable that most of the major contributions to the manipulative conception of bargaining have been formulated with reference to the substantive problems of international bargaining.

no contract zone at all because there is no agreement that both players would prefer to an outcome of conflict. When situations of this kind arise, it is to be expected that the role of bargaining will be relatively restricted[59] and that outcomes will tend to flow either from the unilateral victory of one side or from intervention on the part of one or more of the branches of government.

F. PREPARATORY ACTIVITIES

Bargaining is ordinarily associated with a specified tract of time which has a distinct beginning and end.[60] Consequently, it is possible to separate the period of bargaining from the period prior to the main phase of bargaining and to raise questions about the effects on bargaining of various antecedent activities. Whether such actions are described as preliminary bargaining or as preparatory activities, therefore, they constitute a subject of some importance in the analysis of bargaining.

In fact, a few limited efforts have been made by students of bargaining to analyze preparatory activities of this kind. Perhaps the most important of these efforts is Nash's analysis of threats in his negotiation model of bargaining.[61] In essence, Nash formulates a two-stage analysis of bargaining in which the demand game or main phase of bargaining is preceded by a threat game which resembles a zero-sum game between the bargaining partners. The effect of this threat game is to establish the threat point of the demand game or the outcome that will occur in the event that the demand game terminates in a conflict rather than an agreement on the allocation of the value(s).[62] In addition, there is a sense in which Cross's analysis of pre-agreement costs is relevant to the discussion of preparatory activities, although this case is a little more ambiguous than Nash's threat game.[63] The basic effect of imposing pre-agreement costs on another player in Cross's model is to alter his calculations concerning the demands he should make in the next time period.[64] Even though all these activities take place during the course of a single bargaining process, therefore, it can be argued that the imposition of pre-agreement costs is a preparatory activity from the point of view of the subsequent phases or time periods in the bargaining process.[65]

These efforts are limited, however, because they are bound by the initial

---

[59] But bargaining will not necessarily be eliminated altogether. On this point see the Introduction to Part One of this book.

[60] For a helpful discussion of this issue see Schelling, *The Strategy of Conflict,* Appendix B.

[61] John F. Nash, "Two-Person Cooperative Games," reprinted herein.

[62] For a careful evaluation of Nash's concept of the threat game see Robert L. Bishop, "Game-Theoretic Analyses of Bargaining," reprinted herein.

[63] Cross, *Economics of Bargaining,* Chapters 6 and 7.

[64] *Ibid.,* pp. 153–154.

[65] Cross himself points out the link between his analysis of pre-agreement costs and Nash's analysis of threats, although he rightly argues that this connection should not be overemphasized. See *ibid.,* pp. 123–124.

restrictions of the models with which they are associated. As a result, they do not take into account a wide range of preparatory activities that become relevant when alterations in various structural factors and initial conditions are permitted. A few examples will serve to illustrate these broader prospects for preliminary bargaining. First, an individual who expects to engage in bargaining in the future can take steps to build up his bargaining reputation. Second, preliminary efforts to gather resources may prove useful in making credible threats or promises when bargaining does occur. Unions, for example, often try to increase their strike funds in anticipation of forthcoming bargaining sessions, and firms are likely to seek to maintain a liquid position when they expect hard bargaining in the near future.[66] Third, the players may attempt to determine the time at which bargaining is to occur in such a way as to maximize their own advantages. Compare, for example, the English political system in which such activities are permitted within broad limits with the American political system in which they are largely ruled out by the terms of the electoral arrangements. Fourth, it is sometimes possible to choose the rules to be followed prior to the beginning of the main phase of bargaining itself. And in those famous cases where a given set of rules is widely accepted in advance, such as the Queensberry rules of boxing or the rules of dueling in German fraternities, the origin of this agreement is apt to lie in a general desire to avoid the jockeying for position associated with preliminary bargaining. Fifth, there is often room to influence the definition of the issues that will be at stake in the main phase of bargaining.[67] In some real-world situations, activities of this kind are so important in determining the ultimate outcome of bargaining that they become one of the predominant concerns of the players. This is especially so when it is anticipated that one or more third parties employing some criteria of equity will become involved in the settlement of the interaction.[68]

G. INTERVENTION

It is not uncommon in real-world cases of bargaining for one or more third parties to intervene during the course of the interaction. Sometimes intervention of this kind eliminates the impact of strategic interaction so that it serves to solve the bargaining problem. In other cases, however, the intervention of third parties only influences the course of the interaction without terminating the impact of strategic interaction, with the result that the activities of these parties become an aspect of the bargaining problem itself. Conceptually, it is possible to separate two major types of third-party intervention. Thus, ex-

[66] This does not necessarily mean, however, that they expect strikes or lockouts to occur. In fact, a union or a firm that takes steps of this kind may hope to decrease the chances of a strike or a lockout by doing so.

[67] For some concrete illustrations of this possibility see Young, *Politics of Force*, Chapter 15.

[68] When the third party employs some version of the "split-the-difference" principle, for example, it is obviously advantageous to the individual player to define the issues at stake in such a way as to maximize his own demands.

pansion occurs when a third party's predominant motive in intervening is to help one of the original participants to achieve an improved outcome or payoff. Partial transformation occurs, on the other hand, when the predominant motive of the third party is to facilitate the achievement of a settlement for the issues at stake rather than to improve the outcome for either of the original players. In actual situations, nevertheless, it is frequently difficult to apply this distinction both because third parties may intervene with mixed motives and because such parties may have incentives to manipulate the understanding of others about their motives.[69]

The expansion of a bargaining situation may have a variety of consequences involving the alteration of the issues at stake, the resources available to the players, the tactical flexibility of the parties, and so forth. And in most cases, the effects of these changes will be asymmetrical either because third parties intervene only on one side of the interaction or because there are asymmetries among the intervenors themselves. Consequently, there will sometimes be room for manipulative bargaining on the part of the original players as they attempt to engineer forms of expansion which are favorable to themselves. Such efforts, however, may lead to unexpected results when the intervention of third parties introduces powerful new forces that lead to a radical transformation of the issues at stake in the interaction.[70]

In some cases, partial transformation also has a substantial impact on the subsequent course of bargaining.[71] Thus, even when a third party sticks to service roles and attempts to avoid any actions that would assist one player at the expense of the other, its activities are apt to push the interaction toward some solution other than the one that would have occurred in the absence of intervention. This is why mediators are seldom neutral in their impact on bargaining even though they may be impartial with respect to their attitudes toward the original players. Next, there is generally room for bargaining among the original players about the intervention of third parties interested in facilitating a settlement of the issues at stake. Unless these matters are settled by pre-existing arrangements,[72] bargaining of this kind may deal with such issues as when to permit the intervention of a third party, what third party to accept, and what role to allow the third party to play. In addition, such third parties may become involved in relationships with the original players which are affected by strategic interaction. Accordingly, they may ultimately engage in bargaining activities in their own right.

[69] For a detailed examination of a specific case that illustrates this point see Oran R. Young, "Intermediaries and Interventionists: Third Parties in the Middle East Crisis," *International Journal,* XXII (1967–1968), 52–73.

[70] Under the circumstances, the original players may become minor actors in the subsequent interaction, and their interests may be largely forgotten by the intervenors.

[71] See Oran R. Young, *The Intermediaries* (Princeton, 1967), esp. Part I.

[72] In fact, pre-existing arrangements about such matters are not uncommon. In the United States, for example, there exists a good deal of legislation concerning the roles of such agencies as the National Labor Relations Board (NLRB) as third parties in labor-management negotiations.

H. CONCLUSION

It is apparent that there is a considerable gap between the existing models of bargaining and reality in many real-world situations. This is the basic reason why the principal value of these models lies in the insights and conceptual stimulation which they unquestionably generate rather than in the specific predictions and explanations that can be derived from them. Nevertheless, an important start has been made in the analysis of the bargaining problem. And the progress represented by the existing models is especially marked when they are compared, as a group, with the earlier conclusion that the bargaining problem must inevitably remain indeterminate. In fact, it is the marked progress embodied in the existing models of bargaining which makes it possible to look upon the remaining issues associated with the bargaining problem as stimulating analytic challenges for the future rather than insurmountable barriers.

BIBLIOGRAPHY

Alchian, Armen A., "Uncertainty, Evolution, and Economic Theory," *Journal of Political Economy,* LVIII (1950), 211–221.

Archibald, Kathleen, ed., *Strategic Interaction and Conflict* (Berkeley: Institute of International Studies, 1965).

Arrow, Kenneth J., "Alternative Approaches to the Theory of Choice in Risk-Taking Situations," *Econometrica,* XIX (1951), 404–437.

———, *Social Choice and Individual Values,* 2nd ed. (New York, 1963).

———, "Utilities, Attitudes, Choices: A Review Note," *Econometrica,* XXVI (1958), 1–23.

Aumann, R. J., and M. Maschler, "The Bargaining Set for Cooperative Games," in M. Dresher, L. S. Shapley, and A. W. Tucker, eds., *Advances in Game Theory* (Princeton, 1964).

Axelrod, Robert, "Conflict of Interest: An Axiomatic Approach," *Journal of Conflict Resolution,* XI (1967), 87–99.

———, *Conflict of Interest* (Chicago, 1970).

Becker, Selwyn W., and Fred O. Brownson, "What Price Ambiguity? Or the Role of Ambiguity in Decision Making," *Journal of Political Economy,* LXXII (1964), 62–73.

Bishop, Robert L., "Game-Theoretic Analyses of Bargaining," *Quarterly Journal of Economics,* LXXVII (1963), 559–602, reprinted herein.

———, "A Zeuthen-Hicks Theory of Bargaining," *Econometrica,* XXXII (1964), 410–417, reprinted herein.

Boulding, Kenneth, *Conflict and Defense* (New York, 1962).

———, *The Image* (Ann Arbor, 1956).

Braithwaite, R. B., *Theory of Games as a Tool for the Moral Philosopher* (Cambridge, 1955).

Buchanan, James M., and Gordon Tullock, *The Calculus of Consent* (Ann Arbor, 1962).

Chertkoff, Jerome M., "Sociopsychological Theories and Research on Coalition Formation," in S. Groennings, E. W. Kelley, and M. Leiserson, eds., *The Study of Coalition Behavior* (New York, 1970).

Coddington, Alan, "Game Theory, Bargaining Theory, and Strategic Reasoning," *Journal of Peace Research,* No. 1 (1967), 39–45.

———, *Theories of the Bargaining Process* (London, 1968).

———, "A Theory of the Bargaining Process: Comment," *The American Economic Review,* LVI (1966), 522–530, reprinted herein.

Cross, John G., *The Economics of Bargaining* (New York, 1969).

———, "A Theory of the Bargaining Process," *The American Economic Review,* LV (1965), 66–94, reprinted herein.

———, "A Theory of the Bargaining Process: Reply," *The American Economic Review,* LVI (1966), 530–533, reprinted herein.

Downs, Anthony, *An Economic Theory of Democracy* (New York, 1957).

Dunlop, John T., and Neil W. Chamberlain, eds., *Frontiers of Collective Bargaining* (New York, 1967).

Edwards, Ward, "The Theory of Decision Making," *Psychological Bulletin,* LI (1954), 388–417.

——— and Amos Tversky, eds., *Decision-Making* (Harmondsworth, 1967).

Ellsberg, Daniel, "Reply," *Quarterly Journal of Economics,* LXXVII (1963), 336–342.

————, "Risk, Ambiguity, and the Savage Axioms," *Quarterly Journal of Economics,* LXXV (1961), 643–669.

————, "The Theory and Practice of Blackmail," lecture at the Lowell Institute, Boston, Massachusetts, March 10, 1959, reprinted herein.

————, "Theory of the Reluctant Duelist," *The American Economic Review,* XLVI (1956), 909–923, reprinted herein.

Fellner, William, *Competition among the Few* (New York, 1949).

Flanders, Allan, ed., *Collective Bargaining* (Harmondsworth, 1969).

Foldes, Lucien, "A Determinate Model of Bilateral Monopoly," *Economica,* XXXI (1964), 117–131.

Friedman, Milton, and L. J. Savage, "The Expected-Utility Hypothesis and the Measurement of Utility," *Journal of Political Economy,* LX (1952), 463–474.

————, "The Utility Analysis of Choices Involving Risk," *Journal of Political Economy,* LVI (1948), 279–304.

Frohlich, Norman, Joe A. Oppenheimer, and Oran R. Young, *Political Leadership and Collective Goods* (Princeton, 1971).

Groennings, Sven, E. W. Kelley, and Michael Leiserson, eds., *The Study of Coalition Behavior* (New York, 1970).

Harsanyi, John C., "Approaches to the Bargaining Problem before and after the Theory of Games," *Econometrica,* XXIV (1956), 144–157, reprinted herein.

————, "Bargaining and Conflict Situations in the Light of a New Approach to Game Theory," *The American Economic Review,* LV (1965), 447–457, reprinted herein.

————, "Bargaining in Ignorance of the Opponent's Utility Function," *Journal of Conflict Resolution,* VI (1962), 28–38.

————, "A Bargaining Model for the Cooperative N-Person Game," in R. D. Luce and A. W. Tucker, eds., *Contributions to the Theory of Games,* IV (Princeton, 1959).

————, "Game Theory and the Analysis of International Conflict," *The Australian Journal of Politics and History,* XI (1955), 292–304.

————, "A General Theory of Rational Behavior in Game Situations," *Econometrica,* XXXIV (1966), 613–634.

————, "Notes on the Bargaining Problem," *Southern Economic Journal,* XXIV (1958), 471–476, reprinted herein.

————, "On the Rationality Postulates Underlying the Theory of Cooperative Games," *Journal of Conflict Resolution,* V (1961), 179–196.

Hicks, J. R., *The Theory of Wages* (London, 1932).

Hurwicz, Leonid, "The Theory of Economic Behavior," *The American Economic Review,* XXXV (1945), 909–925.

Iklè, Fred, *How Nations Negotiate* (New York, 1964).

Kahn, Herman, *On Escalation* (New York, 1965).

Kaysen, Karl, "A Revolution in Economic Theory?" *Review of Economic Studies,* XIV (1946–47), 1–15.

————, "The Minimax Rule of the Theory of Games...," *Metroeconomica* (April, 1952), 5–14.

Knight, Frank, *Risk, Uncertainty, and Profit* (Boston, 1921).

Koo, Anthony Y. C., "Recurrent Objections to the Minimax Strategy," *The Review of Economics and Statistics,* XLI (1959), 36–41.

Kuhn, Harold W., "Game Theory and Models of Negotiation," *Journal of Conflict Resolution,* VI (1962), 1–4.

Lindblom, Charles E., " 'Bargaining Power' in Price and Wage Determination," *Quarterly Journal of Economics,* LXII (1948), 396–417.

————, *The Intelligence of Democracy* (New York, 1965).

Luce, R. Duncan, and Howard Raiffa, *Games and Decisions* (New York, 1957).

Marschak, J., "Neumann's and Morgenstern's New Approach to Static Economics," *Journal of Political Economy*, LIV (1946), 97–115.

Mayberry, J. P., J. F. Nash, and M. Shubik, "A Comparison of Treatments of a Duopoly Situation," *Econometrica*, XXI (1953), 141–154.

Mitchell, William C., *Public Choice in America* (Chicago, 1971).

Morgenstern, Oskar, "Oligopoly, Monopolistic Competition, and the Theory of Games," *The American Economic Review*, XXXVIII (1948), 10–18.

Nash, John F., "The Bargaining Problem," *Econometrica*, XVIII (1950), 155–162, reprinted herein.

———, "Non-Cooperative Games," *Annals of Mathematics*, LIV (1951), 286–295.

———, "Two-Person Cooperative Games," *Econometrica*, XXI (1953), 128–140, reprinted herein.

Neisser, Hans, "The Strategy of Expecting the Worst," *Social Research*, XIX (1952), 346–362.

Nicholson, M. B., *Conflict Analysis* (London, 1971).

———, "The Resolution of Conflict," *Journal of the Royal Statistical Society, Series A (General)*, CXXX (1967), 529–540, reprinted herein.

———, "Tariff Wars and a Model of Conflict," *Journal of Peace Research* (1967), 26–38.

Pen, Jan, "A General Theory of Bargaining," *The American Economic Review*, XLII (1952), 24–42, reprinted herein.

———, *The Wage Rate under Collective Bargaining* (Cambridge, 1959).

Raiffa, Howard, "Arbitration Schemes for Generalized Two-Person Games," in H. W. Kuhn and A. W. Tucker, eds., *Contributions to the Theory of Games*, II (Princeton, 1953), 361–387.

———, *Decision Analysis: Introductory Lectures on Choices under Uncertainty* (Reading, Mass., 1968).

Rapoport, Anatol, *Fights, Games, and Debates* (Ann Arbor, 1960).

———, *N-Person Game Theory* (Ann Arbor, 1970).

———, *Strategy and Conscience* (New York, 1964).

———, *Two-Person Game Theory* (Ann Arbor, 1966).

———, and Albert Chammah, "The Game of Chicken," *American Behavioral Scientist*, X (1966), 10–14, 23–28.

——— and ———, *Prisoner's Dilemma* (Ann Arbor, 1965).

———, and Carol Orwant, "Experimental Games: A Review," *Behavioral Science*, VII (1962), 1–37.

Riker, William, *The Theory of Political Coalitions* (New Haven, 1962).

Roberts, Harry V., "Risk, Ambiguity, and the Savage Axioms: Comment," *Quarterly Journal of Economics*, LXXVII (1963), 327–336.

Rothschild, K. W., "Approaches to the Theory of Bargaining," in John T. Dunlop, ed., *The Theory of Wage Determination* (London, 1964), 281–291.

Saraydar, Edward, "A Certainty Equivalent Model of Bargaining," *Journal of Conflict Resolution*, XV (1971), 281–297.

———, "Zeuthen's Theory of Bargaining: A Note," *Econometrica*, XXXIII (1965), 802–813.

Savage, L. J., *The Foundations of Statistics* (New York: 1954).

Sawyer, Jack, and Harold Guetzkow, "Bargaining and Negotiation in International Relations," in H. C. Kelman, ed., *International Behavior* (New York, 1965), 466–520.

Schelling, Thomas C., *Arms and Influence* (New Haven, 1966).

———, "An Essay on Bargaining," *The American Economic Review*, XLVI (1956), 281–306, reprinted herein.

————, "Game Theory and the Study of Ethical Systems," *Journal of Conflict Resolution*, XII (1968), 34–44.

————, *The Strategy of Conflict* (Cambridge, 1960).

Shackle, G. L. S., *Expectation in Economics* (Cambridge, 1949).

————, "The Nature of the Bargaining Process," in John T. Dunlop, ed., *The Theory of Wage Determination* (London, 1964), 292–314.

Shapely, L. S., "A Value for N-Person Games," in H. W. Kuhn and A. W. Tucker, eds., *Contributions to the Theory of Games,* II (Princeton, 1953).

Shubik, Martin, *Competition, Oligopoly, and the Theory of Games* (New York, 1959).

————, "Information, Risk, Ignorance, and Indeterminacy," *Quarterly Journal of Economics*, LXVIII (1954), 629–640.

————, "Information, Theories of Competition, and the Theory of Games," *Journal of Political Economy*, LX (1952), 145–150.

————, "On the Study of Disarmament and Escalation," *Journal of Conflict Resolution*, XII (1968), 83–101.

Siegal, Sidney, and Lawrence E. Fouraker, *Bargaining and Group Decision Making* (New York, 1960).

Simon, Herbert, *Models of Man* (New York, 1957).

Stevens, Carl M., "On the Theory of Negotiation," *Quarterly Journal of Economics*, LXXII (1958), 77–97.

————, *Strategy and Collective Bargaining Negotiation* (New York, 1963).

Tullock, Gordon, *Toward a Mathematics of Politics* (Ann Arbor, 1967).

————, *Private Wants, Public Means: An Economic Analysis of the Desirable Scope of Government* (New York, 1970).

Valavanis, Stefan, "The Resolution of Conflict when Utilities Interact," *Journal of Conflict Resolution*, II (1958), 156–169.

von Neumann, John, and Oskar Morgenstern, *Theory of Games and Economic Behavior* (Princeton, 1st ed., 1944; 2nd ed., 1947).

Wagner, Harvey M., "Rejoinder on the Bargaining Problem," *Southern Economic Journal*, XXIV (1958), 476–482, reprinted herein.

————, "A Unified Treatment of Bargaining Theory," *Southern Economic Journal*, XXIII (1957), 380–397, reprinted herein.

Walton, R. E., and R. B. McKersie, *A Behavioral Theory of Labor Negotiations* (New York, 1965).

Young, Oran R., *The Intermediaries: Third Parties in International Crises* (Princeton, 1967).

————, *The Politics of Force: Bargaining during International Crises* (Princeton, 1968).

Zeuthen, Frederik, "Du Monopole Bilateral," *Revue d'Economie Politique*, XLVII (1933), 1651–70.

————, *Economic Theory and Method* (London, 1955).

————, *Problems of Monopoly and Economic Warfare* (London, 1930), partially reprinted herein.

NOTES ON CONTRIBUTORS

DANIEL ELLSBERG is an economist by training who has worked extensively in the field of public policy analysis.

JOHN F. NASH is a mathematician who specializes in the theory of games. He lives in Princeton, New Jersey.

JOHN C. HARSANYI, Professor of Business Administration and of Economics at Berkeley, is an economist who has made numerous contributions to the theory of games.

ROBERT L. BISHOP is an economist who specializes in theories of imperfect competition. He is Professor of Economics at the Massachusetts Institute of Technology.

FREDERIK ZEUTHEN was a well-known Danish economist who taught at the London School of Economics and Political Science.

JAN PEN is a Dutch economist who has worked extensively in the field of macroeconomics. He is currently Professor of Economics at Groningen University.

JOHN G. CROSS is Assistant Professor of Economics at the University of Michigan.

ALAN CODDINGTON, an economist by training, is Lecturer in Economics at Queen Mary College, University of London.

MICHAEL B. NICHOLSON is Director of the Richardson Institute for Conflict and Peace Research, London.

HARVEY M. WAGNER, an economist by training, is Professor of Administrative Sciences at Yale University.

THOMAS C. SCHELLING, Professor of Economics at Harvard University, is an economist who has done extensive work in the field of public policy analysis.

ORAN R. YOUNG, Professor of Government at the University of Texas, is a political scientist who has a special interest in the analysis of international politics.

DATE DUE